HOW JEWISH CARE MA[KES]

7000
WE SUPPORT
AND CARE FOR
OVER 7000 PEOPLE
AND THEIR FAMILIES
EVERY WEEK

2600
WE HELP AND SUPPORT
OVER 2600 PEOPLE LIVING
IN THEIR OWN HOMES

1 MILLION
WE SERVE OVER 1 MILLION
KOSHER MEALS TO OUR
CLIENTS EACH YEAR

12,000
OUR HELPLINE RECEIVES OVER
12,000 ENQUIRIES EACH YEAR

ONCE UPON
A TIME...

2000
IN THE PAST YEAR, WE SENT OUT
OVER 2000 TALKING BOOKS TO
PEOPLE WITH VISUAL IMPAIRMENT
AND SENSORY DISABILITIES

12,990
OVER 100 VOLUNTEERS
DELIVERED 12,990 HOT,
KOSHER MEALS-ON-WHEELS
TO OUR OLDER MEMBERS
OF THE COMMUNITY IN REDBRIDGE

JEWISH CARE

For information about any of our services,
please contact our helpline on 020 8922 2222,
email helpline@jcare.org or visit jewishcare.org

THE JEWISH YEAR BOOK
2015

Jewish Year Book Editors

1896–1899	Joseph Jacobs
1900–1924	Isidore Harris
1925–1934	Rev. Solomon Levy
1935–1938	Rev. Solomon Levy & Cecil Roth
1939	Cecil Roth
1940–1952	Albert Hyamson
1953–1968	Hugh Harris
1969–1983	Michael Wallach
1984–1989	Roger Japhet
1990–2009	Stephen Massil
2010–	Elkan Levy & Derek Taylor

We are very grateful to the European Jewish Publication
Society and the Jewish Leadership Council for their
generous support for the 2015 Jewish Year Book.

The Jewish Year Book

Founded 1896

2015

5775–5776

Edited by
Elkan D. Levy and Derek Taylor

VALLENTINE MITCHELL
LONDON · PORTLAND, OR

Published in 2015 by Vallentine Mitchell

Middlesex House
29/45 High Street
Edgware, Middlesex HA8 7UU
UK

920 NE 58th Avenue, Suite 300
Portland, Oregon,
97213-3786
USA

www.vmbooks.com
Copyright © 2015 Vallentine Mitchell

British Library Cataloguing in Publication Data
An entry can be found on request

ISBN 978 0 85303 978 5 (cloth)
ISBN 978 0 85303 988 4 (Ebook)
ISSN 0075-3769

Printed by CPI Group (UK) Ltd, Croydon, CR0 4YY

CONTENTS

2014: A LOSE-LOSE SITUATION

In the years to come, those who will want to know what the Jewish community in Britain was like in 2014 might well turn to this résumé. When you've been published since 1896 you tend to become accepted as authoritative. Well, put simply, in the latter half of 2014, the community was in considerable turmoil. The rocket attacks by Hamas in July, to which Israel retaliated, led to an increase in antisemitic incidents, which raised hackles to very high levels. We must, however, start at the beginning.

From 28 December 2013 to 1 January 2014, it became acceptable for United Synagogue rabbis to attend Limmud. Indeed, the Chief Rabbi attended himself. Later in January Ariel Sharon died at 85. In a coma for some years before his death, Sharon was a stout fighter for Israel, if a controversial character outside the country. That same month saw the Oxford University Jewish Society celebrate its 110th anniversary; the oldest JSoc in the country.

There was a debate on Shechita in the House of Lords where the government announced again that Shechita would remain lawful; Lord Sacks and Lord Winston stoutly defended the process. There is still no reliable scientific evidence to suggest that it isn't the most humane way of killing animals. Even so, the British Veterinarian Association, in the amorphous name of animal welfare, continued a campaign to ban it.

Speaking to the Knesset in March, David Cameron pledged that 'Britain's commitment to Israel's security is rock solid', and guaranteed the legal continuance of Shechita. Abroad, the threat to Shechita has been ended in New Zealand and Holland.

Further efforts need to be made to rescue the last Falashas from Ethiopia. There are still a considerable number left after the main body of the community were transported to Israel some years ago.

The Jewish Institute of Policy Research reported in February that the under 40s in the community were more religious than their parents, and that intermarriage was levelling off. Much credit would be due to the Jewish schools, whose academic results continue to be among the best in the country.

In September, however, the Talmud Torah Chaim Meirim Wiznitz in North London was closed by Ofsted for not providing the 250 3–13-year-old pupils with sufficient secular education. The teaching was in Yiddish and, for the older boys, only one and a half hours was allowed for secular studies in a 10-hour day.

The government has created a National Holocaust Commission, whose members include the Prime Minister, the Chief Rabbi, the Leader of the House of Commons, the actress, Helen Bonham-Carter, and Ed Balls for the Labour party.

In February Naftali Bennett, the Knesset Minister for Diaspora Affairs, visited the UK. He described the case for Israel as: 'This is our land and our right to it is set out in the Bible'. For those whose religion does not include the Bible, he might have added that Israel exists because five Arab armies, seeking to nullify a United Nations resolution in 1948, were defeated by the Israel Defense Forces.

If the later results of the 1948, 1956, 1967 and 1973 wars are not justification enough for Israel to exist, then Nice in the South of France goes back to the Italians, Namibia to the Germans, California to the Mexicans, and we have to decide who really ought to have Alsace Lorraine and Schleswig Holstein. As successors to the Romans, the Italians must also have a case for reoccupying Britain.

To add to Israel's problems, more than 50,000 Africans have fled to the Holy Land since the year 2000 to escape impossible living conditions in Eritrea and the Sudan. At the moment they have temporary residence permits.

Throughout the year there have been discussions about the relationship between the Board of Deputies and the Jewish Leadership Council. Accusations and counteraccusations against both bodies and their leadership have been publicised in the Jewish press by senior members of the community, but no final decisions on future cooperation have been agreed.

The new Chief Executive of the Board of Deputies is the former MP, Gillian Merron, a Liberal Jew from the Lincoln community. The Board now has 320 members. There will be new elections in May where Laura Marks, the Senior Vice President, will be a strong candidate. If elected, the two most senior roles in the Board of Deputies would be held by Progressive members. This would lead to more recriminations, as did the fact that none of the Progressives were elected Trustees of the JLC.

In his private capacity, Laurence Brass, the Treasurer of the Board of Deputies, went on record as deploring some of the treatment of Arabs he had seen in Israel. There was a great deal of criticism of his views but four former Israeli ambassadors and former ministers wrote to support him.

Dayan Gelley has been appointed head of the Beth Din to succeed Dayan Ehrentreu. The Beth Din were concerned at the innovation of the sefer torah being paraded in the women's section of London's Dunstan Road Synagogue. The practice was discontinued although there is nothing halachically wrong with the process. It was also pointed out that renowned Rabbi Soloveitchik had advocated boys and girls being taught Torah together. The position of women in the synagogue is discussed in an article in this year's issue by Dina Brawer.

In early July three Jewish youngsters were murdered in Israel by Hamas fanatics, and a young Arab was killed in retaliation, for which several Jewish extremists have been charged. Hamas started firing a large number of rockets across the border and Israel retaliated with air strikes and an army incursion. When a month-long ceasefire was agreed in mid-August, over 2,000 Palestinians were reported by Hamas to have been killed, and Israel lost 65 soldiers.

In Britain the Prime Minister said in the House, 'Those criticising Israel's response must ask themselves how they would expect their own government to react if hundreds of rockets were raining down on British cities'. That's easy. You just have to look back to 1944 to find the answer. Over 7,000 were killed by V2 rockets at that time, including 3,000 Londoners. To stop the onslaught, Bomber Command eliminated the launching sites and the factories manufacturing the rockets. It was estimated that 20,000 civilians were killed in the process, mostly forced labour from occupied countries in the factories. There were no complaints from the British people.

Hamas fired over 4,000 rockets at Israel – more than the 1944 attacks – but the defensive Iron Dome system destroyed those whose trajectory would have reached built-up areas. The Israelis also had shelters to protect them. Gaza citizens had no defences of this nature, and Hamas admitted using them as human shields to try to prevent Israeli shelling schools and hospitals, in which rocket firing bases had been placed. The Greek Orthodox Archbishop in Gaza, for instance, said that the church was used as a launching site for rockets. The chief United Nations representative said that UN schools were used to store weapons.

Colonel Richard Kemp, a former British commander in Afghanistan, said that he had never come across a military attack like Israel's, where so much effort was made to avoid civilian casualties. In his view, by contrast, Hamas was happy to sacrifice its people to get favourable media coverage for what could then be called Israeli atrocities.

Much publicity was given to adverse comments on Israel by fringe politicians. By contrast, the Home Secretary and the Leader of the House of Commons said that any anti-Semitism was abhorrent. The House of Commons has a committee led by non-Jewish MPs to monitor anti-Semitism.

A controversial MP said that Bradford should have nothing to do with Israel. The Israeli ambassador immediately went to Bradford where he was welcomed by members of the Council who said that the MP's views did not represent the feelings of the townsfolk. Indeed, Jewish commercial enterprise has made a very substantial contribution to Bradford over the last 150 years, and part of the town is still known as Little Germany, from the original homes and offices of the Jews who immigrated to the town.

Communities Minister, Stephen Williams, after a meeting with the Community Security Trust on 13 August said, 'Any hostility or harassment directed towards the Jewish community in this country is completely unacceptable, and the government will do everything in its power to prevent the fears and distress such deplorable actions cause'. In addition not only the Prime Minister, but also the Foreign Secretary and the Chancellor of the Exchequer have said they recognize that Israel has a right to defend itself.

There was, however, a substantial increase in the amount of graffiti and anti-Semitic abuse, which will make 2014 the worst year in recording such yobbish behaviour in this country. The Community

Security Trust estimates that the number of incidents this year will be around 1,000, about twice that of last year. There were anti-Israel demonstrations in many parts of the country.

Analysing this figure, there were no fatalities, no need for hospitalization and no arson attacks on Jewish buildings. The vast majority of the incidents were, as usual, graffiti and abusive behaviour. A consistent 7 per cent of the incidents were violent but one of these was considered important enough to receive substantial publicity in the Jewish Chronicle, which reported that, 'A man suffered facial injuries after an egg was thrown at him from a passing car as he walked home from synagogue'. Earlier in the year an anti-Zionist Jew in Salford had his home pelted with eggs and daubed with graffiti.

There have been both pro- and anti-Israel rallies which passed off peacefully, as befits our national traditions. The BBC has been condemned in the Jewish press as non-objective on a number of occasions, though it has also been picketed for its alleged pro-Israel stand. Following a dispute between the Tricycle Theatre and the UK Jewish Film Festival over a funding condition imposed by The Tricycle Theatre, the Festival was held at a variety of new venues this year. Both organisations now hope to work on rebuilding trust so that events may again be held at the Tricycle. The Times has been stalwart in its support for Israel.

One shop in Manchester, which was picketed for selling Israeli products, saw the police move in and restrict the demonstration under the Public Order Act. Nine protesters were arrested in one weekend. Two windows were broken at the Belfast Synagogue and one at Cockfosters. There was substantial vandalism at a Manchester Jewish cemetery, and two 13-year-olds pleaded guilty to causing the damage. The local vicar came with members of his congregation to help clear up the damage. A picketed shop in Brighton closed, though it could have successfully applied for a civil injunction to make its surroundings an exclusion zone under current legislation. Two men were jailed in Gateshead for robbing Charedi homes which had been left unlocked on Shabbat.

The attempts to boycott Israeli products have proved a damp squib. Trade between the two countries improved by 28 per cent, with a value of £2.5 billion. The UK is Israel's largest export market after the United States. There is an article on the subject in the Year Book.

During the conflict with Hamas there were vociferous calls within the community for better leadership. What that was to cover differed according to the advocate. It did make, however, for startling head-lines. A 'straw poll' of 150 Jews by the Jewish Chronicle decided that 63 per cent doubted their future in this country. '63 per cent' made a fine headline but as a study of the community's concerns it is worthless. The view of the Community Security Trust was that, 'Opportunities for Jewish life in Britain are better now than ever before'.

At the moment in Britain, for a community of 270,000, there are 35 Jewish Privy Councillors, eight peers, 71 Life Peers, 21 MPs, 124 Knights and 14 Dames. We are hardly underrepresented in the Establishment.

A panic reaction, however, could well help with Aliyah. Natan Sharansky, a Knesset Minister, announced, 'We are witnessing the end of Jewish history in Europe'. If the Holocaust didn't achieve that, the present isolated incidents are hardly likely to do so either. German Chancellor Angela Merkel was particularly scathing about anti-Semitism at a meeting in Berlin in September.

If one could stand back from the horrors of civilian casualties, the Public Relations results achieved by Hamas were initially considerable. In spite of the 4,000 rockets fired at Israel, the citizens of Gaza were widely portrayed as the victims. This image was substantially nullified, however, by the appalling atrocities committed by Arab extremists throughout the Middle East since the summer, invariably on their own people. In addition, videos of the beheading of innocent hostages, including journalists and aid workers, made support for Hamas far more questionable, and murderous attacks on Christian communities alienated much of the Western world.

In October, however, the House of Commons debated a motion to recognize Palestine as a State. With the Conservative and Liberal MPs abstaining, the vote in favour was 274-12. The tone of the debate was sympathetic to both the Israeli and Palestinian right to live in peace and security, but it is unlikely to move the process forward. Israel has now been at war for 66 years and as the British government has condemned Hamas, the government in Gaza, as a terrorist organization, there are definitely mixed messages coming from Parliament.

In opposing such outrages, the possibility of Western powers and Arab dictatorships becoming allies could make for some very unusual bedfellows. Egypt certainly didn't object to the destruction of Hamas' military capabilities.

In August the National Union of Students narrowly passed a resolution calling for a boycott on almost everything to do with Israel. It managed to produce a very long resolution which didn't once mention 4,000 rockets and what the NUS would have done if the rockets were raining down on their universities.

A similar resolution was passed by the TUC congress, equally one sided. If accepted by the government – which is not within the realms of possibility – the TUC would ban arms sales to Israel but not to Hamas. The Lancet published some virulent anti-Israel sentiments but the Editor partially retracted after discussions in Jerusalem.

The lunatic fringe are always with us. In October a Liverpool man was sentenced to prison for sending an anti-Semitic diatribe to a Jewish MP. As could be expected, the Twitter war flared up again.

Also in October, the Education Minister decided that faith schools would be forced to teach their pupils about other religions, and the need to tolerate those who were not heterosexual. Church schools joined with Jewish ones in objecting strongly.

The campaign for and against independence in Scotland was marred by a degree of violence and intimidation, abusive language and hate-filled graffiti. This might well ensure that Jews are seen as not complaining of anti-Semitism in a vacuum.

This year has deprived us of a number of distinguished centenarians; Elsbeth Juda at 103, Henry Rollin and Camille Wolff at 102, Lady Sainsbury, Natalie Huss-Smickler and Joyce Stone at 101 and Muriel Carvis at 100. Please G-d by us.

We would like to thank Jenni Tinson, Mordaunt Cohen and Elisheva Sokolic for their very valued help in producing the 120th edition of the Year Book.

Elkan Levy and Derek Taylor
Editors

ABBREVIATIONS

Ad. – Address
Admin. – Administrative; administration; administrator
Adv. – Advisory; adviser
Asst. – Assistant

B. – Born
Bd. – Board
BoD – Board of Deputies
Br. – Branch

C. – Council
Ch. – Chairman, chairmen, chair
Cllr. – Councillor
Coll. – College
Com. – Communal; community; commission(er)
Comp. – Company
Cttee. – Committee

Dep. – Deputy
Dept. – Department(s)
Dev. – Development
Dir. – Director
Distr. – District

Eccl. – Ecclesiastical
Ed. – Editor
Educ. – Education; educationist; educational
Emer. – Emeritus
Exec. – Executive

Fdr. – Founder
Fed. – Federation; federal
Fel. – Fellow; fellowship
Fin. – Finance; financial
Form. – Former; formerly

Gen. – General
Gov. – Governor; governing
Govt. – Government

H. – Honorary
Hist. – History; historical; historian
Hd. – Head, Headmaster, Head Teacher
Hon. T. – Honorary Treasurer
Hon. S. – Honorary Secretary

Imm. - Immediate
Instit. – Institute; institution(al)
Intl. – International

Jt - Joint

Lab. – Labour; laboratory
Lect. – Lecturer; lecture(ship)
Libr. – Librarian
Lit. – Literature
LJ – Liberal Judaism

M. – Minister
Man. – Manager; management; managing
Med – Medical; medicine
Mem. - Member/membership
Min. – Ministry; ministerial
MEP – Member of European Parliament
MP – Member of Parliament

Nat. – National; nationalist; nation(s)
NGO - Non Government organisation

Off. – Officer; office
Org. – Organiser

Parl. – Parliament; parliamentary
Pol. – Political
Pres. – President(s)
PM – Prime Minister
Princ. – Principal
Prof. – Professor
Publ. – Publication; publicity; publishing

Reg. – Registrar; register(ed); region(al)
Res. – Research; residence; resource
RM – Reform Movement

SAE - Stamped Addressed Envelope
Sch. – School(s)
Sec. – Secretary
Soc. – Society; social; sociology
Snr. – Senior
Supt. – Superintendent

T. – Treasurer
Tech. – Technical; technology, -ical
Tru. – Trustee(s); trust

UK – United Kingdom
US – United Synagogue

V. – Vice
Vis. – Visitation; visitor; visiting
Vol. – Voluntary; volunteer; volume

GLOSSARY

AJA – Anglo-Jewish Association
AJEX – Association of Jewish Ex-Servicemen and Women

BMA – British Medical Association

CBF-WJR – Central British Fund for World Jewish Relief
CCJ – Council of Christians and Jews
C of E – Council of Europe

IJPR – Institute for Jewish Policy Research

JBS – Jewish Blind Society

JEDT – Jewish Educational Development Trust
JMC – Jewish Memorial Council
JNF – Jewish National Fund
JWB – Jewish Welfare Board

TAC – Trades Advisory Council

ORT – Organisation for Resources and Technical Training

WIZO – Women's International Organisation
WJC – World Jewish Congress
WZO – World Zionist Organisation

Gillian Merron

JEWS IN UNEXPECTED PLACES

A colleague of mine recently moved to York where there has not been a synagogue for 40 years, and the city's twelfth-century pogrom continues to cast its dark shadow. He was determined that with two universities and a teaching hospital, there must be the potential to build a thriving Jewish community.

So far, those hopes look set to be fulfilled with the first Yom Kippur services in the city attracting around 60 participants and services now being held monthly at the Friends Meeting House.

Jews turn up in the most unexpected of places. In the 2011 census, our co-religionists were found in every one of the 347 local authority areas across the UK, including four in Merthyr Tydfil and another four in the Isles of Scilly. The latter had provided the only 'blank' in 2001, as allegedly the only Jewish family living on the Isles were away on the night of the census.

Such comparisons make my own home town of Lincoln, with its 63 Jews, look like Stamford Hill, but of course the reality is somewhat different. Indeed, when I became the Member of Parliament there in 1997 I was only faintly aware that the city had a Jewish community at all. Then one day I was invited to Lincoln Cathedral to view the Anne Frank exhibition at which I got talking to someone from the then relatively recently revived Lincoln Jewish community. Over the following months and years it became a natural and increasingly fulfilling part of my life to play an active role. Despite the other pressures on my time as the local MP, I made a point of attending services and sharing in the hosting of Friday night Chavurah suppers.

The Lincoln Jewish community became my community and I can say, without a shadow of a doubt, that I would not now be in my current role without it. Of course, I am from a Jewish family. Born in Ilford, my parents were members of Barking and Becontree United Synagogue, albeit not very active, and along with my four elder siblings, we were certainly brought up to know we were Jewish. But it was not until I moved to Lincoln that I really began to engage with and explore the role that Judaism played in my life.

When you live beyond the *shtetl*, North Londoners will tip their heads sideways at you and say sympathetically: 'You live in Lincoln? It must be tough being Jewish there!' In fact, for me – and I suspect for my York colleague and others like us from Perth to Penzance – sometimes it is easier to be a Jew away from the intensity and pressure of the Finchley/Edgware/Golders Green triangle. Of course, there are challenges which affect different people in different ways – getting to services, finding Kosher food, introducing children to Jewish friends – but at the same time there is the ability to find your own way without the judgment of others.

At the Board of Deputies, of course, all community voices – big and small – are heard. I am humbled by the pride that my own community has taken in my appointment as Chief Executive, but, in fact, it is a reflection of the Board's ethos and priorities.

The Board exists to protect and promote Jewish life in Britain. That means all Jewish life and while I reject the notion that Jewish life outside London or Manchester is intrinsically harder, Jews in these 'unexpected places' perhaps do need more and different support and we are here to give it, so that Jewish life can flourish throughout the UK.

It is this commitment that has inspired in the past year the launch of Jewish Connection, the Board's programme to support local communities outside London, by helping them to find and work with one another, and access the Board's services and information.

For example, we are talking with the Six Point Foundation and social care provider partners. This is with a view to delivering training for non-Jewish care homes and other facilities in the regions, where Jewish people – and particularly survivors – are cared for. Jewish Connection is also helping local communities access rabbinic support, using the Board's central role to arrange locum services. And Jewish Connection is organizing events which bring Jews in unexpected places together to provide opportunities for them to celebrate their Jewishness.

As I travel Britain in my new role, I am intrigued by how many people I come across who have little knowledge or understanding of Judaism or Jewish life. And it is in those areas in which the fewest Jews live where non-Jews have the least opportunity to learn through osmosis: talking to neighbours and workmates, meeting Jews through schools and clubs or hearing about what we do and believe through local media.

The Board regards it as a key responsibility to provide opportunities for learning, especially to those in outlying communities. It is this which has led us in the past year to rejuvenate our Jewish Living Experience exhibition and tours. This enables thousands of non-Jewish adults and children to learn about our faith each year through role-playing, talks and visiting Jewish communities.

During Operation Protective Edge we saw a significant upturn in anti-Semitic incidents, fuelled no doubt by the relentless media coverage of Israel's military campaign, all too rarely balanced by an explanation of the Hamas rockets and terror tunnels which compelled Israel to act.

In those areas in which the Jewish population is concentrated, the pot frequently reached boiling point as conversations around the dinner table turned to 'packing bags' and thousands turned out for rallies and events in Israel's support. There was – without doubt – huge tension, but there was also comfort in numbers, with grassroots organizations springing up and activists feeling empowered to act.

In contrast, however, in those unexpected places, Jews could feel isolated: discomforted by anti-Semitic chanting on pro-Palestinian marches, or by Palestinian flags fluttering over the local town hall. It fell to the Board to provide support, whether through training in Israel advocacy, or challenging authorities when anti-Zionism lapsed into anti-Semitism. At the height of the conflict the Board was providing strategic and hands-on support to 25 Israel grassroots organizations. We were also in regular contact with political parties, retailers, the media and Government departments to address growing concerns across the community. And this work continues.

But while the Board was providing this support to those smaller communities we were also learning from them. If you live in Lincoln or Liverpool, Oxford or Ongar, let alone Mansfield or Merthyr Tydfil, you do not have the option to shut yourself away, wrap yourself in the cloak of your own Jewish community and wait for the storm to pass. Instead, you live and work in a non-Jewish world, with people for whom Gaza is a distant land and Hamas, just a name in the paper.

Some Jews respond by keeping their heads down and their religion to themselves. Many others, however, in our small communities reach out to their neighbours, share their knowledge and experiences with those of other faiths and of none. They build the relationships on which cohesive communities are founded.

In Bradford, for example, it is the local Muslim community which has sustained the city's remaining nineteenth-century synagogue, while in Bristol, Jews and Muslims jointly operate their own community radio station.

Learning from their example, the Board reaches out to other faiths to strengthen the ties that bind us. Most significantly, at the height of Operation Protective Edge, we issued a joint statement with the Muslim Council of Britain, condemning anti-Semitism and calling for peace and unity amongst our communities and in Israel and Palestine.

At a time of heightened anxiety, to work with a Muslim community organization to make a joint statement was unprecedented and not without controversy. For most, however, the value of reaching out was understood, reflecting the reality of daily lives.

I believe that the challenge to us as a community – as peace returns, at least for now – is to ensure that the relationships we have built during the crisis are sustained and strengthened. Just as we call on others to stand with us, so we must stand with them. So we must support the Bahais in their fight for religious freedom in Iran; the Roma, for fuller equality both here and abroad; and the Yazidi people in Iraq, in their fight for life. To quote Hillel: 'If I am not for myself, who is for me? And if I am only for myself, what am I? And if not now, when?'

The challenge for Jews of living away from their co-religionists plays out in other ways. In 2013, the co-incidence of Rosh Hashanah with the first week of school led to a huge upturn in Jewish teachers being denied the time off necessary for religious observance. In 2014, the clash with the school year was less pronounced, but in 2015 the New Year will fall in the first fortnight back and we might once again expect Jewish teachers and other employees to face problems.

A key role of the Board is to work with Government, unions, employers and others to ensure an understanding of the significance of such festivals for observant Jews and to promote constructive solutions. In the past year the Board's work has yielded the issuing of new guidelines by the Equality and Human Rights Commission. As I look forward, we must build on this to ensure that Jews, and those of other faiths, are able to fulfil their religious obligations wherever they choose to live and work.

It is such issues that inspired the Board last year to establish an All Party Parliamentary Group on British Jews which has taken up concerns on behalf of the community, ranging from the impact of benefit changes on Charedi Jews to the rights to compensation for Holocaust survivors. The group's help and support seems set to be needed again as we explore the future of faith schools in the wake of the Trojan Horse scandal, which engulfed a handful of (ironically) secular Birmingham schools this summer.

These and other communal interests have come together to inform the Board's Jewish Manifesto, which sets out for politicians and policy makers the interests, concerns and aspirations of the UK's 300,000-strong Jewish community in the run up to the 2015 General Election. The Manifesto is divided into 14 sections including Religious Freedom and Observance, Israel and the Middle East, Education, and Health and Social Care. There is also a list of 'Ten Commitments' including, for example, the rights to eat kosher meat, circumcise our sons and educate our children in Jewish schools.

As I look forward to the year ahead, the Board will be encouraging individuals and local Jewish communities to take the Manifesto to candidates, and use it as the centrepiece of lobbying efforts, be it at hustings, in letters or in public debates.

We are approaching an election that could see the first Jewish-born Prime Minister since Disraeli, further gains for an anti-immigration party, or the re-election of a Prime Minister who has been a staunch ally of Israel throughout his time in office. Make no mistake: this is an election that will matter, whichever side you are on.

As I write, I am less than six months into one of the most

challenging roles of a professional life which has included running both my own business and the work of a number of Government departments as a Minister. No stranger to crisis management, I have taken a key role on COBRA, the cross government committee responsible for tackling the most significant public safety crises of the past decade.

The lesson I draw from these experiences is that one's effectiveness directly relates to the quality of the people around you. The greatest strength of the Board of Deputies is its democratic legitimacy, gleaned from the nearly 300 Deputies who give up their time voluntarily to represent the interests of their *shuls*, community groups, youth organizations and such like at the Board's meetings.

Some go further: serving as officers on our divisions dealing with defence, international affairs, community issues and finance and organization. Five go onto become Honorary Officers, representing the Jewish community at every level.

As 2015 will be an election year for the Board, we ask ourselves, who will lead the community into the future? Who will put themselves forward for election? And what will their vision be, in representing the whole community? The effectiveness of the Board will depend on the answer to such questions, as the bottom-line is that in a democracy decisions are made by those who turn up.

For me, even a year ago, I would have been amazed to have been told I would be bringing my experience, knowledge and skills into play by running our community's leading representative body, which I am proud to do.

So now I ask Jews from the most expected and most unexpected of places from Ilford and Ilfracombe, Southgate and Southport – will you turn up? Will you ensure that the Board continues to represent your interests, provides your voice and supports your community? Or will you stay on the sidelines, leave it to others, risking the chance that they, in turn, may be leaving it to you?

Gillian Merron is the Chief Executive of the Board of Deputies of British Jews.

To find out more about being involved with the Board of Deputies contact info@bod.org.uk or visit www.bod.org.uk.

Dina Brawer

WOMEN IN JEWISH LAW

The past few years have witnessed significant change in relation to women in Orthodox Judaism. While the drivers of this change are primarily in Israel and the USA, their effects are starting to be felt in Britain as well. It is no longer uncommon to hear Orthodox women reciting *Kaddish*, publicly chanting the *Megillah* on Purim or addressing a congregation from selective synagogue pulpits. In some *minyanim* (known as partnership *minyanim*) women are even called to the Torah or lead parts of the prayer service. While championed by some, these changes are contested by others. Both sides argue using Jewish sources and Jewish law; halacha. The question I want to address in this essay, and one that I am frequently asked is, if Jewish law is clear cut, why is there such a wide divergence of opinion and such controversy, around the question of women's roles within contemporary Orthodox Judaism?

To answer this question we need to do three things: (i) define the function and process of halacha (Jewish Law); (ii) distinguish between halacha and *Psak Din* (halachic ruling); and (iii) appreciate the influence of meta-halacha on the halachic process

The Function and Process of Halacha

Halacha comes from the Jewish root word *hlch*, which means to move. In other words halacha is a dynamic process and is not as cut and dry as many appear to believe. The dynamic of Jewish law is a constant dialectic between Jewish legal principles and real life situations.

Rabbi Daniel Sperber, Israel Prize laureate in Talmud and the world's expert in the development of halacha, compares the relationship between halachic principles and their contemporary application, to the evolution of a tree through the seasons of the year. While the external parts of tree; trunk, branches, and foliage go through radical changes, with every season all of these parts draw nourishment from the same set of roots. So while the tree undergoes routine superficial change its roots are a constant, unchanging source that determines the tree's specific characteristics. Even though external factors such as the climate, the quantity of rain and quality of the soil will determine how lush the foliage or how plentiful the fruit the tree will bear in any given year, the tree's essential character will not change. The external factors cannot cause it to bear a different type of fruit or sprout a differently shaped leaf. Jewish law similarly is in a constant state of change and adaptation, while at the same time its bedrock principles ensure the core element of continuity and stability. A vibrant halacha is always adapting, while at the same time remaining anchored to its foundational principles.

Distinction between Halacha and *Psak Din*

Halacha refers to a process, while *Psak Din* is the outcome of that process. This distinction can be illustrated by comparison with the methodology of medical diagnosis and treatment. Often, the diagnosis allows for a multiplicity of possible treatments. Before the physician decides on a course of treatment, he or she has to go through the process of examining the patient, gathering information about the symptoms and considering medical history, as well as the patient's psychological state, stamina and pain threshold. It is only through this process of diagnosis and personal consultation that the physician is able to reach a final decision regarding the best course of treatment for that particular patient. Likewise, each halachic question allows for multiple possibilities. The halachic decisor, known as a *Posek*, goes through a diagnostic process of information gathering, weighing circumstantial factors and halachic principles to arrive at the final ruling; the *Psak Din*. The *Psak Din* is the application of a single possibility out of many.

Meta-halachic Considerations

Meta-halacha refers to the non halachic considerations that influence the halachic process. Since a *Posek*'s considerations are by their very nature, subjective, the outcome will depend on the particular *Posek*'s wider point of view. In this sense halachic discussion making is not all that different from mid-twentieth century banking. In the 1950s bank managers considering loan applications would generally have first-hand knowledge of the applicant. Potential lender and borrower would have lived in the same community, possibly attended the same church or synagogue, their children were likely to attend the same school and their spouses often were engaged in the same charitable activities. In assessing the loan application the manager would factor in not just hard financial data, but crucially, his own subjective assessment based on firsthand knowledge of the applicant's character. In such circumstances a manager might decide to extend a loan even if, in terms of hard figures, the loan appeared risky, provided he felt the risk would be mitigated by the strength of the borrower's character.

However, as banks grew and expanded they began assessing credit applications with highly sophisticated but impersonal algorithms, to compute the risk factors and the probability of default. The loss of intimacy and empathy with the borrower meant that credit is now awarded applying the same clear-cut set of rules equally to all applicants. In this highly regulated mathematical process subjective factors that may lead to more comprehensive and accurate judgments are lost.

The true halachic process resembles mid-twentieth century banking with highly subjective decisions based on personal knowledge of particular individuals and their circumstances. The Talmud (B. Bava Batra 131a) makes this point abundantly clear when it states that in coming to a halachic ruling the decisor can only consider what 'his eyes behold', namely the particular subjective circumstances surrounding the case in question. In other words, no *Posek* can completely divorce their worldview from influencing their halachic decisions. This is apparent in the halachic literature of all great *Poskim* throughout the ages.

A halachic process that resembles twenty-first century algorithmic banking is an aberration of what halacha has always been.

These three elements, halacha as dialectic, halacha as process, and halacha as subjective, are clearly apparent in the current debate over the role of women in Orthodoxy. It is only through appreciating these dynamics that one can come to understand why, on this issue, there is such controversy and a multiplicity of views.

Case Study: Rabbinic Ordination for Women

As an example, let us examine the issue of women's rabbinic ordination. There are few areas in the debate over women's roles within Orthodoxy that are as hotly contested as the issue of female rabbis.

One of the leading opponents of women's ordination is Rabbi Hershel Shachter who is the senior Rosh Yeshivah at Yeshiva University in New York. His *Psak* (ruling) is unequivocal: a woman cannot receive ordination. The reasoning he uses to support this ruling is interesting. He argues that a rabbi's role is, by definition, an outward facing one, and that, as such, it contravenes the foundational Jewish value of modesty.[1] Aware that his argument logically points to the elimination of male rabbis as well, he is quick to point out that Jewish life cannot function without such roles and so, to the extent that it is necessary to have rabbis, the role should at least be restricted to men:

We too must therefore strive to be anonymous and maintain strict privacy. We know that Hashem did reveal Himself on rare occasions. This is known as *Gilui Shechinah*. So on occasions we are all called upon to do things in a demonstrative fashion and in a public forum. We need a *shaliach tzibur* (prayer leader) to lead us in *tefillah*; we need a rabbi. But even then we recommend that whenever possible, only the men should compromise on *tznius* (modesty) and take these public positions. Women are always encouraged to avoid compromising their privacy.

The late Sephardic Israeli Chief Rabbi Benzion Uziel (1880–1953), while not discussing the question of female rabbinic ordination, addresses the issue of women's modesty and argues in favour of greater female lay leadership roles in the synagogue.[2]

It is common sense that in any serious meeting and meaningful conversation there is no question of lack of modesty. And sitting in the proximity [of women] when involved in communal affairs, which is work of holiness, does not lead to lightheartedness (i.e. immodesty). 'For all Israel are holy people and her women are holy, and are not to be suspect of breach of modesty and morality' (Responsa Piskei Uziel Siman 44).

What we see from these two positions is a divergence of views regarding the interpretation of modesty in the contemporary world. Both rabbis argue from Jewish sources and yet they come to very different conclusions. While it must be emphasized that Rabbi Uziel does not address the specific question of women's ordination, it is abundantly clear that Rabbi Shachter's principal argument against it (based on modesty) is not one that would resonate with him.

So what causes two rabbis to take such divergent views? This is where meta-halacha comes into play and in this case it is about how the respective rabbis understand feminism.

Rabbi Schachter has consistently and publicly decried feminism as a foreign import and corrosive challenge to traditional Judaism.[3] He is unable to judge the issue of female ordination in a cultural vacuum. Rather the question is tangled up with the wider issue of feminism which he is anxious to keep at bay. Given this cultural bias he is naturally drawn to a particular source which he chooses to interpret in a particular way. Rabbi Uziel, on the other hand, appears to have little or no uneasiness about feminism. His understanding of the role of contemporary woman is far more open and encouraging. His choice and interpretation of sources reflects this worldview.

So aren't the rabbis just choosing the sources that best fit in with their biases? In a word, yes, but that in no way means that they are cynically manipulating the sources. Applying one's subjective view of reality to the vast array of traditional Jewish sources is precisely what the halachic process is all about. And it is also why there is such robust, and at time acrimonious, debate around the halachic interpretation of new realities such as feminism.

If halacha were an objective, algorithmic process, one could just design a computer program to compute the data entered and then spew out consistent rulings. In reality this is not how halacha operates, and its intensely subjective nature is the reason there is such a divergence of views.

So if that is the case, how does one know which halachic view to follow? That is where choosing a rabbi comes in to play. One ought to seek out a rabbi who not only is knowledgeable in halacha, but also understands and empathises with one's worldview. It is not just a matter of the question that the rabbi will have to consider, but also the questioner and his wider social and cultural perspective.

The debate around women's roles within Orthodox Judaism will continue to rage for some time, but that is not a bad thing. Debates are healthy and necessary for the development of halacha and Judaism. For those looking for neat, consistent, clear-cut answers this can be frustrating. But for those who appreciate the complexity, fluidity and subjectivity of the halachic process, the debate over women's roles is an exciting and invigorating one. Rather than silencing those who we disagree with, we should be giving voice to the full spectrum of halachic viewpoints so as to allow the individual Jew to follow a halachic path suitable and inspiring for her life's journey in the service of God.

Notes

1. Hershel Schachter, 'Women Rabbis?', *Hakirah, the Flatbush Journal of Jewish Law and Thought*, 11 (Spring 2011), pp.19–23. http://www.hakirah.org/Vol%2011%20Schachter.pdf.
2. Daniel Sperber, 'On Women in Rabbinic Leadership Positions', *Meorot, A Forum of Modern Orthodox Discourse*, 8 (September 2010), pp.1–12. http://wwwyctorah.org/component/option, com_docman/task,doc_view/gid,1393/.
3. Adam Fertziger, 'Feminism and Heresy: The Construction of a Jewish Metanarrative', *Journal of the American Academy of Religion* (Berman Jewish Policy Archive), 77, no.3 (September 2009), pp.494–546. http://www.bjpa.org/Publications/details.cfm?PublicationID=4807.

Dina Brawer is studying for rabbinical ordination at Yeshivat Maharat, New York and represents the Jewish Orthodox Feminist Alliance (JOFA) in the UK.

Hugo Bieber

UK/ISRAEL TRADE

Introduction

Over the last 66 years, Israel has become a true global success story. Geographically, Israel is a similar size to Wales, with a population of around eight million. Over the decades, Israel's population has grown through waves of immigration from around the world. One group of immigrants in particular has made a significant impact on the transition of the Israeli economy from agriculture to technology – the mass influx of immigrants from the former Soviet Union in the early 1990s. Highly skilled mathematicians and scientists have helped propel Israel forward at an exceptionally fast pace.

Such is Israel's technological prowess that many consider it to be the Silicon Valley for the rest of the world. Israel is also widely known as the 'Start-up Nation', having the second highest concentration of start-ups after Silicon Valley. A unique combination of a highly qualified technology workforce (40 per cent are educated to Masters or PhD level) and military service have spawned tremendous accomplishments for Israel in the global business world. In 2013, global technology giants Apple, Facebook and Google all made acquisitions of hundreds of millions of dollars for Israeli companies. In addition, many multinational companies have Research & Development Centres in Israel.

Israeli Economy

The Israeli economy has been described as having gone from Oranges to Apples in reference to the transition from an agricultural to technology-based economy. This was reflected in Israel's entry into the OECD in 2010, backed by solid economic growth. Indeed, Israel's GDP per capita grew from $30,389 in 2010 to $36,151 in 2013. Since the 1970s, Israel has seen a tremendous growth in GDP and, despite regional tensions, continues to show growth. Such is the resilience of the Israeli economy that when global financial markets were in turmoil in 2008–09, Israel was one of only two countries to show positive growth. This can be in part attributed to the international nature of Israeli businesses.

FIGURE 1. GDP PER CAPITA (CURRENT US$)

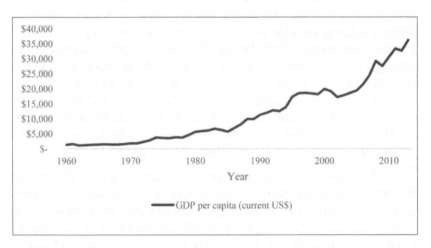

Source: World Bank Data

In 2010, Israel was invited to join The Organisation for Economic Co-operation and Development (OECD). This legitimised Israel's status as an advanced and developed country. Membership of the OECD helped boost Israel's international economic standing and serves as a solid economic benchmark to attract inward investment.

In some areas, Israel is near the top of the OECD rankings. These include Gross Domestic Spending on R&D (second after South Korea) and spending on education and healthcare. However, education standards are ranked towards the bottom of OECD countries. Levels of inequality and poverty, particularly amongst the ultra-orthodox and Israeli-Arab communities, as well as average wages, also see Israel placed towards the bottom of the OECD league tables.

UK Trade Relations

Trade relations between the UK and Israel are strong and Israel is the UK's largest trading partner in the Near East and North Africa. From an Israeli perspective, the UK is Israel's second largest trading partner, with 8.6 per cent of total Israeli exports going to the UK.

One of Israel's most significant exports to the UK is pharmaceuticals, and generic drug supplier Teva accounts for close to a third of Israel's total exports to the UK. Teva is the largest supplier of medicines to the NHS, shipping over 300 million individual packets of medicine to the UK in 2013 and employing 1,300 people across the country.

There is a steady stream of Israeli companies floating on both NASDAQ and on the London Stock Exchange. Currently, there are 20 Israeli companies listed in London, and as of the end of September 2014, six Israeli companies had floated in London in 2014: Crossrider (28 September), Matomy Media (11 July), Marimedia Ltd (28 May), Nomad Holdings Ltd and Bagir Group Ltd (both 15 April), and XL-Media (21 March).

Start-up Nation

Israeli Government funding has played a significant role in the incubation of companies. In 1993, the Government launched the

Yozma programme, which was aimed at stimulating venture capital investment and attracting foreign investment in Israeli companies. The Office of the Chief Scientist (OCS) is part of the Ministry of Economy and tasked with the execution of government policy for support of industrial R&D.

The goal of the OCS is to assist in the development of technology in Israel; this is a means of fostering economic growth and encouraging technological innovation and entrepreneurship. It also aims to leverage Israel's scientific potential, enhancing the knowledge base of industry in Israel, stimulating high value-added R&D and encouraging R&D collaboration both nationally and internationally. A variety of on-going support programmes, developed and offered by the OCS, play a major role in enabling Israel to be a key centre for high tech entrepreneurship.

One of the characteristics of Israel as a start-up nation is the acceptance of failure. In many countries, failed entrepreneurs are often tarnished. Israelis wear a badge of failure with pride, and tend to use the experience of a failed start-up to learn their lessons the second time around. In an interview with the *Financial Times* in February 2014, Avi Hasson, Israel's Chief Scientist, described a company backed by the Office of the Chief Scientist that failed. However, over 30 new start-ups emerged from the failed company.

There is now a sense of maturity in the Israeli start-up eco system, with management often onto their second or third company. An emerging trend sees entrepreneurs re-investing their exit proceeds, both within the Israeli start-up ecosystem as angel investors, and also often using the exit proceeds to start another business.

Particularly given that management of many Israeli companies is now second or even third generation, the need for an early exit is significantly lessened. Consequently, we are starting to see Israeli companies continue to grow into valuations well over $100m. A number of companies have chosen to float in New York or sometimes London, rather than sell to what have generally been large American corporate buyers. In addition, 2014 has seen both Chinese and

Japanese companies start to make large acquisitions of Israeli companies. Chinese food and beverage manufacturing company, Bright Food, is finalising its acquisition of a 56 per cent stake in Israeli dairy company Tnuva from the UK's Apax Partners at a valuation of around $2.6bn. Japanese online retailer, Rakuten, bought Israeli internet messaging and calling service Viber for $900m in February 2014.

Oil and Gas

Since Israel's inception, it has been dependant on external sources for oil and gas. However, this is changing with the discovery and development of offshore gas field finds in recent years.

The gas finds have the potential to transform Israel into an energy exporter, and make Israel energy independent. The Israel Electric Corporation started the process of converting coal and diesel fired power stations to natural gas in 2004. It plans by 2015 to have 64 per cent of Israeli electricity generated by natural gas. Export of natural gas has been approved by the Knesset. In April 2013, the creation of a Sovereign Wealth Fund was also approved by the Knesset, to reinvest the proceeds from the export of gas for the long-term.

In 2009, following exploratory drilling, the Tamar gas field, situated 50 miles west of Haifa was officially discovered. Gas production from the field started in March 2013. The field is estimated to hold 9 trillion cubic feet of natural gas and is expected to contribute 1 per cent to Israel's gross domestic product, according to the Bank of Israel. This improved the nation's current account balance by up to $3bn in 2013.

In 2010, Israel discovered the Leviathan field, the world's largest deepwater natural gas find in the previous decade. The Leviathan field is estimated to cover approximately 125 square miles (325 square kilometres) and total gross mean resources discovered are estimated to be approximately 22 trillion cubic feet of natural gas. Israel's Delek Drilling and Avner Oil Exploration own 45 per cent; US company Noble Energy owns 40 per cent and another Israeli company, Ratio Exploration, has a 15 per cent stake. Production is expected to begin in 2017.

FIGURE 2. EASTERN MEDITERRANEAN OIL AND GAS FIELDS

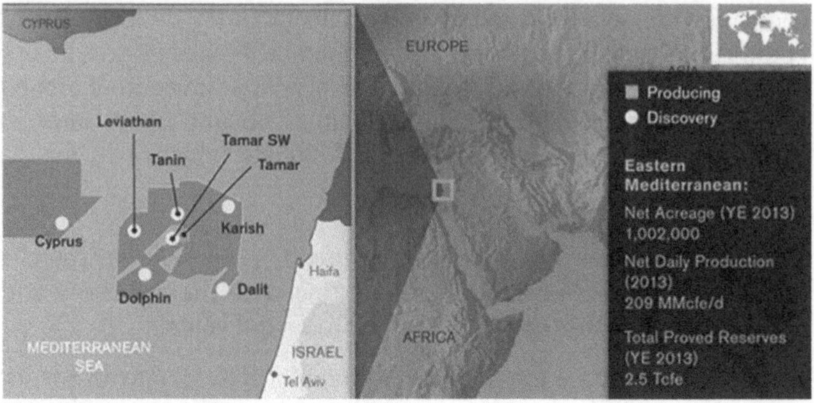

Source: Noble Energy

In September 2014, a deal was announced to sell up to $15bn of natural gas over the next 15 years from the Leviathan field to Jordan. A further preliminary agreement was signed with British oil and gas company BG Group to export gas from Leviathan to BG's liquefied natural gas (LNG) plant in Idku, Egypt. This would see 7bn cubic meters per year supplied for 15 years via an underwater pipeline, a deal worth an estimated $30bn.

Concentration Law

In December 2013, the Knesset passed landmark legislation aimed at reducing the concentration of business ownership in the Israeli economy. These structural reforms created opportunities for non-Israeli investors as, at the time the law was passed, Israel's ten largest concerns controlled over 40 per cent of the equity of Israel's public markets. The passing of the law placed a six-year time frame on the largest concerns to sell-down their holdings.

From a British perspective, all the natural local buyers in Israel would be precluded from purchasing assets put up for sale due to the Concentration Law. As a result a real opportunity exists for foreign entities to invest in what are often solid Israeli businesses, serving either a local or international market.

In March 2014, UK ISRAEL BUSINESS created the Israel Private Equity Opportunity Summit, bringing together UK Private Equity funds to discuss the challenges and practicalities of operating in Israel. Sponsored by Linklaters, KPMG and leading Israeli law firm Herzog Fox & Neeman, with the British Venture Capital Association (BVCA) as an event partner, the event was chaired by Sir Trevor Chinn, Senior Advisor to private equity fund CVC. Dan Gillerman, Senior Advisor to the Blackstone Group, and Sir Ronald Cohen, founder of Apax Partners, delivered keynote speeches.

Around 120 British investors from private equity funds and family offices, each with an ability to invest at least $20 million into a deal, attended the event. They were thus able to understand more about the Israeli economy and potential opportunities arising through the passing of the law. Seasoned investors in Israel, including the Chief Investment Officer of Apax Partners, Nico Hansen, shared their experiences of operating in Israel.

For UK private equity investors looking at Israel, there is the ability to tap into a strong and growing local market. Israel offers a stable economy with strong returns. In addition, there are a number of Israeli companies with a strong international presence making them also attractive to private equity investors.

UK Israel Bilateral Success Stories

We can highlight a number of cross-industry case studies that show-case collaborations between UK and Israeli companies as well as Israeli companies that have successfully entered the UK market.

Arup

Towards the beginning of 2014, Israel's national water company, Mekorot, signed a memorandum of understanding with British infra-structural design firm Arup. The companies agreed to jointly facilitate research and development in the fields of water and wastewater treatment, which will see Israeli technologies being implemented globally by Arup. This memorandum of understanding (MoU) was facilitated by the UK Israel Tech Hub, based in the British Embassy in Tel Aviv.

Mapal Green

Israeli company Mapal Green Energy has a number of UK utility companies as clients. Mapal has developed an innovative solution, using bubble aeration technology, for waste water treatment systems. The Mapal system uses bubbles – water infused with air – to clean water as part of aeration systems, and they are considered very effective in removing pollutants and separating sludge from water.

In May 2013, Mapal signed its first UK client, Anglian Water Services. In February 2014, Mapal launched a trial with Thames Water for an innovative energy-saving pilot scheme at its Chesham sewage works. This will cut the cost of treating wastewater in older biological reactors by up to 50 per cent.

June 2014 saw UK-based United Utilities select Mapal's floating fine bubble aeration (FFBA) technology, making it the largest FFBA installation so far in the UK.

Netafim

Netafim was founded in 1965 at Kibbutz Hatzerim in Israel. Netafim is the global leader in drip and micro-irrigation systems for a sustainable future. Since 2011, Netafim has been owned by UK-based investment company Permira, who acquired the 61 per cent stake owned by the three founding kibbutzim – Hatzerim, Magal and Yiftah.

AposTherapy

AposTherapy is an innovative Israeli company offering a non-surgical and drug-free programme for knee and back pain. AposTherapy is growing into a global business, and has a presence in a number of cities across the UK. In March 2014, AposTherapy announced an investment of 10m in the UK in the next three years by opening clinics and creating hundreds of jobs. This is in addition to the 11m it has already invested.

GSK

In February 2014, GlaxoSmithKline (GSK) signed a joint drug development agreement with Israeli company BioRap Technologies Ltd.

This aims to commercialise the Israeli company's molecule for the treatment of immune-system related diseases.

Teva Pharmaceuticals

Teva pharmaceuticals is a global leader in generic pharmaceuticals. Headquartered in Israel, Teva is the world's largest generic drug maker. In September 2013, Teva signed a multi-project alliance agreement with UK charity Cancer Research's technology arm, Cancer Research Technology Ltd, to research and develop first-in-class cancer drugs. These modulate DNA damage and repair response processes in cancer cells.

In March 2014, Teva agreed to invest $20 million in clinical trials. This is in collaboration with the Office for Clinical Research Infrastructure at the UK National Health Service's National Institute for Health Research.

Conclusion

Ties between the UK and Israel have always been strong. A significant strengthening in business ties between the two nations came about, however, with the appointment of British Ambassador to Israel, Matthew Gould, CMG, MBE in September 2010.

In October 2011, Ambassador Gould founded the UK-Israel Tech Hub, a government-led initiative. This aims to help foster economic growth in both countries by partnering British companies with the best of Israeli innovation. The goal is to create partnerships in which British companies help Israeli innovation go global, and Israeli innovation gives British companies a global competitive edge. This initiative has helped further strengthen business ties.

Israelis commonly look towards the US as their primary marketplace, due both to the population size of the USA and the large pool of capital available for investment. Even so, companies are starting to look more at the UK. For Israeli technology businesses, the UK provides a prime market of technology-savvy consumers and can be utilised as a good testing ground for Israeli companies looking to expand into the US. Further, the UK can serve as an entry point to

Europe for Israeli businesses. The closer flying time and time difference make doing business between the two countries easier than between the US and Israel.

Across all manner of industries, trade between the two countries continues to flourish, to the benefit of both nations. As the central port of call for all trade between the UK and Israel, UK ISRAEL BUSINESS helps facilitate greater connections between businesses in both the UK and Israel. Further, working with both large and small companies, we seek to inform both British and Israeli companies about the opportunities in both countries.

Our events bring together leading business people from both the UK and Israel. Every year we have a number of high-profile speakers at our events, including former prime ministers, government ministers from both countries, ambassadors, FTSE 100 chairmen and CEOs, and industry experts.

As a member-led organisation, UK ISRAEL BUSINESS offers a comprehensive range of services. These include specialist knowledge, networking opportunities, platforms to exchange ideas and share information, as well as professional contacts. Our bespoke market intelligence reports provide comprehensive sector research and analysis, and outline emerging business trends in the UK and Israel.

Hugo Bieber is Chief Executive of UK ISRAEL BUSINESS, the bilateral chamber of commerce between the UK and Israel. UK ISRAEL BUSINESS provides a central port of call for all issues relating to UK and Israel business, trade, industry and investment activities.

For more information regarding UK ISRAEL BUSINESS please contact:

UK ISRAEL BUSINESS
Email: info@ukisraelbusiness.co.uk
Website: www.ukisraelbusiness.co.uk
Phone: 020 3510 0002

Simon Morris

25 YEARS OF JEWISH CARE

This year marks the 25th anniversary of the community's largest social welfare charity, Jewish Care. Any milestone anniversary is an opportunity for the celebration of achievement as well as a fitting moment for reflection.

Jewish Care is an organization born out of a bold partnership, developed thanks to the foresight of leaders in our community 25 years ago. These communal leaders were able to set aside their own personal position in the community and place their current and future clients at the centre of their decision making.

Over the past 25 years Jewish Care has evolved, thanks to subsequent partnerships, into the organization it is today. Our community is, however, changing; social care is changing and with that, we as an organization need to ensure we not only meet today's needs but plan for the future.

In this article I want to look at the formation of our 25-year-old partnership and the growth and changes in Jewish Care since its inception. I will look at the importance of the symbiotic partnership Jewish Care has with the community and the impact this partnership has on our work.

Over 150 Years of History

Established in 1859, The Board of Guardians, which later became known as the Jewish Welfare Board, was a ground-breaking umbrella organization established by communal leaders to enable the provision of social care for those most in need.

At the time, the Jewish community of between 25,000–30,000 was mainly composed of poor immigrants who had fled persecution, leaving their homeland with very little.

It wasn't only the community which established a range of charitable organizations; the entire country had seen a huge growth in charities. Generally charities were established as single cause organizations; for example those serving the poor, blind people, the aged or orphans. Each had their own eligibility criteria and each operated independently of the next.

The Jewish Board of Guardians was born out of the need to provide coordination and an amalgamation of the numerous charitable organizations and 'societies' that had been developed over two centuries to provide support; from food and clothing to health and social care for young and old. The Board's task was to 'carry out case enquiries, administer temporary relief and to direct applications to the appropriate agency for more permanent help; and it would seek to coordinate and promote the amalgamation of the existing agencies'.

Creating a coordinating body with principles based on new accountability was a bold approach. The board was established on the principles of investigation into an individual's circumstances, adequate recording and promptitude (the provision of immediate relief). To us today this may seem like common sense, but over 150 years ago this was a big shift, a professionalization in the handling of relief.

From its very outset, the Board was established to try and reduce overlapping, and 'streamline' the community's charitable organizations, to ensure those in need had access to the right support, in a fair and equal way. With high levels of poverty, funds into communal organizations were limited and the more coordinated, the most cost effective the community could be.

Organizations such as the Jewish Blind Society, founded in 1819 as the Institution for the Relief of the Indigent Blind of the Jewish Persuasion, continued to provide specialized support for individuals in the community. These individuals would often benefit from referrals from the Board as it more often than not became the first port of call.

What strikes me as fascinating, particularly for its time, was the Board's ability, often through adversity, to change and adapt. As the community changed, the Board evolved to ensure it could meet the current and future needs of the community of the time. We have a lot to thank those early pioneers for, and a lot to learn from them too.

The Formation of Jewish Care

By the 1980s both the community and the voluntary sector had changed dramatically. The community was over ten times larger than in the previous century, yet more established. The voluntary sector had evolved, professionalized and become a vital part of the fabric of British society. Despite this, mergers or partnerships in the sector were few and far between. The formation of Jewish Care was one of the first major mergers of its time, not only in the Jewish community but in the wider voluntary sector.

The Board of Guardians, now known as the Jewish Welfare Board, and the Jewish Blind Society, had for some time been working in partnership, notably through the creation of the Sobell Day Centre in Golders Green.

The Jewish Welfare Board was an organization inundated with clients and struggling due to lack of funding. The Jewish Blind Society was a more niche charitable organization, with a substantially smaller client base, yet a large donor base (donors seemed to be more attracted to supporting blind people than the general ageing community). The difference in provision of service was becoming increasingly blurred. As one former chief executive said: 'One organization supported Jewish blind old people, the other Jewish old blind people'.

It was a change in leadership, both professional and lay leaders, that prompted merger discussions, helped by pressure from volunteers who were increasingly questioning the difference between the two organizations and the benefit of partnership, as already demonstrated at the Sobell Centre.

By the mid 1980s discussions about potential opportunities for partnership had begun. Whilst some opposed the idea, on the whole there was agreement that this was a sensible approach. It was a way forward to improve social care services for the community. As I've said, this decision was only possible because both professionals and lay leaders were able to set aside their own personal positions and put the best interests of the community at the centre of their decision making.

Jewish Care was formed on 1 January 1990 from an amalgamation of the Jewish Welfare Board and the Jewish Blind Society. Its objects were set out as 'the relief of persons of the Jewish faith (wherever resident but in particular those residing in the United Kingdom) who are in need, or suffering sickness, hardship or distress, or who suffer visual or other physical or mental impairment resulting in disability or handicap', continuing the work of the three principal organizations it succeeded (The Jewish Welfare Board, the Jewish Blind Society and the Jewish Association for the Protection of Girls, Women and Children).

Jewish Care: The Early Years

Melvyn Carlowe, former chief executive of the Jewish Welfare Board, was appointed as Jewish Care's first chief executive, supported by Tony Krais, former chief of the Jewish Blind Society. Jeffrey Greenwood, former chair of the Jewish Welfare Board was the first chairman of Jewish Care and it was agreed that his first term would be followed by the appointment of former Jewish Blind Society chair, David Lewis.

In its first year, Jewish Care introduced six new services for the community, funded by overhead reductions and a general streamlining of resources.

Within the first month of the organization's formation, Jewish Care was approached by two communal organizations. The first, Waverly Manor (Friends of the London Jewish Hospital), a care home for older people, came to Jewish Care in need of saving. The organization had been declared bankrupt and unless it could find a solution quickly, it faced deregistration that would lead to the 60 residents losing their home. Unsure how the finances would work out, Jewish Care felt an immediate obligation to step in and agreed to take over the home.

The day Jewish Care took over the home, still unsure of how it would finance it, a representative of a charitable foundation approached the organization looking for 'somewhere to support'. Melvyn Carlowe described that day as 'the closest he ever got to experiencing a miracle or winning the lottery'.

In that same year Jewish Care was approached by the Jewish Home & Hospital for Incurables at Tottenham. Another partnership was formed. From the sale of the run down unsuitable home and generous support from the community, Jewish Care was able to relocate the home to modern purpose-built premises in Friern Barnet. The new home was named Lady Sarah Cohen House.

Most organizations which approached Jewish Care in those early years were older charitable organizations in need of modernization, or whose primary purpose was outdated. Not surprisingly, many of them were also strapped for cash, struggling to make ends meet. At times the Jewish Care Board struggled with the challenges of merging these organizations into the relatively new organization. It wasn't always easy and lessons were learnt along the way but in the main, communal leaders, clients, donors, staff and the wider community were supportive, recognising the need for consolidation and modernisation. Subsequent mergers included: Food for the Jewish Poor (Jewish Soup Kitchen) in the East End; the Brighton and Hove

Jewish Home – now Hyman Fine House; Stepney Jewish (B'nai Brith) Clubs and Settlements; and The British Tay-Sachs Foundation.

For many years the Jewish Welfare Board had run a day centre in Sinclair House, the Redbridge Jewish Community Centre, and it was a longstanding and successful partnership. Pressure from key funders in the community, notably Alan Sugar, led to the centre joining the Jewish Care family and the subsequent expansion of Jewish Care services in the area.

During the years, there were some who spoke out in opposition of partnerships and mergers with Jewish Care, seeing a merger as a loss of identity, an eradication of deep-rooted history. Jewish Care was seen as the Goliath verses the David, the small local organization.

The Difference between a Merger and a Partnership

It is important to explain the difference between a merger and a partnership, the reasons for which will become clearer later.

Jewish Care was formed from a merger, a formal joining of two organizations which merged to become one. It was a merger born from a unique and successful partnership. However, the loss of identify of both organizations and a coming together on equal terms was, in my view, a classic example of a merger.

The majority of partnerships Jewish Care embarked upon in the early years resulted in a merger. These organizations subsequently become part of Jewish Care. They didn't retain their own board of trustees, funding, or often their identity. Each merger was structured through a successful partnership between lay leaders and professional staff. Each was unique, taking into careful consideration the history and current situation of the organization. But what every single one had in common was the desire to place the clients at the forefront, to improve or increase service provision for clients. Money, or the lack of it, was of course often a motivator.

The need to coordinate and amalgamate was quite possibly history repeating itself. The Jewish community was again organizing itself in response to changes in our demographic and need.

Jewish Care Today

As Jewish Care has evolved and changed, so too have the needs of the community. As we live longer, people's care needs are more complex. The growing numbers of people living with dementia is, and will continue to be, the single biggest social care challenge for the community. The impact of changes on carers, spouses, children and even grandchildren is immense. Jewish Care supports more people now than ever before. Over 7,000 people use our services each week.

With a reduction of government funding, in real terms, into social care, and increasing pressure on the already cracking system, we in the Jewish community are lucky to have our own social care system. Over the last decade the squeeze on local authorities across the UK has seen the widespread closure of day centres and other lifelines for older and vulnerable people. Whilst the UK has a funded health system for all, it's a very different story when it comes to social care. That is why I often joke that being old and Jewish does have its advantages – something I am constantly reminded of when I talk to other providers in the social care sector. Our community, from its early arrival into this country, has looked after itself and continues to do so.

We are a community that has organized itself to ensure we are ahead of the game, planning for the future, thinking about our resources and the needs of the community. We have evolved and changed. We have recognised the need for and embraced change, seeing it as a positive step forward. If it wasn't for our ancestors' boldness in recognising and embracing change I don't think we would have a community support system like we have today.

In the same vein, Jewish Care would not be here today without the partnership it has with its 3,000 volunteers. The community is responsible for developing, leading and shaping its social care charity. Some 25 years since its inception, the relationship between Jewish Care and the community is deep-rooted, a symbiotic relationship with an understanding that we both need each other. At different stages in their lives, members from across the community turn to Jewish Care for support. In return, Jewish Care relies on the community to support its services. Its work wouldn't be possible without its volunteers and the partnership they have with professional staff, and of course its donors, from those who put a few pennies in a charity box through to its prominent and committed Patrons.

There have been no mergers since 1997 but partnerships of a new nature have emerged. The Otto Schiff Housing Association owned and managed care homes and supported housing projects for the community. Whilst their assets were in prime locations, some of their resources were in need of modernization. Their Chairman, Ashley Mitchell, could see a range of organizations who were doing similar work with specific areas of expertise. He took a bold approach and Otto Schiff embarked on a series of partnerships across the community, handing over responsibility of the development and management to specialist organizations, such as Jewish Care.

Our latest partnership, is again, an altogether different model from anything we have embarked upon in the past. In 2013 Jewish Care entered into an operating agreement with JAMI (Jewish Mental Health Organization). Both Jewish Care and JAMI were providing mental health support services to people living in the community. The two entered into a partnership agreement designed to reduce the duplication of this work whilst also creating an opportunity to have a single strategy to meet the growing needs of mental health services. The partnership saw Jewish Care staff working in community-based mental health projects, becoming part of the JAMI team and JAMI taking on the responsibility for running all community-based mental health services.

JAMI has retained its own identity, senior leadership team, management of finances and is operating as a subsidiary of Jewish Care.

A Rebirth of the Growth of Communal Organizations

Whilst the community has seen consolidation, almost in tandem came the emergence of new organizations responding to new need, different needs, from Israel-focused charities through to the huge new infrastructures developed to meet the need for Jewish education and our thirst for cultural activity. We have more communal buildings than ever before.

The consequence of this growth in infrastructure is that we as a community have more to support.

The Future

The community is changing; it is more fragmented than ever before. The Charedi community continues to grow both in size and distance from the rest of UK Jewry. Take away the Charedi community and synagogue attendance is in decline.

A report published last year by the Institute for Jewish Policy Research found unsurprisingly that increasing numbers of young secular Jews don't have the affinity with Jewish charities that their parents' or grandparents' generations had. This will impact on our future leadership and ability to secure funding from within the community, both of which are a lifeline to organizations working across the community.

Whilst we can celebrate partnerships that have brought improved services and efficiency to the community, there is a long way to go if we are to be a community that can sustain its infrastructure as we look to the future.

We at Jewish Care are continuing to explore partnership opportunities with the recognition that the community needs them. Over the past ten years we have been engaging the Charedi community in East London in particular to encourage them to share resources. They do engage to a point but we are realistic about how limited these partnerships are.

As a community we need to look back at our history and specifically take note of the changes that took place in the nineteenth century as a result of the emergence of an unsustainable community structure. We need to recognize the impact of the work of our forefathers who created the Board of Guardians. We need to commend those who took the bold move to create Jewish Care from two organizations with deep roots in the community and we need to celebrate the subsequent mergers that have taken place.

But we also need to recognize there is so much more to be done. I believe that as a community we need to encourage more partnerships, to ensure we are providing quality services across the community for another 150 years. I foresee these being a hybrid of past mergers and partnerships that allow organizations to maintain their own identity whilst providing a more strategic and cost-effective approach to planning and delivering services for the community.

The partnership model we have developed with JAMI is a shining example of how this could work. The JAMI partnership shows the benefits of an effective partnership, a partnership which enables an organization with its own culture, history and expertise to retain the identity of its organization, its leadership team, and do what it does best.

We as a community need to have our own Pentland or Unilever model. One central organization, sharing back office resources, focused on a coherent strategic approach to the market place. An organization that through the development of successful partnerships can meet the current and future welfare needs of the Jewish community. It won't be easy, but just like our forefathers did, we need to put differences aside and place the community at our core.

Simon Morris is the Chief Executive of Jewish Care

Rabbi Reuben Livingstone LLM CF (Major)

THE FIRST WORLD WAR CENTENARY: THE JEWISH MILITARY CONTRIBURTION

The centenary commemoration of the First World War marks not only an important milestone in modern history. It was also the tumultuous beginning of a century that would change the face of Europe and the world. From a Jewish perspective, the Great War – the so called 'war to end all wars' – would also sow the seeds of the Holocaust and of the utter upheaval of Jewish life on the Continent. But there is another and more optimistic parallel; the British Jewish story – that of proud service and sacrifice for King and Country, and of exemplary commitment and citizenship.

The number of identified Jews who served during the First World War, based on British military records, was around 50,000. But then, as now, it was not entirely uncommon to be reticent in declaring one's Jewish identity. Many Jews also changed their names for fear of anti-Semitism in the ranks. These factors mean that the actual number was likely to have been higher.

Five Jewish soldiers won the Victoria Cross awarded for valour 'in the face of the enemy'. The courage shown by Sergeant Issy Smith (Shmulevitch), Captain Robert Gee, Lieutenant Frank Alexander de Pass, Private Jack White (Weiss), and Lance Corporal Leonard Maurice Keysor still resonates in the annals of Army history. No less than 50 Jewish soldiers received the Distinguished Service Order.

In addition, Jews formed their own unit, the Zion Mule Corps, fighting at Gallipoli and the Dardanelles in 1915. The Zion Mule Corps and the Jewish Legion went on to fight with distinction in Palestine. In 1918, three Jewish units, the 38th, 39th and 40th battalions of the Royal Fusiliers known as the Jewish Legion fought under General Sir Edmund Allenby in Palestine. These unique regiments were disbanded after the First World War.

Many Eastern European Jews served in the Pioneer Corps, working as labourers on the infamous trenches. The number of such foreign Jews in the Labour Corps is estimated (from the British Jewry Book of Honour) at over 4,600, including those who served in the Middlesex Alien Companies and the Egyptian Labour Corps.

Jews, in fact, have a very long and distinguished tradition of military service that goes back to the Torah itself, and continues prominently in the State of Israel. But even our history in the British Forces goes back over 300 years. A common European anti-Semitic fabrication was to accuse Jews of being unwilling to join the military – but the facts tell a different story. During the First World War, a census instituted by the German Military High Command known as Judenzahlung (literally 'Jew-count') was carried out to substantiate claims that Jews were under-represented in the German military and thus unpatriotic. Though suppressed and never publicized, the results roundly disproved the claims.

The Jewish authorities who had conducted a parallel census and found the statistics of Jewish involvement to be very high, were denied access to the official archives. Remarkably, thousands of men of Jewish descent and hundreds of what the Nazis called 'full Jews', served in the German military in the Second World War with Hitler's knowledge and approval. Cambridge University researcher Bryan Rigg has traced the Jewish ancestry of more than 1,200 of Hitler's soldiers, including two field marshals and 15 generals (two full generals, eight lieutenant generals, five major generals ('men commanding up to 100,000 troops'). In approximately 20 cases, Jewish soldiers in the Nazi army were awarded Germany's highest military honour, the Knight's Cross.

Professor Derek Penslar of St Anne's College, Oxford and the University of Toronto, has done extensive research into Jewish military service in the nineteenth century. He notes that, based on archives, it can be seen that in France, Austro-Hungary, Italy, and several other countries during the Victorian era, 4–18% of military officers were Jewish; hugely more than the proportion of Jews in the wider populations. In Russia, under different conditions, the same situation prevailed. This was partly because a military career offered Jews greater equality of opportunity – especially in technical areas such as engineering, artillery and logistics – where they excelled. It also gave them the means to shine as men and put to rights the noxious stereotype of the passive Jew.

In the late nineteenth century the famous Rabbi Israel Meir Kagan of Radin, known as the Chofetz Chaim, wrote a guidebook for Jewish soldiers called *Machane Yisrael*. It is highly significant that, despite offering special leniencies for serving personnel, nowhere in the work does he say that Jews should not serve or that fighting is prohibited. On the contrary, the author reaches out to these men and attempts to recognize their importance and integrate them into the traditional Jewish world.

Later, during the Second World War, out of a Jewish population in Britain estimated at only 400,000, approximately 65,000 Jewish men and women served in all three services of the British Armed Forces. As in the First World War, British Jews bore more than their full share of the War effort in operations around the globe – on sea, land and in the air – and won three Victoria Crosses. They continued to do so in later conflicts including Malaya, Kenya, Korea, Northern Ireland, the Falklands, Iraq and Afghanistan.

In the same way, American Jews served in disproportion to their numbers: nearly 250,000 in the First World War and well over 400,000 in the Second World War. The very same phenomenon was true in the Soviet Red Army.

Remarkably, nearly 200,000 Polish Jews fought against Nazi Germany during the Second World War in the ranks of the Polish Armies – on Polish soil and in exile. Despite this tremendous contribution to the war effort, the official Polish historical bibliography of the Second World War shamefully ignores this contribution (particularly as there were nearly 5,000 Jewish officers).

Jewish military chaplaincy in the British Armed Forces, under the authority of the Chief Rabbi, has been the sustaining spiritual force behind Jewish service for nearly 120 years. Its unique history was very much forged out of the experience of the First World War when Jewish Chaplains first formed part of the British Army on active service.

Jews were officially recognised in the British Armed Forces as a distinct religious body from 1889. Before that the Visitation Committee of the United Synagogue had been responsible for the religious and spiritual welfare of Jews in public institutions. It decided to extend the scope of its activities to serving members of the Forces and applied to the War Office for the formal appointment of a Jewish Chaplain. This request was granted in 1892 and the Reverend Francis L. Cohen, Minister of the Borough Synagogue in London, was appointed as the first Jewish Chaplain to HM Forces.

In 1897 Rev. Cohen obtained the sanction of the British Admiralty and the War Office for a special annual service for Jewish men in the Forces. Every year the event was attended by important representatives of the Fighting Services, including the Chaplain General and senior members of the Army Chaplains Department. The Honorary Officers of the United Synagogue also attended. In those days the order for this parade was Dress as for Church Parade, i.e. Helmet and Side-Arms. Every unit turned out in Full Dress, filling the synagogue with varied coloured uniforms of all types, with all kinds of head-dress including bearskins, busbies, shakos and helmets.

The officers were accommodated in front of the Ark, and the rank and file in the main ground floor of the building. The public, which included friends and family of those present, occupied the gallery. For all civilians, admission was by ticket only. The whole parade would form up under the supervision of a prominent senior officer and, headed by a Regimental Band, would march ceremoniously into synagogue.

Personnel included representatives of the Royal Navy, Royal Marines, Army, Militia, Army Cadets, Volunteers, Yeomanry, British Red Cross and St John Ambulance Detachments; as well as veterans of all the campaigns in India, Egypt, Africa and Canada. The Metropolitan Police were also represented.

Encouraged by the Honorary Officers of the United Synagogue this Parade became an annual event and, for some years, was commanded by Colonel David de Lara Cohen, VD. The adjutant was one of his regimental officers, Major Gordon Kennard, and the RSM was Sergeant-Instructor J.H. Levy of the Scots Guards (said, at one time, to have 'the loudest word of command in the Brigade of Guards'), the latter becoming Lieutenant Colonel, with DSO and OBE – having been mentioned in despatches seven times. This august event was the precursor to what has become the annual Association of Jewish Ex-Servicemen Parade at the Cenotaph.

When Rev. Cohen was called to become Chief Rabbi of Sydney, Australia in 1904, he was succeeded by a remarkable man – Reverend Michael Adler, Minister of the Hammersmith, and later the Central Synagogues. After the War Reverend Arthur Barnett CF, wrote of Michael Adler:

At the outbreak of the First World War he was the only Jewish Chaplain to have held His Majesty's Commission in the Army. He was faced now with the tremendous task of organizing an adequate Jewish Chaplaincy for work in the field as well as at home. The peculiar problems of the Jewish Serviceman scattered in almost every army unit were well nigh insurmountable.

In addition, the War Office was at a loss to know what to do with a Jewish Chaplain in the field and refused to allow Adler to go overseas. It was only his persistence and tenacity which finally overcame the objection, and in January 1915, for the first time in the history of the British Army, a Jewish Chaplain was ministering to Jewish troops in the field.

It is not possible here to continue the story of how he built up the Jewish Chaplaincy during the war. Suffice it to say that it was a *creatio ex nihilo*. With no precedent to guide him, with nothing but his own forcefulness of purpose and growing experience, he organized the department with such efficiency that before the war was over he had received promotion in rank, a twofold mention-in-dispatches and the signal honour of the DSO. He was indefatigable in his energies, infectious in his enthusiasm, dynamic in his influence on his colleagues, and impressive in his devotion to the Jewish soldier's well-being. Many thousands of Jews will remember him with gratitude and honour. During those tragic years he made Jewish history.

Eventually, there were 17 uniformed Jewish Chaplains who served in the Army Chaplains' department between 1914 and 1918 in all theatres of war. By the Second World War, there were at least 38 – including Lieutenant-Colonel Israel Brodie who had also served in the First World War and would later become Chief Rabbi.

One hundred years on, we are all connected to the First World War, either through our own family history, the heritage of our local communities, or because of its long-term impact on society and the world we live in today. From 2014 to 2018, across the world, nations, communities and individuals of all ages will come together to mark, commemorate and remember the lives of those who lived, fought and died in the Great War. The Jewish community will play its full part in the proud knowledge that it made a significant contribution. That selfless commitment continues unto this very day through those numbers of Jews, current members of The Armed Forces Jewish Community, that serve with devotion and sacrifice in Her Majesty's Armed Forces.

Jewish Chaplains Serving in Army Chaplains' Department 1914–1918

1. Rev. Michael Adler, Senior Jewish Chaplain [1909], Deployed January 1915, France

2. Rev. A. Barnett – 30 March 1916 – France

3. Rev. I. Brodie – 8 January 1918 – France

4. Rev. L. Falk – 25 January 1918 – Palestine

5. Rev. I. Frankenthal – 11 June 1916

6. Rev. L.J. Geffen – 21 August 1917 – France

7. Rev. M. Gollop – 26 March 1917 – Salonika, Greece

8. Rev. N. Goldstone – 4 February 1918

9. Rev. D. Hirsch – 14 August 1917 – France

10. Rev. W. Levin – 27 October 1918 – Italy, Egypt, Palestine

11. Rev. N. Levine – 9 July 1918 – France

12. Rev. E. Levy – June 1917 France

13. Rev. B. Lieberman -16 January 1917 France

14. Rev. S. Lipson – 22 January 1915

15. Rev. L. Morris – 22 January 1915 – France,Italy

16. Rev. H. Price – 23 October 1917 – France

17. Rev. V. Simmons – 24 August 1915 – France

TABLE 1. STRENGH OF THE ARMY CHAPLAINS' DEPARTMENT

Strength of the Army Chaplains' Department						
Denomination						
Church of England	89	620	1270	1850	1941	805
Presbyterian	11	110	175	273	298	138
Roman Catholic	17	250	400	583	643	275
Wesleyan		100	160	219	256	108
United Board		75	125	205	248	117
Welsh Clvinist		7	10	11	11	4
Jewish		2	3	13	14	7
Salvation Army					5	2
Totals	117	1164	2143	3154	3416	1456

The War Office - Statistical Abstract of Information regarding the Armies at Home
and Abroad 1914-1920 (June 1920)

Source: The War Office – Statistical Abstract of Information Regarding the Armies at Home and Abroad 1914-1920 (June 1920)

Jewish Chaplains Serving in Army Chaplains' Department 1939–1945

1. Rev. S. Amias

2. Rev. A. Berman

3. Rev. M. Berman

4. Rev. S.M. Bloch

5. Rev. I. Brodie

6. Rev. S. Brown

7. Rev. B.M. Casper

8. Rev. T. Chait

9. Rev. B. Cherrick

10. Rev. P. Cohen

11. Rev. E.M. Davis

12. Rev. L.I. Edgar

13. Rev. M. Elton

14. Rev. B. Epstein

15. Rev. I.N. Fabricant

16. Rev. J. Gill (Lifschitz)

17. Rev. M. Gollop

18. Rev. B. Greenberg

19. Rev. E.T. Hamburger

20. Rev. L.H. Hardman

21. Rev. B. Hooker

22. Rev. S. Hooker

23. Rev. S Isaacs

24. Rev. J. Israelstam

25. Rev. M.A. Jaffe

26. Rev. I. Levy

27. Rev. M.A. Lew

28. Rev. B. Lucki

29. Rev. S. Margulies

30. Rev. A.A.W. Miller

31. Rev. W. Morein [Died in Service]

32. Rev. A.D.S. Pimontel

33. Rev. H.J. Rabinowitz

34. Rev. I. Rapaport

35. Rev. E.E. Urbach

36. Rev. M. Wagner

37. Rev. J. Weintrobe

38. Rev. H. Bornstein [Died in Service]

39. Rev. B. Joseph

40. Rev. A.S. Super

Rabbi Reuben Livingstone LLM CF (Major) is the Jewish Chaplain to HM Forces.

Constance Milman

THE JEWISH FILM FESTIVAL

The Jewish contribution to the film industry is well known. Many of the earlier studio bosses in Hollywood were Jewish, including the founders of Metro-Goldwyn Mayer, Warner Brothers and Columbia. Louis B. Meyer, Sam Goldwyn, Darryl Zanuck, Harry Cohn and Harry Warner shaped the industry. Tony Curtis, Paul Muni, Kirk Douglas, Erich von Stroheim, Sophie Tucker and Lauren Bacall were just some of the great film stars. The Jewish element was often played down, though. Tony Curtis did not keep his original name, Bernard Schwartz, nor Kirk Douglas his patronym of Issur Danielovitch.

The idea of a specifically Jewish Film Festival was, therefore, not one which originally would have been considered. The idea did not come from a film magnate. Nevertheless, it is now over 25 years since the first Jewish Film Festival was conceived in San Francisco. Seven years later the JFF was brought to the UK as the Brighton Jewish Film Festival, the brainchild of a diminutive, 68-year-old, bundle of energy, Judy Ironside, MBE, who lives in Brighton and was previously a Drama Therapist working with children with special needs.

Since 1997 there have been continual developments headed by Judy, Michael Etherton, the Managing Director, and a small team. Over the course of a year, UK Jewish Film (the official title of the charity) holds several film festivals, which include the UK, Tel Aviv and the Geneva International Jewish Film Festival. They are now also programming the Hong Kong Jewish Film Festival.

There are also year round screenings at JW3, the Jewish Community Centre in London, and educational activities for Holocaust Memorial Day UK, as well as their own Hackney Roots, an intergenerational project to explore representations of Jewish identity.

The UK Jewish Film team work tirelessly to develop a culture where Jewish and Israeli film is recognized and enjoyed by the widest possible audience. They also aim to position Jewish related film at the heart of British culture. Their work encourages pride and knowledge amongst the younger generations and promotes understanding and awareness towards Jewish and Israeli people and Jewish culture amongst non-Jews.

When Judy first developed the idea for a Jewish film festival, she approached Sir Sydney Samuelson CBE, the first British Film Commissioner and, at the time, the Chairman of BAFTA, the British Academy of Film and Television Arts, and he agreed to become the Film Festival's first president.

Securing the support of a notable figure in the film world was a very good start, but it was obviously going to be necessary to get support from Jewish charitable trusts, organizations and individuals. The remarkable fact, however, is that the sponsors are both Jewish and non-Jewish. They include the Pears Foundation, Sky, Bank Leumi, the Association of Jewish Refugees and the National Lottery.

The list of sponsors and patrons runs to more than 100 individuals and organizations including the *JC*, *Jewish News*, Marriott and many generous individuals. Two public relations companies are now used to spread the word. There are special privileges for those who become Members of UKJFF, which include designated events during the year, discounts at various companies and priority bookings made available to broaden the support.

The amount of work involved in gathering such support was enormous and Judy Ironside might well have missed her vocation by not becoming Unilever's Sales Director. Looking back over its small beginnings, she has every right to feel very satisfied with the results she has achieved.

Today the content of the Film Festival comes from over 500 submissions every year. About a third come from Israel, which has a flourishing film industry, but the remainder come from all over the world; films with Jewish themes that have been made as far away as the Philippines, Uruguay and China. The topics are also very diverse, though all focused in some way on international Jewish life, history and culture.

The majority of films brought to the UK by the Festival are highly individual, such as the Israeli documentary about three Hungarian sisters called Polgar who were brought up by their parents to become chess champions. Judit Polgar became the youngest ever Grandmaster at 15 – younger than the previous record holder, Bobby Fischer – and was the first woman to compete in the Men's World Championships.

There is always a vibrant and fascinating programme of full length films, dramas, comedies, films about the Holocaust and Israeli films focussing on a wide variety of subjects. The Festival films are shown in 14 cinemas across London every year in November and simultaneously in Manchester, Leeds, Glasgow and several other cities. More than 15,000 people came together to watch a diverse and remarkable programme.

This often included a short film before the main feature, so that a wide variety of Jewish film-making is exhibited, including the work of new young filmmakers with their graduate short films. The UKJFF is held over three weekends in November with international and national guest directors, actors and special guests holding Q&A's and panel discussions after many of the screenings. The Festival runs throughout each week, apart from Shabbat, though films are also shown after Shabbat goes out, and Sunday is always a very popular day.

Some of the highlights of the UKJFF are the gala nights. These are special events with a reception, and these high profile evenings are often sponsored by one of the many Charitable Trusts or Corporate Sponsors of the Festival. However, for individuals and companies or charities, for between £1,000 and £1,500, there is also the opportunity to become a Film Sponsor of a drama or documentary film. This is a powerful way to become part of UKJFF, and offer the charity support to bring these unique films to audiences in the UK.

The films are selected by a Film Programmer, assisted by a panel of 12 experts and lay people. To ensure that nothing is missed, there is also close scrutiny of films shown at other International Film Festivals and a thorough study of worldwide industry journals.

In addition, to encourage the production of films by new enthusiasts, there is the Pears Foundation Short Films Fund at UKJF. The two winners of the annual competition receive £10,000 apiece to finance turning their script into a short film. This initiative is now in its eighth year and more than 60 scripts are submitted each year. Many of the winning films go on to be invited to international film festivals and one winning short film, *Sydney Turtlebaum*, starring Sir Derek Jacobi, was nominated for an Oscar.

The work of the UK Jewish Film Festival is not confined simply to the Festival. You can now rent many of the wonderful Festival films through the 'video on demand' facility on the website, www.ukjewish film.org. In addition there are six screenings a week at JW3.

The overall aim of all the work is to educate, enlighten and entertain Jewish audiences, as well as the British world outside the Jewish community. The aim is to draw attention to Jewish history, life and culture, and also to try to ensure that stereotypical views can be successfully countered.

One of the aspects of the UKJFF which is most noticeable is the quality and professionalism with which it is promoted. So often with organizations, the efforts to bring them to the attention of the general public appears amateurish, but a near 100-page brochure for the UKJFF is stylish, elegant and obviously produced by those who understand the principles of marketing.

Judy Ironside shows us once again that if there is sufficient determination, it is possible to make a difference. That you can do so on your own initiative, without a power base, without an unlimited bank balance, from a starting point at the seaside, and from scratch. It is a remarkable achievement.

Dr Dennis Coppel

BELFAST JEWISH COMMUNITY

It was suggested by Elkan Levy that the average life of a Jewish Community in the UK was 100 years. The Belfast Jewish Community (BJC) will have been in existence in 2015 for 150 years, well past its sell-by date. How have we survived for so long and how much longer will there be a community in Belfast? Chief Rabbi Ephraim Mirvis indicated recently that we must not dwell unduly in the past and we should refrain from looking back at the community highlights. That we should deal with the present and plan for the future. On the other hand, if we don't know where we came from, how do we know where we are going? Said Alice.

Daniel Joseph Jaffe is considered by many to be the founder of BJC. He was born in Mecklenburg in North Germany in 1809. He visited Northern Ireland frequently to purchase Irish linen for worldwide distribution and, in 1845, was advised by prominent local manufacturer J.N. Richardson to open a linen house in Belfast. His business prospered and Daniel took up residence in Northern Ireland, bringing his wife, brothers and nine sons and daughters with him.

Initially they had to travel to Dublin for religious services as there was no *minyan* in Belfast, but it is recorded that the first service was held in the home of Daniel's son, Martin, in Holywood, Co. Down in 1860.

The linen trade expanded and more German merchants, such as Loewenthal, Boas, Betzold and Portheim, joined the Jaffe family. It soon became apparent that a synagogue was required and Daniel Jaffe was responsible for the first one in Great Victoria Street in 1871–72. It remained in existence until 1904. Daniel died in 1874 in Nice and was later buried in Belfast's City Cemetery. His contribution to the commercial and religious life of Belfast was considerable, and is recognized by an ornamental drinking fountain which is in a prominent position in the Victoria Centre in downtown Belfast.

If Daniel Jaffe provided the foundation of the community, it was his son, Otto, who developed and expanded the community's influence and prestige. Otto was born in Denmark in 1846 and came to Belfast at the age of 12. On reaching 16 he joined the family business, Jaffe Brothers Linen Merchants. His progress up the political ladder was a rapid and remarkable achievement, rising from being a City Hall Councillor in 1894 to Lord Mayor in 1899. He was soon knighted and in 1904 became Lord Mayor for a second time. Otto was also the German Consul in Northern Ireland.

He was very generous with his time and money, contributing to the dependents of soldiers and sailors of the Boer War and The Royal Victoria Hospital, where he served as a Governor. He made significant financial contributions to Queens College, and was a member of the senate (now Queens University). He was also involved in the establishment of the first free library. The Jewish Community was not neglected and, apart from being Life President (seldom attending meetings), he provided the finances (£4,000) for a new synagogue, built in Annesley Street in 1904, as well as a school for Jewish and non-Jewish children, appropriately named The Jaffe School.

Jaffe was said to be shrewd, sharp-witted, far-seeing and almost parsimonious in business, but lavish and generous with multiple charities. He built the Jaffe Spinning Mill, which provided employment for 650 people by 1914. Although denaturalized as a German Citizen and becoming a British Citizen, he and his family were viewed with suspicion, verbally abused and intimidated at the onset of the First World War. His son, Arthur Daniel, served in the British army.

Otto was effectively driven from Belfast in 1915, even though he supported the war effort and described Germany's action as horrible and detestable. He moved to London as a broken man, being overwhelmed with pain and sorrow. Sir Otto was a *macher* who contributed so much to Belfast and the BJC. He died in 1929 and never returned to Belfast.

There were of course other German figures that left an imprint on Northern Ireland's Jewish Community. One was Herman Fox, a wealthy merchant who was not only Honorary President, but also President of the Belfast Board of Guardians, which provided free loans or gifts to poor immigrant families in financial distress. In his will he left gifts to the Ladies Benevolent Society as well as the Royal Victoria Hospital and the Mater Hospital. Gustav Wolf deserves a mention as a founder of the famous shipyards Harland & Wolf; although not Jewish, he came from German Jewish lineage.

The introduction of the May Laws by the Russian Parliament in 1882 resulted in an exodus of Russian Jewry fleeing vicious Tsarist persecution, oppression and pogroms. Some families found their way to Belfast, either by accident or because of family connections. They were assisted by the Belfast Board of Guardians to purchase small houses in the Carlisle Circus area of North Belfast and were kindly received by the local non-Jewish inhabitants.

The new Russian arrivals, accompanied by Poles, Lithuanians and Austrians, found the German-Jewish establishment's less orthodox traditions, manners and business ethics, incompatible. They would not worship in the Great Victoria Street Synagogue and, therefore, developed their own synagogue in Regent Street. It soon became clear that despite their distaste for one another, the two communities could not survive independently because of financial pressures, education needs, kosher requirements and rabbinical input. The decline in the linen industry, due to the re-emergence of cotton and later synthetic materials, coincided with a decrease in Jewish German influence. In 1903 amalgamation occurred followed by the building of the new Synagogue in Annesley Street in the heart of Carlisle Circus close by Jewish homes.

In the early part of the twentieth century the community thrived; businesses prospered, such as Goorwitch Department Store, Solomon & Peres Music and Record shops, and EMCO Mattress manufacturers. There were furniture stores such as Berwoods, The Model, and Gilpins, Enlanders (jewellers), and L. Marcus (music). A major furniture manufacturer was Lees Hyman & Lees. There were gents outfitters, such as Milestone and Kay, and many individual, small, but talented tailors. Kosher meat was not a problem and three butcher shops competed with one another: Hodes, Nemtzov and Diamonds. There was even a kosher delicatessen shop (Levey's).

The community grew to 1,500 with weddings, bar mitzvahs, births, *brits* and well-attended synagogue services. The community was able to employ a rabbi and there were many distinguished rabbonim,including Rabbi Hertzog (1916–18), who later became Chief Rabbi of the Dublin Community and then Ashkenazi Chief Rabbi in Israel. His son, Chaim, was born in Belfast and became President of Israel.

Rabbi Shachter was a highly respected figure and remained in Belfast from 1926 to 1953 before retiring to Israel. He was made an honorary MA by Queen's University Belfast. His books and papers are in the University Library and his portrait hangs in the Ulster Museum. Rabbi Alexander Carlebach (1954–65) succeeded Shachter and was largely responsible for university student education, and for creating the *Belfast Jewish Record* which is still in existence today and which has faithfully recorded the history of the BJC since 1950.

Cantors included Lithuanian-born Simcha Myerwitz, Saul Barnett, the Hungarian Rev. Polakoff, and Shmuel Aharoni. Assistant cantors doubled up as teachers and *shochets*, with a *shammas* running the financial and administrative affairs. The *Chevra Gemorrah* met every evening and stalwarts included Berl Cohen, Joseph Hurwitz and Chaim Weinstein, who conducted classes in Yiddish with his eyes closed; he knew vast tracts by heart. The *cheder* was attended six days a week by over 100 pupils and the community employed several teachers; the best known was Albert Fundaminsky.

Unemployment was low, new families appeared and it became apparent that a social centre for the community was required. A purpose-built building was erected in 1926 and provided four tennis hard courts, a kosher restaurant, table tennis, drama, a debating society and facilities for bridge and poker. A large ballroom catered for wedding receptions, bar mitzvah celebrations, dances and public meetings. On Yom Tov it was the venue for an overflow service. It was referred to affectionately as the CLUB. Sadly it burnt down in 1981.

During the Second World War the Belfast Jewish Community established a hostel in Clifton Park Avenue for escaping refugees from Nazi atrocities. As children arrived in Northern Ireland by Kindertransport a larger sanctuary was necessary and the community secured the lease of a 70-acre sea-front farm in Millisle, Co. Down in 1939 for over 300 adults and children. Eventually the farm became self-sufficient, providing dormitories, living spaces, workshops and fields of cattle and crops. The children were made welcome in the local school in Millisle. The farm closed in 1948 and is now privately owned. Sadly, all the buildings have been demolished despite efforts to preserve an area of historical importance. The school created a garden Safe Haven as a permanent reminder for future generations of school children.

During this period of prosperity and growth several outstanding personalities contributed to not only the Jewish Community but also to Belfast. Harold Goldblatt achieved fame as an actor with the Group Theatre and appeared in several Anglo-American films. Harry Towb was another well-known actor and Helen Lewis brought Laban's modern dance to Belfast. Solly Lipsitz was known as Mr Jazz and contributed articles on a regular basis to the local papers, as well as organizing significant concerts. Barney Hurwitz was a very dominant and influential figure, serving as President for 20 years and was made an OBE.

Harold Smith, a Captain in the Royal Navy from Springs in South

Africa, married Rada Hyman, a local girl, and became a Belfast City Councillor and Chairman of the Belfast Library Board. He headed up HMS *Caroline* and was President of the Rose Society. In addition he served as President of the Community for many years. Locally born, Jackie Morris, from North Belfast, became an Israeli Ambassador.

The legal profession was not neglected and the Recorder of Belfast was Judge Bernard Fox. Our present long-time President, Ronald Appleton, was a highly respected Crown Prosecutor. Solicitors that had busy practices in Belfast included Jackie and Leonard Fox, Ivan Selig, Martin Coppel, Brian Apfel, Leslie Morris and Raymond Segal. The medical profession was represented by a neurologist Louis Hurwitz who had a worldwide reputation, Dr Lazarus, a Diabetic Physician, and Dennis Coppel and David Hurwitz, both anaesthetists. There were several Jewish GPs including Joey Lewis, Sonny Hool and Mosey Rosenberg, as well as a few dentists; Henry Coppel, Leslie Leopold, Eddie Price, Ivan Goldblatt, Bernard Jaffe and Harry Herbert. Politics were wisely avoided and only Harold Smith and Sam Daly showed any interest.

In the early 1960s it was realized that the Annesley Street Synagogue was no longer appropriate for the present community which had moved away to the North and South of Belfast. The president, Barney Hurwitz, with Council approval, levied a fee from each member and Barney personally approached each individual and family. So successful was he that the new Synagogue on Somerton Road was opened in 1964 and dedicated by the then Chief Rabbi Israel Brodie. The services of the London firm of architects, Yorke, Rosenberg and Mardell, were employed and it was described as one of the most sophisticated synagogues built in the UK.

The building is round in shape with the traditional layout of central *bimah* and prayer hall. The roof, when viewed from above, is in the shape of the Star of David. The ladies sit in an elevated area on the circle separated from men by a rail. The Ark with rolling metal gates is set in a stone-clad wall, graced by a cantilevered bronze menorah, the work of Israeli artist Nehemiah Aziz. The synagogue is bright and airy with great acoustics and much admired by Jewish and non-Jewish visitors.

The onset of hostilities between the predominant Protestants Loyalists and the minority Catholics Republicans/Nationalists with the British armed forces (30,000) in between, was a major factor in the decline of the BJC. Many Jewish businesses were either fire bombed or just set on fire. The worst incident was the murder of business man Leonard Kaitcer; nobody was ever charged. Leonard Steinberg (later Lord Steinberg of Belfast), also a high profile business man, was shot and on recovery moved with his family to Manchester.

These incidents evoked fear in the community and many left for England and Israel. The so called Troubles and the world wide coverage on TV were major disincentives to migrate to Northern Ireland, invest or set up businesses. Kosher meat no longer was available locally and had to be brought in from Dublin or Manchester. The Jewish delicatessen shop closed from lack of customers. The Community had difficulty in attracting a rabbi and for many months there was no one to *leyen*.

Minyanim proved difficult and only on Thursday morning and Shabbat were services held. The synagogue which could seat 1,000 now became too big and the prayer hall was divided into two by a wall. The area, without the Ark and *bimah*, became the function room for the community, now without the Club which had been burnt to the ground. The community continued to diminish as the aged slipped away and no new blood emerged. The *cheder* has two children.

As we approach our 150th anniversary in 2015 some stability has returned, despite a membership of only 80. We have a dynamic new rabbi in David Singer, a popular club for the elderly which meets every two weeks, a *shiur* conducted by the rabbi twice a week, an active WIZO, the *Belfast Jewish Record* is published three times a year, and CCJ meets in the *shul* on a regular basis. The annual Holocaust Memorial Day is supported by over 400 people and the International Christian Embassy Jerusalem (ICEJ) hosts an annual celebration of Israel's anniversary. A book, *More than a Suitcase of Memories*, was recently published about the Matthews family who left Zhager in Lithuania and settled in Northern Ireland in 1890. Aaron Black wrote, filmed and directed a documentary for the BBC titled *The Last Minyan*. Both were well received and raised the profile of the BJC, which soldiers on.

Dr Dennis Coppel is Joint Vice President of the Belfast Jewish Community.

ANGLO-JEWISH INSTITUTIONS

BOARD OF DEPUTIES OF BRITISH JEWS
6 Bloomsbury Square, London WC1A 2LP
Tel 020 7543 5400 *Fax* 020 7543 0010
Email info@bod.org.uk *Website* www.bod.org.uk
BoD Charitable Foundation (Reg. Charity No. 1058107).
Founded in 1760 as a joint committee of the Sephardi and Ashkenazi communities in London, the BoD of British Jews has flourished in its role as the elected representative body of the British Jewish community. It has been involved in all issues affecting the political and civil rights of British Jewry and, in many cases, in times of crisis, in affairs overseas. It conveys the views of the community to Government and other public bodies on political and legislative matters which affect British Jewry, and provides information about the Jewish community and Israel to the non-Jewish world. The Board examines legislative proposals in Britain and the European Union which may affect Jews, and ensures the political defence of the community. It collects statistics and demographic information and undertakes research on and for the community. It maintains contact with, and provides support for, Jewish communities around the world and promotes solidarity with Israel. It counters bias in the media, defends Jewish religious practice and ensures that Jews enjoy the full rights of all British citizens. It is the political face of the community combatting antisemitism and leads the dialogue with other faith on behalf of the community.
The Board plays a co-ordinating role in key issues affecting the Jewish community, and promotes co-operation among different groups within the community The basis of the Board's representation is primarily synagogal, although the body itself has no religious affiliations. All properly constituted synagogues in Great Britain are entitled to representation, as are other significant communal organisations, such as the Regional Representative Councils, youth organisations and other communal bodies, including major charities. The Charedi community works closely with the Board of Deputies. The Board meets most months in London, but holds one meeting a year in a regional community.
Pres. Vivian Wineman; *Snr. V. Pres.* Laura Marks; *V. Pres.* Jonathan Arkush, Alex Brummer; *T.* Laurence Brass; *Chief Exec.* Gillian Merron
The work of the Board is channelled through four Divisional Boards, each chaired by an Honorary Officer and supported by a professional Director.
International Division *Ch.* Alex Brummer; *Dir.* Philip Rosenberg
Defence Policy and Group Relations: *Ch.* Jonathan Arkush; *Dir.* Philip Rosenberg
Community Issues: *Ch.* Laura Marks
Finance and Organisation: *Ch.* Laurence Brass; *Dir.* Martin Frey
Regional Assembly: *Ch.* Ephraim Borowski
Jewish Connection: Establishes viable and productive links between the small communities within the United Kingdom. *Man.* Tori Joseph
Pikuach: Statutory equivalent of Ofsted for Jewish religious education to inspect and monitor our schools to ensure highest standard are maintained. *Dir.* Sandra Teacher
Public Affairs *Dir.* Elizabeth Harris-Sawczenko
Community Research Unit (CRU): Carries out demographic and other research on various aspects of the community. *Email* research@bod.org.uk
Trades Advisory Council: Affiliated to the Board, the Council seeks to combat causes of friction in industry, trade and commerce, and discrimination in the workplace, where these threaten good relations where Jews are concerned. The TAC offers arbitration and conciliation facilities in business disputes and advice to employees who consider that they have suffered discrimination. *Dir.* Martin Frey
Jewish Community Information: Provides information to the Jewish and non-Jewish public on all aspects of the Jewish community in the UK. *Tel* 020 7543 5421 *Email* jci@bod.org.uk
Communal Diary: Designed to minimise clashes between events organised by different communal organisations. *Email* diary@bod.org.uk
Jewish Community Services: Ombudsman c/o The Board of Deputies of British Jews, *Tel* 020 7543 0105 (answerphone). (Reg. Charity No: 269525). The Ombudsman is available to deal with disputes or complaints concerning Jewish community services, i.e. any institutions in the Jewish community. It is an independent service, for which no fee is charged.
Ombudsman, Paul Shaerf *Email* ombudsman@bod.org.uk

JEWISH REPRESENTATIVE COUNCILS

BERKSHIRE JEWISH REPRESENTATIVE COUNCIL
(Est. 1995). Representing Maidenhead Synagogue, Reading Hebrew Congregation and Reading Liberal Jewish Community. *Contact* Myer Daniels *Email* mdaniels@globalnet.co.uk

REPRESENTATIVE COUNCIL OF BIRMINGHAM & WEST MIDLANDS JEWRY
Email jewishbirmingham@talktalk.net *Website* www.jewishbirmingham.org
(Est. 1937). *Pres.* Sir B. Zissman; *Ch.* R. Jacobs; *Hon. S.* Leonard Jacobs *Tel* 0121 236 1801; *Admin.* c/o BHC, Singers Hill, Ellis Street, Birmingham, B1 1HL *Tel* 07768 761 930

BOURNEMOUTH JEWISH REPRESENTATIVE COUNCIL (incorporating Southampton)
Email info@bournemouthjewishcommunity.co.uk
Website www.bournemouthjewishcommunity.co.uk
Ch. Jonathan Kay *Tel* 01202 557 748

GLASGOW JEWISH REPRESENTATIVE COUNCIL
Jewish Community Centre, 222 Fenwick Road, Giffnock, Glasgow G46 6UE
Tel 0141 577 8200
Email office@glasgowjewishrepcouncil.org *Website* www.jewishglasgow.org
(Reg. Charity No. SCO166). *Pres.* Paul Morron MBE; *Admin.* Orli Schechper; *Hon. S.* Fiona L. Brodie; *Sec.* Frank Angell

HULL JEWISH REPRESENTATIVE COUNCIL
Pres. J. Rose *Tel* 01482 655367; *Hon. S.* Prof. J. Friend, 9 Allanhall Way, Kirk Ella, HU10 7QU *Tel* 01482 658930 *Email* j.friend@cj2f.karoo.co.uk

THE INTERFAITH COUNCIL FOR WALES
c/o Cytûn, 58 Richmond Road, Cardiff CF24 3UR
Website www.interfaithwales.org.uk
Sec. Rev Canon Aled Edwards OBE *Tel* 02920 464 375

LEEDS JEWISH REPRESENTATIVE COUNCIL
Marjorie & Arnold Ziff Community Centre, 311 Stonegate Road, Leeds LS17 6AZ
Tel 0113 269 7520
Website www.leedsjewishcommunity.com
Pres. Simon Jackson; *V. Pres.* Alan Dunwell, Abigail Levin; *Hon. T.* Keith Ackerman; *Hon. S.* (*acting*) Jonathan Rose

JEWISH REPRESENTATIVE COUNCIL OF GREATER MANCHESTER & REGION
Jewish Community Centre, Bury Old Road, M7 4QY
Tel 0161 720 8721
Email office@jewishmanchester.org *Website* www.jewishmanchester.org
Pres. Sharon A. Bannister; *V. Pres.* Jacky Buchsbaum BSc ACA CTA, Jonny Wineberg; *Hon. T.* Philip A. Langer; *Hon. S.* Michael Rubinstein, Rabbi Arnold Saunders; Ex-officio, Frank Baigel BA B.Dent.Sc; *H. Media Analyst,* Frank R. Baigel. *Publ.* Year Book, Newsletter *RepPresents*

MERSEYSIDE JEWISH REPRESENTATIVE COUNCIL
433 Smithdown Road, L15 3JL
Tel 0151 733 2292 *Fax* 0151 734 0212
Email repcouncil@mjccshifrin.co.uk *Website* www.liverpooljewish.co.uk
(Reg. Charity No. 1140569). *Pres.* Prof. Julian Verbov, JP; *Ch. of the Council* Ian S. Cohen; *Hon. S.* Max Marcus. *Publ.* Year Book

REPRESENTATIVE COUNCIL OF NORTH EAST JEWRY
Email repcouncil@northeastjewish.co.uk *Website* www.northeastjewish.org.uk
(Reg. Charity No. 1071515). *Hon. T.* W. Knoblauch *Email* walter@total-accounting.com; *Pres.* Leonard Musat *Tel* 0191 285 7698

SOUTH WALES JEWISH REPRESENTATIVE COUNCIL
9 Holmwood Close, Cyncoed, Cardiff CF23 6BT
Tel 029 2075 5556
Email swjewishrepcouncil@gmail.com
Ch. Stanley Soffa; *Hon. S.* Ruth Levene *Tel* 07920 585 848

SOUTHPORT JEWISH REPRESENTATIVE COUNCIL
Hon. S. R. Jackson 33 The Chesters, 17-19 Argyle Road PR9 9LG *Tel* 01704 532 696

SUSSEX JEWISH REPRESENTATIVE COUNCIL
Tel 07789 491 279
Email info@sussexjewishrepresentativecouncil.org
Website www.sussexjewishrepresentativecouncil.org
Nearly every synagogue, charitable organisation, social and cultural institution, as well as the communities in Eastbourne, Hastings, Bexhill and Worthing, are affiliated to this Council, and meetings are held quarterly. *Pres.* Beryl Sharpe; *Sec.* Jessica Rosenthal *Corr.* P.O. Box 2178, Hove, BN3 3SZ

COMMUNAL ORGANISATIONS

ANGLO-JEWISH ASSOCIATION
11/15 William Road, London NW1 3ER
Tel 020 7449 0909
Email info@anglojewish.org.uk *Website* www.anglojewish.org.uk
(Est. 1871. Reg. Charity No. 256946). Membership of the Association is open to all British Jews who accept as their guiding principle loyalty to their faith and their country. Its aim is to promote the education of Jews in the UK and elsewhere. It offers scholarships to Jewish UK university students who can demonstrate academic excellence and financial need. *Pres.* Jonathan Walker

ASSOCIATION OF JEWISH WOMEN'S ORGANISATIONS IN THE UNITED KINGDOM (AJWO)
108-110 Finchley Road, London NW3 5JJ
Tel 020 7319 9169 *Fax* 020 7431 3671
Email contact@ajwo.org *Website* www.ajwo.org
(Est. 1965). To further communal understanding. To promote the achievement of unity of purpose among Jewish women of differing shades of opinion, belonging to autonomous organisations with different aims. *Affiliate orgs:* Agunot Campaign; B'nai B'rith Women; British Emunah; Chana; Friends of Hebrew University Women's Group; Jewish Women's Aid; League of Jewish Women; Liberal Judaism; Masorti Judaism; Paperweight; Reform Judaism Women; Sephardi Women (Lauderdale Road Synagogue Association); US Women WIZO.uk; Women in Jewish Leadership. *Ch.* Anne Lyons; *V. Ch.* Vivien Freeman; *Hon. S.* Shiela Mann; *Hon. T.* Helen Reisman

BICOM: BRITISH ISRAEL COMMUNICATIONS AND RESEARCH CENTRE
Tel 020 7636 5500 *Fax* 020 7636 5600
Email info@bicom.org.uk *Website* www.bicom.org.uk
(Est. 2001). To provide a better understanding of Israel in the UK; to create a more positive environment for Israel in the UK. *Chief Exec.* Dermot Kehoe *Email* laura@bicom.org.uk *Twitter* @BritainIsrael; *Donor Relations & Events Man.* Ruth Fisher *Email* ruthf@bicom.org.uk; *Hd. of Communications,* Carly Maisel *Email* carlym@bicom.org.uk; *Press Off.* David Walsh *Email* davidw@bicom.org.uk; *Dir. Israel Off.* Richard Pater *Email* richardp@bicom.org.uk *Twitter* @Richard_Pater

COMMUNITY SECURITY TRUST (CST)
Head Office, London and Southern Region P.O. Box 35501, London NW4 2FZ
Tel 020 8457 9999
Manchester and Northern Region P.O. Box 245, Manchester M7 2WY
Tel 0161 792 6666
Email Enquiries@thecst.org.uk *Website* www.thecst.org.uk
(Reg. Charity No. 1042391). CST believes that the fight against antisemitism and terrorism is vital to help ensure a vibrant Jewish community. CST provides physical security, training and advice for the protection of British Jews. CST also assists victims of antisemitism and monitors antisemitic activities and incidents. CST represents British Jewry to Police, Government and media on the subjects of antisemitism, terrorism and security.

JEWISH LEADERSHIP COUNCIL (formerly Jewish Community Leadership Council)
6 Bloomsbury Square, London WC1A 2LP
Tel 020 7242 9734
Email email@thejlc.org *Website* www.thejlc.org
Northwest London Office, Shield House, Harmony Way, NW4 2BZ
(Est. 2006. Reg. Charity No. 1115343). As a 'coalition of organisations', the Jewish Leadership Council helps its member organisations. It does this by organising projects that

all its member organisations can benefit from and by supporting member organisations in their own strategic goals. JLC works to ensure the health of the Jewish voluntary sector, both through internal strategic planning for the future and, where necessary, through external campaigning and lobbying. The JLC plans for the future of the UK Jewish community. It does this through commissioning research, holding seminars and supporting leadership development. The Council also works to ensure that there is a positive public policy environment for the British Jewish community. It coordinates internally so that the Jewish community has a connected and forward-looking approach to policy.

In addition to its central operations the JLC incorporates two subsidiary Divisions. Partnerships for Jewish Schools (PaJeS) and LEAD (Jewish Leadership Excellence and Development). PaJeS Division: *Ch.* Jonathan Goldstein; *Exec. Dir.* Alastair Falk; LEAD Division: *Ch.* Nigel Layton; Exec. Dir. Nicky Goldman

The JLC comprises the heads of the major institutions in each sector of British Jewish life, together with significant individual leaders of British Jewry. *Publ.* The Future of Jewish schools (2008); The Big Society and the UK Jewish Community (2010); The Future of Jewish Schools: Three Years On (2011); Inspiring Women Leaders: Advancing Gender Equality in Jewish Communal Life (2012). *Ch. of Council of Membership,* Vivian Wineman (BoD.); *Ch. of Bd. of Tru.* Mick Davis, Poju Zabludowicz; *V. Pres.* Sir Victor Blank, Sir Trevor Chinn CVO, Michele Vogel, Gilllian Merron, Lord Stanley Fink, Henry Grunwald OBE QC, Lord Greville Janner, Howard Leigh, Leo Noé, Lord Harry Woolf; *Council of Members,* Frank Baigel (Representative Council of Greater Manchester and Region), Bill Benjamin (UJIA), Adrian Cohen (London Jewish Forum), David Dangoor, Spanish & Portuguese Jews Congregation; Rhea Wolfson, Harry Jardine (ZYC); Jonathan Goldstein (PaJeS), Joe Tarsh (UJS), Lucian J. Hudson (Liberal Judaism), Brian Kerner (Cross Communal Group), Debbie Klein (JCC), Nigel Layton (LEAD), Steven Lewis (New Leadership Network/Jewish Care), James Libson (New Leadership Network/World Jewish Relief), Simon Jackson (Leeds Jewish Representative Council), Bernie Myers (Norwood), Stephen Pack (United Synagogue), Robert Weiner (Movement for Reform Judaism), Gerald M. Ronson CBE (CST), Harvey Rosenblatt (Nightingale Hammerson), Jill Shaw (WIZO), Lord David Young (Ch. Jewish Museum), Edward Mizrahi (BICOM), Michael Ziff (Maccabi GB)

LEAGUE OF JEWISH WOMEN
Ort House, 126 Albert Street, London NW1 7NE
Tel 020 7242 8300
Email office@theljw.org *Website* www.theljw.org
(Est. 1943. Reg. Charity No. 1104023). Voluntary service organisation to unite Jewish women of every shade of opinion who live in the UK; to intensify in each Jewish woman her Jewish consciousness and her sense of responsibility to the Jewish community and the community generally; to stimulate her personal sense of civic duty and to encourage her to express it by increased service to the country. *Pres.* Yvonne Brent; *Hon. S.* Marilyn Herman
    Groups operate in the following centres:

Greater London
Barnet; Bushey Heath; Central; Chigwell & Hainault; Coombe & District; Harrow & Kenton; JMUMS; London North West; Newbury Park & District; North & East London; Northwood; Oakwood & Winchmore Hill; Pinner; Radlett; Southgate; Stanmore & Edgware; Surrey; Prime Time (single women).

Outside London
Bournemouth; Cardiff; Glasgow; Leicester.

North West Region (centred at Manchester)
Bowdon & Hale; Brentwood; Bury & Whitefield; Cheadle & Gatley; Fylde; Kingsway; Park & Windsor; Prestwich; Sale & Altrincham.

In addition to groups of women throughout the UK, there are focussed groups for young mums, JMums, and women on their own, Prime Time. Men can join as associate members, League Associate Division (LADS). LJW is the UK Affiliate of the International Council of Jewish Women.

ORT HOUSE CONFERENCE CENTRE
126 Albert Street, London NW1 7NE
Tel 020 7485 5847 *Fax* 020 7446 8651
Email ort@pavpub.com *Website* www.orthouse.co.uk
(Est. 1996). A Jewish conference centre and IT Suite. Capacity 120. Suitable for business, community or social events. *Org.* Natalie Campbell

WORKING PARTY ON JEWISH MONUMENTS IN THE UK & IRELAND
c/o Board of Deputies, 6 Bloomsbury Square, London WC1A 2LP
Email heritage_wp@bod.org.uk
(Est. 1991). To act as a forum, bringing together people with a wide interest, expertise, and involvement in maintaining and supporting Jewish Heritage Institutions in the UK. *Ch.* David Jacobs

INTERFAITH REPRESENTATIVE BODIES

COUNCIL OF CHRISTIANS AND JEWS
21 Godliman Street, London EC4V 5BD
Tel 020 7015 5160
Email cjrelations@ccj.org.uk *Website* www.ccj.org.uk
(Est. 1942. Reg. Charity No. 238005). Patron: Her Majesty the Queen. The Council brings together the Christian and Jewish Communities in a common effort to fight the evils of prejudice and intolerance, especially antisemitism. It is neither a missionary nor a political organisation. It runs projects nationally and through its 35 regional branches. *Pres.* The Archbishop of Canterbury; The Chief Rabbi; The Archbishop of Westminster; The Greek Orthodox Archbishop of Thyateira and Great Britain; The Moderator of the Church of Scotland; The Free Churches' Moderator; The Head of the Movement for Reform Judaism, The Chief Executive of LJ, and The Spiritual Head of the Spanish and Portuguese Jews' Congregation. *Ch.* The Lord Bishop of Manchester; Rt. Rev. Nigel McCulloch. *Dir.* Dr Jane Clements. *Publ.* Common Ground.

3FF (formerly The Three Faiths Forum)
Star House, 104-108 Grafton Road, London NW5 4BA
Tel 020 7482 9549
Email info@3ff.org.uk *Website* www.3ff.org.uk
(Est. 1997. Reg. Charity No. 1092465). 3FF, the Three Faiths Forum builds understanding and lasting relationships between people of all faiths and beliefs; It runs education, engagement and action programmes that bring diverse communities together. Its main focus is in the UK, but it also works internationally to create new models for intercultural cooperation, particularly in the EU, USA and Middle East. Its work involves teachers, students and young professionals, faith organisations, artists and galleries, political leaders in Parliament and upcoming leaders still at university. *Trustees: Co. Fdr*. Sir Sigmund Sternberg KC*SG; *Co. Fdr.* Revd. Dr. Marcus Braybrooke MA MPhil, *Ch.* Michael Sternberg QC FRSA KFO, Solicitor of the Senior Courts of England and Wales, Farmida Bi MA (Cantab), Barbara Mills LLB, Dilwar Hussain, Professor Mike Hardy CMG OBE

JOSEPH INTERFAITH FOUNDATION
75 North End Road, London NW11 7RL
Tel 020 8458 9081 *Mobile* 07816 814 691
Email info@josephinterfaithfoundation.org *Website* www.josephinterfaithfoundation.org
(Est. 2006. Reg. Charity 1119284). An officially registered joint Muslim-Jewish interfaith organisation. It is committed to fostering constructive and sustained interaction through academic and educational programmes and a deeper understanding of both faiths in Britain. *Tr.* Sir David Michels, Judge Khurshid Drabu; *Exec. Dir.* Mehri Niknam, MBE

JEWISH PRESS, RADIO AND INFORMATION SERVICES

The following is a selection of the major national publications. Many synagogues and communal organisations publish newsletters and magazines.

JEWISH PRESS

BELFAST JEWISH RECORD (Quarterly)
14 Norton Drive, Belfast BT9 6ST
Tel 07533 324 618
(Est. 1953). *Soc. Sec.* M. Black

BIMAH (Three issues annually)
18 St Edeyrns Road, Cyncoed, Cardiff CF23 6TB
Tel 0292 076 2689
(Est. 1994). The Platform of Welsh Jewry. *Ed.* Barbara Michaels
Email barbara.michaels@btopenworld.com

BIRMINGHAM JEWISH RECORDER (Monthly)
P.O. Box 13512, Birmingham B32 9BX
Tel 0121 428 3347
Email admin@recorder.org.uk
(Est. 1935).

EDINBURGH STAR (Two issues a year)
31/3 Rattray Grove, Edinburgh EH10 5TL
(Est. 1989). Community journal. *Ed.* M. Brannan

ESSEX JEWISH NEWS (Three issues a year)
Ed. Email editor@ejnews.org.uk; *Accounts Email* office.ejn@gmail.com

EUROPEAN JUDAISM (Two issues a year)
Leo Baeck College, 80 East End Road, London N3 2SY
Tel 020 8349 5600 *Fax* 020 8349 5619
Email editorial@journals.berghahnbooks.com *Website* www.journals.berghahnbooks.com/ej/
(Est. 1966). *Ed.* Rabbi Prof. J. Magonet

JEWISH CHRONICLE (Weekly)
28 St Albans Lane, London NW11 7QE
Website www.thejc.com
(Est. 1841). *Ed.* Stephen Pollard

JEWISH NEWS (Weekly)
Unit 611, Highgate Studios, 53-79 Highgate Road, London NW5 1TL
Tel 020 7692 6929
Website www.totallyjewish.com
Ed. Richard Ferrer

JEWISH QUARTERLY (incorporating Jewish Book News and Reviews) (Quarterly)
c/o 93 South Hill Park, London NW3 2SP
Email info@jewishquarterly.org *Website* www.jewishquarterly.org
Twitter @JewishQuarterly
(Reg. Charity No. 268589). The Jewish Quarterly is a London-based literary journal of ideas and culture boasting among its contributors the greatest writers and minds of the Jewish and non-Jewish world. Founded in 1953, it is loved for its fine writing and editorial integrity. *Ed.* Keith Kahn-Harris

JEWISH RENAISSANCE: MAGAZINE OF JEWISH CULTURE (Four issues a year)
P.O. Box 28849, London SW13 0WA
Email editor@jewishrenaissance.org.uk *Website* www.jewishrenaissance.org.uk
(Est. 2001). *Ed.* Janet Levin; *Ch.* Lionel Gordon

JEWISH SOCIALIST (Quarterly)
JS Publications, BM3725, London WC1N 3XX
Website wwwjewishsocialist.org.uk
(Est. 1985). Magazine of the Jewish Socialists' Group

JEWISH TELEGRAPH (Published weekly)
Telegraph House, 11 Park Hill, Bury Old Road, Prestwich, Manchester M25 OHH
Tel 0161 741 2631 (Newsdesk) *Tel* 0161 740 9321 (Switchboard) *Fax* 0161 740 9325
Email manchester@jewishtelegraph.com *Website* www.jewishtelegraph.com
Facebook Jewish Telegraph *Twitter* @jewishtelegraph
(Est 1950). In Glasgow: glasgow@jewishtelegraph.com Leeds: leeds@jewishtelegraph.com
and Liverpool: liverpool@jewishtelegraph.com *Ed.* P. Harris

JEWISH TRIBUNE (Weekly)
97 Stamford Hill, London N16 5DN
Tel 020 8800 6688 *Fax* 020 8800 5000
(Est. 1962). English and Yiddish. *Ed.* Dan Levy (Agudas Yisroel of Great Britain)

LEO BAECK INSTITUTE YEAR BOOK (Annually)
2nd Floor, Arts Two Building, Queen Mary, University of London, Mile End Road,
London E1 4NS
Email info@leobaeck.co.uk
(Est. 1956). *Ed.* Professor R. Gross, Dr. Cathy Gelbin

MENORAH
A magazine for Jewish members of H.M. Forces and Friends of Jewish Servicemen and
Women. *Ed.* Col. M. Newman DL
Tel 0161 766 6479 *Email* martin.newman@armymail.mod.uk

THE SCRIBE: JOURNAL OF BABYLONIAN JEWRY (Annually)
4 Carlos Place, London W1K 3AW
Tel 020 7399 0850
Email scribe@dangoor.com *Website* www.thescribe.info
(Est. 1971). *Ed.* Dr. N.E. Dangoor, CBE

SUSSEX JEWISH NEWS (Monthly)
P.O. Box 2178, Hove BN3 3SZ,
Tel 07906 955 404
Email sjneditor@sussexjewishnews.com
Website www.sussexjewishrepresentativecouncil.org
Admin. Bernard Swithern subscription £24 p.a./£18 online

WESSEX JEWISH NEWS (Five issues a year)
3 De Lisle Road, Bournemouth, BH3 7NF
Email edwjn@onetel.com

JEWISH RADIO PROGRAMMES

JEWISH HOUR

Radio weekly show for and about the Jewish Community in Manchester. Every Monday evening from 7-8pm online, and on 94.4 FM. Listen again at www.jewishhour.co.uk
Editor and *Producer* Basil Herwald *Email* Herwald_law@hotmail.com

TIKKUN SPECTRUM JEWISH RADIO

4 Ingate Place, Battersea, London SW8 3NS
Tel 020 7627 4433 Phone-In: 020 7627 8383 *Fax* 020 7627 3409
Email tikkunspectrum@spectrumradio.net *Website* www.spectrumradio.net
Facebook spectrum radio *Twitter* @spectrumradio
Producer and Presenter Michael Milston. Other Presenters Jon Kaye, Laurence Kilshaw, Ervin Landau and Joanne Simmons. One weekly hour programmes of news, views and discussion. Programme accessible for one week on the internet, Smart Phone and Tablet. See Website for programme details weekly.

INFORMATION SERVICES

BRIJNET

Website www.brijnet.org

Provider of UK Jewish communal internet services. Creates awareness of the use and benefits of the Internet in the community through training and assistance with all Internet tools. Creates and maintains a useful, quality, communal, electronic information database. Published electronic listings including: brij-announce, daf-hashavua.

JEWISH COMMUNITY INFORMATION

6 Bloomsbury Square, London WC1A 2LP
Tel 020 7543 5421 *Fax* 020 7543 0010
Email jci@bod.org.uk

A service of the Board of Deputies, providing information to the Jewish and non-Jewish public on all aspects of the Jewish community in the UK.

RELIGIOUS ORGANISATIONS

THE CHIEF RABBINATE

The Chief Rabbinate of Britain has evolved from the authority of the Rabbi of the Great Synagogue in London. From the early years of the 18th century he was acknowledged as the spiritual leader of the majority of the London community, a recognition also accorded by the provinces and overseas. Ephraim Mirvis was inducted into office in 2013. Previous holders of the office were: Aaron Hart (1709–1756); Hart Lyon (1756–1764); David Tevele Schiff (1765–1791); Solomon Hirschell (1802–1842); Nathan Marcus Adler (1845–1890); Hermann Adler (1891–1911); Joseph Herman Hertz (1913–1946); Israel Brodie (1948–1965); Immanuel Jakobovits (1967–1991); Jonathan Sacks (1991-2013).

The formal designation (1845–1953) of the office was 'Chief Rabbi of the United Hebrew Congregations of the British Commonwealth of Nations' and subsequently 'Chief Rabbi of the United Hebrew Congregations of the Commonwealth'.

Chief Rabbi Ephraim Mirvis
Office of the Chief Rabbi: 305 Ballards Lane, London N12 8GB
Tel 020 8343 6301
Email info@chiefrabbi.org *Website* www.chiefrabbi.org
Chief Exec. Ari Jesner

Marriage Authorisation Office of the Chief Rabbi, 305 Ballards Lane, London N12 8GB
Tel 020 8343 6313 *Dir.* Rabbi Dr J. Shindler

UNITED SYNAGOGUE

305 Ballards Lane, London N12 8GB
Tel 020 8343 8989
Website www.theus.org.uk
Tru. Stephen Pack, Stephen Fenton, Russell Kett, Jacqui Zinkin, Leonie Lewis, Stephen Goldman, Claire Lemer, Doreen Samuels, Brian Markeson; *Chief Exec.* Dr Steven Wilson (Reg. Charity No. 242552). For accurate contact information for all our synagogues and for further information about the US, please visit the website.

While the Act of Parliament under which it was created bears the date July 14, 1870, the US had its origin much earlier in the history of London Jewry. Of the five Constituent Synagogues which joined to form the US, the oldest – the Great Synagogue – was early 18th Century; the Hambro dated from 1707, while the New Synagogue was founded in 1761. The Member Synagogues now number 45, there is also one associate and a small number of affiliate communities within the London area, providing religious facilities for over 100,000 Jews in the greater London area. For Member and Affiliated Synagogues, *See* London and the Home Counties.

The US is the main contributor towards the maintenance of the Chief Rabbinate.

The **Community Services Division** *Tel* 020 8343 5680. This department is the interface between the US Centre and the local synagogue communities. The department provides a range of activities including US Cares, Project Chesed and Tribe – Young US.

Tribe *Tel* 020 8343 5656 provides a range of activities for its members, including After School activities at Tribe Clubs across London. There are Residential Summer camps and Summer Day schemes, as well as comprehensive training and support for member synagogues, with their youth provision and employees. **Project Chesed** carries out a wide range of activities, including its annual Pesach food parcel delivery to members. *Dir.* David Collins

The **Kashrut Division** *Tel* 020 8343 6255 *Fax* 020 8343 6254
Website www.kosher.org.uk *Dir.* Rabbi J. Conway, BA; *Kashrut Admin.* N. Lauer
Publ.: The Really Jewish Food Guide, Kosher Nosh Guide, Passover Supplement.

The **Visitation Committee** provides a caring service for all Jews who unfortunately find themselves in hospital, in prison or who are bereaved (*See* p. 169). The Jewish Bereavement Counselling Service has a team of trained bereavement counsellors available to meet the needs of all members of the Jewish community. *Tel* 020 8457 9710

The **External Services Division** The Division includes the US Legal department as well

as Burial, Hospital and Prison visitation. *Tel* 020 8343 8989 *Dir.* David Frei
Burial Society *Tel* 020 8950 7767
(All Cemeteries) *Dir.* Melvyn Hartog; *Man.* Bushey Office Marcia Wohlman

CEMETERIES
Willesden, Beaconsfield Road, NW10 2JE *Tel* 020 8459 0394 *Fax* 020 8830 4582 (Opened 1873); East Ham, Marlow Road, High Street South, E6 3QG *Tel* 020 8472 0554 *Fax* 020 8471 2822 (Opened 1919);
Bushey, Little Bushey Lane, Herts, WD2 3TP *Tel* 020 8950 7767 *Fax* 020 8420 4973 (Opened 1967);
Waltham Abbey, Upshire Hall, Honey Lane, Essex, EN9 3QT *Tel* 01992 714 492 *Fax* 01992 650 735 (Opened 1960);
Plashet, High Street North, E12 6PQ (Opened 1896);
West Ham, Buckingham Road, Forest Lane, E15 1SP *Tel* 020 8472 0554 (Opened 1857);
Alderney Road, E1 (Opened for Great Synagogue in 1696. Disused);
Brady Street, E1 (Opened for the New Synagogue, in 1761; subsequently used also by Great Synagogue. Disused);
Hackney, Lauriston Road, E9 (Opened for Hambro' Synagogue in 1788. Disused).

BETH DIN (COURT OF THE CHIEF RABBI)
305 Ballards Lane, London N12 8GB
Tel 020 8343 6270 *Fax* 020 8343 6257
Email info@bethdin.org.uk
Dayanim Rabbis Menachem Gelley, Ivan Binstock, BSc., Yonason Abraham, Shmuel Simons, *Registrar* D. Frei, LLB
The Beth Din fulfils the following functions: (i) dispute arbitration and mediation; (ii) supervision of Jewish religious divorces, adoptions and conversions; (iii) certification of religious status; (iv) supervision of shechita and kashrut.
General enquiries may be made from 9am-5pm (Monday to Thursday). You need an appointment to attend the Beth Din. Messages left on the answerphone will be dealt with as soon as possible.
The London Beth Din (Court of the Chief Rabbi) is an integral part of the US.

INITIATION SOCIETY
Website www.initiationsociety.org.uk
(Est. 1745. Reg. Charity No. 207404). To train Mohalim and to supply Mohalim in cases where they are needed. For a list of Mohalim practising in the British Isles and registered with the Society, you should contact the Secretary.
Pres. Dr Shalom Springer BSc PhD; *Med. Off.* Dr. J. Spitzer *Tel* 020 8802 2002 *Email* j.spitzer@doctors.org.uk *Sec.* M. Levenson 22 Wentworth Road, London NW11 0RP *Tel* 020 8455 5059 *Email* mlev@parl.org.uk

JEWISH COMMITTEE FOR H.M. FORCES
12 Conisborough Place, Manchester M45 6EJ
Tel 0161 766 6479
Email afjc@armymail.mod.uk
The Committee is officially recognised by the Minister of Defence for appointing Jewish chaplains and to provide for the religious needs of Jewish members of H.M. Forces.
Pres. Lt. Cdr. Alan Tyler RN; *V. Pres.* Brig. Simon Bell TD, Rear Admiral Lord Sterling, Capt. Solomon Levy MBE ED; *Ch.* Col. Martin Newman DL FCIPR; *V. Ch.* Judge Stuart Taylor; *Hon. T.* Major Rob Pollock; *Jewish Chaplain to H.M. Forces* Rabbi Major Reuben Livingstone CF(V); *Hon. S.* Brian Bloom; *Faith Adv.* Rabbi Dr. Abraham Levy OBE *Publ.* Menorah.

JEWISH MEMORIAL COUNCIL
Begbies Chettle Agar, Epworth House, 25 City Road, London, EC1Y 1AR
Tel 020 7628 5801 *Fax* 020 7628 0390
Email admin@begbiesaccountants.co.uk *Website* www.begbieschettleagar.co.uk

(Est. 1919). To commemorate the services rendered by Jews in the UK and British Empire in the war of 1914-18 by establishing an organisation which will carry on Jewish tradition as a permanent ennobling force in the lives of Jews in this country.
Ch. E. Astaire; *Tru.* J. Guttentag, S. Bentley, S. Cohen

JMC PENSIONS FUND
Admin 25 Enford Street, London W1H 1DW
Tel 020 7724 7778
Email jmcpf@btinternet.com
JMC Pension Fund is separate from the Jewish Memorial Council and now is a closed scheme for Jewish Communities. *Tru. Ch.* T. Simon

NATIONAL COUNCIL OF SHECHITA BOARDS
Elscot House, Arcadia Avenue, London N3 2JU
Tel 0800 035 0466 *Fax* 0800 035 0467
Email ncsb@shechita.co.uk *Website* www.shechitauk.org
Shechita UK PR Office: *Tel* 020 7284 6969 *Email* shechita@theproffice.com
Provides information on all matters relating to the performance and administration of Shechita. It also acts as liaison between all Shechita Boards and the Government and agencies affecting shechita and the kosher meat and poultry industry, throughout the UK and abroad. The National Council registered a trade mark in 1955, and re-registered in 1995 a warranty of Kashrus. This testifies that the holder of this trade mark is a purveyor of kosher meat and/or poultry and is licensed by a recognised Shechita Board affiliated to the Council and under the supervision of a Rabbinical Authority. Shechita UK is its information arm. *Ch.* Shlome Sinitsky; *V. Ch.* Benjamin Mire, David Pine; *Hon. T.* Leo Winter, *H. Life Pres* J. Lobenstein MBE, Rev B. Sandler, R. Singer

RABBINICAL COMMISSION FOR THE LICENSING OF SHOCHETIM
Established in respect of Welfare of Animals Regulations (1995). This provides for the shechita of animals and poultry by a shochet, duly licensed for the purpose by the Rabbinical commission. Membership of the Rabbinical Commission is as follows: The Chief Rabbi, who is the permanent Chair; one member appointed by the Spanish and Portuguese Synagogue (London), who is a Vice Chair; three members appointed by the Beth Din (London); two members appointed by the Federation of Synagogues (London); one member appointed by the Union of Orthodox Hebrew Congregations (London); two members appointed by the Pres. of the BoD to represent regional congregations. *Ch.* The Chief Rabbi; *Hon. S.* Stuart Taylor 305 Ballards Lane, London N12 8GB *Tel* 020 8343 6301
Email info@chiefrabbi.org

SHATNEZ CENTRE TRUST
22 Bell Lane, Hendon, London NW4 2AD
Tel 020 8202 4005
(Est. 1990. Reg. Charity No. 1013840). To provide Shatnez checking at the Shatnez Centre and promote Shatnez observance in the community. *T.* A. E. Bude, David Rabson

SMALL JEWISH COMMUNITIES COUNCIL
c/o Board of Deputies, 6 Bloomsbury Square, London WC1A 2LP
Tel 020 8459 4372
To provide appropiate help to small communities that do not have a Minister. *M.* The Rev Malcolm Weisman OBE, MA

SPANISH AND PORTUGUESE JEWS' CONGREGATION
Website www.sandp.org
The community of Spanish and Portuguese Jews in London was founded by Marranos in the middle of the seventeenth century. The congregation 'Sahar Asamaim', worshipped in Creechurch Lane (where a tablet records the site) from 1657 to 1701, when the Bevis

Marks Synagogue was built. It is the oldest extant synagogue building in Britain except for the medieval synagogue of Lincoln. The first branch synagogue of the congregation in the West End was established in Wigmore Street in 1853, and in 1861 removed to Bryanston Street; in 1896 the existing building in Lauderdale Road, Maida Vale was opened. In 1977 another branch of the Spanish & Portuguese Jews' Congregation was opened in Wembley. The congregation is run by a board of Elders as well as a Mahamad (six members) who act as an Executive. An assessment (Finta) is levied on the Yehidim, and congregational affairs are regulated by laws, termed Ascamot, the first code of which was drawn up in 1663.

The congregation maintains the Medrash of Heshaim (founded in 1664). Hebrew religious instruction is given at the Communal Centre, Ashworth Road, W9

A brotherhood Mikveh Israel (Lavadores), established 1678, and a Burial Society, Hebrat Guemilut Hassadim (1665), attend to the last rites to the dead. A number of charitable and educational trusts exist for the benefit of Sephardim. Previous holders of the office of Haham were: Jacob Sasportas (1664-65); Joshua da Silva (1670-79); Jacob Abendana (1681-5); Solomon Ayllon (1689-1700), David Nietto (1702-28), Isaac Nietto (1733-41), Moses Gomez de Mesquita (1744-51); Moses Cohen Dazevedo (1761-84); Raphael Meldola (1805-28); Benjamin Artom (1866-79); Moses Gaster (1887-1917); Solomon Gaon (1947-77).

Pres. of Elders, D. Dangoor; *V. Pres. of Elders,* R. Leon; *Exec. Dir.* Alison Rosen *London Sephardi Trust.* Office, 2 Ashworth Road, Maida Vale, W9 1JY
Tel 020 7289 2573 *Fax* 020 7289 2709 *Admin.* A. Rosen *Email* alisonrosen@spsyn.org.uk
Rosh Beth Din Dayan S. Amor.
(Reg. Charity No. 212517). Synagogues and organisations are listed in the London and the Home Counties section. *Snr. Rabbi,* Dayan Joseph Dweck

Burial Society
2 Ashworth Road, W9 1JY
Tel 020 7289 2573

CEMETERIES
253 Mile End Road, E1 4BJ. (Opened in 1657. Disused), The oldest Jewish burial ground in the United Kingdom
329 Mile End Road, E1 4NT (Opened 1725. Disused)
Dytchleys, Coxtie Green, Brentwood. (Disused)
Hoop Lane, Golders Green, NW11 7EU *Tel* 020 8455 2569 *Email* director@ejbb-jbc.org.uk
Edgwarebury Lane, Edgware HA8 8QP *Tel* 020 8958 0090 *Email* director@ejbb-jbc.org.uk

FEDERATION OF SYNAGOGUES
65 Watford Way, NW4 3AQ
Tel 020 8202 2263 *Fax* 020 8203 0610
Email info@federationofsynagogues.com *Website* www.federationofsynagogues.com

The Federation of Synagogues, then embodying 16 small Synagogues in the East End of London, was established in 1887. It now comprises 14 Constituent Synagogues and 10 Affiliated congregations situated in most parts of Greater London and Manchester. The objects of the Federation include: To provide the services of Orthodox rabbis, ministers and Dayanim; the provision of a Burial Society; to assist synagogues in the erection, reconstruction or redecoration of their Houses of Worship, to assist in the maintenance of Orthodox religious instruction in Talmud Torahs and Yeshivot; to obtain and maintain Kashrut; to support charitable and philanthropic works; to further the progress of Eretz Yisrael. *Pres.* A. Finlay; *V. Pres.* H. Dony, B. Mire; *T.* L. Newmark, M. Greenbaum; *Chief Exec.* Dr. Eli Kienwald
Constituent and affiliated synagogues are listed in the London and the Home Counties and Manchester sections.
Associated Bodies
Beth Din of the Federation of Synagogues
Dayan Yisroel Yaakov Lichtenstein, Rosh Beth Din, Dayan M.D. Elzas; *Reg.* Rabbi S. Z. Unsdorfer

Kashrus Board
Kashrus Dir. Dayan M. D. Elzas; *Pres.* A. Finlay
Federation Burial Society
Tel 020 8202 3903 *Fax* 020 8203 0610
Office: 65 Watford Way, Hendon NW4 3AQ *Tel* 020 8202 3903 *Fax* 020 8203 0610
Admin. T. Zelmanovits; *Sexton* N. Kahler; *T.* Rabbi J. Cohen, M. Ezra
Hamaor Magazine (Two issues a year)
Federation of Synagogues, 65 Watford Way, London NW4 3AQ
(Est. 1962). *Ed.* E. Chapper

CEMETERIES
Montagu Road, Edmonton, N18 2NF *Tel* 020 8807 2268
Foreman Paul Beasley *Tel* 020 8807 2268
416 Upminster Road North, Rainham, Essex RM13 9SB *Supt.* Rev. M. Brown *Tel* 01708 552
825; *Foreman* Mark Stonely *Tel* 01708 552 825, Mobile 07960 349 382

UNION OF ORTHODOX HEBREW CONGREGATIONS
140 Stamford Hill, N16 6QT
Tel 020 8802 6226 *Fax* 020 8809 6590
(Est. 1926. Reg. Charity No. 249892). The Union of Orthodox Hebrew Congregations was
founded by the late Rabbi Dr. Victor Schonfeld to protect traditional Judaism. It comprises
synagogues and institutions, which retain their independence but accept the authority of
the rabbinate of the union. Synagogues are entitled to representation on the Council of the
Union, through their delegates who elect the executive committee.
　Rabbinate Rabbi Ephraim Padwa (Principal Rabbinate Authority), Dayan A. D. Dunner,
Rabbi Z. Feldman, Dayan S. Friedman, Dayan D. Grynhaus, Rabbi Ch. Halpern, Rabbi E.
Halpern, Rabbi P. Roberts, Dayan J. Padwa; *Court Registrar* J. R. Conrad, *Pres.* Rabbi D.
Frand, *Exec. Co-ord.* Chanoch Kesselman, *Gen. Sec.* C. Z. Schneck
Constituent and affiliated synagogues are listed in the London and the Home Counties
section.
Details of the Eruv in Edgware are given on p.157

Associated Bodies
Kashrus Committee-Kedassia
140 Stamford Hill, N16 6QT *Tel* 020 8800 6833 *Fax* 020 8809 7092
Ch. Sinitsky; *Admin.* Y. Feldman, Y. Y. Frankel
Central Mikvaot Board
140 Stamford Hill, N16 6QT
Tel 020 8802 6226
Adath Yisroel Burial Society
40 Queen Elizabeth's Walk, N16 0HH *Tel* 020 8802 6262/3 *Fax* 020 8800 8764
Sec. D. Lobenstein

CEMETERIES
Carterhatch Lane, Enfield *Tel* 020 8363 3384; Silver Street, Cheshunt, Herts *Tel* 01707 874 220

MASORTI

MASORTI JUDAISM
Alexander House, 3 Shakespeare Road, Finchley, London N3 1XE
Tel 020 8349 6650
Email enquiries@masorti.org.uk *Website* www.masorti.org.uk
Masorti means Traditional Judaism for Modern Jews. Masorti Judaism is the umbrella body
that serves all Masorti communities in Britain. It acts as a central co-ordinating body with
responsibility for developing Masorti communities, providing social, cultural and
educational opportunities for youth, students and young adults, and for promoting
Masorti values. Masorti Judaism provides a network of welcoming, inclusive Jewish

Communities, Noam - Masorti Youth, Marom - Masorti Young Adults, the European Masorti Bet Din, a range of leadership training programmes, adult education courses, and resources for educators. *Jt. Ch.* Clive Sheldon QC, Nick Gendler; *Ch. Exec.* Matt Plen. Constituent synagogues are listed in the London and the Home Counties section. *See also* Bournemouth, Leeds and Oxford.

European Masorti Beth Din (form. **Bet Din of the Assembly of Masorti Synagogues**)
Alexander House, 3 Shakespeare Road, Finchely, London N3 1XE
Tel 020 8349 6650
Email office@europeanmasortibetdin.org *Website* www.europeanmasortibetdin.org
(Est. 2005). Provides Bet Din services (conversion, Divorce, Kashrut Supervision) in Masorti communities in the UK and across Europe. *Av Bet Din and Dir.* Rabbi Chaim Weiner *Email* director@europeanmasortibetdin.org

REFORM

THE MOVEMENT FOR REFORM JUDAISM

The Sternberg Centre for Judaism, 80 East End Road, London N3 2SY
Tel 020 8349 5640 *Fax* 020 8349 5699
Email admin@reformjudaism.org.uk *Website* www.reformjudaism.org.uk
The Movement for Reform Judaism was formed in 2005 as successor to the Reform Synagogues of Great Britain, founded in 1942 with just 6 synagogues. The Movement for Reform Judaism in Britain now consists of 42 synagogues with more than 35,000 members (approximately 20 per cent of UK synagogue affiliations). The Movement is a major supporter of the Leo Baeck College where its rabbis and educators are trained. Akiva Primary School is under the auspices of the Reform and Liberal Movements and Clore Tikva and Clore Shalom Primary School are under Reform, Liberal and Masorti auspices. The Movement sponsors the RSY-Netzer Youth Movement and supports the Jewish Cross Communal Secondary School. The Movement for Reform Judaism seeks to reach out to and engage with Jews 'where they are', understand their Jewish needs and facilitate a wide range of continuing Jewish journeys. It offers pluralist Judaism, rooted in tradition yet in dialogue with modernity.
Life Pres. Sir Sigmund Sternberg; *Pres.* Rabbi Dr. Tony Bayfield; *Movement Rabbi*, Laura Janner-Klausner
Constituent Synagogues are listed in the London and home counties section. *See also* Blackpool; Bournemouth; Bradford; Brighton & Hove; Cambridge; Cardiff; Cheshire; Glasgow; Hull; Liverpool; Maidenhead; Manchester; Milton Keynes; Newcastle; Leeds; N. Manchester; Sheffield & District; Southend & District; South Hampshire; Southport; Thanet & District; Coventry; Darlington; Swindon; Totnes; Cornwall.

Assembly of Rabbis *Ch.* Rabbi Sybil Sheridan
Rabbinical Court (Beit Din) *Tel* 020 8349 5657 *Convenor,* Rabbi Jaqueline Tabick
Associated Schools Akiva Finchley, Clore Shalom Shenley, Clore Tikva Redbridge
RSY-Netzer (The Movement for Reform Judaism's Youth Movement)
See under Organisations Concerned with Jewish Youth

Jewish Joint Burial Society (serving Reform & Masorti communities)
1 Victory Road, Wanstead E11 1UL
Tel 020 8989 5252 *Fax* 020 8989 6075
Email admin@jewishfunerals.org.uk
(Est. 1968; Reg. Charity No. 257345). *Sexton* C.R. Joseph, *Asst. Sexton* M. Kalinsky

THE STERNBERG CENTRE FOR JUDAISM

80 East End Road, N3 2SY
Tel 020 8349 5640 *Fax* 020 8349 5699
Email admin@manorhousetrust.org.uk
(Manor House Trust, Est. 1982. Reg. Charity No. 283083). A European centre for the

promotion of Jewish religious, educational, intellectual and cultural matters. The Centre includes a Holocaust Memorial garden and a mikveh; it houses the Akiva School; Assembly of Reform Rabbis UK; Leo Baeck College; Manor House Books; Manor House Centre for Psychotherapy & Counselling; The Association of Reform and Liberal Mohalim; The Movement for Reform Judaism; Offices of the Reform Beit Din, the Masorti New North London Synagogue, European Union for Progressive Jewry, the Strudel Cafe and the Art Stables. *Ch. of Trs.* Sir Sigmund Sternberg KCSG JP; *T. D.* Leibling; *Movement Ch.* Robert Weiner; *V. Ch.* Dr Jonathan Oppenheimer

LIBERAL JUDAISM (formerly **ULPS**)
The Montagu Centre, 21 Maple Street, London W1T 4BE
Tel 020 7580 1663 *Fax* 020 7631 9838
Email montagu@liberaljudaism.org *Website* www.liberaljudaism.org
(Reg. Charity No. 1151090). Est. 1902 for the advancement of Liberal Judaism and to establish and organise Congregations, Groups and Religion Schools on Liberal Jewish principles. *Ch.* Lucien J. Hudson; *Chief Exec.* Rabbi Danny Rich *Tel* 020 7631 9830 *Email* d.rich@liberaljudaism.org; PA to Chief Exec. Tracy Harris *Tel* 020 7631 9830 *Email* t.harris@liberaljudaism.org
Constituent Synagogues are listed in the London and the Home Counties section. *See also* Bedfordshire; Birmingham; Brighton & Hove; Bristol & West; Crawley; Dublin; East Anglia; Eastbourne; Edinburgh; Gloucestershire; Herefordshire; Kent; Leicester; Lincolnshire; Manchester; Nottingham; Peterborough; Norwich; Suffolk; Reading; Amersham (South Bucks), Wessex.

LJY Netzer
Liberal Judaism's Youth Department LJY-Netzer
Tel 020 7631 0584 *Email* ljynetzer@liberaljudaism.org *Admin* Selina O'Dwyer
Rabbinic Conference
The Montagu Centre, 21 Maple Street, London W1T 4BE
Tel 020 7580 1663
Email montagu@liberaljudaism.org
Ch. Rabbis Charley Baginsky
Associate Communities
Oxford, Beit Ha'Chiddush (Amsterdam) and Wessex Liberal Jewish Group (Bournemouth)
For further information look at the respective headings.

CEMETERIES
Funeral-Dir. Martin Broad and Son. *Tel* 020 8445 2797 *Fax* 020 8343 9463
Edgwarebury Lane, Edgware, Middlesex HA8 8QP *Cemetery Dir.* Lester Harris *Tel* 020 8958 0090/07967 656 733 *Email* director@ejbb-jbc.org.uk
Liberal Jewish Cemetery, Pound Lane, Willesden, NW10 *Supt.* A. O'Brian *Tel* 020 8459 1635
Western Cemetery, Bulls Cross Ride, Cheshunt, Herts EN7 5HT *Supt.* A. Harris *Tel* 01992 717 820

ASSOCIATION OF REFORM AND LIBERAL MOHALIM
The Sternberg Centre for Judaism, 80 East End Road, London N3 2SY
Tel 020 8349 5645 *Fax* 020 8349 5699
(Est. 1988). You can get a full list of Mohalim from constituent synagogues, from Reform Judaism (020 8349 5657), LJ (020 7580 1663) or by writing to the Association at the Sternberg Centre.

WELFARE ORGANISATIONS

BRITISH TAY-SACHS FOUNDATION
Now under the administration of Jewish Care.

CHAI CANCER CARE
142-146 Great North Way, London NW4 1EH
Tel Office 020 8202 2211 *Helpline Freephone* 0808 808 4567 *Fax* 020 8202 2111
Email info@chaicancercare.org *Website* www.chaicancercare.org
(Reg. Charity No. 1978956). Chai Cancer Care is the community's cancer support organisation, providing a range of services including: counselling for families, individuals and couples; complementary therapies; children, teenage and family services; Medical Outpatient Rehabilitation and Palliative Care Service; home support services; group activites and support groups. Services are available to patients in the flagship North West London centre, South London Hackney, Essex, South Manchester, North Manchester, Liverpool, Leeds and Glasgow. *Pres.* Lord Young; *Ch.* L. Hager; *Chief Exec.* Lisa Steele

CHILDREN'S AID COMMITTEE CHARITABLE FUND
P.O. Box 68019, Hendon, NW4 9HN
Email info@thecac.org.uk *Website* www.thecac.org.uk
(Est. 1955. Reg. Charity No. 302933). *Ch.* M. Herman; *Sec.* A. Littman; *Admin* Michele Stern

EZER LEYOLDOS LTD
Unit 2, 2a Northfield Road, London N16 5RN
Tel 020 8880 2488 *Fax* 020 3137 5708
Email mail@ezerleyoldos.co.uk *Website* www.ezerleyoldos.co.uk
(Est. 1986. Reg. Charity No. 1132971). Based in the Hackney and Haringey area, Ezer Leyoldos's aim is to provide support to families with short term difficulties; enable families with ongoing difficulties to function; educate and empower parents by teaching parenting skills; provide support to dysfunctional families. *Dir.* Malke Sterlicht 136 Stamford Hill London N16 6QT; *Ch.* Aron Emanuel Bude 10 Parkway London NW11 0EX; *V. Ch.* Rabbi Abraham Pinter 6 Northdene Gardens London N15 6LX; *Sec.* Michael Posen 46 Riverside Road London N15 6DA

FINNART HOUSE SCHOOL TRUST
Radius Works, Back Lane, London NW3 1HL
Tel 07804 854 905
Email info@finnart.org *Website* www.finnart.org
(Est. 1901. Reg. Charity No. 220917). A charitable trust that provides scholarships and bursaries to Jewish young people. *Ch. of Tru.* Dame Hilary Blume

JAT (Jewish Action and Training for Sexual Health)
c/o 2a Dunstan Road, London NW11 8AA
Tel 07546 429 885
Website www.jat-uk.org
(Reg. Charity No. 327936). JAT is the only charity in the UK providing support for Jewish people from across the whole Jewish community and their families/carers who are living with HIV and AIDS. *Patrons* Prof. Michael Adler, CBE, Clive Lawton, Lady Morris of Kenwood, Lord Sacks of Aldgate; *Client Support,* Janine Clements; *Ch.* Ruth Hilton

JEWISH ASSOCIATION FOR MENTAL ILLNESS – JAMI
Olympia House, Armitage Road, London NW11 8RQ
Tel 020 8458 2223 *Fax* 020 8731 7395
Email info@jamiuk.org *Website* www.jamiuk.org
(Est. 1980. Reg. Charity No. 1003345). JAMI provides mental health services to the Jewish community. These range from day services for those with severe and enduring ill-health,

to education for our children, to ensure they seek help quickly and effectively and so help to prevent just such problems. Other services include befriending; cultural and religious activities; advice and information; social events; outreach and hospital visiting. One in four people will experience mental health difficulties at some time. JAMI helps people to recognise the symptoms and know where and how to seek help. JAMI runs a range of activities to help regain confidence and vital skills, and offers what is for many the only hot, nutritious daily meal that they will eat. JAMI provides a lifeline by enabling people to come to a place which is free of judgement, prejudice and stigma.

JEWISH CARE
Amélie House, Maurice and Vivienne Wohl Campus, 221 Golders Green Road, London NW11 9DQ
Tel 020 8922 2000 Jewish Care Direct (Helpline) 020 8922 2222 *Fax* 020 8201 3897
Email jcdirect@jcare.org *Website* www.jewishcare.org
(Est. 1990. Reg. Charity No. 802559). Jewish Care is the largest social care and health charity for the Jewish community in London and the South-east. Staff and volunteers help and support over 7,000 people every week through a range of 70 services. Jewish Care wants to make a positive impact on the lives of Jewish people by creating and providing excellent social care that enhances wellbeing and inspires them to stay connected to their community. Its ambition is to work collaboratively, initiate debate, be a catalyst for change, a channel for advancement and a voice across the sector. Jewish Care – promoting meaningful lives for our community.
   Jewish Care was formed on 1 January 1990 by the merger of the Jewish Blind Society and the Jewish Welfare Board. Jewish Care has since merged its activities with a number of other Jewish organisations. These include: the Jewish Home and Hospital at Tottenham, Food for the Jewish Poor, British Tay Sachs Foundation, Waverley Manor (Friends of the London Jewish Hospital), Brighton & Hove Jewish Home, Stepney Jewish (B'nai Brith) Clubs and Settlements, and the Redbridge Jewish Community Centre (Sinclair House), and most recently a collaboration with JAMI. *Pres.* Lord Levy; *Ch.* Steven Lewis; *Chief Exec.* Simon Morris

JEWISH CHILD'S DAY (JCD)
707 High Road, London N12 0BT
Tel 020 8446 8804
Email info@jcd.uk.com *Website* www.jcd.uk.com
(Est. 1947. Reg. Charity No. 209266). Raises funds to distribute to agencies providing services to Jewish children in need of special care throughout the world. Provides equipment of all kinds and supports specific projects for children who are blind, deaf, mentally or physically disabled, orphaned, neglected, deprived, abused, refugee or in need of medical care. *Life Pres.* J. Jacobs; *Ch.* J. Moss MBE; *T.* S. Moss, CBE; *Exec. Dir.* Melanie Klass

JEWISH GENETIC DISORDERS UK (JGD UK)
P.O. Box 65520, London, N3 9BU
Tel 020 8123 5022
Email info@jgduk.org *Website* www.jewishgeneticdisordersuk.org
(Est. 2010. Reg. Charity No.1134935). JGD UK is dedicated to making a real difference to the prevention, diagnosis and management of Jewish genetic disorders in the UK. It focuses on genetic conditions that are more common among people of Jewish ancestry relative to the general population - including disorders that are fatal in childhood and others associated with chronic disability.
JGD UK aims to raise awareness of Jewish genetic disorders across the Jewish and healthcare professional communities; and to help those affected and at risk, to access the best available information, services and support.
Its core activities include: awareness raising, information provision and referral, and facilitating access to responsible genetic testing services. *Exec. Dir.* Katrina Sarig; *Ch. of Tru. Bd.* Peter Jacobs

JEWISH HELPLINE LTD (formerly **MIYAD**)
(*Admin. Office*) Studio 2, No. 2 Downshire Hill, London NW3 2NR
Tel 0800 652 9249
Email jewishhl@live.co.uk
(Est. 1988. Reg. Charity No. 1101612). Professionally trained volunteers offer free telephone support to individuals who are struggling to cope with life's challenges. Through listening and talking, the Jewish Helpline offers a lifeline at a time when someone may be feeling very alone, anxious, depressed or suicidal. Jewish Helpline reaches people of all ages across the entire spectrum of the community. Sunday - Thursday 12pm-12am, Friday 12-3pm. *Tru.* T. Zenios, A. Kamiel, D. Davies

JEWISH MARRIAGE COUNCIL
23 Ravenshurst Avenue, NW4 4EE
Tel 020 8203 6311
Email info@jmc-uk.org *Website* www. jmc-uk.org
(Est. 1946). The Council provides the following services: a counselling service for couples, individuals and families - nobody is turned away through lack of funds. Divorce Mediation. (*Tel* 020 8203 6311); support group for divorced/divorcing women *Tel* 020 8203 5207

JEWISH WOMEN'S AID (JWA)
JWA, P.O. Box 2670, London N12 9ZE
Tel Office, 020 8445 8060 *Fax* 020 8445 0305
Confidential Helpline Freephone 0808 801 0500 Monday-Thursday 9.30am-9.30pm
Email info@jwa.org.uk For *Email* advice advice@jwa.org *Website* www.jwa.org.uk
(Est. 1992. Reg. Charity No. 1047045). Jewish Women's Aid (JWA) is a charity for Jewish Women, and their children, who are affected by domestic violence. JWA has two core aims; First, to provide confidential, accessible, empowering and culturally sensitive advocacy and support for Jewish women and children who are affected by domestic violence. Second, through education, training and awareness raising, to ensure that all sectors of the Jewish community recognise and speak out against domestic violence.
JWA has a team of dedicated professional staff and volunteers who run the organisation's core services; a national freephone helpline; a refuge for Jewish women and their children; a community support and children's service, free counselling services, and education and awareness raising programmes.
Hon. Pres. Judith Usiskin; *Ch.* Francis Turner; *Exec. Dir.* Naomi Dickson

JSENSE
9 Leicester Avenue, Salford M7 4HA
Tel 0161 850 3330
Email services@jsense.org.uk *Website* www.jsense.org.uk
(Reg. Charity No. 1151197). Support for education of Jewish Children with special educational needs. *Admin.* Michelle Conrad

LANGDON
PO Box 640, Edgware, Middlesex HA8 4GL
Tel 0845 600 6562 (ext. 4, admissions), (ext. 5, fundraising/events)
Email info@langdonuk.org *Website* www.langdon.info
(Est. 1992. Reg. Charity No. 1142742). Langdon provides education, employment and supported living for Jewish young and adults with learning disabilities in Manchester and London.
CEO, Alison Rosen; *Ch.* Jonathan Pfeffer; *V. Ch.* Jonathan Joseph; *Tru.* Geoffrey Berger, Michael Blane, Jeremy Bolchover, Ross Fabian, Paul Goodman, Nigel Henry, Carole Joseph, Gareth Kreike, Jonny Manson, Samuel Shaerf, Laurence Tish

London Centre: Maccabi House, Gideon Close, Manor Park Crescent, Edgware, Middlesex HA8 7FR

Manchester Office: 44 Rectory Lane, Prestwich, Manchester, M25 1BL
Langdon College: 9 Leicester Avenue, Salford, Manchester, M7 4HA *Princ.* Christopher Mayho

THE MANOR HOUSE CENTRE FOR PSYCHOTHERAPY AND COUNSELLING (MHCPC)
The Sternberg Centre, 80 East End Road, N3 2SY
Tel 020 8371 0180
Email admin@manorhousecentre.org.uk *Website* www.manorhousecentre.org.uk
(Reg. Charity No. 1131804). The Centre provides counselling training for people working
or planning to work, in both paid and voluntary positions in the community. A counselling
service is also provided for those seeking help for emotional distress.

RESOURCE (formerly **Employment Resource Centre**)
8 Dancastle Court, 14 Arcadia Avenue, London N3 2JU
Tel 020 8346 4000 *Fax* 020 8346 4433
Email office@resource-centre.org *Website* www.resource-centre.org
(Est. 1992. Reg. Charity No. 1106331). A service for the Jewish community offering
opportunities for the unemployed to gain skills and training for the job market.
Ch. Exec. Victoria Sterman

TAY-SACHS SCREENING CENTRE
Genetics 7th Floor, Borough Wing, Guy's Hospital, Great Maze Pond, London SE1 9RT
Tel 020 7188 1364 *Fax* 020 7188 1369
Website www.guysandstthomas.nhs.uk
Provides information, carrier testing and genetic counselling for Tay-Sachs disease, and a
walk-in clinic on Monday morning. Additional private test now offered for 8 other genetic
conditions that are common in the Ashkenazi Jewish population. *Sec.* Debbie Wyndham;
Genetic Counsellor Sara Levene

REFUGEE ORGANISATIONS

45 AID SOCIETY
10 York House, Royal Connaught Drive, Bushey, Herts WD23 2RF
Tel 07786 240 309
Email max.kim@hotmail.co.uk
(Est. 1963). The Society consists mainly of Holocaust survivors who came to England in 1945/6 and others who have immigrated subsequently. It maintains close links with members who have emigrated to Israel, USA, Canada and other countries. The Society is active in the community, helps members as well as others in need. It furthers Holocaust education and other charitable causes. *Pres.* Sir Martin Gilbert; *Ch.* Ben Helfgott MBE D.Univ; *V. Ch.* Angela Cohen; *T.* Alan Greenberg; *Sec.* Kim Stern

ACJR (Association of Children of Jewish Refugees)
Tel 020 8201 7986
Email info@acjr.org.uk *Website* www.acjr.org.uk
A cultural and social group for those whose parents were victims of, or who fled from, Nazi persecution in the 1930s and 1940s. *Publ.* Monthly newsletter. *Ch.* Anthony Abbey

➤ ASSOCIATION OF JEWISH REFUGEES (AJR)
(Head Office) Jubilee House, Merrion Avenue, Stanmore, Middlesex HA7 4RL
Tel 020 8385 3070 *Fax* 020 8385 3080
Email enquiries@ajr.org.uk *Website* www.ajr.org.uk
(The Association of Jewish Refugees (AJR) is a company limited by guarantee (8220991) and a charity registered with the Charity Commission for England and Wales (1149882). The AJR provides social and welfare services to Holocaust refugees and survivors and their families. Alongside its team of dedicated social care workers, the AJR operates a nationwide network of regional groups for members to enjoy entertainment. The AJR Volunteers department looks after the interests of many AJR members who still live in their own homes, including arranging for regular visits from a befriender and helping out at regional groups and Head Office. The AJR offers advice and assistance with claims for Holocaust-era compensation and the restitution of appropriated assets. The AJR arranges frozen kosher meals to be delivered once a week to members in the North West London area. The Kindertransport and the Child Survivors Association (CSA) are Special Interest Groups of the AJR. All members receive the monthly *AJR Journal*, which combines topical news analysis with feature articles as well as book, theatre and film reviews.
Chief Exec. Michael Newman; *Dir.* David Kaye. *Publ.*: *AJR Journal* (monthly), *Kindertransport Newsletter* (quarterly), *Child Survivors Association* (bi-monthly).

➤ HOLOCAUST SURVIVORS' CENTRE (HSC)
(Jewish Care with the support of World Jewish Relief)
Corner of Parson Street/Church Road, London NW4 1QA
Tel 020 8202 9844 *Fax* 020 8202 2404
Email hsc@jcare.org
A Jewish social centre for survivors who were in Europe during the Second World War, or came to the UK as refugees after November 1938 and on the Kindertransport.
It offers a friendly, safe place where elderly survivors can meet and socialise, and where they can benefit from a full therapeutic programme. The centre offers a wide range of social activities for members, six days a week, Sunday-Friday. Testimonies are also recorded and survivors visit schools, colleges and universities to talk about their experiences. It is the only centre designed specifically for Holocaust survivors in the UK.
Dir. Aviva Trup; *Co-ord.* Rachelle Lazarus, Melanie Gotlieb

SHALVATA
Parson Street/Corner of Church Road, London NW4 1QA
Tel 020 8203 9033 *Fax* 020 8201 5534
Email shalvata@jcare.org

Associated with the Holocaust Survivors' Centre. Testimonies are recorded. Shalvata is a counselling and social work service. It is also known as a training and consultation service for professionals working with war trauma. In conjunction with World Jewish Relief, Shalvata is currently working with a group of Bosnian refugees.

ORGANISATIONS CONCERNED WITH THE JEWS OF EASTERN EUROPE

COMMUNITY CONNECTIONS (Formerly **Exodus 2000**)
European Union for Progressive Judaism, Sternberg Centre, 80 East End Road, London N3 2SY
Tel 020 8349 5651
Email communityconnections@eupj.org *Website* www.eupj.org/en/communityconnections
Community Connections' aims to support Progressive Judaism in Eastern Europe. It works under the aegis of the European Union for Progressive Judaism (part of the WUPJ). Community Connections has a national executive and groups in many Reform and Liberal synagogues. Its major areas of work are: (i) supporting the growth of Progressive Judaism in the former Soviet Union; (ii) establishing and facilitating twinnings between UK Progressive Communities and those in Russia, Ukraine and Belarus; (iii) sending Rabbis and lay educators to teach. Community Connections works closely with the World Union of Progressive Judaism in Israel and America.

ZIONIST ORGANISATIONS

ISRAEL EMBASSY
2 Palace Green, Kensington, W8 4QB
Tel 020 7957 9500 (Consulate telephone hours: Monday-Thursday 2.30-5pm)
Email info@london.mfa.gov.il *Website* www.embassyofisrael.co.uk
Consulate opening hours Monday-Thursday 9.30am-12.45pm, Friday and eve of festivals.
9.30am-11.30pm (See website for full details). *Ambassador to the Court of St James's, HE* Daniel Taub; *Min. Plenipotentiary* Eitan Na'eh

➤ JEWISH AGENCY FOR ISRAEL
7th Floor, Central House, 1 Ballards Lane, London N3 1LQ
Aliyah and Youth Community Services: *Tel* 020 8371 5250 *Fax* 020 8371 5251
Treasury & Administration: *Tel* 020 8371 5300 *Fax* 020 8371 5301
Email londonoffice@jafi.org *Website* www.jewishagency.org
Since 1929, The Jewish Agency for Israel has been working to secure a vibrant Jewish future. It is instrumental in founding and building the State of Israel and continues to serve as the official link between the Jewish state and Jewish communities everywhere. This global partnership has enabled The Jewish Agency For Israel to address the Jewish People's greatest challenges in every generation.
Today, The Jewish Agency For Israel connects the global Jewish family, bringing Jews to Israel, and Israel to Jews, by providing meaningful Israel engagement and facilitating Aliyah. It builds a better society in Israel - and beyond - energizing young Israelis and their worldwide peers to rediscover a collective sense of Jewish purpose. The Jewish Agency continues to be the Jewish world's first responder, prepared to address emergencies in Israel, and to rescue Jews from countries where they are at-risk. *Ch. of the Exec.* Natan Sharansky; *Ch. of the Bd. of Gov.* Richard L. Pearlstone; *Dir. Gen.* Alan Hoffman

JEWISH LABOUR MOVEMENT (incorporating Poale Zion)
P.O. Box 695, Harrow, HA3 0HF
Tel/Fax 020 8621 4574
Website www.jlm.org.uk
The Jewish Labour Movement, launched officially in July 2004, is the successor to Poale Zion. As such it retains its Labour Zionist ideals and affiliation to the Labour Party, where it acts as a link between Labour and the Jewish community. It also works within communal organisations, such as the Board of Deputies. Its main campaigning activities focus on the peaceful conclusion of the Israel-Palestine conflict, on the basis of a two-state solution, and combating racism and antisemitism. *Ch.* Louise Ellman MP; *V. Ch.* Neil Nerva, Jerry Lewis; *Hon. S.* Dr Judith Bara; *Hon. T.* Edwin Strauss

JNF UK
Head Office, JNF House, Spring Villa Park, Spring Villa Road, Edgware, Middlesex HA8 7ED
Tel 020 8732 6100 *Fax* 020 8732 6111
Website www.jnf.co.uk
CEO Matan Toledano; *Ch.* Samuel Hayek; *V. Ch.* Dr. Michael Sinclair

KKL Executor & Trustee Co. Ltd
JNF House, Spring Villa Park, Spring Villa Road, Edgware, Middlesex HA8 7ED
Tel Freephone 0800 358 3587 *Fax* 020 8732 6111
Email wills@kkl.org.uk
Will writing, Estate planning and Executorship services.

SmartGiving
Head Office, Unit 6, Spring Villa Park, Spring Villa Road, Edgware, Middlesex HA8 7ED
Tel Freephone 0800 358 1191 *Fax* 020 8732 6111
Email info@smartgiving.org.uk
Admission of charity accounts, payroll giving and online fundraising platform

LIKUD-HERUT MOVEMENT OF THE UNITED KINGDOM

Email mail@Likud-Herut.org.uk *Website* www.likud-Herut.org.uk

(Est. 1970). To promote the Zionist ideology as conceived by Ze'ev Jabotinsky. Member of World Likud. *Life Pres.* Eric Graus; *Ch.* Zalmi Unsdorfer

Affiliated Organisations: Young Likud-Herut; (Brit Nashim Herut Women's League); Betar-Tagar, Brit Hashmonayim.

MERETZ UK For equality, human rights and peace (part of World Union of Meretz) Hashomer House, 37A Broadhurst Gardens, London NW6 3BN

Tel 020 7328 5451/020 3286 1616

Email info@meretz.org.uk *Website* www.meretz.org.uk

Social, cultural, educational and political programme, stressing humanistic values of Judaism and progressive Zionist elements.

NEFESH B'NEFESH

65 Watford Way, Hendon, London NW4 3AQ

Tel 0800 075 7200

Website www.nbn.org.il

Established in 2002 with the aim of revitalising western Aliyah (immigration to Israel) from USA and Canada. In May 2006, in response to numerous requests from British Jewry, Nefesh B'Nefesh expanded its services to the UK. Working together with the Jewish Agency and the Government of Israel, Nefesh B'Nefesh assists Olim (immigrants to Israel) throughout the entire Aliyah process, from the planning stage to well beyond arrival in Israel. By removing or minimising the financial, professional, logistical and social obstacles that potential Olim face, Nefesh B'Nefesh helps ensure their successful absorption in Israel. To date, the organisation has brought over 35,000 Olim (new immigrants) from North America and the UK.

Dir. of UK Aliyah Dov Newmark *Email* dov@nbn.org.il

PRO-ZION: PROGRESSIVE RELIGIOUS ZIONISTS

The Sternberg Centre for Judaism, 80 East End Road, N3 2SY

Tel 020 8349 5640

Email info@prozion.org.uk *Website* www.prozion.org.uk

(Est. 1978). To work for full legal and religious rights for Progressive Judaism in Israel, to affirm the centrality in Jewish life of the State of Israel. Affiliated to the Zionist Federation, LJ and the Movement for Reform Judaism. Associated with the Israel Movement for Progressive Judaism. A constituent of Arzenu. *Co-Ch.* D. Needlestone, C. Gluckman; *Hon. S. M.* Silverman; *Hon. T. S.* Michaels; *Admin.* P. Lewis *Publ.* Shema, Progressive Jewish News

UJIA (United Jewish Israel Appeal)

37 Kentish Town Road, London NW1 8NX

Tel 020 7424 6400 *Fax* 020 7424 6401

Email central@ujia.org *Website* www.ujia.org

(Reg. Charity No. 1060078. Reg. Company No. 3295115). UJIA changes lives by investing in young people in Israel and in our Jewish community. In the under-resourced Galil region, UJIA is creating new educational and employment opportunities through schools, colleges and community projects. In the UK it underpins the crucial ladder of Jewish and Israel engagement, by supporting youth movements and organisations, schools and educational programmes in Israel. *Hon. Pres.* The Lord Levy, The Rt. Hon. The Lord Woolf; Chief Rabbi Ephraim Mirvis; *Hon. V. Pres.* Lord Janner of Braunstone QC, Gerald M. Ronson CBE; *Pres.* Sir Trevor Chinn CVO, David M. Cohen, Mick Davis, Brian Kerner; *V. Pres.* Michael Bradfield, Stanley Cohen OBE, Alan Fox, Michael Goldstein FCA, Dov Hamburger, Ronald Preston, Stephen Rubin OBE, Sir Harry Solomon, Anthony Spitz, Prof. Anthony Warrens, Michael Ziff; *Ch.* Bill Benjamin; *Chief Exec.* Michael Wegier; *Company Sec.* Maurice Stone FCA; *Fin. Dir.* Eyal Samuel

WIZOUK

Charles House, 108-110 Finchley Road, London NW3 5JJ
Tel 020 7319 9169 *Fax* 020 7486 7521
Email central@wizouk.org *Website* www.wizouk.org
(Est. 1918. Reg. Charity No. 1125012. Reg. Company No. 6634748). The largest women's society in the UK and Ireland. WIZOUK is the UK Branch of World WIZO, the leading provider of social welfare and educational services for disadvantaged families and children in Israel. It has over 90 affiliated women's groups with over 9,000 members. Its mission is to help support and strengthen Israeli citizens through fundraising. *Pres.* Loraine Warren; *Ch.* Jill Shaw; *Hon. S.* M. Pollock; *T.* Helen Reisman, Hanni Seifert; *Exec. Dir.* Linda Boxer *Publ.* WIZOUK newsletter (Two issues a year).

WORLD ZIONIST ORGANISATION

BM Box 1948, London WC1N 3XX
Tel 020 8202 0202 *Fax* 020 8202 0233
Website www.zionist.org.uk
The WZO was established by the first Zionist Congress, which met in Basle on August 29, 1897. The aim of the Organisation, as defined in the programme adopted by the Basle Congress, was to secure for the Jewish people a home in Palestine guaranteed by public law. At the Congress, a constitution providing for a self-governing World Organisation, with the Zionist Congress as the supreme body, was adopted.
The aims of Zionism, as enunciated in the 'New Jerusalem Programme' adopted by the 27th World Zionist Congress in June, 1968, are:
The unity of the Jewish People and the centrality of Israel in Jewish Life;
The ingathering of the Jewish people in its historic homeland, Eretz Israel, through Aliya from all countries;
The strengthening of the State of Israel which is based on the prophetic vision of justice and peace;
The preservation of the identity of the Jewish people through the fostering of Jewish and Hebrew education and of Jewish spiritual and cultural values. *UK contact,* Alan Aziz

ZIONIST FEDERATION OF GREAT BRITAIN AND IRELAND

Box 1948, 116 Ballards Lane, London N3 2DN
Tel 020 8202 0202
Email office@zfuk.org *Website* www.zionist.org.uk
(Est. 1899). The Zionist Federation was founded in 1899 and helped create support for the establishment of the State of Israel. Today the ZF is the UK's leading Israel advocacy organisation countering false and unfair criticisms of Israel and educating and empowering people to promote a better understanding of the country by highlighting Israel's positives. We are supported by over 70 affiliated organisations, representing a wide range of political and religious views and ages. Each year the ZF initiates more than 200 events, ranging from educational seminars, university programmes, advocacy campaigns and media training sessions, to lobbies of Parliament, all designed to present the truth about Israel and demonstrate the country's diversity.
Exec. Ch. Paul Charney; *V. Ch.* Howard Ross, David Duke Cohan; *Hon. T.* Jerrold Bennett; *Pres.* Prof Eric Moonman OBE, Harvey Rose; *Dir.* Alan Aziz; *Dir. Young ZF,* Royi Gutkin; *Fin.* Rowena Rosenberg; *Campaigns off.* Chris Lawes; *P.A.* Louise Rose
Cttee. Chairmen Constitution, Jonathan Kramer; *Fin.* John Barnett; Yom Ha'atzmaut, Estelle Gilston; Young ZF, Jerrold Bennett

ORGANISATIONS CONCERNED WITH ISRAEL AND ISRAELI ORGANISATIONS

EMIC STUDY GROUP ON ISRAEL AND THE MIDDLE EAST
42763, London N2 0YJ
8444 0777 *Fax* 020 8444 0681
Email info@foi-asg.org
(Reg. Charity No. 801772). An academic organisation which aims at forging and expanding research contacts between academics in this country and their colleagues in Israel. Organises Anglo-Israel Research Workshops in Israel and the UK. *Pres.* Sir Walter Bodmer, Oxford University; *T.* Aviva Petrie, Eastman Dental Instit.; *Dir.* J. D. A. Levy

AKIM
(Est. 1964. Reg. Charity No. 241458). To assist with the rehabilitation of mentally handicapped children in Israel. *Pres.* Sir Sidney Samuelson CBE. *V. Pres.* Judge B. Lightman; *Ch.* A. Broza; *V. Ch.* J. Samad; *Hon. T.* V. Cohen. *Corr.* 22 Golf Close, Stanmore, Middlesex HA7 2PP *Tel* 020 8954 2772 *Email* info@akim.org.uk *Hon. S.* B. Kober

ALL-PARTY-BRITISH ISRAEL PARLIAMENTARY GROUP
c/o Louise Ellman, House of Commons, London, SW1A 0AA
Tel 020 7219 3000
Email louise.ellman@parliament.uk *Ch.* Louise Ellman MP; *T.* Mike Freer MP; *Sec.* Matthew Offord MP; *V. Ch.* Bob Blackman MP

ANGLO-ISRAEL ARCHAEOLOGICAL SOCIETY
2nd Floor, Supreme House, 300 Regents Park Road, London N3 2JX
Tel 020 8349 5754
Email sheilarford1@sky.com *Website* www.aias.org.uk
(Reg. Charity No. 220367). Lectures on recent archaeological discoveries in Israel, publishes an annual research bulletin entitled Strata and awards travel grants to students to participate in excavations in Israel. *Ch.* Prof. Martin Goodman, Oriental Institute, Pusey Lane, Oxford OX1 2LE; *Admin.* Sheila Ford

ANGLO-ISRAEL ASSOCIATION
P.O. Box 47819, London NW11 7WD
Tel 020 8458 1284 *Fax* 020 8458 3484
Email info@angloisraelassociation.com *Website* www.angloisraelassociation.com
(Est. 1949. Reg. Charity No. 313523). The purpose of the Association is to promote a wider and better understanding of Israel in the UK; to encourage exchanges in both directions; and generally to support activities which foster goodwill between British and Israeli People. The AIA administers two educational Trust Funds. The Wyndham Deedes Memorial Travel Scholarship provides British Students with the opportunity to study in Israel. The Kenneth Lindsay Scholarship Trust provides scholarships for Israeli students to study in the UK. *Fdr.* The late Brigadier-General Sir Wyndham Deedes, CMG, DSO; *Hon. Pres.* The Israeli Ambassador; *Ch. of C.* Lady Sainsbury; *Ch. Exec. Cttee.* Lord Bew; *Hon. T.* H. Lewis; *Exec. Dir.* R. Saunders

THE BALFOUR DIAMOND JUBILEE TRUST
67 Addison Road, London W14 8JL
Tel 020 7603 5847
Email strage@compuserve.com
(Est. 1977. Reg. Charity No. 276353). To consolidate and strengthen cultural relations between the UK and Israel. Provides the community with a diverse programme of topical activities throughout the year in literature and the arts. Makes financial support available to individuals and small organisations – both in the UK and Israel – whose work will make an enduring cultural contribution.

BANK LEUMI (UK) plc
London Office, 20 Stratford Place, London W1C 1BG
Tel 020 7907 8000
Email info@bankleumi.co.uk *Website* www.bankleumi.co.uk
Bank Leumi (UK) is a subsidiary of Bank Leumi Le-Israel B.M., which was established in London in 1902 as the financial instrument of the Zionist Movement (under the name of Jewish Colonial Trust). Today the bank specialises in providing corporate and private banking services via its offices in London (Head Office) and Leeds. The bank has two subsidiaries in Jersey, C.I., Bank Leumi (Jersey,) Ltd. and Leumi Overseas Trust Corp. Ltd. and an asset based lending subsidiary in Brighton, Leumi ABL Ltd. *Ch.* Y. Mintz; *CEO,* Eli Katzav

BEN-GURION UNIVERSITY FOUNDATION
Ort House, 126 Albert Street, London NW1 7NE
Tel 020 7446 8558
Email bengurion.foundation@bguf.org.uk *Website* www.bguf.org.uk
(Est. 1974. Reg. Charity No. 276203). Promoting and raising awareness of Ben-Gurion University of the Negev (number one choice of Israeli undergraduates - *National Union of Israeli Students Survey 2012*), Israel's youngest University founded in 1969 with a special mandate to develop the Negev. BGU is a University with a conscience, where high standards of research are integrated with community involvement. The University has five Faculties: Health Sciences, Humanities and Social Sciences, Natural Sciences, Engineering Sciences and the Guilford Glazer Faculty of Business and Management. There is also the Kreitman School of Advanced Graduate Studies. Ben-Gurion University is privileged to have the only National Jean Monnet Centre of Excellence in European Studies in Israel. *Ch. V. Pres.* Lord George Weidenfeld, Suzanne Zlotowski, the Countess of Avon, Arnold Bengis; *Ch.* Harold Paisner; *Tr.* Eric Charles; *Chief Exec.* Jeremy Kelly; *Admin. Dir.* Hannah Allen

BRITISH & EUROPEAN MACHAL ASSOCIATION
3 Moorcroft Court, Bibsworth Road, London N3 3RE
Tel/Fax 020 8343 3508
Email stanleymedicks@email.uk.com *Website* www.machal.org.il
To inform and publicise the inaugeration of a Machal Exhibition at Beit Hatfusot (Museum of Diaspora) on the Campus of Tel Aviv University. The exhibition depicts the heroic endeavour and sacrifice of Machal (Volunteers from the Diaspora) in the 1948 Israel War of Independence. *Co-ordinator* Stanley Medicks

BRITISH FRIENDS OF THE ART MUSEUMS OF ISRAEL
Euston Tower, Floor 33, 286 Euston Road, London NW1 3DP
Tel 020 3463 8715
Email info@bfami.org *Website* www.bfami.org
(Est. 1948. Reg. Charity No. 313008). BFAMI raises funds to help support art museums in Israel. The main focus is on educational activities and the projects sponsored enrich the lives of children from Israel's multi-cultural backgrounds. The versatility of these projects engages individuals as well as communities and offers activities which are open to everyone especially the disadvantaged. BFAMI also acquires works of art and antiques for the museum as well as sponsoring exhibitions. *Patrons* H.E. The Ambassador of Israel, Sir Anthony Caro OM CBE, Dame Vivien Duffield DBE, Sir Anish Kapoor, Sir Timothy Sainsbury PC; *Ch.* Wendy Fisher; *Exec. Dir.* Michelle Hyman

BRITISH FRIENDS OF BAR ILAN UNIVERSITY
109 Baker Street, London W1U 6RP
Tel 020 7486 7394 *Fax* 020 7935 1192
Email info@bfbiu.org *Website* www.bfbiu.org
(Est. 1957. Reg. Charity No. 314139). (*See* p. 266). (BFBIU) promotes Israel's fastest-growing university through a variety of activities designed to advance its academic

programmes, research, and continued growth. The Bar-Ilan family numbers 33,000 students pursuing their BA, MA and PhD degrees on the University's award-winning campus just outside Tel Aviv and its four regional colleges throughout the country. Recently Bar-Ilan opened a new Medical School in Sfat, This is a National Israeli project. Combining academic excellence with a commitment to Jewish enrichment and values, Bar-Ilan has achieved an international reputation in the sciences and humanities. *Ch.* Romie Tager QC; *Exec. Dir.* Shlomo Rechtschaffen; *Asst. Dir.* Nadia Nathan; *Chancellor* Rabbi Joseph H. Lookstein; *Pres.* Rabbi Prof. Daniel Hershkowitz; *Rector* Prof. Teitelbaum

BRITISH FRIENDS OF BOYS TOWN JERUSALEM
6 Bloomsbury Square, London WC1A 2LP
Tel 020 7404 1437
Email office@boystownjerusalem.co.uk
(Est. 1963. Reg. Charity No. 1100332). To help and enrich the lives of over 900 disadvantaged Jewish students who study and live at Boys Town Jerusalem (Kiryat Noar, Bayit Vegan). *Ch.* L. Reuben

BRITISH FRIENDS OF HAIFA UNIVERSITY
c/o Jewish memorial Council, 26 Enford Street, London W1H 1DW
Tel 020 7724 3777
Email friends@haifa-univ.org.uk *Website* www.haifa-univ.org.uk
(Reg. Charity No. 270733). To further the interests and development of Haifa University (*See* p.266) by donations, books, equipment and subscriptions. The British Founders are represented on the board of Governors of Haifa University *Co.-Ch.* Peter Kadas, Jonathan Lux; Exec *Dir.* Tali Sayar

BRITISH FRIENDS OF THE HEBREW UNIVERSITY OF JERUSALEM
Supreme House, 300 Regents Park Road, London N3 2JX
Tel 020 8349 5757 *Fax* 020 8349 5750
Email friends@bfhu.org *Website* www. bfhu.org.uk
(Est. 1926. Reg. Charity No. 209691. Reg. Company No. 6350828). To promote and fundraise on behalf of the Hebrew University of Jerusalem, Israel's leading academic and research centre. The Hebrew University works for the benefit of all Israel's citizens while benefiting nations across the globe and enhancing Israel's reputation. The University boasts an impressive 8 Nobel Prize Laureates, over 273 Israel Prize winners, 14 Wolff Prizes and ranks in the Top 60 of world universities (Shanghai Jiao Tong Rankings). *Pres.* John Sacher CBE; *Ch.* Isaac Kaye; *Chief Exec.* Nigel Salomon. The British and Irish Friends are represented on the Hebrew University Board of Governors. **Groups** Legacies; Students/Alumni; Women's Group; Legal; Young Profession and various Regional Groups including Glasgow friends.

BRITISH FRIENDS OF THE ISRAEL FREE LOAN ASSOCIATION
c/o K.C. Keller FCA, 25 Lodge Avenue, Elstree, Herts WD6 3NA
Tel 020 8207 2627
Email ifla@freeloan.org.il *Website* www.freeloan.org.il
(Reg. Charity No. 1009568). Provides interest-free loans to Russian and Ethiopian immigrants in Israel and other needy Israelis, including small business loans, emergency housing, medical loans, and loans to families with handicapped children.
Established in Jerusalem in 1990, and in 1992 in London. *Ch.* Kenneth Keller *Email* kennethk53@gmail.com; *Hon. T.* D. Druce; *Patrons,* Lord Sacks.

BRITISH FRIENDS OF THE ISRAEL GUIDE DOG CENTRE FOR THE BLIND
P.O. Box 756, Borehamwood, Herts WD6 9JE
Tel 07702 316 423
Website www.israelguidedog.org
(Reg. Charity No. 1027996). Office hours Monday-Thursday 9.30am-3.30pm *Projects Co-ord.* Jess Green *Email* bfigdcb-jessgreen@sky.com

BRITISH FRIENDS OF ISRAEL WAR DISABLED
45 Ealing Road, Wembley, Middlesex HA0 4BA
Tel 020 8903 8746 *Fax* 020 8795 2240
(Est. 1974. Reg. Charity No. 269269). A non-political organisation dedicated to helping disabled soldiers rebuild their lives. Aid is given in purchasing rehabilitation equipment at Beit Halochem. Working with the ZAHAL Disabled Veterans' Organisation, we bring groups of injured soldiers to the UK to stay with caring families. *Ch.* F. M. Weinberg; *H. Solicitor* L. Curry; *Hon. T.* C. Niren

BRITISH FRIENDS OF PEACE NOW
P.O. Box 35583, London NW4 4QY
Tel 020 8621 7172
Website www.peacenowuk.org
(Est. 1982. Reg. Charity No. 297295). Peace Now is a grass roots Israeli movement dedicated to Israeli–Palestinian and Israeli–Arab peace. Peace Now organises pro-peace activities and monitors Israel's settlement policy on the West Bank and Gaza Strip. The first and primary goal of Peace Now is to press the Israeli government to seek peace – through negotiations and mutual compromise – with Israel's Arab neighbours and the Palestinian people. British Friends of Peace Now mobilises support for the Israeli peace movement and the peace process among British Jews and the wider community. It is a membership organisation. Membership expresses support for the many Israelis actively working for peace, security, justice and reconciliation in the Middle East.

BRITISH FRIENDS OF RAMBAM MEDICAL CENTRE
1 Opal Court, 120 Regents Park Road, London, N3 3HY
Tel 020 8371 1500
Email anita@rambamuk.co.uk *Website* www.rambamuk.co.uk
(Reg. Charity No. 028061). Raising funds for the purchase of medical equipment for all hospital departments and in particular for Paediatric Nephrology, Oncology, Intensive Care and Incubators for at risk babies in the Neo Natal Department. Also funding scholarships for research. *Dir.* Anita Alexander-Passe

BRITISH FRIENDS OF SARAH HERZOG MEMORIAL HOSPITAL (EZRATH NASHIM), JERUSALEM
37 The Avenue, Radlett, WD7 7DQ
Tel 01923 850 100
(Reg. Charity No. 1024814). Israel's foremost centre for geriatric and mental health care, Sarah Herzog Hospital offers exceptional medical care and has outstanding research achievements. The Hospital, with over 100 years experience, treats the effects of advancing age and mental instability with the best medical technologies. With 350 beds, the Hospital is the third largest in Jerusalem. Its Israel Centre for the Treatment of Psychotrauma and Community Mental Health Centre have leading roles in helping individuals affected by terrorist attacks. *Ch.* D. Halpern, QC

BRITISH FRIENDS OF SHUVU
Investing in Jewish Children in Israel
17 Golders Court, Woodstock Road, London NW11 8QG
Tel 020 8209 3010 *Fax* 0870 460 4997
Email shuvuuk@aol.com *Website* www.shuvu.org
(Est. 2003. Reg. Charity No. 1100984). Shuvu is an educational and welfare network. It provides disadvantaged immigrant and native Israeli children with excellence in secular and Jewish Studies within a supportive, warm and nurturing environment. Shuvu's network spans 68 schools and kindergartens, educating some 15,000 children and assisting families through counselling, financial, and medical assistance. *Ch.* David Blachman

BRITISH FRIENDS OF UNITED HATZALAH OF ISRAEL (formerly Hatzolah Jerusalem)
c/o Joseph Kahan Associates, 923 Finchley Road, London, NW11 7PE
Tel 020 8209 0159
(Reg. Charity No. 1101329)

BRITISH FRIENDS OF ZAKA
223a Golders Green Road, London NW11 9ES
Tel 020 8458 5391 *Fax* 020 8458 5398
Email info@zaka.org.uk *Website* www.zaka.org.uk
(Est. 2003. Reg. Charity No. 1099639). Raises vital funds for the Israel Emergency & Humanitarian NGO – ZAKA ('Chessed Shel Emet') – whose purpose is the search, rescue & recovery of victims of natural and unnatural disasters. *Patrons* Chief Rabbi Ephraim Mirvis, Sir Victor Blank, Sir Trevor Chinn, The Kirsh Foundation, Gerald Ronson; *Tru.* Joshua Wahnon, Flora Frank, Herbert N. Frank; *Exec. Dir.* David Rose

CONSERVATIVE FRIENDS OF ISRAEL
45b Westbourne Terrace, W2 3UR
Tel 020 7262 2493 *Fax* 020 7224 8941
CFI works to promote its twin aims of supporting Israel and promoting Conservatism. It organises numerous events in and around Westminster, takes Conservative parliamentarians and candidates on delegations to Israel, campaigns hard for Tory candidates in target seats, and works to ensure that Israel's case is fairly represented in Parliament. *Exec. Ch.* Andrew Heller; *Exec. Dir.* Stuart Polak

FEDERATION OF JEWISH RELIEF ORGANISATIONS
HRS, Danescroft Avenue, Hendon, London NW4 2NA
Tel 020 8457 9169
Email fjro@btinternet.com
(Reg. Charity No. 250006). *Tr.* Alfred Garfield FCA, A. Lando; *Gen. Sec.* B. Shepherd

FRIENDS OF ALYN
88 Ossulton Way, London N2 0LB
Tel 020 8883 4716
Email alynuk@ip3.co.uk *Website* www.alyn.org
(Est. 1962. Reg. Charity No. 232689). To financially assist in the work of the Alyn Pediatric and Adolescent Rehabilitation Centre in Jerusalem, *Hon. S.* Maureen Lowry

FRIENDS OF THE BIKUR CHOLIM HOSPITAL, JERUSALEM & BRITISH AID COMMITTEE
c/o G. Rose, 34 Cleveland Square, London W2 6DD
Tel 020 7706 2666
Bikur Cholim, Jerusalem's oldest hospital, is now the largest medical centre in the heart of the city. *Ch.* G. Rose

FRIENDS OF THE ISRAEL CANCER ASSOCIATION
c/o Berwin Leighton Paisner LLP, Adelaide House, London Bridge, EC4R 9HA
Tel 020 3400 2361 *Fax* 020 3400 1111
Email jonathan.morris@blplaw.com
(Est. 1955. Reg. Charity No. 260710). Raises funds for the Israel Cancer Association (ICA). ICA plays a prominent role in the fields of detection, research, treatment and education. It supports oncological institutes, nationwide screening, patient care and information services. *Pres.* Vered Aaron; *V. Pres.* Dame Vivien Duffield, CBE, Lady Alliance; *Hon. T.* Jonathan Morris

FRIENDS OF ISRAEL EDUCATIONAL FOUNDATION
PO Box 42763, London N2 0YJ
Tel 020 8444 0777 *Fax* 020 8444 0681

Email info@foi-asg.org
(Reg. Charity No. 1095303). To promote and advance the education of the public in the knowledge of the country of Israel and its citizens. F.O.I.E.F. undertakes an extensive UK education programme and sponsors a variety of young adult and professional scholarships in Israel. *Bd.* Jeremy Manuel, Hon. Gerard Noel, Peter Oppenheimer, David Kaye, Larry Levine, Marcus Rebuck; *Dir.* John D. A. Levy

FRIENDS OF ISRAEL SPORT CENTRE FOR THE DISABLED
1 Marylebone High Street, London W1U 4LZ
Tel 020 7935 5541 *Fax* 020 7935 6638
Email fiscd@fiscd.co.uk
(Est. 2001. Reg. Charity No. 1086205). Building hope and renewal through sporting achievement. Formed in 1961, the Israel Sports Centre for the disabled in Ramat Gan is a world-leading facility for rehabilitation. Spread over four acres, the facilities offer everything from swimming pools and gymnasiums to cultural activities. The centre is currently rehabilitating over 2,500 people per week from all denominations, most of them children, including many victims of terrorists attacks. It is the Centre's goal to help everyone into full integration and involvement in Israeli society. The Centre's funding comes almost entirely from kind and generous donations. *Ch.* Brian Harris; *V. Ch.* Irwyn Yentis; *T.* Jeremy Harris; *Sec.* Jane C. Jukes

FRIENDS OF JERUSALEM BOTANICAL GARDENS
Upper Unit, 100 Green Lane, Edgware, Middlesex HA8 8EJ
Tel 020 8238 2779
Email friendsjbg@gmail.com *Website* www.friendsjbg.org.uk
(Reg. Charity No. 1151347). To provide annual scholarships for horticultural graduates from around the world to work and study at the Jerusalem Botanical Gardens; organising working holidays there, supporting educational programmes and special projects.

FRIENDS OF YESHIVAT DVAR YERUSHALAYIM (Jat: The Jerusalem Academy Trust)
Office, 1007 Finchley Road, London NW11 7HB
Tel/Fax 020 8458 8563
(Reg. Charity No. 262716). London Cttee: *Jt. Ch.* A. Maslo, BCom; FCA, and M.A. Sprei, MA (Cantab), MSc; *Patrons* Lord Sacks; *Princ.* Rabbi B. Horovitz, MA

FUNDING FOR PROGRESSIVE JUDAISM (FPJ)
PO Box 3998, Gerrards Cross, Bucks, SL9 1AS
Tel 01753 886220
Email admin@fpjie.org.uk *Website* www.fpjie.org.uk
(Reg. Charity No. 241337). Friends of Progressive Judaism in Israel and Europe.
Admin. Neil Drapkin

HADASSAH
26 Enford Street, London W1H 1DW
Tel 020 7723 1144
Email uk.office@hadassah.org *Website* www.hadassahuk.org
(Reg. Charity No. 1040848). Hadassah UK is a registered charity, dedicated to supporting the Hadassah Medical Organisation in Jerusalem and promoting its medical and scientific excellence. *H. Pres.* Lady Wolfson; *Ch.* Carolyn Simons; *Dir.* Mark Addleman

HOLYLAND PHILATELIC SOCIETY (formerly British Association of Palestine Israel Philatelists)
Email holylandphilatelicsociety@yahoo.com
(Est. 1952). For the study and encouragement of all branches of the philately of Palestine and the State of Israel, and of other countries connected with the postal

history of the region. *H. Mem. Sec.* A. Tunkel 3 Stone Buildings, Lincoln's Inn, London WC2A 3XL *Tel* 020 7242 4937 *Fax* 020 7405 3896 *Email* atunkel@3sb.law.co.uk

ISRAEL DISCOUNT BANK, London Branch
65 Curzon Street, London W1J 8PE
Tel 020 7499 1444 *Fax* 020 7499 1414
Website www.israeldiscountbank.co.uk
The London branch is part of the Israeli Discount group, a major financial group in Israel, with subsidiaries in Switzerland, the US and South America. The branch first opened as a representative office in 1982 and achieved full branch status in 1999. It offers various services such as: property lending, corporate and trade finance as well as treasury services. It also operates an Israeli desk for Hebrew-speaking clients based in Israel and the UK. Authorised and regulated by the Bank of Israel and the Prudential Regulation Authority. Subject to regulation by the Financial Conduct Authority and limited regulation by the Prudential Authority. Details about the extent of their regulation by the Prudential Regulation Authority are available on request.

ISRAEL GOVERNMENT TOURIST OFFICE
Tel 020 7299 1100
Email info@igto.co.uk *Website* www.thinkisrael.com
Facebook Visitisrael
(Est. 1954). *Dir.* N. Oryan-Kaplan. The office provides information about Israel as a tourist destination, and assistance to the British and Irish travel trade wishing to promote Israel as a holiday destination.

ISRAEL PHILATELIC AGENCY IN GREAT BRITAIN
P.O. Box 5, Poole, Dorset BH12 9GF
Tel 01202 711 371 *Fax* 01202 711 372
Email enquiries@harryallen.com
Official Agents of the Philatelic Service, Israel Postal Authority, Tel Aviv-Yafo, Israel, for the distribution and promotion of postage stamps and related products of Israel (in the UK). *New Issues Man.* Aileen Walshe, on behalf of Harry Allen (Intl. Philatelic Agencies).

THE JERUSALEM FOUNDATION
Administered by Prism the Gift Fund, 20 Gloucester Place, London W1U 8HA
Tel 020 009 9649 *Fax* 020 7224 2744 *Website* www.jerusalemfoundation.org
(Reg. Charity No. 258306). The Jerusalem Foundation works toward creating an open, equitable and modern society by responding to the needs of residents and improving their quality of life through a comprehensive approach centred on community vitality, cultural life and coexistence for all Jerusalem's residents. *Ch.* Peter Halban; *Admin, Prism The Gift Fund,* Anna Josse; *UK Dir.* Susan Winton

JEWISH BLIND IN ISRAEL ASSOCIATION
c/o K. C. Keller F.C.A., 25 Lodge Avenue, Elstree, Herts WD6 3NA
Tel 020 8207 2627
Email kennethk53@gmail.com
(Reg. Charity No. 1006756). Provides financial support and equipment to the Jewish registered blind in Israel. *Adv:* Prof. Lutza Yanko & Prof. Eliezer D. Jaffe, Dr. Ben-Zion Silverstone (Jerusalem), Joseph S. Conway, F.R.C.S. (London). *Ch.* K.C. Keller

JEWISH INSTITUTE FOR THE BLIND (British Aid Committee)
71 Eyre Court, Finchley Road, London NW8 9TX
Tel 0207 722 0887
Email info@jewishblind.org *Website* www.jewishblind.org
(Est 1964. Reg. Charity No. 222849). The British Aid Committee for the Jewish Institute

for the Blind, Jerusalem (Est. 1902) has provided aid to the Institute since 1964 and undertakes work and support through legacies and donations.

LABOUR FRIENDS OF ISRAEL
BM LFI, London, WC1N 3XX
Tel 020 7222 4323
Email mail@lfi.org.uk *Website* www.lfi.org.uk

LANIADO HOSPITAL UK
2nd Floor, Shield House, Harmony Way, London NW4 2BZ
Tel 020 8201 6111 *Fax* 020 8201 6222
Email admin@laniado.co.uk *Website* www.laniado.co.uk
(Reg. Charity No. 1126356). Raising vital funds for Laniado Hospital in Netanya, Israel. *Ch.* Jerry Kohn; *Chief Exec.* Simon Silver; *Manchester Ch.* Dov Hamburger; *Leeds Ch.* Carl Evans

LIBERAL DEMOCRAT FRIENDS OF ISRAEL
LDFI, PO Box 57769, London NW11 1GF
Corres: 1 View Point, 1475 High Road, London NZ0 9PL
Tel 020 8455 5140 *Email* admin@ldfi.org.uk
Open to all supporters of the Liberal Democrats in the UK who recognise the right of Israel to a free, independent, permanent and prosperous existence as a member state of the United Nations. The Association exists to foster good relations and understanding between Britain and the State of Israel. *Pres.* Rt. Hon. Sir Alan Beith, MP; *V. Pres.* Lord Monroe Palmer OBE, Sarah Ludford MEP; *Ch.* G. Stollar; *V. Ch.* J. Davies

LIFELINE FOR THE OLD
(Reg. Charity No. 232084). To assist the work of Lifeline for the Old in Jerusalem, which aims to help the aged in Israel by providing training in occupational skills. Also to improve the welfare and quality of life of Jerusalem's elderly and disabled. *Leeds Branch: Jt. Ch.* Dr. Marjorie E. Ziff, 626 Harrogate Road, Leeds LS17 8EW, *London Branch* Denise Cohen, 3 Bryanston Court, George Street, London W1H 7HA

MAGEN DAVID ADOM UK
Shield House, Harmony Way, off Victoria Road, London NW4 2BZ
Tel 020 8201 5900 *Fax* 020 8201 5901
Email info@mdauk.org *Website* www.mdauk.org
(Reg. Charity No. 1113409). Magen David Adom is Israel's only National ambulance and medical emergency service. For over 60 years Magen David Adom UK has raised funds for medical equipment, ambulances, bloodmobiles and stations to benefit all the citizens of Israel - Arabs, Christians, Druze and Jews. The organisation also collects and supplies 300,000 units of blood each year and is responsible for all Israel's first aid and pre-hospital medical emergency training. As a member of the International Federation of Red Cross and Red Crescent Societies, Magen David Adom works internationally to give its support and share its expertise with those in need around the world. Magen David Adom is a non-Governmental, not-for-profit organisation that depends on the generosity of its supporters to save more lives. Magen David Adom UK also provides first aid training and equipment to schools, youth and community groups throughout the UK. *Ch.* D. Curtis; *Jt. Hon. T.* J. Ward, FCA, T. Shasha; *Chief Exec.* Daniel Burger. Groups in many districts of London and the Regions.

MEDICAL AID COMMITTEE FOR ISRAEL (MAC-I)
(Est. 1969. Reg. Charity No. 258697). To provide medical and laboratory equipment and offer technical and professional advice. To assist and promote health and welfare projects in Israel. Applications from the Director of International Relations, Israel Min. of Health, 2 Ben Tabai Street, Jerusalem 93591. *Chief Exec.* Prof. David Katz

MIZRAHI TEFAHOT BANK LTD
30 Old Broad Street, London EC2N 1HQ
Tel 020 7448 0600 *Fax* 020 7448 0610
Email umb.main@umtb.co.uk *Website* www.umtb.co.uk
Branch of Mizrahi Tefahot Bank in Israel. *Branch Man.* Itzik Coriat

NEW ISRAEL FUND
25-26 Enford Street, London W1H 1DW
Tel 020 7724 2266 *Fax* 020 7724 2299
Email info@uknif.org
(Est. 1992. Reg. Charity No. 1060081). The New Israel Fund (NIF) supports Israelis who work to realise Israel's founding vision of a free and democratic society by protecting civil and human rights, fostering religious tolerance, tackling poverty and disadvantage, promoting Jewish-Arab coexistence and preserving the environment. NIF provides hundreds of Israeli non-profit organisations with financial support and professional training each year, thus assisting them in building a brighter future within the framework of the best Jewish and democratic values. *Ch.* Nicholas Saphir; *CEO* Adam Ognall

ONE TO ONE PROJECT (formerly **Jewish AID Committee**)
Carradine House, 237 Regents Park Road, London N3 3LF
Tel 020 8343 4156 *Fax* 020 8343 2119
Email admin@one-to-one.org *Website* www.one-to-one.org
(Reg. Charity No. 801096). The JAC (formerly the 35's) formed the One to One project in 1991. It was responding to the mass immigration of Soviet Jews to Israel and to the economic situation of some of Israel's poorest families (Druse, Bedouin, Muslim, Christian and Jewish). Funds are raised through sponsored treks, the Annual Backgammon/Poker Event in May, individual donations and grant making trust/foundations. *Co-Ch.* Rita Eker MBE, Margaret Rigal

OPERATION WHEELCHAIRS COMMITTEE
1 Opal Court, 120 Regents Park Road, London, N3 3HY
Tel 020 8371 1500
Email alexanderpasse@tiscali.co.uk
(Est. 1970. Reg. Charity No. 263089). Voluntary organisation providing rehabilitation and general medical equipment to hospitals in Israel and in particular for children and adults who need help to walk and use their hands through neuro stimulation. *Ch.* Anita Alexander-Passe

POALE AGUDAT ISRAEL
Unites Orthodox religious workers to build up Eretz Yisrael in the spirit of the Torah. **World Central Office:** 64 Frishman Street, Tel Aviv *Pres.* Rabbi A. Werdiger. **European Office and Great Britain:** P.A.I., 2A Alba Gardens, NW11 9NR *Tel/Fax* 020 8458 5372 *Corr.* D. Winter

REUTH
Email info@reuth.org.uk *Website* www.reuth.org
Reuth is one of Israel's oldest and most respected non-profit healthcare and social welfare organisations. Guided by a commitment to professional excellence and the preservation of human dignity, the organisation has become the nation's leader in the fields of elder care, rehabilitation, and treatment of the chronically ill. From humble beginnings as a provider of social and housing assistance to Holocaust survivors in Tel Aviv, Reuth has grown into a multi-disciplinary umbrella organisation that provides a comprehensive range of medical, rehabilitative and community services for all sectors of Israeli society, with a focus on children, wounded soldiers, victims of terror, senior citizens, and the indigent. *Patrons* Chief Rabbi Rabbi Mirvis, Lord Pannick QC, Peter Sheldon OBE; *Ch.* N. Ferber; *Projects Co-ord.* J. Dayan

SHAARE ZEDEK UK
766 Finchley Road, London NW11 7TH and P.O. Box 202, Salford, M7 4WS
Tel 020 8201 8933 *Fax* 020 8201 8935
Email office@shaarezedek.org.uk *Website* www.shaarezedekuk.com
(Hospital est. Jerusalem 1902. Reg. Charity No. 1143272). Shaare Zedek UK's sole purpose is to raise much needed funds for The Shaare Zedek Medical Centre in Jerusalem. This is Jerusalem's busiest hospital and it is imbued throughout with the warmth of traditional Jewish values. The hospital cares equally for anyone and everyone regardless of race, religion or financial circumstances - treating all with the same unparalleled degree of care, compassion and medical excellence. Shaare Zedek does not receive any government funding for the equipment and development which is vital to enabling the world class medical staff to save lives on a daily basis and so it is only with the support of the hospital's friends from around the world that these essential elements can be provided. *Ch.* M. Sorkin; *Hon. T.* A. Stechler, ACA

STANDWITHUS UNITED KINGDOM
Email uk@standwithus.com
Websites www.standwithus.co.uk   www.standwithus.co.il
(Reg. Charity No. 1115343). StandWithUs is an international organisation based in Los Angeles and Jerusalem. StandWithUs UK is one of 16 regional offices around the world. Its mission is to counter misconceptions and prejudices about Israel and the Arab-Israel conflict through education about Israel. Using print materials, speakers, programmes, conferences, missions to Israel, campaigns, social media and internet resources, StandWithUs brings Israel's story of achievements and its on-going challenges to campuses, communities, the media, churches and schools around the world.
StandWithUs UK office is part of the Jerusalem based team, but serves the whole of the UK. It has three main strands of activity, work with students, work in the community (Jewish and non Jewish) and pro Israel campaigning. The StandWithUs team is available to create Israel education and advocacy events with students and communities. *Ch.* Joy Wolfe MBE; *Leadership Team: Community Dir.* Irene Naftalin; *Campus Dir.* Shlomie Liberow

STATE OF ISRAEL BONDS
Development Company for Israel (UK) Ltd
ORT House, 126 Albert Street, London NW1 7NE
Tel 020 7446 8670 *Fax* 020 7446 8675
Email info@israelukbonds.com *Website* www.israelukbonds.com
(Est. 1981). Promotes and sells State of Israel Bonds (Israel's gilt-edged securities). *Man. Dir.* Moti Besser

TECHNION UK
62 Grosvenor Street, London W1K 3JF
Tel 020 7495 6824 *Fax* 020 7355 1525
Email info@technionuk.org   *Website* www.technionuk.org
also on Facebook and Twitter
(Est. 1951. Reg. Charity No. 1092207). Technion UK supports the Technion, Israel Institute of Technology in Haifa, one of the world's leading technology universities. The society brings Technion expertise to the UK through a series of events, seminars and networking sessions with Israel's foremost scientific, education and business leaders. Our funds have provided research centres and equipment, as well as student facilities and scholarships. *H. Patron* The Ambassador of Israel; *V. Pres.* L. Peltz, Sir Michael Heller, *Exec. Dir.* A. Bernstein; *Ch.* D. Peltz; *Sec.* S. Posner

TEL AVIV UNIVERSITY TRUST
126 Albert Street, London NW1 7NE
Tel 020 7446 8790
Email info@tau-trust.co.uk

(Reg. Charity No. 314179). The principal aim of the Trust is to raise funds to promote the work of Tel Aviv University and to encourage support for academic projects, scholarships and campus development. The Trust also advises those who may wish to study at the University. *Acting Ch.* William Shaul; *Chief Exec.* Cara Case

TRADE UNION FRIENDS OF ISRAEL (TUFI)
BCM TUFI, London, WC1N 3XX
Tel 020 7222 4323 *Fax* 020 7222 4324
Website www.tufi.org.uk
Established to strengthen the links between the Histadrut (the Israeli TUC), the Palestinian General Federation of Trade Unions (PGFTU) and the British Trade Union Movement.
It aims to build support for the Middle East peace process in the UK Labour movement, promote efforts towards finding a just and lasting peace settlement for both Israelis and Palestinians, initiate dialogue by taking British delegations to meet with both Israeli and Palestinian trade unionists, build support for the Peace Process in the UK by providing meetings and briefings for British Trade Unionists, engage trade unionists on a variety of issues beyond the Israeli-Palestinian conflict and aims to provide practical assistance that helps Israeli and Palestinian workers. *Pres.* Lord Clarke of Hampstead, CBE, KSG; *Ch.* Roger Lyons

UK FRIENDS OF THE ASSOCIATION FOR THE WELLBEING OF ISRAEL'S SOLDIERS
Tel 020 3210 3060 *Fax* 020 3210 3075
Email ukawis@ukawis.net *Website* www.ukawis.co.uk
(Est. 2001. Reg. Charity No. 1084272). To support the work of the Association in Israel, by raising funds for the wellbeing, education and culture of Israel's soldiers. *Tr.* Peter Sussmann, Julian Kemble, Zeev Remez, David Tucker; *Exec. Dir.* E. Hellerstein

UK ISRAEL BUSINESS
Tel 020 3510 0002
Email info@ukisraelbusiness.co.uk *Website* www.ukisraelbusiness.co.uk
UK Israel Business is a member-led organisation promoting bilateral business, trade, industry and investment between the UK and Israel. It works closely with the UK Embassy in Tel Aviv and the Israeli Embassy in London. Its network includes more than 2,000 companies and an extensive database of over 10,000 entrepreneurs, investors, senior executives, professional advisers and financiers. It organises and provides a host of activities and services in the UK and Israel, aimed at creating new business opportunities for members. *Hon. Pres.* Sir Victor Blank, Sir Trevor Chinn CVO. *Bd. Members*, Marc Worth (*Ch.*), Hugo Bieber (*CEO*) Yitz Applbaum, Stuart Lewis, avital Lobel, Jonathan Morris, Neil Stone, Larry Weiss, Paul Winter

UK SOCIETY FOR THE PROTECTION OF NATURE IN ISRAEL
P.O. Box 67678, London NW11 1LD
Tel 020 8731 9208
Email ukspni@spni.org.il *Website* www.natureisrael.org
(Est. 1986. Reg. Charity No. 327268). To generate interest in the beauty of Israel's natural landscapes and to muster support for the conservation lobby in Israel. *Trs.* Michael Green, John D. A. Levy

WEIZMANN UK
9 Hampstead Gate, 1a Frognal, London NW3 6AL
Tel 020 7424 6860 *Fax* 020 7431 2165
Email post@weizmann.org.uk *Website* www.weizmann.org.uk
(Est. 1956. Reg. Charity No. 232666). To stimulate financial, scientific and cultural support in the UK for the Weizmann Institute of Science in Rehovot. *Ch. of Exec. Cttee.* Martin Paisner CBE; *V. Ch.* Dame Vivien Duffield, DBE; *Hon. S.* J. Kropman; *Hon. T.* Howard Stanton; *Dir.* S. Gould

YAD VASHEM - UK FOUNDATION
Contact, Stirling House, Breasy Place, 9 Burroughs Gardens, London NW4 4AU
Tel 020 8359 1146
Email office@yadvashem.org.uk *Website* www.yadvashem.org.uk
(Est 1978. Reg. Charity No. 1099659). Incorporated in 2003, to represent Yad Vashem, Jerusalem (*See* p. 271). *Life Pres.* Ben Helfgott MBE; *Ch.* Simon Bentley; *Operational Man.* Evelynne Garbacz

YOUTH ALIYAH-CHILD RESCUE
Trojan House, 34 Arcadia Avenue, Finchley, London N3 2JU
Tel 020 8371 1580
Email info@youthaliyah.org.uk *Website* www.youthaliyah.org.uk
(Est. 1933. Reg. Charity No. 1077913). Object: to offer a secure home for under-privileged and deprived refugee, immigrant and native Israeli children. Six Youth Villages offer residential community care.
Ch. Melvin Robinson; *Admin. Exec. Dir.* Nelly Ebert *Email* nelly@youthaliyah.org.uk; *Dir. of Develpopment,* Martin Mason *Email* martin@youthaliyah.org.uk; *Communications,* Nicola Noah *Email* nicola.noah@hotmail.com

NAL AND CULTURAL ORGANISATIONS
Religion Classes are attached to most of the synagogues listed.
ty Centres and Organisations *See* pp. 103-106.

NK TRUST UK

Star House, 104-108 Grafton Road, London NW5 4BA
Tel 020 7284 5858 *Fax* 020 7428 2601
Email info@annefrank.org.uk *Website* www.annefrank.org.uk
(Est. 1990, Reg. Charity No. 1003279). The Anne Frank Trust draws on the power of Anne Frank's life and diary to challenge antisemitism, racism and all forms of prejudice and discrimination. Working in some of the UK's most difficult areas, the Trust does this by taking exhibitions and educational programmes into schools, prisons and community venues. The exhibitions are enhanced by educational activities such as workshops and peer educator training for teenagers. The Trust's Anne Frank Ambassador Scheme, with over 200 participants a year, increases knowledge and confidence in young people.

CHAZAK

379 Hendon Way, London NW4 3LP
Tel 020 8457 4444
Email info@chazak.org.uk
There exists a proud established network of Sephardic communities spanning the UK who have successfully guarded and transmitted the grand traditions of Spain, Portugal, India, Aden, Syria, Egypt, Iraq, Persia, Tunisia and Morocco. Chazak's goal is to work alongside and in conjunction with all existing communities and organisations in order to further inspire young British Jews of Sephardic descent with a pride and commitment to their culture, heritage and continuity. *Dir.* Rabbi S. Farhi; *Man.* Rabbi M. Levy

DAVAR, The Jewish Institute in Bristol and the South West

Suite 431, 179 Whiteladies Road, Clifton, Bristol, BS8 2AG
Tel/Fax 0117 970 6594
Email davarbristol@yahoo.co.uk *Website* www.davarbristol.com
DAVAR provides a wide programme of cultural, educational and social activities. A regular newsletter is available, and Jewish groups in the area advertise their own events via the mailing list. *Ch.* Martin Weitz

HOLOCAUST EDUCATIONAL TRUST

BCM Box 7892, London WC1N 3XX
Tel 020 7222 6822 *Fax* 020 7233 0161
Email info@het.org.uk *Website* www.het.org.uk
(Est. 1988. Reg. Charity No. 1092892 England and Wales, SC042996 Scotland). The Holocaust Educational Trust works with schools, colleges and communities across the UK to educate about the Holocaust and its contemporary relevance. Work includes the *Lessons from Auschwitz* project for post-16 students, which includes a one-day visit to Auschwitz-Birkenau. The Trust arranges for Holocaust survivors to speak in schools, delivers innovative educational and teacher training programmes and produces groundbreaking resources. *Patrons* Most Rev. and Rt. Hon. Lord Carey of Clifton, Lord Dholakia OBE, Rt. Hon. Lord Mackay of Clashfern, Lady Merlyn-Rees JP, Prof. Elie Wiesel KBE; *Bd. of Tru.* Founding *Patron.* Lord Janner of Braunstone QC; *Pres.* R. Stephen Rubin OBE; *H. V. Pres.* Rt. Hon Lord Hunt of Wirral MBE; *T.* Paul Berlyn; *Ch.* Paul Phillips, Oliver Blechner, David Gryn, Richard Harrington MP, Kitty Hart-Moxon, OBE, Ben Helfgott MBE, Helen Hyde, Michael Karp, Sir Ivan Lawrence QC, Nigel Layton, Edward Lewin, Kirsty McNeill, Lord Jon Mendelsohn, Martin Paisner CBE, Alberta Strage; *C.* James Clappison MP, Louise Ellman MP, Rt. Hon Andrew Lansley CBE, MP, Sir Antony Sher KBE, Stephen Twigg MP; *Chief Exec.* Karen Pollock MBE

INCLUSIVE JEWISH SCHOOLS PARTNERSHIP (IJSP)
c/o, Akiva School, The Sternberg Centre For Judaism, 80 East End Road, N3 2SY
Tel 020 8349 4980 *Fax* 020 8349 4959
Email ijsp@akivaschool.org
(Est. 2012). A network of schools that teach the full range of Jewish values, beliefs and practises with equivalence and include all memebrs of hte Jewish community. Schools included in the partnership: JCoSS, Akiva, Clore Shalom, Clore Tikva, Eden Primary, South London Jewish Primary School, Finchley Jewish Primary School. Co-ord. Susy Stone MA

ISRAEL ZANGWILL MEMORIAL FUND
c/o, The Sternberg Centre For Judaism, 80 East End Road, N3 2SY
Tel 020 8349 5640
Email admin@reformjudaism.org.uk
(Est. 1929). To assist poor Jews engaged in research into special areas of Jewish music or art.

ISRAELI DANCE INSTITUTE
Suite 8, Time House, 56b Crewys Road, NW2 2AD
Tel 020 8209 3155
Email info@idi.org.uk *Website* www.idi.org.uk
The Israeli Dance Institute uses dance as a tool to promote Jewish and Israeli culture. It does this through an annual training seminar, Machol Europa, and training and support programmes that include an annual dance festival for schools across the country. The Institute's performance troupes represent the community in interfaith and multi-cultural events. *Ch.* M. Stone

JEWISH BOOK COUNCIL
ORT House, 126 Albert Street NW1 7NE
Tel 020 7446 8771
Email Info@jewishbookweek.com *Website* www.jewishbookweek.com
Admin. Pam Lewis *Tel* 020 7446 8771
(Est. 1947. Reg. Charity No. 293800). To stimulate and encourage the reading of books on Judaism and on every aspect of Jewish thought, life, history and literature; organises an annual Jewish Book Week, now Europe's largest Jewish literary festival, and associated events. Administers a triennial prize for Hebrew translation and an annual children's poetry prize. *Pres.* Anne Webber; *Co-Ch.* Gail Sandler, Lucy Silver

JEWISH COMMUNITY DAY SCHOOL ADVISORY BOARD
c/o Leo Baeck College, Sternberg Centre, 80 East End Road, London N3 2SY
Tel 020 8349 5620 *Fax* 020 8349 5639
Email sharon@silver-myer.com
(Est. 1998). Promotion and development of Jewish cross-community day schools throughout the UK. *Ch.* Jon Epstein; *Admin.* S. Silver-Myer

JEWISH GENEALOGICAL SOCIETY OF GREAT BRITAIN
33 Seymour Place, London W1H 5AU
Membership: *Email* membership@jgsgb.org.uk *Website* www.jgsgb.org.uk
(Est. 1992. Reg. Charity No. 1022738). To promote and encourage the study of Jewish genealogy. The Society organises lectures, seminars and family history workshops; it publishes *Shemot*, and guides to the study of Jewish genealogy; it promotes research; and operates a library. *Pres.* Dr Saul Issroff; *Pres. Emer.* Dr Anthony Joseph; *Ch.* Doreen Berger; *T. P.* Roth; *Sec.* Martin Hill; *Membership Sec.* Hazel Atlass. *Regional Groups:* Leeds (Judith Williams), Manchester (Lorna Kay), South West London (Ena Black), East of London (Raymond Montanjees), Chilterns and the Home Counties (S. Rose), Midlands (David Harrison), South East Essex (Anne Marcus)

JEWISH HERALDIC FOUNDATION
73 Newberries Avenue, Radlett WD7 7EL
Tel 0845 519 3451 *Fax* 0845 519 3452
The Jewish Heraldic Foundation runs Jewish Identity Projects, benefiting young people with interactive sessions of educational value aimed at strengthening Jewish identity. *Dir.* Rabbi Ariel Abel, MSc, MCMI

JEWISH HERITAGE UK
Room 204, Ducie House, 37 Ducie Street, Manchester, M1 2JW
Tel 0161 238 8621
Email director@jewish-heritage-uk.org *Website* www.jewish-heritage-uk.org
(Est. 2004. Reg. Charity No. 1118174). To care for the historic synagogues, cemeteries and sites of Britain's Jewish community and to promote the Jewish built heritage through education and public access. *See* pp. 315-318. *Dir.* Dr. Sharman Kadish; *Consult. Architects,* Viorica Feler-Morgan, Lynda Jubb, Daniel Leon, Hedy Parry-Davies; *Admin.* Sharon Hood

JEWISH HISTORICAL SOCIETY OF ENGLAND
33 Seymour Place, W1H 5AP
Email info@jhse.org *Website* www.jhse.org
(Est. 1893. Reg. Charity No. 217331). *Pres.* Dr. Piet van Boxel; *Exec. Ch.* David Jacobs
Branches: Birmingham Dr.Anthony Joseph *Email* birmingham@jhse.org; **Essex** Sheila Lassman *Email* lassmans@aol.com; **Herts and Middlesex** Norman Gerald *Email* geraldn@btinternet.com; **Israel** Dr.Kenneth Collins *Email* drkcollins@gmail.com; **Leeds** Murray Winer *Email* murraywiner@ntlworld.com; **Liverpool** Arnold S. Lewis. *Email* arnoldslewis@gmail.com; **Sussex** Godfrey Gould *Email* g.gould915@btinternet.com

JEWISH LITERARY TRUST
ORT House, 126 Albert Street, London NW1 7NE
Tel 020 7267 9442
Website www.jewishquarterly.org
(Est. 1984. Reg. Charity No. 268589). Established on the death of Jacob Sonntag, (founding Ed.), to ensure the continuity of the Jewish Quarterly. *Patrons* David and Marion Cohen, The John S. Cohen Foundation, Elizabeth and Stanley Corob, Sir Trevor Chinn, Daniel and Elizabeth Peltz, Robin and Inge Hyman, The Dorset Foundation, The Humanitarian Trust, Lord Kalms, Simon Ryde, Roger Wingate; *Co-Ch.* Mark Goldberg, Lance Blackstone; *Hon. T.* Stanley Salter; *Exec. Cttee.* James Freedman, Michael Green, Andrew Renton, Jodie Myers; *Ed.* Rachel Lasserson; *Man. Ed.* Susannah Okret. *Publ.* Jewish Quarterly (*See* Jewish Press).

—JEWISH MUSIC INSTITUTE
SOAS University of London, Thornhaugh Street, Russell Square, London WC1H 0XG
Tel 020 7898 4307
Email jewishmusic@jmi.org.uk *Website* www.jmi.org.uk
(Reg. Charity No. 328228). JMI is the home of Jewish music in the UK. It is dedicated to the celebration, preservation and development of the living heritage of Jewish music for the benefit of people of all ages and backgrounds.
Jewish Music Institute's goal is to inform and inspire audiences with an exciting original programme of live performances, educational events and collaborative projects and to support musicians playing Jewish music across the UK enabling them to preserve this traditional heritage, create new work and reach the widest audience.
Artistc Dir. Sophie Solomon; *Ch.* Jennifer Jankel; *Man.* Laura Phillips, Gil Karpas

THE JEWISH TEACHERS' ASSOCIATION (JTA)
C/o Board of Deputies of British Jews, 6 Bloomsbury Square, London WC1A 2LP
Tel 020 7543 5400 *Fax* 020 7543 0010

Email info@jewishteachers.org.uk *Website* www.jewishteachers.org.uk
Twitter @jewishteacher *Facebook* UK Jewish Teachers
(Est. 2007). The Jewish Teachers' Association (JTA) is a membership organisation for Jewish teachers, trainee teachers, teaching assistants and educational psychologists as well as those working in informal education, such as youth workers and tutors. The JTA exists to protect the rights of Jewish teachers; provide continual professional development through training and resources; offer support on issues of discrimination in the work place and encourage balanced teaching about Judaism and the state of Israel. *Ch.* FRH. Richards

KESHER – THE LEARNING CONNECTION
933 Finchley Road, London NW11 7PE
Tel 020 8458 5836 *Fax* 020 8201 9537
Email connect@kesher.org.uk *Website* www.kesher.org.uk
(Est. 1997. Reg Charity No. 1061689). Social, educational, communal and outreach programming for Jews of all backgrounds. *Dir.* Rabbi Rashi Simon, MA. International, Shabbat and Festival Services. (Orthodox)

LEO BAECK COLLEGE
The Sternberg Centre for Judaism, 80 East End Road, London N3 2SY
Tel 020 8349 5600
Email info@lbc.ac.uk *Website* www.lbc.ac.uk
(Est. 1956. Reg. Charity No. 209777). Established for the study of Judaism and the training of rabbis and educators serving the Movement for Reform Judaism and Liberal Judaism. *Princ.* Rabbi Dr Deborah Kahn-Harris; *Ch. and Bd. of Govs.* Noeleen Cohen; *Exec. Dir.* Stephen Ross; *Dir. Jewish Studies*, Rabbi Dr Charles Middleburgh; *Dir. Jewish Education*, Jo-Ann Myers; *Hd. of Academic Services*, Gabriela Ruppin; *Hd. of HR* and *Support Services*, Rhona Lesner

Rabbinic and Higher Jewish Studies
Offers a five-year programme leading to Rabbinic Ordination, full-time and part-time degrees. It also caters for those wishing to further their Jewish knowledge, and supports Progressive communities in developing their own programmes.

Jewish Education
The College provides various Jewish Educational services to the Progressive movements and independent Progressive communities. It offers teacher training and consultancy for Hebrew in Jewish supplementary schools. It also offers a BA (Hons) in Jewish Education and MA in Jewish Education validated by the University of Winchester. In addition, the College offers courses in Adult Jewish learning.

LIMMUD
1A Hall Street, North Finchley, London N12 8DB
Tel 020 3115 1620
Email office@limmud.org *Website* www.limmud.org
(Reg. Charity No. 1083414). Limmud is a volunteer-led cross-communal, multi-dimensional education organisation. Its flagship event is the week long winter residential Limmud Conference. It also organises Limmud in the Woods in the summer; Regional Day Limmuds in 14 communities across the UK; the Limmud on One Leg weekly cross-communal parasha commentary; and the annual Chavruta project. Through its Limmud International team, Limmud supports the development of 65 Limmud communities in over 40 countries outside of the UK. *Ch.* Kevin Sefton; *Exec. Dir.* Shelley Marsh; *Admin.* Cathryn Sweid

LONDON ACADEMY OF JEWISH STUDIES
2-4 Highfield Avenue, NW11 9ET
Tel 020 8455 5938/020 8458 1264
(Est. in 1975). To assist post-Yeshiva students to further their Jewish education and engage

in advanced Talmudic research. Graduates are expected to take up rabbinical and teaching posts in the community. The Kolel also serves as a Torah-study centre for laymen. Its specialised library is open to the general public throughout the year including Shabbat and Yom Tov. *H. Princ.* Rabbi G. Hager

LONDON JEWISH CULTURAL CENTRE
Ivy House, 94-96 North End Road, London, NW11 7SX
Tel 020 8457 5000 *Fax* 020 8457 5024
Email admin@ljcc.org.uk *Website* www.ljcc.org.uk
(Est 2000. Reg. Charity No. 1081014). The London Jewish Cultural Centre is a vibrant centre of education, the Arts and cultural activity throughout the year. Inclusive and independent, the centre welcomes c2,000 people of all ages each week to engage with Jewish life, language, identity and heritage through the broadest range of courses, events and activities, including tours to places of Jewish interest. The Holocaust Education department works to challenge prejudice wherever it is found; represents the UK on the Task Force for International Cooperation on Holocaust Education, educates teachers around the world in how to teach the Holocaust and provides survivor enrichment programmes. The LJCC has also developed a unique Holocaust education website for secondary school children www.theholocaustexplained.org. FUSION, the Centre's innovative youth programme, offers creative, interactive schemes and activities both during term and during school holidays. *Publ.* Prospectus, LJCC FUSION and Ivy House Music and Dance. *Chief Exec.* Louise Jacobs

LONDON SCHOOL OF JEWISH STUDIES (formerly Jews' College)
Schaller House, Wohl Campus for Jewish Education, 44A Albert Road, London NW4 2SJ
Tel 020 8203 6427 *Fax* 020 8203 6420
Email info@lsjs.ac.uk *Website* www.lsjs.ac.uk
London School of Jewish Studies is a world-class Centre of Jewish Scholarship and teaching that inspires our community with lifelong love of Jewish learning and practices. *Pres.* Chief Rabbi Ephraim Mirvis; *Dep. Pres.* Rabbi Joseph Dweck OBE; *Ch. of the C.* Prof. Anthony Warrens; *Dean* Rabbi Dr. Raphael Zarum; *CEO* Jason Marantz

MAROM (MASORTI YOUNG ADULTS)
Alexander House, 3 Shakespeare Road London N3 1XE
Tel 020 8349 6650
Email students@masorti.org.uk
Twitter @MaromUK
Facebook Marom Coordinator (*Young Adults*)   Marom Fieldworker (*students*)
Marom builds grassroots communities, whilst developing young adults and engaging them with positive Masorti experiences. Marom is composed of two parts: Marom on Campus and Marom Young Adults. It supports many social events, initiatives, such as communal Shabbat dinners, Masorti programming on UK campuses, and learning experiences in Israel and Europe. Marom is part of an international movement of young Masorti Jews, empowering young emerging leaders within the Masorti movement.

NATIONAL HOLOCAUST CENTRE AND MUSEUM
Laxton, Newark, Notts NG22 0PA
Tel 01623 836 627 *Fax* 01623 836 647
Email office@holocaustcentre.net *Website* www.holocaustcentre.net
(Est. 1978, as Beth Shalom Limited. Reg. Charity No. 509022). Holocaust education, museum and memorial site. *Pres. and Bd. of Tru.* Dr. James Smith CBE; *Chief Exec.* Phil Lyons MBE

ORT UK
126 Albert Street, London NW1 7NE
Tel 020 7446 8520 *Fax* 020 7446 8654

Email info@ortuk.org *Website* www.ortuk.org
Facebook ORT UK

(Est. 1921. Reg. Charity No. 1105254). British ORT is the UK arm of World ORT, the world's largest Jewish education and training charity. Currently operating in 56 countries, ORT helps vulnerable communities to become self-sufficient by educating and training their members in skills they need for life. *Pres.* Sir David Sieff; *Ch.* Simon Alberga; *Exec. Dir.* Dan Green

POLACK'S HOUSE EDUCATIONAL TRUST CLIFTON COLLEGE

32 College Road, Bristol BS8 3JH
Tel 0117 315 7000
Email jgreenbury@cliftoncollege.com
Website www.cliftoncollege.com www.polackshousetrust.org

(Reg. Charity No. 1040218). The Trust supports the education of Jewish pupils at Clifton College, and in so doing continues a tradition going back to 1878. Jewish Studies, Jewish Worship and kosher food for boys and girls aged 3-18. Scholarships and bursaries available. *Hd. Jewish Studies,* Jonathan Greenbury (Hd. Sixth form)

SCOPUS JEWISH EDUCATIONAL TRUST (formerly ZFET)

38 Wigmore Street, London W1U 2RU
Tel 020 7935 0100 *Fax* 020 7935 7787

(Est. 1953. Reg. Charity No. 313154). To raise funds by way of endowment, legacy, bequest, gift or donation in order to provide a first-class education in Jewish Studies and Hebrew throughout its national network of day schools; all of which have a Zionist ethos and emphasise the centrality of Israel in Jewish life. *H. Pres.* Stanley S. Cohen, OBE; *Ch.* Peter Ohrenstein; *Hon. T.* Jonathan M. Kramer; *Hon. S.* Brenda Hyman. School: **London** Harry & Abe Sherman Rosh Pinah Primary School, Mathilda Marks-Kennedy Jewish Primary School, Simon Marks Jewish Primary School

Seed UK

Mowbray House, 58-70 Edgware Way, Edgware, Middlesex, HA8 8DJ
Tel 020 8958 0820 *Fax* 020 8958 0821
Email info@seed.uk.net *Website* www.seed.uk.net

(Est. 1980. Reg. Charity No. 281307 Project SEED). To provide Jewish adult education through courses, weekend residential seminars and one-to-one study throughout the year. Working also with school and parents - specialising in the interests of parents and young children. *Dir.* Rabbi J. Grunfeld; *London contact* for One to One Rabbi A. Lazarus; *Manchester* contact Rabbi A. Hassan: *Educ. London Programmes,* Rabbi M. Herman, Manchester A. Bar Ilan *Tel* 0161 792 4457

THE SEPHARDI CENTRE

2 Ashworth Road, Maida Vale, London W9 1JY
Tel 020 7266 3682 *Fax* 020 7289 5957
Email scadmin@spsyn.org.uk

(Est. 1994. Reg. Charity No. 1039937). The Centre's aim is to promote Sephardi culture. Courses, open to all, focus on Religion, History, Music, Art and Cuisine. A library and reading room, specialising in Sephardi literature, is open to the public (*See* p. 119). *Admin.* Joanne Reich

SOCIETY FOR JEWISH STUDY

1A Church Mount, London N2 0RW
Website www.sjslondon.org.uk

(Est. 1946. Reg. Charity No. 283732). The Society presents academic research in Jewish religion, literature, history and the arts. *Sec.* Rosemary Goldstein

THE SPIRO ARK
788-790 Finchley Road, London NW11 7TJ
Tel 020 7289 6321 *Fax* 020 7289 6825
Email education@spiroark.org *Website* www.spiroark.org
(Est. 1998 Reg. Charity No.1070926). The Spiro Ark was established to continue the educational and cultural work of Nitza and Robin Spiro at the Spiro Institute (now known as the London Jewish Cultural Centre). It uses innovative teaching methods in order to encourage a learning community mainly based on Jewish History and Culture. Hebrew and Yiddish are taught at all levels. The Spiro Ark also specialises in providing extremely enjoyable Hebrew learning programmes to children of all ages. In addition there are regular outstanding cultural events, plus tours of Jewish interest. *Fdrs and developers, The Spiro Institute and Spiro Ark,* Nitza and Robin Spiro; *Admin.* Alon Hutter

SPRINGBOARD EDUCATION TRUST
32 Foscote Road, London NW4 3SD
Tel 020 8202 7147 *Fax* 020 8203 8293
Email aumie@hotmail.co.uk
(Est. 1979. Reg. Charity No. 277946). Specialising in reminiscence and stimulation programmes for senior citizens, Springboard has extended its range of audio-visual and film productions to cover Jewish and Zionist history, synagogue and home traditions and interfaith projects.
    Springboard also produces low-cost DVD/film programmes for other organisations and provides seminars for teachers and welfare workers in the use of its programmes, with substantial back-up materials. *Dirs.* Aumie and Michael Shapiro

UK JEWISH FILM
5.09 Clerkenwell Workshops, 27-31 Clerkenwell Close, London EC1R 0AT
Tel 020 3176 0048
Email info@ukjewishfilm.org *Website* www.ukjewishfilm.org
(Est. 1997. Reg. Charity No. 1072914). UK Jewish Film is the largest exhibitor of films in the UK and Europe that engage with Jewish and Israeli life and culture. The annual UK Jewish Film Festival is held over 2 ½ weeks in November in cinemas across London and cities around the UK, and comprises around 100 screenings and events including Q&As with filmmakers and actors and panel discussions. UK Jewish Film also organises the Geneva International Jewish Film Festival, now in its 4th edition, and in 2014 was selected to programme the Hong Kong Jewish Film Festival. Additionally the organisation programmes six films per week, year round, at the JW3 Cinema in London. Its education programmes includes the inter-generational Hackney Roots project using film to explore Jewish heritage, and a Holocaust education programme. *Fdr. and Exec. Dir.* Judy Ironside; *Man. Dir.* Michael Etherton; *Ch.* Stephen Margolis

UNIVERSITY CENTRES AND ORGANISATIONS
(*See also* Organisations concerned with Jewish students and Libraries).

BRITISH ASSOCIATION FOR JEWISH STUDIES
Email h.spurling@southampton.co.uk *Website* www.britishjewishstudies.org
(Est. 1975). Membership is open to scholars concerned with the academic pursuit of Jewish studies in the British Isles. The Association promotes and defends the scholarly study of Jewish culture in all its aspects and organizes an annual conference. *Pres.* (2015) Daniel Langton, Samuel Alexander Building-WG20A, School of Arts, Languages and Cultures, The University of Manchester, Manchester M13 9PL *Sec.* Dr. Helen Spurling, Building 65, Faculty of Humanities, University of Southampton, Avenue Campus, Highfield, Southampton SO17 1BF; *T.* Dr. Maria Diemling, Theology and Religious Studies, Canterbury Christ Church University, North Holmes Road, Canterbury CT1 1QU

CENTRE FOR GERMAN-JEWISH STUDIES
University of Sussex, Falmer, Brighton, East Sussex BN1 9QN
Website www.sussex.ac.uk/cgjs
Dir. Dr. Gideon Reuveni *Tel* 01273 877 344 *Email* g.reuveni@sussex.ac.uk; *Centre Man.* Diana Franklin *Tel* 01273 678 771 *Email* d.franklin@sussex.ac.uk; London Office *Tel/Fax* 020 8455 4785

CENTRE FOR JEWISH STUDIES (University of Leeds)
Leeds LS2 9JT
Tel 0113 343 5197 *Fax* 0113 245 1977
Email e.frojmovic@leeds.ac.uk *Website* www.cjs.leeds.ac.uk
(Est. 1995). Teaching Jewish Studies at undergraduate and postgraduate level and supervising research degrees. *Dir.* Dr Eva Frojmovic

CENTRE FOR JEWISH STUDIES (University of London)
School of Oriental and African Studies, Thornhaugh Street, Russell Square, London WC1H 0XG
Tel 020 7898 4358
Email cs52@soas.ac.uk *Website* www.soas.ac.uk/centres/jewish
The Centre seeks to promote modern Jewish and Israeli studies. It seeks to foster research seminars and to collaborate with other institutions of higher education. Through public lectures and conferences, the Centre endeavours to bring areas of academic interest to the wider community. In the multi-cultural atmosphere that is unique to the SOAS, it provides a forum for discussion and dialogue. In 2008 it staged an International Conference 'Israel and the Great Powers 1948–2008'. In 2009, the centre staged a weekly series of lectures to commemorate the founding of Tel Aviv in 1909, in conjunction with Tel Aviv University. In 2010, its speakers have included Anthony Julius, Mohammed Dara Washe, Ed Husain, Sami Zubeida, Robert Fine; *Ch.* Dr. Y. Wallach

CENTRE FOR JEWISH STUDIES (University of Manchester)
University of Manchester, Oxford Road, Manchester M13 9PL
Tel 0161 275 3614
Email cjs@manchester.ac.uk *Website* www.manchesterjewishstudies.org
(Est. 1997). The Centre seeks to maximise the teaching - undergraduate and postgraduate - of Jewish Studies in the University of Manchester, to foster collaborative research between staff of the University of Manchester and others in the region, through research seminars and research projects, to bring the results of academic work in Jewish Studies to the wider community through public lectures (including the Sherman Lectures in Jewish Studies and the Bogdanow Lectures in Holocaust Studies) and conferences; and to disseminate the results of these activities on the internet, and through its on-line journal: Melilah. *Co-Dirs* Prof. Daniel Langton, Prof. Alexander Samely

CENTRE FOR MODERN HEBREW STUDIES
Faculty of Asian and Middle Eastern Studies, Sidgwick Avenue, Cambridge CB3 9DA
Tel 01223 335 117 *Fax* 01223 335 110
The Centre functions within the Faculty of Asian and Middle Eastern Studies where degree courses include options in classical, medieval and modern Hebrew studies. The Centre's principal activities include the provision of open language classes in Modern Hebrew, seminars on Israeli literature and culture, and weekly screenings of Israeli films; also, an annual ten-day summer Ulpan. *Contact* R. Williams, Dr. M. Marzanska-Mishani

INSTITUTE OF JEWISH STUDIES
University College London, Gower Street, WC1E 6BT
Tel 020 7679 3520 *Fax* 020 7679 2766
Email ijs@ucl.ac.uk *Website* www.ucl.ac.uk/ijs
Twitter @Inst.JewishStudy
(Est. 1953. Reg. Charity No. 213114). Founded by the late Prof. Alexander Altmann, IJS is now located within the Department of Hebrew and Jewish Studies at University College, London, while retaining its autonomous status. It is funded by the private sector. The programme of activities is dedicated to the academic study of all branches of Jewish history and civilisation, including public lectures, seminars, symposia, major international conferences, and publications, especially of its conference proceedings. It brings together scholars, students, and academic institutions from all sections, inside and outside the University of London and the scholarly scene in the UK and worldwide. All activities are free and open to the public. The conference topic for 2015 is Depicting Jewish Thought. A publications and events programme is available by email or on the website. *Patrons* Lord Moser, Lord Woolf; *Bd. of Govs: Ch.* Edward M. Lee BSc (Econ); *Hon. T.* Daniel Peltz MA FKC, David J. Lewis BSc FRICS, Stuart Roden, J. Caplan FCA (also *Hon. S.*); *Dir.* Prof. Mark J. Geller. The Tr. of the Institute of Jewish Studies, a non-profit making company limited by guarantee, registered in England No. 2598783.

LEO BAECK INSTITUTE
Second Floor, Arts Two Building, Queen Mary, University of London, Mile End Road, London E1 4NS
Tel 020 7882 5690 *Fax* 020 7882 6901
Email info@leobaeck.co.uk *Website* www.leobaeck.co.uk
(Est. 1955. Reg. Charity No. 235163). Research and publications on history of Central European German-speaking Jewry. *Ch.* Prof. Peter Pulzer; *Dir.* Prof. R. Gross; *Hon. T. D.* Goldsmith; *Dep. Dir.* Dr. D. Wildmann. *Publ.:* Year Book (*Ed.* Prof. R. Gross, Dr. Cathy Gelbin), symposia, lectures, etc.

OXFORD CENTRE FOR HEBREW AND JEWISH STUDIES
Clarendon Institute Building, Walton Street, Oxford OX1 2HG
Tel 01865 377 946
Email enquiries@ochjs.ac.uk *Website* www.ochjs.ac.uk

Hebrew and Jewish Studies Unit
Oriental Institute, University of Oxford, OX1 2LE
01865 288216 *Fax* 01865 278190
Website www.orinst.ox.ac.uk/nme/hjs/index.shtml
The Centre, together with the Unit which it funds, is one of Europe's leading teaching and research institutions in the area of Jewish studies. Its work includes Jewish history and literature, ancient, medieval and modern; Jewish/Christian relationships in all periods; Hebrew and Yiddish language and literature; and Jewish theology. It provides instruction in Jewish studies towards the Oxford University BA, M.St., M. Phil, M.Litt and D. Phil degrees. The Centre initiated and runs the one-year Masters of Studies (M.St.) in Jewish Studies at Oxford.

Publ.: Journal of Jewish Studies (half-yearly); and numerous books and articles by Fellows past and present. The termly listing of lectures, seminars and classes, Newsletter and the Annual Report of the Centre are available on request. *Pres.* David Ariel; *Co-Ch. Bd. Gov.* Stanley Fink. G. Pinto (The Centre also houses the Leopold Muller Memorial Library, *See* p.117).

PARKES INSTITUTE FOR THE STUDY OF JEWISH/NON-JEWISH RELATIONS
History, School of Humanities, Avenue Campus, University of Southampton, SO17 1BJ
Tel 02380 592 261 *Fax* 02380 593 131
Website www.parkes.soton.ac.uk

The Parkes Institute is an inter-disciplinary community of scholars, librarians, students and curators, whose work is based around the resources of the Parkes Library and archive. This is dedicated to the study of Jewish/non-Jewish relations throughout the ages and to the development of Jewish Studies with the School of Humanities at the University of Southampton. Through our research, publications, conferences, teaching and outreach work, we seek to bring the vision of James Parkes, pioneering campaigner against antisemitism and historian of Jewish/non-Jewish relations, to new generations; to provide a world-class centre for the study of Jewish culture and history; to study the experience of minorities, refugees and outsiders; and to examine the power of prejudice from antiquity to the contemporary world. A new area of research, in accordance with the School of Humanities, is dedicated to Jewish Maritime Studies. Members teach courses in Jewish history, literature, religion and cultural practice at undergraduate level. We offer an innovative MA programme in Jewish History and Culture in Southampton and London. PhD studies in the broad field of Jewish/non-Jewish relations from antiquity to the present. Publications linked to the Institute include three journals (*Patterns of Prejudice, Jewish Culture and History,* and *Holocaust Studies*). *Hd. of Instit.* Prof. Tony Kushner

SCHOOL OF ORIENTAL AND AFRICAN STUDIES (SOAS)
Department of the Languages and Cultures of the Near and Middle East, Thornhaugh Street, Russell Square, London WC1H OXG
Tel 020 7898 4320 *Fax* 020 7898 4359
Website www.soas.ac.uk/nme

SOAS has one of the world's greatest concentrations of expertise on Africa and Asia. The Near & Middle East Department offers a B.A. in Hebrew & Israeli Studies and degrees combining Hebrew with Law, Economics, Management, Arabic and with many other subjects – all affording a year's study at the Hebrew University of Jerusalem. The one-year MA in Israeli Studies caters for postgraduates from around the world seeking an entrée into the field. Doctorates in Israeli and Modern Jewish Studies can be researched. These programmes have the benefit of one of the largest open-stack Jewish Studies libraries in Europe. Also based at SOAS is the Centre for Jewish Studies, which hosts lecture series and symposia on a wide range of issues (*See* p. 103). In 2011, the European Association of Israeli Studies was established and is currently based at SOAS. *Contact* Professor Colin Shindler *Tel* 020 7898 4358 *Email* cs52@soas.ac.uk

STANLEY BURTON CENTRE FOR HOLOCAUST STUDIES
School of History, University of Leicester, Leicester LE1 7RH
Tel 0116 2522800 *Fax* 0116 2523986
Website www.le.ac.uk/hi/centres/burton

To promote the study of, and research, into the Holocaust. *Acting Dir.* Dr A. Korb; *Dep. Dir.* Dr. O. Jensen

UNIVERSITY COLLEGE LONDON
Department of Hebrew and Jewish Studies
Gower Street, WC1E 6BT
Tel 020 7679 7171 *Fax* 020 7679 2766
Email jewish.studies@ucl.ac.uk *Website* www.ucl.ac.uk/hebrew-jewish/home/index.php

The largest University department in the UK and Europe for obtaining honours degrees in Hebrew and Jewish Studies. There are single subject BA degrees in Hebrew and Jewish Studies; Jewish Studies or Jewish History; combined degrees in History (Central and East European) and Jewish Studies, Modern Languages, Modern Languages Plus and Language and Culture; MA in Hebrew and Jewish Studies, Holocaust Studies; Israeli Studies or Jewish History; MPhil or PhD. Fields of teaching and research include: the Ancient Near East; Biblical Languages and Literature; Rabbinic Literature; Ancient, Medieval and Modern Jewish History and Culture; Jews in Central and Eastern Europe; Comparative European Jewish History; Modern Hebrew Judeo-Spanish (Ladino) and Yiddish Language and Literature; Modern Israeli Politics; Jewish Mysticism and Spirituality, especially Hasidism, Women in the Jewish Tradition; the Holocaust in Historical Perspective. Undergraduate students spend a year of the course at the Hebrew University of Jerusalem. All degrees are available as full- or part-time programmes. The department often hosts visiting staff from abroad on an annual basis. It comprises nine full-time and seven part-time members of staff and hosts the Institute of Jewish Studies (*See* p. 104) *Hd.* Prof. Sacha Stern

WOOLF INSTITUTE
12-14 Grange Road, Cambridge CB3 9DU
Tel 01223 741 048
Email enquiries@woolf.cam.ac.uk *Website* www.woolf.cam.ac.uk
(Reg. Charity No. 1069589). The Woolf Institute is a global leader in addressing one of the most pressing and rewarding challenges of our time: the current historical relationships that exist between the faith-traditions of Judaism, Islam and Christianity, with special reference to Europe and the Middle East. Established in Cambridge (UK) in 1998, with close links to the city's famous University, the institute comprises the Centres for the study of Jewish-Christian Relations and Public Education. Its work highlights the importance of shared values whilst acknowledging difference in order to further understanding between the communities and enhance the wider public good. *Exec. Dir.* Dr E. Kessler MBE; *Dep. Dir.* Dr Shana Cohen

ORGANISATIONS CONCERNED WITH JEWISH YOUTH

━BBYO
Shield House, Harmony Way, London NW4 2BZ
Tel 020 8202 6698
Email bbyo@bbyo.org.uk *Website* www.bbyo.org.uk
BBYO UK & Ireland is part of the global BBYO family - the world's largest Jewish youth movement. We have ten chapters across the country, meeting on a weekly basis with innovative activities based on our five ideologies of Zionism, Judaism, Activism, Pluralism and Peer-Leadership. Our chapters are run for teens, by teens, giving you the opportunity to make your mark. We also run exciting camps in the UK, trips to Israel, Europe and North America and an incredible gap year experience in Israel.

FJL (Forum for Jewish Leadership)
379 Hendon Way, London NW4 3LP
Tel 020 8457 2115
Email info@jewish-leadership.com
(Reg. Charity No. 1139858). FJL offers outstanding educational opportunities to intelligent and ambitious future leaders of the Jewish community. Its range of courses and programmes provide an in-depth understanding of the theory and practice of Jewish leadership, as well as Jewish perspectives on a host of legal, political and social issues associated with the modern world. *Dir.* Rabbi A. Savage

FRIENDS OF JEWISH YOUTH (formerly Old Boys' Association)
Martin Shaw, c/o A.J.Y., 128 East Lane, Wembley, Middlesex HA0 3NL
Tel 020 8908 4747 *Fax* 020 8904 4323

GIFT
379 Hendon Way, London NW4 3LP
Tel 020 8457 4429
Email info@jgift.org *Website* www.jgift.org
(Est. 2003, Reg. Charity No. 1153393). GIFT (Give It Forward Today) inspires and educates young people in the value of 'Giving' and 'volunteering'. GIFT finds tailor-made opportunities for young people in the community including rescuing and redistributing food to over 1,700 people every week, helping children from disadvantaged families with homework etc and arranging group visits to old age homes to provide entertainment. *Dir.* Michelle Barnett; *Man.* Shimon Gillis

━ J-ROOTS
379 Hendon Way, London NW4 3LP
Tel 020 8457 2121
Email info@jroots.org.uk
(Est. 2006, Reg. Charity No. 1136532). J-Roots was established to empower today's generation of Jews, to meaningfully connect with its past in order to shoulder responsibility for its future. J-Roots offers an all-inclusive journey through our heritage, looking at the past, the present and future. J-Roots combines the collective expertise and experience drawn from the most prolific educational tour operators and providers of informal education in the Jewish world. The J-Roots executive team is comprised of individuals responsible for facilitating over 200 Jewish journeys to destinations such as Poland, Belarus, Lithuania, Morroco, Prague, Israel and Ukraine, involving thousands of Jewish students and members of the community. *Dir.* Tzvi Sperber, Rabbi N. Schiff

JENERATION (Students and Young Adults)
The Sternberg Centre, 80 East End Road, N3 2SY
Tel 020 8349 5666
Email aly@jeneration.org *Website* www.jeneration.org

JEWISH GUIDE ADVISORY COUNCIL (JGAC)

JGAC furthers Girl Guiding within the Jewish community.
National Ch. Lucinda Glasser 21 West Avenue, London NW4 2LL *Tel* 07967 110 028
Email lucindaglasser@yahoo.co.uk

JEWISH LADS' AND GIRLS' BRIGADE (JLGB)

HQ: Camperdown, 3 Beechcroft Road, South Woodford, E18 1LA
Tel 020 8989 8990 *Fax* 020 8530 3327
Email getinvolved@jlgb.org *Website* www.jlgb.org
(Est. 1895. Reg. Charity No. 286950). JLGB has trained and developed tens of thousands of young people to reach their potential through active citizenship, within both the Jewish and wider community, empowering them to become future leaders. Through local weekly groups across the UK, the JLGB encourages friendship through achievement, recognition and personal development programmes. The JLGB helps to prepare and enable young Jewish people to develop the essential life skills needed to help their transition from young person to adult life.

It is the only Jewish Operating Authority for the Duke of Edinburgh's Award and works with almost every Jewish school in the UK promoting the Award scheme. *Pres.* Lord Levy; *Colonel Commandant* B/Col Jill Attfield; *Ch.* Norman Terrett, JP; *Chaplain* Rabbi A. Plancey; *Chief Exec.* N.S. Martin, BSc (Hons), MA

JEWISH SCOUT ADVISORY COUNCIL

Furthers Scouting in the Jewish community. Mrs Ellis *Tel* 01923 855 514

JEWISH YOUTH FUND

C/o 3rd Floor, Chiswell Street, London, EC1Y 4YX
Tel 020 7449 0909
Email info@jyf.org.uk *Website* www.jyf.org.uk
(Est. 1937. Reg. Charity No. 251902). Provides funds to promote the social education of Jewish young people through the provision of leisure time facilities to clubs, movements and other Jewish youth organisations in the UK. *Co-Ch.* Stephen Spitz, Philippa Strauss; *Dir.* Julia Samuel

LJY–NETZER (Liberal Jewish Youth, Progressive Zionist Youth)

The Montagu Centre, 21 Maple Street, W1T 4BE
Tel 020 7631 0584
Email ljynetzer@liberaljudaism.org *Website* www.ljy-netzer.org
The Liberal Jewish youth movement, offering events and leadership training for young people aged eight to 23, all within a Progressive Zionist framework.
Movement Workers, G. Webber *Email* g.webber@liberaljudaism.org; Tom Francies *Email* t.francies@liberaljudaism.org; Tamara Silver *Email* t.silver@liberaljudaism.org

MACCABI GB

Shield House, Harmony Way, Hendon, London NW4 2BZ
Tel 020 8457 2333 *Fax* 020 8203 3237
Email enquiries@maccabigb.org *Website* www.maccabigb.org
To support the long-term future of British Jewry by engaging and developing the entire community, and especially young people, in a broad range of Jewish sporting, educational and social activities, whilst actively promoting the centrality of Israel.
Ch. M. Ziff; *CEO* M. Berliner

NOAM (NOAR MASORTI)

Alexander House, 3 Shakespeare Road, London N3 1XE
Tel 020 8349 6650
Email noam@masorti.org.uk *Website* www.noam.org.uk

(Est. 1985. Reg. Charity No. 801846). NOAM is the Zionist youth movement of Masorti Judaism. It runs a wide variety of fun educational and social activities for 4-18 year olds. These range from summer camps, both residential and Kaytana day camp, Shabbat services for kids, weekend outings, clubs, Israel tour, and more. NOAM also runs the MERKAZ NOAM Teenage Centre for years 9-13, which develops and trains young Jewish leadership. Over the summers, participants become *madrichim* (leaders) on Noam camps, go on Israel Tour, or run the Kaytana day camp. Each year Noam undertakes a charity fundraiser project for the Ruth Schneider Memorial Trust and another charity chosen by the movement. In July 2012, Noam leaders cycled to Brighton and in May 2013, each member of the NOAM office ran 10km. Mazkir 2012-13: Sam Schryer.

OXFORD & ST. GEORGE'S
120 Oakleigh Road North, N20 9EZ
Tel 020 8446 3101
(Est. in 1914. Reg. Charity No. 207191). Oxford & St George's Jewish Youth Trust, formerly known as Oxford & St George's Jewish Youth & Community Centre, was established with the sole aim of running a Jewish youth and community centre. Over the years, because of a decline in membership, these activities have ceased and it is now a grant making organisation. The closure of the vast majority of Jewish youth clubs in the UK has restricted the grant making potential of the charity. The few Jewish youth clubs that still exist are aware of the facilities available and many have successfully applied for grants.

RSY-NETZER (Movement for Reform Judaism Youth Movement)
The Sternberg Centre, 80 East End Road, N3 2SY
Alyson Joseph *Tel* 020 8349 5666
Email admin@rsy-netzer.org.uk *Website* www.rsy-netzer.org.uk
RSY-Netzer is the Youth Movement of The Movement for Reform Judaism. Every year, it runs events and activities for over 800 10-18 year olds, offering fun and social experiences in a safe and supportive environment. RSY-Netzer is proud of its reputation for high quality fun events, Shemesh summer and Sheleg winter camps, leadership course, Israel tour and Shnat gap year and activities in local Reform Synagogues.

TRIBE (Young United Synagogue)
305 Ballards Lane N12 8GB
Tel 020 8343 5656
Email info@tribeuk.com *Website* www.tribeuk.com
Tribe is the youth arm of the United Synagogue, built on authentic Jewish Values of living, learning and caring.
Exec. Dir. David Collins *Email* davidcollins@tribeuk.com
Tribe Central Rabbi, Rabbi Yisroel Binstock *Email* rabbibinstock@tribeuk.com; *Kids Projects Exec.* Andrew Goldman *Email* andrewgoldman@tribeuk.com; *Young US Events Exec.* Natasha Hurwitz *Email* natashahurwitz@tribeuk.com; *Events Coord.* Nomi Goldberg *Email* nomigoldberg@tribeuk.com; *Snr. Tribe Admin.* Lynne Helman *Email* kids@tribeuk.com

UJIA Informal Education Department
37 Kentish Town Road, London NW1 8NX
Tel 020 7424 6472
The UJIA Informal Education houses world-class educators who assist volunteers and professionals in the fields of Jewish Education and youth work in partnership with the Jewish Agency for Israel. It is the community's main centre for youth leadership training, offering seminars, conferences, mentoring and training and support for Israel engagement programmes and strategies. The Department also supports Jewish activities in mainstream schools and runs the University campus preparation programme in partnership with the Union of Jewish Students. *Dir.* A. Ashworth-Steen

YOUNG JEWISH CARE (YJC)
Tel 020 8922 2822
Email jwilson@jcare.org *Website* www.jewishcare.org
Young Jewish Care is a dynamic and interactive part of Jewish Care, playing a key role in the fundraising successes of the charity through a mixture of initiatives and events. YJC supports and encourages young people to develop committees and fulfill their leadership potential through organising events that cover a wide range of interests.

The following groups are associated with the Zionist Movement.

BNEI AKIVA
2 Hallswelle Road, London NW11 0DJ
Tel 020 8209 1319 *Fax* 020 8209 0107
Email mazkir@bauk.org *Website* www.bauk.org
Facebook bneiakivauk *Twitter* @bneiakivauk
(Est. 1939). Bnei Akiva inspires and empowers young Jews with a sense of commitment to the Jewish people, the Land of Israel and the Torah. As the largest Jewish youth movement in the UK, Bnei Akiva runs weekly activities, summer and winter camps, tours and gap years to Israel and so much more. It is an inclusive youth movement, so whilst it has high religious standards, everyone is welcome. Bnei Akiva has branches in 37 countries all over the world. *Mazkir* Ben Dov Salasnik; *Rabbi* Rav Ari Faust; *Admin.* Sharon Kenley
   Regional centres: 72 Singleton Road, Salford M7 4LU *Tel* 0161 740 1621 *Fax* 0161 740 8018 *Email* north@bauk.org Shlichim Mickey & Ortal Flaumenhaft

EZRA YOUTH MOVEMENT
British and European Office: 2a Alba Gardens, London, NW11 9NR
Tel/Fax 020 8458 5372
Associated with Poale Agudat Israel. An Orthodox Jewish movement based in London, with a branch in Manchester and in Israel and other parts of the world.

—FEDERATION OF ZIONIST YOUTH (FZY)
25 The Burroughs, Hendon, London NW4 4AR (Head Office)
Tel 020 8201 6661 (Head Office) *Tel* 0161 721 4782 (Northern Office)
Email office@fzy.org.uk *Website* www.fzy.org.uk
FZY is a Zionist youth movement for those aged 14 and above. It operates within a pluralist framework and educates its members around Jewish and Zionist themes, with the intention of fulfilling the four aims of FZY: Aliyah Nimshechet, Magen (defence of Jewish rights), Tzedakah and Tarbut (Jewish culture). FZY trains its members in leadership skills and encourages them to involve themselves as leaders in the wider Jewish community. The movement is part of the Atid partnership which also incorporates Young Judaea in USA and the Israeli Scouts. *Pres.* Paul Lenga; *Mazkir* Darren Wogman; *Dir. of Summer Programmes,* Nikki Horesh; *Dir. of 12-16 Programming,* Katie Frankel; *Shaliach,* Matan Hemo; *Northern Shaliach* Or Katzman; *Office Man.* Louise Jacobs; *Year Course Co-ord.* Vivienne Stone; *Tour Admin.* Fiona Prince. *Publ.* The Young Zionist.

FRIENDS OF BNEI AKIVA (BACHAD) (formerly **Bachad Fellowship**)
2 Hallswelle Road, London NW11 0DJ
020 8458 9370 *Fax* 020 8209 0107
(Est. 1942 Reg. Charity No. 1109706). To promote and organise Jewish religious educational activities in the UK and Israel, with a view to preparing the youth of Bnei Akiva for a life in Israel. To provide scholarships for students wishing to attend Bnei Akiva's gap year programme in Israel, and grants for children wishing to go to Bnei Akiva's activities. Maintains Youth Centres in London and Manchester. *Hon Pres.* Chief Rabbi Lord Sacks, Arieh L. Handler z"l; *Ch.* D. Kestenbaum; *V. Ch.* Lawrence Susser; *T. S.* Renshaw

HABONIM–DROR
Platinum House, Gabriel Mews, Crewys Road, London NW2 2GD
Tel 020 8209 2111 *Fax* 020 8209 2110
Website www.habodror.org.uk
(Est. 1929). Habonim was founded in the East End of London, and became the leading international socialist Zionist Jewish youth movement, merging with Dror in 1979. Habonim-Dror's ideology is centred around meaningful, cultural Judaism, socialism and Zionism. It educates members, aged 9–23, towards strong Jewish identities, striving for a more equal and compassionate Israeli society. Weekly activities around the UK focus on informal education. Habonim Dror's Shnat Hachshara involves living together as a community in Israel and engaging in social activism projects, intensive educational and leadership-training seminars, and tours of Israel. *Pres.* Ruth Lady Morris of Kenwood; *Admin.* Rosey Daniels; *Nat. Sec.* Ethan Schwartz. *Publ.* Koleinu.

Offices
London Platinum House, Gabriel Mews, Crewys Road, London NW2 2GD
Tel 020 8209 2111   *Email* ethan@habodror.org.uk
Manchester
(Socialist-Zionist Youth Movement) 28 Wilton Road, Crumpsall, Manchester M8 4WQ
Email michael@habodror.org.uk
(North Manchester Ken) Whitefield Hebrew Congregation, Park Lane, Manchester M45 7PB
Tel 0161 795 9447
(South Manchester Ken) Yeshurun Synagogue, Coniston Road, Gatley
Birmingham c/o Central Office; **Glasgow** c/o Central Northern Office **Leeds** c/o Central Northern Office; **Oxford** c/o Central Office

HANOAR HATZIONI
37 Kentish Town Road, London NW1 8NX
Tel 020 7424 6535
Email office@hanoar.co.uk *Website* www.hanoar.co.uk
Hanoar Hatzioni is a non-political Zionist Youth Movement catering for people between the ages of 7 and 23. Groups are run all over the country. Annual events include Summer and Winter Camps, Israel Tours for 16 year olds, outings, educational and social programmes. Hanoar Hatzioni also run the Shnat Sherut Year Scheme in Israel.
Admin. Hannah Kleinfeld; Joel Meyer

KIBBUTZ REPRESENTATIVES
16 Accommodation Road, London NW11 8ED
Tel 020 8458 9235 *Fax* 020 8455 7930
Website www.kibby.org.uk
(Reg. Charity No. 294563). Representing all the Kibbutz movements in Israel. The organisation arranges Working Visits on Kibbutz for those aged 18–40; Enquirers are requested to send SAE for information packs.

ORGANISATIONS CONCERNED WITH JEWISH STUDENTS

UJS - UNION OF JEWISH STUDENTS (UK and Ireland)
Office 1, 353-359 Finchley Road, London NW3 6ET
Tel 020 7424 3288
Email office@ujs.org.uk *Website* www.ujs.org.uk
(Est. 1919. Reg. Charity No. 313503). *Ch.* Sir Victor Blank; *Hon. T. P.* Keane; *Exec. Dir.* David Brown; *Dir. of Finance and Operations*, Lindsay Davidson; *Pres.* Ella Rose
  Residential and social facilities are available at **Hillel Houses** in the following locations:
  Birmingham: Bella Lupasco *Tel* 0121 777 3505; **Cardiff:** Lisa Gerson *Tel* 029 2075 9982; **Liverpool** Gareth Jones *Tel* 0151 280 0551; **London:** *Golders Green* Debbie Jackson *Tel* 020 8731 0914; **Manchester:** Sydney Baigel *Tel* 0161 740 2521; **Sheffield:** Jeffrey Shaw *Tel* 0114 266 9936

UNIVERSITY JEWISH CHAPLAINCY
305 Ballards Lane, London N12 8GB
Tel 020 8343 5678
Email office@mychaplaincy.co.uk *Website* www.mychaplaincy.co.uk
(Reg. Charity No. 1126031). Our Chaplains and Chaplaincy couples are building student communities and invigorating Jewish life at Universities across the UK. Chaplains and Chaplaincy couples live in the heart of the campus and provide emotional and welfare support, practical help and spiritual and educational guidance as well as being the formal representatives for Jewish students at the Universities. *Pres.* Chief Rabbi Ephraim Mirvis; *H. Life Pres.* Emeritus Chief Rabbi Lord Sacks; *Ch.* Uri Goldberg; *Chief Operating Officer*, Suzy Richman *Email* suzy@mychaplaincy.co.uk; *Chaplains* Birmingham & West Midlands, Rabbi Fishel Cohen *Tel* 07771 653 717 *Email* fishel@mychaplaincy.co.uk; Brighton and South Coast, Rabbi Joe Kaye *Tel* 07929 953 511 *Email* joe@mychaplaincy.co.uk; Bristol & Western, Rabbi Josh Zaitschek, *Tel* 07969 318 699 *Email* josh@mychaplaincy.co.uk; Cambridge & East Anglia; Rabbi Yisrael & Elisheva Malkiel *Tel* 07916 139 974 *Email* yisrael@mychaplaincy.co.uk; Leeds & Yorkshire, Rabbi Eli & Rivka Magzimof *Tel* 07815 108 260 *Email* eli@mychaplaincy.co.uk; London, Rabbi Gavin Broder *Tel* 07811 286 664 *Email* rabbibroder@mychaplaincy.co.uk; Manchester, Rabbi Ephraim Guttentag *Tel* 07817 250 557 *Email* ephraim@mychaplaincy.co.uk; Liverpool and North West, Rabbi Dan Lieberman *Tel* 07975 834 471 *Email* rabbidan@mychaplaincy.co.uk; Newcastle, Rabbi Aaron Lipsey *Tel* 07793 746 454 *Email* aaron@mychaplaincy.co.uk; Nottingham & East Midlands, Rabbi Zvi and Esther Bloom *Tel* 07980 955 026 *Email* zvi@mychaplaincy.co.uk; Oxford, Rabbi Michael & Tracey Rosenfeld-Schueler *Tel* 07717 742 835 *Email* michael@mychaplaincy.co.uk; Scotland, Rabbi Yossi and Sarah Bodenheim *Tel* 07791 292 790 *Email* yossi@mychaplaincy.co.uk; *Chaplaincy Ambassador*, Rabbi Jonny Hughes *Tel* 07817 202 209 *Email* rabbijonny@mychaplaincy.co.uk

WINGATE YOUTH TRUST
(Est. 1975. Reg. Charity No. 269678). To provide facilities for youth, for recreation and leisure. *Ch.* Martin Stone; 135-137 The Broadway, Mill Hill, London NW7 4TD *Sec.* Peter Rebak

LIBRARIES, MUSEUMS AND EXHIBITIONS

ANGLO-JEWISH ARCHIVES

A registered charity under the auspices of the Jewish Historical Society of England. The genealogical collections have been deposited at the Society of Genealogists and the main archive collection has been deposited with the Hartley Library, University of Southampton (*See* p. 115). For information, please email info@jhse.org

BEN URI ART, IDENTITY AND MIGRATION

The London Jewish Museum of Art, 108a Boundary Road, off Abbey Road, London NW8 0RH
Tel 020 7604 3991 *Fax* 020 7604 3992
Email reply@benuri.org.uk *Website* www.benuri.org.uk (for opening times and programmes)
(Est. 1915. Reg. Charity No. 280389. Reg. Museum No. 973). Founded by Lazar Berson as an Art society in Whitechapel in London's East End to collect works by Jewish artists and provide support to Jewish (often émigré) artists who were outside the British mainstream. Today a proud representative of the Jewish Community in Britain's cultural mainstrean, the objectives of the museum are to promote learning of the Jewish experience through art, enjoyment and outreach between communities. This is achieved through exhibitions that tour internationally; publications that are distributed internationally; learning modules for schools and special needs, accessible to 25,000 Schools nationwide through the National education Network; social health 'art' for the elderly and those with Dementia; an extensive artist development programme and wide use of the internet and Social Media. Ben Uri explores and tells the stories of the life and work of artists of European Jewish descent, alongside their artist peers, within both the artistic and social history contexts. *Ch.* David Glasser (Exec.); *Deputy Ch.* Mike Posen; *Fin. Dir. Co. Sec.* Keith Graham, Simon Bentley; *Advisor*, David Franks; *Ch. of Exhibitions Cttee.* Rachel Dickson; *Ch. of Collection Cttee.* Sarah MacDougall; *Education Man.* Alix Smith; *Development Management*, Kate Ferrie, Stephen Goldman; *Business Man.* Tania Talaga

BIESENTHAL COLLECTION

Special Collections Centre, Univeristy Library, Bedford Road, Aberdeen, AB24 3AA
Tel 01224 272 598
Email speclib@abdn.ac.uk
Consists of some 2,000 volumes. It has one of Britain's finest Rabbinical collections acquired in 1872. The Special Libraries and Archives also feature the collections and papers of Malcolm Hay of Seaton, which include material on Zionism and correspondence in Hebrew.

BODLEIAN LIBRARY

Broad Street, Oxford OX1 3BG
Tel 01865 277000
Email cesar.merchan-hamann@bodleian.ox.ac.uk
The Hebrew and Yiddish collections has 3,000 manuscript volumes and 60,000 printed books, including many incunabula, fragments from the Cairo Genizah and the Oppenheimer Library, the finest collection of Hebrew books and manuscripts ever assembled. Intending readers should always contact the Admissions Office in advance. Open to holders of a reader's ticket Monday to Friday 9am–7pm, Saturday 10am–4pm *Hebrew Specialist Libr.* Dr. Cesar Merchan-Hamann

THE BRITISH LIBRARY

African and Asian Studies, 96 Euston Road, London NW1 2DB
Tel 020 7412/7646 *Fax* 020 7412 7641
Email opac-enquiries@bl.uk *Website* http://www.bl.uk/reshelp/findhelplang/hebrewcoll/index.html
The Hebrew collection has over 3,000 manuscript volumes and 10,000 fragments (incl. Moses Gaster's collection and many fragments from the Cairo Genizah). Its Hebrew

printed books, amount to about 73,000 titles, incl. some 100 incunabula, rabbinic and modern Hebrew literature; Yiddish, Ladino, Judeo-Arabic and Judeo-Persian books; some 1,000 Hebrew and Yiddish periodicals and newspapers. The Asian and Africa Studies Reading Room is open to holders of readers' passes. (Opening hours may be revised at any time. Normal opening: Monday 10am–5pm; Tuesday-Saturday 9.30am–5pm). Some Hebrew manuscripts are on permanent display in the British Library Exhibition Galleries, open (free of charge): Monday, Wednesday to Friday 9.30am–6pm, Tuesday 9.30am–8pm, Saturday 9.30am–5pm, Sunday and English public Holidays 11am–5pm. The Golden Haggadah and Lisbon Bible are included in the electronic 'Turning the Pages' programme on www.bl.uk By 2016, 1250 manuscripts from the Hebrew collection will be digitised and made freely accessible on-line. The British Library has already digitised 49 manuscripts which can be viewed at www.bl.uk/manuscripts/ A further 351 Hebrew manuscripts will be uploaded by September this year. This Hebrew Manuscript Digitisation Project will enable free universal online access to these unique objects, and will enrich people's study of Judaism across different regions and in different times.
Hebrew Specialist, Ilana Tahan M.Phil. OBE *Email* ilana.tahan@bl.uk

BROTHERTON LIBRARY
University of Leeds, Leeds LS2 9JT
Tel 0113 3435518 *Fax* 0113 3435561
Email special-collections@library.leeds.ac.uk *Website* www.leeds.ac.uk/library
Holdings include substantial materials for Hebrew and Jewish studies and the Travers Herford Collection on Judaism and Talmudic studies. The primary Judaica collection is the Roth Collection which has the manuscripts and printed books from the Library of Cecil Roth, including 350 manuscripts, 900 printed books (pre-1850) 6,000 modern books and other archival material. Available to bona fide scholars, who should write to the library in the first instance, enclosing an appropriate recommendation. *Libr.* Margaret Coutts; *Asst. Libr. Publ.* Selig Brodetsky lecture series.

CAMBRIDGE UNIVERSITY LIBRARY
West Road, Cambridge CB3 9DR
Tel 01223 333 000 *Fax* 01223 333 160
Email library@lib.cam.ac.uk *Website* www.lib.cam.ac.uk
Dir. A. Jarvis. The Hebraica and Judaica collections have c. 190,000 Cairo Genizah fragments; 1,000 complete Hebrew codices (*See* S. C. Reif, Hebrew Manuscripts at Cambridge University Library, CUP, 1997); approximately 40,000 printed books. Available to members of the University and bona fide scholars by application. Reading rooms open Monday-Friday 9am–7pm, Saturday 9am-4.45pm; Admissions Office Monday-Thursday 9am–12.45pm, 2–5pm, Friday 9am–12.45pm, 2–4.45pm, Saturday 9am–1pm, 2–4pm. For more information see www.lib.cam.ac.uk/admissions *Hd. Genizah Res. Unit.* Dr B. M. Outhwaite; *Hebraica Librarian* Ms Y. Faghihi

DAUBE COLLECTION
Special Collections Centre, Univeristy Library, Bedford Road, Aberdeen, AB24 3AA
Tel 01224 272 598
Email speclib@abdn.ac.uk
Consists of some 30,000 printed volumes dating from 16th to 20th centuries on ancient law (especially Roman and Jewish), rabbinical subjects and history. Personal working library of David Daube, (1909-1999), jurist and scholar. Daube, who spent much of his career as a law professor at University of California Berkeley, served as professor or Jurisprudence at Aberdeen from 1951-1955. The printed collection was donated by Daube's family with a substantial body of archival material in 2004, and is currently being catalogued.

THE HARTLEY LIBRARY

University of Southampton, Highfield, Southampton SO17 1BJ
Contact *Tel* 023 8059 3335 (Parkes), 023 8059 2721 (Archives) *Fax* 023 8059 3007
Email libenqs@soton.ac.uk (Parkes); archives@soton.ac.uk (Archives)
Website www.southampton.ac.uk/archives
Holdings of the Special Collections Division include (i) the **Parkes Library**, founded by the late Revd. Dr. James Parkes in 1935 to promote the study of relations between the Jewish and the non-Jewish worlds. It now contains 27,000 books and periodicals; (ii) more than 950 collections of manuscripts, of around 3.5 million items, relating to Anglo-Jewry (incorporating the collections of the **Anglo-Jewish Archives**). These manuscript collections encompass the papers of the Anglo-Jewish Association; records of the London Board of Shechita; archives of the Jewish Board of Guardians and the Jewish Association for the Protection of Girls, Women and Children; papers of the International Military Tribunal and the Nuremberg Military Tribunals; Zangwill and Henriques family papers,; papers of Sir Robert Waley Cohen, Lady Swaythling and Rabbi Solomon Schonfeld; the archives of Leo Baeck College, the Reform Synagogues of Great Britain and the West London Synagogue; the archives of the British Section of the World Jewish Congress and of the Institute of Jewish Affairs (now the Institute for Jewish Policy Research). The holdings of the Parkes Library are listed in the library WebCat http://www-lib.soton.ac.uk/ A guide to the archive collections is available at www.southampton.ac.uk/archives Visits to the Archives and Manuscripts reading room need to be arranged in advance. *Snr. Archivist,* K. Robson

HEBRAICA LIBRARIES GROUP

Website http://www.lib.cam.ac.uk/hebraica/hebraicam2.htm
(Est. 1976). The Group brings together representatives of all the major Judaica and Hebraica collections in Great Britain and Ireland, together with other academic libraries with an interest in the field. Membership is open to specialist librarians in academic libraries, specialists in public or private institutions, as well as scholars and researchers with an interest in the Hebrew book. It holds an annual meeting as well as visits to libraries and collections in the area of Hebraica and Jewish studies, and is affiliated to the National Committee for Information Resources on Asia (NACIRA). It offers expertise in all aspects of Hebraica collections, their preservation, security, conservation, cataloguing, computer systems and collection development. *Convenor* Vanessa Freedman, Hebrew and Jewish Studies Librarian, UCL *Tel* 020 7679 2598 *Email* v.freedman@ucl.ac.uk

THE HIDDEN LEGACY FOUNDATION

Kent House, Rutland Gardens, London SW7 1BX
Tel 020 7584 2754 *Fax* 020 7584 6896
(Est. 1988. Reg. Charity No. 326032). Devoted to promoting the awareness of provincial (English) and rural (German) Jewish history, as seen through buildings and artefacts. It has become particularly identified with German Genizot. It organises exhibitions: Genizah (1992), Mappot (1997), The Jews of Devon and Cornwall (2000). Having been active in Germany, it is now working in England, cataloguing Judaica. Library, slide and photo archives on rural German Jewry. *Exec. Dir.* Evelyn Friedlander

IMPERIAL WAR MUSEUM HOLOCAUST EXHIBITION

Lambeth Road, London SE1 6HZ
Dept. of Research *Tel* 020 7416 5286
Website www.iwm.org.uk
Holocaust Exhibition Hd. of Research, Suzanne Bardgett; *Curator,* Emily Fuggle; *Founding Patrons* Lord Bramall, Sir Martin Gilbert, Ben Helfgott, Lord Moser, Lord Rothschild, Lord Weidenfeld, Lord Wolfson of Marylebone, Stephen Rubin; *Advisory Gp.* Prof. D. Cesarani, Sir Martin Gilbert, Ben Helfgott, Antony Lerman, Martin Smith. This major national exhibition was opened by H.M. the Queen in 2000. To discuss any exhibition-related enquiries please contact *Curator,* Emily Fuggle *Tel* 020 7416 5286

JEWISH MILITARY MUSEUM
Shield House, Harmony Way, Hendon, London NW4 2BZ
Tel 020 8201 5656
Email visit@thejmm.org.uk *Website* www.thejmm.org.uk
Curator, Roz Currie; *Museum Ch.* Ron Shelley MBE; *Fdr. Pres.* Henry Morris; *Archivist* Martin Sugarman. A History of the Jewish contribution to the Armed Forces of the Crown over three centuries. Displays of unique medals, photos, badges, letters, documents, uniforms and much other personal memoribilia of all kinds and a large archive available to reseachers by appointment. Please ring if you would like to visit.

JEWISH MUSEUM - LONDON
Raymond Burton House, 129-131 Albert Street, Camden Town, London NW1 7NB
Switchboard Tel 020 7284 7384
Email admin@jewishmuseum.org.uk *Website* www.jewishmuseum.org.uk
(Est. 1932. Reg. Charity No. 1009819). The Jewish Museum opened in 2010 following a £10 million investment. Here you can explore Jewish culture, heritage and identity. The Jewish story is placed in the wider context of British history. There are exhibitions, education programmes and activities available. The additional objectives are to build interfaith understanding, inspire people to take a stand against racism and to look at the world from a different point of view.
Open: daily, 10am–5pm, except Friday 10am-2pm. *Chief Exec.* Abigail Morris; *Ch.* Lord Young of Graffham; *T.* Mike Frankl

JEWS' COLLEGE LIBRARY
London School of Jewish Studies, Schaller House, 44A Albert Road, London NW4 2SJ
Tel 020 8203 6427 *Fax* 020 8203 6420
Email info@lsjs.ac.uk
150th anniversary in 2010. This is one of the most extensive Judaica and Hebraica libraries in Europe. With about 70,000 volumes and manuscripts. Open, free of charge: Monday 9am-4pm, Tuesday to Thursday, 9am-1pm. *Consultant Libr.* Erla Zimmels

JOHN RYLANDS LIBRARY
150 Deansgate, Manchester M3 3EH
Tel 0161 306 0555
Email jrul.special-collections@manchester.ac.uk
Website www.manchester.ac.uk/library/deansgate
Admission is free to all visitors and readers. Visitor opening hours are Sunday and Monday 12-5pm, Tuesday-Saturday 10am-5pm. Those wishing to consult rare books, manuscripts or archives should provide a suitable letter of introduction as well as proof of their address; advance notice of any visit is advisable. The Hebraica and Judaica has over 10,500 fragments from the Cairo Genizah; manuscripts and codices from the Crawford and Gaster collections; Samaritan manuscripts from the Gaster collection; 6,600 items of printed Hebraica and talmudic literature in the Marmorstein collection; 1,000 volumes of the Haskalah collection; the Moses Gaster collection; and some 5,000 volumes in the Near Eastern collection in the Main University Library dealing with Hebrew language and literature. *Hd. of Special Collection and Research Service Man.* (archives and manuscripts) John Hodgson

KEREN HATORAH BOOK LIBRARY AND TAPE LIBRARY
97 Stamford Hill, London N16 5DN
Tel 020 8800 6688
A comprehensive collection of Torah literature for the whole family, and over ten thousand cassette recordings including the complete Talmud in English and Yiddish and a range of other Torah and Jewish topics. Operates as a lending library.
Book Library open Sunday, Tuesday, Thursday, 10am-12.30pm, Monday 3.30-5.30pm
Tape Library for opening hours please phone.

LEO BAECK COLLEGE LIBRARY
80 East End Road, N3 2SY
Tel 020 8349 5610/1 *Fax* 020 8349 5619
Email Library@lbc.ac.uk
Est. 1956 to provide a library for Jewish Studies and research. Holdings: 60,000 vols; 40 current periodicals; 10,000 pamphlets; 180 rabbinic and MA theses; 500 rare books; Hyams collection of Jewish Children's literature. Range: Bible, rabbinic literature, codes, liturgy, education, literature, history, Holocaust and post-Holocaust studies, Israel and Zionism, Interfaith, historic children's books. Open to members and occasional readers from Monday–Thursday 10am–5pm, Friday 10am–1pm. Closed on Jewish Festivals, bank holidays and during the last week of December. During July and August, visits can be made only by appointment with the library For regular access to the library a yearly contribution of £40 is charged. *Hd. Libr.* Annette M. Boeckler, PhD; *Asst. Libr.* P. Claiden and volunteers

LEOPOLD MULLER MEMORIAL LIBRARY
Oxford Centre for Hebrew & Jewish Studies, Yarnton Manor, Yarnton, Oxford OX5 1PY
Tel 01865 377 946 (library office ext. 117; library ext. 120) *Fax* 01865 375 079
Email muller.library@ochjs.ac.uk *Website* www.ochjs.ac.uk
(Reg. Charity No. 309720). The Leopold Muller Memorial Library is an open access lending library of about 90,000 volumes and 80 current periodicals, covering the full range of Hebrew and Jewish studies, with special focus on Hebrew literature of the 19th and 20th centuries, Haskalah, modern Jewish history, Zionism, Israeli and Hebrew bibliography. Special collections: the Foyle-Montefiore Library, including the library of Leopold Zunz; the Louis Jacobs collection; the Copenhagen Collection (on Dutch Jewry and the Holocaust); the largest collection of *Yizkor* books in Europe; the Arthur Sebag-Montefiore Archive and the Shandel-Lipson Archive, containing materials on Sir Moses Montefiore; the Western Hebrew Library; the Hugo Gryn collection; an extensive microfiche collection containing the Montefiore collection of Manuscripts, the manuscripts and rare books collections of the Jewish Theological Seminary of America and the Harvard College Library, the *Dokumentation zur jüdischen Kultur in Deutschland 1840–1940: Die Zeitungsausschnittsammlung Steiniger* and the *Jüdisches Biographisches Archiv*; an archive of 40,000 newspaper cuttings on 12,000 Jewish personalities and on the early Yishuv in Palestine, as well as representative samples of the Hebrew and Yiddish press. For opening times, access and borrowing rights, see website. *Dir.* Dr César Merchán-Hamann; *Dep. Dir.* Milena Zeidler; *Assist. Libr.* Jane Barlow, Dr Zsófia Buda

LONDON METROPOLITAN ARCHIVES
40 Northampton Road, London EC1R 0HB
Tel 020 7332 3820 *Fax* 020 7833 9136
Email ask.lma@cityoflondon.gov.uk *Website* www.cityoflondon.gov.uk/lma
LMA is the regional archive for Greater London. The collections within it of Jewish interest include: BoD of British Jews, Office of the Chief Rabbi, US, London Beth Din, Jews Free School, Jews Temporary Shelter, London School of Jewish Studies, World Jewish Relief and the Spanish & Portuguese Jews' Congregation. Many collections are available to researchers only with the prior permission of the depositor, so please contact LMA in advance for the relevant addresses. Opening Hours: Monday 9.30am-4.45pm; Tuesday, Wednesday, Thursday 9.30am-7.30pm; closed Friday, selected Saturdays 9.30am-4.45pm (Please call for open dates or see website).

LUBAVITCH LENDING LIBRARY
1 Northfield Road, London N16 5RL
Tel 020 8800 5823
Email library@lubavitch.co.uk
Established in 1972 to help the Jewish public study traditional Jewish culture and aid scholarship. The library contains 18,000 volumes in Hebrew, English and Yiddish. Services

include a reference library, a children's library and postal lending. Lectures and displays organised anywhere. New expanded Library opened in Summer 2010. Loans free. Normal opening times Sunday 11am-8pm; Monday-Thursday 10.30am-5.45pm, 7.15pm-8.30pm; Friday 8.30am-1pm (Winter), 9.30am-4.30pm (Summer). *Librarian*, Z. Rabin MBE

MEMORIAL SCROLLS TRUST
Kent House, Rutland Gardens, London SW7 1BX
Tel 020 7584 3741
Email info@memorialscrollstrust.org *Website* www.memorialscrollstrust.org
(Reg. Charity No. 278900). This permanent exhibition tells the unique story of the rescue from Prague, in 1964, of 1,564 Torah Scrolls and of their restoration and distribution on permanent loan to communities throughout the world. The exhibits include some of the scrolls, a display of Torah binders, some dating from the 18th century, and other reminders of the vanished Czech communities of Bohemia and Moravia. The centre is open on Tuesdays and Thursdays from 10am-4pm. Other times and Sundays are by arrangement. *Admin.* Rabbi Ariel J. Friedlander

NATIONAL LIFE STORIES at The British Library
96 Euston Road, London, NW1 2DB
Tel 020 7412 7404
Email oralhistory@bl.uk *Website* www.bl.uk/nls
(Est. 1987. Reg. Charity No. 327571). To 'record first-hand experiences of as wide a cross-section of present-day society as possible'. As an independent charitable trust within the Oral History Section of the British Library, NLS's key focus and expertise has been oral history fieldwork. To listen to selected recordings online visit www.sounds.bl.uk/oral-history *Lead Curator, Oral History and Dir. of National Life Stories*, Rob Perks *Tel* 020 7412 7405; *Oral History Curator and Deputy Dir. of National Life Stories*, Mary Stewart *Tel* 020 7412 7406;

LIVING MEMORY OF THE JEWISH COMMUNITY (C410) is a major collection with a primary focus on pre-Second World War Jewish refugees to Britain, those fleeing from Nazi persecution during the Second World War and Holocaust survivors. The collection has recently expanded to include interviews with children of survivors. The collection complements other sound archive material on Jewish life, notably the Holocaust Survivors' Centre interviews (C830), Central British Fund Kindertransport interviews (C526), Testimony: Video Interviews with British Holocaust Survivors (C533) and London Museum of Jewish Life oral history interviews (C525).

PORTON COLLECTION OF JUDAICA
Business and Research Department, Central Library, Calverley Street, Leeds LS1 3AB
Tel 0113 2478282 *Fax* 0113 395 1833
Email informationandresearch@leeds.gov.uk *Website* www.leeds.gov.uk/libraries
The Porton Collection of Judaica has its roots in volumes originally housed in Rabbi Moses Abrahams Memorial Library in Leeds. The collection was enlarged over the years and presented to Leeds City Council in 1965 by Mr Porton's son Leslie, along with Mr Joseph Porton's Judaica collection. The collection covers all aspects of the religion and culture of the Jewish people and includes works in English, Hebrew and Yiddish, in all some 3,500 items. The collection is strong in theological works and religious texts, Jewish and Anglo-Jewish History and biography and also contains archives of the Jewish Year Book, Jewish Chronicle and Jewish Gazette. Rare books and pamphlets, largely in Hebrew and Yiddish, and published in the nineteenth century, are a feature of the collection. Some items are available for loan.

SCHOOL OF ORIENTAL AND AFRICAN STUDIES (University of London)
Thornhaugh Street, Russell Square, London WC1H 0XG
Tel 020 7898 4154 *Fax* 020 7898 4159
Website www.soas.ac.uk/library

The Ancient Near East, Semitics and Judaica Section of the SOAS Library. The Semitics and Judaica collections comprise about 15,000 Hebrew items, covering the fields of modern Hebrew language and literature (one of the finest collections in Europe), biblical and intertestamental studies, Judaism, the Jewish people, and the land of Israel. There are also a considerable number of books in Western languages covering these fields. In addition, largely owing to the acquisition of the Stencl and Leftwich collections in 1983 and some books from the Whitechapel collection in 1984, there are about 3,000 books on Yiddish language and literature. Periodicals, of which the library holds about 200 Hebrew titles, are shelved separately. The transfer of the Joe Loss Lectureship in Jewish Music from the City University to SOAS has also brought the Harry Rosencweig Collection of Jewish Music to the library. For details of services, please refer to the Library's web pages.

SPANISH & PORTUGUESE JEWS' CONGREGATION ARCHIVES
2 Ashworth Road, W9 1JY
Tel 020 7289 2573 *Fax* 020 7289 2709
Archives The archives of the Spanish & Portuguese Jews' Congregation, London, and its institutions, which date from the mid-17th century, include Minute and Account Books, Registers of Births, Circumcisions, Marriages and Burials. Most of the Registers have now been published and copies may be purchased from the Congregation's office. The archives are not open to the public. Most of the Congregation's archive material is now located at London Metropolitan Archives. Queries and requests for access to the material at LMA from bona fide researchers should be submitted in writing to the Hon. Archivist. Advice and help will be given to general enquirers wherever possible. A search fee may be charged. *Hon. Archivist* Miriam Rodrigues-Pereira. **Shasha Library** (Est 1936) Designed to contain books on Jewish history, religion, literature and kindred interest from the Sephardi standpoint. It contains over 1,200 books. These collections are available at the Sephardi Centre by appointment only. (*See* p. 101).

UNIVERSITY COLLEGE LONDON LIBRARY (UCL)
University College London, Wilkins Building, Gower Street, WC1E 6BT
Tel 020 7679 2598 *Fax* 020 7679 7373
Email library@ucl.ac.uk *Website* www.ucl.ac.uk/library
The Hebrew and Jewish Studies collection comprises around 29,000 volumes in the fields of Jewish history, Israel and Zionism, Hebrew and Semitic languages, Bible, Rabbinic literature, mysticism, Jewish philosophy, Hebrew literature and Yiddish language and literature. In addition there are over 185,000 items of rare and archival material. The collection incorporates the Mocatta Library, Altmann Library and the William Margulies Yiddish Library. See website for opening times and access arrangements. *Hebrew and Jewish Studies Libr.* Vanessa Freedman

THE WIENER LIBRARY FOR THE STUDY OF HOLOCAUST AND GENOCIDE
29 Russell Square, London WC1B 5DP
Tel 020 7636 7247 *Fax* 020 7436 6428
Email info@wienerlibrary.co.uk *Website* www.wienerlibrary.co.uk
(Reg. Charity No. 313015). Founded by Dr. A. Wiener in Amsterdam, 1933, and since 1939 in London. Research library and Institute on contemporary European and Jewish history, especially the rise and fall of the Third Reich; survival and revival of Nazi and fascist movements; antisemitism; racism; the Middle East; post-war Germany. Holds Britain's largest collection of documents, testimonies, and books on the Holocaust. Active educational programme of lectures, seminars and conferences. *Ch. of Bd.* A. Spiro; *Dir.* B. Barkow

PROFESSIONAL ORGANISATIONS

ASSOCIATION OF MINISTERS (CHAZANIM) OF GREAT BRITAIN
Ch. Rev. S. I. Brickman 3 Chatsworth Close, Borehamwood, Herts WD6 1UE *Tel* 020 8387 9962; *T.* Rev. M. Haschel

ASSOCIATION OF ORTHODOX JEWISH PROFESSIONALS OF GREAT BRITAIN
53 Wentworth Road, London NW11 0RT
(Est. 1962). To promote research in matters of common interest, and the general acceptance of Torah and Halacha as relevant and decisive in all aspects of modern life and thought. *Ch.* H. J. Adler

JEWISH NURSES & MIDWIVES ASSOCIATION
32 Wykeham Road, London NW4 2SU
Tel 020 8203 2241 *Mobile* 07932 730 944
Email sara@smbarnett.com
(Est. 1993). A social, educational and support group for all Jewish nurses, midwives and members of allied professions. *Ch.* Sara Barnett

RABBINICAL COUNCIL OF NORTH-EAST LONDON
Co-ord. Rev G. Newman *Tel* 07932 166 733 *Email* reverendnewman613@hotmail.co.uk

RABBINICAL COUNCIL OF THE PROVINCES
Pres. Rabbi Lord Sacks; *Ch.* Rabbi Shlomo Odze; *Hon. T.* Rabbi Yoinosson Golomb; *M.* Rev. N. Fagelman 1 Sale Synagogue, 12a Hesketh Road, Sale, Cheshire M33 5AA *Tel* 0161 222 4478

RABBINICAL COUNCIL OF THE UNITED SYNAGOGUE
305 Ballards Lane, London N12 8GB
Tel 020 8343 6313 *Fax* 020 8343 6310
Email rabbi.shindler@chiefrabbi.org
Ch. Rabbi B. Davis; *V. Ch.* Rabbi N. Liss, Rabbi N. Wilson; *Exec. Dir.* Rabbi Dr J. Shindler, MSc; *Hon. T.* Rabbi D. Mason; *Hon. S.* Rabbi S. Odze

UNITED SYNAGOGUE ADMINISTRATORS' ASSOCIATION
305 Ballards Lane, London N12 8GB
Tel 020 8343 8989 *Fax* 020 8343 6236
Ch. Charles Loeb

VAAD HARABBONIM
Organisation of all the rabbis of the synagogues under the auspices of the Union of Orthodox Hebrew Congregations. *Hon. S.* Rabbi D. Halpern 3 The Approach, London NW4 2HU

MISCELLANEOUS ORGANISATIONS

◄ALAN SENITT MEMORIAL TRUST
13 Chestnut Avenue, Edgware, Middlesex HA8 8AB
Tel 07714 960 212
Email admin@alansenitt.org *Website* www.alansenitt.org
Facebook Alan Senitt Memorial Trust *Twitter* @senitttrust
(Est. 2006. Reg Charity No. 1117111). A Trust established to be a testimony to and the perpetuation of the life, work and aspirations of Alan Charles Senitt (1978-2006) for the benefit of future generations. The Trust runs a Community Leadership Programme for Year 10 pupils, of all faiths, running in 8 High Schools, provides funding for innovative educational programmes in Youth work, Community Leadership, Interfaith and Israel Programmes. It also partners UJS-Hillel in many activities, including the Alan Senitt Student Hardship Fund and the UJS Student Award for Outstanding Achievement. *Ch.* Emma Senitt; *V. Ch.* Jamie Senitt; *Hon. T.* R. Chaplin; *Hon. S.* Karen Senitt

ASSOCIATION OF JEWISH EX-SERVICEMEN AND WOMEN (AJEX)
Shield House, Harmony Way, Hendon, London NW4 2BZ
Tel 020 8202 2323 *Fax* 020 8202 9900
Email headoffice@ajex.org.uk *Website* www.ajex.org.uk
(Est. 1923). *Nat. Ch.* J. Fox; *Exec. Dir.* J. Weisser; *H. Chaplain* Rabbi Reuben Livingstone CF (U). A list of London and Regional Branches can be obtained from the Office. For the Jewish Military Museum contact the Curator, Roz Currie; *Museum Ch.* Ron Shelley MBE; *Fdr. and Pres.* Henry Morris; *Archivist*, Martin Sugarman (*See* p. 116).

ASSOCIATION OF JEWISH GOLF CLUBS & SOCIETIES
Pres. Clive Leveson, 4 College House, South Downs Road, Bowden, Cheshire WA14 3DZ *Email* clive@thelevesons.co.uk; *Sec./T.* Alan Simons 12 Purcells Avenue, Edgware HA8 8DT *Email* alsimcon@gmail.com; *Tournament Sec.* David Futerman 24 The Ridgeway, Finchley, London N3 2PH *Email* david.futerman@virgin.net

THE BIG GREEN JEWISH WEBSITE
25-26 Endford Street, London W1H 1DW
Tel 020 3603 8120
Email info@biggreenjewish.org *Website* www.biggreenjewish.org
The Big Green Jewish Website is a resource for Jewish People. It is the on-line meeting point between Jewish and environmental ethics. It seeks to educate about climate change and aims to inspire you to make a difference to the planet. *Staff* Oliver Marcus, David Brown

THE BURNING BUSH
19 Patshull Road, London NW5 2JX
Tel 020 7485 3957
Email lucieskeaping@hotmail.com *Website* www.theburningbush.co.uk
(Est. 1990). 3–6 musicians, traditional Klezmer, Yiddish, Sephardi, Israeli music and song. Weddings, Barmitzvahs, private parties and concerts. *Dir.* Lucie Skeaping

CAMPAIGN FOR THE PROTECTION OF SHECHITA
Elscot House, Arcadia Avenue, London NW3 2JU
Tel 0800 035 0466
Email david@shechita.co.uk
(Est. 1985). To protect the freedom of Jews to perform Shechita; to make representations to Government on proposed legislation or other measures which may affect the proper performance of Shechita. *Nat. Co-ord. and Hon. Solicitors* Neville Kesselman; *Reg. Coord.* Chanoch Kesselman, London; *Rabbinical Adv.* Rabbi Benjamin Vorst and Rabbi Dr David Miller, MA, MSc, DPhil (Oxon)

CELEBRITIES GUILD OF GREAT BRITAIN
The Studio, 16 Covert Way, EN4 0LT
Tel 020 8449 1234 weekdays 10am–4pm *Fax* 020 8441 8430
Email info@celebritiesguild.org.uk *Website* www.celebritiesguild.org.uk
(Est. 1977. Reg. Charity No. 282298). A social and fund-raising Guild of prominent people in British Jewry who organise events to raise funds to provide equipment for disabled and handicapped people. *H. Exec. Dir.* Ella Glazer MBE; *Master Guilder* Mike Sarne

EDGWAREBURY JOINT BURIAL BOARD (EJBB)
Edgwarebury Cemetery, Edgwarebury Lane, Edgware, HA8 8QP
Edgwarebury Cemetery comprises 23 acres and was opened in 1973, it is owned by the Spanish & Portuguese Jews' Congregation, West London Synagogue, Liberal Judaism and Belsize Square Synagogue. *Tel* 020 8958 0090

FRIENDS OF JEWISH SERVICEMEN AND WOMEN
Freepost RSHG-JLJH-XZYY, JCHMF, 12 Conisborough Place, Manchester M45 6EJ
Email afjc@armymail.mod.uk
(Est. 1956. Reg. Charity No. 267647). Supports the Jewish Committee for H.M. Forces *(See* p. 68) in funding and ministering to the religious needs of serving Jewish personnel. *Ch.* Dr P. Wagerman; *Pres.* Lt Col. Mordaunt Cohen TD DL; *Hon. T.* Major Rob Pollock; *Hon. S.* Brian Bloom; *Tru.* Col. M. Newman DL, Lt. Cdr. A. Tyler RN; *Tru.* Dr P. Wagerman

INDEPENDENT JEWISH VOICES (IJV)
Tel 020 8883 7063
Email info@ijv.org.uk *Website* www.ijv.org.uk
(Est. 2007). To promote expression of alternative Jewish voices, particularly with respect to Israel, based on commitment to universal human rights and social justice. *Sec.* Ann Jungman

JEWISH ASSOCIATION FOR BUSINESS ETHICS
2nd Floor, Mowbray House, 58-70 Edgware Middlesex HA8 8DJ
Tel 020 8905 4048 *Fax* 020 8905 4658
Email info@jabe.org *Website* www.jabe.org
(Reg. Charity No. 1038453). JABE aims to encourage honesty, integrity and social responsibility in business and the professions, operating within the corporate world and the education system to achieve this. JABE regularly delivers high-profile seminars, educational events and thought provoking publications, in addition to its highly successful 'Money and Morals' School Programme. *Ch.* Alan Tapnack; *Exec. Dir.* Lorraine Spector

JEWISH ASSOCIATION OF SPIRITUAL HEALERS
Email jashhealing@hotmail.com *Website* www.jashhealing.com
(Est. 1966. Reg. Charity No. 275081). Aims: (1) To attempt to relieve sickness and suffering; (2) To demonstrate that Spiritual Healing is in keeping with the teachings of Judaism. *Ch.* Stephen Sharpe *Tel* 020 8866 9332; *Sec.* Francine Benjamin *Tel* 07956 261 738; *News Ed.* Yetta and Maurice Powell *Tel* 020 8954 0787

THE JEWISH COUNCIL FOR RACIAL EQUALITY
P.O. Box 47864, London NW11 1AB
Tel 020 8455 0896
Email admin@jcore.org.uk *Website* www.jcore.org.uk
(Est. 1976. Reg. Charity No. 1132666). JCORE provides a Jewish voice on race and asylum issues in the UK and works with both the Jewish and wider community to promote a positive, multi-ethnic UK, free from all forms of racism. JCORE delivers race-equality education and publications for all ages; campaigns for the right of asylum seekers and refugees; and provides practical support for destitute asylum seekers, unaccompanied

child refugees and refugee doctors. JCORE works closely with other ethnic minority, refuge, anti-racism and interfaith organisations, bringing together people from Black, Jewish and Asian communities for dialogue, joint projects and campaigning. *Exec. Dir.* Dr Edie Friedman

JEWISH FRIENDLY SOCIETIES
Grand Order of Israel and Shield of David
11 The Lindens, Prospect Hill, Waltham Forest, London E17 3EJ
Tel 020 8520 3531
Email info@goisd.org.uk *Website* www.goisd.org.uk
(Est. 1896). The membership is contained in three Lodges in the Metropolitan area and one in Birmingham.

JEWISH GAY AND LESBIAN GROUP
BM-JGLG, London WC1N 3XX
Tel 07504 924 742
Email info@jglg.org.uk *Website* www.jglg.org.uk
(Est. 1972). Social group for the Jewish LGBT community. *Pres.* Sonia Lawrence

JEWISH SOCIALISTS' GROUP
BM 3725, London WC1N 3XX
Email jsg@jewishsocialist.org.uk *Website* www.jewishsocialist.org.uk
(Est. 1974). Political, cultural and campaigning organisation committed to socialism, diasporism and secularism, aiming to unite the Jewish community with other oppressed/persecuted minorities. Active on local, national and international issues. National Committee (collective leadership). Publ. Jewish Socialist Magazine.

JEWISH VOLUNTEERING NETWORK (JVN)
The Wohl Campus for Jewish Education, 44a Albert Road, London NW4 2SJ
Tel 020 8203 6427
Email info@jvn.org.uk *Website* www.jvn.org.uk
Facebook JewishVolunteeringNetwork *Blog* www.jvnblog.com
(Est. 2007). JVN helps to match Jewish volunteers with volunteering opportunities in charities and organisations across England; provides training and support to Volunteer Co-ordinators and Trustees in the community and raises the profile of volunteers and volunteering across the UK Jewish community generally. *Pres.* Rosalind Preston OBE; *Dir.* Leonie Lewis; *Ch.* David Lazarus; *Fdr.* Judy Citron z'l

JEWS FOR JUSTICE FOR PALESTINIANS
P.O. Box 46081, London W9 2ZF
Email jfjusticefp@yahoo.co.uk *Website* www.jfjfp.com
(Est. 2002). JFJFP is a network of Jews who are British or live in Britain, practising and secular, Zionist and not. JFJFP opposes Israeli policies that undermine the livelihoods, and human, civil and political rights of the Palestinian people, while supporting the right of Israelis to live in freedom and security within Israel's 1967 borders. JFJFP is the largest group of British Jews openly critical of Israeli alleged human-rights abuses and transgressions of international law. JFJFP draw on Jewish values of justice, tolerance and mutal respect, and is motivated by concerns to combat antisemitism and to protect the long-term future of both peoples. JFJFP rejects any routine labeling of Israel's critics as antisemitic and promotes factually-based, open discourse on the conflict within British society, cooperating with other organisations on specific issues, without necessarily endorsing everything they do. JFJFP is a founding member of *European Jews for a Just Peace* and is a member of the Jewish Human Rights Network. *Contact* Deborah Maccoby

JOINT BURIAL COMMITTEE (JBC)
Hoop Lane Cemetery, London NW11 7EU
Hoop Lane cemetery is owned by the Spanish & Portuguese Jews' Congregation and West London Synagogue, The cemetery opened in 1897 and is one of the oldest operational Jewish cemeteries in London.
There are many notable interments within the grounds. *Tel* 020 8455 2569

JW3 - THE NEW POSTCODE FOR JEWISH LIFE
341-351 Finchley Road, London, NW3 6ET
Tel 020 7433 8989 *Box Office Tel* 020 7433 8988
Email info@jw3.org.uk *Website* www.jw3.org.uk
(Reg. Charity No. 1117644) JW3's aim is to transform the Jewish landscape in London by helping to create a vibrant, diverse and proud community inspired by and engaged in Jewish arts, culture and community. JW3 offers events, activities, classes and courses that increase the quality, variety and volume of Jewish conversation. Their goal is to encourage greater understanding between sections of the community and different faiths.
Ch. Michael Goldstein; *Chief Exec.* Raymond Simonson

LONDON CANTORIAL SINGERS
c/o 166 Regal Way, Harrow, Middx HA3 0SQ
Tel/Fax 020 8907 0616
Email info@tlcs.org.uk *Website* www.tlcs.org.uk
(Est.1995). Choir performing Synagogue, Israeli and Yiddish music. *Musical Dir.* David Druce; *Chazanim,* David Shine; *Rev Cantor,* David Rome; *Patron,* Rev Reuben Turner

NE'IMAH SINGERS
c/o St. John's Wood United Synagogue, 37-41 Grove End Road, London NW8
Tel 020 7286 3838
Email info@neimah.com *Website* www.neimah.com
(Est. 1993). Choir performing Synagogue music. *Fdr. and Conductor,* Marc Temerlies; *Co-Fdr. and Co-Conductor,* Jonathan Weissbart *Tel* 07973 424 306; *Asst. Chazan,* Moshe Haschel

OPERATION JUDAISM
95 Willows Road, Birmingham B12 9QF
Tel 0121 440 6673 (24 hour ansaphone) *Fax* 0121 446 4199
Email operationjudaism@lubavitchuk.com
(Est. 1986). The community's defence against missionary attack. It operates nationally an information and counselling service. Information and support for those involved with cults. Management committee consists of representatives from: Office of the Chief Rabbi, BoD and Lubavitch Foundation.

PARENTS OF JEWISH GAYS AND LESBIANS
Tel 07806 636089
Email parentsjgl@gmail.com *Website* www.parentsofjewishgaysandlesbians.co.uk
(Reg Charity No. 1079918). Affiliated to FFLAG (Families & Friends of Lesbians & Gays) A support Group to help the parents of Jewish Gays and Lesbians.

PAVEL HAAS FOUNDATION UK
7 Roma Read Close, London SW15 4AZ
Tel 020 8785 4772
(Est. 2002). To promote the performance of the works of Pavel Haas (1899-1944) and Holocaust education. *Exec. Dir.* Jacqueline Bowen Cole

START YOUR DAY THE TORAH WAY
c/o Kehillas Ohel Moshe, 102 Leeside Crescent, London NW11 0LA
Email info@torahway.org.uk *Website* www.torahway.co.uk

(Est. 2005). Morning courses for men. Sunday and Bank Holiday 9.20-9.50am, Monday to Friday 8.30-9am. *Dir.* M. D. Salczman

SUPPORT GROUP FOR PARENTS OF JEWISH GAYS AND LESBIANS
59 Mowbray Road, Edgware, Middlesex HA8 8JL
Tel 020 8958 4827
Email kenmowbray@aol.com
(Est. 1996). To give support and help to parents of Jewish gays and lesbians. *Hon. S.* Kenneth Morris

SZYMON LAKS FOUNDATION UK
7 Roma Road Close, London SW15 4AZ
Tel 020 8785 4772
Email szymonlaks@viktorullmann.freeserve.co.uk *Website* www.musiciansgallery.com
(Est. 2005). To honour and celebrate the life and work of composer Szymon Laks (1901-1983). *Fdr. and Artistic Dir.* Jacqueline Bowen Cole *Tel* 07508 876 194; *Hon Patron* Dr. Y. Bauer. *Hon. Adr. Exec. Cttee.* Dr. G. Fackler, F.H. Wuthenow, Prof. Andre Laks

TJSPN
P.O. Box 33317, London NW11 9FR
Tel 020 8632 0216 *Fax* 020 8458 3261
Email jr6287@yahoo.co.uk
The Jewish Single Parent Network aims to assist single parents with a range of services focusing on the practical difficulties of single parenting. Enquiries to R. Zrihen

TZEDEK (Jewish Action for a Just World)
25-26 Enford Street, London W1H 1DW
Tel 020 3603 8120
Email info@tzedek.org.uk *Website* www.tzedek.org.uk
(Est. 1990. Reg. Charity No. 1016767). Tzedek is an overseas development and educational charity working in some of the poorest countries in Africa and Asia. It aims to provide direct support to small-scale, self-help, sustainable development projects, regardless of race or religion, whilst educating the UK Jewish community about the causes and effects of poverty and the Jewish obligation to respond. *Chief Exec.* Jude Williams; *Ch.* Jonny Persey

UNITED KINGDOM ASSOCIATION OF JEWISH LAWYERS & JURISTS
The Administrator, UKAJLJ, PO Box 63349, London NW4 9FL
Tel 07946 403 627
Email ukajlj@jewishlawyers.co.uk *Website* www.jewishlawyers.co.uk
(Est. 1990). The objectives of the Association are: to contribute towards the establishment of an international legal order, based on the Rule of Law, in relations between all nations and states; to promote human rights and the principles of equality of all and the right of all states and peoples to live in peace; to act against racism and antisemitism, where necessary, by legal proceedings; to promote the study of legal problems affecting the world's Jewish communities; to promote, in consultation with the legal profession within Israel, the study of legal problems of particular concern; to promote the study of Jewish law in comparison with other laws, and facilitate the exchange of any information resulting from research among member groups; to collect and disseminate information concerning the *de facto* and *de jure* status of the Jewish communities and other minority ethnic and religious groups throughout the world, to give help and support pursuant to human rights treaties; to promote and support co-operation and communication between the Association's member groups; to concern itself with any other matter of legal interest considered of relevance by any of the member groups.
Pres. Lord Woolf; *V. Pres.* Lord Neuberger, Lord Justice Rix, HH D. Levy QC; *Ch.* Sir Gavin Lightman; *Hon. S.* Deanna Levine; *Admin.* Liza Tilley

VIKTOR ULLMANN FOUNDATION UK
7 Roma Read Close, London SW15 4AZ
Tel 07936 268 804
Website www.viktorullmannfoundation.org.uk
(Est. 2002). To remember and celebrate the genius of Viktor Ullmann, (1898–1944), and to promote his music in association with the Terezin Music Memorial Foundation, the Jewish Music Institute, the International Forum for Suppressed Music and other bodies. *Exec. Cttee.* Anita Lasker-Wallfisch, Father Yves Dubois, Alexander Knapp, Gloria Tessler; *Artistic Dir.* Jacqueline Cole

INTERNATIONAL ORGANISATIONS

JEWISH ORGANISATIONS HAVING CONSULTATIVE STATUS WITH THE ECONOMIC AND SOCIAL COUNCIL OF THE UNITED NATIONS

Agudas Israel World Organisation; Coordinating Board of Jewish Organisations (comprising the British BoD, the South African BoD, and the B'nai B'rith); Consultative Council of Jewish Organisations (comprising the Anglo-Jewish Association, the Alliance Israélite Universelle, and the Canadian Friends of the Alliance); W.J.C. International Council on Jewish Social and Welfare Services (comprising American Joint Distribution Committee, World Jewish Relief, Jewish Colonization Association, European Council of Jewish Community Services, United Hias Service, World ORT Union); International Council of Jewish Women.

AGUDAS ISRAEL WORLD ORGANISATIONS

The organisation was founded in Kattowitz in 1912. Its programme was defined as being 'the solution – in the spirit of the Torah – of problems which periodically confront the Jewish people in Eretz Yisroel and the Diaspora'. This object was to be fulfilled 'by coordination of Orthodox Jewish effort throughout the world ... by the representation and protection of the interests of Torah-true Jewish communities'. The programme was formulated by our ancestors for the unconditional acceptance by all Jewish generations of the Biblical injunction 'And ye shall be unto Me a kingdom of priests and a holy nation'. The organisation seeks to implement this injunction by its endeavours. It opposes assimilation and different interpretations of Jewish nationhood. Consultative status with United Nations, New York and Geneva, and Unesco in Paris.
Main contact 42 Broadway, 14th Floor, New York NY 10004
Tel +1 (212) 797 9000 *Fax* +1 (646) 254 1640

Agudas Israel of Great Britain
97 Stamford Hill, N16 5DN
Tel 020 8800 6688 *Fax* 020 8800 5000
Presidium, Rabbi Y. M. Rosenbaum *Publ.* Jewish Tribune (weekly).

Zeire Agudas Israel
95 Stamford Hill, N16 5DN; 35a Northumberland Street, Salford 7
Ch. J. Schleider

Agudas Israel Community Services
97 Stamford Hill, N16 5DN
Tel 020 8800 6688 *Fax* 020 3240 0110
(Est. 1980. Reg. Charity No. 287367), To help find suitable employment for observant Jews, including immigrants and Yiddish speakers. Also an advice centre dealing with welfare benefits and immigration advice, plus other social services. *Dirs.* Y. Silkin, M. M. Posen

Jewish Rescue and Relief Committee
215 Golders Green Road, NW11 9BY
Tel 020 8458 1710
(Reg. Charity No. 1120311). *Ch.* A. Strom

Society of Friends of the Torah Ltd
97 Stamford Hill, London N16 5DN
Tel 020 3240 0106 *Fax* 020 8800 5000
215 Golders Green Road, London NW11 9BY
Tel 020 8458 9988 *Fax* 020 8458 8425
Email accounts@softorah.com
(Reg. Charity No. 1140838). *Ass. Dir.* S. Bowden

ALLIANCE ISRAELITE UNIVERSELLE
45 rue La Bruyère, Paris 75009
Tel +33 (01) 53 32 88 55 *Fax* +33 (01) 48 74 51 33

Email info@aiu.org *Website* www.aiu.org   *Library Website* www.aiu.org/bibli
(Est. 1860). This educative and cultural-oriented organisation essentially works through its network of schools in France, but also in Belgium, Canada, Israel, Morocco, Spain and North America. Active in the field of European Jewish Education, with the Alliance Europe Project, as well as with the European Emmanuel Levinas Institute. It has defended human rights before governmental and international institutions all over the world. Its library with more than 150,000 books in the field of Hebraica-Judaica, and its College des Etudes Juives, make it one of the most important Jewish centres in Europe. *Pres.* Marc Eisenberg; *Dir.* J. Tolédano.

AUSTRALIA/ISRAEL AND JEWISH AFFAIRS COUNCIL (AIJAC)
Level 1, 22 Albert Road, South Melbourne, Victoria 3205
Tel +61 (3) 9681 6660 *Fax* +61 (3) 9681 6650
Email aijac@aijac.org.au
The AIJAC is the premier public affairs organization for the Australian Jewish Community Through research, commentary, analysis and representation, AIJAC promotes the interests of the Australian Jewish Community to Government and other community groups and organizations. It has professionals dedicated to analysis and monitoring development in the Middle East, Asia and Australia. AIJAC is associated with the American Jewish Committee. in a global partnership designed to bring about a greater understanding of the issues and challenges lying ahead for Jewry. The former Australian Institute of Jewish Affairs, now operating as a division of AIJAC, maintains its programme of social and cultural activities, and holds important public functions and briefings throughout Australia. It also retains a role in South East Asia. *Publ.* Australia/Israel Review (monthly); *Exec. Dir.* Dr. Colin Rubenstein, AM; *Contact* L. Kahn

B'NAI B'RITH INTERNATIONAL
(Est. 1843). The world's largest Jewish human rights, philanthropic and community action group, bringing Jews to work in harmony for the common good, to help the poor and oppressed, and to become active in cultural and humanitarian projects. It is active in 58 countries around the world, with its head office in Washington DC. It has NGO status at the United Nations in New York, an office at the European Union in Brussels, and a World Centre in Jerusalem.

B'nai B'rith UK
A division of B'nai B'rith Europe, with headquarters in Brussels and comes under the overall umbrella of B'nai B'rith International in Washington.
The Core Objectives of B'nai B'rith in the United Kingdom are:
• to foster friendship through social, cultural and recreational programmes;
• to support the State of Israel and World Jewry;
• to work for charitable endeavours;
• to initiate and develop community projects;
• to strengthen B'nai B'rith links across Europe.
   B'nai B'rith UK's London Bureau of International Affairs visits Embassies and the Foreign Office on a regular basis to advance the cause of Jews and Israel. It works with corresponding B'nai B'rith groups in Brussels, Paris and Washington.
   B'nai B'rith UK's annual European Days of Jewish Culture and Heritage arranges for synagogues and places of Jewish interest to be open to the public. The rich Jewish history is showcased by cultural events, guided walks and heritage trails. B'nai B'rith works with other Jewish organisations across Europe.
   B'nai B'rith UK is actively involved in a number of projects to help disadvantaged Jews and Righteous Gentiles in other countries. It raises funds and takes a keen interest in making sure that those funds are put to the best possible use. Each fund has a project leader and there are regular visits for members to see how the funds benefitting recipients.
   B'nai B'rith UK has three lodges in the North of England and 12 in London. The lodges and the new BB2545 group offer social events to enable Jews across the whole spectrum of observance to meet and enjoy a wide range of activities.

B'nai B'rith International HQ 2020 K Street, NW, 7th Floor, Washington, DC 20006, USA
Tel + 1 (202) 857 6600
Website www.bnaibrith.org
B'nai B'rith Europe Rue Dautzenberg 36, B-1050 Brussels, Belgium
Tel +32 (2) 646 9298
Email secretariat@bnaibritheurope.org *Website* www.bnaibritheurope.org
Pres. Ralph Hofmann
B'nai B'rith UK ORT House, 126 Albert Street, London NW1 7NE
Tel 020 7446 8660
Email office@bnaibrithuk.org *Website* www.bbuk.org
(Reg Charity No. 1061661). *Nat. Pres.* Eve Swabe

   London Bureau of International Affairs ORT House, 126 Albert Street, London NW1 7NE
   Ch. Richard Sotnick; *Dir.* Helene Briskman *Email* lbia2000@hotmail.co.uk

CCJO. René Cassin
The JHub, 152 West End Lane, London NW6 1SD
Tel 020 7443 5130
Email info@renecassin.org *Website* www.renecassin.org
(Est. 2000. Reg. Charity No. 1117472). René Cassin is a human rights, non-governmental organisation that works to promote and protect universal human rights drawing on Jewish experience and values. It does this this by campaigning for change in defined human rights areas through a combination of advocacy, policy analysis, public campaigning and education; and building the capacity of activists and lawyers to promote and protect human rights. *Dir.* Shauna Leven; *Ch.* Danny Silverstone

CENTRAL REGISTRY OF INFORMATION ON LOOTED CULTURAL PROPERTY 1933–1945
76 Gloucester Place, London W1U 6HJ
Tel 020 7487 3401 *Fax* 020 7487 4211
Email info@lootedart.com *Website* www.lootedart.com
(Est. 2001. Reg. Charity No. 309720. IRS No. 13-2943469). Provides a centre of research, expertise and information on cultural objects looted by the Nazis and their collaborators between 1933 and 1945 - paintings, drawings, books, manuscripts, Judaica, silver, porcelain, etc. *Dir.* Anne Webber

COMMISSION FOR LOOTED ART IN EUROPE
76 Gloucester Place, London W1U 6HJ
Tel 020 7487 3401 *Fax* 020 7487 4211
Email info@lootedartcommission.com *Website* www.lootedartcommission.com
(Est. 1999). Non-profit, expert representative body which negotiates restitution policies and procedures, and assists families, communities and institutions internationally to locate and recover Nazi-looted cultural property. Represents the European Council of Jewish Communities and the Conference of European Rabbis. *Co-Ch.* Anne Webber, David Lewis

COMMITTEE FOR THE PRESERVATION OF JEWISH CEMETERIES IN EUROPE
34a Fairholt Road, London N16 5HW
Tel 020 8802 6853 *Fax* 020 8802 3756
Email cpjce@btconnect.com
(Est 1991. Reg. Charity No. 1073225). Preservation of Jewish burial sites in Europe to ensure that they are maintained according to Jewish law and tradition. *Pres.* Rabbi E. Schlesinger; *Hon. S.* Y. Marmorstein; *Hon. T.* A. Goldman. *Exec. Dir.* A. Ginsberg

COMMONWEALTH JEWISH COUNCIL AND TRUST
BCM Box 6871, London WC1N 3XX
Tel 020 7222 2120

Email info@cjc.org.uk *Website* www.cjc.org.uk
(Est. 1982, Reg. Charity No. 287564). To provide links between Commonwealth Jewish communities; to provide a central representative voice for Commonwealth Jewish communities and to help preserve their religious and cultural heritage; to seek ways to strengthen Commonwealth Jewish communities in accordance with their individual needs and wishes and to provide mutual help and cooperation. The Council undertakes charitable projects in Jewish communities throughout the Commonwealth, with special emphasis on the smaller communities. *Fdr. and Pres.* Lord Janner of Braunstone, QC; *Pres.* Michael Ellis MP; *V. Pres.* Paul Secher, Rev. Malcolm Weisman, OBE; *Tru.* Marlene Bethlehem (South Africa), Mitchell Coen, Jason Holt, Samuel Marshall (India), Dorothy Reitman (Canada), Gideon Wittenberg; *Dir.* Maureen Gold; *Co-ord.* Alanna Cawston
  There are 38 members, including those in Antigua, Australia, Bahamas, Barbados, Belize, Bermuda, Botswana, Canada, Cayman Islands, Cyprus, Gibraltar, Guernsey, India, Isle of Man, Jamaica, Jersey, Kenya, Mauritius, Namibia, New Zealand, Seychelles, Singapore, Sri Lanka, Trinidad & Tobago, Turks & Caicos Islands, United Kingdom, Zambia. Obeservers: Hong Kong and Zimbabwe.

CONFERENCE OF EUROPEAN RABBIS
Website www.confeurorabbis.org
(Est. 1957). To provide a medium for co-operation on matters of common concern to rabbis of European communities.
Pres. Rabbi Pinchas Goldschmidt; *Ch. of the Presidium,* Rabbi Joseph Sitruck; *Ch. European Rabbinical Court,* Dayan Chanoch Ehrentreu; *Mem. of Presidium,* Rabbi Lord Dr Sacks; *V. Pres.* Dayan Menachem Gelley, Rabbi Yaakov Dov Bleich, Rabbi Riccardo DiSegni, Rabbi Rene Sirath; *Assoc. Pres.* Chief Rabbi Ephraim Mirvis

CONFERENCE ON JEWISH MATERIAL CLAIMS AGAINST GERMANY, Inc
1359 Broadway, Room 2000, New York, NY 10018
Tel +1 (646) 536 9100 *Fax* +1 (212) 679 2126
Email info@claimscon.org *Website* www.claimscon.org
(Est. 1951). Represents world Jewry in negotiating for compensation and restitution for victims of Nazi persecution and their heirs. More than 500,000 Holocaust survivors in 67 countries have received payments from Germany and Austria due to the work of the Claims Conference. Administers compensation funds, recovers unclaimed Jewish property and allocates funds to institutions that provide social welfare services to Holocaust survivors, and preserves the memory and lessons of the Shoah. *Ch.* Julius Berman; *Exec. V. Pres.* Greg Schneider

EAST EUROPEAN JEWISH HERITAGE PROJECT
25 Plantation Park, Keele, Staffs ST5 5NA
Email eejhp@voluntas.org *Website* www.eejhp.netfirms.com
(Reg. Charity No. 10616229). The East European Jewish Heritage project is active in Belarus, Lithuania and Ukraine. In addition to its humanitarian assistance programmes, it encourages Jewish leadership in civil society through participation in projects which benefit the broader community. The EEJHP provides travel programmes for those interested in their ancestral past as well as genealogy services. Over the past ten years the EEJHP has engaged with many western organisations and universities in the restoration of derelict Jewish cemeteries. *Exec. Dir.* F. J. Swartz; *Dirs.* D. Solomon, K. G. Cushing

EMUNAH (British Emunah Fund)
Shield House, Harmony Way, off Victoria Road, London NW4 2BZ
Tel 020 8203 6066 *Fax* 020 8203 6668
Email info@emunah.org.uk *Website* www.emunah.org.uk
(Est. 1933. Reg. Charity No. 215398). Emunah cares for those children in Israel whose lives are at risk, and whom no one else wants. Through its network of residential children's homes, therapy centres, day care and community centres, Emunah is recognised as one of Israel's leading provider of family welfare services. Emunah's members in the UK work tirelessly in a voluntary capacity to raise funds to support the vital projects in Israel. British

Emunah currently helps to support 36 projects in Israel. *H. Pres.* Valerie Mirvis; *H. Life. Pres.* Lady Sacks; *Found. Pres.* Gertrude Landy; *Exec. Pres.* Guggy Grahame, Daphne Kaufman; *Exec. V. Pres.* Vera Garbacz, Gertrude Compton, Rochelle Selby; *Ch.* Hilary Pearlman; *Israel Projects Ch.* Lilian Brodie; *Admin. Ch.* Rosalyn Liss; *Hon. S.* Judith Sheldon; *Hon. T.* Joanna Benarroch; *Dir.* Deborah Nathan

EUROPEAN ASSOCIATION FOR JEWISH CULTURE
Paris office: 19 Rue de la Tour d'Auvergne, 75009 Paris Tel +33 (0)1 4878 5892
London office: 12 Rosemont Road, Richmond, TW10 6QL
Email london@jewishcultureineurope.org
Website www.jewishcultureineurope.org   www.judaica-europeana.eu
(Est. 2001). An independent grant-making body, which fosters and supports artistic creativity and promotes digital access to Jewish culture in Europe. *Pres.* Peter L. Levy OBE; *Sec.* Jean-Jacques Wahl; *Dir.* Lena Stanley-Clamp

EUROPEAN ASSOCIATION FOR JEWISH STUDIES
Oxford Centre for Hebrew and Jewish Studies, The Clarendon Institute, Walton Street, Oxford OX1 2HG
Tel 01865 377 946 (x111) *Fax* 01865 375 079
Email admin@eurojewishstudies.org *Website* www.eurojewishstudies.org
Admin. Dr. G. Gilmour; *Pres.* Prof. Judith Olszowy-Schlanger; *Sec.* Prof. Daniel Langton; *T.* Prof. Gad Freudenthal *Publ.* European Journal of Jewish Studies.

EUROPEAN COUNCIL OF JEWISH COMMUNITIES (ECJC)
Oscar Joseph House, 54 Crewys Road, London, NW2 2AD
Tel 020 8455 8392 *Fax* 0 208 209 0583
Email info@ecjc.org *Website* www.ecjc.org www.presidents-meeting.ecjc.org
www.arachim.ecjc.org, www.jewisheritage.org www.european-encounters.ecjc.org
ECJC is a non-government organisation (NGO) established as a non-profit association in accordance with the laws of Belgium as a "Vereniging Zonder Winstoogmerk". It has its registered office at Centraal Beheer van Joods Weldadigheid, Antwerp. The first statutes were adopted in 1968 in London. ECJC represents Jewish national communal organisations from over 40 countries in Europe. The ECJC enjoys participative NGO status with the Council of Europe and has consultative NGO status recognition with the European Union. *Pres.* Jonathan Joseph; *Chief Exec.* Neville Kluk. *Contact.* Michelle Kathan *Email* michelle@ecjc.org Full list of board members on websites.

EUROPEAN JEWISH CONGRESS (previously The European Branch of the World Jewish Congress)
78 Avenue des Champs-Elysées, 75008 Paris
Tel +33 (01) 43 59 94 63 *Fax* +33 (01) 42 25 45 28
Website www.eurojewcong.org
(Est. 1986). Federates and co-ordinates the initiatives of 38 communities in Europe and acts as their spokesman. Has consultative status with the Council of Europe, European Commission and Parliament. Current concerns are the democratic development of Eastern Europe and the problems of racism and antisemitism throughout Europe. *Pres.* Moshe Kantor; *Sec. Gen.* Serge Cwajgenbaum

EUROPEAN UNION OF JEWISH STUDENTS
3 ave Antoine Depage, B-1000, Brussels, Belgium
Tel 010 32 2 647 72 79 *Fax* 010 32 2 648 24 31
Email info@eujs.org *Website* www.eujs.org
(Est. 1978). For co-ordination purposes between nat. unions in the 36 countries of Europe (and Turkey). It represents more than 180,000 European Jewish students in international Jewish and non-Jewish forums, dealing with cultural and political matters, and opposes all forms of racism and fascism. The EUJS is also a 'service organisation' for students. It helps

with courses abroad, supplies material on different subjects for university students and organises visits and seminars. *H. Pres.* Simone Veil, Maram Stern; *H. Mems.* Lord Janner, David Susskind (Belgium), Suzy Jurysta (B.), Laslov Kadelburg (Yu.); *Pres.* Benjamin Zagzag; *Exec. Dir.* Deborah Abisror; *Programme Dir.* Adam Mouchtar

HIAS
333 Seventh Avenue, 16th Floor, New York, NY 10001-5019, USA
Tel +1 (212) 613 1438
Website www.hias.org
(Est. 1881). HIAS, the Hebrew Immigrant Aid Society, is America's oldest international migration and refugee resettlement agency. In 1909, the Hebrew Immigrant Aid Society merged with the Hebrew Sheltering House Association and became universally known as HIAS. HIAS assists Jewish and other migrants and refugees to countries of freedom and security, helps newcomers to integrate into their new communities, and reunites family members. It advocates for, and works with government and other agencies to promote fair migration policies and increased opportunities. HIAS activities have always mirrored world events. In the past decade alone, the organisation has worked to help refugees and immigrants from Afghanistan, Bosnia, Bulgaria, Czech Republic, Democratic Republic of the Congo, Ethiopia, Haiti, Hungary, Iran, Morocco, Nigeria, Poland, Romania, Sudan, Tunisia, Vietnam, successor states to the former Soviet Union, and other countries where persecution and absence of liberty have forced people to seek new lives in America and other welcoming nations. *Pres.* Mark Hetfield; *Ch.* Dale Schwarz

INSTITUTE FOR JEWISH POLICY RESEARCH (JPR)
ORT House, 126 Albert Street, London NW1 7NE
Tel 020 7424 9265
Email jpr@jpr.org.uk *Website* www.jpr.org.uk
JPR is a London-based independent research organisation, consultancy and think-tank. It aims to advance the prospects of Jewish communities in Britain and across Europe by conducting research and developing policy in partnership with those best placed to influence Jewish life. *Hon. Pres.* Lord Rothschild, OM; *Pres.* Lord Haskel; *Ch.* Harold Paisner; *T.* Brian Smouha; *Exec. Dir.* Dr Jonathan Boyd; *Development Dir.* Judith Russell. *Publ.* JPR Reports and Policy Debate papers

INTERNATIONAL COUNCIL OF CHRISTIANS AND JEWS
Martin Buber Haus, Werlestrasse 2, Postfach 1129, D-64646, Heppenheim, Germany
Tel +49 6252 689 6810 *Fax* +49 6252 68331
Email info@iccj.org *Website* www.iccj.org
Established 1947 to strengthen Jewish–Christian understanding on an international basis and to co-ordinate and initiate programmes and activities for this purpose. Now increasingly engaged in trilateral dialogue of Jews, Christians and Muslims. *Pres.* Dr. Deborah Weissman; *Patron* Sir Sigmund Sternberg

INTERNATIONAL COUNCIL OF JEWISH WOMEN
5655 Silver Creek Valley Road #480, San Jose, CA 95138, USA
Tel +1 408 274 8020 *Fax* +1 408 274 0807
Website www.icjw.org
ICJW is made up of 43 Jewish women's organisations in 40 countries, covering between them almost the whole spectrum of the Jewish world. The core purpose of ICJW is to bring together Jewish women from all walks of life in order to create a driving force for social justice for all races and creeds. ICJW has consultative status with ECOSOC at the United Nations and is represented on many international organisations. *Pres.* Sharon Gustafson

INTERNATIONAL COUNCIL ON JEWISH SOCIAL AND WELFARE SERVICES
The Forum, 74-80 Camden Street, London NW1 0EG
Tel 020 7691 1771 *Fax* 020 7691 1780
Email info@wjr.org.uk

(Est. 1961). Member Organisations: American Joint Distribution Committee; WJR; European Council of Jewish Community Services; HIAS; World ORT Union. *Chief Exec.* P. Anticoni

INTERNATIONAL JEWISH GENEALOGICAL RESOURCES (IJGR(UK))

Judith Joseph 344 Quinton Road, Birmingham B17 0RE *Email* josephj-2007@hotmail.co.uk
Dr. A.P. Joseph 3 Edgbaston Road, Smethwick, West Midlands, B66 4LA
(Est. 1988). Provides guidance on Jewish genealogy; has a library including material on Anglo-Jewry/Anglo-Australasian Jewry; microfilm of Jewish Chronicle, etc. Research undertaken.

INTERNATIONAL JEWISH VEGETARIAN SOCIETY

Bet Teva, 853/855 Finchley Road, NW11 8LX
Tel 020 8455 0692
Email info@jvs.org.uk *Website* www.jvs.org.uk
Facebook The Jewish Vegetarian Society *Twitter* JewishVegSoc
(Est. 1965. Reg. Charity No. 258581). Affiliated to the international Vegetarian Union. Branches: North and South America, South Africa, Israel, Australia. *Dir.* Lara Smallman; *Hon. T.* Michael Freedman FCA; *Tru.* Adam Jackson, Rabbi David Rosen, Stanley Rubens, Dan Jacobs; *Patron*, Rabbi Jonathan Wittenberg

IRANIAN JEWISH CENTRE

1 Dukes Mews, London W1U 3ET
Tel 020 7414 0069 *Fax* 020 7491 4804
Email ijc@ijc.org.uk *Website* www.ijc.org.uk
(Est. 1981. Reg. Charity No. 287256). Fundraising to support Iranian Jewish communities in Britain, Iran and the USA. Promotion of Iranian/Jewish heritage and culture. *Ch.* Hamid Sabi

JCA CHARITABLE FOUNDATION

c/o Victoria Palace Theatre, Victoria Street, SW1E 5EA
Tel 020 7828 0600 *Fax* 020 7828 6882
Email thejcafoundation@aol.com *Website* www.ica-is.org.il
(Reg. Charity No. 207031). Charitable company established in 1891 by Baron Maurice de Hirsch to assist poor and needy Jews. The JCA was instrumental in promoting the emigration from Russia of thousands of Jews who were settled in farm 'colonies' in North and South America, Palestine/Israel and elsewhere. Today JCA's main efforts are in Israel in rural areas where it supports schools, institutes of higher learning, agricultural research and helps to promote the subsistence of needy Jews. *Pres.* Sir Stephen Waley-Cohen Bt; *Man.* Y. Lothan

JEWISH AFFILIATES OF THE UNITED NATIONS ASSOCIATION AND PRO-ACTIVE GROUP

Email davidmjacobs@waitrose.com
(Est. 1971). A co-ordinating group of Jewish organisations and individuals affiliated to the United Nations Association. Members of the group represent their organizations at the UNA where they have two functions. First, to promote the interests of Israel and the Jewish People, and second, to present the Jewish view on general international and humanitarian issues. In addition the group acts as an umbrella organization for opposing Anti-Israel activity. *Ch.* David M. Jacobs; *Hon. S.* Prof. Gerald Adler

MACCABI WORLD UNION

Kfar Maccabiah, Ramat Gan 52105, Israel
Website www.maccabi.org
(Est. 1921). The union is a co-ordinating body for the promotion and advancement of sports, educational and cultural activities among Jewish communities worldwide. *Pres.* R. Bakalarz; *Pres.* Jeanne Futeran (South Africa); *Ch.* Oudi Recanati; *Ch. European Maccabi Confederation* Leo Dan-Bensky; *Ch.* Igal Carmi (Israel); *Exec. Dir.* E. Tiberger; *V. Ch. Hd. of European Confederation*, Stuart Lustigman. Maccabi GB, *See* p. 108.

MEMORIAL FOUNDATION FOR JEWISH CULTURE
50 Broadway, 34th Floor, New York, NY 10004
Tel +1 (212) 425 6606 *Fax* +1(212) 425 6602
Email office@mfjc.org *Website* www.mfjc.org
(Est. 1965). Supports Jewish cultural and educational programmes all over the world in co-operation with educational research and scholarly organisations, and provides scholarship and fellowship grants in Jewish fields. The Memorial Foundation for Jewish Culture sponsors the International Nahum Goldmann Fellowship (www.ngfp.org). *Pres.* Prof. I. Schorsch; *Exec. V. Pres.* Dr. J. Hochbaum

SIMON WIESENTHAL CENTRE
European office: 66 rue Laugier, 75017 Paris, France
Tel +33 (1) 4723 7637 *Fax* +33 (1) 4720 8401
London office: Simon Wiesenthal Centre UK, 27 Old Gloucester Street, WC1N 3XX
Tel 020 7419 5014 *Fax* 020 7831 9489
Email csweurope@gmail.com *Website* www.wiesenthal-europe.com
(Est. Los Angeles, 1979. Reg. Charity No. 1030966). To study the contemporary Jewish and general social condition in Europe by drawing lessons from the Holocaust experience. To monitor, combat and educate against antisemitism, racism and prejudice. *H. Ch.* Graham Morris; *Ch.* David Dangoor; *Int. Dir.* Rabbi Marvin Hier; *Ch. Board of Tru.* Larry Maizel; *Dir. for Int. Relations* Dr. Shimon Samuels. 400,000 members. Headquarters: Los Angeles. Offices in: New York, Washington DC, Toronto, Jerusalem, Paris and Buenos Aires

WORLD COUNCIL OF CONSERVATIVE/MASORTI SYNAGOGUES
Israel: 32 Pierre Koenig Street, Jerusalem, Israel 93469
Tel +972 (02) 624 7106 *Fax* +972 (02) 624 7677
Email mail@masortiolami.org
USA: 3080 Broadway, New York, NY 10027
Tel +01 (212) 280 6039 *Fax* +1 (212) 678 5321
Email worldcouncil@masortiworld.org
(Est. 1957). To build, renew and strengthen Jewish life throughout the world, focusing on Europe, Latin America, the FSU, Africa, Asia and Australia. It works with all arms of the Conservative/Masorti movement. Emphasizing the study of Torah in its fullest sense, and its transmission from generation to generation. It is also concerned with the centrality of the synagogue, Israel and the Hebrew language and centrist, dynamic Jewish practice, based on *halacha* and *mitzvot*. It encourages the values of egalitarianism, pluralism and tolerence within this framework

WORLD JEWISH CONGRESS
Email info@worldjewishcongress.org *Website* www.worldjewishcongress.org
(a) To co-ordinate the efforts of its affiliated organisations, in respect of the political, economic, social, religious and cultural problems of the Jewish people; (b) to secure the rights, status and interests of Jews and Jewish communities and to defend them wherever they are denied, violated or imperilled; (c) to encourage and assist the creative development of Jewish social, religious and cultural life throughout the world; (d) to represent and act on behalf of its affiliated organisations before governmental, intergovernmental and other international authorities in respect of matters which concern the Jewish people as a whole. *Fdr Pres.* Late Dr N. Goldmann; *Pres.* Ronald S. Lauder; *Ch. Gov. Bd.* David de Rothschild; *CEO*, Robert Singer; *Ch. of Regional affiliates:* **North America** Evelyn Sommer, **Latin America** Jack Terpins, **Europe** Moshe Kantor; **Israel** Shai Hermesh MK; **Euro-Asia** Julius Meinl.
   Principal Offices New York: 501 Madison Avenue, New York, NY 10022 *Tel* +1 (212) 755 5770; Brussels: 84 rue de Stassart, 1050 Brussels *Tel* +32 (02) 552 09 00 *Fax* +32 (02) 552 09 11 *Email* protocol@wjc.eu; Jerusalem: P.O.B. 4293, Jerusalem 91042. *Tel* +972 (02) 633 3000 *Email* wjc@wjc.co.il. *Publ.* World Jewry Digest (monthly), WJC Email Newsletter (daily).

WORLD JEWISH RELIEF
Oscar Joseph House, 54 Crewys Road, London NW2 2AD
Tel 020 8736 1250 *Fax* 020 8736 1259
Email info@wjr.org.uk *Website* www.wjr.org.uk
(Est. 1933. Reg. Charity No. 290767 Member: Fundraising Standards Board). World Jewish Relief (WJR) is the leading UK Jewish international agency, responding to the needs of primarily, but not exclusively Jewish communities at risk or in crisis, outside the UK and Israel. At times of major international disaster, it leads the UK Jewish community's emergency response to others in need. *Ch.* James Libson; *Chief Exec.* Paul Anticoni; *Pres.* Henry Grunwald OBE QC

WORLD ORT
1 Rue de Varembé, 1211 Geneva 20, Switzerland
Tel +41 (22) 919 4234 *Fax* +41 (22) 919 4232
(Est. 1880, Reg. Charity No. 1042541). Over three and a half million students have been trained since 1880, and currently some 300,000 students are being trained in more than 60 countries in different parts of the world.
Operational Headquarters in UK World ORT Trust, 126 Albert Street, London NW1 7NE
Tel 020 7446 8500
Email wo@ort.org *Website* www.ort.org

WORLD UNION FOR PROGRESSIVE JUDAISM
13 King David Street, 94101 Jerusalem
Tel +972 (02) 6203 447 *Fax* +972 (02) 6203 467
Email wupjadmin@wupj.org.il *Website* www.eupj.org
(Est. 1926). To foster the international growth and practice of Progressive Judaism, and to co-ordinate the activities of its autonomous constituent organisations.
European Union for Progressive Judaism (EUPJ): The Sternberg Centre, 80 East End Road, London N3 2SY *Tel* 020 8349 5651 *Fax* 020 8349 5699 *Email* administrator@eupj.org *Website* www.eupj.org *Ch.* Miriam Kramer

ZIONIST COUNCIL OF EUROPE
Box 1948, 116 Ballards Lane, Finchley, London N3 2DN
Tel 020 8202 0202 *Fax* 020 8202 0233
Email zion-fed@dircon.co.uk
(Est. 1980). An umbrella organisation, consisting of the Zionist Federations from around Europe, with the aim of co-ordinating Zionist activities and developing young leadership on the continent. *Ch.* Harvey Rose; *Dir.* Alan Aziz

AGOGUES

United Synagogue
For contact details: *See under* Religious Organisations.
Member and Affiliated Synagogues of the United Synagogue.

MEMBER SYNAGOGUES
Alei Tzion
LSJS, 44a Albert Road, Hendon, London NW4 2SJ
Email info@aleitzion.co.uk aleitzion@theus.org.uk *Website* www.aleitzion.co.uk
M. Rabbi D. Roselaar; *Admin.* J. Cowen *Tel* 020 8343 5691
Barnet Synagogue
Eversleigh Road, New Barnet, Herts EN5 1ND
Tel 020 8449 0145
Email administrator@barnetsynagogue.org.uk *Website* www.barnetsynagogue.org.uk
Office hours: Sunday-Thursday 9.30am-12.30pm *M.* Rabbi Barry Lerer; *Admin.* Susie Shaw
Belmont Synagogue
101 Vernon Drive, Stanmore, Middlesex HA7 2BW
Tel 020 8426 0104
Email office@belmontsynagogue.org.uk *Website* www.belmont.theus.org.uk
M. Rabbi Elchonon Feldman; *Admin.* C. Fletcher
Borehamwood & Elstree Synagogue
P.O. Box 47, Croxdale Road, Borehamwood, Herts WD6 4QF
Tel 020 8386 5227
Email info@borehamwoodshul.org *Website* www.borehamwoodshul.org
(Est. 1955). Mikveh on the premises. *Emer. M.* Rabbi A. Plancy; *Snr. M. Rabbi* C. Kanterovitz;
Associate M. Rabbi B. Boudilovsky; *Fin. Mem.* N. Arnold; *Snr. Admin.* H. Phillips; *Comm. Care
Co-ord.* R. Brummer
Brondesbury Park Synagogue
143 Brondesbury Park, NW2 5JL
Tel 020 8459 1083 *Fax* 020 8459 5927
(Est. 1934). *R.* Rabbi B. Levin; *Admin.* S. Littner
Bushey & District Synagogue
177/189 Sparrows Herne, Bushey, Herts WD23 1AJ
Tel 020 8950 7340
Email adminstrator@busheyus.org
Daily Services held. *M.* Rabbi Z. M. Salasnik, BA, FJC, *Email* zm@salasnik.net; *Snr. Admin.*
M. Chambers; *Associate Rabbi.* Rabbi Y. Richards *Email* rabbi.richards@busheyus.org
Central Synagogue
(Great Portland Street), 36-40 Hallam Street, W1W 6NW
Tel 020 7580 1355 *Fax* 020 7636 3831
Email administrator@centralsynagogue.org.uk *Website* www.centralsynagogue.org.uk
(Consecrated 1870, destroyed by enemy action May 1941, rebuilt 1958). *Admin. Office*
36 Hallam Street, W1W 6NW; *M.* Rabbi B. Marcus; *R.* S. Leas; *Admin.* C. Levison
Chigwell and Hainault Synagogue
Limes Avenue, Chigwell, Essex IG7 5NT
Tel 020 8500 2451 *Fax* 020 8500 4345
Email chshul@btinternet.com *Website* www.chigshul.net
Regular Services held. *M.* Rabbi B. Davis; *Admin.* W. Land
Clayhall Synagogue
Sinclair House, Woodford Bridge Road, Ilford, Essex IG4 5LN
Tel 020 8551 6533 *Fax* 020 8551 9803
Email office@clayhallsynagogue.co.uk *Website* www.clayhallsynagogue.org.uk
M. Rabbi N. Wilson; *Admin.* A. Petar

Cockfosters & North Southgate Synagogue
Old Farm Avenue, Southgate, N14 5QR
Tel 020 8886 8225
Email office@cnss.co.uk *Website* www.cnss.co.uk
(Est. 1948. Consecrated Dec. 1954). *M.* Rabbi Daniel Epstein; *Admin.* L. Cohen

Dollis Hill Synagogue
No longer functioning (Sept 2011). All enquiries to United Synagogue, 305 Ballards Lane,
London N12 8GB

Ealing Synagogue
15 Grange Road, Ealing, W5 5QN
Tel 020 8579 4894 *Fax* 020 8567 2348
Email office@ealingsynagogue.org.uk *Website* www.ealingsynagogue.org.uk
M. Rabbi H. Vogel, MA; *Admin.* M. Levitt

—Edgware Synagogue
Parnell Close, Edgware, Middlesex HA8 8YE
Tel 020 8958 7508 *Fax* 020 8905 4449
Email office@edgwareu.com *Website* www.edgwaresynagogue.org www.edgwareu.com
M. Rabbi D. Lister; *Asst. Rabbi*, Rabbi B. Kurzer; *Admin.* T. Harman; *Asst. Admin.* N. Herman

Enfield & Winchmore Hill Synagogue
53 Wellington Road, Bush Hill Park, Middlesex EN1 2PG
Tel 020 8363 2697
(Est. 1950). *Ch. Bd.* Tony Flacks *Email* tflacks@hotmail.com; *M.* Rabbi I.H. Sufrin
Email yitzips@gmail.com

—Finchley Synagogue
Kinloss Gardens, London N3 3DU
Tel 020 8346 8551 *Fax* 020 8349 1579
Email office@kinloss.org.uk *Website* www.kinloss.org.uk
(Consecrated 1935). *M.* Rabbi Michael Laitner

Finsbury Park Synagogue
220 Green Lanes, London N4 2JG
Tel 020 8802 7004
Email fpsynagogue@yahoo.co.uk *Website* www.finsburyparksynagogue.co.uk
R. Rev. E. Kraushar; *Admin.* H. Mather

—Golders Green Synagogue
41 Dunstan Road, London NW11 8AE
Tel 020 8455 2460 *Fax* 020 8731 9296
Email office@ggshul.org.uk
(Consecrated 1922). *M.* Rabbi H. Belovski *Tel* 020 8458 8824; *Community Man.* C. Janet; *Youth Dir.* Gavriel Rosen

Hadley Wood Synagogue
Email office@hwjc.org.uk
M. Rabbi Yoni Birnbaum; *Admin.* J. Gubbay *Tel* 07850 638 326

Hackney & East London Synagogue
2a Triangle Road, E8 3RP
Tel 020 7254 0183 *Fax* 020 7249 8210
Email office@hackneysynagogue.org.uk
M. Rev. N. Tiefenbrun; *Admin.* M. Fraser

—Hampstead Garden Suburb Synagogue
Norrice Lea, N2 0RE
Tel 020 8455 8126 *Fax* 020 8201 9247
Email office@hgss.org.uk *Website* www.hgss.org.uk
(Consecrated 1934). *M. Rabbi* D. Kaplan; *Associate M.* Rabbi M. Levene, R. Chazan, A. Freilich; *Office Man.* S. Drucker

—Hampstead Synagogue
Dennington Park Road, West Hampstead, NW6 1AX

Tel 020 7435 1518 *Fax* 020 7431 8369
Email admin@hampsteadshul.org.uk www.hampsteadshul.org
(Consecrated 1892). *M.* Rabbi Dr M. J. Harris; *R.* Rabbi S. R. Gerzi; *Community Man. C.* Janet

Highams Park and Chingford Synagogue
81a Marlborough Road, London E4 9AJ
Tel 020 8523 1609
M. Rabbi A. Kahan; *Sec.* S. Smokler

Hendon Synagogue
18 Raleigh Close, Hendon, London NW4 2TA
Tel 020 8202 6924 *Fax* 020 8202 1720
Email admin@hendonus.org.uk
(Consecrated 1935). *M.* Rabbi M.S. Ginsbury; *Exec. Sec.* L. Cohen

Highgate Synagogue
57 North Road, Highgate, N6 4BJ
Tel/Fax 020 8340 7655
Email office@highgateshul.com
(Est. 1929). *M.* Rabbi N. Liss *Tel* 020 8341 1714; *Admin.* Rachel Cohen

Ilford Synagogue
22 Beehive Lane, Ilford, Essex IG1 3RT
Tel 020 8554 5969 *Fax* 020 8554 4543
Email office@ilfordsynagogue.co.uk *Website* www.ilfordsynagogue.co.uk
(Est. 1936). *M.* Rabbi G. Hyman; *Admin.* Simone Mazin, Marian Myers

Kenton Synagogue
Shaftesbury Avenue, Kenton, Middlesex HA3 0RD
Tel 020 8907 5959 *Fax* 020 8909 2677
Email admin@kentonsynagogue.org.uk *Website* www.kentonsynagogue.org
M. Rabbi Y. Black; *Admin.* Ivan Gold

Kingsbury Synagogue
Hool Close, Kingsbury Green, NW9 8XR
Tel 020 8204 8089
Email kinsyn@btinternet.com *Website* www.brijnet.org/kingsyn
M. Rabbi Z. Cohen; *Admin.* Ivan Gold

— **Mill Hill Synagogue**
Station Road, Mill Hill NW7 2JU
Tel 020 8959 1137 *Fax* 020 8959 6484
Email office@millhillsynagogue.co.uk *Website* www.shul.co.uk
M. Rabbi Y. Y. Schochet; *Admin.* Charles Loeb, Alyson Sharron, Gerry Shaer

— **Muswell Hill Synagogue**
31 Tetherdown, N10 1ND
Tel 020 8883 5925
Email office@muswellhillsynagogue.org.uk *Website* www.muswellhillsynagogue.org.uk
(Est. 1911). *M.* Rabbi D. Mason; *Admin.* Joanna Cowen

New Synagogue
Victoria Community Centre, Egerton Road, Stamford Hill, N16 6UB
Office: 2a Triangle Road, London E8 3RP *Tel* 020 8880 2731 *Fax* 020 7249 8210
(Est. Leadenhall Street, 1761). Morning services held, throughout Shabbat and Yom Tov as
well as every weekday morning. *Admin.* Michelle Fraser; *Fin. Representative,* J. Yeshooa
Tel 07812 394 267

New West End Synagogue
St Petersburgh Place, Bayswater, W2 4JT
Tel 020 7229 2631 *Fax* 020 7229 2355
Email nwes@newwestend.org.uk *Website* www.newwestend.org.uk
(Consec. 1879). Services held weekdays 7am, Sunday and Bank Holidays 8.30am, Shabbat
9.15am. *M.* Rabbi G. Shisler; *Beadle* Eli Ballon; *Admin.* Mesod Wahnon

Newbury Park Synagogue
23 Wessex Close, off Suffolk Road, Newbury Park, Ilford, Essex IG3 8JU

Tel 020 8597 0958
M. Rev. G. Newman; *Admin.* A. Redland *Email* office@newburyparksynagogue.org.uk

Northwood Synagogue
21-23 Murray Road, Middlesex HA6 2YP
Tel 01923 820 004 *Fax* 01923 820 020
Email admin@northwoodus.org
M. Rabbi Dr Moshe Freedman; *Admin.* E. Granger

Palmers Green and Southgate Synagogue
Brownlow Road, N11 2BN
Tel 020 8881 0037
Email office@palmersgreensynagogue.org.uk
M. Rabbi E. Levy, BA(Hons); *Admin.* L. Cohen

Pinner Synagogue
1 Cecil Park, Pinner, Middlesex HA5 5HJ
Tel 020 8868 7204
Website www.pinnershul.org
Regular daily services held. Rabbi D. Bergson; *Community Admin.* Carolyn Abrahams
Email admin@pinnershul.org

Potters Bar Synagogue
PO Box 466, Potters Bar, Herts EN6 9EE
Tel/Fax 01707 656 202
Email office@pottersbarshul.org.uk *Website* www.pottersbarshul.org.uk
M. Rabbi A. S. Hill

Radlett
P.O. Box 28, Herts. WD7 7PN
Tel 01923 856 878
Email office@radlettus.org *Website* www.radlettus.org
Admin. A. Primhak, R. Hart

Richmond Synagogue
Lichfield Gardens, Richmond-on-Thames, Surrey TW9 1AP
Tel 020 8940 3526 *Fax* 020 8945 6586
(Est. 1916). *M.* Rabbi Hughes; *Admin.* The Hon. Mrs J.M. Fellows JP

St Albans United Synagogue
Oswald Road, Herts AL1 3AQ
Tel 01727 854 872
Email info@stalbanssynagogue.org.uk *Website* www.stalbanssynagogue.org.uk
M. Rabbi D. Sturgess; *Admin.* M. Levitt

St John's Wood Synagogue
37/41 Grove End Road, St John's Wood, NW8 9NG
Tel 020 7286 3838
Email office@shulinthewood.com *Website* www.shulinthewood.com
(Est. in Abbey Road 1876; present building consecrated 1964). *M.* Dayan I. Binstock BSc;
R. Rev. M. Haschel; *Associate Rabbi,* Rabbi Ari Shainfield; *Admin.* Jennifer Weider

Shenley Synagogue
c/o 305 Ballards Lane, London N12 8GB
Tel 020 8343 5671
Email shenley@theus.org.uk *Website* www.shenleyunited.org
Shabbat and Yom Tov services only

South Hampstead Synagogue
21-22 Eton Villas, Eton Road, NW3 4SG
Tel 020 7722 1807 *Fax* 020 7586 3459
Email rachel@southhampstead.org *Website* www.southhampstead.org
M. Rabbi S. Levin, Rabbi E. Levin; Rabbi S. Odze; *Admin.* R. Perez-Arwas

South London Synagogue
45 Leigham Court Road, SW16 2NF

Tel 020 8677 0234
Email admin@sls1.org.uk *Website* www.sls1.org.uk
M. Rabbi Y. Grunewald, M.A.; *Admin.* T. Goldman

South Tottenham Synagogue
111-113 Crowland Road, N15 6UR
Tel 020 8809 2555
Email admin@stsynagogue.org.uk
(Est. 1938). *M.* Rabbi C. M. Biberfeld; *Snr. Warden.* M. Milner

⪦ **Stanmore and Canons Park Synagogue**
London Road, Stanmore, Middlesex HA7 4NS
Tel 020 8954 2210
Email mail@stanmoresynagogue.org
M. Rabbi M. Lew; *R. J.* Turgel; *Community Dev. Rabbi* Rabbi A. Shaw; *Asst. Community Rabbi* Rabbi B. Landau; *Man.* Jodie Sinyor

Sutton & District Synagogue
14 Cedar Road, Sutton, Surrey SM2 5DA
Tel 020 8642 5419
Email sutton@theus.org.uk *Website* www.suttonsynagogue.org.uk
M. Rabbi M. Lev; *Admin.* W. Land *Tel* 020 8343 5684

Wanstead and Woodford Synagogue
20 Churchfields, London, E18 2QZ
Tel 020 8504 1990
Email office@wwshul.org *Website* www.wwshul.org/
M. Rabbi B. Fleischer; *Admin.* L. Appleby

⪦ **Watford Synagogue**
16 Nascot Road, Watford, Herts WD17 4YE
Tel 01923 222 755
Email secretary@watfordsynagogue.org.uk
(Est. 1946). *M.* Rabbi E. Levine; *Admin.* C. Silverman

⁻**Wembley Synagogue**
Forty Avenue, Wembley, Middlesex HA9 8JW
Tel 020 8904 6565 *Fax* 020 8908 2740
Email office@wembleysynagogue.org.uk *Website* www.wembleysynagogue.org.uk
M. Rabbi S.Y. Harris, BA Hons, Mst. (Oxon); *Admin.* E. Weiner

⁻ **Woodside Park Synagogue**
Woodside Park Road, N12 8RZ
Tel 020 8445 4236 *Fax* 020 8446 5515
Email admin@woodsidepark.org.uk *Website* www.woodsideparksynagogue.org.uk
Regular daily services held. *M.* Rabbi P. Hackenbroch; *Asst. M.* Rabbi G. Wayland; *Ch. D.* Conway; *Community Man.* N. Sommer, D. Bruce

AFFILIATE SYNAGOGUE
—**Western Marble Arch Synagogue**
32 Great Cumberland Place, W1H 7TN
Tel 020 7723 9333 *Fax* 020 7224 8065
Email office@marblearch.org.uk *Website* www.marblearch.org.uk
Successor to the Western Synagogue (Est. 1761) and the Marble Arch Synagogue. *M.* Rabbi L. Rosenfeld; *Pres.* Stanley Simmonds; *Admin.* Gina Drew-Davis. Affiliated for burial rights with United Synagogue and Western Charitable Foundation.
Affiliated Organisations: Western Charitable Foundation. *Ch.* H. Pasha; *V. Ch.* D. Winton; *T.* A.H. Yadgaroff

AFFILIATED SYNAGOGUES
These are synagogues. belonging to US by means of a scheme for small and newly established congregations.

Catford & Bromley Affiliated Synagogue
6 Crantock Road, SE6 2QS
Enq. P.O. Box 4724, London SE6 2YA
Tel 020 8698 9496
(Est. 1937). *M.* Rev. D. G. Rome *Email* minister@catfordsynagogue.org.uk *Admin.* P. Tomlinson
Tel 020 8658 0090 *Email* administrator@catfordsynagogue.org.uk

Chelsea Affiliated Synagogue
Smith Terrace, Smith Street, Chelsea, SW3 4DL
Tel 020 7351 6292
Email office@chelseasynagogue.co.uk
(Reg. Charity No. 1101862). *M.* Rabbi Y. Efune *Tel* 07972 261 229; *Admin.* G. Gean *Tel* 020
7351 6292/ 07980 965 171

Harold Hill and District Affliliated Synagogue
Trowbridge Road, Harold Hill, Essex RM3 8YW
(Est. 1953). *T.* D. Jacobs *Tel* 020 8924 8668; *Hon. S.* Miss D. Meid, 4 Portmadoc House,
Brosely Road, Harold Hill, Essex RM3 9BT *Tel* 01708 348 904

Kingston, Surbiton and District Affiliated Synagogue
33-35 Uxbridge Road, Kingston on Thames, Surrey KT1 2LL
Tel 020 8339 2689
Email admin@kingston-synagogue.org.uk *Website* www.kingston-synagogue.org.uk
(Est. 1947). *M.* Rabbi Samuel Landau; *H. Admin.* C. Abrahams 15 Albany Reach, Queens
Road, Thames Ditton, KT7 0QH *Tel* 020 8224 2073 *Email* carol.abrahams@btinternet.com

Peterborough Affiliated Synagogue
Tel 01733 264 151 *Admin.* C. Salamon

Romford and District Affiliated Synagogue
25 Eastern Road, Romford, Essex RM1 3NH
Tel 01708 741 690
(Est. 1929). *M.* J.R. Rose, *M.* Rabbi L. Sunderland

Ruislip and District Affiliated Synagogue
9 Shenley Avenue, Ruislip Manor, Middlesex HA4 6BP
Tel 01895 622 059 *Fax* 01895 622 059
Email secretary@ruislipsynagogue.org.uk *Website* www.ruislipsynagogue.org.uk
(Est. 1946). *M.* Rabbi S. Coten; *Admin.* Michelle Davis

Staines Synagogue
Westbrook Road, South Street, Middlesex TW18 4PR
Tel 020 8890 0016
Email staines.synagogue@btinternet.com *Website* www.staines-synagogue.org.uk
Officiant David Kale; *Admin.* Eric Fenton

Welwyn Garden City Affiliated Synagogue
Barn Close, Handside Lane, Herts AL8 6ST
Tel 01707 322 443
Email info@wgcshul.org.uk
M. Rabbi H. Gruber; *Hon. S.* H. Rosenberg

Federation of Synagogues

For contact details: *See under* Religious Organisations.
Constituent and Affiliated Synagogues of the Federation of Synagogues

CONSTITUENT SYNAGOGUES

Beis Hamedrash Nishmas Yisroel
62 Brent Street, Hendon, London NW4 2ES
Tel 07931 575 292
Website www.bhny.co.uk
Daily services held. *M.* Rabbi D. Tugendhaft; *Sec.* A. Krausz; *Ch.* S. Unsdorfer

Clapton Federation Synagogue (Sha'are Shomayim). (Incorporating Yavneh Synagogue) (in association with Springfield Synagogue). Services held at Springfield Synagogue 202 Upper Clapton Road, E5 9DH *Sec. R.* Jacobs *Tel* 020 8530 5816

Croydon & District Synagogue
The Almonds, 5 Shirley Oaks Road CRO 8YX
Website www.croydonsynagogue.org.uk
(Est. 1908; present synagogue consecrated 1995). Services held Friday night and Shabbat morning at 10am *M.* Rabbi Natan Asmoucha; *Hon. S.* Beila Harris *Tel* 020 8726 0179

East London Central Synagogue
30/40 Nelson Street, E1 2DE
Tel 020 7790 9809
Regular Shabbat Services at 10am *M.* Rabbi Y. Austin *Sec.* J. Beninson *Tel* 07983 931 178; *Pres.* L. Silver

Finchley Central Synagogue
Redbourne Avenue, N3 2BS
Tel 020 8346 1892
Website www.finchleyfed.org.uk
Regular weekday services: Shacharit Sunday 8am, Monday and Thursday 7.05am, Tuesday, Wednesday, Friday 7.15am; Mincha/Maariv 7.30pm; Shabbat services at Pardes House School, Hendon Lane, N3; Friday night 7.15pm or start of Shabbat if earlier; Shabbat morning 9.15am. *Rav.* Rabbi Y. Hamer; *Sec.* P. Wittner

Hendon Beis Hamedrash
65 Watford Way NW4 3AQ
Mincha and Ma'ariv services Monday - Friday at 1.40pm and Shabbat *M.* Dayan Y.Y. Lichtenstein; *Contact* P. Burns *Tel* 020 8203 7757

Ilford Federation Synagogue
2a Clarence Avenue, Ilford, Essex IG2 6JH
Tel 020 8554 5289 *Fax* 020 8554 7003
Email ilfordfedsynagogue@btconnect.com *Website* www.ilfordfeds.org
(Est. 1927). Daily services held. *M.* Rabbi A. Chapper; *Sec.* L. Klein

Machzike Hadath Synagogue
1-4 Highfield Road, NW11 9LU
Tel 020 8455 9816
Email secretary@machzikehadath.com *Website* www.machzikehadath.com
Services held daily morning and evening. *M.* Rabbi C. Z. Pearlman

Netzach Israel Community Centre
281 Golders Green Road, NW11 9JJ
Daily services held. *M.* Rabbi D. Ahiel *Admin.* Rabbi Adam Mather *Tel* 020 8455 7725

Ohr Yisrael Synagogue
31-33 Theobald Street, Borehamwood, Herts WD6 4RN
Website www.ohr-yisrael.org.uk
Daily services held. *M.* Rabbi R. Garson *Tel* 020 8953 8385 *Sec.* Jo Kay *Tel* 020 8207 4702

Shomrei Hadath Synagogue
64 Burrard Road, NW6 1DD
Website http://shomrei-hadath.com
Services held Shabbat, Yom Tov, Rosh Chodesh, Taanis. *Sec.* P. Schotten *Tel* 020 7435 6906; Rabbi Moshe Mayerfeld *Tel* 07977 291 567 *Email* rabbim@shomrei.org.uk

Sinai Synagogue
54 Woodstock Avenue, NW11 9RJ
Tel 020 8455 6876
(Est. 1935). Daily services held. *Rab.* Rabbi B. Knopfler; *Sec.* E. Cohen *Tel* 020 8458 8201

Yeshurun Synagogue
corner of Fernhurst Gardens and Stonegrove, Edgware, Middlesex HA8 7PH
Tel 020 8952 5167 *Fax* 020 8905 7439
Email admin@yeshurun.org *Website* www.yeshurun.org

(Est. 1946). Daily services held. *Emer. Rab.* Dayan G. Lopian; *Rab.* Rabbi A. Lewis; *Sec.* Lisa Denby

AFFILIATED SYNAGOGUES
Aish Community Synagogue
379 Hendon Way, NW4 3LP
M. Rabbi J. Roodyn *Tel* 020 8457 4444
Congregation of Jacob
351/353 Commercial Road, E1 2PS
Tel 020 7790 2874
Email info@congregationofjacob.org *Website* www.congregationofjacob.org
(Est. 1903). Regular Shabbat and Yom Tov services held. Contact D. Brandes, D. Behr
Fieldgate Street Great Synagogue
41 Fieldgate Street, E1 1JU
Tel 020 7247 2644
Secs. F. Treep, L. Michaels; *Pres.* H. Michaels
Finchley Road Synagogue (Sassover)
1a Helenslea Avenue, NW11 8NE
(Est. 1941). *Rab.* Rabbi S. Freshwater *Tel* 020 8455 2588
Contact S. Halpern *Tel* 020 8455 1814
Leytonstone & Wanstead Synagogue
2 Fillebrook Road, E11 4AT
Sec. Cllr. L. Braham *Tel* 020 8989 0978
Loughton Synagogue
Borders Lane, Loughton, Essex IG10 1TE
Email admin@loughtonsynagogue.com *Website* http://loughtonsynagogue.com
Regular Shabbat services are held Friday evening at 7pm and Shabbat morning at 9am *Ch.* B. Cohen; *Rav* Rabbi Zvi Portnoy; *Admin.* M. Lewis *Tel* 020 8508 0303
Springfield Synagogue
202 Upper Clapton Road, E5 9DH
Tel 020 8806 3167 (office)
(Est. 1929). Regular daily services held. *Rab.* Dayan I. Gukovitski
Stamford Hill Beis Hamedrash
50 Clapton Common, London E5 9AL
M. Dayan D. Grynhaus; *Ch.* M. Chontow *Tel* 020 8800 7369
Waltham Forest Hebrew Congregation
140 Boundary Road, E17 8LA
Tel 020 8509 0775 *Fax* 020 8518 8200
Email secretary@wfhc.co.uk
(Est. 1902) *M.* Rev. S. Myers; *Ch.* Mark Phillips; *Admin.* B. Rose
West End Great Synagogue
32 Great Cumberland Place, W1H 7TN
Tel 020 7724 8121 *Fax* 020 7723 4413
Email wegs@clara.co.uk
Regular Shabbat morning services are held in the Mintz Beth Hamidrash on the first floor at 9.45am. *M.* Rev. Ari Cohen; *Admin. N. Singer*
East End synagogues are served by Rev. Gingold *Tel* 020 7790 5287

Union of Orthodox Hebrew Congregations
For contact details: *See under* Religious Organisations.
Synagogues Associated with the Union of Orthodox Hebrew Congregations or the Burial Society.

Adath Yisroel Synagogue
40 Queen Elizabeth's Walk, N16 0HT

Tel 020 8802 6262 *Fax* 020 8800 8764
Rabbi Dovid Lewis; *Delegates*, M. T. Bibelman, M. Lobenstein

Adath Yisroel Tottenham Beth Hamedrash
55/57 Ravensdale Road, N16 6TJ
Tel 020 8800 3978
Dayan A.D. Dunner; *Delegate*, Dr S. Springer

Ahavat Israel Chasidey Wiznitz Synagogue
Wiznitz House, 89 Stamford Hill, N16 5TP
Tel 020 8800 9359
Rabbi A. Weiss; *Delegates*, R. Bergman JP LLB, Y. Feldman, Y. Zieg

Beis Gavriel Lubavitch
54 Parsons Street, NW4 1TP
Rabbi M. M. Junik; *Delegate*, M. Freundlich

Beis Hamedrash Avreichim Golders Green
211 Golders Green Road, NW11 9BY
Rabbi Y. Y. Lev

Beis Hamedrash Biala (Birkas Zvi)
45-47 Moundfield Road, N16 6DT
Rabbi B. L. Rabinowitz; *Delegate*, A. Schechter

Beis Hamedrash Maharim Dushinsky
1b Braydon Road, N16 6QL
Delegate, S. Z. Reizner

Beis Hamedrash Noam Hatorah
38a Braydon Road, N16 6QB
Delegate, Y. N. Schimanowitz

Beis Hamedrash 'Oraysoh'
102 Darenth Road, N16 6ED
Tel 020 8802 0103
Rabbi M. D. Weiss; *Delegate*, Y. Reichman

Beis Hamedrash Sharei Shulem Tchabe
23 Portland Avenue, N16 6HD
Rabbi A. E. Schwartz; *Delegate*, Y. Moster

Beis Kossov
96 Lewis Gardens, N16 5PJ
Tel 020 8809 6534
Rabbi M. Monderer; *Delegate*, B. Z. Goldstein

Beis Sholem D'Shotz
42 St. Kilda's Road, N16 5BZ
Rabbi S. Deutsch; *Delegates*, F. Gluck, Z. Singer

Beis Yitzchak Dovid, Avreichei Gur
26 Amhurst Parade, Amhurst Park, N16 5AA
Tel 020 8800 6615
Delegates, D. Piller, A. M. Royde

Beth Abraham (Goschalks Synagogue)
46 The Ridgeway, NW11 8QS
Tel 020 8455 2848
Rabbi C. Schmahl; *Delegate*, S. Chonton

Beth Chodosh Synagogue
51 Queen Elizabeth's Walk, N16 5UG
Tel 020 8809 4820
Rabbi H. Frankel; *Delegate*, Rabbi H. Frankel

Beth Hamedrash Cheishev Hoeifod
Brenner Centre, 91-93 Stamford Hill, N16 5TP
Rabbi Y. Padwa; *Delegate*, Y. M. Mann

Beth Hamedrash D'Chasidei Wiznitz
126 Stamford Hill, N16 6QT
Rabbi G. Spitzer; *Delegate*, E. Bretler
Beth Joseph Zvi
Schonfeld Square, Lordship Road, N16 0QQ
Tel 020 8802 7477
Delegate, Ch Konig
Beth Shmuel Synagogue
171 Golders Green Road, NW11 9BY
Tel 020 8458 7511
Rabbi E. Halpern; *Delegates*, S. Feiner, L. Frankel, I. Gabay, A. Heilpern
Beth Talmud Centre
78 Cazenove Road, N16 6AA
Tel 020 8806 8103
Delegate, N. Freedman
Beth Yisochor Dov Beth Hamedrash
4 Highfield Avenue, NW11 9ET
Tel 020 8458 1264
Rabbi G. Hager; *Delegates*, W. Grant, W. Held, Dr P. Mett
Biala Chelkas Yehoshua Beth Hamedrash
110 Castlewood Road, N15 6BE
M. Glausiusz
Bridge Lane Beth Hamedrash
44 Bridge Lane, NW11 0EG
Tel 020 8458 8364
Rabbi S. Winegarten *Burial Society Affiliate*
Chasidey Alexander Me'oron Shel Yisroel Beth Hamedrash
99 Clapton Common, E5 9AB
Delegate, S. Leichtag
Chasidey Belz Beth Hamedrash
99 Bethune Road, N16 5ED
Tel 020 8802 2151
Rabbi E. D. Friedman; *Delegates*, B. Bard, Rabbi D. Frand, Y. Gluck
117 Clapton Common, N16 6AB
Delegate, L. Weiser
Chasidey Belz Beth Hamedrash
96 Clapton Common, E5 9AL
Tel 020 8802 8233
Rabbi J. D. Babad; *Delegates*, M. Grosskopf, N. Merlin, B. Roth
49 St. Kilda's Road, N16 5BS
Tel 020 8211 0213
Rabbi N. B. Eckstein; *Delegates*, D. Y. Gluck, Y. S. Grosz
26 Lampard Grove, N16 6XZ
Rabbi M. Galitsky; Delegate, G. Schwartz
Chasidey Bobov Beth Hamedrash
73 Clapton Common, E5 9AA
Delegates, A. M. Lensky, C. Rudzinski
Chasidey Bobov D'Ohel Naphtoli including **Yeshiva Bnei Zion Beth Hamedrash**
87 Eagerton Road, N16 6UE
Tel 020 8809 0476
Rabbi B. Z. Blum; *Delegates*, Y. C. Blau, M. Just, M. Rothfeld
Chasidey Ryzhin Beth Hamedrash
33 Paget Road, N16 5ND
Tel 020 8800 7979
Delegate, M. Erlich

Chasidey Ryzhin-Sadigur Or Yisroel Beth Hamedrash
269 Golders Green Road, NW11 9JJ
Rabbi Y. M. Friedman; *Delegates*, N. Bude, P. Smus

Chasidey Sanz-Klausenburg Beth Hamedrash
124 Stamford Hill, N16 6QT
Tel 020 8802 1149
Delegate, Y. M. Klein

Chasidey Skver Beth Hamedrash
47 East Bank, Stamford Hill, N16 5PZ
Tel 020 8800 8448
Rabbi Y. Friesel; *Delegate*, M. Ciment

Chasidey Wizintz-Monsey Imrei Chaim Beth Hamedrash
121 Clapton Common, E5 9AB
Tel 020 8800 3741
Rabbi D. Hager; *Delegates*, Y. M. Cohen, Rabbi Zishe Fuchs

Cheishev Sofer D'Pressburg Beth Hamedrash
103 Clapton Common, E5 9AB
Tel 020 8809 1700
Rabbi S. Ludmir; *Delegate*, U. Low

Chevras Shass Zichron Shlomo Beth Hamedrash
11 Elm Park Avenue, Tottenham, N15 6UE
Tel 020 8809 7850
Rabbi S. Meisels; *Delegate*, Y.Y. Meisels

Congregation Chovevei Torah
76 Princes Park Avenue, NW11 0JX
Tel 020 8381 4227
Rabbi Y. Levenberg

Divrei Chaim Beth Hamedrash
71 Bridge Lane, NW11 0EE
Tel 020 8458 1161
Rabbi Chaim A. Z. Halpern; *Delegates*, M. Aisenthal, P. M. Grossnass

Etz Chaim Yeshiva
83-85 Bridge Lane, NW11 0EE
Rabbi Z. Rabi; *Delegate*, B. Manson

Golders Green Beth Hamedrash Congregation
The Riding, NW11 8HL
Tel 020 8455 2974
Rabbi Y. M. Greenberg

Gur Beiss Hachasidim
98 Bridge Lane, NW11 0ER
Tel 020 8458 6243
Delegate, A. Weingarten

Gur Beiss Hachasidim
2 Lampard Grove, Stamford Hill, N16 6UZ
Tel 020 8806 4333
Delegates, Y. M. Cymerman, Y. S. Goldman, Y. Traube

Heichal Hatorah
27 St. Kilda's Road, Stamford Hill, N16 5BS
Tel 020 8809 4331
Rabbi L. Rakow; *Delegate*, A. M. Schwartz

Heichal Leah
62 Brent Street, NW4 2ES
Tel 020 8203 6210
Rabbi M. Nissim; *Delegates*, C. Kohali, Rabbi M. Nissim

Heichal Menachem
209 Golders Green Road, NW11 9BY
Rabbi Y. M. Hertz; *Delegate*, Rabbi N. Cohen
Hendon Adath Yisroel Congregation
11 Brent Street, Hendon, London NW4 2EU
Sec. M. Moller *Tel* 020 8202 9183; *Rabbi* Rabbi P. Roberts
Hendon Beth Hamedrash
3 The Approach, Hendon, London NW4 2HU
Tel 020 8202 5499
Rabbi D. Halpern; *Delegate*, J. Gertner
Kehal Chareidim Beth Hamedrash
99 Clapton Common, E5 9AB
Rabbi A. Y. Rubinfeld; *Delegates*, S. B. Gluck, D. Margulies
Kehal Chasidim D'Munkatch Synagogue
85 Cazenove Road, Stamford Hill, N16 6BB
Delegate, C. L. Lipschitz
Kehal Chassidim Beth Hamedrash
213 Golders Green Road, NW11 9BY
Tel 020 8731 9583
Rabbi Y. E. Brief; *Delegate*, D. Ost
Kehillas Ohel Moshe
102 Leeside Crescent, NW11 0JN
Tel 020 8800 3868
Rabbi Dovid Stern; *Delegate*, M. Berger
Kingsley Way Beth Hamedrash
3-5 Kingsley Way, Hampstead Garden Suburb N2 0EH
Tel 020 8458 2312
Rabbi Y. M. Hertz; *Delegate*, F. Hager
Knesset Yehezkel Beth Hamedrash
187 Golders Green Road, NW11 9BY
Tel 020 8455 4722/3591
Rabbi A. Bassous
Knightland Road Synagogue
50 Knightland Road, Upper Clapton E5 9HS
Tel 020 8802 7684 (Office)
Rabbi M. Halpern; *Delegate*, Y. Taub
Kol Ya'akov Beth Hamedrash
47 Mowbray Road, Edgware, Middlesex HA8 8JL
Tel 020 8905 3853
Rabbi S. Joseph
Lieger Beth Hamedrash Torath Chaim
37 Craven Walk, Stamford Hill, N16 6BS
Tel 020 8800 3868
Rabbi J. Meisels; *Delegate*, A. Reifer
Lieger Beth Hamedrash Torath Chaim
145 Upper Clapton Road, E5 9DB
Tel 020 8806 8405
Rabbi M. Meisels
Lubavitch Synagogue
107-115 Stamford Hill, N16 5RP
Tel 020 8800 0022
Rabbi N. Sudak, Dayan L. Y. Raskin; *Delegates*, B. Hackner, S. Herzog
Lubavitch of Edgware
230 Hale Lane, Edgware, Middlesex HA8 9PZ

Tel 020 8905 4141
Rabbi L. Y. Sudak; Delegate, T. Brooks
Machzikei Hadass Edgware Beth Hamedrash
296 Hale Lane, Edgware, Middlesex HA8 8NP
Tel 020 8958 1030
Rabbi E. Schneelbalg; Delegates, B. Gordon, H. L. Sacks
Mesifta Synagogue
82-84 Cazenove Road, Stamford Hill, N16 6AB
Tel 020 8806 1775
Delegate, P. Ostreicher
Nachlei Emunah Chasidey Kretchnif
122 Cazenove Road, N16 6AH (Rav Tov)
Rabbi L. Kahane; Delegate, M. B. Kraus
Nadvorna Beth Hamedrash
45 Darenth Road, Stamford Hill, N16 6ES
Tel 020 8806 3903 Fax 020 8806 9590
Rabbi M. Leifer; Delegate, M. Z. Landau
North Hendon Adath Yisroel Synagogue
Holders Hill Road, NW4 1NA
Tel 020 8203 2390
Rabbi D. Cohn; Delegate, A. H. Ehreich
Ohel Israel (Skolyer) Beth Haedrash
11 Brent Street, NW4 2EU
Rabbi Y. Royde; Delegate, K. Kessleman, M. Meyer
Ohel Yaakov Beiss Hamedrash (Pshevorsk)
26 Lampard Grove, N16 6XB
Rabbi N. E. Leiser; Delegate, S. Z. Berger
Sasover Finchley Road Synagogue
1 Henslea Avenue, NW11 8ND
Tel 020 8455 4305
Rabbi S. Y. Freshwater; Delegates, B. Freshwater, N. Rokach
Beth Hamedrash Satmar Kehal Yetev Lev
86 Cazenove Road, N16 6AB
Tel 020 8806 2633
Delegates, B. Berger, Y. Z. Gross, S. Laufer, Sh. Seidenfeld
Beis Hamedrash Kehal Yetev Lev
42 Craven Walk, N16 6BU
Tel 020 8806 2932
Delegates, C. Y. Gluck, B. Kisch
Beis Hamedrash D'Chasidei Satmar
57 Bethune Road, N16 5EE
Delegates, A. Grunhut, S. Matyas
Beis Hamedrash Tehillois Yoel
148 Upper Clapton Road, E5 9JZ
Delegate, Y. Reiner
Beth Hamedrash Satmar Kehal Yetev Lev
26 Clapton Common, E5 9BA
Tel 020 8880 8930
Dayan S. Low, Dayan Ch. Inzlicht
Beis Hamedrash V'Yoel Moshe
(67 Heathland Road, Stamford Hill) 91 Amhurst Park, N16 5DL
Tel 020 8809 0446
Harav S. B. Krausz; Dayan M. Markovits
Sdei Chemed D'Nitra Beth Hamedrash
113 Clapton Common, E5
Tel 020 8806 4828

Rabbi L. Braun; *Delegate*, L. Weiss
Spinke Beth Hamedrash
36 Bergholt Crescent, Stamford Hill, N16 6JE
Tel 020 8809 6903
Rabbi M. M. Kahana; *Delegate*, Y. Tunk
Stamford Hill Beth Hamedrash
50 Clapton Common, E5 9AL
Tel 020 806 8070
Dayan D. Grynhaus; *Delegate*, M. Chontow
Stanislowa Beth Hamedrash
93 Lordship Park, N16 5UP
Tel 020 8800 2040
Rabbi E. Aschkenazi; *Delegate*, M. Spiegel
Stolin Karlin
4 Castlewood Road, N16 6DW
Tel 020 8809 7454
Delegate, Y. Dreyfus
Tiferes Amrom Beth Hamedrash
3 Northdene Gardens, Stamford Hill, N15 6LX
Rabbi A. Jungreis; *Delegate*, B. Stroh
Torah Etz Chayim Beth Hamedrash
69 Lordship Road, N16 0QX
Tel 020 8800 7726
Rabbi Z. Feldman; *Delegates*, I. Hoffman, R. Spitzer
Yeshivas Ahavas Torah
10-18 Craven Park Road, N15 6AB
Tel 020 8809 5884
Rabbi B. Weisz; *Delegate*, M. Block
Yeshivas Horomoh Beth Hamedrash
100 Fairholt Road, N16 5HN
Tel 020 8800 6778
Rabbi E. Schlesinger; *Delegate*, S. Singer
Yeshivas Ohr Torah
Wellbury House, Great Offley, near Hitchin, Herts
Tel 01462 768 698 & 768 925
Rabbi Y. M. Stern; *Delegate*, B. Z. Weissman
Yeshivas Toras Chesed
118 Cazenove Road, London N16
Tel 020 8880 8026
Rabbi C. Y. Babad; *Delegate*, Y. Kornbluh
Yeshuath Chaim Synagogue
45 Heathland Road, N16 5PQ
Tel 020 8800 2332
Rabbi C. Pinter; *Delegates*, Rabbi A. Pinter, A. Rand
Yesodey Hatorah Beth Hamedrash
2-4 Amhurst Park, N16 5AE
Delegate, J. Teller
Zeire Agudath Yisroel Beth Hamedrash
69 Lordship Road, N16 0QX
Delegate, Ch. Kesselman
Zeire Agudath Yisroel Beth Hamedrash
95 Stamford Hill, N16 5DN
Rabbi M. J. Kamionka; *Delegates*, S. C. Grussgott, S. Just
ADATH YISROEL CHEVRA KADISHA
Adath Yisroel Synagogue, 40 Queen Elizabeth's Walk, London N16 0HH

8802 6262; Mobile 07973 622 350 *Fax* 020 8800 8764
K. Berkovits; *V. Gabbai* M. M. Brief; *Ch.* E. M. Hochhauser, *T*. S.B. Stern; L Wosner,
D. Lobenstein; *Cttee.* N. Berkovitz, A. Gluck, S. Grosz, C. L. Lieber, S. Sinitsky

꜒꜒ꜞRS GREEN BETH HAMEDRASH CHEVRA KADISHA
Tel 020 8455 5918

Masorti Judaism

For contact details: *See under* Religious Organisations.

Buckhurst Hill Masorti Synagogue
The Woollard Centre, Loughton Way, Buckhurst Hill, Essex IG9 4AB
Tel 07922 090 180
Email office@bhmasorti.org.uk *Website* www.bhmasorti.org.uk

Edgware Masorti Synagogue
Synagogue Office/Post/Weekly entrance: Pearl Community Centre, Stream Lane, Edgware
HA8 7YA
Shabbat entrance: Bakery Path (off Station Road), Edgware HA8 7YE
Tel 020 8905 4096
Email admin@masorti.org.uk
(Reg. Charity No. 1117623). Rabbi Mijeal Even-David; *Co-Ch.* J. Mitchell, M. Schraer; *T.*
S. Maisel; *Admin.* L. Lassman

Elstree & Borehamwood Masorti Community
Borehamwood & Elstree Childrens Centre (BECC), Shakespeare Drive, Borehamwood,
Herts WD6 2FD
Tel 07843 792 133
Email info@ebmc.org.uk *Website* www.ebmc.org.uk

Hatch End Masorti Synagogue
39 Bessborough Road, Harrow, Middlesex HA1 3BS
Tel 020 8864 0133
Email office@hems.org.uk *Website* www.hems.org.uk
Ch. Neil Mendoza

Kol Nefesh Masorti Synagogue
Jewish Care, Rectory Lane, Edgware, Middlesex HA8 7LF
Enq. *Tel* 07768 117 145
Email convenor@kolnefesh.org.uk *Website* www.kolnefeshmasorti.org.uk
(Reg. Charity No. 1081444). *Co-ord.* Brenda Simmonds; *M.* Rabbi Joel Levy

New London Synagogue
33 Abbey Road, NW8 0AT
Tel 020 7328 1026
Email office@newlondon.org.uk *Website* www.newlondon.org.uk

New North London Synagogue
80 East End Road, N3 2SY
Tel 020 8346 8560
Email office@nnls-masorti.org.uk *Website* www.nnls-masorti.org.uk
(Est. 1974). *M.* Rabbi J. Wittenberg; *Co-Ch.* D. Raff, T. Isaacs; *T.* A. Bogod; *Off.* C. Mandel;
Com. Co-ord. R. Gottlieb

New Stoke Newington Shul
Website www.newstokenewingtonshul.org
New Stoke Newington Shul (NSNS) is a growing Masorti community serving Stoke
Newington and the wider Hackney area as well as Highbury, Islington, Shoreditch, Hoxton,
Tower Hamlets, Haringey and beyond. We welcome newcomers of all generations, affiliations
or levels of knowledge. *Contact* Paul Craven *Email* pcraven@pcraven.net

St Albans Masorti Synagogue
Unit 9, The Dencora Centre, Campfield Road, St Albans, Herts AL1 5HN
Email info@e-sams.org *Website* www.e-sams.org
Tel 01727 860 642

Sephardi

For contact details: *See under* Religious Organisations

SYNAGOGUES

Bevis Marks
EC3A 5DQ
Tel 020 7626 1274
Website www.bevismarks.org.uk
(Est. 1701).

⟶ Lauderdale Road Synagogue
Maida Vale, W9 1JY
Tel 020 7289 2573 *Fax* 020 7289 2709
Website www.lauderdaleroadsynagogue.org
(Est.1896). Daily services held. *Rabbi* Rabbi I. Elia

⟶ Wembley Spanish and Portuguese Synagogue
46 Forty Avenue, Wembley, Middlesex HA9 8LQ
Tel 020 7289 2573
Email secretary@wsps.org.uk *Website* www.wsps.org.uk
M. Rabbi Danny Kada

OTHER INSTITUTIONS

Welfare Board
2 Ashworth Road, W9 1JY
Tel 020 7432 1305
(Est. 1837)

Sephardi Kashrut Authority
2 Ashworth Road, W9 1JY
Tel 020 7432 1321
Ch. E. Cohen; *Dir.* D. Steinhof

Communal Centre
Montefiore Hall, 2 Ashworth Road, W9 1JY
Tel 020 7289 2573

Beth Hamedrash Heshaim
2 Ashworth Road, W9 1JY
Tel 020 7289 2573
(Instituted 1664). *T.* Dr. J. Schonfield

Montefiore Endowment (incorporating the **Judith Lady Montefiore College Trust**)
2 Ashworth Road, W9 1JY
Tel 020 7289 2573

Established by Sir Moses Montefiore in 1866. The purpose of the Endowment (reviewed by the Charity Commission in 1989) 'is the maintenance of the Synagogue, the Mausoleum and the Jewish Cemetery in Ramsgate'. Also 'the promotion of the advanced study of the Holy Law as revealed on Sinai and expounded by the revered sages of the Mishna and Talmud' through its own Semicha programme and by making grants to charitable institutions and Rabbis and by awarding scholarships to trainees.

The Mausoleum, with the remains of Sir Moses and Lady Montefiore is situated next to the Synagogue in Ramsgate (*See* Regions). Sir Moses's seats in Bevis Marks and Ramsgate Synagogues are still preserved.

Edinburgh House (Beth Holim)
36/44 Forty Avenue, Wembley
Tel 020 8908 4151
Email enquiries@edinburghhouse.org.uk
(Est. 1747). Home for the Aged. *Hd. of Home* Paula Peake

ent Sephardi Synagogues

s' Congregation

ton Common, E5

Jacobs *Tel* 020 8806 1320

David Ishag Synagogue
Neveh Shalom Community, 352-4 Preston Road, Harrow, Middlesex HA3 0QJ
Hon. S. E. Myers *Tel* 020 8346 8744, M. Rose *Tel* 020 8907 0572

Heichal Leah
62 Brent Street, NW4 2ES
Tel 07966 258 160 (Gabbai-Haim Kohali)
Rabbi, Rabbi Assaf Portal

Jacob Benjamin Elias Synagogue
140 Stamford Hill, N16 6QT
(Reg. Charity No. 291531). *M.* Rabbi C. Tangy; *Hon. S. E.* Solomon

Levy Kelaty Synagogue OD Yosef Hai
50 Finchley Lane, NW4 1DJ
Dayan A. David *Tel* 020 8202 8374/020 8203 5701
Nancy Reuben Banqueting Suite Moshe King *Tel* 07969 959 933

Ohel David Eastern Synagogue
4-14 Broadwalk Lane, Golders Green Road, NW11 8HD
Tel 020 8455 3491, 07989 387 881
Email info@oheldavid.org *Website* www.oheldavid.org
(Reg. Charity No. 243901). Services held Monday and Thursday 6.30am, 6.45am; during
week, Mincha and Arbit 7.30pm. *M.* Rabbi Asher Seebag

Persian Hebrew Congregation
5a East Bank, Stoke Newington, N16 5RX
Tel 020 8802 7339

Spanish & Portuguese Synagogue, Holland Park
8 St James's Gardens, W11 4RB
Tel 020 7603 7961/3232 *Fax* 020 7603 9471
Email admin@hollandparksynagogue.com *Website* www.hollandparksynagogue.com
(Est. 1928 under Deed of Association with Spanish and Portuguese Jews' Congregation.
Reg. Charity No. 248945). Services are held Shabbat and Yamim Tovim. *M. Rabbi*
Avraham Lavi

Reform

(Constituents of the Movement for Reform Judaism).
For contact details: *See under* Religious Organisations

West London Synagogue of British Jews
34 Upper Berkeley Street, W1; Office: 33 Seymour Place, W1H 5AU
Tel 020 7723 4404 *Fax* 020 7224 8258
Email admin@wls.org.uk
(Reg. Charity No. 212143). The congregation was organised April 15, 1840, to establish
a synagogue 'where a revised service may be performed at hours more suited to our habits
and in a manner more calculated to inspire feelings of devotion, where religious instruction
may be afforded by competent persons, and where, to effect these purposes, Jews generally
may form a united congregation under the denomination of British Jews.'
Snr. Rabbi Rabbi Julia Neuberger; *Principal Rabbi* Rabbi Helen Freeman; *Rabbis*, Rabbi
David Mitchell and Rabbi Sybil Sheridan; *Ch.* Jill Todd; *Exec. Dir.* Simon Myers
Funerals: Tel 020 7723 4404 *Fax* 020 7224 8258
Cemeteries:
Golders Green, Hoop Lane, NW11 7EU *Tel* 020 8455 2569 *Email* linda@ejbb-jbc.org.uk
Edgwarebury, Edgwarebury Lane, Edgware, Middlesex HA8 8QP *Tel* 020 8958 0090
Email irene@ejbb-jbc.org.uk

Bromley Reform Synagogue
28 Highland Road, Bromley, Kent BR1 4AD
Tel 020 8460 5460
M. Rabbi Jason Holtz; *Admin.* J. Burlem *Email* janet@bromleyshul.org.uk
✂ **Edgware and District Reform Synagogue**
118 Stonegrove, Edgware, HA8 8AB
Tel 020 8238 1000
Email admin@edrs.org.uk *Website* www.edrs.org.uk
(Est. 1934. Reg. Charity No. 1038116). Shabbat services Friday 6.30pm and Sundays
10.30am. Regular Children's/Youth Services, Nagila Nursery School, regular Youth Clubs and
holiday play schemes, children's and adult education. Halls available for hire. *M.* Rabbi A.D.
Smith, MA; *Assoc. M.* Rabbi N. S. Kraft MA; *Admin.* K. B. Senitt
▬ **Finchley Reform Synagogue**
101 Fallow Court Avenue, North Finchley, N12 0BE
Tel 020 8446 3244
Email frs@frsonline.org
Princ. Rabbi Miriam Berger; *Cantor* Zöe Jacobs; Rabbi Howard Cooper; *Emer. Rabbi* Jeffrey
Newman; *Office.* Annie Simmons
Harlow Jewish Community
Harberts Road, Hare Street, Harlow, Essex CM19 4DT
Tel 01279 432503; 01279 792926
Email admin@harlowjewishcommunity.org.uk *Website* www.harlowjewishcommunity.org.uk
M. Rabbi Irit Shillor; *Sec.* Scott Pollack
◂ **Hendon Reform Synagogue**
Danescroft Avenue, NW4 2NA
Tel 020 8203 4168 *Fax* 020 8203 9385
Email rosb@hendonreform.org.uk *Website* www.hendonreform.org.uk
(Est. 1949). *Snr. M.* Rabbi Steven Katz; *Synagogue Man.* R. Bloom; *Asst. M.* Rabbi Lisa Barnett
Cemeteries: Edgwarebury Lane, New Southgate Cemetery, Brunswick Park Road, N11
Tel 020 8203 4168
▬ **Kol Chai-Hatch End Jewish Community**
434 Uxbridge Road, Hatch End, Middlesex HA5 4RG
Tel 020 8421 5482
Email admin@kolchai.org *Website* www.kolchai.org
(Reg. Charity No. 299063). Services held weekly Friday night 7pm, Shabbat morning
10.30am. *M.* Rabbi Dr. M. Hilton; *Admin.* D. Levy
▬ **Mosaic Reform** (form. **Middlesex New Synagogue**)
39 Bessborough Road, Harrow, HA1 3BS
Tel 020 8864 0133
Email admin@mosaicreform.org.uk
(Est. 1959). *M.* Rabbi K. de Magtige-Middleton; *Sec.* A. Simon
North West Surrey Synagogue
Horvath Close, Rosslyn Park, Oatlands Drive, Weybridge, Surrey KT13 9QZ
Tel/Fax 01932 855400
Email admin@nwss.org.uk *Website* www.nwss.org.uk
(Est. 1956. Reg Charity No. 256232). *M.* Rabbi Jacqueline Tabick; *Hon. S.* S. Barnett;
Admin. L. Bateman
▬ **North Western Reform Synagogue**
Alyth Gardens, Finchley Road, NW11 7EN
Tel 020 8455 6763 *Fax* 020 8731 8175
Email mail@alyth.org.uk *Website* www.alyth.org.uk
(Est. 1933; Reg. Charity No. 247081). Regular services held Friday 6.30pm, Saturday 10.30am
and daily. *M.* Rabbi M. Goldsmith, Rabbi J. Levy; *Cantor,* C. Wunch, M. Michaels

Radlett Reform Synagogue
118 Watling Street, Radlett, Herts. WD7 7AA
Tel 01923 856 110
Email office@radlettreform.org.uk *Website* www.radlettreform.org.uk
Snr. Rabbi, Rabbi Paul Freedman; *Assoc. Rabbi*, Rabbi Celia Surget; *Synagogue Man.* Madeleine Turner

Sha'arei Tsedek: North London Reform Synagogue
120 Oakleigh Road North, Whetstone N20 9EZ
Tel 020 8445 3400
Email info@shaarei-tsedek.org.uk *Website* www.shaarei-tsedek.org.uk
(Reg. Charity No. 1076670). *Snr. Min.* C. Eimer; *Synagogue Man.* Perry Newton; *Rabbis*, James Baaden, Judith Levitt; *Admin.* Antonia Reed.
    Alonim Kindergarten *Tel* 020 3115 1610 *Email* info@alonim.co.uk

Shir Hayim (Hampstead Reform Jewish Community)
37a, Broadhurst Gardens, NW6 3QT
Email mail@shirhayim.org.uk
M. Rabbi L. Tabick; *Contact* M. Teper *Tel* 020 7794 8488

South West Essex and Settlement Reform Synagogue
Oaks Lane, Newbury Park, Essex IG2 7PL
Tel 020 8599 0936
Email admin@swesrs.org.uk *Website* www.swesrs.org.uk
(Est. 1956. Reg. Charity No. 236663). *Emer.* Rabbi H. Goldstein; M.A. Michaels, *M.* Rabbi Nancy Morris

Sukkat Shalom Reform Synagogue
1 Victory Road, Hermon Hill, Wanstead, E11 1UL
Tel 020 8530 3345
Email admin@sukkatshalom.me.uk *Website* www.sukkatshalom.org.uk
(Reg. Charity No. 283615). *Rabbi*, Rabbi Larry Becker; *Admin.* Frank Godson

Wimbledon and District Synagogue
1 Queensmere Road, Wimbledon Parkside, SW19 5QD
Tel 020 8946 4836 *Fax* 020 8944 7790
Email office@wimshul.org *Website* www.wimshul.org
(Est. 1949. Reg. Charity No. 1150678). *Admin.* Ms J. Penn

Liberal Judaism

For contact details: *See under* Religious Organisations

Beit Klal Yisrael
c/o The Montagu Centre, 21 Maple Street, London W1T 4BE
Tel 07505 477459
Email bkymail@gmail.com *Website* www.bky.org.uk

Bet Tikvah Synagogue (Barkingside)
129 Perrymans Farm Road, Ilford, Essex IG2 7LX
Tel 020 8554 9682 office hours Tuesday and Wednesday 10am-4pm, Thursday 10am-3pm, Sunday 10am-12pm
Email bettikvah@talktalkbusiness.net *Blog* http://bettikvah.blogspot.com
(Reg. Charity No. 283547). Services held every Friday night and Shabbat morning and on the evening and first morning of every festival. Phone Shul office for times. Bet Tikvah welcome non-members to all High Holy Day Services. Please contact the synagogue office. *M.* Rabbi D. Hulbert; *Admin.* Anne Fishman

Ealing Liberal Synagogue
Lynton Avenue, Drayton Green, Ealing, W13 0EB
Tel 020 8997 0528
Email office@ealingliberalsynagogue.org.uk *Website* www.ealingliberalsynagogue.org.uk
(Est. 1943. Reg. Charity No. 1037099). *M.* Rabbi J. Burden; *Admin.* D. Martin

Finchley Progressive Synagogue
54 Hutton Grove, N12 8DR
Tel 020 8446 4063
Email administrator@fps.org *Website* www.finchleyprogressivesynagogue.org
(Est. 1953. Reg. Charity No. 1071040). *M.* Rabbi R. Qassim Birk

Harrow & Wembley Progressive Synagogue
39 Bessborough Road, Harrow, HA1 3BS
Tel 020 8864 5323
Email info@hwps.org *Website* www.hwps.org
(Est. 1947. Reg. Charity No. 251172). *M.* Rabbi Frank Dabba Smith; *Admin.* A. Simon

Kehillah North London (formerly **North London Progressive Jewish Community**)
Postal Add. Office 8, 10 Buckhurst Road, Bexhill on Sea TN40 1QF
Tel 020 7403 3779
Email nlpjc@liberaljudaism.org *Website* www.nlpjc.org.uk
(Est. 2002). Services held first and third Saturday of each month and fourth Friday evening.
M. Rabbi Shulamit Ambalu *Admin.* Melanie Young

Kingston Liberal Synagogue
Rushett Road, Long Ditton, Surrey, KT7 0UX
Tel 020 8398 7400
Email office@klsonline.org *Website* www.klsonline.org
(Reg. Charity No. 270792). *M.* Rabbi C. Baginsky; *Ch.* S. Farrer; *Admin.* H. Mendelson

The Liberal Jewish Synagogue
28 St. John's Wood Road, London, NW8 7HA
Tel 020 7286 5181 *Fax* 020 7266 3591
Email ljs@ljs.org *Website* www.ljs.org
(Reg. Charity No. 235668). Established 1910 by the Jewish Religious Union, the LJS, as it is known, was the first Liberal synagogue in the UK. Synagogue rebuilt 1991. *Ch.* M. Hart; *Rabbi Emer.* Rabbi D.J. Goldberg OBE; *Snr. Rabbi* Rabbi A. Wright; *M.* Rabbi N. Janes; *Dir.* C. A. Bach

The Liberal Synagogue Elstree (formerly **Hertsmere Progressive**)
Elstree High Street, Elstree, Herts WD6 3EY
Tel 020 8953 8889
Email office@tlse.org.uk *Website* www.tlse.org.uk
M. Rabbi P. Tobias; *Hon. S.* D. Bennett; *Man.* R. Davey

Northwood and Pinner Liberal Synagogue
Oaklands Gate, Green Lane, Northwood, Middlesex HA6 3AA
Tel 01923 822 592
Email admin@npls.org.uk *Website* www.npls.org.uk
(Est. 1964. Reg. Charity No. 243618). Services held Erev Shabbat, Shabbat and Yom Tovim.
M. Emer Rabbi Dr. A. Goldstein; *Snr. Rabbi* A. Goldstein; *Rabbi,* Rabbi L. Mühlstein; *Hon. S.* S. Frais

South London Liberal Synagogue
P.O. Box 14475, 1 Prentis Road, Streatham, SW16 1ZW
Tel 020 8769 4787 (admin. office: Tuesday and Friday 11am-4.30pm) *Fax* 020 8664 6439
Email office@southlondon.org *Website* www.southlondon.org
(Est. 1929. Reg. Charity No. 2367711). Services: Friday evening Kabbalat Shabbat 7.30pm (6.30pm on the first Friday of the month); first and third Fridays are bring and share Chavurah suppers; Shabbat morning service 11am; Religion school is on Shabbat morning at 9.45am, toddlers group to Kabbalat Torah class. *Rabbi* Janet Darley

Southgate Progressive Synagogue
75 Chase Road, N14 4QY
Tel 020 8886 0977
Email sps@liberaljudaism.org *Website* www.sps.uk.com
(Est. 1943. Reg. Charity No. 239096). *Rabbi,* Rabbi Yuval Kerron; *Sec.* B. Martin

West Central Liberal Synagogue
The Montagu Centre, 21 Maple Street, W1T 4BE
Tel 020 7636 7627 *Fax* 020 7631 9838
Email wcls@liberaljudaism.org *Website* wwwwcls.org.uk
(Congregation Est. 1928; present synagogue opened 1954). Services held every Saturday
3pm, programmes for families at intervals throughout the year, Kabbalat Shabbat on some
Friday nights. Please check website for details. *Cantor*, Rev. A. Harman ALCM; *Ch.* Dr Julia
Wendon; *Hon. S.* Dr. Peter Philips

Woodford Liberal Synagogue
Marlborough Road, South Woodford, E18 1AR
Tel 020 8989 7619
Email info@woodfordliberal.org.uk *Website* www.woodfordliberal.org.uk
(Est. 1960. Reg. Charity No. 232980). Weekly Shabbat and Erev services held. *M.* Rabbi
R. Jacobi; *Ch.* B. Kamall; *Hon. S.* S. Muscovitch; *Hon. T.* M. Millenbach, J. Rabin

Independent Congregations

Belsize Square Synagogue
51 Belsize Square, London NW3 4HX
Tel 020 7794 3949 *Fax* 020 7431 4559
Email office@synagogue.org.uk *Website* www.synagogue.org.uk
(Est. 1939. Reg. Charity No. 1144866). An Independent Synagogue combining traditional
forms of worship with progressive ideals. *M.* Rabbi Dr. Stuart Altshuler; *Admin.* Lee Taylor;
Co-Ch. Suzanne Goldstein, John Abramson; *Hon. S.* V. Pollins; *T.* Steve Abbott

Edgware Adath Yisroel Congregation
265 Hale Lane, Edgware, Middlesex HA8 8NW
Tel 020 8238 2491
Email admin@eayc.org *Website* www.eayc.org
Rabbi Z. H. Lieberman *Burial Society Affiliate*

Ner Yisrael
The Crest (off Brent Street), Hendon, NW4 2HY
Tel 020 8202 6687 *Fax* 020 8203 5158
Email louise@neryisrael.co.uk *Website* www.neryisrael.co.uk
Services held three times a day. *M.* Rabbi A.A. Kimche. *Tel* 020 8202 6687; *Admin.* L. Brayam

Porat Yosef Synagogue and Community Centre
3 Bell Lane, London, NW4 2BP
Tel 020 8202 6058
Email info@poratyosef.com *Website* www.poratyosef.com
(Est. 1988). Moroccan Hebrew Congregation. *Pres.* Jacques Onona; *Sec.* B. Benarroch

Saatchi Synagogue
37-41 Grove End Road, NW8 9NG
Tel 020 7289 2367
Email hayley@saatchishul.org *Website* www.saatchishul.org
(Est. 1998. Reg. Charity No. 289066). Rabbi Mendel Cohen; *Admin.* H. Bartman

Sandys Row Synagogue, Spitalfields
4a Sandy's Row, E1 7HW
Tel 0207 377 6196
Email info@sandysrow.org.uk *Website* www.sandysrow.org.uk
(Est. 1854). Services: Mincha Monday-Thursday 1.30pm; Shabbat every two weeks. See
website for details. *Pres.* H. Rifkind; *T.* H. Freedman FCA; *Admin* E. Granger; *Warden* H. Gilbert

Sarah Klausner Synagogue
10A Canfield Gardens NW6
Tel 020 7722 6146

Synagogue Française de Londres (La)
101 Dunsmure Road, N16 5HT; Le Grand Rabbin Henri Brand, 54 Bethune Road, N16 5BD
Tel 020 8800 8612
Hon. T. Rabbi C. Pinter; *Hon. S.* I. Kraus

Walford Road Synagogue
99 Walford Road, Stoke Newington, N16 8EF
Tel 020 7249 1599
(Reg. Charity No. 1101200). Rabbi Avraham Citron; *Sec.* S. Raymond

Waltham Forest Hebrew Congregation
140 Boundary Road, E17 8LA
Tel Office 020 8509 0775 *Fax* 020 8518 8200
Email secretary@wfhc.co.uk
(Est. 1902). *M.* Revd. S. Myers; *Pres.* Mark Phillips; *Admin.* B. Rose

West End Great Synagogue (formerly in Dean Street, now in Great Cumberland Place)
32 Great Cumberland Place, W1H 7TN
Tel 020 7724 8121 *Fax* 020 7723 4413
Email wegs@clara.co.uk
(Est. 1880). *M.* Ari Cohen; *Admin.* N. Singer

Westminster Synagogue
Rutland Gardens, Knightsbridge, SW7 1BX
Tel 020 7584 3953 *Fax* 020 7581 8012
Email secretary@westminstersynagogue.org *Website* www.westminstersynagogue.org
(Est. 1957). *M.* Rabbi Dr T. Salamon; *Hd. Education,* N. Young; *Pres.* Lord Leigh of Hurleigh;
Ch. J. Ohrenstein

Religious Organisations

The London Eruvim

The North West London Eruv Committee was inaugurated in February 2003. The area covered by the eruv includes virtually all of NW4 and NW11, most of N2 and N3; and small parts of NW2, NW3 and NW7. This Eruv is under the supervision of the Dayanim of the London Beth Din. *Contact*: Judith Bornstein, 13 Holmfield Avenue, NW4 2LP
Tel 020 8202 ERUV/020 8202 3788 (recorded message with Eruv status)
Email info@nwlondoneruv.org *Website* www.nwlondoneruv.org *Twitter* @nwlondoneruv
The **Edgware Eruv** was inaugurated in 2006. The area covered by the eruv includes parts of HA8 and NW7. This eruv is under the supervision of Rabbi Zvi Lieberman of the Edgware Adath Yisroel Congregation and has the support and approval of the London Beth Din and local Edgware synagogues.
Contact: Edgware Eruv Committee, P.O. Box 594, Edgware, Middlesex HA8 4EE
Website www.edgwareeruv.org
(Reg. Charity No. 1111850). Both websites offer detailed maps of their jurisidictions. The Eruvim are inspected every week to check they are intact. This can be ascertained by visiting the respective websites after 12 noon on Friday. Observers of the Eruvim are invited to subscribe to the respective services maintained.

London Board for Shechita

Elscot House, Arcadia Ave, London N3 2JU
Tel 020 8349 9160 *Fax* 020 8346 2209
Email info@shechita.co.uk *Website* www.shechita.org
(Est. 1804. Reg. Charity No. 233467). Administer the affairs of Shechita in London, having an elected membership from the United Synagogue, the Federation of Synagogues and the Spanish and Portuguese Jews' Congregation. *Rabbinical Authority*, Dayan Y.Y. Lichtenstein, Dayan M. Gelley, Dayan S. Amor; *Ch. Exec.* Mark Goldwater

Sabbath Observance Employment Bureau

Unit 2, 107 Gloucester Place, London W1U 6BY
Tel 020 7224 3433
(Est. 1909. Reg. Charity No. 209451). To obtain employment for those who want to observe the Sabbath and Holy-days. *Tr.* I. M. Katz, S.D. Winegarten; *Man.* E. Statham; *Ch.* D. Winter, FCA

United Synagogue Women
c/o United Synagogue, 305 Ballards Lane, London N12 8GB
Tel 020 8343 5698
Email uswomen@theus.org.uk *Website* www.theus.org.uk/uswomen
(Est. 1968, rebranded 2009). US Women is the representative organisation for women members of the United Synagogue. It liaises directly with the United Synagogue Trustees in all matters relating to women in the United Synagogue. It promotes, facilitates and communicates the interests and full involvement of women as an integral part of the United Synagogue, and at local United Synagogue/Community level. It has representation on other Jewish organisational bodies. *Jt. H. Life Pres.* Stella Lucas MBE JP, Lady Elaine Sacks; *Co-Ch.* Dalia Cramer, Leonie Lewis

Ritual Baths (Mikvaot)

Central Mikvaot Board
See under Religious Organisations

Borehamwood & Elstree Mikveh
Croxdale Road, Borehamwood, WD6 4QF
Tel 07504 927 066; 020 8387 1945
Email mikveh@borehamwoodshul.org *Website* www.borehamwoodshul.org

Edgware & District Communal Mikveh
Edgware United Synagogue, Edgware Way, Edgware, Middlesex
Tel 020 8958 3233 *Fax* 020 8958 4004
Email mikveh@estrin.co.uk
(Reg. Charity No. 281586). Enquiries: Mandy Estrin *Tel* 020 8958 4488, 0780 133 2508

Ilford Mikveh
463 Cranbrook Road, Ilford, IG2 6EW
Appointments and correspondence 367 Cranbrook Road, Ilford, IG1 4UQ *Tel* 020 8554 8532

Kingsbury Mikveh *See* United Synagogue Mikveh
   Friends of the Kingsbury Mikveh – Educational and Support Group
Kingsbury United Synagogue, Hool Close, NW9 8UG
Tel 020 8204 6390 *Enquiries* 07890 932 340 (daytime only)
(Reg. Charity No. 1041629). *Hon. T.* Helene Leigh, 474 Kenton Road, Kenton, Middlesex HA3 9DN *Tel* 020 8206 1512

Mikveh of the Movement for Reform Judaism
Sternberg Centre, 80 East End Road, N3 2SY
Appointments essential. *Tel* 020 8349 5645

New Central London Mikveh
21 Andover Place, NW6 5ED
Appointments *Tel* 07870 696 570, 07989 858 615

North London Mikveh
adjoining 40 Queen Elizabeth's Walk, N16 (entrance Grazebrook Road)
Tel 020 8802 2554 *Fax* 020 8800 8764
Hon. S. M. Mannes

North West London Communal Mikvah
40 Golders Green Crescent, NW11 8LD
Tel 020 8457 5900, 020 8731 9494
10a Shirehall Lane, Hendon, NW4
Tel 020 8202 1427 (only open Friday nights and Yom Tov, by appointment)

Satmar Mikveh
62 Filey Avenue, N16
Tel 020 8806 3961

South London Mikveh
42 St. George's Road, Wimbledon SW19 4ED
Tel 07985 757 517

Email s@dubov.org
(Reg. Charity No. 1009208). By appointment only. *Hon. S. L.* Cohen. *Contact:* S. Dubov
Stamford Hill Mikveh
26 Lampard Grove, N16 (entrance in Margaret Road)
Tel 020 8806 3880
United Synagogue Mikveh
Kingsbury United Synagogue, Hool Close, NW9 8UG
Tel 020 8204 6390
Ch. F. Frank; *General Enq. Tel* 07890 932 340 (*See also* Friends Group, p.158)

Cemeteries

US = United Synagogue. F = Federation of Synagogues. UO = Union of Orthodox Hebrew Congregations. SP = Spanish and Portuguese Synagogue. W = Western Marble Arch Synagogue. WG = West End Great Synagogue. R = Reform. L = Liberal.

Alderney Road Cemetery (historic). Alderney Road, E1
Tel 020 8790 1445 Opened 1696–1853. Opening hours by appointment only (US)
Brady Street Cemetery (historic). Brady Street, E1
Opened 1761–1858. Opening hours by appointment only. (US)
Bullscross Ride Cemetery (current). Bulls Cross Ride, Cheshunt, Herts
Tel 01992 717820 Opened 1968. Opening hours 8am–4pm (W, L and WG)
Bushey Cemetery (current). Little Bushey Lane, Bushey, Herts
Tel 020 8950 7767 Opened 1947. Opening hours 8am–5pm (US)
East Ham Cemetery (reserves only). Marlow Road, E6 3QG
Tel 020 8471 2822 Opened 1919. Opening hours 9am–4.30pm (US)
Edgwarebury Lane Cemetery (current). Edgwarebury Lane, Edgware, HA8 8QP
Opened 1973. *Cemetery Dir.* Lester Harris 020 8958 0090/07967 656 733
Email director@ejbb-jbc.org.uk (SP, R, L, Independent (Belsize Square))
Edmonton Cemetery (current) Montagu Road, Edmonton, N18 2NF
Tel 020 8807 2268. Opened 1889. Opening hours 9am–3.30pm (F)
Enfield Cemetery (current), Carterhatch Lane, Enfield, Midlesex
Tel 020 8363 3384. Opened 1920s. Opening hours 8am–6pm (UO)
Hackney Cemetery (historic). Lauriston Road, E9
Tel 020 8985 1527. Opened 1788–1886 (US)
Hoop Lane Cemetery (current) Hoop Lane, NW11 7EU
Tel 020 8455 2569. Opened 1897. *Cemetery Dir.* Paul Van der Hulks *Tel* 020 8455 2569/
07967 656 733 *Email* director@ejbb-jbc.org.uk Opening hours 8.30am–5pm. (SP and R)
Kingsbury Road Cemetery Kingsbury Road (off Balls Pond Road), N1
Opened 1840–1951 (R)
Liberal Jewish Cemetery (current) The Lodge, Pound Lane, NW10 2HG
Opened 1914. Opening hours 8am–5pm (L)
Mile End Road (Velho) (historic) behind 253 Mile End Road, E1
Tel 020 8958 3388 Opened 1657–1735. Opening hours by appointment. Key available
from Superintendent (SP)
Mile End Road (Novo Beth Chaim) (historic) 329 Mile End Road, E1
Tel 020 8958 3388 Opened 1733–1918. Opening hours by appointment. Key available
from Superintendent (SP)
Plashet Cemetery (reserves only) 361 High Street North E12 6PQ
Tel 020 8472 055 Opened 1896. Opening hours 9am–3pm. Nobody available on site.
Call East Ham to confirm open (US)
Queen's Elm Parade Cemetery (historic) Queen's Elm Parade, Chelsea SW3
Opened 1815–1884. Opening hours by appointment. Key available from Head Office *Tel* 020
7724 7702 (W)
Rainham Cemetery (current) Upminster Road North, Rainham, Essex
Tel 01708 552 825 Opened 1936. Opening hours 9am–3.30pm (F)

Rowan Road Cemetery (current) 3 Rowan Road, SW16 5JF
Opened 1915. Opening hours 8am–4pm. Head Office Tel 020 7724 7702 (WG)
Silver Street Cemetery (current) Silver Street, Goffs Oak, Cheshunt, Herts
Tel 020 8802 6262, 01707 874 220. Opened 1963. Opening hours 8am–6pm (UO).
Waltham Abbey Cemetery (current) Skillet Hill (Honey Lane), Waltham Abbey, Essex,
EN9 3QS
Tel 01992 714492 Fax 01992 650735 Opened 1857. Opening hours 9am–2.30pm. There
is nobody available on site. Call East Ham to confirm open (US).
West Ham Cemetery (reserves only) Buckingham Road, Forest Gate, E15
Tel 020 8472 0554 (US).
Western Synagogue Cemetery (current) Montagu Road, Edmonton N18 2NF
Opened 1890s. Opening hours 8am–4pm. Next to Federation cemetery. Head Office
Tel 020 7724 7702 (W).
Willesden Cemetery (reserves only) Glebe Road, NW10 2JE
Tel 020 8459 0394. Opened 1873. Opening hours 9am–5pm (US).

Memorials

Battle of Britain Memorial, Embankment, Westminster
Contains names of over 40 Battle of Britain Jewish Airmen.
Boer War Memorial Union Jack Club, Waterloo Road
Firefighters Memorial Peter's Hill, Embankment, South Side
Names of 50 Jewish Firemen and Firewomen.
Holocaust Memorial and Garden Hyde Park, near Hyde Park Corner
Opened in July 1983, on a site given to the BoD by the British Government.
Holocaust Memorial Waltham Abbey Cemetery, Upshire Hall, Honey Lane, Essex, EN9 3QS
Consecrated 1985 under United Synagogue auspices.
Holocaust Memorial Rainham Cemetery, Upminster Road North, Rainham, Essex
Holocaust Memorial Sternberg Centre, 80 East End Road, Finchley N3
Kindertransport Statues Liverpool Street Station
Kindertransport Plaque House of Commons
Memorial to the 5000 German and Austrian Jewish refugee soldiers, who fled the Nazis,
who trained at Richborough Camp, nearby, in 1939-41 Barbican arch in Sandwich, Kent.
Memorial with Magen David and description of his act of bravery, to Major Simmon
Latutin, GC holder, Royal Academy of Music foyer, Marylebone Road.
Memorial to General Wingate (and Chindits), Embankment/MoD
Inscribed 'Inspiration of the Israel Defence Forces'.
Memorial in Willesden Jewish Cemetery Beaconsfield Road, NW10
To Jewish Servicemen and Women in the British Armed Forces who died in the two World
Wars and have no known graves. Annual service organised by Ajex.
Memorial Plaque Arthaus Hackney, Richmond Road, E8
In memory of the Israeli athletes murdered at the 1972 Olympics.
The National Inventory of War Memorials, Imperial War Museum
Lists all WWI and WWII Jewish Memorials to War dead located in the UK, in Synagogues,
Cemeteries, Clubs etc.
Prisoners' Memorial Gladstone Park, Dollis Hill Lane, NW2
To those who died in prisoner-of-war camps and concentration camps during WWII.
Annual service jointly organised by Ajex and the Royal British Legion.
Plaque entrance foyer of Homerton Hospital, Hackney
Twinning of Homerton with Rambam Hospital Haifa and St George's Grenada. Unveiled by
Ambassador of Israel 2006.
RAF Church crypt of St Clements Danes, Strand
Memorial plaque with 12 tribes emblems to British and Israeli RAF personnel in the
Second World War.
Raoul Wallenberg Statue Great Cumberland Place, London W1
Royal Fusiliers City of London Regiment Memorial High Holborn, by City boundary

The names of the 38th, 39th and 40th Jewish Battalions are inscribed on the monument, together with all other battalions who served in the First World War. Ajex is represented at the annual service. For Memorials in the rest of the UK, see page 178.

Educational Organisations

Withdrawal on Friday Afternoons

When the Sabbath begins at 5pm or earlier, parents of Jewish children attending either State or State-aided schools can request that their children be withdrawn at such time as to reach their homes before the commencement of the Sabbath. Such requests should be submitted to the Head in writing.

GENERAL

Ackerman Resource Centre

Redbridge JCC, Woodford Bridge Road, Ilford, Essex, IG5 4LN
Tel 020 8551 0017 *Fax* 020 8551 9027
The Resource Centre was created for informal Jewish and Israel education. The Centre has operated in the community for 20 years as a resource for educators who need support and advice in this field. The Resource Centre is a focus for leadership training in the community. *Com. Res. Worker,* Mia Davis

Aish UK

379 Hendon Way, NW4 3LP
Tel 020 8457 4444 *Fax* 020 8457 4445
Email info@aish.org.uk *Website* www.aish.org.uk
(Est 1992; Reg. Charity No. 1069048). Nationwide innovative and dynamic social, educational and leadership opportunities for otherwise unaffiliated young Jews aged 17-35. Including Jewish identity travel to Israel and other destinations for hundreds of participants annually. Independently authenticated by MORI as effectively combating intermarriage and assimilation in the UK. Igniting Jewish commitment and the shouldering of responsibility in the community amongst its graduate student body. Hundreds of alumni subsequently involved in Jewish leadership/pursuing careers in community. Full time branches in Birmingham, Essex, Manchester and London. *Dir.* Rabbi N. Schiff; *Ch.* J. Faith

Binoh (part of Norwood's Education Service)

Tel 020 8457 4745 *Fax* 020 8203 8233
Email binoh@norwood.org.uk *Website* www.norwood.org.uk
(Registered as Hope Charity. Reg. Charity No. 1056674). Binoh is a specialist education and therapy service, run by Norwood, which provides specialist multi-professional support to children with additional and/or special education needs. Binoh works with children within their own school environment or through services provided from Norwood's Children & Family Centres in Hendon and Hackney. Binoh also provides early years services for the under-fives and a transition programme for students aged 16-19. Binoh offers art therapy, educational psychology, occupational therapy, teaching services (including religious studies) and speech and language therapy. In addition to directly supporting children, Binoh also supports schools, professionals and families. Services include consultations, INSET (in-service training) and mentoring.

The Hope Centre

228 Walm Lane, London NW2 3BS
Tel 020 8809 8240
Email hope@norwood.org.uk *Website* www.hope-centre.org.uk
(Reg. Charity No. 1056674). The Hope Centre is run by Norwood and provides services for children and young people, aged 3-19, with a wide range of learning disabilities and educational needs. Hope's multi-professional staff specialise in developing children's thinking skills and give students the tools to become confident and independent learners. Hope offers a wide range of services, including dynamic assessment, speech and language therapy and occupational therapy. Tuition is provided either on a one-to-one basis or in small groups. Training packages are also available for professionals and parents. *Hd. of Service* Luci Austin

Interlink Foundation
Fourth Floor Offices, 97 Stamford Hill, N16 5DN
Tel 020 8802 2469 *Fax* 020 8800 5153
Email admin@interlink-foundation.org.uk *Website* www.interlink-foundation.org.uk
(Reg. Charity No. 1079311, Company Limited by guarantee Reg. No. 3852756). The
Interlink Foundation is the Association of Orthodox Jewish charities. Membership services
include: consultancy and training, regular information bulletin, representation and policy
work. *Chief Exec.* Chaya Spitz

J-Link
c/o Aish, 379 Hendon Way, Hendon, London NW4 3LP
Tel 020 8457 2117 *Fax* 020 8457 4445
Email info@jlink.org.uk
(Est. 1993; Reg. Charity No. 1062551). Schools' J–Link aims to raise the sense of identity
and commitment of Jewish pupils in non-Jewish secondary schools. It runs school assemblies
and classes, less formal Jewish society meetings and lunch-and-learn sessions, and totally
informal parties at Succot, Purim and other occasions. It offers a broad Jewish input by co-
opting rabbis, youth workers, representatives of Jewish organisations and visiting speakers
from abroad. It also runs training programmes for non-Jewish teachers who are teaching
Judaism. Schools' J-Link operates in 60 schools in the London area and several provincial
towns, and communicates with upwards of 6,000 Jewish youngsters each year. *Dir.* Rabbi
B. Landau

Jewish Community Centre for London
6 Park End, NW3 2SE
Tel 020 7431 9866 *Fax* 020 7431 6483
Email info@jcclondon.org.uk *Website* www.jcclondon.org.uk
(Reg. Charity No. 1105622). *Ch.* Debbie Klein; *Chief Exec.* Nick Viner

Jewish Learning Exchange (JLE)
152-154 Golders Green Road, NW11 8HE
Tel 020 8458 4588 *Fax* 020 8458 4587
Email jle@jle.org.uk *Website* www.jle.org.uk
(Est. 1988. Reg. Charity No. 292886). The JLE is an educational and social centre for Jews of
all backgrounds between the ages of 18-35. Through its wide variety of classes, events
and trips, it allows its students to connect to their traditional roots and to meet like-minded
people in a warm and welcoming environment. *Dir.* Rabbi Danny Kirsch; *Dir. Education,*
Rabbi Reuven Stepsky; *Dir. Young Professionals*, Rabbi Benjy Morgan; *Snr. Lecturer*, Rabbi
David Akiva Tatz

Jewish Resource Centre (JRC)
University of Roehampton, The Froebel College, School of Education, Roehampton Lane,
SW15 5PJ
www.roehampton.ac.uk/jrc
(Est. 1996). Serves as a resource for all sections of the Jewish community in South London,
as well as for the non-Jewish teaching community. The JRC has one of the University's Special
Collections which can be accessed online or for research, study and personal interest if you
make an appointment. The JRC hosts educational and cultural events. Staff are available
to visit synagogues, religion schools/hederim and schools in the area to run events.

SCHOOLS

Akiva School
The Sternberg Centre, 80 East End Road, N3 2SY
Tel 020 8349 4980 *Fax* 020 8349 4959
Email admin@akivaschool.org *Website* www.akivaschool.org
(Est. 1981). Voluntary aided State Primary with a progressive Jewish Ethos. Education
for pupils, aged 4-11 years. *Hd.* Susy Stone MA

Avigdor Hirsch Torah Temimah Primary School
Parkside, Dollis Hill, London NW2 6RJ
Tel 020 8450 4377 *Fax* 020 8208 7998
Email admin@torahtemimah.brent.sch.uk
(Est. 1989. Reg. Charity No. 100146). Voluntary-aided (London Borough of Brent)
Orthodox Jewish Primary School and Nursery for boys aged 3-11. *Menahel* Rabbi E. Klyne
MA(Ed); *Hd.* Rabbi Y. Freeman B.Sc; *Ch. of Govs.* U. Kaplan

Beth Jacob Seminary of London
196–198 Lordship Road, N16 5ES
Tel 020 8800 4719 *Fax* 020 8800 6067
Email admin@londonsem.org.uk
(Reg. Charity No. 312913). Teacher Training College and finishing school for Hebrew
Studies and vocational qualifications. *Princ.* Rabbi B. Dunner

Bushey Gan Nursery and Pre School
177–189 Sparrows Herne, Bushey, Herts, WD23 1AJ
Tel 020 8386 1515 *Mobile* 07733 068 358
Email head@busheyganim.org
Website www.busheyganim.org.uk
(ages 2-rising 5). *Hd.* Ms D. Boder-Cohn Cert. Ed. AETC

Clore Shalom School
Hugo Gryn Way, Shenley, Herts WD7 9BL
Tel 01923 855 631 *Fax* 01923 853 722
Email admin@cloreshalom.herts.sch.uk
(Est. 1999). Voluntary-aided primary school (3-11). Pluralist Jewish day school. *Hd.*
Sheree Oxenham

Clore Tikva School Redbridge
115 Fullwell Avenue, Ilford, Essex IG6 2JN
Tel 020 8551 1097 *Fax* 020 8551 2070
(Est. 1999). Community, state-aided primary school (4-11), under Reform, Masorti and
Liberal auspices. *Hd.* L. Rosenberg; *Admin.* Valerie Garnelas

Hasmonean High School:
 Boys' Campus, 11/18 Holders Hill Road, NW4 1NA *Tel* 020 8203 1411 *Fax* 020 8202 4526
 Girls' Campus, 2/4 Page Street, NW7 2EU *Tel* 020 8203 4294 *Fax* 020 8202 4527
Website www.hasmonean.co.uk
Voluntary Aided, London Borough of Barnet. *Exec. Hd.* Rabbi D. Meyer, BA, MBA, NPQH

Hasmonean Pre-Nursery
8-10 Shirehall Lane, NW4 2PD
Tel 020 8201 6252 *Fax* 020 8202 1605
(children ages 2-3). *Man.* J. Truman

Hasmonean Primary School
8-10 Shirehall Lane, NW4 2PD
Tel 020 8202 7704 *Fax* 020 8202 1605
Email admin@hasmonean-pri.barnet.sch.uk
(Boys and Girls ages 3-11) *Princ.* Rabbi M. Ginsbury; *Hd.* A. Shaw, BA (Hons.), MA Cert Ed.

Hertsmere Jewish Primary School
Watling Street, Radlett, Herts WD7 7LQ
Tel 01923 855857 *Fax* 01923 853399
Email admin@hjps.herts.sch.uk
Hd. Steven Isaacs; *Admin.* K. Thomas. Voluntary-aided primary school for ages 3-11.

Ilford Jewish Primary School
Forest Road, Ilford, Essex IG6 3HB
Tel 020 8498 1350/1351
Email admin@ijpsonline.co.uk *Website* www.ijpsonline.co.uk
Exec. Hd. Denise Hughes

Immanuel College (The Charles Kalms, Henry Ronson Immanuel College)
Elstree Road, Bushey, Herts WD23 4EB
Tel 020 8950 0604 *Fax* 020 8950 8687
Email enquiries@immanuel.herts.sch.uk *Website* www.immanuelcollege.co.uk
(Reg Charity No. 803179). Founded by Chief Rabbi Jakobovits, Orthodox. Immanuel College opened in 1990 with a pupil roll of 38. The Immanuel College Preparatory School opened in September 2011. The college is characterised by academic excellence, expert pastoral care and inspiring Jewish education. *Hd.* Charles Dormer MA (Cantab); *Dep. Hd. Pastoral* Beth Kerr (BSc); *Dep. Hd. Jewish Life and Learning*, Rabbi David Riffkin BA, MA

Independent Jewish Day School
46 Green Lane, NW4 2AH
Tel 020 8203 2299
Email office@ijds.co.uk
(Est. 1979). Orthodox Primary School & Kindergarten. *Ch.* A. Levey; *Princ.* A. A. Kimche, BA; *Hd.* Rabbi J. Ebrahimoff

JCOSS (Jewish Community Secondary School)
Castlewood Road, New Barnet, Herts EN5 9GE
Tel 020 8344 2220
Email admin@jcoss.barnet.sch.uk *Website* www.jcoss.org
(Reg. Charity No. 1107705). Secondary School for 11-19 year olds.

Jewish Secondary Schools Movement
11/18 Holders Hill Road, NW4 1NA
Tel 020 8203 1411 *Fax* 020 8202 4526
(Est. 1929).

J.F.S. School
The Mall, Kenton HA3 9TE
Tel 020 8206 3100
Email admin@jfs.brent.sch.uk
(Est. 1732). *Hd.* J. Miller, BSc (Hons), MA, NPQH; *Clerk to Govs.* Dr. A. Fox

Kerem School (including **Kerem Early Years Unit**)
Norrice Lea, N2 0RE
Tel 020 8455 0909
Email admin@kerem.org.uk
(Boys and Girls rising 4-11) *Hd.* A. Burns

King Solomon High School
Forest Road, Barkingside, Ilford, Essex IG6 3HB
Tel 020 8498-1300 *Fax* 020 8498 1333
Email info@kshsonline.com
Acting Hd. Dr P. Doherty; *Ch. of Govs.* S. Sollosi; *Denominational Body:* United Synagogue; *Authority* London Borough of Redbridge

Kisharon Organisation
Head Office, 54 Parson Street, NW4 1TP
Tel 020 8203 2233 *Fax* 020 8731 7005
Email info@Kisharon.org.uk *Website* www.kisharon.org.uk
(Reg. Charity No. 271519). *Chief Exec.* Dr Beverley Jacobson; *Ch. of Govs.* Phillip Goldberg

Kisharon Day School
1011 Finchley Road, Golders Green, NW11 7HB
Tel 020 8455 7483
Sora Kopfstein *Email* kisharondayschool@kisharon.org.uk

Tuffkid Nursery
3 Western Avenue, London NW11 9HG
Tel 020 8201 8488
Janice Marriott *Email* tuffkid@kisharon.org.uk

Law of Truth Talmudical College
50 Knightland Road, E5 9HS *Corr.* 31 Leadale Road, London N16 6BZ
Tel 020 8802 7684 *Fax* 020 8806 9318. Students: 020 8806 6642
Email schneidersyeshivah@gmail.com
(Est. by Rabbi M. Szneider in Memel, 1911, Frankfurt 1918, London 1938. Reg. Charity No. 312845). *Princ.* Rabbi M. Halpern

Lubavitch Children's Centre
1 Northfield Road, N16 5RL
Tel 020 8809 9050
Website www.lubavitchchildrenscentre.com
Admin. D.L. Sudak

Lubavitch Foundation
107-115 Stamford Hill, N16 5RP
Tel 020 8800 0022 *Fax* 020 8809 7324
Email mail@chabad.org.uk *Website* www.chabad.org.uk
(Est. 1959). To further Jewish religious education, identity and commitment. Separate departments for adult education, summer and day camps, youth clubs and training, university counsellors, publications, welfare, and organisations concerned with Israel. *Princ.* Rabbi N. Sudak, OBE; *Admin.* Rabbi I. H. Sufrin. Lubavitch House School *Tel* 020 8809 7476; Girls' Senior, 107/109 Stamford Hill, N16 *Tel* 020 8800 0022; *Hd.* Rabbi S. Lew. Boys', 133/135 Clapton Common E5 *Tel* 020 8800 1044; Girls' Primary, 111-115 Stamford Hill, N16 5RP *Tel* 020 8800 0022 *Fax* 020 8809 7324; *Hd.* F. Sudak. Kindergarten, 107 Stamford Hill, N16 5RP *Tel* 020 8800 0022; *Admin.* B. Raskin; *Libr.* Zvi Rabin, ALA *Tel* 020 8800 5823; Vista Vocational Training, 1 Northfield Road, N16 5RL *Tel* 020 8802 8772; *Man.* H. Lew. Women's Centre, 19 Northfield Road, N16 5RL *Tel* 020 8809 6508; *Admin.* R. Bernstein

Menorah Foundation School
Abbots Road, Burnt Oak, Edgware HA8 0QS
Tel 020 8906 9992 *Fax* 020 8906 9993
Orthodox. *Hd.* C. Neuberger, BSc, PGCE, NPQH; *Princ.* Rabbi D. Roberts; *Ch.* Joe Holder

Menorah Primary School (and Menorah Nursery)
The Wohl Campus, 1-3 The Drive, NW11 9SP
Tel 020 8458 1276
(Est. 1944). Voluntary Aided (London Borough of Barnet) for Boys & Girls ages 3-11. *Princ.* Rabbi Y. M. Greenberg; *Hd.* J. Menczer

MST College
240-242 Hendon Way, NW4 3NL
Tel/Fax 020 8202 2212
Orthodox teacher training college offering a range of accredited Degree courses leading to Qualified Teacher Status. *Princ.* Michael Cohen BA, M.Phil, PGCE; *Reg.* Dr. Abbott Katz MA Ph.D; *College Man.* Bernice Black

Naima Jewish Preparatory School (Independent)
21 Andover Place, NW6 5ED
Tel 020 7328 2802 *Fax* 020 7624 0161
Website www.naimajps.co.uk
(Reg. Charity No. 289066). For children aged 2-11 years offering a broad secular curriculum together with rich programme of Orthodox Jewish studies. Catering for children of all abilities through flexible learning programme. *Hd. Princ.* Rabbi Dr A. Levy; *Hd.* B. Pratt

Nancy Reuben Primary School
48 Finchley Lane, Hendon NW4 1DJ
Tel 020 8202 5646
Email office@nrps.co.uk
Princ. A. Haye

North West London Jewish Day School
180 Willesden Lane, NW6 7PP
Tel 020 8459 3378 *Fax* 020 8451 7298
Email admin@nwljds.org.uk *Website* www.nwljds.org.uk

(Est. 1945). Voluntary Aided. Modern Orthodox Primary school and nursery for boys and girls, 3-11 *Princ.* Dayan I. Binstock; *Hd.* Rabbi D.S. Kerbel MA, NPQH; *Ch. of Govs.* P. Gottlieb; *Patron,* Chief Rabbi Ephraim Mirvis

Pardes House Grammar School
Hendon Lane, N3 1SA
Tel 020 8349 4222
Email admin@phgrammar.co.uk
Hd. Princ. Rabbi E. Halpern; *Hd. M.* Rabbi D. Dunner

Pardes House Kindergarten
Hendon Lane, N3 1SA
Tel 020 8371 8292
Hd. Y. Wajnstock

Pardes House Primary School
Hendon Lane, N3 1SA
Tel 020 8343 3568
Email office@pardeshouse.com
H. Princ. Rabbi E. Halpern; *Hd.* J. Sager; *Menahel* Rabbi G. Abeless

Rosh Pinah Primary School
(Est. 1956). Glengall Road, Edgware, Middlesex HA8 8TE
Tel 020 8958 8599 *Fax* 020 8905 4853
Email admin@rpps.org.uk *Website* www.rpps.org.uk
H. Princ. Rabbi D. Lister; *Hd.* A. Gartland; *Admin.* S. Stern. Voluntary aided Orthodox Jewish Primary School in the London Borough of Barnet for boys and girls aged 3-11.

Sharon Kindergarten
Finchley Synagogue, Kinloss Gardens, N3 3DU
Tel 020 8346 2039
Email info@sharonkindergarten.org
(For children ages 2½-5) *Man.* T. E. Elek

Side by Side Kids Ltd
9 Big Hill, E5 9HH
Tel 020 8880 8300 *Fax* 020 8880 8341
Side by Side is an integrated nursery and special needs school providing therapy and education for children and a support network for their families. *Hd.* Gerald Lebrett

Sinai Jewish PrimarySchool
Shakespeare Drive, Kenton, Harrow, Middlesex HA3 9UD
Tel 020 8204 1550
Email admin@sinai.brent.sch.uk *Website* www.sinaischool.com
(Est. 1981). Orthodox. Voluntary aided primary school for boys & girls, aged 3-11. *Ch. Govs.* L. Glassar; *Hd.* R. Leach *Denominational body* Board of Religious Education; *Authority* London Borough of Brent. *School Rabbi* Rabbi Geoffrey Shisler

Tashbar Primary School
47-49 Mowbray Road, Edgware, Middlesex HA8 8JL
Tel 020 8958 5162
Email secretary@tashbar.co.uk
(Est. 2005. Reg. Charity No. 1110737). Independent Strictly Orthodox primary school for boys aged 3-11. *Princ.* Rabbi N Yaffe; *Associate Hd. Teacher,* A. Wolfson B.Ed(Hons); MA, M.Ed, NPQH

Torah Centre Trust
84 Leadale Road, N15 6BH
Tel 020 8802 3586
(Est. 1975). To provide full or part-time facilities for children, in particular those from uncommitted families, to enable them to further their secular and Hebrew education *Educ. Dir.* Rabbi M. Bernstein, B.Ed

Wolfson Hillel Primary School
154 Chase Road, Southgate, N14 4LG

Tel 020 8882 6487 *Fax* 020 8882 7965
Email schooloffice@wolfsonhillel.enfield.sch.uk *Website* wwwwolfsonhillel.enfield.sch.uk
(Est. 1992). Voluntary aided primary school for boys & girls aged 3-11. *Ch. Govs.* H. Cohen;
Hd. K. Jowett (*Authority* London Borough of Enfield)

Yeshiva Gedola Lubavitch
3/5 Kingsley Way, N2 0EH
Tel 020 8458 3212
Rosh Yeshiva Rabbi I. M. Hertz

Yeshivah Ohel Moshe Etz Chaim
85 Bridge Lane, NW11
Tel 020 8458 5149
(Reg. Charity No. 312232). *Princ.* Rabbi Z. Rabi

Yesodey Hatorah Schools
2 and 4 Amhurst Park, N16 5AE
Tel 020 8800 8612
(Est. 1943). Chassidish. *Princ.* Rabbi A. Pinter; *V. Pres.* Rabbi C. Pinter
Nursery, 2 Amhurst Park, N16 SAE *Tel* 020 8800 9221 *Hd.* Shine
Kindergarten, 2 Amhurst Park, N16 5AE *Tel* 020 8800 8612 *Matron* Mrs Shine.
Primary School (Boys), 2 Amhurst Park, N16 5AE *Tel* 020 8800 8612 *Princ.* Rabbi A.
Pinter; *Menahel* Rabbi P. Rosenberg
Senior School (Boys), 4 Amhurst Park, N16 5AE *Tel* 020 8800 8612 *Princ.* Rabbi A. Pinter;
Menahel Rabbi D. Weiler
Primary School (Girls), 153 Stamford Hill, N16 5LG *Tel* 020 8800 8612 *Princ.* Rabbi A.
Pinter; *Hd.* D. Luria
Senior School (Girls), Egerton Road, N16 6UB *Tel* 020 8826 5500 *Princ.* Rabbi A. Pinter;
Hd. R. Pinter

Welfare Organisations

Abbeyfield Camden (Jewish) Society
59 Belmont Road, Bushey, Herts WD23 2JR *Tel* 01923 213 964
House Man. Margaret Kazanecka *Email* belmontlodge@virginmedia.com *Admin.* G. Benson
Tel 020 8423 1351
Website wwwjewishabbeyfield.org.uk
The Society runs one small supported sheltered home for elderly residents.
House: Belmont Lodge, 59 Belmont Road, Bushey, Herts WD23 2JR

Agudas Israel Housing Association Ltd
206 Lordship Road, N16 5ES
Tel 020 8802 3819/0161 708 0559 (Manchester) *Fax* 020 8809 6206
Email info@aihaltd.co.uk
(Reg. Charity No. 23535). *Chief Exec.* Ita Symons, MBE

Schonfeld Square Foundation
1 Schonfeld Square, Lordship Road, N16 0QQ
Tel 020 8802 3819 *Fax* 020 8809 6206
Email info@aihaltd.co.uk
(Reg. Charity No. 1049179). *Co-ord.* Ita Symons, MBE
Includes ownership of: **Beenstock Home** (Home for the Frail and Elderly)
19–21 Northumberland Street, Salford, M7 4RP *Tel* 0161 792 1515 *Fax* 0161 792 1616
Email admin@beenstock.plus.com *Care Man.* C. Laurence
Beis Brucha (Mother and Baby Home)
208 Lordship Road, N16 5ES
Tel 020 8211 8081
Man. M. Hirschler *Email* management@beisbrucha.co.uk
Beis Pinchos (Residential and Nursing Home for the Frail and Elderly), and
Fradel Lodge (Sheltered Accommodation for the Frail and Elderly)
Schonfeld Square, Lordship Road, N16 0QQ

Tel 020 8802 7477 *Fax* 020 8809 7000
Email schonfeld@aihaltd.co.uk
Care Man. Barbara Carzolio; *Social Man.* H. Pesach
  Beis Rochel (Supported Housing for Vulnerable Women)
52 Lordship Park, N16 5UD
Tel 020 8802 2160 (Office), 020 8802 2909 (Residents)
Email lordship52@btinternet.com
  4 Rookwood Road
N16 6SS (Supported Housing for Vulnerable Men)
Tel (Office) 020 8800 2860, (Residents) 020 8802 0073
Email info@aihaltd.co.uk

Ahada Bereavement Counselling
370 Cranbrook Road, Gants Hill, Ilford, Essex IG2 6HY
Tel 07758 727 328
Email admin@empathy.uk.net *Website* www.empathy.uk.net
(Est. 1986. Incorporated into Empathy Counselling Services, 2012. Reg. Charity No. 1118894).
Offers free confidential counselling and support for members of the Jewish community
who are experiencing difficulties as a result of bereavement. Provides trained voluntary
counsellors who are professionally supervised. Covers Redbridge, neighbouring boroughs
and other areas of Essex. *Tru.* Dr. David Hamilton, Robert Jackson, Rabbi Maurice
Michaels, Marc Preston

Arbib Lucas Charity
(Reg. Charity No. 208666). Arbib Lucas responds to requests for small grants to help needy
women in the community with specific practical items to benefit their day-to-day living in the
long term. *Hon. S.* Marianne Temple, 17 Heronsforde, W13 8JE

Brenner Jewish Community Centre
Raine House, 91-93, Stamford Hill, N16 5TP
Tel 020 8442 7750
Email brenner@jcare.org *Website* www.jewishcare.org
(Reg. Charity No. 802559). Administered by Jewish Care. Community Centre for the local
Jewish community *Centre Man.* L. M. Harris

Camp Simcha
The House, 12 Queens Road, NW4 2TH
Tel 020 8202 9297
Email office@campsimcha.org.uk www.campsimcha.org.uk
(Charity No. 1044685). Camp Simcha exists to improve the quality of life for Jewish
children and their families in the UK with cancer and other life-threatening illness. *Chief
Exec.* N. Goldschneider

Chevrat Bikkur Cholimx (Chevrat Bikkur Cholim)
463a Finchley Road, NW3 6HN
Tel 020 7435 0836
Email info@ukfos.org *Website* www.ukfos.org
(Est. 1947. Reg. Charity No. 91468A). Provides home helps/carers to the sick, needy and
elderly. *Pres.* S. Sackman; *Hd.* M. Wechsler; *Gen. Sec.* N. Brotzen

Empathy Counselling Services
370 Cranbrook Road, Gants Hill, Ilford, Essex IG2 6HY
Tel 07758 727 328
Email admin@empathy.uk.net *Website* www.empathy.uk.net
(Reg. Charity No. 1118894). Incorporating Ahada Bereavement Counselling. Offers free
confidential counselling for members of Jewish families affected by loss, bereavement,
separation and divorce, economic loss, loss of expectations, and of potential. Counsellors
are fully qualified and professionally supervised. Covers Redbridge and neighbouring
boroughs. *Tru.* Dr David Hamilton, Robert Jackson, Rabbi Maurice Michaels, Marc Preston;
Dir. Andrea Wershof

Finchley Kosher Lunch Service (Meals-on-Wheels for the housebound and disabled)
Covers Edgware, Finchley, Golders Green, Hampstead Garden Suburb, Hendon, Mill Hill.

Hon. T. Ruth Freed, Tel 020 8202 8129. *Admin.* by the League of Jewish Women. (*See* p. 49)

Food for the Jewish Poor
To provide (a) food throughout the year; (b) groceries during Passover; (c) special relief for approved emergency cases. (*See* Jewish Care).

Hagadolim Charitable Organisation
(Est. 1950). To provide financial assistance to Homes and charities in England and Israel, and to visit and provide comforts in private homes in the Home Counties. *Ch.* L. Dunitz; *Jt. T.* B. Wallach, R. J. Dunitz; *Sec.* S. Levy, 4 Edgwarebury Court, Edgwarebury Lane, Edgware, Middlesex HA8 8LP *Tel* 020 8958 8558

Hospital Kosher Meals Service
Lanmor House, 370/386 High Road, Wembley, Middlesex HA9 6AX
Tel 020 8795 2058 *Fax* 020 8900 2462
Email hkms@btconnect.com *Website* www.hkms.org.uk
(Reg. Charity No. 1025601). Provides supervised kosher meals to patients in hospitals throughout Greater London. *Ch.* M.G. Freedman, MBA, FCA; *V. Ch.* H. Glyn, BSc, FRICS; *Sec.* G. Calvert; *Admin.* E. Stone; *Hospital Liaison Off.* S. Patashnik

The Industrial Dwellings Society (1885) Ltd
Head Office Ockway House, 41 Stamford Hill, London N16 5SR
Tel 020 8800 9606*Fax* 020 8800 5990
Email housing@ids.org.uk *Website* www.ids.org.uk
(Industrial & Provident Society Reg. No. 14044; Homes and Communities Agency Reg. No. L0266). IDS is a housing association founded by the Rothschild family and other Jewish philanthropists. Direct applications can be made for sheltered housing schemes including Ajex House where priority is given to Jewish Ex-service men and women and their dependants. *Ch.* Jonathan Davies; *Chief Exec.* Paul Westbrook

Jewish Aged Needy Pension Society
(Est. 1829. Reg. Charity No. 206262). Provides pensions for members of the Jewish community aged 60 or over, who have known better times and who, in their old age, find themselves in reduced circumstances. Also supplements income provided from statutory sources. Services to the middle-class of society who find themselves in greater financial need and who do not seem to fall within the purview of any other charitable organisations. *Pres.* M.E.G. Prince; *T.* A.H.E. Prince; *Hon. S.* G. B. Rigal; *Sec./Admin.* Sheila A. Taylor 34 Dalkeith Grove, Stanmore, Middlesex HA7 4EG *Tel* 020 8958 5390 *Fax* 020 8958 8046

Jewish Bereavement Counselling Service (JBCS)
c/o Martin B. Cohen Centre, Deansbrook Road, Edgware, Middlesex HA8 9BG
Tel 020 8951 3881
Email enquiries@jbcs.org.uk *Website* jbcs.org.uk
(Est. 1980. Reg. Charity No. 1047473). The Jewish Bereavement Counselling has for over 30 years offered confidential counselling to individuals, couples, families and children in the Jewish Community who are experiencing loss. Bereavement counselling and support is offered on a one-to-one basis by trained and experienced volunteer counsellors in the client's own home or in designated venue. Group counselling may also be offered where available. JBCS also has two support groups, Butterflies (support group of mums and dads (of young children) who have lost a parent) and Aftershock (support group for young adults (18-30 year olds) who have lost a parent). JBCS is an Independent organisation, which relies on donations and bequests. *Ch.* Keith Simons; *Man.* Trisha Curtis; *Admin.* Barbara Freed

Jewish Blind & Disabled
35 Langstone Way, Mill Hill East, NW7 1GT
Tel 020 8371 6611 *Fax* 020 8371 4225
Email info@jbd.org
(Est. 1969. Reg. Charity No. 259480). Jewish Blind & Disabled is the only Jewish charity providing mobility apartments for people of all ages with physical disabilities or impaired vision. Tenants range from their early 20's, and encompass a wide spectrum of disabilities. Whatever their individual circumstances, the life of each tenant is transformed by being

enabled to live independently with the safety net of knowing that support is always on hand 24/7 if required. *Ch.* John Joseph; *Pres.* Malcolm Ozin; *Chief Exec.* Hazel Kaye

Jewish Blind & Disabled Projects
Assisted Living Schemes: Fairacres, 164 East End Road, Finchley, N2 0RR; Cherry Tree Court, Roe Green, Kingsbury, NW9; Milne Court, Churchfields, South Woodford, E18; Hilary Dennis Court, Sylvan Road, Wanstead, E11 1QX; Aztec House, 163 Tomswood Hill, Ilford, IG6; Frances and Dick James Court, Mill Hill, NW7; and Cecil Rosen Court, Bushey Heath, WD23 1GB.

Jewish Care
Amélie House, Maurice & Viviene Wohl Campus, 221 Golders Green Road, London NW11 9DQ *Tel* 020 8922 2000
Jewish Care Direct (helpline) *Tel* 020 8922 2222 *Fax* 020 8201 3897
Email jcdirect@jcare.org *Website* www.jewishcare.org
(Est. 1990. Reg. Charity No. 802559).
Services managed by Jewish Care:
   Care Homes – Clore Manor, Hendon; Ella & Ridley Jacobs House, Hendon; Hyman Fine House, Brighton; Lady Sarah Cohen House, Friern Barnet; Otto Schiff, Golders Green; The Princess Alexandra Home, Stanmore; Raymond House, Southend on Sea; Rela Goldhill Lodge, Golders Green; Rosetrees, Friern Barnet; Rubens House, Finchley; Vi & John Rubens House, Redbridge
   Community Centres – Brenner Community Centre at Raine House, Stamford Hill; Redbridge Jewish Community Centre (formerly Sinclair House), Redbridge; Southend and Westcliff Community Centre, Southend and Westcliff; Michael Sobell Community Centre, Golders Green.
   Connect@centres – (Monday) connect@kenton; (Tuesday) connect@southgate; (Thursday) connect@southend
   Day Centres – Edgware & Harrow Jewish Day Centre, Edgware; Stepney Jewish Day Care Centre, Stepney.
   Centres for people living with Dementia – The Dennis Centre, Redbridge; Leonard Sainer Centre, Edgware; Sam Beckman Centre, Hendon.
   Mental Health Wellbeing Centres – Kadimah Centre for Wellbeing, Stamford Hill; Mitkadem Centre for Wellbeing, Redbridge; Martin B. Cohen Centre for Wellbeing, Edgware.
   Mental Health Residential Homes – Jack Gardener House (ages 18-50), Golders Green; Sidney Corob (ages 50+), Hampstead.
   Other Services – Holocaust Survivors' Centre & Shalvata, Hendon; Various Support and social groups, The Karten CTEC Centre, Golders Green & Stamford Hill; The KC Shasha Centre for Talking News & Books, Golders Green; Tay Sachs Screenings; Homecare; Community support and social work services.
   Independent Living Apartments – Selig Court, Golders Green
   Sheltered Housing – Shebson Lodge, Westcliff on Sea.
   Youth Services – Redbridge Jewish Community Centre (formerly Sinclair House).

Jewish Children's Holidays Fund (formerly **Jewish Branch of the Children's Country Holidays Fund**)
JCHF, P.O. Box 1206, Enfield, EN1 9SH
Tel 020 7100 5097
Email secretary@jchf.org *Website* www.jchf.org
(Est. 1888. Reg. Charity No. 295361). *Pres.* Joyce Kemble, JP; *Ch.* Ian Donoff; *Sec.* Nicole Conway, JCHF, P.O. Box 1206, Enfield, EN1 9SH *Tel* 020 7100 5097

Jewish Community Housing Association
Harmony Close, Princes Park Avenue, London NW11 0JJ
Tel 020 8381 4901 *Fax* 020 8458 1772
Website www.jcha.org.uk
Ch. B. Reback; *Chief Exec.* S. Clarke. The Association owns and manages sheltered housing in London, Hertfordshire and Kent. Supported housing for people with special needs is managed on the Association's behalf by Jewish Care and Norwood. Short-term accommodation for students and young people is located in Golders Green.

Jewish Crisis Help Line Miyad
Tel 0800 652 9249
Website www.jewishhelpline.co.uk
Confidential listening service for those experiencing stress in their lives. Open Sunday-Thursday noon-midnight; Friday noon-3pm (winter), 6pm (summer). To help assist, please email jewishhl@googlemail.com

Jewish Deaf Association
Julius Newman House, Woodside Park Road, London N12 8RP
Tel 020 8446 0502 (voice), 020 8446 4037 (text) *Fax* 020 8445 7451
Website www.jewishdeaf.org.uk
(Reg. Charity No. 1105845). Full range of information and support services for people with all levels of hearing loss and hearing people living/working with deaf and hard of hearing people. Includes professional guidance on coping with hearing loss, Tinnitus management, weekly Hear to Help aid maintenance service, impartial information on audiology in the NHS and private sector. Vibrant programme of discussion groups enabling participants to become more socially active, more confident and thereby more connected to those around them. Deaf awareness training courses and lip-reading classes also available. Technology and Information Centre features wide range of latest specialist equipment and aids to facilitate independence. *Tel* 020 8446 0214 for appointments or email info@hearingconnect.org.uk. *Pres.* E. Gee, JP; *Ch.* Trudy King; *Exec. Dir.* Susan Cipin

Jews' Temporary Shelter
Amelie House, 221 Golders Green Road, London NW11 9DQ
Tel 07546 519 043
(Reg. Charity No. 1098798). *Admin.* R. Lewis

Kinneret Trust
127-129 Clapton Common, E5 9AB
Tel 020 8809 4844
Email ginaabrahams1@hotmail.com
Supporting the Aden Jews community of the Stamford Hill area. *Ch.* G. Abrahams; *Cttee.* G. Mahalla, G. Nissim, N. Mansoor

Kisharon Services (For Head Office and Administration *See* p.164).

Asher Loftus Business Centre - comprising the **Print Shop** and **Bus Stop Bikes**
27-31 Church Road, Hendon NW4 4EB
Tel 020 8202 3936 *Fax* 020 8203 6071
Email raymond.bonham@kisharon.org.uk

Hackney Community Inclusion Project
(Women) Brenner Community Centre, 91-93 Stamford Hill, London N16 5TP *Tel* 020 3393 0164
(Men) 9 Amhurst Park, N165DH (Scheme Address) *Tel* 020 3393 0164
For more details contact Head Office at 54 Parson Street NW4 1TP
Email aviva.braunold@kisharon.org.uk
The Hackney Community Inclusion Project was established in collaboration with Hackney Local Authority and provides young people with learning difficulties with an opportunity to develop independence skills within their own community. The people supported are encouraged to become self-supporting in accessing local facilities, travelling, shopping and cooking.
The project is in the heart of the Stamford Hill community and comprises separate male and female sites. Work opportunities in the community are actively sourced for both groups. Home industries have also been developed and Kisharon runs a horticulture business as well as a toy library with several new projects underway
Residential Services

Hanna Schwalbe Residential Home
48 Leeside Crescent, Golders Green NW11 0LA
Tel 020 8458 3810
Email petronajohnson@kisharon.org.uk

Kisharon Supported Living Services
Contact Hadassa Kessler *Tel* 020 3393 0167 *Email* hadassa.kessler@kisharon.org.uk

Necessitous Ladies' Fund
(Reg. Charity No. 266921 A3L1). Founded by the Union of Jewish Women. For the relief of Jewish women who are in need, hardship or distress *Ch.* J. Nathan; *H. Admin.* H. Davis, c/o 1 Martlett Lodge, Oakhill Park, London NW3 7LE *Email* admin@nelfwanadoo.co.uk

Nightingale Hammerson
Nightingale House, 105 Nightingale Lane, SW12 8NB
Tel 020 8673 3495
Email info@nightingalehammerson.org *Website* www.nightingalehammerson.org
Hammerson House, 50A The Bishops Avenue, N2 OBE
Tel 020 8458 4523
Email info@nightingalehammerson.org *Website* www.nightingalehammerson.org
(Est. 1840. Reg. Charity No. 207316). Nightingale Hammerson runs two care homes, Nightingale House in Clapham South West London and Hammerson House in North West London. It provides quality care for older members of the Jewish community on both sites and it offers residential, nursing, dementia and respite care. All rooms in both homes have private facilities, in addition to which there are cafes, lounges and other facilities. Fundraising Cttees., Literary Lunch Cttee.; Dinner Cttee.; The Young Nightingales; Business Group; Bridge Cttee.; Relatives Entertainment Cttee. *Life Patron* Dame Vivien Duffield DBE; *H. Patron*, Chief Rabbi Ephraim Mirvis; *Pres.* G. Lipton MBE; *V. Pres.* Patricia Beecham; *Ch.* Harvey Rosenblatt; *Dep. Ch.* David Winton; *CEO*, Helen Simmons.

Norwood
Broadway House, 80/82, The Broadway, Stanmore, HA7 4HB
Tel 020 8809 8809
Email info@norwood.org.uk *Website* www.norwood.org.uk
(Est. 1795. Reg. Charity No.1059050). Norwood is a leading UK charity which each year supports over 7,000 people with learning disabilities and children and families in need. It provides a wide range of Family Services and Learning and Disability Services which help people to live the life they choose and reach their full potential. Delivered by 1,200 staff, and supported by 800 dedicated volunteers, these vital services are provided to the Jewish and wider communities in London and the South East as follows: *Family Services*: family centres, children and family support, social work, an inclusive nursery, adoption. *Learning and Disability Services*: education, after-school clubs and holiday schemes, short breaks, transition, supported living, residential care, work skills and employment, life skills and learning, leisure, health and wellbeing. *Patron* Her Majesty The Queen; *Pres.* Richard Desmond; *Ch.* Bernie Myers; *Chief Exec.* Elaine Kerr

Norwood Drugsline Drop-In Centre
The Kennedy Leigh Centre, Edgworth Close, Hendon, London NW4 4HJ
Telephone Helpline 07850 949 477 (Thursday 6.30-8.30pm), 020 8809 8810 (all other times). Leave a message and someone will get back to you asap
Email drugsline@norwood.org.uk *Website* www.norwood.org.uk/drugsline
(Reg. Charity No. 109050). Norwood Drugsline is a crisis, information and support charity that provides free and confidential information and support for people with drugs, alcohol and addiction issues, their families and friends. Thursday 6-8pm. No appointment necessary. *Chief Consultant,* Rabbi Aryeh Sufrin MBE CASAP

Raphael - The Jewish Counselling Service
P.O. Box 172, Stanmore HA7 3WB
Tel 0800 234 6236 (24 hour)
Email info@raphaeljewishcounselling.org *Website* www.raphaeljewishcounselling.org
(Reg. Charity No. 278522). London, Home Counties and the Redbridge area based professional Jewish Counsellors provide confidential counselling for individuals and couples. Donations, grants and bequests enable us to continue this important work in the community and to further professional training.

Sunridge Housing Association Ltd
76 The Ridgeway, NW11 8PT
Tel 020 8458 3389
Ch. Linda Stone; *Hon. S.* Richard Levy. *Man.* P. Peterkin

Westlon Housing Association
850 Finchley Road, NW11 6BB
Tel 020 8201 8484 *Fax* 020 8731 8847
Providers of affordable housing for the elderly. *Ch.* Bernard Graham; *Chief Exec.* J.W. Silverman **Annette White Lodge**, 287/289 High Road, N2 8HB; **Deborah Rayne House**, 33b Sunningfields Road, NW4 4QX; **The Woodville**, 1a Woodville Road, W5 2SE Applications to 020 8201 8484

Yad Voezer
9 Amhurst Park, London N16 5DH
Tel 020 8809 4303/9060 *Fax* 020 8809 9061
Email enquiries@yadvoezer.com *Website* www.yadvoezer.com
(Est. 1975. Reg. Charity No. 1032490). Residential care and support for people with learning disabilities, mental health problems and their families. *Ch.* Rabbi E. Landau; *Chief Exec.* Z. Landau

Clubs and Cultural Societies

See also under Synagogues and Organisations concerned with Jewish Youth

London Jewish Forum
Shield House, Harmony Way, NW4 2BZ
Tel 020 7242 9734
Email info@londonjewishforum.org.uk
The London Jewish Forum is an advocate for the capital's Jewish Community, campaigning and influencing change in the public institutions that make decisions which affect Jewish lives. Rooted within Jewish Values, London Jewish Forum works across the Community regardless of religious, cultural or political affiliations or beliefs, and with our neighbours. It works to identify the issues and concerns of London's Jewish community and ensure that City Hall and Town Halls understand and are responsive to them. These are often the same issues and concerns of London's wider community. Our wellbeing is tied to that of our neighbours, so working with communities across the city, the London Jewish Forum strives to deliver a cohesive, inclusive and tolerant London that all communities can enjoy. *Ch.* Adrian Cohen; *Public Affairs Dir.* Jay Stoll; *Admin.* Gemma Freeman

Alyth Choral Society
North Western Reform Synagogue, Alyth Gardens, NW11 7EN
Tel 020 8455 6763
Email alythchoralsociety@gmail.com *Website* www.alythchoralsociety.org
(Est. 1983). Rehearsals 8pm every Tuesday during term time. *Musical Dir.* Robin Osterly; *Ch.* Felicity Dirmeik; *Sec.* Linda Perez; *Chorus Master,* Viv Bellos

Centre for Jewish Life
Media House, 4 Stratford Place, W1C 1AT
Tel 020 7495 6089 *Fax* 020 7495 6099
Email info@thecjl.org *Website* www.thecjl.org
(Est. 2008). The Centre is dedicated to providing social, educational and business events for young unaffiliated Jews of all backgrounds and nationalities, enabling them to connect with each other and their heritage. *Hon. Pres.* Dr. Sam Peltz; *Ch.* Rabbi F. Vogel; *Advisory Bd.* Eduardo Azar, Keith Breslauer, Colin Gershinson, Dennis Levine, Edward Mishrahi, Conrad Morris, Martin Moshal, Alan Samson

Chabad Lubavitch Centres of North East London and Essex
Imperial Chambers, 10-17 Sevenways Parade, Gants Hill, Ilford, Essex IG2 6JX
Tel 020 8554 1624 *Fax* 020 8518 2126
Email rabbisufrin@chabadilford.co.uk *Website* www.chabadilford.co.uk
(Est. 1986. Reg. Charity No. 1123001). *Exec. Dir.* Rabbi A.M. Sufrin, MBE; *Asst. Dir.* Rabbi M. Muller

Chabad Wimbledon
42 St. George's Road, Wimbledon, SW19 4ED
Tel 020 8944 7770

Email rabbi@dubov.org *Website* www.chabadwimbledon.com
(Est. 1988. Reg. Charity No. 227638). Chabad Hebrew School, Adult Jewish education, Chabad Shul, library, food and bookshop, mailings, mikvah, Bar/Bat Mitzvah, tuition, Mitzva campaigns, youth activities, mothers and toddlers groups and camps. *Dir.* Rabbi Nissan Dubov

Friends of Jewish Youth *See under* Organisations concerned with Jewish Youth

Jewish Appreciation Group Tours
32 Anworth Close, Woodford Green, Essex IG8 0DR
Tel 020 8504 9159
(Est. 1960). Full history tours of the Jewish East End, the Jews in England from 1066 etc. Historic walks and tours throughout the year. *Tours Org.* Adam Joseph

Jewish Association of Cultural Societies (J.A.C.S.)
Edgware Synagogue, Parnell Close, Edgware, Middlesex HA8 9YE
Tel 020 8958 7508 *Fax* 020 8905 4449
Email office@edgwareu.com
(Est. 1978). Twenty-three clubs located throughout the Greater London area, with two in Surrey, one in Brighton, one in Westcliff-on-Sea, providing weekly meetings for the 65+, embracing cultural and social programmes. *H. Pres.* Cyril Gordon; *H. Nat. Ch.* Harold Newman MBE; *Nat. Sec.* Sheila Levitt; *Hon. S. S.* Pizer

JHSE Essex Branch
Email jhseessex1@aol.com *Website* www.jhse.org
Lectures will start at 8.15pm at the King Solomon High School.
Contact S. Lassman *Tel* 020 8554 9921

JW3 - The New Postcode for Jewish Life
341-351 Finchley Road, London, NW3 6ET
Tel 020 7433 8989 (Box Office) 020 7433 8988
Email info@jw3.org.uk *Website* www.jw3.org.uk
(Reg. Charity No. 1117644). JW3's aim is to transform the Jewish landscape in London by helping to create a vibrant, diverse and proud community inspired by and engaged in Jewish arts, culture and community. JW3 offers events, activities, classes and courses that increase the quality, variety and volume of Jewish conversation. Their goal is to encourage greater understanding between sections of the community and different faiths.
Ch. Michael Goldstein; *Chief Exec.* Raymond Simonson

KabbalahUK.com
42 St George's Road Wimbledon SW19 4ED
Tel 020 8944 7770
Email rabbi@dubov.org
(Est. 2005). To disseminate Kabbalistic and Chassidic teaching in the UK. *Dir.* Rabbi N.D. Dubov

Kadimah Youth Club *See under* Organisations concerned with Jewish Youth

London Jewish Male Choir
Tel 07889 465 417
Email info@ljmc.org.uk *Website* www.ljmc.org.uk
For over 85 years, The London Jewish Male Choir has entertained audiences throughout the world with high quality performances of a broad range of Jewish Music, encompassing Liturgical music through to Broadway and Yiddish. Regular rehearsals on Thursday evenings, and new members welcome, especially those with sight reading ability. *Mus. Dir.* Joseph Finlay; *Ch.* David Renton; *T.* Tony Margolis

Lubavitch of Edgware
230 Hale Lane, Edgware, Middlesex HA8 9PZ
Tel 020 8905 4141 *Fax* 020 8958 1169
Email rabbi@lubavitchofedgware.com *Website* www.lubavitchofedgware.com
(Est. 1986). Pioneers in Street Youth Work programmes: Kindergarten, Synagogue (affiliated to the Union of Orthodox Hebrew Congregations), Gan Israel Day Camp, Library, Tel Torah: telephone learning service. *Dir* Rabbi L. and F. Sudak. *Publ.* Central, *Ed.* F. Sudak

The Maccabaeans
(Est. 1891). Consisting primarily of those engaged in professional pursuits, its aims being to provide 'social intercourse and co-operation among its members with a view to the promotion of the interests of Jews, including the support of any professional or learned body and charities'. *Pres.* Prof. D. Latchman; *Hon. T.* R. Michaelson; *Hon. S.* L. Slowe 4 Corringway, NW11 7ED

Museum of Immigration and Diversity
19 Princelet Street, E1 6QH
Tel 020 7247 5352
Email office@19princeletstreet.org.uk *Website* www.19princeletstreet.org.uk
(Reg. Charity 287279). Grade II* heritage building incorporating a Victorian synagogue. Occasional public openings are held in celebration of immigration and diversity; private tours for educational groups by advance arrangement.

Redbridge Jewish Cultural Society
(Est. 1965). Meetings held at South West Essex & Settlement Reform Synagogue Oaks Lane, Newbury Park. *Contact* Isabel Morris *Tel* 020 8599 1746. Monthly meetings on Sunday evenings 8pm. Call for further details.

Redbridge Jewish Community Centre
Sinclair House, Woodford Bridge Road, Ilford, Essex, IG4 5LN
Tel 020 8551 0017 *Fax* 020 8551 9027
(Reg. Charity No. 3013185). *Ch.* P. Leigh; *Centre Man.* R. Shone. Redbridge JCC, home of the Redbridge Jewish Community Centre, meets the social, educational and welfare needs of all sections of the Redbridge and District Jewish Community. More than 2,500 people make use of the Centre's facilities each week. The Redbridge Jewish Day Centre provides a high level of essential care for over 350 elderly and disabled people. A Meals-on-Wheels service provides approx. 250 kosher meals each week. There are programmes and services for young people, including those with special needs. There are also social, educational, welfare and active sports programmes for the young and adults alike. The Centre is also the base for the Community Shlicha, Clayhall Synagogue, Ackerman Resource Centre, and many communal events and activities. The Redbridge Jewish Community Centre is part of Jewish Care.

Stepney Jewish Community Centre
2-8 Beaumont Grove, E1 4NQ
Tel 020 7790 6441 *Fax* 020 7265 8342
Administered by **Jewish Care**. Community Centre for the Elderly; Special care centre for physically and mentally frail; Kosher Meals on Wheels; outreach and support services; and Friendship Clubs. *Centre Man.* Philippa Paine

Tribe (Young United Synagogue) *See under* Organisations concerned with Jewish Youth

Western Charitable Foundation
32 Great Cumberland Place, W1H 7TN
Tel 020 7724 7702
Ch. Harold Pasha; *V. Ch.* David I. Winton; *T.* Anthony H. Yadgaroff; *Exec. Sec.* S. Garcia

Zemel Choir
Contact Anthony Cohen
Tel 07770 345 679
Email marketing@zemelchoir.org *Website* www.zemelchoir.org
(Reg. Charity No. 252572/ACL). The UK's leading mixed voice Jewish Choir performing a varied repertoire, with an emphasis on Hebrew, Yiddish, Israeli and liturgical music, and contemporary compositions of Jewish interest. Overseas tours, prestige concerts in London and provinces, recordings, and social events. Zemel welcomes enthusiastic and committed singers with some experience of reading music. Rehearsals most Mondays 8-10.30pm. North London. *Musical Dir.* Benjamin Wolf

scellaneous Organisations

ALL ABOARD SHOPS LIMITED
(Reg. Charity No. 1125462). All Aboard operate Charity Shops for the benefit of UK-based Jewish Charities. All Aboard welcome donations of clothing, bric-a-brac etc, and welcome volunteers to assist in the shops and at Head Office. *Life V. Pres.* Stella Lucas; *Ch. of Tru.* Howard Brecker; *Tru.* Irving H. Brecker FNAEA FICBA (*Ch.*), Brian Finch MA (Cantab)MBA FCCA, Flo Kaufmann, Robert Lipson, Harvey Rose FCA, Michael Wernicke; Life Pres. Stella Lucas MBE; *H. V. Pres.* Michael Green FCA, Alan Millet, Jeffrey Pinnick FCA; *Company Sec.* Carol Marks
Tel 020 8381 1717 *Fax* 020 8381 1718
Email admin@allaboardshops.com *Website* www.allaboardshops.com
Head Office Stella Lucas House, 105 High Street, Edgware, Middlesex HA8 7DB
Shops located at **Barnet** 67 High Street, EN5 5UR; **Borehamwood** 120 Shenley Road WD6 1EF; **East Finchley** 124 High Road, N2 9ED; **Edgware** Unit 1, Boot Parade, 88 High Street, HA8 7HE, 224 Station Road, HA8 7AU; **Finchley Central** 102 Ballards Lane, N3 2DN; **Finchley Road** 150 Finchley Road NW3 5HS; **North Finchley** 369 Ballards Lane, N12 8LJ; **Golders Green** 616 Finchley Road NW11 7RR and 125 Golders Green Road NW11 8HR; **Hendon** 98 Brent Street NW4 2HH; **Manchester** Unit 10, The Longfield Centre, Prestwich MA25 5AY; **Mill Hill** 51 The Broadway, NW7 3DA; **Paddington** 12 Spring Street, W2 3RA; **Ruislip** 98 High Street, Ruislip HA4 8LS; **Stamford Hill** 2a Regent Parade, Amhurst Park N16 5LP; **Streatham** 83 Streatham High Road SW16 1PH; **Temple Fortune** 1111 Finchley Road NW11 0QB; **West Hampstead** 224 West End Lane NW6 1UU

JEWISH POLICE ASSOCIATION
Non Charter Mail, Peel Centre, Aerodrome Road, Hendon, London NW9 5JE
Tel 07770 492 782
Email info@jewishpoliceassociation.org.uk *Website* www.jewishpoliceassociation.org.uk
(Est. 2001). Provides a network for support and advice to Jewish staff within the Metropolitan Police Service; to promote understanding of the Jewish faith within the Police Service; and to act as a resource reference for Police Services regarding religious and cultural issues, in particular those that affect front-line policing. *Ch.* Tim Williams; *Dep. Ch.* Michael Loebenberg; *T.* Sara Levene; *Sec.* Danny Phillips; *Asst. Sec.* Nicholas Goldwater; *Youth Officer,* Daniel Morris; *Chaplain,* Dr. Rabbi Jonathan Romain

JEWISH VISITING
Admin. United Synagogue Visitation Committee, 305 Ballards Lane, London N12 8GB
Tel 020 8343 6238
Email admin@jvisit.org.uk
The Visitation Committee, while under the administration of the United Synagogue, includes Hospital Visiting and Prison Chaplaincy services for anyone Jewish, irrespective of synagogue affiliation. The Committee is recognised by the National Health Service as the provider of hospital chaplaincy for Jewish patients, servicing hospitals within London and the Home Counties. Visits by chaplains and lay visitors are made in those hospitals where there is a regular intake of Jewish patients, and information is given to other hospitals for emergency situations and occasional visits. The Jewish Prison Chaplaincy department, is officially recognised by the Ministry of Justice as the sole provider for religious, spiritual and pastoral needs of all Jewish prisoners throughout England and Wales. Its director is the Jewish Faith Advisor to HM Prison Service.
Ch. Keith D. Simons; *Snr. Hospital Chaplain,* Rabbi Zorach Meir Salasnik; *Dir. of Jewish Prison Chaplaincy* Rev. Michael Binstock MBE
Bereavement Counselling Service (*See* p.169).

JEWISH MEDICAL ASSOCIATION (UK)
Administrator, PO BOX 38278, London NW3 4YG
Tel 07929 633 108 *Website* www.jewishmedicalassociationuk.org
The Jewish Medical Association (UK) combines several previous Jewish Medical groups in the UK, including the former British Chapter of the Israel Medical Association and the London Jewish Medical Society. Its aim is to support the UK's Jewish medical professionals

and informing on Jewish and Israeli medical approaches and achievements.
Exec. Ch. Prof David R Katz; *Hon. S.* Dr Simon Nadel; *Hon. T.* Dr Mervyn Jaswon; *London Pres.* Prof Daniel Hochhauser; *Israel Liaison,* Dr Simon Cohen; *BoD Representative,* Dr Simon Nadel; *Admin. Sec.* Hilary Cane; *Admin. T.* Helene Gordon; *Fdr. Patron,* The Late Lady Jakobovits; *Patrons,* Henry Grunwald QC, Rabbi Dr Abraham Levy, The Israel Ambassador, His Excellency Daniel Taub, Rabbi Lord Sacks, Lord Turnberg, Lord Winston

LONDON SOCIETY OF JEWS AND CHRISTIANS
21 Maple Street, London W1T 4BE
Tel 020 7580 1663
Email m.solomon@liberaljudaism.org
(Est. 1927). The oldest public interfaith organisation of its kind in the UK. It was established to give an opportunity to Jews and Christians to confer together on the basis of their common ideals and with mutual respect for differences of religion. It holds several lectures each year. *Jt. Pres.* Rabbi Dr. D.J. Goldberg OBE, Revd. Dr. A. Harvey; *Jt. Ch.* Rabbi M. L. Solomon, Rev. Dr. A. Bergquist; *Hon. S.* Paula Flynn

There are disused cemeteries at a number of towns in the British Isles, including Bath, Canterbury, Dover, Falmouth, Ipswich, King's Lynn, Penzance, Sheerness, and Yarmouth. General enquiries about these and other locations should be addressed to the Board's Community Issues Division, or to Jewish Heritage (*See* page 315–318).

Mikvaot are maintained in the following towns: Birmingham, Bournemouth, Brighton, Cardiff, Edinburgh, Gateshead, Leeds, Leicester, Liverpool, Manchester, Newcastle, Sheffield, Southend, Southport, Sunderland and Glasgow.

Memorials
Blue Plaque Memorial to Muriel Byck (SOE) Bayfort Mansions, Warren Road, Torquay
Memorial Lincoln Cathedral.
Memorials Hutchinson Square (Park Square), Douglas, Isle of Man
By local art students to the hundreds of Jewish refugee artists and musicians who were interned in the camp 1940-42.
Memorial Stone Clifford's Tower, Yor. Remembering the York massacre of Jews in 1190.
National Jewish Memorial (AJEX Memorial) and **Special Forces plot** with a Magen David shaped table in memory of Vera Atkins aka Rosenberg and all the Jewish SOE and SAS/Special Forces men and women served in British and Israeli Forces in WW2, Arboretum at Alrewas, staffordshire.
Sea Wall Aberdovey West Wales.
Memorial to No. 3 'Jewish' Troop, No. 10 Commando, WW2. Plaque opposite on sea wall explains the Jewish refugee make-up of the troop.

AMERSHAM
South Bucks Jewish Community (LJ)
P.O. Box 826, Amersham, HP6 9GA
Tel 0845 644 2370
Email info@sbjc.org.uk *Website* www.sbjc.org.uk
Eruv Shabbat services every week in Amersham; monthly Shabbat morning services; High Holy days and festivals; Cheder; adult education services; Rosh Chodesh Group.
M. Rabbi R. Benjamin. Cemetery: *See* Edgwarebury Cemetery

BASILDON (Essex)
Merged with Southend. Burials arranged through Southend & Westcliff Hebrew Congregation at their cemetery in Southend.

BATH
The last synagogue closed in 1910. Services are currently being revived under the auspices of the Bristol and West Progressive Jewish Congregation (*See* p.185) at The Friends' Meeting House, York Street.

BEXHILL-ON-SEA
Bexhill and District
Jewish Friends, P.O. Box 198, TN40 9BG *Ch.* G. Lee; *T.* R. Caidan; *Sec* J. Caidan; *Asst. Sec.* M. Phillips *See also under* Hastings

BIRMINGHAM
This Jewish community is one of the oldest in the provinces, dating from 1730, if not earlier. Birmingham manufacturing attracted early Jewish settlers. In the Anglo-Jewish economy Birmingham's position was similar to a port, a centre from which Jewish pedlars covered the surrounding country week by week, returning to their homes for the Sabbath. The first synagogue of which there is any record was in The Froggery in 1780. But there was a Jewish cemetery in the same neighbourhood in 1730, and Moses Aaron is said to have been born in Birmingham in 1718. The history of the Birmingham community has been investigated by the Birmingham Jewish History Research Group under the leadership of the late Zoë Josephs.

REPRESENTATIVE BODIES
Representative Council of Birmingham and West Midland Jewry
Email jewishbirmingham@talktalk.net *Website* www.jewishbirmingham.org
(Est. 1937). *Pres.* Sir B. Zissman; *Ch.* R. Jacobs; *Hon. S.* Leonard Jacobs *Tel* 0121 236 1801; *Admin.* c/o BHC, Singers Hill, Ellis Street, Birmingham, B1 1HL *Tel* 07768 761 930

SYNAGOGUES
Birmingham Central Synagogue
4 Speedwell Road, B5 7PA
Tel 0121 440 4044 *Fax* 0121 440 5405
Website www.centralshul.com
M. Rabbi C. Atlas; *Sec.* C. Jennings
Birmingham Hebrew Congregation
Singers Hill, Ellis Street, B1 1HL
Tel 0121 643 0884 Fax 0121 643 2273
Email office@singershill.freeserve.co.uk *Website* www.singershill.com
The present synagogue was consecrated on September 24, 1856 and celebrated its 150th anniversary in 2006. *M.* Rabbi Y. Jacobs; *Admin.* B. Gingold
Birmingham Progressive Synagogue (LJ)
Bishopsgate Street, 1 Roseland Way, B15 1HD
Tel 0121 634 3888
Email office@bps-pro-syn.co.uk *Website* www. bpsjudaism.com
Hon. S. Yvonne Stollard *Tel* 01905 775 972; *M.* Rabbi Dr. Margaret Jacobi

CEMETERIES
Brandwood End Cemetery
(Entrance Broad Lane) Woodthorpe Road, Kings Heath, Birmingham, West Midlands B14 6EQ Enquiries to Hebrew Congregation *Tel* 0121 643 0884
Witton Cemetery
Warren Road, B44 8QH
The Ridgeway, College Road, Erdington *Tel* 0121 382 9900

EDUCATIONAL
King David School
244 Alcester Road, B13 8EY
Tel 0121 449 3364
Email enquiry@kingdavidschool.co.uk
Hd. S. Langford

RELIGIOUS ORGANISATIONS
Lubavitch Centre & Bookshop
95 Willows Road, B12 9QF
Tel 0121 440 6673 *Fax* 0121 446 4299
M. Rabbi S. Arkush. Also at this address: Operation Judaism (*See* p. 111).
Midlands Centre for Liberal Judaism
c/o Birmingham Progressive Synagogue, Bishopsgate Street, Roseland Way, B15 1HD
Mikveh
at Central Synagogue, For appointments *Tel* 0794 664 2265

SOCIAL, CULTURAL & INTERFAITH
Jewish Historical Society
(Branch Est. 1968). *Ch.* Dr A. P. Joseph

WELFARE
Birmingham Jewish Community Care
Bill Steiner Suite, Riverbrook Drive, B30 2SH
Tel 0121 459 3819 *Fax* 0121 459 1487
Email admin@bhamjcc.co.uk *Website* www.bhamjcc.co.uk
Pres. Dr B. Roseman; *Dir.* I. Myers
Care Home with Residential, Nursing, and Respite Care
Andrew Cohen House, Riverbrook Drive, Stirchley, B30 2SH
Tel 0121 458 5000
Email admin@bhamjcc.co.uk

YOUTH & STUDENTS

Birmingham Union of Jewish Students
c/o Hillel House, 26 Somerset Road, Edgbaston, B15 2QD
Tel 0121 454 5684
Email ujs@ujs.org.uk

Hillel House
26 Somerset Road, Edgbaston, B15 2QD
Tel 0121 454 5684
Email birminghamhillel@hotmail.co.uk
Website www.ujshillel.co.uk/hillel-facilities/accomodation/midlands/birmingham
Applications for admission to Bella Lupasco, 10 East Drive, Edgbaston, Birmingham, B5 7RX
Tel 0121 471 4370

BLACKPOOL

SYNAGOGUES

United Hebrew Congregation
Leamington Road, FY1 4HD
Now closed.

Blackpool Reform Jewish Congregation
40 Raikes Parade, FY1 4EX
Tel 01253 623 687
A constituent of the Movement for Reform Judaism. Services: Erev Shabbat 8pm,
Shabbat morning 11am. *Pres.* E. Ballam *Tel* 01253 319 334; *V. Pres.* S. Tax *Tel* 01253 315 700

SOCIAL, CULTURAL & INTERFAITH

Fylde League of Jewish Women
Hon. S. A. Poston, 100 St Thomas Road, Lytham St Annes, Lancashire FY8 1JR
Tel 01253 711 078 *Email* abposton123@btinternet.com

BOGNOR REGIS

Bognor Regis and District Hebrew Congregation
Elm Lodge, Sylvan Way, PO21 2RS
Ch. and *Hon. S. J. S.* Jacobs, *Tel* 01243 823 006 *Email* jackneve@talktalk.net

BOURNEMOUTH

The Bournemouth Hebrew Congregation was established in 1905 and met in the
Assembly Rooms, where the Bournemouth Pavilion now stands. A synagogue, built in
Wootton Gardens in 1911, was rebuilt in 1961 to seat some 950 congregants. The
Menorah suite was added in 1974, and a mikveh in 1976. The congregation has many
educational and social activities each week of which details can be supplied through
the synagogue office.

Bournemouth Reform Synagogue was started by a small band of enthusiasts in 1947.
Ten years later the congregation was large enough to build the present synagogue building
at 53 Christchurch Road. It was extended in 1980 and now has a membership of over 700,
with a voluntary mixed choir, an active Cheder, and many social activities. It is host to the
Jewish Day Centre every Monday.

Chabad Lubavitch has been an integral part of Bournemouth Jewish community for the
past twenty years. In 2009 they opened their million pound centre which houses a shul,
library, classrooms and catering facilities. They have Shabbos and weekday minyanim and
hold numerous events throughout the year.

Bournemouth is the religious and social centre for the fast growing community in
Dorset, West Hampshire.

REPRESENTATIVE BODIES

Bournemouth Jewish Representative Council (incorporating Southampton)
Website www.masorti-bournemouth.co.uk

SYNAGOGUES

Bournemouth Masorti Group
Tel 07810 854 673
Email masortibmth@btinternet.com *Website* www.masorti-bournemouth-masorti.co.uk

Bournemouth Hebrew Congregation
Synagogue Chambers, Wootton Gardens, Dorset BH1 1PW
Tel 01202 557 433 *Fax* 01202 557 578
Tel 07984 427 375 (Ladies Mikveh)
Email office1@bhcshul.co.uk *Website* www.bhcshul.co.uk
M. Rabbi Adrian Jesner
  Bournemouth Jewish Social Services *Tel* 01202 298 877

Reform Syngagogue
53 Christchurch Road, BH1 3PA
Postal address P O Box 8, BH1 3PN
Tel 01202 557 736
Website www.bournemouthreform.org
(Est. 1947). A Constituent of the Reform Movement. It now has a membership of over 400, with an active Cheder, art group, Bridge club, educational classes and many social activities.

Chabad Lubavitch of Bournemouth
20 Lansdowne Road, BH1 1SD
Tel 01202 555 367
Website www.bournemouthchabad.org
Rabbi, Rabbi Yosef Alperowitz; *Co-Dir,* Rabbi Yosef Alperowitz, Chanie Alperowitz

CEMETERIES
Kinson Cemetery (used by both the Hebrew Congregation and the Reform Synagogue)
Boscombe Cemetery (used by old established members Hebrew Congregation)
Throop Cemetery (Hebrew Congregation)

EDUCATIONAL
Yavneh Kindergarten
Gertrude Preston Hall, Wootton Gardens, BH1 3PW
Tel 07831 530 216
Email yavnehkindergarten@gmail.com
Supervisor, Jan Knapp

RELIGIOUS ORGANISATIONS
Bournemouth Sephardi Association
69 Orchard Avenue, Poole, BH14 8AH
Tel 01202 745 168 after 8pm
Ch. Simon Tammam; *T.* David Kalfon

Lubavitch Centre
Chabad House, 20 Lansdowne Road, BH1 1SD
Tel 01202 555 367
Mikva Gertrude Preston Hall, Wootton Gardens Rebbetzin Jesner *Tel* 07984 427 375

SOCIAL, CULTURAL & INTERFAITH
Wessex Jewish News (6 issues a year)
3 De Lisle Road, BH3 7NF
Email edwin@onetel.com

WELFARE
Home for Aged
Hannah Levy House, 15 Poole Road, Dorset
Tel 01202 765 361
Email hlhtrust@btconnect.com

YOUTH & STUDENTS
Bournemouth University Jewish Society
Wallisdown Road, Poole
Tel 01202 524 111

BRADFORD
Jews of German birth, who began settling in Bradford in the first half of the nineteenth century, were in a large measure responsible for the development of its wool yarns and fabrics exports to all parts of the world. Jewish services, first held in the 1830s in private houses, were held in 1873, on Reform lines, in a public hall. About the same period saw the beginnings of the Orthodox community.

SYNAGOGUE

Bradford Synagogue
7a, Bowland Street, Bradford, BD1 3BW
Website www.bradfordsynagogue.co.uk
(Est. 1880). A constituent of the Reform Movement. Ad hoc Shabbat morning services about once a month and High Holy Days and Chanukah services. *Ch.* R. Leavor, 76 Heaton Park Drive, BD9 5QE *Tel* 01274 544 198 *Email* leavor@onetel.com

CEMETERIES
Scholemoor, Necropolis Road, Cemetery Road, Bradford (both Orthodox and Reform).

WELFARE

Jewish Benevolent Society
Contact, 1 Fern Chase, Scarcroft, Leeds LS14 3JL
Pres. A.A. Waxman; *Hon. T.* W. Behrend

BRIGHTON & HOVE
There were Jews living in Brighton in the second half of the eighteenth century, and by the beginning of the nineteenth century there was an organised community (The earliest synagogue was founded in Jew Street in 1792).

REPRESENTATIVE BODIES

Sussex Jewish Representative Council
Tel 07789 491 279
Email info@sussexjewishrepresentativecouncil.org
Website www.sussexjewishrepresentativecouncil.org
Nearly every synagogue, charitable organisation, social and cultural institution, as well as the communities in Eastbourne, Hastings, Bexhill and Worthing, are affiliated to this Council, and meetings are held quarterly. *Pres.* Beryl Sharpe; *Sec.* Jessica Rosenthal *Corr.* P.O. Box 2178, Hove, BN3 3SZ

SYNAGOGUES

Brighton & Hove Hebrew Congregation
West Hove Synagogue: 29-31 New Church Road, Hove BN3 4AD /66 Middle Street, BN1 1AL
Tel 01273 888 855
Email office@bhhc-shul.org *Website* www.bhhc-shul.org
(Reg. Charity No. 1115092). Open monthly Sundays for viewing; contact Admin for details. *M.* Rabbi H. Rader

Brighton & Hove Progressive Synagogue (LJ)
6 Lansdowne Road, Hove, BN3 1FF
Tel 01273 737 223
Email bhps@freenetname.co.uk
(Est. 1935). *M.* Rabbi Elizabeth Tikvah Sarah; *Admin* Chandra Wishart

Brighton & Hove Reform Synagogue
Palmeira Avenue, Hove, BN3 3GE

Tel 01273 735 343
Email accounts@bh-rs.org
(Est. 1955). *Admin.* L. Shaw

Hove Hebrew Congregation
79 Holland Road, Hove, BN3 1JN
Tel 01273 732 035
Email hollandroadshul@btconnect.com *Website* www.hollandroadshul.com
Ch. Stanley Cohen; *T.* Michele Cohen; *M.* Rabbi V. Silverman

CEMETERIES
Cemetery (Orthodox) Meadow View Cemetery, Bear Road, Brighton BN2 4DA
Contact Rabbi P. Efune *Tel* 01273 321 919
Cemetery (Non-Orthodox) Old Shoreham Road, Hove BN3 7EF
Contact either the Reform or Progressive Synagogues.

EDUCATIONAL
Torah Nursery
29 New Church Road, Hove BN3 4AD
Tel 01273 328 675
Centre for German-Jewish Studies
University of Sussex, Sussex House, BN1 9RH

RELIGIOUS
Joint Kashrut Board
Contact Rabbi H Rader *Tel* 01273 888 855 or Rabbi V. Silverman *Tel* 01273 732 035
Lubavitch Brighton
15 The Upper Drive, East Sussex BN3 6GR
Email rabbiefune@lubavitchbrighton.com
Rabbi P. Efune *Tel* 01273 321 919

SOCIAL, CULTURAL & INTERFAITH
AJEX
Ch. Aubrey Cole, 61 Langdale Road, Hove BN3 4HR
Tel 01273 737 417
Ben Gurion University Foundation
Ch. & Delegate Sam Barsam 47 Woodruff Avenue, Hove BN3 6LH *Contact Tel* 01273 508 323
Email sambarsam@hotmail.com
Brighton & Hove Interfaith Contact Group IFCG
c/o Community Base, 113 Queens Road, BN1 3XG
Website www.interfaithcontactgroup.com
Contact Charlotte Gravestock *Email* mail@jcgravestock.plus.com
Brighton & Hove Jewish Centre
Ralli Hall, 81 Denmark Villas, Hove BN3 3TH
Tel 01273 202 254
Email rallihall@tiscali.co.uk
(Reg. Charity No. 269474). Incorporating Ralli Hall Lunch and Social Club, Film Club, Ralli Hall Israeli Dance Group, Jewish Arts Society, SARID (Holocaust Survivors Group). *Man.* Norina Duke; *Ch.* Roger Abrahams.
Meeting centre for various senior clubs, mother & baby club, youth clubs and communal groups. Facilities include committee rooms, theatre facilities, library/reading room, cafeteria, etc. Kosher kitchen (lunch available on Tuesdays and Thursdays). Function rooms and Ballrooms for hire.
JAS - Jewish Arts Society
Ch. Rochelle Oberman 23 Hove Park Road, Hove BN3 6LA
Sussex Jewish Golfing Society
Pres. Roland Moss *Tel* 01273 502 221; *T.* Michael Marks 9 Woodlands, Hove BN3 6TJ
Tel 01273 541 299 *Email* michael@marksand.co.uk

Sussex WIZO-Ziona
Ch. Claire Barsam 47 Hove Park Road, Hove BN3 6LH *Tel* 01273 508 323
Email sambarsam@hotmail.com

WELFARE
Brighton & Hove Jewish Housing Association
61 Furze Croft, Furze Hill, Hove BN3 1PD
Tel 01273 738 463
Email bahjha@googlemail.com
Brighton & Hove Jewish Welfare Board
Tel 07952 479 111
Contact, Ch. Fiona Sharpe *Email* sussexjwb@googlemail.com or info@bhjwb.org
Helping Hands
3/80 Langdale Road, Hove BN3 4HP
Email helping-hands@helping-hands.org *Website* www.helping-hands.org
(Reg. Charity No. 1117001). Provide care and assistance both in practical and emotional terms for all members across the community. ie visiting or phoning someone who is lonely, shopping for house bound transport for medical appointments and much more.
Hyman Fine House (Jewish Care residential home)
20 Burlington Street, Brighton BN2 1AU
Website www.jewishcare.org
Hd. of Home, Natasha Carson *Tel* 01273 688 226 *Email* ncarson@jcare.org
Sussex Tikvah (Home for Jewish adults with learning difficulties)
25 Chatsworth Road, Brighton BN1 5DB
Tel 01273 564 021
Man. Peter Senker

YOUTH & STUDENTS
Hillel House
18 Harrington Road, Brighton BN1 6RE
Tel 01273 503 450
Ch. & Delegate Aileen Hill 2/9 Adelaide Crescent, Hove BN3 2JH *Tel* 01273 727 979
Brighton Union of Jewish Students
Adam *Email* jsoc@ussu.sussex.ac.uk

BRISTOL
There was an established Jewish community in the city by 1140 and, probably unique in Europe, the synagogue was in the crypt of a church. Close to the site of the pre-expulsion cemetery, in Jacob's Well Road, a medieval rock cut chamber with a Hebrew inscription was rediscovered in 1987. Thought to be either a beit tahara or possibly a mikveh, this historic feature is presently inaccessible.

After the expulsion of 1290, there was an intermittent Jewish presence in the city, and there is record of an established community of Spanish origin, living near the waterfront in the 1520s.

The community was re-established by 1743, the year in which a burial ground was leased. The community employed a rabbi by 1744, and services were conducted in a hall known as the Stone Kitchen, situated behind a medieval merchant's house in Temple Street. Bankrolled by Lazarus Jacobs of Bristol Glass fame, the community leased the adjacent medieval Weavers' Hall as a synagogue in 1786. The community moved again to a refurbished former Quaker meeting house in Temple Street, in 1842. Contemporary guide books described this synagogue as 'one of the smallest but also one of the most beautiful appointed places of worship in the city'.

The Stone Hall, The Weavers' Hall and the 1842 synagogue all disappeared in a massive redevelopment in 1870-71, and the present Park Row Synagogue was consecrated in September 1871. However, it contains many of the fittings and fixtures from earlier synagogues in the city. The building was listed Grade II in 2012.

The Bristol and West Progressive Jewish Congregation was founded in 1961. Its present synagogue, in Bannerman Road, Easton, Bristol, was consecrated in 1971. It was extended in 1988 and again in 2003.

There are cordial relations between the two communities, and both are welcoming to visitors and newcomers to the city.

The university has a thriving and growing Jewish Student population and an active Jewish Students' Society.

SYNAGOGUES

Bristol Hebrew Congregation (I)
9 Park Row, BS1 5LP
Tel 07845 288 897
Email bristolhebrewcongregation@btinternet.com *Website* www.bristoljewishcommunity.org
Chabad Contact *Email* bristolchabad@gmail.com

Bristol & West Progressive Jewish Congregation (LJ)
43-47 Bannerman Road, Easton BS5 0RR
Email bwpjc@bwpjc.org *Website* www.bwpjc.org
(Reg. Charity No. 73879). *Ch.* Gary Webber; *Rabbi*, Rabbi Monique Mayer

CEMETERIES
Oakdene Avenue, Fishponds, Bristol BS5 6QQ
Memorial Woodlands, Earthcott Green, Alveston, Bristol, BS35 3TA
Canford, Canford Lane, Westbury-on-Trym, Bristol, BS9 3PQ
South Bristol, Bridgwater Road, Bedminster Down, Bristol, BS13 7AS

EDUCATIONAL
Davar
Suite 413, 179 Whiteladies Road, Clifton BS8 2AG
See under Educational and Cultural Organisations chapter

YOUTH & STUDENTS
Bristol University Jewish Society (JSoc)
Website www.bristoljsoc.co.uk
Pres. Natasha Isaac *Email* chair@bristoljsoc.org.uk
Hillel
The Ark & Dove, 36 Oakfield Road, Clifton, BS8 2BA

CAMBRIDGE

The present congregation was founded in 1888, but an organised community was present from 1774. There is extensive Jewish life in Cambridge. The Cambridge Jewish Residents Association (CJRA) was the original resident organisation set up in 1940-41 following the influx of evacuees and refugees into Cambridge and the need for a Jewish Burial Ground. The Jewish section of the Newmarket Road City Cemetery dates from this time.

A variety of religious services are held on a regular basis, there are also extensive cultural and educational programmes held across and for the whole community. The School of Divinity also has a regular programme of activities and there is extensive Interfaith work carried out in the Woolf Institute.

SYNAGOGUES
Cambridge Traditional Jewish Congregation
3 Thompson's Lane, CB5 8AQ
Tel 01223 501 916
(Est. 1937. Reg. Charity No. 282849). *Ch.* Prof. S. Goldhill
Email sdg1001@cam.ac.uk *Website* www.ctjc.org.uk
Beth Shalom Reform Synagogue
Email info@beth-shalom.org.uk *Website* www.beth-shalom.org.uk
(Est. 1978). Services, cheder, pre-cheder, adult education and welfare programmes. *Ch.* Mike Frankl

RELIGIOUS

Cambridge & Suffolk Jewish Community (Hama'ayan)
Correspondence, *Sec.* D. Gilinsky 101 Perse Way, Cambridge, CB4 3SB
Tel 01223 354825
Website www.jewishcambridge.org.uk
(Reg. Charity No. 1111197). Mikveh and children's nursery at 268 Milton Road, CB4 1LQ
Cambridge Commmunity Mikveh Charitable Trust (CCMC)
(Reg. Charity No. 1067075). *Enquiries* Dr S. Goldhill, Kings College, Cambridge CB2 1ST
Chabad of Cambridge
37a Castle Street, CB3 0AH
Website www.cuchabad.org
Tel/Fax 01223 354 603
Rabbi Reuven Leigh; *Dir.* Rochel Leigh

SOCIAL, CULTURAL & INTERFAITH

Cambridge Jewish Residents' Association (CJRA)
Email admin@cambridgejewishresidents.org *Website* www.cambridgejewishresidents.org
(Est. 1940. Reg. Charity No. 289724). The CJRA acts as an umbrella group for the whole community, concentrating on social, educational, cultural and welfare activities that encompass Jews of all persuasions in Cambridge. Membership is open to all Jews, irrespective of their Jewish religious affiliation. Non-Jewish partners are encouraged to join in all activities. In September 2011 the CJRA celebrated its 70th anniversary with a special event and tea at Girton College at which the Chief Rabbi, Lord Sacks, gave an address.

Cambridge Jewish Cultural Association
The Cambridge Jewish Cultural Association is an offshoot of the CJRA and the cross communal welfare group (Cambridge Jewish Community Support) and meets on a monthly basis on a Monday afternoon.

YOUTH & STUDENTS

Cambridge University Jewish Society
3 Thompson's Lane, CB5 8AQ
Website www.cujs.org

CANTERBURY & DISTRICT
The history of the Canterbury community, 'The Jews of Canterbury, 1760–1931' by Dan Cohn-Sherbok, was published in 1984.

SOCIAL, CULTURAL & INTERFAITH

Canterbury and District Jewish Community
c/o 10 Durnford Close, Canterbury, Kent CT2 7RY
(Est. 1974). To provide social and cultural events for Jewish people in East Kent. *Ch.* Cedric Rebuck *Email* cedric.rebuck@btinternet.com; *T.* Ian Smiler *Tel* 07798 555 391

CHATHAM
There was an organised Jewish community in Chatham from the first half of the eighteenth century. The present synagogue was erected in 1869 in memory of Captain Lazarus Simon Magnus, by his father, Simon Magnus. It is on the site of its predecessor, erected about 1740. It is an independent traditional orthodox congregation holding regular services and events. A Centenary Hall and Mid-Kent Jewish Youth Centre was consecrated in 1972. Instigated 'Jewish Kent', Social organisation, incorporating all Jewish communities in Kent. The old cemetery, dating back to about 1790, is behind the synagogue.

Chatham Memorial Synagogue
366 High Street, Rochester ME1 1DJ
Website www.chathamshul.org.uk
Enquiries David Herling *Email* d.a.herling@city.ac.uk

CHELMSFORD
Chelmsford Jewish Community
Suite 6, Springfield Lyons House, Springfield Lyon Approach CM2 5LB
Tel 01245 475 444
Email info@jewishcommunitychelmsford.co.uk *Website* ww.jewishcommunitychelmsford.co.uk
(Est. in 1974. Reg. Charity No. 281498). The community holds regular services, religion classes and social activities. It has burial arrangements through the Jewish Joint Burial Society.

CHELTENHAM
The congregation was established in 1823 and the cemetery in Elm Street was consecrated the following year. The present synagogue in St. James's Square opened in 1839. The furniture, Ark and Bimah came from the New Synagogue, Leadenhall Street, London, when it relocated to Great St Helen's in 1837. The furniture is thus the oldest extant Ashkenazi synagogue furniture in the country. The Community dwindled and the synagogue closed in 1903. Evacuees and Refugees helped the few residents to re-open the synagogue in 1939. *The History of the Community of Cheltenham, Gloucester and Stroud* by Rev Brian Torode was issued in 1989, reprinted in 1999 and again in 2011.

Hebrew Congregation
The Synagogue, Synagogue Lane, St James's Square, Cheltenham GL50 3PU
Email info@cheltenhamsynagogue.org.uk *Website* www.cheltenhamsynagogue.org.uk
(Reg. Charity No. 1135352). *Contact* J. Silverston *Email* chair@cheltenhamsynagogue.org.uk

CHESTER
Jewish Congregation
Ian and Lesley Daniels Porthouse, 6 South Crescent Road, Queens Park, CH4 7AU
Tel 01244 677 776

COLCHESTER
Colchester and District Jewish Community
The Synagogue, Fennings Chase, Priory Street, CO1 2QG
Tel 01206 860 0107 (not always manned)
Website www.cdjc.org.uk
(Est. 1969. Reg. Charity No. 237240). An independent shul, serving North Essex and Suffolk. The community has close links with the University of Essex. Services are held on Friday nights at 8pm and are conducted by a lay readers as the shul has no Rabbi. For information about services, cheder and social events, please contact the Chairman, Roy Fox *Tel* 01787 310 352 *Email* royfoxfap@btconnect.com

COVENTRY
There were Jews settled in and around Coventry from at least 1775. The watchmaking industry was instrumental in the growth of the community in the late 1800's.
The synagogue was built in 1870 and has been in (almost) continual use to the present day. The Reform community started in 1993.

SYNAGOGUES
Synagogue
Barras Lane, Coventry CV1 3AF
Grade II Listed Building. Currently disused.

SOCIAL, CULTURAL & INTERFAITH
Coventry Reform Jewish Community
24 Nightingale Lane, Coventry CV5 6AY
Sec. Ros Johnson *Tel* 02476 672 027 *Email* ros.johnson@gmail.com

CRAWLEY
Jewish Community (LJ)
Ch. Lynda Bloom *Tel* 01293 534 294; *T.* Joyce de Ath *Tel* 01444 811 825; *Sec.* Shirley
Livingstone *Tel* 01403 791 753

DARLINGTON
CEMETERIES
Contained in a consecrated section of: The West Cemetery, Carmel Road, Darlington DL3 8RY
SOCIAL, CULTURAL & INTERFAITH
Hebrew Congregation (Movement for Reform)
13 Bloomfield Road, DL3 6RZ
(Est. 1904). *Ch.* P. Freitag, 237 Parkside, DL1 5TG *Tel* 01325 468 812

EASTBOURNE
SYNAGOGUES
Hebrew Congregation
22 Susans Road, BN21 3TJ
Hon. S. Tel 01323 484 135
Services every Saturday at 10am and on festivals.

CEMETERIES
Eastbourne Borough Cemetery
A section is set aside for the community in conjunction with the Brighton Chevra Kadisha.
SOCIAL, CULTURAL & INTERFAITH
Eastbourne Liberal Jewish Community
c/o 'Jaybirds', 39 Mountbatten Drive, Langney Point, BN23 6AX
Enquiries Tel 01323 725 650/07258 155 135
Website www.eljc.org.uk
(Reg Charity No. 1115670). Please call for information on services. *Ch.* Suzanne King
Email malka.seltzer@gmail.com; *V. Ch.* Yvonne Greene *Email* aviva.greene@gmail.com;
Admin./Hon. S. Angela Jay *Email* eljcommunity@gmail.com

EXETER
The historic Georgian Synagogue off Mary Arches Street was built in 1763. Jews are
known to have lived in Exeter 30 years earlier and the community is said to have been
founded as early as 1728. The cemetery at Bull Meadow dates from 1757. The Synagogue is
home to a small, inclusive, non-affiliated, very diverse, lively community. There are regular
Shabbat and Festival Services, a parents and toddlers group, and educational and cultural
activities. *The Jews of Exeter* by Helen Fry was published in 2013.

Exeter Hebrew Congregation
Synagogue Place, Mary Arches Street, EX4 3BA
Tel 01392 251 529
Email mail@exetersynagogue.org.uk *Website* www.exetersynagogue.org.uk
Pres. Stella Tripp *Email* president@exetersynagogue.org.uk
CEMETERIES
Historic cemetery at Bull Meadow (Magdalen Road)
Exwick Cemetery (municipal) has a part set aside for Jewish Burials.

GATESHEAD
SYNAGOGUES
Beis Hatalmud
1 Ashgrove Terrace, NE8 1RL
Princ. Rabbi S. Steinhaus *Tel* 0191 478 4352

Kolel Synagogue
22 Claremont Place, NE8 1TL
Constituent of the Union of Orthodox Hebrew Congregations. *Sec.* S. Ehrentreu *Tel* 0191 477 2189

Gateshead Hebrew Congregation
180 Bewick Road, NE8 1UF
Tel 0191 477 3552 (Mikveh) *Rabbi*, Rabbi S. Zimmerman

EDUCATIONAL

Gateshead Girls High School
6 Gladstone Terrace, NE8 4DY
Tel 0191 477 3471
Princ. Rabbi D. Bowden; *Sec.* R. Dunner

Gateshead Jewish Boarding School
10 Rydal Street, Gateshead NE8 1HG
Tel 0191 477 1431 *Fax* 0191 477 1432
Email admin@gjbs.gateshead.sch.uk
(Reg. Charity No. 527371)

Institute for Higher Rabbinical Studies (Kolel Harabbonim)
22 Claremont Place, NE8 1TL
Sec. S. Ehrentreu *Tel* 0191 477 2189

Jewish Primary School
18 Gladstone Terrace, NE8 4EA
Tel 0191 477 2154 *Fax* 0191 478 7554
(Reg. Charity No. 527372). *Hon. S.* C. Rabinowitz

Ohel Rivka Kindergarten
Alexandra Road, NE8 1RB
Tel 0191 478 3723
Hon. S. Esofsky, 13 Grasmere Street *Tel* 0191 477 4102

Sunderland Kolel – Centre for Advanced Rabbinical Studies
139 Prince Consort Road, NE8 1LR
Tel 0191 477 5690
Princ. Dayan Ch. Ehrentreu

Sunderland Talmudical College and Yeshiva
Prince Consort Road, NE8 4DS
Tel 0191 490 0195 (Office); 0191 490 0193 (Students)
Princ. Rabbi J. Ehrentreu

Yeshiva
88 Windermere Street, NE8 1UB
Tel 0191 477 2616 *Fax* 0191 490 0480
Email talmudical@btopenworld.com
Students, 179 Bewick Road *Tel* 0191 478 3048/1351 *Sec.* S. Esofsky

Yeshiva Lezeirim
36-38 Gladstone Terrace, NE8 4EF
(Office) *Tel* 0191 477 1317 *Fax* 0191 381 0250
Email yltyuk@yahoo.co.uk
(Reg. Charity No. 514963). *Princ.* Rabbi E. Jaffe *Tel* 0191 477 0744

GLOUCESTER
Gloucestershire Liberal Jewish Community
Mailing address c/o Phoenix Centre, 86-90 Winchmore Street, Cheltenham, GL52 2NW
Email info@gljc.org.uk *Website* www.gljc.org.uk
(Est. 2008). To provide an egalitarian form of Judaism for the people of Gloucestershire.
Pres. David Naydorf; *Ch.* Jill Rosenheim; *Sec.* Maureen Campion; *T.* Alex May; *Burial Off.*
David Naydorf

GRIMSBY

There are records of Jews living here prior to 1290 and a community of sorts existed in the early 1800s. Mass immigration came from Eastern Europe when Grimsby, like so many East coast ports, was the first landfall for these 'escapees' from persecution. It saw many passing through *en route* for the larger northern cities and even further onward to Canada and the United States. A fair number remained, though and a proper community was created. The synagogue and cemetery were consecrated in 1885. The community reached its numerical peak in the 1930s, when it numbered between 450/500, but its gradual decline began in the immediate post-war years. The history of the community has been published: D. and L. Gerlis, 'The Story of the Grimsby Jewish Community', 1986. Regular services are held every Friday evening at 7pm, and also on all the major festivals and holidays.

SYNAGOGUES

Sir Moses Montefiore Synagogue

Holme Hill, Heneage Road, DN32 9DZ
Pres. L. Solomon *Tel* 01472 824 463; *T.* H. S. Kalson; *Hon. S.* M. Saunders 29 Manor Drive, Waltham DN37 ONS

CEMETERIES

Chevra Kadisha First Avenue, Nunsthorpe, Grimsby
Sec. R. Resner, 14 Welholme Avenue, DN32 0EA *Tel* 01472 342 521; *T.* H. Kalson, 12A Welholme Avenue, DN32 0HP

GUILDFORD

In 1995 archaeologists from Guildford Museum discovered an unusual stone chamber beneath a High Street shop that may have been a medieval synagogue. Built in the late 12th century and demolished in the late 13th century, the chamber has features that fit in with what is known about medieval synagogues. The only object found in the building, was a coin depicting Henry III. It was of a type minted about 1272 and taken out of circulation in 1279.

Although there is no definitive proof that the chamber was a synagogue, Jews were known to have lived in Guildford before their expulsion from England in 1290.

Further information about the Medieval and Contemporary Guildford Jewish Community can be seen at www.guildfordjewish.com

SYNAGOGUES

Guildford and District Hebrew Congregation (1979)

York Road, GU1 4DR
The community has grown up since the Second World War. Regular services, Cheder and social activities. *Ch.* Prof. R. Spier *Tel* 01483 560 074; Cheder, Silke Goldberg *Tel* 07809 200 255; *Contact* B. Gould *Tel* 01483 576 470

CEMETERIES

Cemetery: Consecrated section of municipal cemetery.

YOUTH & STUDENTS

University of Surrey Jewish Society and Chaplaincy

Jewish Common Room, Wey Flat, University of Surrey, Guildford GU2 7XN *Website* http://www.surrey.ac.uk/currentstudents/faith/jewish/
(90 Jewish Students, 30 Jewish members of staff). The University of Surrey has a Jewish community numbering over 100. On the campus there is both the University and the world-famous Guildford School of Acting, where there has traditionally been a strong Jewish presence. The Jewish community have the use of a newly opened Jewish Common Room in the Chaplaincy Centre and will be building more permanent facilities as part of a new Chaplaincy Centre to open in 2015. There are weekly Jewish roundtables at the Common Room. Services take place on campus.

BBC Radio: The Jewish Chaplain co-hosts the BBC Surrey and Sussex Sunday Breakfast show live from the BBC studios at University of Surrey campus every month.

Jewish Chaplain, Rev. Alex Goldberg *Tel* 07939 594 212 *Email* a.goldberg@surrey.ac.uk
Website http://www.alexgoldberg.eu; *Jewish Society Ch.* Daniel Muller (2014)

HARLOW
Jewish Community
Harberts Road, Hare Street, Essex CM19 4DT
Tel 01279 432 503
Movement for Reform. *Life Pres.* C. Jackson; *Ch.* Ms H. Garnelas, Rabbi I. Shillor; *Sec.*
S. Pollack

HARROGATE
'The History of the Harrogate Jewish Community' by Rosalyn Livshin was published in 1995.
SYNAGOGUES
Harrogate Hebrew Congregation
St. Mary's Walk, HG2 0LW
Website www.harrogatehebrewcongregation.co.uk
(Est. 1918). Services every Shabbat at 10am, Kiddush every week. All festivals have
services, details on application. Visitors very welcome. *Sec.* P.E. Morris *Tel* 01423 871 713
Email morris.philip2@gmail.com; *Warden*, L. Shrago *Tel* 01423 886 713 *Email*
l.shrago@ntlworld.com

HASTINGS
Hastings and District Jewish Society
Hon S. Sheila Stanley 55a Sea Road, Bexhill-on-Sea, East Sussex TN40 1JJ
Tel 077 4399 2295
(Reg. Charity No. 273806). Regular meetings of the Society, including a short service are
held on the first Friday of the month in Bexhill, at 7pm.

HEMEL HEMPSTEAD
SYNAGOGUES
Hebrew Congregation (affiliated to US)
Lady Sarah Cohen Community Centre, Midland Road, Hemel Hempstead, Herts HD1 1RP
(Est. 1956). *Hon. S.* H. Nathan *Tel* 01923 32007

WELFARE
Morton House (Jewish Care residential home)
Midland Road, HP2 5BJ

HITCHIN
Yeshivas Toras Chessed
Wellbury House, Great Offley, Hitchin, Herts SG5 3BP
Rab. A. S. Stern *Tel* 01462 768 698

HOVE (*See* Brighton & Hove)

HULL
In Hull, as in many English port towns, a community was formed earlier than in inland
areas. The first recorded resident was in 1766. The first synagogue was used in 1780,
which is about when the first cemetery was acquired. After London, Hull was the principal
port of entry for Jews from Continental Europe. Of the 2.2 million immigrants who
came through Hull between 1850 and 1914, 500,000 were Jews. Today there are 130 in
the Orthodox congregation and 70 in the Reform.

REPRESENTATIVE BODIES
Hull Jewish Representative Council
Pres. Judah Rose *Tel* 01482 655 367; *Hon. S.* Prof. J. Friend, 9 Allanhall Way, Kirk Ella, HU10
7QU *Tel* 01482 658 930 *Email* j.friend@cj2f.karoo.co.uk

SYNAGOGUES

Hull Hebrew Congregation
30 Pryme Street, Anlaby HU10 6SH
Website www.hullhebrewcongregation.co.uk
(Reg. Charity No. 1035451). *Hon. S.* D. Lewis; *M.* Rabbi N. Lifschitz (part time) *Tel* 07917 468 659

Hull Reform Synagogue
Great Gutter Lane, Willerby HU10 7JT
Website www.hull-reform.com
Constituent of RSGB. *Hon. S.* Joanne Kearsley 29 Copse Road, Ashby, Scunthorpe DN16 3JA
Tel 01724 340 506

SOCIAL, CULTURAL & INTERFAITH

Mikveh, Cemeteries, Jewish Archive, Kosher food
Contact Hull Hebrew Congregation.

WELFARE

Hull Jewish Community Care
Ch. H. Flasher Tel 07766 416 605; *Hon. S.* D. Lewis *Tel* 01482 650 282
(Est. 1880).

ISLE OF WIGHT

Isle of Wight Jewish Society
IWJS, 10 Old School Court, Appulduncombe Road, Wroxall, PO38 1DL
Tel 01983 855 051
Email jan_tavill@lineone.net
(Est. 2005). Encourages Jewish people living on the island to enjoy their Jewish heritage, to socialise with each other and to establish and maintain contact with other Jewish Communities. *Publicity,* Howard Kalley; *Membership Sec.* Jan Tavill *Tel* 01983 562 565

KENT

Kent Liberal Jewish Community
Correspondence c/o Liberal Judaism, The Montagu Centre, 21 Maple Street, London W1T 4BE
Tel 07952 242 432
Email kljc@liberaljudaism.org *Website* http://tinyurl.com/kentljc
Monthly Shabbat morning services in Maidstone, High Holyday services, Seder, social events.

LANCASTER

Lancaster and Lakes Jewish Community
Covering North Lancashire and Cumbria up to the Scottish border, we are open to all who are Jewish, have Jewish connections, or who wish to learn about Judaism and the Jewish way of life. There are occasional services in the Jewish rooms at Lancaster University on festivals and occasionally on Shabbat. Our Havurah group meets monthly and there are other social and cultural events. We also work closely with the Lancaster University Jewish Society, which runs regular Friday night meals and bagel brunches.
Ch. Prof. Stanley Henig *Email* stanhenig@googlemail.com; *Sec.* Fiona Frank *Tel* 07778 737 681
Email lancslakesjc@gmail.com; *M.* Rev Malcolm Weisman (also Chaplain for the Lancaster University Jewish Society).

Lancaster University Jewish Society
Chaplain, Rev Malcolm Weisman *Email* jsoc@lancaster.ac.uk

LEEDS

Leeds has the third largest Jewish community in Britain. Jews have lived in Leeds at least from the middle of the eighteenth century, but it was only in 1840 that a Jewish cemetery was acquired. The first so-called synagogue was a converted room in Bridge Street, where services were held up to 1846. Thereafter the place of worship was transferred to the Back Rockingham Street Synagogue, which was replaced by the Belgrave Street Synagogue built in 1860. Another synagogue was built in 1877, but this closed in 1983.

The Leeds Jewish community is mainly the product of the persecution of Russian Jewry in the latter half of the nineteenth century. The bulk of the immigrants settled in Leeds between 1881 and 1905, enhancing the growth of the clothing industry which developed from woollen and worsted manufacturing in the West Riding of Yorkshire. This industry was made world famous by John Barran, a non-Jew, and his Jewish associate Herman Friend, who were responsible for introducing the division of labour into the clothing industry. While the sweating system existed in Leeds, both wages and working conditions were better than in London or Manchester. Trade unionism was successful and the first recorded strike by Jewish industrial workers took place spontaneously in Leeds in 1885.

During the early decades of this century the old Leylands area where most of the immigrants lived, began to break up. The main move of the Jewish people was to northern districts of Leeds, first to Chapeltown, which flourished in the 1940s, and then to the Moortown and Alwoodley suburbs. The Leeds Representative Council republished in 1985 the late Louis Saipe's 'A History of the Jews of Leeds'.

Today, this well-organised, strong community of over 8,000 provides Leeds Jews with over 100 organisations which are affiliated to the Leeds Jewish Representative Council, the official spokesman of the Leeds Jewish community.

REPRESENTATIVE BODIES

Leeds Jewish Representative Council
Marjorie & Arnold Ziff Community Centre, 311 Stonegate Road, LS17 6AZ
Tel 0113 269 7520
Website www.leedsjewishcommunity.com
Nearly every synagogue, charitable organisation, social and cultural instititution and Zionist Society is affiliated to this council and on its executive committee. Serves ex-officio all local Jewish magistrates, public reps. and BoD members. *Pres.* Simon Jackson; *V. Pres.* Alan Dunwell, Abigail Levin; *Hon. T.* Keith Ackerman; *Hon. S.* (*acting*) Jonathan Rose

SYNAGOGUES

Beth Hamidrash Hagadol Synagogue
399 Street Lane, LS17 6HQ
Email office@bhhs.co.uk *Website* www.bhhs.co.uk
(Est. 1874). *M.* Rabbi J. Kleiman, Rabbi M. Sufrin; *Exec. Off.* Wendy Tobias *Tel* 0113 269 2181

Chassidishe Synagogue
Donisthorpe Hall, Shadwell Lane, LS17 6AW
(Est. 1897).

Etz Chaim Synagogue
411 Harrogate Road, LS17 7BY
Email admin@etzchaim.co.uk
Rab. Rabbi S. Kupperman; *R.* Rabbi A. Gilbert; *Sec.* Sandhill Parade, 584 Harrogate Road, LS17 8DP
Tel 0113 266 2214 *Fax* 0113 237 1183

Leeds Masorti
Contact Eva Frojmovic *Email* eva.frojmovic@ntlworld.com

Queenshill Synagogue
Contact Hon. S. 49 Queenshill Drive, Moortown, LS17 6BG

Shomrei Hadass Congregation
368 Harrogate Road, LS17 6QB
Tel 0113 268 1461/7611
M. Dayan Y. Refson

Sinai Synagogue, Leeds
Roman Avenue, Street Lane, LS8 2AN
Tel 0113 266 5256

Email info@sinaisynagogue.org.uk *Website* www.sinaisynagogue.org.uk
(Est. 1944). Constituent of the Movement of Reform Judaism. *Snr. Rabbi*, Rabbi I. Morris
Email rabbi@sinaisynagogue.org.uk; *Asst. Rabbi*, Rabbi Esther Hugenholtz *Email*
rabbihugenholtz@sinaisynagogue.org.uk; *Ch.* Elsje Prins *Email* chair@sinaisynagogue.org.uk;
Dir. of Education, Gwynneth Lewis *Email* gwynneth_education@sinaisynagogue.org.uk;
Admin Heidi Sizer. Monday-Friday 9.30am-2.30pm, Thursday 10am-12pm.

United Hebrew Congregation
151 Shadwell Lane, LS17 8DW
Tel/Fax 0113 269 6141
Email office@uhcleeds.com *Website* www.uhcleeds.com
(Reg. Charity No. 515316). *M.* Rabbi D. Levy. *Tel* 0113 266 4772

EDUCATIONAL

Brodetsky Jewish Primary School
Wentworth Avenue, LS17 7TN
Hd. Jeremy Dunford, School *Tel* 01132 930 578; Deborah Taylor Nursery. *Tel* 0113 293 0579

Leeds Jewish Education Authority (Talmud Torah)
(Est. 1879). Providing top quality education for children, teens and adults. In addition,
providing assemblies in local non-Jewish schools. *Pres.* Rabbi Anthony Gilbert, BA Hons
Tel 0113 268 5657; *Ch. of Education,* Rabbi Daniel Levy, BA Hons, MA *Tel* 0113 266 4772

Makor–Jewish Resource Centre and Israel Information Centre (JPMP)
311 Stonegate Road, LS17 6AZ
Tel 0113 268 0899

Leeds Menorah School
399 Street Lane, LS17 6HQ
Tel 0113 237 0360 *Fax* 0113 320 0770
Independent school for boys and girls aged from 3 to 16. *Co-Dir.* Rabbi Yehuda Refson,
Ettel Refson; *Teacher*, Rabbi Chaim Bell, Rabbi Menachem Mendel Sufrin, S. Angyalfi

RELIGIOUS

Beth Din
Tel 0113 269 6902 *M.* Dayan Y. Refson; Rabbi A. Gilbert BA

Chevra Kadisha: Reform
Convenors Rabbi Morris, Maxine Brown *Tel* 0113 266 5256

Leeds Joint Chevra Kadisha
Admin./Co-ord. Linda Schulman 21 Linton Rise, LS17 8QW
Tel 0113 237 0159 *Mobile* 0771 387 9759 *Email* leedsjointchevrakadisha@gmail.com
    On call Deputy Registrars for the Leeds Jewish Community. This is a voluntary service
available for Sundays and Bank Holidays. Linda Schulman *Tel* 0113 237 0159, Susan Cohen
Tel 0113 269 3815

Mikveh
411 Harrogate Road, LS17 7BY
M. Morris *Tel* 0113 269 4377

SOCIAL, CULTURAL & INTERFAITH

AJEX *Ch.* Leonard Fineberg; *Hon. S.* Leonard Cohen, 72 High Ash Drive, LS17 8RB

Emunah
  Shoshanah
  Ch. Sylvia Baum, Lynda Gilmore; *Hon. S.* Cynthia Myerson 37 Primley Park Road, LS17 7HR
  Tel 0113 268 6984
  Tzfia Goren
  Ch. Maureen Brooke, Monica Gay; *Hon. S.* Margaret Gothelf 37 Primley Park Crescent,
  LS17 7HY *Tel* 0113 268 2374

Makor Leeds Jewish Resource and Cultural Centre
311 Stonegate Road, LS17 6AZ
Tel 0113 268 0899 *Fax* 0113 268 8419

M.B. Sender Administrator
12 Plantation Gardens, LS17 8RY
Tel 0113 318 6403
Email msender101@gmail.com
Jt. Sec. Anita Buxbaum, Peter Brostet; *Jt. T.* Gerald Leonard, Murray Winer

Jewish Telegraph
The Gatehouse Business Centre, Mansion Gate, Chapel Allerton LS7 4RF
Tel 0113 295 6000 *Fax* 0113 262 2384
Email leeds@jewishtelegraph.com

Leeds Council of Christians and Jews
(Reg. Charity No. 238005). *Ch.* A. M. Conway *Tel* 0113 268 0444; *Hon. S.* Rabbi Morris, S. Crowther *Tel* 0113 256 1407

Leeds Zionist Federation
311 Stonegate Road, LS17 6AZ
Tel 0113 218 5865 *Fax* 0113 218 5880
District Org. S. Cohen

Porton Collection
The Information Centre, Central Library, Calverley Street, LS1 3AB (*See* p.118).
Tel 0113 247 8282 *Fax* 0113 395 1833

UJIA Office
Balfour House, 299 Street Lane, LS17 6HQ
Tel 0113 269 3136 *Fax* 0113 269 3961

Women's International Zionist Organisation (WIZOuk)
311 Stonegate Road, LS17 6AZ
Tel 0113 268 4773
Admin. Shelley Peel

WELFARE
Leeds Jewish Welfare Board
Marjorie & Arnold Ziff Community Centre, 311 Stonegate Road, LS17 6AZ
Tel 0113 268 4211
Pres. E. Ziff; *Chief Exec.* R. Weinberg

Care Home for the Elderly
Donisthorpe Hall, Shadwell Lane, LS17 6AW
Tel 0113 268 4248
Website www.donisthorpehall.org
(Est. 1923). *CEO* Carol Whitehead

YOUTH & STUDENTS
Chaplaincy Board–Yorkshire & Humberside
Tel 0113 278 9597
Hon. Ch. Ivan Green *Tel* 0113 269 6610

Community Shaliach
311 Stonegate Road, LS17 6AZ
Tel 0113 268 0899 *Fax* 0113 266 8419

Jewish Students' Association
Hillel House, 2 Springfield Mount, LS2 9NE
Tel 0113 243 3211
(Est. 1912). *Sec.* c/o Leeds University Union, LS2

LEICESTER
There have been Jewish communities in Leicester since the Middle Ages, but the first record of a Synagogue appears in the 1861 Leicester Directory and the first marriages were consecrated in 1875. The present synagogue dates from 1897.

SYNAGOGUES
Synagogue
Highfield Street, P.O. Box 6836, LE2 1WZ

Website www.Jewish-leicester.co.uk
M. Rabbi S. Pink *Email* rabbipink@btinternet.com *Tel* 0116 270 6622; *Hon. S.* Ian Simons *Tel* 0116 288 4887 For synagogue tours, contact Howard Freeman *Tel* 0116 271 5538
Leicester Progressive Jewish Synagogue (LJ)
24 Avenue Road, LE2 3EA
(Est. 1950). *Ch.* R. King *Email* robcking@aol.com

CEMETERIES
Leicester Hebrew Congregation uses a section of the Gilroes Cemetery, Groby Road LE3 9QG
Contact Rabbi S. Pink *Tel* 0116 270 6622. The Progressive congregation uses a section of the Loughborough Municipal Council

EDUCATIONAL
Jewish Library
Communal Centre, 39 Highfield Street, LE2 1AD
Tel 0116 254 0477

RELIGIOUS
Mikveh
Synagogue Building, Highfield Street LE2 1AB
Contact Rivie Pink *Tel* 07515 422 072

SOCIAL, CULTURAL & INTERFAITH
Communal Centre
39 Highfield Street, LE2 1AD
Tel 0116 254 0477

Maccabi Association
Communal Centre, 39 Highfield Street, LE2 1AD
Tel 0116 254 0477

YOUTH & STUDENTS
Jewish Students' Society
c/o The Union, Leicester University, LE1 7RH
Email su-jewish@le.ac.uk
Pres. Charlotte Agran

LINCOLN
Lincolnshire Jewish Community (Affiliated to LJ)
Email ljc@liberaljudaism.org
Sec. Allan Levene *Tel* 01427 628 958

LIVERPOOL
Liverpool, for centuries an important port, first for Ireland, later also for America, had a natural attraction for Jews looking for a place in which to start their new lives. There is evidence of an organised community before 1750. It appears to have had a burial ground attached. Little is known of this early community. It declined, but about 1770 was reinforced by a new wave of settlers chiefly from Europe, who worshipped in a house in Frederick Street, near the river front, with a Mikveh and a cemetery. In 1807 a synagogue of some size was built in Seel Street, the parent of the present synagogue in Princes Road, one of the handsomest in the country. At this time Liverpool was already one of the four leading regional communities. The site for the Seel Street Synagogue was a gift from the Liverpool Corporation.

REPRESENTATIVE BODIES
Merseyside Jewish Representative Council
433 Smithdown Road, L15 3JL
Tel 0151 733 2292 *Fax* 0151 734 0212
Email repcouncil@mjccshifrin.co.uk *Website* www.liverpooljewish.co.uk
(Reg. Charity No. 1140569). *Pres.* Prof. Julian Verbov, JP; *Ch. of the Council* Ian S. Cohen; *Hon. S.* Max Marcus *Publ.* Year Book

SYNAGOGUES
Allerton Hebrew Congregation
207 Mather Avenue, L18 9UB
Tel 0151 724 4811
Email admin@allertonshul.org.uk *Website* www.allertonshul.org.uk
M. Rabbi Daniel Lieberman; *Admin.* D. A. Coleman
Childwall Synagogue
Dunbabin Road, L15 6XL
Email rabbi@theshul.co.uk *Website* www.theshul.co.uk
Tel 0151 722 2079
(Est. 1935. Consecrated 1938). *M.* Rabbi M. Wollenberg; *Admin.* A. Reuben
Liverpool Old Hebrew Congregation
Synagogue Chambers, Princes Road, L8 1TG
Tel 0151 709 3431 *Fax* 0151 709 4187
Email lohc1@aol.com *Website* www.princesroad.org
(Congregation founded c. 1780; Synagogue consecrated 1874). *Admin.* P. Nevitt
Liverpool Progressive Synagogue & Cheder
28 Church Road North, L15 6TF
Tel 0151 733 5871
(Est. 1928). Affiliated to the Movement for Reform Judaism. *M.* Rabbi M. Mayer; *Hon. S.*
E. Kearney

CEMETERIES
Springwood; Lowerhouse Lane; Broad Green; Long Lane

EDUCATIONAL
King David and Harold House Foundation
King David Campus, 120 Childwall Road, LI5 6WU
Tel 0151 235 1584 *Fax* 0151 737 1752
Email admin@kdf.org.uk
Pres. M. Fraenkel; *Clerk* S. Heaps
King David High School
Childwall Road, L15 6WU
Tel 0151 235 1428
Clerk to Govs. King David High School - Jean McMeakin
King David Kindergarten
King David Campus, Childwall Road, L15 6WU
Email kdk@kdf.org.uk
Teacher-in-charge R. Shiffman *Tel* 0151 235 1586 *Fax* 0151 737 1752
King David Primary School
Childwall Road, L15 6WU
Tel 0151 7235 1420
Clerk to Govs. Jean McMeakin King David Campus, Childwall Road, L15 6WU *Tel* 0151
235 1428 *Fax* 0151 737 1752
Hon. T. Rachel Rick, MA (Ed), NPQH
Merseyside Amalgamated Talmud Torah
Cheder Etz Ghayim, Harold House
Ch. M. Levitt

RELIGIOUS
Liverpool Kashrut Commission
c/o Shifrin House, 433 Smithdown Road, L15 3JL
Tel 0151 733 2292 *Fax* 0151 734 0212
Rab. Under the Liverpool Rabbonim
Mikveh
Childwall Synagogue
Ch. Rebbetzin Wollenberg *Tel* 07794 907 284

SOCIAL, CULTURAL & INTERFAITH

Jewish Telegraph
Tel 0151 475 6666
Email liverpool@jewishtelegraph.com
Facebook Jewish Telegraph *Twitter* @jewishtelegraph
Liverpool Jewish Historical Society
(Branch). *Ch.* A. Lewis, 61 Menlove Avenue, L18 2EH
Tel 0151 722 5021
Email arnoldslewis@gmail.com
Liverpool Jewish Resource Centre
King David Campus, Childwall Road, L15 6WU
Tel 0151 235 1594
Email ljrc@btconnect.com
Monday and Thursday 1-4pm, Tuesday and Wednesday 11am-5pm. *Dir.* A. Lewis

WELFARE

Merseyside Jewish Community Care
Shifrin House, 433 Smithdown Road, L15 3JL
Tel 0151 733 2292 *Fax* 0151 734 0212
Email info@mjccshifrin.co.uk *Website* www.merseysidejewishcommunitycare.co.uk
(Est. 1875). *Chief Exec.* L. Dolan
Merseyside Jewish Women's Welfare Society
433 Smithdown Road, L15 3JL
Tel 0151 733 2292
Email info@mjccshifrin.co.uk
Hon. S. P. Talisman
Stapely Jewish Residential and Nursing Home
North Mossley Hill Road, L18 8BR
Admin. Tel 0151 724 3260; 0151 724 4548 (Hospital wing)

YOUTH & STUDENTS

Hillel House
101 Ullet Road, L17 2AB
Applications to *Tel* 0151 280 0551 (office hours)
Chaplain Rabbi Y. Y. Rubinstein *Tel* 0151 721 4066
Jewish Community Centre
King David Campus, 118-120 Childwall Road, L15 6XL
Tel 0151 235 1587
University Jewish Students' Society
101 Ullet Road, L17 2AB
Email liverpool.jsoc@hotmail.co.uk *Website* www.liverpooljsoc.org
Co-Ch. Stuart Lesser, Naomi Kudren

LUTON, DUNSTABLE & DISTRICT

SYNAGOGUES
Bedfordshire Progressive Synagogue (Rodef Shalom) (LJ)
c/o Liberal Judaism, The Montagu Centre, 21 Maple Street, W1T 4BE
Tel 01234 218 387
Email info@bedsps.org.uk *Website* www.bedfordshire-ps.org.uk
(Reg. Charity No. XN22769). Based in Luton and Bedford. Friday night services and twice monthly Shabbat morning services. *Ch.* David Young; *T.* Rosie Comb; *Sec.* Hilary Fox
Luton United Synagogue
656 Dunstable Road, Luton, Bedfordshire LU4 8SE
Tel 020 8343 5851
Email secretary@lutonhebrew.co.uk *Website* www.lutonhebrew.co.uk
M. Rabbi Y. Schwei

MAIDENHEAD

Maidenhead started in 1940 as an evacuee congregation during the Blitz. It experienced a rapid growth in the 1980s as younger families moved out of London, obliging it to move into larger premises in 2001. Its membership now covers a wide area of Berks and Bucks, numbering 800 households, with regular services and a religious school.

Royal Jews: A Thousand Years of Jewish Life in and around the Royal County of Berkshire by J. Romain was published in 2013.

SYNAGOGUES

Synagogue
Grenfell Lodge, Ray Park Road, SL6 8QX
Tel 01628 673012
Email admin@maidenheadsynagogue.org.uk *Website* www.maidenheadsynagogue.org.uk
Reform. *M.* Rabbi Dr. J. A. Romain *Tel* 01628 671058

CEMETERIES
Braywick Cemetery, Maidenhead.

MANCHESTER

The Jewish community of Greater Manchester is the largest community outside London numbering approximately 30,000 and, in contrast with other communities in the UK, is still growing. The greater part of the community lives to the north of the city in Salford, Broughton Park, Prestwich, Whitefield and Bury, and to the south of the city in Altrincham, Cheadle, Gatley, Hale and Sale.

The community is very diverse: there are more than 44 congregations, of which four are Sephardi, three Reform, and one Liberal and a growing number of 'shtieblach'.

There are more than 400 different communal organisations, including yeshivot, schools, charities, and welfare, Zionist, social and youth groups.

The strictly observant and large Charedi community is centred on Broughton Park, Salford, and is the fastest-growing part of the community. The Charedi community is very well-served by its own network of charities and gemachs.

The Jewish Representative Council of Greater Manchester and Region (JRC) acts as the umbrella representative body of the community; each year it publishes a Year Book, which is a valuable guide to communal infrastructure and organisations. The JRC forges links with local councils, other faith communities, hospital trusts and other bodies in order to protect and defend the Jewish community and its interests. It coordinates its efforts with the Board of Deputies of British Jews and the Jewish Leadership Council.

Manchester's Jewish community is staunchly Zionist; over the years many members of the community have made aliyah. Manchester-based charities raise funds to purchase ambulances and support hospitals in Israel; and to support needy families and children with special needs. Other groups work to promote bilateral trade between Israel and the UK, and to promote collaboration between Israeli and British universities.

Manchester Jewish Museum
The history of Manchester's Jewish community from its earliest beginnings has been meticulously researched and documented by Bill Williams in his book The Making of Manchester Jewry 1740–1875 (Manchester: Manchester University Press, 1985), and subsequent works. Bill's scholarship and vision were the foundation upon which Manchester Jewish Museum was created by converting the Spanish and Portuguese Synagogue, which has been beautifully restored and is now a Grade II* listed building.

In 1865 there were 4,500 Jewish Mancunians. The rapid and great increase came between 1883 and 1905, a consequence of the intensified persecution of the Jews in Russia. Newcomers to England in the eighteenth century were encouraged by their co-religionists in London to go farther afield. This they did, as pedlars in the countryside, generally financed by their longer-settled fellow Jews in London. As these newcomers prospered they settled in the ports, for their part sending out a wave of later arrivals similarly supplied with stock to peddle in the inland towns and villages, where this new wave ultimately settled. Thus was laid the foundation of the Jewish community of Manchester.

The middle of the 1780s saw the first signs of an organised community, when two pedlar brothers, Jacob and Lemon Nathan, opened small shops in the centre of Manchester.

In 1794 a plot for Jewish burials was rented just outside the city, and in 1796 a large warehouse was hired for public worship. This period coincided with Manchester's development as a major centre of industry and commerce, and Manchester Jewry steadily increased in number, attracting many enterprising settlers, including merchants and men of substance from the European mainland. Among these was Nathan Mayer Rothschild, the first of that family to settle in England.

A later influx was from North Africa and the Levant, lands closely connected with the cotton industry of which Manchester was then the centre. This was the origin of the Sephardi community still prominent in Manchester. The last two decades of the nineteenth century saw the mass immigration to Manchester of Eastern European Jews, fleeing from poverty and persecution. By the end of the 19th century Manchester had the largest Jewish population in the provinces, reaching a peak of 35,000 just before the First World War.

REPRESENTATIVE BODIES

Jewish Representative Council of Greater Manchester and Region (Incorporating the Trades Advisory Council). The Representative body for the Jewish community of Manchester, Salford and the surrounding region, including Stoke, Blackpool and St Annes. Made up of representatives from all synagogues and other organisations, local Jewish MPs and MEPs, local members of the Board of Deputies, magistrates and town councillors. *Office* Jewish Community Centre, Bury Old Road, M7 4QY
Tel 0161 720 8721
Email office@jewishmanchester.org *Website* www.jewishmanchester.org
Pres. Sharon A. Bannister; *V. Pres.* Jacky Buchsbaum BSc ACA CTA, Jonny Wineberg; *Hon. T.* Philip A. Langer; *Hon. S.* Michael Rubinstein, Rabbi Arnold Saunders; Ex-officio, Frank Baigel BA B.Dent.Sc; *H. Media Analyst*, Frank R. Baigel. *Publ.* Year Book, Newsletter *RepPresents*

SYNAGOGUES
Adass Yeshurun Synagogue
Cheltenham Crescent, Salford, M7 4FP
Tel/Fax 0161 740 3935
M. Rabbi Y. Cohen; *Sec.* M. Goldman
Adath Yisrael Synagogue (formerly **Kahal Chassidim Synagogue**)
Upper Park Road, Salford M7 4GL
(present building opened in 1957) *Tel* 0161 740 3905
M. Rabbi S Liberow; *Sec.* Rev. S. Simon
Beis Hamedrash Chanichei Hayeshivos
106 Kings Road, Prestwich, M25 0FY
Tel 07977 178 384
M. Dayan Y.O. Steiner
Beis Hamedrash Eitz Chaim
29 Tewkesbury Drive, Prestwich, M25 0HR
Tel 0161 773 5932
Pres. S. Schwalbe, *M.* Rabbi D. Ortzel
Beis Hamedrash Shaarei Mordechai
80 Bury New Road, Prestwich M25 0JU
Tel 0161 798 7374
M. Rabbi L Rabinowitz
Beis Mordechai
90 Kings Road, Prestwich M25 0FY
M. Rabbi Y. Wreschner
Beis Yisroel
Manchester Jewish Community Centre, Bury Old Road, M7 4QY
M. Rabbi Y.A. Sopher

Belz Communities
28 Broom Lane, Salford, M7 4FX
Tel 0161 740 9210
M. Dayan A. Grinfeld
Bury Hebrew Congregation
Sunnybank Road, Bury, BL9 8ET
Tel/Fax 0161 796 5062
Email mirrelbhc@hotmail.co.uk *Website* buryhc.org.uk
M. Rabbi B. Singer; *Admin.* M. Wilson, M. Rappaport
Chaim v'Tikvah Independent Congregation
Chaim v'Tikvah is a small, independent Progressive congregation based in Prestwich with traditional values and a family friendly atmosphere.
It has a good attendance at services where everyone is welcome, and men and women sit together. For further information, contact the office by email or phone. *Tel* 07976 419 654
Email chaimvtikvah@onetel.com
Chassidei Gur Centre
1 Legh Road, M7 4RT
Tel 0161 708 8864
M. Rabbi S.Z. Suffrin

Cheetham Hebrew Congregation
Jewish Cultural Centre, Bury Old Road M7 4QY
Tel 0161 740 7788
Pres. B. M. Stone. *M.* Rabbi Y. Abenson
Menorah Synagogue - Cheshire Reform Congregation
198 Altrincham Road, M22 4RZ
Tel 0161 428 7746 *Fax* 0161 428 0937
Email office@menorah.org.uk *Website* www.menorah.org.uk
(Est. 1964. Reg. Charity No. 1124560). *Ch.* Howard Barlow; *Hon. S.* J. Krell
Chortkov Beis Hamedrash
42 Broom Lane, Salford M7 4FJ
Tel 0161 792 7870
M. Rabbi Y. Friedman
Damesek Eliezer Synagogue
74 Kings Road, Prestwich M25 0LN
Tel 0161 798 9298
M. Rabbi S. Goldberg
Hale and District Hebrew Congregation
11 Shay Lane, Hale Barns, Cheshire WA15 8NZ
Tel 0161 980 8846
Email admin@hale-community.org.uk
(Est. 1976). *M.* Rabbi J. Portnoy; *Pres.* N. Rosenthal
Heaton Park Hebrew Congregation
Ashdown, 84 Middleton Road, M8 4JX
Tel 0161 740 4766
Email corinne@hphc.org.uk
M. Rabbi Daniel Walker; *Pres.* A. Levy
Higher Crumpsall and Higher Broughton Hebrew Congregation
Bury Old Road, Salford, M7 4PX
Tel 0161 740 1210
M. Emer. Rabbi A. Saunders, Rev. A. Hillman *Tel* 0161 740 4179; *Admin.* E. Somers *Tel* 0161 740 8155
Higher Prestwich Hebrew Congregation
445 Bury Old Road, Prestwich M25 1QP
Tel 0161 773 4800
Email hphc@btinternet.com
M. Rabbi A. Z. Herman; *Pres.* P.W. Reed

Hillock Hebrew Congregation
Beverley Close, Ribble Drive, Whitefield, M45 8LB
Email hillock.shul@ntlworld.com
Hon. S. R. Walker, 13 Mersey Close, Whitefield, M45 8LB *Tel* 0161 959 5663
Holy Law South Broughton Congregation
Bury Old Road, Prestwich M25 0EX
Tel 0161 740 1634 *Fax* 0161 720 6623
Email admin@holylaw.org.uk
(Est. 1865, present building opened 1935, merged with South Broughton Synagogue, 1978).
M. Rabbi Y. Chazan *Tel* 0161 792 6349 (Study 0161 721 4705); *Pres.* I. Ingleby; *Admin.* N. Bor
Burial Bd. Tel 0161 740 1634
Kahal Chassidim Lubavitch Synagogue
62 Singleton Road, Salford M7 4LU
Corr. G.R. Rose 20 Woodhill Drive, Prestwich, M25 0AD *Tel* 0161 773 9581
M. Rabbi A. Jaffe *Tel* 0161 740 3632; *Sec.* D. Lipsidge *Tel* 0161 740 1629
Ohr Yerushalayim Synagogue
470 Bury New Road, Manchester M7 4NU
Tel 07813 326 423
Website www.ohryerushalayim.org.uk
Rabbi, Rabbi Berel Cohen; *Pres.* Avi Stern
Kol Rinoh Horodenka
64 Waterpark Road, Salford M7 4JL
Tel 0161 720 6659
M. Rabbi Y.A. Weiss
Machzikei Hadass Communities
17 Northumberland Street, Salford M7 4RP
Tel 0161 792 1313
Email admin@mhmanchester.org.uk
Kashrus, Burial Board, Shul, Kolel, Mikvah, Beis Hoiroel, charity vouchers *Rov.* Rabbi M.
M. Schneebalg; *Dayonim* Rabbi A. Grunfeld; Rabbi M. Mehler; Rabbi D. Orzel; Rabbi P.
Weiss; Rabbi C. M. Zahn
    Manchester & District Mikva Sedgley Park Road, Prestwich *Tel* 0161 773 1537/795 2852/
    708 8989 (facilities for the disabled available)
Manchester Great New and Central Synagogue
'Stenecourt', Holden Road, Salford, M7 4LN
Email shul@stenecourt.com *Website* www.stenecourt.com
(Est. 1740). *M.* Rabbi B. Simmonds *Tel* 0161 773 9667; *Pres.* M. Livshin; *Admin.* K. Levy *Tel*
0161 792 8399 Monday-Friday 9.30am-12.30pm
Manchester Liberal Jewish Community
c/o Cross Street Chapel, Cross Street, M2 1NL
Tel 0161 796 6210
Email mljc@mljc.org.uk *Website* www.mljc.org.uk
(Reg. Charity No. 1120548). We actively seek to include those who have experienced
exclusion and discrimination on account of their gender, sexuality, disability or Halakhic
status (interfaith, marriage, adoption, patrilineal descent etc). Based on the central Jewish
values of truth (Emet), Social Justice (Tzedek) and loving kindness (Chesed). *Ch.* Andrew
Chandler; *Rabbi* Mark Solomon *Email* m.solomon@liberaljudaism.org
Manchester Reform Congregation
Jackson's Row, M2 5NH
Tel 0161 834 0415
Email admin@jacksonsrow.org
(Est. 1856). Former synagogue in Park Place was destroyed by enemy action in 1941; present
premises occupied since 1953. 150 Years of Reform Judaism in the Heart of Manchester. *M.*
Rabbi Dr. R. Silverman; *Sec.* Mandy Bernhardt *Tel* 0161 834 0415
Meade Hill Shul (formerly **United Synagogue Manchester**)
88 Meade Hill Road, M8 4LP

Tel 0161 740 9586
Email office@meadehillshul.co.uk *Website* www.meadehillshul.co.uk
Pres. Col. Martin Newman; *M.* Rabbi J. Lever, Rabbi Y. Prijs
North Salford Synagogue
2 Vine Street, Kersal, Salford M7 3PG
c/o Tel 0161 792 3278
Jt. Pres. R. Smith, E. Pine; *M.* Rabbi Elozor Stefansky
Ohel Torah Synagogue
132 Leicester Road, Salford M7 4GB
Tel 0161 792 3442
M. Rabbi S.Z. Hoff; *Hon. S.* Z. Cope
Prestwich Hebrew Congregation
Bury New Road, Prestwich M25 9WN
Tel 0161 773 1978
Email office@shrubberies.org.uk
Rev. Rabbi D. Eisenberg; *Admin.* W. Cohen-Wilks
Sale and District Hebrew Congregation
12a Hesketh Road, Sale, Cheshire M33 5AA
Tel 0161 973 2172
M. Rev Natan Fagelman; *Sec.* M. Clyne *Tel* 0161 973 4565
Satmar Cultural Centre
37 Nothumberland Street, Salford M7 4DQ
Tel 0161 792 9421
M. Rabbi Y.C. Horowitz
Sedgley Park Synagogue (Shomrei Hadass)
Parkview Road, Prestwich M25 5FA
Email shomreihadass@googlemail.com *Website* www.shomreihadass.com
Tel 0161 773 4828
Rabbi, Rabbi D. Kestenbaum; *Pres.* Steven Baddiel
Sephardi Congregation Zichron Yitzchak
2 New Hall Road, Salford M7 4EL
Tel 0161 792 3716
M. Rabbi S. Amor
Sha'arei Shalom Synagogue North Manchester Reform Congregation Ltd
Elms Street, Whitefield, M45 8GQ
Tel 0161 796 6736
Email office@shaareishalommanchester.org.uk *Website* www.shaareishalommanchester.org.uk
(Est. 1977. Reg. Charity No. 506117). A Constituent of the Movement for Reform Judaism.
Ch. W. Rashman; *Admin.* H. Harrison
Shaare Hayim Sephardi Congregation
8 Queenston Road, West Didsbury M20 2WZ
Tel 0161 445 1943
Email shaarehayim@clara.co.uk
(Reg. Charity No. 1067759). (Shaare Hayim). Amalgamated with the former Sha'are Sedek
Synagogue. *M.* Rabbi S. Ellituv *Tel* 0161 434 6903 *Email* ellituv@aol.com, Rabbi Amir
Ellituv 18 Wicker Lane, WA15 0HQ *Tel* 07869 134 917 *Email* aellituv@hotmail.com
Shaarei Shamayim (Sephardi)
Situated at Manchester Jewish Community Centre
Tel 0161 773 3233 *Fax* 0161 773 3381
M. Rabbi S. Chocron
Shaare Tepillah (Spanish and Portuguese Jews) Synagogue
18 Moor Lane, Salford, M7 3WX
Tel 0161 792 4168
Email synagogue@moorlane.org *Website* www.moorlane.org
(Est. 1873). *M.* Rabbi N. Nadav; *Pres.* A.N. Bitton

South Manchester Synagogue
The Firs, Bowdon, Altrincham, WA14 2TE
Tel 0161 928 2050 *Fax* 0161 924 0344
Email info@southmanchestersynagogue.org.uk
Website www.southmanchestersynagogue.org.uk
(Est. 1872. Reg. Charity No. 1124507). *M.* Rabbi D.Y. Lewis MA; *Admin.* T. Hyams; *Office Man.* J. Samuels

Talmud Torah Chinuch N'orim Synagogue
11 Wellington Street, East, Salford M7 2AU
Tel 0161 792 9292
Constituent of the Union of Orthodox Hebrew Congregations. *M.* Rev. P. Koppenheim; *Hon. S.* J. Waldman

Whitefield Hebrew Congregation
Park Lane, M45 7PB
Tel 0161 766 3732
Email office@thewhc.co.uk *Website* www.thewhc.co.uk
(Est. 1959). *M.* Rabbi J. Guttentag, BA Hons; *Admin.* A. Rodrigues-Pereira

Yeshurun Hebrew Congregation
Coniston Road, Gatley, Cheadle, Cheshire SK8 4AP
Tel 0161 428 8242
Email office@yeshurun.org.uk *Website* www.yeshurun.org.uk
(Reg. Charity No. 236420). *M.* Rabbi Chanan Atlas; *Admin.* M. Pawlowski

Zerei Agudas Israel Synagogue
35 Northumberland Street, Salford M7 4DQ
Tel 0161 708 9228
M. Rabbi O.Y. Westheim

CEMETERIES

North Manchester Jewish Cemeteries Trust
Manchester Jewish Community Centre, Bury Old Road, Manchester M7 4QY
Tel 0161 795 0735
Email admin@nmjct.org *Website* www.mdcs.org.uk

Rainsough Charitable Trust
Established to ensure that Jewish cemeteries in Greater Manchester are safe, secure and properly maintained. They have already refurbished the Ohel and repaired very extensive damage caused by repeated bouts of mindless vandalism. Further works are in progress to provide more grave spaces and enhance security. Contributions to help with further work and improvements should be addressed to:
Rainsough Charitable Trust, c/o Brian White, 26 Danesway, Prestwich, Manchester M25 0FS

Agecroft Cemetery Langley Road, Pendelbury, M27 8SS *Tel* 0161 737 0947 Admin. Central and North Manchester Burial Board *Sec.* K. Levy *Tel* 0161 792 8399

Agecroft Liberal Cemetery *Tel* 0870 991 7327 Admin. Manchester Liberal Community

Blackley Cemetery Rochdale Road, Manchester, M9 8JP Admin. Central and North Manchester Burial Board *Sec.* K. Levy *Tel* 0161 792 8399

Cheadle Cemetery Brookfield Road, Cheadle, SK8 2PN *Tel* 0161 428 8242 Admin. Yeshurun Synagogue Burial Board *Sec.* S. Goldich *Tel* 0161 491 4774, S. Cohen *Tel* 0161 428 9923

Crumpsall Cemetery Crescent Road, M8 5UR *Tel* 0161 740 2876 Admin. Manchester Great and New Burial Board *Sec.* K. Levy *Tel* 0161 792 8399

Dunham Lawn Cemetery Whitehouse Lane, Altrincham, WA14 5RH *Tel* 0161 980 8846 Admin. Hale and District Hebrew Congregation Burial Board

Failsworth Cemetery Cemetery Road, M35 0SN *Tel* 07974 268 565 Admin. Holy Law South Broughton Burial Board *Sec.* N. Bor *Tel* 0161 740 1634

Great Synagogue Cemetery Bury New Road, Prestwich (historic).

Mill Lane Cemetery Manchester Road, Cheadle, SK8 2PX *Tel* 0161 428 7746 Admin. Menorah Synagogue Burial Board and Manchester Reform Synagogue Burial Board

Tel 0161 834 0415

Philips Park Cemetery *Tel* 0161 766 2065 Admin. United Synagogue Burial Board *Tel* 0161 740 9586; Whitefield Synagogue Burial Board *Tel* 0161 766 3732; Machzikei Hadass Communities Burial Board *Tel* 0161 792 1313

Rainsough Cemetery *Tel* 0161 773 2641Admin. Rainsough Joint Burial Board - Central and North Manchester Burial Board, Higher Crumpsall and Higher Broughton Synagogue, Manchester Communal Burial Board *Sec.* Rabbi Y. Brodie BA(Hons) *Tel* 0161 740 9711

Southern Cemetery Barlow Moor Road, Chorlton, M21 7GH *Tel* 0161 227 3204 Admin. South Manchester Synagogue *Tel* 0161 928 2050; Shaare Hayim Synagogue *Tel* 0161 445 1943; Manchester Reform Congregation *Tel* 0161 834 0415

Urmston Cemetery Chapel Grove, Urmston, M41 9BB *Tel* 01706 840 642 Admin. Manchester Great and New Burial Board *Tel* 0161 792 8399; Whitefield Synagogue Burial Board *Tel* 0161 766 3732

Whitefield Cemetery Higher Lane, Whitefield, M45 *Tel* 0161 834 0415 Admin. Manchester Reform Congregation

EDUCATIONAL

Academy for Rabbinical Research (Manchester Kollel)
134 Leicester Road, Salford M7 4GB
Tel 0161 740 1960 (Students) 0161 740 2231
(Reg. Charity No. 526665). *Princ.* Rabbi W. Kaufman; *Sec.* D. Cohen

Beis Yaakov High School
Hubert Jewish High School for Girls, 69 Broom Lane, Salford, M7 4FF
Tel 0161 708 8220 *Fax* 0161 708 9968
Princ. Rabbi Y. Goldblatt, MA (Oxon), PGCE

Bnos Yisroel School - Fayge Sufrin Kindergarten
Leicester Road, Salford, M7 4DA
Tel 0161 792 3896
Infant, Junior and Senior

Broughton Jewish Cassel Fox Primary School
Legh Road, Salford M7 4RT
Tel 0161 921 2500 *Fax* 0161 921 2510
Email admin@bjps.net *Website* www.bjcfps.co.uk
Nursery *Tel* 0161 921 2512; Kindergarten *Tel* 0161 921 2513
Acting Hd. S. Caplan; *Princ.* Rabbi Y. Pearlman; *Ch.* D Black

Bury & Whitefield Jewish Primary School
School Close, Parr Lane, Bury, Lancs BL9 8JT
Tel 0161 766 2888
Email bwjp@bury.gov.uk
Hd. Claire Simon; *Ch. of Govs.* Rabbi A. J. Jaffe; *Hd. Jewish Studies* B. Z. Lewis *Tel* 0161 796 3341

Private Nursery School, Parr Lane, Bury, Lancs
Tel 0161 767 9390 (from birth upwards). *Hd.* Miri Weisz

Jewish Senior Boys School - Kesser Torah
Hubert House, 4 New Hall Road, Salford M7 4EL
Tel 0161 708 9175

King David Schools (Est. 1838. Reg. Charity No. 526631)

King David Schools, Administration Centre
Eaton Road, Crumpsall, M8 5DY
Tel 0161 741 5056 *Fax* 0161 741 5081
Campus Bursar D. Rose *Email* droseds@aol.com

King David High School
Eaton Road, Crumpsall, M8 5DY
Tel 0161 740 7248 *Fax* 0161 740 0790
Email admin@kingdavidhigh.manchester.sch.uk *Website* www.kdhs.org.uk

Hd. B. N. Levy, BEd; *Yavneh Girls Tel* 0161 740 3184 S. Eden; *Yavneh Boys Tel* 0161 741 5029
Ramim Rabbi P. Cohen, Rabbi Y. Joseph, Rabbi S. Schwalbe

King David Primary School
Wilton Polygon, Bury Old Road, Crumpsall, M8 6DR
Tel 0161 741 5090
Hd. N. Nelson

King David Private Nursery & Crèche
Wilton Polygon, Bury Old Road, Crumpsall, M8 6DR
Tel 0161 740 3481
Man. L. Balaban

Lubavitch Yeshiva
Lubavitch House, 62 Singleton Road, Salford M7 4LU
Tel 0161 792 3495
Email manchesty@aol.com
Dir. S. Weiss

Manchester Junior Girls School
64 Upper Park Road, Salford, M7 4JA
Tel 0161 740 0566

Manchester Mesivta
Beechwood, Charlton Avenue, Prestwich M25 0PH
Tel 0161 773 1789 *Fax* 0161 772 9170
Email mesivta@bury.gov.uk
Princ. Rabbi B. Sulzbacher

Mechinoh L'Yeshiva
13 Upper Park Road, Salford M7 4HY
Tel 0161 795 9275
Princ. Rabbi N. Baddiel

North Cheshire Jewish Primary School
St. Anns Road North, Heald Green, Cheadle, Cheshire SK8 4RZ
Tel 0161 282 4500 *Fax* 0161 282 4501
Website www.ncjps.org.uk
Hd. Joseph Kelly *Email* headteacher@northcheshire.stockport.sch.uk

OYY Lubavitch Boys School
4 Upper Park Road, Salford, M7 4HL
Tel 0161 740 0923

Seed Manchester
Park Gates, Bury New Road, Prestwich, M25 0JW
Tel 0161 792 4457 *Fax* 0161 210 2995
Email info@seedmanchester.com *Website* www.seed.uk.net
(Reg. Charity No. 281307).

T'Mimei Lev/Torah Tots
Manchester Jewish Community Centre, Bury Old Road, M7 4QY
Tel 0161 795 2253 (office)
Snr. Man. Y. Cochron

Talmud Torah
33 Northumberland Street, Salford M7 4OQ
Tel 0161 792 7841

Talmud Torah Chinuch N'orim
11/13 Wellington Street, East, Salford M7 2AU
Tel 0161 792 9292
Ch. Bd. of Govs. J. Waldman

Talmud Torah Toras Emes
2a Back Hope Street, Salford, M7 2FR
Tel 0161 792 1368

Whitefield Community Kollel
c/o Whitefield Hebrew Congregation, Park Lane, Whitefield, M45 7PB
Email office@theforumwck.org *Website* www.thewhc.co.uk
Admin. B. Woolfstein *Tel* 0161 766 2150
The Forum runs a wide selection of programmes for adults and youth
Yeshiva and Kollel
Saul Rosenberg House, Seymour Road, Higher Crumpsall, M8 5BQ
Tel 0161 740 0214
Yesoiday HaTorah School
Sedgley Park Road, off Bury New Road, Prestwich M25 0JW
Tel 0161 773 6364 *Fax* 0161 773 3914
Email info@yhs.org.uk
Yocheved Segal Kindergarten
Sedgley Park Road, Prestwich M25 0JW
Tel 0161 773 6364

RELIGIOUS
Aguda Keren L'Dovid
2 Castlefield Avenue, Salford M7 4GQ
Tel 0161 721 4365/740 7892
Extra Torah lessons for children. Ethics lectures for professionals dealing with potential
conflicts between State & Torah laws.
Communal Mikveh (under Beth Din authority)
Broome Holme, Tetlow Lane, Salford, M8 9HF
Appointments Tel 0161 740 4071/5199 (ladies) *Tel* 0161 792 3970 (during opening hours)
Supt. D. Fhima *Tel* 0161 795 2272
Hershel Weiss Children and Family Centre (inc. Aguda Community Services)
35 Northumberland Street, Salford M7 4DQ
Tel 0161 778 0700/0071
Sure Start childrens centre services, Citizens Advice Bureau and health services
Lubavitch South Manchester Community Programmes
3 The Firs, Altrincham WA14 2TN
Tel 0161 929 9999
Email southmanchester@lubavitchuk.com Website www.lubavitchsouthmanchester.com
Chabad Lubavitch Providing Education and Support. Youth programmes, welfare and sup-
port, crisis funding, day camp for the kids, day centre for the elderly, support for kids in
crisis, people with special needs, lending libraries, computer resources, Festival and
Shabbos programmes and guides.
Manchester and District Council of Synagogues (Orthodox)
8 Castlefield Avenue, Salford M7 4GQ
Ch. S. Lopian *Tel* 0161 832 8721 *Email* sal@lopiangb.co.uk; *Sec.* M. Green *Tel* 0161 792 2275
Sunday-Friday 9am-12.30pm
Manchester and District Mikvah
Sedgley Park Road, Prestwich, M25 0JW
Tel 0161 773 1537 / 07855 683 049
Email david.simon49@btinternet.com
Facilities for the disabled are available
Manchester Beth Din Ltd
MBD Shechita Services Ltd and MBD Kosher Certification Services Ltd
Jewish Community Centre, Bury Old Road, M7 4QY
Tel 0161 740 9711 *Fax* 0161 721 4249
Email info@mbd.org.uk *Website* www.mbd.org.uk
Pres. J. Nussbaum; *Chief Exec.* Rabbi Y. Brodie, BA (Hons)
Naomi Greenberg South Manchester Mikveh and South Manchester Keilim Mikveh
Hale Synagogue, Shay Lane, Hale Barns, WA15 8NZ
By Appointment Tel 0161 904 8296

Tevilas Keilim Mikveh
Broome Holme
Tel 0161 795 2272
Whitefield Hebrew Congregation Mikveh
By appointment only *Tel* 0161 796 1054
Whitefield Keilim Mikveh
Park Lane, Whitefield M45 7PB
Email mikva@thewhc.co.uk *Website* www.thewhc.co.uk
By arrangement office *Tel* 0161 796 1054
Yeshiva L'Zeirim
33 Legh Street, Salford M7 4EF   *Tel* 0161 792 8612 / 07914 424 514
Rosh Yeshiva, Rav Yosef Brandeis *Email* ylzmcr@gmail.com
Yeshivas Lubavitch
62 Singleton Road, Salford M7 4LU
Tel 0161 740 4243
Rosh HaYeshiva, Rabbi A Cohen; *Admin.* S Weiss
Yeshivas Shaarei Torah
38-40 Upper Park Road, Salford M7 4GZ
Tel 0161 740 3129
Email admin@yst613.co.uk
Dean Rabbi G. Knopfler
A traditional yeshiva and kollel comprising some 250 students.
Zeire Agudas Yisroel
35 Northumberland Street, Salford M7 4DG
Tel 0161 708 9228

SOCIAL, CULTURAL & INTERFAITH
B'Nai Brith Lodge (Whitefield, Prestwich, Salford, Higher Crumpsall)
Email office@bnaibrithuk.org
Hon. S. Leila Yesner *Tel* 0161 796 9906
Club Thursday
Jewish Social and Cultural Society
Ch. R. Kushner *Tel* 0161 445 0152
Meet at 2pm every Thursday at Manchester Bridge Club, 30 Palatine Road, Manchester.
Faith Network 4 Manchester
Ch. Rev Bob Day; *Adv.* Jonny Wineberg; *Community Development Worker,* Revd Andy Williams
Manchester Multifaith Centre, Ada House, 77 Thompson Street, Manchester M4 5FY
Tel 0161 833 8822
Email jonny@fn4m.org *Website* www.fn4m.org
Hillel House Manchester
Contact Dr Neil Joseph *Tel* 0161 795 7894
Israel Information Centre
85 Middleton Road, Manchester M8 4JY
Tel 0161 721 4344
Email iicmcr@clara.co.uk
Information and public relations on behalf of Israel. *Exec. Dir.* Doreen Gerson
Jewish Agency Aliyah Dept
Oakhill Court, 171 Bury New Road, M25 9ND
Consultant, Eitan Sadeh *Tel* 0161 773 9733 *Email* eitansa@jafi.org
Jewish National Fund - JNF UK
Tel 020 8732 6100
Email info@jnf.co.uk *Website* www.jnf.co.uk
Jewish Telegraph
11 Park Hill, Bury Old Road, Prestwich M25 0HH
Tel 0161 740 9321 *Fax* 0161 740 9325
Email manchester@jewishtelegraph.com *Website* www.jewishtelegraph.com

Jewish Theatre Company
Sec. Deborah Finley *Email* deborahjtg@aol.com; *Co-Ch.* Lorna Brown *Email* lornabrown39@gmail.com, Sam Black *Email* samblack2000@gmail.com
150 adult and junior members put on shows, plays and concerts.

Lubavitch Community and Youth Centre
62 Singleton Road, Salford M7 0LU
Tel 0161 720 9514
Youth Dir. Rabbi L. Wineberg; *Ch.* A. Jaffe

Manchester Jewish Community Centre
Jubilee School, Bury Old Road, M7 4QY
Tel 0161 795 4000 *Fax* 0161 720 6222
(Reg. Charity No. 1089467). Centre provides recreational facilities for all ages, reference and lending library, function room, swimming pool and kosher fitness. *Admin.* M. Allweis

Manchester Jewish Museum (MJM)
190 Cheetham Hill Road, M8 8LW
Tel 0161 834 9879
Website www.manchesterjewishmuseum.com
Facebook www.facebook.com/manchesterjewishmuseum *Twitter* @manjewishmuseum
(Est. 1984 Reg. Charity No. 508278). MJM is for Jewish and non-Jewish people offering a unique experience as both a social history museum and as a resource for learning.
The museum tells the story of Manchester's Jewish community from the 1780s to the present day. It has over 30,000 items in its collections, and explores the cultural and religious evolution of Manchester's Jewish community - the largest Jewish community in the UK (outside London). The museum galleries reveal the political and industrial legacies of this community on a local, regional, national and international scale. MJM is the only UK museum housed in an original synagogue and, built in 1874, it is Manchester's oldest surviving synagogue building. The building provides a unique and powerful learning space for all ages. From schoolchildren to adult learners, the museum helps over 15,000 people a year discover, explore and celebrate Jewish faith and culture.
The museum is situated in a spectacular Grade II* listed building and through its displays, exhibitions and event programme it offers an experience that will inspire, inform and educate everyone. Opening hours: Sunday-Thursday 10am-4pm, Friday 10am-1pm. Admission charges apply.

Manchester Maccabi Community & Sports Club
Brooklands, Bury Old Road, Prestwich, Manchester M25 0EG
Tel 0161 492 0040
Website www.manchestermaccabi.org.uk
Ch. Bradley Feld; *Sec.* David Nadler
Activities on offer include: Pilates, Yoga, Personal Safety for Women, First Aid for Parents, Bridge, Quiz nights, Youth Club, 3G All Weather Pitches available

Muslim Jewish Forum Manchester
c/o Manchester Multifaith Centre, Ada House, 77 Thompson Street, Manchester M4 5FY
Tel 0161 833 8822 *Email* mail@muslimjewish.org.uk *Website* www.muslimjewish.org.uk
Co-Ch. Jonny Wineberg, Mohammed Amin; *Sec.* Heather Fletcher

Sam Herwald JNF Wednesday Club
Ch. M. Reuben *Tel* 0161 796 9449
Senior citizens and JNF fundraisers meeting at Maccabi Community & Sports Club.

Second Generation
Ch. T. Nelson, 44 Park Road, Prestwich M8 4HU *Tel* 0161 795 0731
V Ch. M. Rubinstein *Tel* 0161 766 7683
The Second Generation group in Manchester constitutes the children of Holocaust survivors. Membership is open to all children/2nd Generation whose parents were victims of Nazi persecution. Primary objective is to preserve, perpetuate and protect the memory and testimonies of those who perished and those who survived but sadly are no longer with us. Provide support group both for survivors and 2nd Generation. Second Generation aims to raise Holocaust education and awareness.

UJIA
P.O. Box 800, Altrincham WA15 5GD
Tel 0161 740 1825
Pres. J. Rowe, D. Hamburger

WIZO
Suite 7, Sulaw House, 1 Chapel Street, Bury New Road, Prestwich M25 1AE
Hon. Life Pres. J Woolfe MBE *Tel* 0161 425 5018 *Email* manchester@wizouk.org

Zionist Central Council of Greater Manchester
C/o Bnei Akiva, 72 Singelton Road, Salford M74LU
Email zcc.man@zen.co.uk *Website* www.zcc.org.uk
Dir. Karen Solomon *Tel* 0161 740 8835

WELFARE

Aim Habonim Special School for Special Kids
401 Bury New Road, Salford M7 2BT
Tel 0161 705 0020
Email info@aimhabonim.com
Facility for Jewish Children with Special Needs. It aims to educate the children to the highest standards of their abilities. *Co-ord.* D. Cohen

Binoh of Manchester
Binoh Education Centre, Broadhurst, Bury Old Road, Salford M7 4QX
Tel 0161 720 8585
Email binohmanchester@tiscali.co.uk
Educational Consultant, S. Lewis; *Dir. Services*, Rabbi S. Grant; *Ch. Man. Cttee.* A. Henry
Specialists in special educational needs assistance, advocacy, assessment, advice, training and tuition. Recent additions include a Parental Support Scheme, a Teenage Outreach Worker, and a Community Resource Centre to assist groups with funding and infrastructure needs.

Brookvale
Simister Lane, Prestwich, M25 2SF
Tel 0161 653 1767 *Fax* 0161 655 3635
Email admin@brookvale.org
(Reg. Charity No. 526086). Under supervision of Manchester Beth Din. Caring for People with Special Needs. *Exec. Dir.* L. Richmond; *Fin. Dir.* M. Walters

Chabad Community Care
12a Hesketh Road, Sale M33 5AA
Tel 0161 929 9999
Website www.chabadcare.org
Provides day centre services including yoga, exercise classes, manicures, shiurim and luncheon club at the Centre in Sale Shul.
Home visits, meals-on-wheels, hospital visits, counselling, benefit advocacy service and shopping assistance provided.
For more information contact Roxanne Stross or Tracy Labaton *Tel* 0161 710 3450/07979 862 453

Council of Manchester Emunah Societies (incorporating Prestwich, Assata, Kiryat Gat and Zehava Groups)
Ch. B. Bookin *Tel* 0161 773 3527

Delamere Charitable Trust
132-134 Great Ancoats Street, M4 6DE
Tel 0161 773 2580
Email charity@delamereschool.org.uk *Website* www.delamereschool.org.uk
(Reg Charity No. 1117339). For Jewish children with special needs. *Ch. of Dir.* M. Joels

Eshel UK Friends of Colel Chabad
UK Office: Manchester Jewish Community Centre, Bury Old Road, Manchester M7 4QY
Tel 0161 720 9992
Website www.colelchabad.org

(Est. 1788. Reg. Charity No. 327485). One of the biggest providers of humanitarian aid in Israel outside of the government. It runs 22 food halls serving one million meals a year and aims to help 500,000 children a year by delivering over 8500 tons of food, and also runs 12 dental clinics and 12 daycare centres. The only centre for adults with MS and other debilitating illnesses. Highly respected Orphans programmes caring for nearly one thousand orphans and 600 single parents, widow and widowers. For more information contact *Campaign Dir.* Russell Conn *Email* russell@colelchabad.org or russell@esheluk.org; *National Pres.* Daniel Levy; *Life Pres.* Mark Adlestone

Ezer Layeled Children's Therapy Centre
400-404 Bury New Road, Salford M7 2BT
Tel 0161 708 0606 *Fax* 0161 708 2059
Email info@ezerlayeled.org

The Fed
The Federation of Jewish Services (formerly **The Fed** and **Heathlands Village**)
Head Office Heathlands Village, Heathlands Drive, Prestwich, M25 9SB
Tel 0161 772 4800 *Fax* 0161 772 4934
Email info@thefed.org.uk *Website* www.thefed.org.uk
South Manchester Branch 207a Ashley Road, Hale, Cheshire WA15 9SQ
Tel 0161 941 4442 *Fax* 0161 941 5039
Email southside@thefed.org.uk
(Reg. Charity No. 1117126). *Ch.* Mark Adlestone; *Chief Exec.* Karen Phillips MBE, DL. The Fed is the leading social care agency for the Greater Manchester Jewish Community, serving people of all ages. Its services are based at its main multigenerational care centre at Heathlands Village in North Manchester and its South Manchester branch office. It looks after over 1,000 people at any one time offering among other things: residential, nursing, dementia, end-of-life and respite care, supported living tenancies and day services for older people, mental health, carer and volunteer support, social work assessment and support, respite for children with special needs, care at home and a community cafe.

The Interlink Foundation
400-404 Bury New Road, Salford M7 4EY
Tel 0161 740 1877
Email office@interlinknw.org.uk
Strengthening the Orthodox Voluntary Sector. Dir. N. Kestenbaum

JADDS - Jewish Autistic & Deficit Disorders Support
Tel 0161 660 9124
Email volunteer@jadds.org.uk *Website* www.jadds.org.uk
(Reg. Charity No.1144158). Supports parents and children with disabilities such as Autism, ADHD, Dyspraxia, Dyslexia and other related conditions. It runs regular monthly support groups for parents as well as events with speakers.

Jewish Mental Health Alliance of Greater Manchester
A consortium of local Jewish charities involved in supporting people with a wide range of health problems from depression to severe clinical conditions. Involved in the Alliance are all the principal voluntary sector organisations in this field including the Federation of Jewish Services (The Fed), Neshoma, Nicky Alliance Centre, Orthodox Jewish Forum, Interlink Northwest and Binoh plus representatives of the statutory sector. For further details contact *V. Ch.* Dr Yaakov Wise *Tel* 0161 720 9588 *Email* yaakovwise@aol.com

Jewish Soup Kitchen (Meals-on-Wheels Service)
Rita Glickman House, Ravensway, Prestwich M25 0EX
Tel 0161 795 4930
(Reg. Charity No. 226424). *Ch.* Phil Langer; *Hon. S.* H. Amdurer *Tel* 0161 773 5229

Manchester Jewish Community Care (The Nicky Alliance Day Centre)
85 Middleton Road, M8 4JY
Tel 0161 740 0111 *Fax* 0161 721 4273
Email info@mjcc.org.uk *Website* www.mjcc.org.uk
(Reg. Charity No. 257238). Provides day care for those with visual impairment, physical

disability, elderly, frail, lonely or suffering from dementia-related illness. *Pres.* N. Alliance OBE; *Ch.* B. White; *Ch. Exec.* M. Wiseman

Misaskim Manchester
Website www.misaskim.co.uk
(Reg. Charity No. 1100134). Gives support for bereaved families, and deliver and set up everything for a shiva house. *Contact* D. Liefman *Tel* 0161 798 4999

Morris Feinmann Home (Care Home for older people)
C/o Allingham House, Stockdean Close, Deansgate Lane, Timperley, Altrincham, WA15 6SQ
Tel 0161 929 1783
Website www.allinghamhouse.com
Ch. Alan Wilkins; *Gen. Man.* H. Naylor

Newlands Care with Nursing Home
18 Tetlow Lane, Salford M7 4BU
Tel 0161 792 0993
Website www.newlandscare.org.uk
A Jewish care and nursing home that provides round-the-clock care. All residents are encouraged to be as independent as possible, within a caring and comfortable environment. Entertainment and activities are arranged by Activities Organiser. The home is strictly kosher and is under the supervision of the Manchester Beth Din.

Outreach Community & Residential Services
Redbank House, 4 St Chads Street, Cheetham, Manchester M8 8QA
Tel 0161 740 3456 *Fax* 0161 740 5678
Email jennifer@outreach.co.uk *Website* www.outreach.co.uk
(Reg. Charity No. 509119). *Ch. Exec.* A. Akinola; *Ch.* P. Elton

YOUTH & STUDENTS

B'nos Agudas Yisroel – Girls Groups
64 Upper Park Road, Salford M7 0JA
Tel 0161 740 0566
All enquiries to D. Adler 32 Waterpark Road, Salford M7 4ET *Tel* 0161 740 1776
Activities at weekends, summer camp, outings, lectures, rambling club, handicraft group – for girls between the ages of 4 and 24 years.

Bnei Akiva Northern Youth Centre
72 Singleton Road, Salford M7 4LU
Tel 0161 740 1621
Email north@bauk.org *Website* www.bauk.org
Shaliach Mickey Flaumenhaft

The Forum/Whitefield Community Kollel
C/o Whitefield Hebrew Congregation, Park Lane, Manchester M45 7PB
Tel 0161 766 2150 *Email* info@theforumwck.org
Tru. Rabbi J Guttentag (*Ch.*), Rabbi M Kupetz, G. Nussbaum
(Reg. Charity No. 1004263). Whitefield Community Kollel: Academy of higher Jewish Learning and rabbinical training college; The Forum: Informal Jewish education and outreach for the community.

Hillel House Manchester
Contact Dr Neil Joseph *Tel* 0161 795 7894/07764 170 620

Jerusalem Academy Study Groups
43 Stanley Road, Salford M7 4FR
Tel 0161 740 2506
Ch. Rev. G. Brodie

Junior Stage 80
Contact M. Blank *Tel* 0161 928 0324 *Email* marilyn.blank@mcif.co.uk
An award winning stage group based in South Manchester for adults and year 6 children upwards. Musical show put on annually in December at the Waterside Theatre, Sale.

Keren Mamosh, Whitefield (Our Future)
(Reg. Charity No. 1103219). Dedicated centre for young people and for the benefit of the whole community. Rabbi S. Jaffe *Tel* 0161 766 1812 The Willows, 54a Hawkstone Avenue, Whitefield, Manchester M45 7PG

Manchester Jewish Students
Wilbraham Road, Jewish Student Centre, M14 6JS
Email president@manchesterjsoc.com *Website* www.manchesterjsoc.com
Co-Pres. Emily Deaner, Arthur Caplin

Streetwise
Website www.streetwisegb.org
A partnership between the Community Security Trust and Maccabi GB working with children aged 8-18 years, focusing on personal safety and personal development. Sarah Polak *Tel* 0161 705 7080 *Email* sarah@streetwisegb.org

UJIA JAMS (Jewish Activities in Mainstream Schools)
Provides Jewish experiences to Jewish pupils in Mainstream Schools in the form of Jewish discussion groups and talks, lunches and social events. For more information please contact *Co-ord.* Petra Rodrigues-Pereira *Tel* 0161 740 1825 Ext. 2 *Email* petra@ujia.org

UJIA JLEC (UJIA Jewish Life Education Centre) (Makor)
PO Box 800, Altrincham WA15 5GD
Tel 0161 740 1825
Contact Community Shlicha, Liat Greenberg *Email* liat.greenberg@ujia.org

Whitefield Jewish Youth Centre
Whitefield Hebrew Congregation, Park Lane, Whitefield M45 7PB
Tel 0161 796 8564; *Fax* 0161 796 3878
Email wjyc@hotmail.co.uk
Manchester Contact: Rodney Ross *Tel* 0161 767 8890
Northern office Email stevenweller@jlgb.org; *Facebook* www.facebook.com/JLGBHQ
Twitter www.twitter.com/JLGBHQ

Wilbraham Road Jewish Student Centre (The GE Centre)
Wilbraham Road, Manchester M14 6JS
For times of Services and information contact *Wardens* G. Cohen *Tel* 0161 248 7602, Adam Prais *Tel* 07835 420 298

MARGATE

SYNAGOGUES
Margate Hebrew Congregation
Synagogue, Albion Road, Cliftonville, CT9 2HP
(Est. 1904; new synagogue consecrated 1929; Reg. Charity No. 273506). *Pres.* Dr N. Jacobs. Enquiries to *Hon. S.* David Gradus, 11 Dalmeny Avenue, CT9 3NL *Tel* 01843 226 983

CEMETERIES
For Margate Hebrew Congregation & Thanet Reform at Manston Road, Margate.

MIDDLESBROUGH
Linthorpe Cemetery, Ayresome Green Lane, Middlesbrough TS5 5AP

MILTON KEYNES & DISTRICT
Reform Synagogue (Beit Echud) (Movement for Reform)
1 Hainault Avenue, Giffard Park, MK14 5PQ
Tel 01908 617 790
Email info@mkdrs.org.uk *Website* www.mkdrs.org.uk
(Est. 1978. Reg. Charity No. 1058193) Rabbi Shulamit Ambalu *Email* rabbi@mkdrs.org.uk; T. S. Friedman *Tel* 01908 560 714

NEWCASTLE UPON TYNE
The community was established in the 1820s, when services were held and a Shochet employed. A cemetery was acquired in 1831. Jews, however, had been resident in

Newcastle since before 1775. In the Middle Ages Jews are known to have been established in Newcastle in 1176.

REPRESENTATIVE BODIES

Representative Council of North East Jewry
Email repcouncil@northeastjewish.co.uk *Website* www.northeastjewish.org.uk
(Reg. Charity No. 1071515). *Hon. T. W.* Knoblauch *Email* walter@total-accounting.com; *Pres.* Leonard Musat *Tel* 0191 285 7698

SYNAGOGUES

United Hebrew Congregation
The Synagogue, Graham Park Road, Gosforth NE3 4BH
Tel 0191 284 0959
Email secretary@uhc-newcastle.org
(Est. 1973). *Pres.* A. Ross; *M.* Rabbi A. Lipsey; *Sec.* M. Conway. Mikveh on premises.

   Burial Committee *Ch.* P. Gold *Tel* 0191 285 1680

Newcastle Reform Synagogue
The Croft, off Kenton Road, Gosforth, NE3 4RF
Tel 07971 853 102 (24 hour answerphone)
Email admin@nertamid.org.uk *Website* www.nertamid.org.uk
(Est. 1963). A Constituent of Movement for Reform Judaism. *Ch.* Tony Wortman

   Burial Committee *Ch.* P. Gold *Tel* 0191 285 1680

CEMETERIES

Hazelrigg and Heaton (UHC)
North Shields (Reform)

SOCIAL, CULTURAL & INTERFAITH

AJEX
Tel 01661 824 819
Ch. J. Fox *Tel* 0191 213 0304; *Sec.* Mr. Topez *Tel* 01661 824 819

North East Council Of Christians and Jews
Contact D. Van der Velde *Tel* 0191 285 1253 *Email* clivando@hotmail.com

Newcastle Jewish Leisure Group
(Founded in 1981) A senior citizen's group, which meets in the Marion Abrahams Hall two afternoons every month except July and August. There is a varied programme of entertainment, talks, bingo, and bus outings during the summer. Tea is provided as well as transport facilities.

Newcastle WIZO
Co-Ch. Pam Peterson *Tel* 0191 285 4302 and Monica Stern *Tel* 0191 284 2502
Email monica@sternmail.co.uk

WELFARE

North East Jewish Community Services
NEJCS offers a wide range of services to those who are in need and live in the North East. Counselling, meals-on-wheels, voluntary visiting and work with the voluntary and statutory sector are the key components. *P/T Community Worker* Pamela Muscat *Tel* 0191 285 7698; *Ch.* Henry Ross *Tel* 0191 285 4043 *Email* henry.ross@dsl.pipex.com

Philip Cussins House (Residential Care for Jewish Aged in the North East)
33/35 Linden Road, Gosforth NE3 4EY
Tel 0191 213 5353 *Fax* 0191 213 5354
Email christine@philipcussinshouse.co.uk *Website* www.philipcussinshouse.co.uk

YOUTH & STUDENTS

Education and Youth Committee
c/o United Hebrew Congregation
Email secretary@uhc-newcastle.org
Ch. A. Ross

Jewish Students' Society and Hillel House
Ilford Road, Gosforth
Email info@newcastlejsoc.com *Website* www.newcastlejewish.co.uk
Pres. Tamma; *T.* Jack; *Sec.* Jo

NORTHAMPTON

The community marked its centenary in 1988. For a history of the medieval and modern settlement in the town See *A Short History of the Jews of Northampton, 1159–1996* (1996), by M. Jolles.

SYNAGOGUES
Northampton Hebrew Congregation
Overstone Road, Northampton, NN1 3JW
Website www.northantshc.org
Sec. G. Goldcrown *Tel* 01604 633 345

CEMETERIES
Towcester Road Cemetery

NORWICH

There was an important medieval community in Norwich which is well documented. The first recorded small community after the return in 1656 was in 1759, followed by the first Synagogue in 1828. A significant Synagogue was built and consecrated in 1849 and was destroyed by bombing in 1942. The present building was consecrated in 1969. It serves a large area, having members in King's Lynn, Great Yarmouth, Lowestoft and Cromer.

SYNAGOGUES
Norwich Hebrew Congregation Synagogue
3a Earlham Road, NR2 3RA
Email enquiries@norwichsynagogue.org.uk *Website* www.norwichsynagogue.org.uk
M. Daniel Rosenthal *Tel* 07828 205 997; *Pres.* M. Leveton; *Hon. S. F.* Cadywould

SOCIAL, CULTURAL & INTERFAITH
Chevra Kadisha 3a Earlham Road, NR2 3RA *Pres.* B. Leveton *Tel* 01603 749 796; *Sec.* M. Prinsley
Jewish Ladies' Society
3a Earlham Road, NR2 3RA
Jt. Pres. P. Simons, F. Cadywould *Tel* 01362 850 515

Norfolk and Norwich Branch of the Council of Christians and Jews
(Est. 1991). *Ch.* A. Bennett *Tel* 01263 710 726; *Sec.* Jill Gower *Tel* 01508 491 770
Email jill@jill495.orangehome.co.uk
Norwich Israel and Social Society (NISS)
Email enquiries@norwichsynagogue.org.uk
Ch. Jo Cummin

Norwich Liberal Jewish Community
Website www.norwichljc.org.uk
Affiliated to LJ. Regular services at The Old Meeting House, Colegate, Norwich NR3 1BN
Ch. S. Boosey *Tel.* 07460 849 472 *Publ.* Norwich Liberal Jewish Community Newsletter.

NOTTINGHAM

A small community has lived in Nottingham since the early 19th century, and in 1890, with a community increased by immigrants to some 100 families, the Hebrew Congregation built its first synagogue in Chaucer St. During the Second World War, there was a sharp growth in the community, and the congregation acquired its present synagogue in 1954. With the closure of the Derby synagogue in 1986, many of its members joined the Nottingham Hebrew Congregation. The Progressive Jewish Congregation was established in 1959.

SYNAGOGUES
Nottingham Hebrew Congregation
Shakespeare Villas, NG1 4FQ
Tel 0115 947 2004
Email info@officenhc.co.uk *Website* www.nottinghamsynagogue.co.uk
Pres. L.N. Goodman
Progressive Liberal Synagogue
Lloyd Street, NG5 4BP
Tel 0115 962 4761
Email info@nottinghamliberalsynagogue.com
Website www.nottinghamliberalsynagogue.com
Ch. Peter Gordon; *Sec.* Philip Kaye; *T.* David Leigh

WELFARE
Nottingham Jewish Women's Benevolent Society
c/o 4 Levens Close, West Bridgford, NG2 6SN
Ch. Natalie Bogod *Tel* 0115 945 2170 *Email* natalie@bogod.eu

YOUTH & STUDENTS
University of Nottingham Jewish and Israel Society
c/o The University of Nottingham, NG7 2RD

OXFORD
An important centre in the medieval period – see www.oxfordjewishheritage.co.uk for
the history of the Jews in Oxford. The modern community was established in 1842 and
in 1974 the Oxford Jewish Centre was built on the site of the earlier synagogue. The
Centre underwent a major refurbishment and extension in 2004. It serves a resident
community of some 400 families, with a fluctuating number of University students,
graduates and visitors. The Centre is available for Orthodox, Masorti and Liberal forms
of worship. The following are available to all members (including students who are honorary
members during their time in Oxford): Mikveh; Oxford WIZO; Marriage and Burial
Services; Playshul (0-5) Cheder (5+) and Barmitzvah preparation; Mosaic Adult Education
Programme including Hebrew, lectures and films; Friendship club (over 60's); Midweek
Lunch club (over 60's) and midweek social and cultural activities; Counselling services
(BLESS); Oxford Shir Choir; Helping Hand; Oxford Jewish Heritage Group; Oxford Social
Action Group; Oxford CCJ; shop and Kosher Cafe (Sunday mornings in termtime). For
information on all of these, please contact Oxford Jewish Congregation.

SYNAGOGUES
Oxford Jewish Congregation
The Oxford Jewish Centre, 21 Richmond Road, OX1 2JL
Tel 01865 514 356
Email connections@ojc-online.org *Website* www.ojc-online.org
Oxford Orthodox
(under the auspices of the United Synagogue). Services Friday evenings, Saturday mornings,
and daily morning minyan, plus all festivals. *Contact* Barry Freilich *Tel* 01865 559 899
Oxford Masorti Group
The Synagogue, 21 Richmond Road, Oxford OX1 2JL
Email connections@ojc-online.org *Website* www.ojc-online.org
Services usually held once a month on Shabbat morning at the Oxford Jewish Centre, usually
on the last Shabbat of the (secular) month. The service follows the Sacks Siddur. Families
can sit together and women and men lead the services. Visitors are welcome to attend and
participate. Please email for further information. *Contact* Wendy Fidler
Oxford Progressive
Email progressive@ojc-online.org *Website* www.ojc-online.org
Contact Katherine Shock *Tel* 01865 515 584
Services usually held on the second Shabbat of each month, from 11am and High Holy Day
festivals held.

EDUCATIONAL
Oxford Chabad Society
75-75A Cowley Road, Oxford OX4 1HR
Tel 01865 200 158
Serving Oxford Jewish Students. *Co-Dir.* Rabbi Eli Brackman, Freida Brackman
University Jewish Societies (Oxford University and Oxford Brookes University)
(Est. 1903). *Snr. Member* J Getzler, St Hugh's *Tel* 01865 557 058/375 942; *JSoc Pres. Email*
presidents@oxfordjsoc.co.uk; *Student Chaplains* Rabbi Daniel, Hannah Braune Friedman

PETERBOROUGH

SYNAGOGUES
Hebrew Congregation (Affiliated to the US)
142 Cobden Avenue, PE1 2NU
Tel 01733 264151
(Congregation Est. 1940. Synagogue opened 1954). *Admin.* C. Salmon Services Kabbalat
Shabbat 7pm.

SOCIAL, CULTURAL & INTERFAITH
Liberal Jewish Community (LJ)
c/o The Montagu Centre, 21 Maple Street, London W1T 4BE
Enquiries Elisabeth Walker *Tel* 020 7580 1663

PLYMOUTH

The Plymouth community was founded in 1745, when a cemetery was opened. Jews lived
in the city even earlier. The synagogue, built in 1762, is the oldest Ashkenazi house of worship still standing in the English-speaking world, still in regular use, with services every
Erev Shabbat, Shabbat morning and all festivals. Its 250th anniversary in May 2012 was
marked by a service conducted by Reverend Elkan Levy in the presence of the Chief Rabbi
Lord Sacks, representatives of the United Synagogue, the Board of Deputies and the Civic
Authorities. In the early 19th century, Plymouth was one of the four most important
provincial centres of Anglo-Jewry. The history of the community, 'The Plymouth
Synagogue 1761–1961' by Doris Black, was published in 1961.

Plymouth Hebrew Congregation
Catherine Street, Synagogue Chambers, Devon PL1 2AD
Tel 01752 263 162
Email imannahi@hotmail.com *Website* www.plymouthsynagogue.com
(Est. 1762. Reg. Charity No. 220010). *Hon. S.* A. Kelly *Tel* 01822 614 203

PORTSMOUTH

The community was established in 1746 and opened a synagogue in Oyster Row, later to
move to a building in White's Row, off Queen St. which was occupied for over 150 years.
The present synagogue was built in 1936. The cemetery was acquired in 1749 and is the
oldest in the Regions still in use. It is situated in Fawcett Road, which was known for more
than 200 years as Jews' Lane. By 1815 Portsmouth was one of the four main Jewish centres outside London, the others being Plymouth, Liverpool and Birmingham. Portsmouth's
prosperity declined after the Napoleonic Wars. For South Hampshire Reform Jewish
Community *See under* Southampton.

SYNAGOGUES
Portsmouth & Southsea Hebrew Congregation Synagogue
The Thicket, Elm Grove, Southsea PO5 2AA
Tel 023 9282 1494
(Reg. Charity No. X50585). Officers of the Board of Guardians (Est. 1804), the Chevra
Kadisha, Friendship Club, and the Jewish Ladies' Benevolent Society (Est. 1770) may be
contacted through the synagogue.

CEMETERIES
Fawcett Road, Kingston, New Road; Catherington

PRESTON
Synagogue established 1882, now closed.

RAMSGATE
SYNAGOGUES
Sir Moses Montefiore Synagogue
Honeysuckle Road, Ramsgate, Kent CT11 8AA
Website www.montefioreendowment.org.uk
Thanet and District Reform Synagogue
293A Margate Road, Ramsgate, Kent CT12 6TE
Tel 01843 851 164
Website www.tdrs.org.uk

READING
The community began in 1886 with the settlement of a number of tailors from London. They attracted the help of such personages as Lord Swaythling, Claude Montefiore, Sir Hermann Gollancz and Lady Lucas to build and support a synagogue in 1900, and the synagogue has been in continuous use ever since. This flourishes today as the centre of the Reading Hebrew Congregation, and is the only Orthodox congregation in Berkshire. The Sir Hermann Gollancz Hall next to the synagogue is the venue of many social groups. The Progressive Community was founded in 1979 and attracts membership from across the Thames Valley. (*See also under* Maidenhead).

REPRESENTATIVE BODIES
Berkshire Jewish Representative Council
(Est. 1995). Representing Maidenhead Synagogue, Reading Hebrew Congregation and Reading Liberal Jewish Community. *Contact*, Myer Daniels *Email* mdaniels@globalnet.co.uk

SYNAGOGUES
Reading Hebrew Congregation Synagogue
Synagogue, 7 Goldsmid Road, RG1 7YB
Tel 0118 957 3954
Website www.rhc.org.uk *Email* secretary@rhc.org.uk
(Reg. Charity No. 220098). *M.* Rabbi Z. Solomons

SOCIAL, CULTURAL & INTERFAITH
Reading Liberal Jewish Community (LJ)
2 Church Street, Reading RG1 2SB
Email readingliberaljewishcommunity@gmail.com *Website* www.readingljc.org.uk
(Est. 1979). For details of services, religious/social events, please contact Gill Switler
Tel 0118 375 3422

YOUTH & STUDENTS
University Jewish Society
c/o Hebrew Congregation.

ST. ANNE'S ON SEA
SYNAGOGUES
Hebrew Congregation
Orchard Road, FY8 1PJ
Tel 01253 721 831
(Charity No. 66492). *Pres.* R. Pinkus; *Hon. T.* J. Hecht

CEMETERIES
Consecrated section of municipal cemetery at Regents Avenue, Lytham, and consecrated

section of municipal cemetery at Carleton, Blackpool.

SHEFFIELD

The earliest records of an organised Jewish community in Sheffield date from 1850, but the congregation had already been in existence for some time and Jews are known to have been living in the city from the eighteenth century. At its peak in the 1960s, the community numbered over 2,000. A study of the community, 'Sheffield Jewry' by Armin Krausz, was published in 1980. In 2000, the Orthodox congregation moved from the large Wilson Road synagogue (built 1929) into a new and smaller synagogue within the grounds of the Jewish Centre which was consecrated by the Chief Rabbi in 2000. The Reform congregation was founded in 1989 and was admitted as a full constituent member of the RSGB in 2000. Though now a smaller community, Sheffield has an exceptional range of societies and groups, covering all varieties of Jewish interests.

SYNAGOGUES
Sheffield Jewish Congregation and Centre (Orthodox)
Kingfield Synagogue, 3 Brincliffe Crescent, S11 9AW
Tel 0114 255 2296 (synagogue) 0114 281 7459 (home)
Email ycgolomb@gmail.com *Website* www.jewishsheffield.org.uk
(Reg. Charity No. 250281). Mikveh on premises. *M.* Rabbi Y. Golomb; *Pres.* Frada Wilenski

EDUCATIONAL
Sheffield Jewish Education Organization
Sheffield Jewish Community Centre, 3 Brincliffe Crescent, S11 9AW
(Reg. Charity No. 529362). *Pres.* Dr A. Anderson *Tel* 0114 235 1041

SOCIAL, CULTURAL & INTERFAITH
Sheffield & District Reform Jewish Congregation
For information contact P.O. Box 675, SW PDO, S11 8TE
Email enquiries@shef-ref.co.uk *Website* www.shef-ref.co.uk
Ch. Mrs Kay *Tel* 07719 209 259

WELFARE
Sheffield Jewish Welfare Organisation in association with SJCC
Pres. A. Kaddish *Tel* 0114 236 7958 *Email* tony.kaddish@talktalk.net

YOUTH & STUDENTS
Sheffield Hillel House
1 Guest Road, S11 8UJ
Office Tel/Fax 0114 268 7638/0845 108 0109
Email jss@netheredgelaw.co.uk
(Reg. Charity No. 529385). *Pres.* Jeffrey Shaw

SOLIHULL

The community began in 1962. The synagogue was built in 1977. Its close proximity to Birmingham means that many of the facilities of the Birmingham community are shared with Solihull.

SYNAGOGUES
Solihull & District Hebrew Congregation
Solihull Jewish Community Centre, 3 Monastery Drive, Solihull, West Midlands B91 1DW
Tel/Fax 0121 706 8736
Email rabbi@solihullshul.org *Website* www.solihullshul.org
M. Rabbi Y. Pink *Tel* 0121 706 8736; *Pres.* S. Fisher; *Admin.* H. Woolf

EDUCATIONAL
Solihull & District Cheder
Hon. T. Rabbi Y. Pink *Tel* 0121 706 8736

SOCIAL, CULTURAL & INTERFAITH
Hakol – Community Magazine
3 Monastery Drive, B91 1DW
Email rabbi@solihullshul.org

Mother and Toddler's Group
Solihull Jewish Community Centre, 3 Monastery Drive, Solihull, West Midlands B91 1DW
Email dinapink@gmail.com *Website* www.solihullshul.org
Every Monday 11am-1pm. Dina Pink *Tel* 0121 706 8736

Stanley Middleburgh Library
3 Monastery Drive, B91 1DW
Email rabbi@solihullshul.org
Open Thursday 11am-2pm, Sunday 9.30am–1pm or by appointment.

WELFARE
The Thursday Club
Solihull Jewish Community Centre, 3 Monastery Drive, Solihull, West Midlands B91 1DW
Website www.solihullshul.org
For the over 60s. Every Thursday 11am-2pm. *Co-ord.* Ruth Abrahams *Tel* 0121 705 5287

SOUTH SHIELDS
Cemetery: Consecrated section of the municipal cemetery.

SOUTHAMPTON
The orthodox congregation dates from 1833 when the first synagogue in East Street was founded. The synagogue built in 1864 in Albion Place was demolished in 1963, when the present one was consecrated. There were Jewish residents in Southampton in 1786. Since 1838, when Abraham Abraham was elected to the Town Council, they have shared in civic affairs. The South Hampshire Reform Jewish Community was formed in 1983.

SYNAGOGUES
Orthodox Synagogue
Mordaunt Road, Inner Avenue, SO14 6GP
Tel 023 8022 0129
Website www.sotonhebrew.org.uk
Pres. M. Rose

South Hampshire Reform Jewish Community
Email shrj2@hotmail.com *Website* www.southhantsreform.wordpress.com
(Est. 1983; Reg. Charity No. 1040109). For Hampshire and the Isle of Wight. *Pres.* I. Elia
Tel 02380 220 034; *Sec.* J. Badley *Tel* 01489 783 385

CEMETERIES
Cemetery: Consecrated section at the municipal Hollybrook cemetery.

SOCIAL, CULTURAL & INTERFAITH
Hartley Library
University of Southampton, Highfield, SO17 1BJ
Houses the Anglo-Jewish Archives and Parkes Library (*See* p.115).

SOUTHEND, WESTCLIFF & LEIGH-ON-SEA
Jewish families settled in the Southend area in the late nineteenth century, mainly from London's East End. In 1906 the first temporary synagogue was built of wood in Station Road, Westcliff. In 1912 a synagogue was built in Alexandra Road, which served the community until February 2001 when it was sold. A second synagogue was built in Ceylon Road, Westcliff, in 1928, but when a new synagogue was built in Finchley Road, the Ceylon Road premises were converted into a youth centre. The Ceylon Road premises have now been sold and a new youth centre has been opened at the Talmud Torah premises.

SYNAGOGUES

Southend and District Reform Synagogue
851 London Road, Westcliff-on-Sea SS0 9SZ
Tel 01702 711 663 (answerphone)
Email admin@southendreform.org.uk *Website* www.southendreform.org.uk
M. Rabbi Warren Elf *Email* rabbielf@southendreform.org.uk; *Ch.* D. Carr; *Hon. T.* K. Phillips;
Hon. S. S. Levitas

Southend and Westcliff Hebrew Congregation
Finchley Road, Westcliff-on-Sea, Essex SS0 8AD
Email swhc@hotmail.com *Website* www.swhc.org.uk
Pres. S. Salt; *M.* Rabbi Bar *Tel* 01702 344 900 *Fax* 01702 391 131
Gen. Man. Janice Steel *Email* swhcmanager@hotmail.co.uk; *Admin.* Pamela Freedman

CEMETERIES
Orthodox Jewish Cemetery, Sutton Road, Southend SS2 5PX (Entrance Stock Road)
Tel 01702 344 900
Reform Jewish Cemetery, Sutton Road, Southend SS2 5PX (Entrance Stock Road)

EDUCATIONAL
Coleman & Lilian Levene Talmud Torah (Orthodox)
Finchley Road, Westcliff-on-Sea SS0 8AD
Tel 01702 344 900
Princ. Rabbi B. Bar

Hebrew Education Board
Email admin@southendreform.org.uk *Website* www.southendreform.org.uk
Ch. Paul Winston (Synagogue)

Chedar (Reform)
851 London Road, Westcliff, SS0 9SZ *Princ.* B. Barber *Tel* 01702 297 238

RELIGIOUS
Kashrut Commission
Ch. M.Nelkin

Mikveh
44 Genesta Road, Westcliff-on-Sea SS0 8DA
Tel 01702 344 900
Supt. R. Samuel

SOCIAL, CULTURAL & INTERFAITH
Council of Christians and Jews
Terry Mendoza *Tel* 01702 478 789; Jack De Metz *Tel* 01702 391 535

Myers Communal Hall
Finchley Road, Westcliff-on-Sea, Essex SS0 8AD
Tel 01702 344 900

Southend & District AJEX
An active branch of the Association of Jewish Ex-Servicemen and Women. For more information contact Sid Barnett, Jeffrey Barcon via the Shul office *Tel* 01702 344 900 or visit the national website www.ajex.org.uk

Tuesday Nighters
For the over 55s. For more information, contact Lewis Herlitz *Tel* 01702 715 676

WIZO
A local branch of national organisation. *Ch.* Jackie Kalms *Tel* 01702 437 801
Email jackiekalms@live.co.uk or central@wizouk.org

WELFARE
Kosher Meals-on-Wheels Service
Delivery to Jewish residents in Southend. For more information contact Tony Rubin *Tel* 01702 345 568 (24 hours)

Raymond House
7 Clifton Terrace, SS1 1DT
Man. Tel 01702 352 956
Southend Aid Society
Jewish Care's support group in Southend, working closely with Raymond House, a Jewish Care residential home for the elderly, Shebson Lodge, Jewish Care's warden assisted flats and the community centre. *Ch.* Norman Zetter; *Sec.* Janice Linden *Tel* 01702 478 375
Southend & Westcliff Community Centre
1 Cobham Road, Westcliff-on-Sea, SSO 8EG (a Jewish Care Community Centre)
Tel 01702 334 655
Website www.jewishcare.org
Man. H. Demartino *Email* hdemartino@jcare.org

YOUTH & STUDENTS
The Buzz Youth Club (Orthodox)
Finchley Road, Westcliff-on-Sea SS0 9SZ *Tel* 01702 432 067
Email sjyc.thebuzz@gmail.com
Youth Co.-ord. Paul Winston

SOUTHPORT
The first Synagogue was consecrated in 1893 and the congregation moved to Arnside Road, in 1924. The New Synagogue (Reform) was established in 1948. The community grew between and during the First and Second World Wars, but is now decreasing.

REPRESENTATIVE BODIES
Jewish Representative Council
Hon. S. R. Jackson 33 The Chesters, 17-19 Argyle Road PR9 9LG *Tel* 01704 532 696

SYNAGOGUES
Southport Hebrew Congregation
Arnside Road, PR9 0QX
Tel 01704 532 964
Website www.jscn.org.uk/southport-hebrew-congregation
(Est. 1893). *Ch.* Ray Roukin; *Snr. Warden* Adrian Fletcher; *Admin.* Mrs S Roukin
Southport Reform Synagogue
Princes Street, PR8 1EG
Tel 01704 535 950
Website www.southportreform.org.uk
Office Hours Tuesday, Thursday, Friday 10am-1pm. *Office Admin.* Lisa Sachs

RELIGIOUS
Mikveh
Arnside Road, PR9 0QX
Tel 01704 532 964

SOCIAL, CULTURAL & INTERFAITH
Southport Hebrew Philanthropic Society
(Est. 1897). *Sec.* M.P. Braham *Tel* 01704 563 665

WELFARE
Southport Rest Home
81 Albert Road, PR9 9LN
Tel 01704 531 975 (office); 01704 530 207 (visitors)
Email office@sjah.freeserve.co.uk
Ch. B. King
Manchester House
83 Albert Road, Southport, PR9 9LN
Tel 01704 534 920 (office); 01704 530 436 (visitors)

STOKE-ON-TRENT AND NORTH STAFFORDSHIRE
Hebrew Congregation
London Road, Newcastle, Staffs, ST5 1LZ
(Est. 1873. Reg. Charity No. 232104).
Pres. M.D. Morris *Tel* 01782 616 417 *Email* martin@mmorris01.wanadoo.co.uk; *Hon S.* Ray Elias *Tel* 01782 318 110

SUFFOLK
Suffolk Liberal Jewish Community (LJ)
Suffolk Jewish Community is a very small and friendly community. We try to meet once a month in Ipswich (generally last Friday of the month), and have a few Shabbatons throughout the year. We meet in people's houses, or local village halls, but at present, do not have a fixed base. We hold a communal Seder service, and services for Erev Rosh Hashanah and other festivals. We are affiliated to LJ. *Enquiries* Beverley Levy *Tel* 01473 250 797 *Email* sjc@liberaljudaism.org

SUNDERLAND
The first Jewish settlement was in 1755. The first congregation was established about 1768; it was the first regional community to be represented at the BoD.
A synagogue was erected in Moor Street in 1862; rebuilt in 1900.
In 1928 the congregation moved to Ryhope Road, The Beth Hamedrash, which was established in Villiers St. in 1899, and which moved to Mowbray Road in 1938, closed in December 1984.
Arnold Levy published *History of the Sunderland Jewish Community, 1755-1955* (1956). There is also *The Sunderland Beth Hamedrash 1889 - 1999*, written by Derek Taylor and Harold Davis (2010).

CEMETERIES
Bishopwearmouth Cemetery, Hylton Road, Sunderland.

SWINDON
The community formed by Second World War evacuees has dispersed, but a community was re-formed in 1983.
Swindon Jewish Community (Associated Community of the Movement for Reform Judaism) c/o Reform Judaism, Sternberg Centre, 80 East End Road, London N3 2SY *Tel* 020 8349 5643 (Est.1983). *Contact Tel* 01793 831 335

TORQUAY (TORBAY)
SYNAGOGUES
Synagogue
Old Town Hall, Abbey Road
The synagogue was closed at the end of 2000 and the congregation dissolved.

RELIGIOUS
Chevra Kadisha Cemetery, Colley End Road, Paignton, Torbay TQ3 3QX *Ch.* E. Freed 11 Kestor Drive, Paignton TQ3 1AP *Tel* 01803 553 781

TOTNES
Totnes Jewish Community (Movement for Reform)
We are a small, open-hearted community representing a diverse range of Jewish expression, and offering regular spiritual, social and cultural events. For all enquiries contact Marc Frank *Tel* 07508 806 770 *Email* marcfrank12@googlemail.com

TRURO
The Jews of Cornwall: A History; Tradition and Settlement to 1913 by Keith Pearce was published in 2014.

Kehillat Kernow

Website www.kehillatkernow.com

(Est. 1999 Reg. Charity No. 1090562). Kehillat Kernow is a thriving Jewish community in Cornwall which has recently celebrated its fifthteenth anniversary. Kehillat Kernow is a growing congregation of over 50 families who live all over Cornwall. They meet fortnightly for Shabbat Services and cheder followed by a kiddush lunch at Three Bridges School in Blackwater near Truro. We also celebrate all major holidays and festivals together including a very popular and delicious communal seder. Holiday makers and visitors are warmly welcome. For service dates, times and directions please refer to our website. *Ch.* Harvey Kurzfield Owl Cottage, Mill Road, Penponds, Cornwall *Tel* 01209 719 672; *T.* Leslie Lipert *Tel* 01736 762 675; *Sec.* Rachel Brown *Tel* 01872 862 665

WALLASEY
Hebrew Congregation
28 Grant Road, Wirral, Merseyside, L46 2RY
Tel 0161 638 6945
(Est. 1911). *Pres.* D. Daniels; *T.* D. J. Waldman; *Hon. S.* L.S. Goldman

WORTHING
Worthing & District Jewish Community
The Friends Meeting House, 34 Mill Road, Worthing BN11 5DR
Meet for social and cultural events. *Outreach Chaplain,* Rev. Malcolm Weisman. *Ch.* Ian Gordon *Tel* 01903 779 720 *Email* barbaraian@talktalk.net

YORK
A memorial stone was consecrated at Clifford's Tower, York Castle, in 1978 in memory of the York Jewish community massacred there in 1190. A small community resettled and continued to live in York until the 1290 expulsion. There is now a small community in the city and a Jewish Society at York University.

York Jewish Community
York Jewish Community welcomes all the many shades of Judaism. It organises events usually around food and festivals such as Chanukah, Pesach and Shabbat.

It no longer has a synagogue, nor does it organise regular services, although the get-togethers usually encompass some relevant rituals. It runs a communal Seder and Chanukah. For more information, please email shalom@yorkjewishcommunity.org.uk For activities across a wider part of Yorkshire please go to the following website: www.leedsjewishcommunity.com

WALES

CARDIFF
Jews settled in Cardiff about the year 1787. The present community was founded in 1840.

REPRESENTATIVE BODIES
The Interfaith Council for Wales
c/o Cytûn, 58 Richmond Road, Cardiff CF24 3UR
Website www.interfaithwales.org.uk
Sec. Rev Canon Aled Edwards OBE *Tel* 02920 464 375

South Wales Jewish Representative Council
9 Holmwood Close, Cyncoed, Cardiff CF23 6BT
Tel 029 2075 5556
Email swjewishrepcouncil@gmail.com
Ch. Stanley Soffa; *Hon. S.* Ruth Levene *Tel* 07920 585 848

SYNAGOGUES
Cardiff United Synagogue
Cyncoed Gardens, Cyncoed Road, Penylan, CF23 5SL
Tel 029 2047 3728
Website www.cardiffshul.org
Rabbi R. Rose *Email* rabbi@cardiffshul.org
  Mikveh Appointments *Tel* 07928 669 536

Cardiff Reform Synagogue (Movement for Reform)
Moira Terrace, CF24 0EJ (opposite Howard Gardens)
Tel 029 2049 1689
Email info@cardiffreformsyn.org.uk *Website* www.cardiffreformsyn.org.uk
Ch. M. Odey; *Sec.* J. Golten

Cathedral Road Synagogue
(Opened 1871). Closed 1997. *Tel* 01633 810 013 *Ch.* A. Davidson *Email* abd321@onetel.com

CEMETERIES
Old Cemetery – High Fields Road, Roath Park
New Cemetery – Greenfarm Road, Ely
Reform: at Cowbridge Road Entrance, Ely Cemetery

RELIGIOUS
Kashrus Commission
Cyncoed Gardens, Cyncoed Road, Penylan, CF23 5SL
Tel 029 2047 3728

SOCIAL, CULTURAL & INTERFAITH
Bimah (Three issues annually)
18 St Edeyrns Road, Cyncoed, Cardiff CF23 6TB
Tel 0292 076 2689
(Est. 1994). The Platform of Welsh Jewry. *Ed.* Barbara Michaels
Email barbara.michaels@btopenworld.com

Israel Information Centre Wales & the West of England
P.O.B. 98, CF2 6XN
Tel/Fax 02920 461 780
Dir. Jean A. Evans

WELFARE
Cardiff Jewish Helpline (formerly **Cardiff Jewish Board of Guardians**)
23 Solva Avenue, CF14 0NP
Tel 029 2075 0990
Ch. A. Schwartz

Penylan House, Jewish Residential and Nursing Home
Penylan Road, CF23 5YG
Tel 029 2048 5327 *Fax* 029 2045 8409
Nursing Office 029 2049 2574
Email penylanhouse@aol.com
Dir. Paul Evans; *Pres.* Judy Cotsen; *Matron/Nursing Man.* Geraldine Paterson

YOUTH & STUDENTS
Hillel House
89 Crwys Road, Cardiff CF24 4NF
Applications for admission: L. Gerson *Email* lisa.gerson@ymail.com
Hillel House is located in the heart of Cardiff's student area, among many local shops including a large supermarket. It is within walking distance from Cardiff University and Cardiff City Centre and is close to Medical School, UWIC campuses and Atrium and accesses major bus, rail and road routes with roadside resident parking. Each room is spacious and comes complete with its own kitchenette and ensuite shower facilities. Additionally

the house has a large living room with flat screen tv and is the meeting place of the JSoc where Friday night meals are regularly held.

Union of Jewish Students
c/o Hillel House
Website www.groups.cardiffstudents.com/jewish/about/
Facebook Cardiff Jewish Society

Hillel House and Cardiff Jewish Society are open to all Jewish students in South Wales. To get involved, please go to the Facebook page.

Contact for South Wales university students, Rabbi Michoel Rose *Email* Rabbi@cardiffshul.org

LLANDUDNO AND COLWYN BAY

Hebrew Congregation
28 Church Walks, Llandudno LL30 2HL
(Est. 1905). Llandudno serves as the centre for the communities of North Wales, including Bangor, Rhyl, Colwyn Bay and Caernarvon.

MERTHYR TYDFIL

The synagogue is now closed. The community was established before 1850. The cemetery is still being maintained. Apply to the Cardiff Jewish Representative Council.

NEWPORT (Gwent)

CEMETERIES
Cemetery: Risca Road, Newport

RELIGIOUS
Burial Society c/o Cardiff United Synagogue, Penylan, Cardiff

SOCIAL, CULTURE & INTERFAITH
Synagogue (opened 1871). Now closed.
Tel 01633 810 013
Ch. A. Davidson *Email* abd321@onetel.com

SWANSEA

The Jewish community dates at the latest from 1768, when the Corporation granted a plot of land for use as a cemetery. In 1780 a synagogue was built. Probably its history is even older, for Jews are known to have been living in the town from about 1730. The synagogue in Goat Street was destroyed in an air raid in Feb. 1941, but another was erected in the Ffynone district. The former Llanelli congregation is now part of the Swansea community.

SYNAGOGUES
Swansea Hebrew Congregation
(Est. 1780). Synagogue, Ffynone Road, c/o 17 Ffynone Drive, SA1 6DB

CEMETERIES
There are cemeteries at Oystermouth and Townhill.

RELIGIOUS
Chevra Kadisha
S. Franks 4 The Causeway, Parc Wern Road, Sketty, Swansea SA2 0SX *Tel* 01792 205 298

WELSHPOOL

Welshpool Jewish Group
c/o M. and S. Michaels, 10 Corndon Drive, Montgomery, Powys SY15 6RE
Tel 01686 668977
Email markjmichaels@googlemail.com

SCOTLAND

REPRESENTATIVE BODIES

Scottish Council of Jewish Communities (SCoJeC)
Jewish Community Centre, 222 Fenwick Road, Giffnock, Glasgow G46 6UE
Tel 0141 638 6411 *Mobile* 07887 488 100
Email scojec@scojec.org *Website* www.scojec.org
(Est. 1987 as the Standing Committee of Scottish Jewry. Charity SCO 29438). A Democratic umbrella body representing all the Jewish Communities in Scotland to the Scottish Parliament and Executive churches and other faith communities, educational, health and welfare organisations. An educational charity to promote understanding of the Jewish religion and community. JSoJeC also supports isolated and unaffiliated Jewish people outside the main Jewish communities in Scotland. *Ch.* H. Rifkind; *Dir.* Ephraim Borowski; *Research and Publications*, Leah Granat; *Public Affairs Officer*, Nicola Livingston; *Outreach and Projects*, Fiona Frank

SOCIAL, CULTURAL & INTERFAITH

The Scottish Jewish Archives Centre
Garnethill Synagogue, 129 Hill Street, Glasgow G3 6UB
Tel 0141 332 4911
Email info@sjac.org.uk *Website* www.sjac.org.uk
(Est. 1987). Aims to: collect, catalogue, preserve and exhibit records of communal interest, stimulate study of the history of the Jews of Scotland, heighten awareness, in the Jewish communities of Scotland, of their cultural and religious heritage. Exhibition on Jewish history in Scotland. *Ch.* Dr Kenneth Collins; *Dir.* Harvey L. Kaplan; *Hon. T.* Fiona L. Brodie, Harvey Livingston; *Hon. S.* Marcia Goldman, Dianna Wolfson; *Curator*, Deborah Hass

ABERDEEN

Refurbished synagogue and community centre opened in 1983.

Hebrew Congregation
74 Dee Street, AB11 6DS
Email aberdeenhebrew@gmail.com *Website* www.aberdeenhebrew.org.uk
(Est. 1893. Reg. Charity No. SC002901). *Pres.* Yonni Shoshan; *V. Pres.* Chris Fynsk; *Hon S.* Sarah Bronzite; *T.* Chrissie Nyssen

DUNDEE

Tayside and Fife Jewish Community
9 St. Mary Place, DD1 5RB
Email dundeehebrewcongregation@gmail.com   taysideandfife@scojec.org
Website www.scojec.org/dundee.index.html
(Est. 1874. New synagogue opened 1978. Scottish Charitable Incorpated Org. 12108). *Ch.* Dr P. Spicker. In an emergency, the Scottish Council of Jewish Communities can be contacted on our behalf *Tel* 0141 638 6411
Dundee University Jewish Society is centred at the synagogue.

EDINBURGH

The Edinburgh Town Council and Burgess Roll, Minutes of 1691 and 1717, record applications by Jews for permission to reside and trade in Edinburgh. Local directories of the eighteenth century contain Jewish names. There is some reason to believe that there was an organised Jewish community in 1780 but no cemetery, and in 1817 it removed to Richmond Ct. where there was also for a time a rival congregation. In 1795, the Town Council sold a plot of ground on the Calton Hill to Herman Lyon, a Jewish dentist, to provide a burying place for himself and members of his family. In 1816, when a synagogue was opened, a cemetery was also acquired. The present synagogue in Salisbury Road was consecrated in 1932 and renovated in 1980.

SYNAGOGUES
Edinburgh Hebrew Congregation
Synagogue Chambers, 4 Salisbury Road, EH16 5AB
Website www.ehcong.com
(Est. 1816, Present Synagogue built 1932). *Ch. of the Board of Management*, Raymond Taylor
Tel 0131 667 3144 *Email* ray.taylor1@blueyonder.co.uk; *M.* Rabbi D. Rose; *Sec./Admin.*
Jackie Taylor Email secretary@ehcong.com
   Board of Guardians *Ch. M.* Kaplan c/o 4 Salisbury Road, EH16 5AB

RELIGIOUS
Edinburgh Jewish Burial Friendly Society
Edinburgh Eastern Cemetery Co. Ltd, 204a Piersfield Terrace, Midlothian EH8 7BN
Tel 0131 620 7025

SOCIAL, CULTURAL & INTERFAITH
The Edinburgh Star (2 times a year)
31/3 Rattray Grove, EH10 5TL
Community Journal. *Ed.* M. Brannan
Jewish Literary Society
Email h.holtschneider@gmail.com
Ladies' Guild
37 Cluny Drive, Edinburgh EH10 6DU
Tel 0131 447 7386
Pres. Hilary Rifkind
Wizo
Synagogue Chambers, 4 Salisbury Road, EH16 5AB
The shop, manned by volunteers, is open on Sunday mornings before each festival and at other times by arrangements.

YOUTH & STUDENTS
Edinburgh University Jewish Society (JSoc)
Email edinburghjsoc@gmail.com *Website* www.jsoc.eusa.ed.ac.uk
The Edinburgh University Jewish Society (JSoc) is a pluralist, active, apolitical and inclusive community for all students interested in the Jewish faith and culture.
Pres. Jacob Pearson; *Sec.* Rachel Rubin; *T.* Hunter Weinsheink

GLASGOW AND WEST OF SCOTLAND
The Glasgow Jewish community was founded in 1823 although there are records of Jewish activity in the city for many years prior to that. The first Jewish cemetery was opened in the prestigious Glasgow Necropolis in 1831 and the community was housed in a variety of synagogues in the city centre for many years. The community grew in the 1870s and the Garnethill Synagogue, the oldest Jewish building in Scotland and home of the Scottish Jewish Archives Centre, was opened in 1879. At the same time Jews began settling in the Gorbals district, just south of the River Clyde, where there was a substantial Jewish community with many synagogues and Jewish shops and communal institutions until the 1950s. None of these now remain. In more recent years the community has been centred in the southern suburbs, such as Giffnock and Newton Mearns, where most Jewish institutions are now situated.
   Details of Jewish history in Glasgow in the early days (1790–1919) can be found in 'Second City Jewry' and 'Scotland's Jews' by Dr. Kenneth Collins, available from the Glasgow Jewish Representative Council.

REPRESENTATIVE BODIES
Glasgow Jewish Representative Council
Jewish Community Centre, 222 Fenwick Road, Giffnock, Glasgow G46 6UE
Tel 0141 577 8200
Email office@glasgowjewishrepcouncil.org *Website* www.jewishglasgow.org

(Reg. Charity No. SCO166). *Pres.* Paul Morron MBE; *Admin.* Orli Schechper; *Hon. S.* Fiona L. Brodie; *Sec.* Frank Angell

SYNAGOGUES
Garnethill Synagogue
129 Hill Street, G3 6UB
Tel 0141 332 4151
Email greenhillm@btinternet.com *Website* www.sjac.org.uk/archives/garnethill.html
Senior congregation in city. Victorian 'A' listed building. Groups of visitors shown round by appointment. Scottish Jewish Archives have completed a renovation and upgrading of their museum housed in the building. We are a friendly congregation who welcome visitors on Shabbat and Yom Tov.
Garnethill Synagogue was the first purpose-built synagogue in Scotland. Its inaugural service was held on 9 September, 1879 and a massive refurbishment was completed in 1998. To arrange a visit, please write to the synagogue enclosing a stamped addressed envelope. Shabbat services begin at 10am. *Ba'al Torah*, Stanley Kaye; *Snr. Warden,* Errol Hornstein; *Cantor,* Eddie Binnie; *Co-Ch.* Bernard Goodman, Tony Silverdale (and *Hon T.)*; *Sec.* Dr Michael Greenhill *Email* mdg121@sky.com

Giffnock and Newlands Synagogue
222 Fenwick Road, Giffnock G46 6UE
Tel 0141 577 8250
Email admin@giffnockshul.co.uk *Website* www.giffnockshul.co.uk
M. Rabbi A.M. Rubin; *Ch.* J. Freedman; *Admin.* H. Livingstone

Glasgow Reform Synagogue - Or Chadash
147 Ayr Road, Newton Mearns G77 6RE
Tel 0141 639 4083
Email shul@grs.org.uk *Website* www.grs.org.uk
Rabbi, Kate Briggs; *Ch.* Eileen Carroll; *V. Ch.* Jonathan Green; *Admin.* Tracey Jacobs

Langside Hebrew Congregation
125 Niddrie Road, G42 8QA
Tel 0141 649 2962/ 0141 423 4062
M. Ch. J. Levingstone; *Hon. S.* P. Morron

Newton Mearns Synagogue
14 Larchfield Court, G77 5PL
Tel 0141 639 4000
Email office@nmhc.org.uk *Website* www.nmhc.org
Ch. Bradley Kay; *V. Ch.* C. Cowan; *Hon. S.* J. Fischer; *Admin,* S. Tobias

Shul in the Park (Lubavitch)
Tel 0141 638 5613
Email lubofscot@aol.com *Website* www.lubofscot.co.uk
Founder, M. Rabbi Mendel Jacobs

EDUCATIONAL
Calderwood Lodge Jewish Primary School
28 Calderwood Road, G43 2RU
Tel 0141 570 7060
Hd. M. Johnson

RELIGIOUS
Hebrew Burial Society
Tel 0141 577 8226/ 07748 676 429
Email hebrewburialsociety@gmail.com
Mikveh
Giffnock & Newlands Synagogue, Maryville Avenue, Giffnock G46 7NE
Mikveh appointments: Margalit Borowski *Tel* 07831 104 110 (between mid-August and last week of June). Synagogue office *Tel* 0141 577 8250 *Email* office@giffnockshul.co.uk (between end of June and approx 12th August).

West Scotland Kashrut Commission
Tel 0141 221 1827
Ch. M. Livingstone

SOCIAL, CULTURAL & INTERFAITH

Glasgow Zionist Federation
222 Fenwick Road, Giffnock G46 6UE
Tel 0141 577 8222

Israel Scottish Information Service
222 Fenwick Road, Giffnock, G46 6UE
Tel 0141 639 3294
Email ezra@isrinfo.demon.co.uk *Website* www.isrinfo.demon.co.uk
Provides online news services about Israel.

Jewish Telegraph
May Terrace, Giffnock G46 6LD
Tel 0141 621 4422 (classified ads) *Tel* 0141 621 4433 (Newsdesk) 0141 621 4455 (Display Ads)
Email glasgow@jewishtelegraph.com *Website* www.jewishtelegraph.com

Lubavitch of Scotland
8 Orchard Drive, Giffnock G46 7NR
Tel 0141 638 6116
Email lubofscot@aol.com *Website* www.lubofscot.co.uk
Dir. Rabbi Chaim Jacobs, Sora Jacobs

Maccabi GB Scotland
May Terrace, Giffnock, G46 6LD
Tel 0141 638 6177
Email info@maccabigbscotland.org
Ch. D. Shenkin; *Operations Man.* Sue Faber

UJIA (incorporating Glasgow Jewish Continuity)
222 Fenwick Road, Giffnock, G46 6UE
Tel 0141 530 5340
Fundrasing, Ruth Grace

WELFARE

Arklet Housing Association
Barrland Court, Barrland Drive, Giffnock, G46 7QD
Tel 0141 620 1890 *Fax* 0141 620 3044
Email arklet@arklet.org.uk *Website* www.arklet.org.uk
Dir. Maureen Paterson

Cosgrove Care
The Walton Community Care Centre, May Terrace, Giffnock, G46 6LD
Tel 0141 620 2500
Email care@cosgrove.co.uk *Website* www.cosgrovecare.org.uk
Cosgrove Care supports people with learning disabilities and their families within the Jewish community. It offers a comprehensive range of support, including supported independent living for adults, holiday play schemes for children, and daily and weekly group activities. One of its two charity shops offers supported employment and volunteering opportunities to service users. *Ch.* John Dover; *Hon T.* Paul Shafar; *Chief Exec.* Walter Hecht; *Board,* Colin Black, Gary Clark, Nicola Livingston, Walter Hecht

Jmind
222 Fenwick Road, G46 6UE
Tel 0141 577 8246
Email jwatters@cosgrovecare.org.uk
Mental health service within Cosgrove Care and provides support to adults with mental health issues. It offers a comprehensive range of person-centred support, including talking therapy and individual support at home to enable people to manage their long term conditions more effectively.

Jewish Blind Society (Scotland)
Walton Community Care Centre, May Terrace, Giffnock, G46 6LD
Tel 0141 620 3339
Email jbs@jcarescot.org.uk
(Reg. Charity No. SCO11789). *Ch.* L. Sellyn; *Sec.* C. Blake

Jewish Care Scotland
The Walton Community Care Centre, May Terrace Giffnock, G46 6DL
Tel 0141 620 1800 *Fax* 0141 620 1409
Email admin@jcarescot.org.uk *Website* www.jcarescot.org.uk
Just Giving Page www.justgiving.com/jcarescot
(Caring for the Community since 1858. Reg. Charity No. SCO 05267). Jewish Care Scotland is Scotland's leading Jewish welfare charity dedicated to providing professional social work and social care services to individuals and families in need. The charity runs a registered day-care centre, kosher meals-on-wheels, a lunch club for older people, a club for those with long-term illness or disability, a weekly drop-in for adults with mental health problems, a kosher foodbank and a hardship fund. Support ranges from welfare rights advice and debt counselling to specialist help for people with enduring mental health problems. Please call in confidence to speak to a member of the social work team, for information about the clubs and services or to find out more about volunteering opportunities. *Ch.* George Hecht CA

Newark Care
32 Burnfield Road, Giffnock, G46 7PZ
Tel 0141 621 2560 *Fax* 0141 621 2569
Email info@newarkcare.org.uk *Website* www.newarkcare.org.uk
Provides residential and nursing care within a Jewish environment for those no longer able to continue in their homes. *Ch.* M. Jackson; *Chief Exec.* M. Joshi

YOUTH & STUDENTS
UJIA Programmes (UJIA Scotland)
Based at UJIA, Jewish Community Centre, 222 Fenwick Road, Giffnock, Glasgow, G46 6UE
(Reg. Charity No. Sc039181) *Tel* 0141 530 5340
Scottish Programmes Dir. Joanna Hyman *Tel* 0141 530 5343 *Email* Joanna.hyman@ujia.org
Scottish Youth Worker, Julie-Rae King *Tel* 0141 530 5344 *Email* glasgow.youthworker@ujia.org
Northern Region Chaplaincy
Chaplain, Yossi Bodenheim *Email* yossi@mychaplaincy.co.uk

HIGHLANDS
Jewish Network of Argyll and The Highlands (JNAH)
Contact Lochaline, Morvern PA80 5XT
Tel 07527 040 501
Email linda@scojec.org

NORTHERN IRELAND

BELFAST
There was a Jewish community in Belfast from 1864. The first synagogue was erected in 1871 on Great Victoria Street.

SYNAGOGUES
Hebrew Congregation
49 Somerton Road, BT15 3LH
(Est. 1871; Second synagogue was erected in 1904 on Annesley Street. Present synagogue on Somerton Road was erected in 1964). Rabbi D. Singer *Tel* 028 9077 5013

SOCIAL, CULTURAL & INTERFAITH
BELFAST JEWISH RECORD (Quarterly)
14 Norton Drive, Belfast BT9 6ST
Tel 07533 324 618
(Est. 1953). *Soc. Sec.* M. Black
Jewish Community Centre
49 Somerton Road, BT15 3LH
Tel 028 9077 7974 / *Tel* 02890 775 013 (Rabbi)

ISLE OF MAN

CEMETERIES
Consecrated section of the Douglas Cemetery, Glencrutchery Road IM2

SOCIAL, CULTURAL & INTERFAITH
Hebrew Congregation
Contact Carol Jempson, 8 Mountain View, Douglas IM2 5HU; *Visiting M.* Rev. Malcolm Weisman OBE, MA (Oxon)

CHANNEL ISLANDS

JERSEY
A synagogue existed in St. Helier, the capital of the island, from 1843 until about 1870. The present community was founded in 1962.

Jersey Jewish Congregation
La Petite Route des Mielles, St Brelade, JE3 8FY
Tel 01534 44946
Pres. S. J. Regal; *Hon. S.* M. Morton, 16 La Rocquaise, La Route des Genets, St Brelade, JE3 8HY *Tel* 01534 742819; *Hon. T.* M. Kalman; *Visiting M.* Rev. M. Weisman, OBE, MA. Seven families of the Jersey congregation live in Guernsey.

OTHER COUNTRIES

AFGHANISTAN

Jews have lived in Afghanistan since antiquity. Just over 100 years ago they reportedly numbered 40,000. Since 1948 there has been a mass emigration to Israel. Zebulon Simantov is believed to be the sole remaining Afghan Jew in Afghanistan since 2005. There is an old synagogue on Flower Street, in Kabul.

ALBANIA

There have been Jews living in the area, now known as Albania, since Roman times, and there are remains in Dardania, in the north, of an ancient synagogue. The community was re-established by Jews from Iberia escaping the Spanish Inquisition in the fifteenth and early sixteenth centuries.

By 1930, the Jewish population had grown to 200, but was soon augmented by refugees escaping the Nazis. Most Jews were helped to hide from Italian occupiers, and then from the Nazis.

Post–war communism isolated Jews until the regime fell. In 1991 almost the entire community, about 300, was airlifted to Israel. The few Jews who remained in Albania live in the capital Tirana.

Albania Israel Friendship Society
Contact Refik Veseli
Rruga Barriskatave 226, Tirana
Tel +355 (4) 222 611

ALGERIA

It is believed that there were Jews in Algeria as early as the fourth century, BCE. The fortunes of the community varied under the Turkish regime, which began in 1519. After the French conquered Algeria the community was reorganised and, in 1870, most Jews were granted French citizenship. However, there have been anti-Jewish excesses even in the present century. After Algeria's bitter fight for independence, the Jews, like other French nationals, lost their possessions when they left the country. About 120,000 at Independence in 1962, there remain less than 50 today: almost all fled to France.
Contact Mme L. Meller-Saïd, 12 Ave Louis Pasteur, 92220 Bagneux France
Email linemeller@wanadoo.fr

Jewish Community Office and Synagogue
6 Rue Hassena Ahmed, Algiers
Tel +213 (2) 62 85 72
Pres. Maitre Roger Said *Tel* +213 (3) 49 26 57

ANDORRA

Andorra, which is governed by two co-princes – the Bishop of Urgell in Spain and the President of France – does not have a Jewish history. There are currently, however, around 15 Jewish families, mostly of Moroccan origins.

A synagogue and community centre was established in 1997 in Escaldes and is the first in Andorra's 1,100 year history.

CONTACT INFORMATION
Isaac Benchluch Ayach *Tel* +376 341 282, Baruj Rodriquez *Tel* +376 324 724, Mercedes Abitbol *Tel* +376 335 306 Community Email *Email* aciv.ad@gmail.com

ANTIGUA AND BARBUDA (West Indies)

A few Jewish residents live permanently on the island.
Correspondence B. Rabinowitz, Cedar Valley, P.O.B. 399 *Tel* +268 461 4150

ARGENTINA

The early Jewish settlers in Argentina were Marranos, who were gradually absorbed in the general population. The present community grew through immigration (beginning in 1862) from Germany, the Balkans, and North Africa. Immigrants began to arrive from Eastern Europe in 1889, many of them going to the agricultural settlements established by the Jewish Colonization Association. The community is estimated to number 300,000, including 60,000 Sephardim, who have their own separate institutions, according to D.A.I.A., the representative organisation of Argentine Jews. The Jewish population of Greater Buenos Aires is estimated at 220,000. A survey conducted by the Hebrew University of Jerusalem however estimates the Jewish population at 240,000, of whom 210,000 are Ashkenazim and 30,000 are Sephardim.

There are nine other major communities in Parana, Rosario, Cordoba, Bahia Blanca, Posadas, Resistencia, Tucuman, Mendoza and La Plata. There is a small but very active community in Mar del Plata, south of Buenos Aires. Very few Jewish families remain on the former J.C.A. settlements. There are about 100 synagogues (80 Orthodox, one Reform, the rest Conservative or Liberal), and a well-organised network of communal and educational institutes. There are community offices in Cordoba at Alvear 254, and in Rosario at Paraguay 1152.

BUENOS AIRES
Congreso Judio Latinoamericano
Larrea 744, 1030
Tel +54 (11) 4962 5028
Representative Organisation of Argentine Jews
DAIA, Pasteur 633, 5th floor
Argentine Jewish Community (AMIA)
Pasteur 633, C1028AAM
Tel +54 (11) 4959 8800
Email amia@amia.org.ar *Website* www.webamia@amia.org.ar
(Est. 1894) A victim of terrorism in 1994, the reconstructed Community Centre has now re-opened in the service of the life and culture of the Jewish community of Argentina
Central Sephardi Community
FESERA, Las Heras 1646

ARMENIA

Jews have lived in Armenia for over 2,000 years and the various communities were spread around different parts of the country. There was a synagogue in Yerevan, but in the 1930s it was destroyed. Nowadays, nearly all the Armenian Jews live in Yerevan, with only a few families living in Vanadzor (Kirovakan) and Gjumri (Leninakan). Others are scattered in some small towns and villages. When 'perestroika' was introduced in 1989, the Jewish community organised itself and in 1991 was registered as a non-formal organisation. Perestroika opened the doors, so that a large number of the population emigrated to Israel. In 1991 a Jewish Sunday school was opened both for children and adults. In 1992 the Israeli embassy in Moscow financed the school. Over 60 per cent of the population is over 60 years of age and there are about 40 children below the age of 16.

CONTACT INFORMATION
Pres. Willi Weiner *Tel* +374 (1) 525 882; *Dir. of Educ.* Dr. George Fajvush *Tel* +374 (1) 735 852; *Rabbi* Gersh-Meir Burchstein *Tel* +374 (1) 271 115
Chabad Lubavitch of Yerevan Synagogue
23 Nar-Dosa Street, Yerevan, Armenia 375018 *Tel* +374 (1) 571 677

ARUBA

Today, the Jewish community has about 85 members, and 150 Overseas Members.
Due to its small size, and the intimate, close-knit nature of the community, one joint organization was formed, blending the Sephardic with the Ashkenazic traditions, respecting their common culture, and enjoying the differences. monthly newsletter, that is mailed to

local and overseas members. It portrays significant events in the life of the community, and connects all members.

Beth Israel Synagogue (Independent Conservative/Reform)
A. Laclé Blvd. #2, P.O. Box 655, Oranjestad
Tel +297 582 3272 *Fax* +297 886 264
Rabbi Mario Gurevich *Email* rabbi.aruba@yahoo.com
The synagogue of Aruba is an independent Conservative/Reform style congregation.

CEMETERY
There is an Old Jewish Cemetery in Oranjestad, on Petronia Street, which contains eight gravestones dating back to 1563. The cemetery did not begin to be utilized by Jewish settlers regularly until 1837. These gravestones are the only indication of a Jewish presence on the island in the past centuries.

AUSTRALIA

The earliest organisation of Jews in Australia was in 1817 when 20 Jews in New South Wales formed a burial society. In 1828 a congregation was formed in Sydney and the first specially erected synagogue was opened in 1844. The first Jewish service was held in Melbourne in 1839, four years after the beginning of the colonisation on the banks of the River Yarra. A synagogue was opened in 1847. A permanent congregation was formed in Adelaide in 1848. Congregations were established at Ballarat (1853) and Geelong (1854) in South Australia. A congregation in Brisbane was established in 1865. In Western Australia the first congregation (now ended) was formed at Fremantle in 1887, and the present Perth congregation established in 1892, with Kalgoorlie in 1895. In Tasmania a synagogue was opened in Hobart in 1845 and another at Launceston in 1846. Organised Jewish communities were established in other States a few years later.

In Australia's public life Jews have played a distinguished part. Many have risen to high office in the Federation and State Parliaments or on the Judicial bench. Two Governors-General of Australia have been Jews; The late Sir Zelman Cowen and the late Sir Isaac Isaacs. Sir John Monash, the Commander of the Australian Expeditionary Forces in the First World War, was a Jew. The Exec. Council of Australian Jewry represents the central Jewish organisations in each State. The Australian census has an optional question on religious affiliation. In 2001, 88,993 people declared themselves Jews by religion. If a proportionate number of 'no religion/religion not stated' replies are regarded as Jewish, the number of Jews rises to 105,000. Recent demographic res. indicated that there are probably about 92,000 people in Australia who are religiously or ethnically Jewish. The main Jewish coms. are in Melbourne; Sydney; Perth; Brisbane; Adelaide; The Gold Coast, Queensland; Canberra and Hobart.

KASHRUT CONTACTS
Kosher Australia
P.O. Box 2247 Caulfield Junction, 3161, Victoria
Tel +61 (3) 8317 2555 *Fax* +61 (3) 9527 5665
Email info@kosher.org.au *Website* www.kosher.org.au
The Kashrut Authority
Office hours Monday to Thursday 9am-5pm, Friday 9am-2pm
Tel +61 (2) 9365 2933 *Fax* +61 (2) 9365 0933
Email office@ka.org.au *Website* www.ka.org.au

MAIN JEWISH ORGANISATIONS
Australasian Union of Jewish Students
306 Hawthorn Road, Caulfield, Victoria 3162
Tel +61 (3) 9272 5622
Australia/Israel and Jewish Affairs Council (AIJAC)
See under International Organisations
B'nai B'rith Australia/New Zealand
71 Kooyong Road, Caulfield North, Victoria 3161
Tel +61 (3) 9756 1116 *Fax* +61 (3) 9756 0339
Website www.bnaibrith.org.au

Jewish Community Council of Victoria
306 Hawthorn Road, South Caulfield, Victoria 3162
Email community@jcc.org.au *Website* www.jcc.org.au
Pres. John Searle *Tel* +61 (3) 9272 5566
NSW Jewish Board of Deputies
146 Darlinghurst Road, Darlinghurst, NSW 2010
Tel +61 (2) 9360 1600
Pres. Yair Miller
Sephardi Federation of Australian Jewry
40-42 Fletcher Street, Bondi Junction, NSW 2022
Tel +61 (2) 9130 3192
Pres. A. Gubbay
Union for Progressive Judaism (Australia, New Zealand, Asia)
Email upj@upj.org.au *Website* www.upj.org.au
Victorian Office P.O. Box 347, Balaclava, Victoria 3183
Tel +61 (3) 9533 8587 *Fax* +61 (3) 9529 1229
NSW Office *Tel* +61 (2) 9328 7644 *Fax* +61 (2) 9327 8715

MAIN SYNAGOGUES AND COMMUNAL CENTRES

ADELAIDE
See B.K. Hyams, *Surviving: A History of The Institutions and Organisations of the Adelaide Jewish Community* (1998).
Beit Shalom Synagogue
41 Hackney Road, P.O. Box 47, Stepney, SA 5069
Tel +61 (8) 8362 8281 *Fax* +61 (8) 8362 4406
Email info@bshalomadel.com
Admin. L. Willis
Hebrew Congregation
13 Flemington Street, P.O. Box 320, Glenside, SA 5065
Tel +61 (8) 8338 2922 *Fax* +61 (8) 9379 0142
Email office@adelaidehebrew.com

BRISBANE
Brisbane Hebrew Congregation (Orthodox)
98 Margaret Street, Brisbane, Qld. 4000
Tel +61 (7) 3229 3412 *Fax* +61 (7) 3366 8311
Beit Knesset Shalom (Conservative)
15 Koolatah Street, Carina, Qld. 4152
Email info@bks.org.au

MELBOURNE
Melbourne Hebrew Congregation (Orthodox)
One Toorak Road, South Yarra, Victoria 3141
Tel +61 (3) 9866 2255
Email mhc@mhc.org.au *Website* www.melbournesynagogue.org.au
Temple Beth Israel (Liberal)
76 Alma Road, St. Kilda, Victoria 3182
Tel +61 (3) 9510 1488 *Fax* +61 (3) 9521 1229
Email info@tbi.org.au

PERTH
Chabad of Western Australia (Inc) (Orthodox)
396 Alexander Drive, Dianella, WA 6059
M. Rabbi Shalom White; Office *Tel* +61 (8) 9275 13500
Email info@chabadwa.org
Perth Hebrew Congregation
Corner Plantation Street and Freedman Road, Menora, WA 6050
Tel +61 (8) 9271 0539
Email phc@theperthshule.asn.au *Website* www.theperthshule.asn.au

Mikvah on premises.
Pres. K. Blitz; *M.* Rabbi D. Freilich
SYDNEY
Central Synagogue (Orthodox)
15 Bon Accord Avenue, Bondi Junction, NSW 2022
Tel +61 (2) 9389 5622 *Fax* +61 (2) 9389 5418
Email central@centralsynagogue.com.au

TASMANIA
Hobart Hebrew Congregation (Orthodox and Progressive)
59 Argyle Street, 7000
Tel +61 (3) 6234 4720
Email shule@hobart.org *Website* www.hobartsynagogue.org
The synagogue is the oldest in Australia, having been consecrated in July 1845. *See* H. Fixel, 'Hobart Hebrew Congregation: 150 Years of Survival Against All Odds' (1999); P. and A. Elias, 'A Few from Afar: Jewish Lives in Tasmania from 1804' (2003).

AUSTRIA

Jews arrived in this area of Europe more than one thousand years ago. The community was expelled from Austria between 1420 and 1421, but Jews were allowed to return in 1451. The Jews were granted their own quarter of Vienna in 1624, but were expelled again in 1670. The economy declined after the expulsion and so they were asked to come back.

It was not until 1782 that the situation became more stable, when Joseph II began lifting the anti-Jewish decrees that his mother, Maria Theresa, had imposed on her Jewish subjects. The Jews received equal rights in 1848 and, in 1867, legal and other prohibitions were lifted.

Antisemitism did continue, however, and many influential anti-semitic publications were available in Vienna and were keenly read by many people, including the young Adolf Hitler. After the First World War Austria lost its empire (which included Czech lands and Galicia, which had a very large Jewish community), and the Jewish population fell accordingly. At the time of the Nazi take-over in 1938, 200,000 Jews lived in the country. Some 70,000 were killed in the Holocaust, the rest escaped or were hidden.

Today there are several synagogues in Vienna. The city has an active Ultra-Orthodox community and kosher food is available. There are prayer rooms in some provincial cities.

Visitors to Vienna should not miss the new Jewish Museum opened in 2001. It combines Rachel Whiteread's memorial, the Museum of Medieval Jewish Life and details of the excavation of a medieval synagogue built around the middle of the thirteenth century.

VIENNA
Chief Rabbi Rabbi Paul Chaim Eisenberg *Tel* +43 (1) 5310 4111
Jewish Community Centre
Israelitische Kulturgemeinde, Seitenstettengasse 4, 1010 Vienna
Tel +43 (1) 5310 4104
Pres. Dr. A. Muzicant; *Sec. Gen.* R. Fastenbauer, F. Herzog
Jewish Welcome Service
A-1010 Vienna, Stephansplatz 10
Tel +43 (1) 533 2730
Dir. Dr. L. Zelman
The Viennese Yeshiva
College for Jewish social occupations & Boarding School.
Offers three year courses for 14 to 16 year olds.
1020 Vienna, Grosse Mohrengasse 19
Tel +43 (1) 216 06 79
Rabbi Chayim Stern

MAIN SYNAGOGUES
Baden Synagogue, Grabengasse 14, Baden 2500 (Modern Orthodox); **Bet Hamidrash Torah Etz-Chayim**, Grosse Schiffgasse 8, Vienna (Orthodox); **Khal Israel**, Tempelgasse 3,

1020 (Orthodox); **Machsike Hadass,** Grosse Mohrengasse 19, 1020 (Orthodox); **Ohel Moshe,** Lilienbrunngasse 19, 1020 (Orthodox); **Or Chaddasch Congregation** (Reform), Robertgasse 2, 1020 **Stadttempel,** Seitenstettengasse 4 (Traditional)

AZERBAIJAN

Azerbaijan has a remarkable Jewish history, which can be better explored now that the country is independent from the former Soviet Union. The Tats (mountain Jews) believe that their ancestors arrived in Azerbaijan at the time of Nebuchadnezzar. They lived in several mountain villages and adopted the customs of their non-Jewish neighbours. They spoke a north Iranian language known as Judeo-Tat, to which they added some Hebrew words. The Soviets clamped down on their way of life after 1928, changing the alphabet of their language from Hebrew to Latin, and then in 1938, to Cyrillic. Some of their synagogues were also closed down. Zionist feeling is high, with almost 30,000 emigrating to Israel since 1989.

The other strand in Azerbaijan's Jewish population are the Ashkenazis who arrived in the nineteenth century from Poland and other countries to the west.

The largest synagogue in Baku is the Tat synagogue, but there are also Ashkenazi and Georgian synagogues. Synagogues are found in other towns as well.

BAKU
Mountain Jews Synagogue
Dmitrova Street 39 370014
Tel +994 (12) 892 232 8867
Chabad Lubavitch Synagogue
18 D. Alieva str. apt. 6, C. Mustafayev kuc., dalan 4 ev 1, Baku 370014
Tel +994 (12) 4945297

KUBA
Kuba Synagogue
Kolkhoznaya Street 46

BAHAMAS

Luis de Torres, the official interpreter for Columbus, was the first Jew in the Bahamas, as well as being one of the first Europeans there. He was a *converso.* The British arrived in 1620 and eventually gained control of the islands. Although there was a Jewish Attorney-General and Chief Justice in the islands in the eighteenth century, few Jews settled there until the twentieth century. They came from Eastern Europe and the UK after the First World War, and settled in the capital Nassau.

There are approximately 300 Jewish residents in the Bahamas. However, it is estimated that about 350,000 Jews visit the islands each year as tourists. There are congregations in Nassau and Freeport. Both cities have Jewish cemeteries, that in Nassau being the more historic.

Luis de Torres Synagogue
East Sunrise Highway, P.O. Box F-41761, Freeport Grand Bahama
Tel +1242 373 2008 Please contact for times of services.
Pres. Anthony Gee *Tel* +1242 373 8994 *Email* goldylocks@coralwave.com
Sec. Jean Berlind *Tel* +1242 373 9457 *Email* jberlind@coralwave.com

BARBADOS

Jewish history in Barbados starts in 1628, a year after the British first settled there. Jewish settlers came from Brazil, Suriname, England and Germany, and were mainly Sephardi. The first synagogue was established in the capital, Bridgetown, in 1654. Early settlers were engaged in cultivating sugar and coffee.

The Jewish population was well treated. In 1831 Barbados was the first British possession in which Jews were granted full political emancipation. Despite a largely favourable climate the community suffered losses from hurricanes, which destroyed sugar plantations, and the Jewish population fell to 70 by 1848. In 1925 no Jews remained, but a new influx (30 families escaping Nazism) came shortly after.

The synagogue was restored in 1987, and postage stamps were produced which commemorated its restoration. The Jewish population remains small, but it was a group of Barbadian Jews who founded the Caribbean Jewish Congress. The Jewish cemetery, one of the oldest in the Americas, is now back in use.

Jewish Community Council
P.O.B. 256, Bridgetown
Tel +1246 809 432 0840
Contact Benny Gilbert

BELARUS

For the adventurous traveller who has a keen interest in Jewish history, Belarus (also known as White Russia) makes an interesting and unusual destination. Situated on the western side of the former Soviet Union, this largely flat country borders Poland and Lithuania to the west, Ukraine to the south and Russia to the east. Belarus finally achieved independence in 1991, and within its present borders are many towns and villages of Jewish interest, such as Minsk, Pinsk and Grodno. One of the most famous villages in Belarus is Lubavitch, a hamlet in the far east of the country, near the Russian border, where the worldwide Lubavitch movement had its origins.

During WWII over 800,000 Belarusian Jews were massacred, and in the following years emigration to Israel was very high. However, the community has slowly started to rebuild itself and in the late 1980s an Ulpan (class to study Hebrew) and a Jewish Sunday School were opened. In 1992 the first Rabbi to Belarus arrived and the community continued to flourish with the publication of the first Jewish newspaper and openings of the first Kindergarten, Secondary school and an Israeli Embassy.

Religious Union for Orthodox Judaism in Belarus
Tel/Fax +375 (17) 334 5612
Pres. Yuri Dorn; Chief Rabbi Avraam Benenson
Religious Union for Progressive/Reform Judaism in Belarus
Beit Simcha Centre, Shornaya Str. 20, 220004, Minsk
Tel +375 (17) 226 4069
Email roopi@mail.ru
Rabbi Grigory Abramovich

BELGIUM

Jewish settlement in the area now called Belgium dates back to the thirteenth century, and suffered a similar fate to other medieval European Jewish communities, taking the blame for the Black Death and suffering expulsions. The Sephardim were the first to resettle in Belgium, mainly in Antwerp. After independence in 1830, conditions for the Jews improved and more Jews began to settle there. The diamond centre of Antwerp later developed rapidly, attracting many Jews from Eastern Europe.

By 1939 the Jewish population had grown to 100,000, a large proportion of whom were refugees hoping to escape to America. Some succeeded, but many became trapped after the German invasion. Some 25,000 Belgian Jews were deported and killed in the Holocaust. A national monument listing the names of the victims stands in Anderlecht in Brussels. The present Jewish population includes a large Hassidic community in Antwerp, where there are some 30 synagogues. There are also more than ten synagogues in Brussels. There are Jewish schools and newspapers in Antwerp and Brussels.

International Jewish Center of Belgium (IJC)
Services and other activities held in the Brussels region
Avenue Louise 149, 1050 Brussels
Tel +32 477 281 678
Email info@ijc.be *Website* www.ijc.be
(Est. 2003) The IJS is Belgium's only liberal, English-speaking reform Jewish community. It has more than 150 members. Rabbi Nathan Alfred. A Belgian ASBL/VZW non-profit organization. Officially recognised by the World Union of Progressive Judaism.

Sunday school is held for children starting at kindergarten to Bar/Bat Mitzvah level. There is a Talmud Torah, Shabbat services are held twice a month, regular Shabbat dinners are also held twice a month and in the IJC satellite site in Leuven once a month. All major Jewish holidays are celebrated. A cultural women's group meets every two months. Many Jewish cultural events are hosted here.

ANTWERP
Central Jewish Welfare Organisation
Jacob Jacobsstr. 2, 2018 Antwerpen
Tel +32 (3) 232 3890
Machsike Hadass (Orthodox)
Jacob Jacobstr. 22. Main synagogue: Oostenstr. 42-44, 2018 Antwerpen
Sephardi Synagogue
Hovenierstr. 31, 2018 Antwerpen
Shomre Hadas
Israëlitische Gemeente van Antwerpen, Terliststraat 35, 2018 Antwerpen
Tel +32 (3) 232 0187 *Fax* +32 (3) 226 3123
Email info@shomre-hadas.be *Website* www.shomre-hadas.be

BRUSSELS
Centre Communautaire Laic Juif
52 Rue Hotel des Monnaies, 1060 Brussels
Comité de Coordination des Organisations Juives de Belgique (C.C.O.J.B.)
Av. Ducpétiaux 68, 1060 Brussels
Tel +32 (2) 537 1691 *Fax* +32 (2) 539 2295
Consistoire Central Israélite de Belgique
2 rue Joseph Dupont, 1000 Brussels
Tel +32 (3) 512 2190
Machzikei Haddass
Rabbinat Av. St. Augustin 40, 1190 Bruxelles
Tel +32 (2) 345 4518 *Fax* +32 (2) 347 5222
Website www.ciob.be

BERMUDA

The small community of 120 members, has just opened the first Jewish Community Centre ever in Bermuda, at 75 St. Johns Road, Pembroke. Friday night services are held once a month and there is also an active Hebrew school and some adult education classes. A visiting Rabbi has conducted High Holy day services for the last 10 years.

Jewish Community of Bermuda
P.O. Box HM 1793, Hamilton, HMHX Bermuda
Tel +1441 291 1785
Website wwwjewishbermuda.com

BOLIVIA

The history of the Jews of Bolivia dates back to the Spanish colonial period. *Conversos* came with the Spaniards in the seventeenth century.
The main influx of Jews occurred in 1905 with immigrants from Eastern Europe, but the number entering Bolivia was much smaller than that going to other South American countries. In 1933 there were only some 30 Jewish families. At the end of the decade, however, there was a small increase in Jewish immigration as German and Austrian Jews fled from Europe. Ironically, the Jewish community did not grow that much, even though the government granted every Jew an entry visa.
Many Jews started to leave Bolivia in the 1950s because of political instability and the apparent lack of educational opportunities. The present-day community has a central organisation known as the Circulo Israelita de Bolivia in La Paz.

COCHABAMBA
Asociación Israelita de Cochabamba
P.O.B. 349, Calle Valdivieso
Pres. Ronald Golan
Synagogue Calle Junin y Calle Colombia, Casilla 349

LA PAZ
Comunidad Israelita Synagogue
Calle Canada Stronguest 1846, P.O.B. 2198
Tel +591 (2) 232 5925 *Fax* + 591 (2) 234 2738
Israel Tourist Information Office
Centro Shalom, Calle Canada Stronguest 1846, La Paz Country Club, Quinta J.K.G.
Obrajes. Calle 1, esquina calle Hector Ormachea Casilla 1545, La Paz
Synagogue
Circulo Israelita de Bolivia, Casilla 1545 *Tel* +591 (2) 278 5083 Calle Landaeta 346, P.O.B.
1545 Services Saturday morning only. *Pres.* Dr Miguel

SANTA CRUZ
Circulo Israelita de Santa Cruz
P.O.B. 7087, WIZO, Casilla 3409 *Tel* +591 (3) 3435848 *Pres.* Sra Guicha Schwartz

BOSNIA AND HERZEGOVINA

Sephardi Jews were the first to arrive in the area in the late sixteenth century. They established a Jewish quarter in Sarajevo, and this was home for the poorer Jews until the Austrians conquered the area in 1878. It was the Turks, however, who emancipated the Jews in the nineteenth century when Bosnia and Herzegovina was under Ottoman rule.

When Bosnia and Herzegovina became part of the newly formed Yugoslavia, after the First World War, the community maintained its Sephardi heritage and joined the all-Yugoslav Federation of Jewish Religious Communities. The Jewish population numbered 14,000 in 1941. This number dropped sharply after the Germans conquered Yugoslavia.

After the war the survivors were joined by many who had decided to return. The Sephardi and Ashkenazi communities became unified. La Benevolencija, founded 100 years ago, is a humanitarian organisation which ameliorated the plight of the community and became well known in the early 1990s at the time of the civil war. After the Yugoslav civil war, many made aliyah to Israel, reducing the community still further.

Sarajevo Jewish Community
Hamdije Kresevljakovica 59, Sarajevo, Bosnia, 71000
Tel +387 (33) 229 666

BRAZIL

The first Jewish settlers in Brazil came with the Portuguese in 1500. They were mainly *Conversos* escaping persecution in Portugal, and initially worked on the sugar plantations. In due course they played important roles as traders, artisans and plantation owners. The huge area which is called Brazil today was in the process of being conquered by the Dutch and the Portuguese. Two synagogues were opened in Recife during the 1640s when many Jews came from Holland. When the Dutch left Brazil in 1654 one of the terms of surrender allowed the Jews who had been on their side to emigrate. Many fled and some went on to found the first Jewish community in New York, then known as New Amsterdam. A seventeenth-century Mikveh was discovered in 2000 in the basement of the Tsur Israel Synagogue in Recife.

With Brazilian independence in 1822, conditions became more favourable for Jews and many came from North Africa and Europe. The majority of Jews in Brazil today, however, originate from the immigration of East European Jews in the early twentieth century. From about 6,000 Jews in 1914, the community grew to 30,000 in 1930. After 1937 Brazil refused to allow Jewish immigrants into the country, but some limited immigration managed to continue despite the restrictions.

A central organisation was established in 1951 (the CONIB), and this includes 200 various Jewish organisations. Brazilian Jews live in an atmosphere of tolerance and prosperity, and

assimilation is widespread.
There are synagogues in all the major cities.

RIO DE JANEIRO
Congrecão Beth El
Rua Barata Ribeiro 489 (Sephardi)
Federacão Israelita & Fundo Communitario
R. Buenos Aires 68, AN15
Orthodox Rabbinate
R. Pompeu Loureiro No.40
Tel/Fax +55 (21) 236 0249

SYNAGOGUES
Agudat Israel, Rua Nascimento Silva, 109 Beth Aron, Rua Gado Coutinho, 63 Kehilat Yaacov Copacabana, Rua Capelao Alvares da Silva 15; Templo Uniao Israel, Rua Jose Higino, 375-381

SÃO PAULO
Escola Beit Yaacov
Av Marques de São Vicente, 1748 Cep 01139-002
Tel +55 (11) 361 1060
Federacao Israelita do Estado de São Paulo
Av. Paulista 726, 2nd floor
Tel +55 (11) 288 6411

SYNGOGUES AND RELIGIOUS CENTRES
Centro Judaico Religioso de Sao Paulo (Orthodox)
Tel 220 5642; Beit Chabad, Rua Chabad 56/60; Communidade Israelita Sefaradi, Rua da Abolicao 457; Congregacão Israelita Paulista, "Einheitsgemeinde" (Liberal), Rua Antonico Carlos 653. Sinagoga Beit Yaacov (Congregação e Beneficência Sefardi Paulista) Rua Dr. Veiga Filho, 547 Cep 01229-000 São Paulo *Tel* +55 (11) 366 2215

BULGARIA

Dating back to the Byzantine conquest, the community in Bulgaria was established by Greek Jews in Serdica (Sofia, the capital). The Jewish community grew when the Bulgarian state was founded in 681. Czar Ivan Alexander (1331–71) had a Jewish wife who converted to Christianity.

The community has included eminent rabbinic commentators, such as Rabbi Dosa Ajevani and Joseph Caro, the codifier of the Shulchan Aruch, who escaped to Bulgaria after the expulsion from Spain. The various Jewish groups joined to form a unified Sephardi community in the late seventeenth century.

About 50,000 Jews lived in Bulgaria in 1939. Bulgaria joined the war on the side of Germany but, despite much pressure from the Nazis, the government and general population refused to allow Bulgarian Jews to be deported. Only Jews from Macedonia and Thrace, then occupied by Bulgaria, were deported. Despite being saved, most of the community emigrated to Israel after the war. The 10 per cent who remained were then under the control of the communists and had little contact with the outside world.

Since the fall of communism, the community has been reconstituted and now has synagogues in Sofia and Plovdiv. The community is ageing, although 100 children attend a Sunday school run by the Shalom Organisation, the central Jewish organisation for Bulgaria.

Central Jewish Religious Council and Synagogue
16 Exarch Joseph Street, Sofia 1000
Tel +359 (2) 983 1273
Pres. Robat Djerassi

Beit Ha'am
50 Stambolijski
Tel +359 (2) 926 5301

Organization of the Jews in Bulgaria
"Shalom", 50 Al. Stambolijski Street, Sofia 130

Tel +359 (2) 4006 301 *Pres.* Dr. Maxim Benvenisti. Publishes newspaper "Evrejski Vesti" and research compendium "Annual". Jewish museum in the Synagogue: Sofia, 16 Exarch Joseph St. Joseph. Caro permanent exhibition in the city. Museum and a memorial stone in the town of Nikopol. Publishing house "Shalom", Jewish Sunday School, Jewish Resource Centre, Memorial stone dedicated to the Salvation of the Bulgarian Jews near the Parliament, B'nai Brith, Maccabi and other Jewish organizations.

BURMA (Myanmar)

The first Jews came to Myanmar in the early eighteenth century from Iraq and other Middle Eastern countries. A synagogue was built in 1896. In the first years of the twentieth century Rangoon and Bassein both had Jewish mayors. The Jewish population swelled to 2,000 before 1939, but most of these fled to Britain and India before the Japanese invasion in the Second World War. Only a few hundred more returned after the war, and the community began to decline through intermarriage and conversion. The handful of remaining Jews are elderly and services are held only on the High Holy Days, when a minyan is made up with help from the Israeli embassy.

There is also a tribe of Jews in the north of the country (the Karens), who have their own prayer houses and who believe that they are descended from the tribe of Menassah.

YANGON
Israel Embassy
15 KhaBaung Street, Hlaing Township, Yangon
Tel +95 (1) 515 115 *Fax* +95 (1) 515 116
Email info@yangon.mfa.gov.il
Musmeah Yeshua Synagogue
85 26th Street, P.O. Box 45, Yangon
(Est. 1896). *Man. Tr.* Moses Samuels *Email* samuels@mptmail.net.mm

CANADA

Jews were prohibited by law from living in Canada as long as it remained a French possession. Nevertheless, Jews from Bordeaux – David Gradis, a wealthy merchant and shipowner, and his son Abraham Gradis, in particular – had a large share in the commercial development of the colony.

Jews played some part in the British occupation of Canada. Half a dozen Jewish officers, were suppliers to the expeditionary force which occupied Quebec. They included Aaron Hart, and their descendants played important roles in Jewish and Canadian life for several generations.

A number of Jews settled at an early date in Montreal, where the Spanish and Portuguese Synagogue, Shearith Israel (still flourishing), was established in the 1770s. A congregation of 'German, Polish and English' Jews was granted a charter in 1846. A burial society was formed in Toronto in 1849. Montreal Jews were also among the fur traders in the Indian territories.

In the 19th century, Jewish immigrants arrived in Canada in some numbers, and in 1832 – a quarter of a century earlier than in Britain – the Lower Canada Jews received full civil rights. A fresh era in the history of Canadian Jewry opened at the close of the century, when emigration on a large scale from Eastern Europe began. Montreal, Toronto, and, to a lesser degree, Winnipeg became the seats of Jewish communities of some importance.

On the history of the Jews in Canada generally, *See* A. D. Hart, *The Jew in Canada*, 1926; L. Rosenberg, *Canada's Jews*, 1939; B. G. Sack, *The History of the Jews in Canada*, 1945; and I.M. Abella, *A Coat of Many Colours: Two Centuries of Jewish Life in Canada*, 1990. The early colonial period in North America is covered in Sheldon and Judith Godfrey, *Search Out the Land*, 1995.

Association for Canadian Jewish Studies
c/o Dept of Religion, Concordia University, 1455 De Maisonneuve Blvd West, Montreal H3G 1MP

Tel +1 (514) 848 2424/2074 *Fax* +1 (514) 848 4541
Contact Dr. I. Robinson *Website* www.acjs-aejc.ca
Canada-Israel Committee
130 Slater Street, Suite 630, Ottawa K1P 6E2
Exec. Dir. Shimon Fogel *Tel* +1 (613) 234 8271
Ontario Office 2221 Yonge Street #502, Toronto M4S 2B4 *Tel* +1 (416) 489 8889
Canadian Zionist Federation
5250 Decarie Boulevard #550, Montreal, H3X 2H9
Tel +1 (514) 486 9526
(Est. 1967).

NATIONAL INSTITUTIONS
Canadian Jewish Congress
(Est. 1919. reorganised 1934)
National Office 100 Sparks Street, Suite 650, Ottawa, Ontario K1P 5B7
Tel +1 (613) 233 8703 *Fax* +1 (613) 233 8748
Website www.cjc.ca
Nat. Co-Pres. Rabbi Dr. Reuven Bulka and Sylvain Abitobol
Chief Exec. Bernie M. Farher 4600 Bathurst Street Fourth Floor, Toronto Ontario M2R 3V2
Tel +1 (416) 635 2883 ext. 5186 *Fax* +1 (416) 635 1408 *Email* bfarber@on.cjc.ca
Dir. of Operations Joshua Rotblatt National Office address *Email* joshr@cjc.ca
Nat. Gen. Counsel Jonathan Schwartz 4600 Bathurst Street, 4th Floor, Toronto Ontario M2R
3V2 *Tel* +1 (416) 635 2883 ext. 5265 *Fax* +1 (416) 635 1408 *Email* jschwartz@on.cjc.ca
Nat. Archives Janice Rosen. Archives Director, Canadian Jewish Congress Charities
Committee, 1590 Avenue Doctor Penfield, Montreal, Quebec H3G 1C5 *Tel* +1 (514) 931
7531 ext. 271 *Fax* +1 (514) 931 0548 *Email* janicer@cjccc.ca
CJC Atlantic Region
Tel +1 (902) 422 7491 *Fax* +1 (902) 422 7372
Reg. Dir Jon M. Goldberg *Email* jgoldberg@theajc.ns.ca
CJC Ontario Region
Tel +1 (416) 638 1991 ext. 5147
Regional Dir. Len Rudner
CJC Pacific Region
Tel +1 (604) 622 4240 *Fax* +1 (604) 622 4244
Regional Dir. Romy Ritter
CJC Quebec Region
Tel +1 (514) 345 6411 ext. 3162 *Fax* +1 (514) 345 6412
Regional Director/Directeur général Daniel Amar Email damar@cjq-qjc.ca
CJC Saskatchewan Region - North
Tel +1 (306) 343 7023 *Fax* +1 (306) 343 1244
June Aviva *Email* ajaviva@shaw.ca
CJC Saskatchewan Region-South
Tel +1 (306) 569 8166 *Fax* +1 (306) 569 8166

CAYMAN ISLANDS

There are approx. 60 Jewish residents in the 3 Cayman Islands, nearly all living on Grand
Cayman. They are joined by about 40 others who are regular visitors. Services in private
homes. *Contact* Harvey De Souza P.O. Box 72, Grand Cayman, KY1 1102

The Jewish Community of the Cayman Islands (JCCI)
P.O. Box 292, Grand Cayman KY1-1104
Tel +345 526 0572
Email info@jccicayman.org *Website* www.jccicayman.org

CHILE

The original Jewish settlers in Chile were *Conversos*. Rodrigo de Organos, a *Converso*, was the
first European to enter the country in 1535. The Inquisition, however, curtailed the growth

of the community.
The first legal Jewish immigration, albeit small, occurred only after Chile's independence in 1810. In 1914 the Jewish community numbered some 500, but this increased in the late 1930s with those refugees from Nazism who were able to avoid the strict immigration laws. Antisemitism, however, also grew, and the *Comite Representativo* was formed to respond to it. There is an umbrella organisation and a large Zionist body in Chile. Most of the community is not religious, but some keep kosher and there are several synagogues in the capital Santiago and a few kosher shops. There are two Jewish schools, and several Jewish newspapers are published.

SANTIAGO
B'nai Brith
Ricardo Lyon 1933 *Tel* +56 (2) 274 2006
Comunidad Israelita de Santiago
Tarapaca 870 (Ashkenazi)
Tel +56 (2) 633 1436
Comunidad Israelita de Santiago Congregacion Jafetz Jayim
Miguel Claro 196 (Orthodox)
Tel +56 (2) 274 5389
Comunidad Israelita Sefaradi de Chile
R. Lyon 812
Tel +56 (2) 209 8086
Comité Representativo de las Entidades Judias de Chile (CREJ)
Miguel Claro 196
Tel +56 (2) 235 8669

CHINA

In recent years, Jewish tourists from a number of countries, including Britain and the United States, have visited the ancient city of Kaifeng, 300 miles south of Peking. There they met people who claim descent from a sizeable community which lived there for centuries and dispersed in the 19th century. Some experts believe the Kaifeng Jews to have originated from Persia or Yemen. Few are left of the communities formed by other immigrants from Asia at the end of the 19th century and by the Russian and German refugees of the First and Second World Wars.

A comprehensive bibliography on the Jews of China was published in 1998: *Jews and Judaism in Traditional China: A Comprehensive Bibliography*, Donald Daniel Leslie (Sankt Petersburg: Steyler Verlag, 1998) (Monumenta serica, XLIV).

HONG KONG

Although there were some Jewish merchants trading out of Hong Kong over the centuries, the first permanent community consisted of Jews who came from Baghdad in the early nineteenth century. The first synagogue was not established until 1901, the early settlers preferring to organise communal events from their homes. The majority of the community were Sephardi, but Nazi persecution led to more Ashkenazi settlers arriving in Hong Kong, via Shanghai. Since the Second World War many Chinese Jews have emigrated through Hong Kong to Australia and the USA, although some have remained in Hong Kong. Following the reversion to Chinese control in mid-1997, the Jewish community is still thriving, and the mood is optimistic.
The Jews have contributed greatly to the building of the infrastructure of Hong Kong and, since the 1960s, many Western Jews, attracted by the success of this major financial centre, have made their homes there. The first communal hall was founded in 1905, but a new, multi-purpose complex (the Jewish Community Centre) has recently been opened, which is one of the most luxurious in the world. The Centre includes everything from a library and a strictly kosher restaurant to a swimming pool and sauna.

Chabad of Hong Kong
7-9 Macdonnell Road, Hoover Court 1st Floor, Hong Kong
Tel +852 2523 9770 *Fax* +852 2845 2772

Website www.chabadhongkong.org
Rabbi Mordechai Avtzon
Chabad-Lubavitch in the Far East
Website www.chabadhk.org
Israel Consulate-General
Admiralty Centre, Tower II, Room 701, 18 Harcourt Road
Tel +852 2529 6091 *Fax* +852 2865 0220
The Jewish Community Centre
1 Robinson Place, 70 Robinson Road, Mid-levels
Tel +852 2868 0828, (Information)*Tel* +852 2801 5440 *Fax* +852 2877 0917
Website www.jcc.org.hk
Gen. Man. Michael Sheppard
Mikveh
Contact Revital Ben Yishai *Tel* +852 2140 6475
Shanghai Jewish Centre
Shang-Mira Garden Villa #1, 89 South Shui Cheng Road, Shanghai, 200336
Tel +862 6278 0225 *Fax* + 862 6278 0223
Email info@chinajewish.org *Website* www.chinajewish.org
Rabbi Shalom Greenberg
The United Jewish Congregation of Hong Kong
1 Robinson Place, 70 Robinson Road, Mid-levels
Tel +852 2523 2985 *Fax* +852 2523 3961
Email ujc@ujc.org.hk *Website* www.ujc.org.hk
(Liberal/Reform) (Est. 1991). Rabbi L. Diamond

COLOMBIA

The first Jews in Colombia were *Conversos*, as was common in South America. However, they were soon discovered by the Inquisition when it was established in Colombia.
The next influx of Jews came in the nineteenth century, followed by mass immigration from Eastern Europe and the Middle East after 1918. Jews were banned from entering after 1939, but this restriction was eased after 1950.
The present community is a mix of Ashkenazi and Sephardi elements, each having their own communual organisations. There are also Youth and Zionist organisations. There is a central organisation for Colombian Jewry in the capital Bogota. There are also Jewish schools and synagogues, and Jewish publications and radio programmes.

Centro Israelita de Bogota
Carrera 29 No. 126, Bogota or: Apartado Aereo 12.372
Santa Fe de Bogota
Tel +011 (571) 626 4367, +011 (571) 625 4377 *Fax* +011 (571) 274 9069
Email centrocib@tutopia.com
Kosher Meals available by calling Rabbi Goldschmidt *Tel* +011 (571) 218 2500
Embassy of Israel in Bogota
Edificio Caxdac, Calle 35, No. 7-25 14 Piso, Bogota
Tel +011 (571) 287 7962 or +011 (571) 232 0764 *Fax* +011 (571) 287 7783
Email Bogota@israel.org

CONGO, DEMOCRATIC REPUBLIC (Formerly Zaire)

Today, Congo has approximately 320 Jews living predominately in Lubumbashi. Most of the Jews are of Sephardic descent and speak Ladino, a Spanish-Jewish dialect. There is a synagogue in Lubumbashi that is served by a rabbi. There is also a small Jewish community in Kinshasa called Congregation Israelite. The Jewish community in Congo is represented by the Communaute Israelite du Shaba. There is a Jewish cemetery under the control of the Chief Rabbi of Zaire, Rabbi Levy.

Chief Rabbi of Zaire
Rabbi Moishe Levy 50 W. Churchill Avenue, Box 15, 1180 Brussels, Belgium

Chabad-Lubavitch of Central Africa
251 Avenue de la Mission, Kinshasa
Tel +243 999 770 *Fax* +212 504 2621
Exec. Dir. Rabbi Shlomo Bentolila; *Co-Dir.* Miriam Bentolila
Embassy of Israel
12 Avenue des Aviateurs, P.O. Box 8343 KIN 1, Kinshasa
Tel +243 122 1955 *Fax* +243 884 5055
Synagogue
Congregation Israelite, Baite Postale No. 931, Kinshasa

COSTA RICA

The first Jews arrived in Costa Rica in the nineteenth century from nearby islands in the Caribbean, such as Jamaica. The next wave of immigrants came from Eastern Europe in the 1920s. Thereafter Costa Rica did not welcome new Jewish immigrants, and passed laws against foreign merchants and foreign land ownership. However, the Jewish community in Costa Rica established a communal organisation in 1930. There is a monthly newsletter, and a synagogue in San Jose. Most Jewish children attend the Haim Weizmann School, which has both primary and secondary classes.
It is interesting to note that the Costa Rican embassy in Israel is in Jerusalem and not Tel Aviv, where most other embassies are situated.
Centro Israelita Sionista de Costa Rica
Orthodox Commmunity Carretera a Pavas, San Jose 1007
Tel +506 2520 1013 *Fax* +506 2520 1951
Website www.centroisraelita.com
Pres. S. Aizenman; *Exec. Dir.* Guita Grynspan; *Chief Rabbi* Rabbi Gershon; *Sec.* M. Froimzon

CROATIA (Formerly constituent republic of Yugoslavia)

Jews were in the land now known as Croatia before the Croats themselves. The Croats arrived in the seventh century, the Jews some centuries before with the Romans: there are the remains of a third-century Jewish cemetery in Solin (near Split).
The first Jewish communites were involved in trade with Italy across the Adriatic Sea, and also in trade along the River Danube. Their success was brief, however, and they were expelled in 1456, only returning more than 300 years later. The area became part of the newly formed Yugoslavia after the First World War, and the Jewish community became part of the Federation of Jewish Communities in Yugoslavia.
The Croatian Jews suffered greatly under the German occupation in the Second World War when the local *Ustashe* (Croatian Fascists) assisted the Germans. Despite their efforts some Jews survived and even decided to rebuild their community when peace returned.
Today, after the civil war, there are synagogues in towns across the country. There are some Hebrew classes and newsletters are published. There are also many places of historical interest, such as Ulicia Zudioska (Jewish Street) in Dubrovnik. This street has recently been renamed Jewish Street.
There is an impressive monument to Jewish victims of the Holocaust in the Jewish cemetery of Mirogoj and a monument to Jewish soldiers who fell in the First World War.
There is a plaque in Praška Street 7 on the site of the pre-war Central synagogue of Zagreb. Before 1941 the community numbered over 12,000 Jews. Today there are 1,500 members.

DUBROVNIK
Jewish Community and Synagogue
Zudioska Street 3 (Jewish Street)
Tel +385 (20) 321 028
This is the second oldest synagogue in Europe, dating back to the 14th century. It was damaged in the 1991-2 war. There are 47 Jews in the city and services are held on Jewish holidays. *Pres.* S. Horovic
ZAGREB
Bet Israel Jewish Community of Croatia and Synagogue
Židovska Vjerska Zajednica Bet Israel u Hrvatskoj, Mažuranićev trg 6, 10 000 Zagreb,

Hrvatska
Tel +385 (1) 4851 008 *Fax* +385 (1) 4851 376
office Email ured@bet-israel.com *Website* www.bet-israel.com
Chabad of Croatia
Rabbi Pinchas Zaklas
Gunduliceva 49, Zagreb, Croatia
Tel +385 (1) 4812 227

CEUTA
Ceuta Kashrut Information and Synagogue
Calle Sargento Coriat 8

CUBA

The first Jew to set foot in Cuba (1492) was Luis de Torres. Although hundreds arrived following the Spanish Inquisition, they were prohibited from practising their religion. This changed in 1898 following Cuba's liberation from Spain. With the end of Spanish colonial rule in that year, Jews from nearby areas, such as Jamaica and Florida, and Jewish veterans of the Spanish American War, began to settle in Cuba. A congregation was established in 1904. Later, Turkish Sephardim formed their own synagogue. The community was then augmented by immigrants from eastern Europe who had decided to stay in Cuba, which was being used as a transit camp for those seeking to enter America. A central committee was established for all Jewish groups in the 1930s. Cuba imposed severe restrictions on immigration at that time, and the story of the German ship St Louis (full of Jewish refugees), which was refused entry into Cuba, is well known.

About 12,000 Jews lived on the island in 1952. Havana had by far the largest community, and 75 per cent of the Cuban community was Ashkenazi. Although the Cuban revolution did not target Jews, religious affiliations were initially discouraged and many Jews emigrated (as did many non-Jews). The remaining community has synagogues and a Sunday school. Kosher food and Judaica are imported, mainly from Canada and Panama. Cuba broke off diplomatic relations with Israel in 1973, although in 1998/99 a number of Jews were allowed to emigrate to Israel.

Cuban Jewish Community - Comunidad Hebrea de Cuba
Calle 1, #259, Esquina 13, Vedado, Ciudad de la Habana 10400
Tel +53 (7) 832 8953
Email beth_shalom@enet.cu or
Website www.chcuba.org/english/index.thm
Pres. Dr Jose Miller; *V. Pres.* Adela Dworin

CYPRUS

During the Roman Empire, Jewish merchants made their home on Cyprus. However, after a revolt that destroyed the town of Salamis, they were expelled. In medieval times small Jewish communities were established in Nicosia, Limassol and other towns, but the community was never large.

It is interesting to note that Cyprus was seen as a possible 'Jewish Homeland' by the early Zionists. Agricultural settlements were established at the end of the nineteenth century, but they were not successful. Herzl himself tried to persuade the British government to allow Jewish rule over Cyprus in 1902, but met with failure.

Some German Jews managed to escape to Cyprus in the early 1930s. After the war, many Holocaust survivors who had tried to enter Palestine illegally were deported to special camps on the island. Some 50,000 European Jews were held there. Since the establishment of the State of Israel, the Jewish community on the island has become small; the Israeli embassy serves as a centre for community activities.

CJCC - Cyprus Jewish Community Centre
Diogenous 7b, Larnaca, 6020 Cyprus
Tel +357 (24) 828 770/1
Website www.koshercyprus.com

A full list of kosher products in Cyprus, as well as details for the mikveh, synagogue services and the Jewish school can be found on the chabad Cyprus website. There is also a list of recommended hotels within walking distance of the synagogue and chabad centre.
Rabbi Arie Zeev and Sheindel Raskin

CZECH REPUBLIC

Prague, the capital of this small central European country, has become a major tourist attraction. It is one of the few cities to actively promote its Jewish heritage, which dates from early medieval times. The oldest (still functioning) synagogue in Europe is there (the Altneuschul), as well as other interesting Jewish sites.

After the arrival of the first Jews in the country in the tenth century, they suffered similar tragedies to those of other medieval Jewish communities: forced baptism by the Crusaders and expulsions, although occasionally there was some tolerance. Full emancipation was reached in 1867 under the Habsburgs. The celebrated Jewish writer, Franz Kafka, lived in Prague and did not neglect his Judaism, unlike many other Czech Jews who assimilated and intermarried. The German occupation led to 85 per cent of the community (80,000 people) perishing in the Holocaust. Further difficulties were faced in the Communist period after the war, but since the 1989 'Velvet Revolution', Judaism is being rediscovered. The community (mostly elderly) has several synagogues around the country, a kindergarten and a journal, and there are kosher restaurants in the old Jewish Quarter in Prague.

CONTACT INFORMATION
Federation of Jewish Communities in the Czech Republic
Maiselova 18, 110 01, Prague
Tel +420 (2) 2480 0824 *Fax* +420 (2) 2481 0912
Email sekretariat@fzo.cz *Website* www.fzo.cz
Sec. JuDr. Tomas Kraus
Orthodox
Chabad Prague, U Milosrdných 6, Prague 1, Jewish Quarter
Tel +420 (2) 2232 0200/(7) 2818 6832 *Fax* +420 (2) 2232 0200
Email jewishprague@gmail.com *Website* www.chabadprague.cz/
Dir. Rabbi Manis Barash *Email* chabadprague@gmail.com
Liberal
BEJT SIMCHA, Maiselova 4, 110 00 Praha 1
Tel +420 (7) 2402 7929
Website www.bejtsimcha.cz
Jewish Museum
U Staré školy 1, 110 00 Prague 1
Tel +420 (2) 2171 1511 *Fax* +420 (2) 2274 9300
Email office@jewishmuseum.cz
Please email for information on the Jewish museum, the Jewish cemetery, and any research activities.

DENMARK

Jews were allowed to settle in Denmark in 1622, earlier than in any other Scandinavian country. Thereafter the community grew, with immigration largely from Germany. The Danish King allowed the foundation of the unified Jewish community of Copenhagen in 1684, and the Jews were granted full citizenship in 1849.

In the early part of the twentieth century many refugees arrived from eastern Europe, and Denmark welcomed refugees from Nazi Germany. When the Germans conquered Denmark and ordered the Jews to be handed over, the Danish resistance managed to save 7,200 (90% of the community) by arranging boats to take them to neutral Sweden. Some Jews did, however, stay behind and were taken to the transit ghetto of Theresienstadt (Terezin), where many died. After the war most of the Jews returned, and there is now a central Jewish organisation based in Copenhagen. There are also homes for the elderly, synagogues and a mikveh.

COPENHAGEN
Chief Rabbi Rabbi Bent Lexner Bomhusvej, 18, DK 2100
Tel +45 3929 9520 *Fax* +45 3929 2517
Email bent@lexner.dk Private Oestbanegade 9, DK 2100 *Tel* +45 3526 3540
Det Mosaiske Troessamfund i Kobenhavn (Jewish Congregation of Copenhagen)
Ny Kongensgade 6, DK 1472
Tel +45 3312 8868 *Fax* +45 3312 3357
Email mt@mosaiske.dk *Website* www.mosaiske.dk
Great Synagogue
Krystalgade 12, DK 1172
Tel +45 3312 8868
Progressive Judiasm of Denmark
Website www.shirhatzafon.dk/

DOMINICAN REPUBLIC

Jewish settlement in the Dominican Republic was comparatively late; the oldest Jewish grave dates back to 1826. Descended from central European Jews, the community was not religious and many married Christians. President Francisco Henriquez y Carvajal (1916) traced his ancestry back to the early Jewish settlers.

In 1938 the republic decided to accept refugees from Nazism (one of the very few countries of the world that did so freely), and even provided areas where they could settle. As a result, there were 1,000 Jews living there in 1943. This number declined as, once again, the Jewish community assimilated and married the local non-Jewish population. Despite this, many non-Jewish husbands, wives and children take part in Jewish events.

Two synagogues and a rabbi who divides his time between them, are features of Jewish life. There is also a Sunday school in Santo Domingo and a bi-monthly magazine is produced. There is a small Jewish museum in Sosua.

Chabad Lubavitch of Dominican Republic
Avenida Sarasota 71 Apt # 702, Santo Domingo
Chabad House *Tel* +1 (809) 533 8770 *U.S. Tel* 718 504 1990
Email chabaddominican@gmail.com *Website* www.chabadominican.com/
Dir. Rabbi Shimon Pelman

SANTO DOMINGO
Centro Israelita de la República Dominicana
Avenida Sarasota #21, (between Av. Lincoln & Av. Churchill)
Tel +1 (809) 535 6042 La Julia, Santo Domingo.

ECUADOR

As in most Latin American countries, *Conversos* comprised the earliest Jewish settlers in Ecuador. It was not until 1904 that Eastern European Jews began to arrive, and numbers increased further following the Nazi take-over in Germany, as Ecuador granted refuge to more Jews than other neighbouring countries. About 3,000 Jews entered Ecuador in the 1930s. The Jewish population peaked in 1950 at 4,000, but this number declined owing to emigration. In recent years, some Jews have moved to Ecuador from elsewhere in South America.

There are no Jewish schools, but children do have access to Jewish education.

Comunidad Judia del Ecuador
Calle Roberto Andrade OE3-580 y Jaime Roldos, Urbanizacion Einstein, P.O. Box 17-03-800
Tel +593 (2) 483 800/927 *Fax* +593 (2) 486 755
Website www.cje-ec.com
Beit Jabad del Ecuador
Chabad of Ecuador, Los Cabildos #135, Edif. Paola Apt. 2 y Afganistan Quito
Telfax +1 (593) 2243 3481 *U.S. Tel* +1 (770) 884 6113 *Mobile* +1 59392 666 954
Email jabadecuador@gmail.com *Website* www.jabad.org.ec

EGYPT

The history of the Jewish community in Egypt goes back to Biblical times. Following the establishment of the State of Israel in 1948 and the subsequent wars, only about 200 Jews remain, about 150 in Cairo and 50 in Alexandria. Services are conducted in Shaar Hashamayim Synagogue during the High Holy Days.

ALEXANDRIA
Great Synagogue Eliahu HaNabi
69 rue Nebi Daniel, Ramla Station
Pres. Dr. Max Salama

CAIRO
Jewish Community Headquarters
13 rue Sebil el Khazendar, Midan el Gueish, Abbasiya
Tel +20 (2) 2482 4613
Email bassatine@yahoo.com *Website* www.bassatine.news
Pres. C. Weinstein *Tel* +20 (2) 2393 5896

EL SALVADOR

The Jewish connection to El Salvador is not a strong one. It is believed that some Portuguese *Conversos* crossed the country a few hundred years ago. After that, some Sephardis from France moved to Chaluchuapa. Other Jews came from Europe, but in smaller numbers than those settling in other Latin American countries. There were only 370 Jews in 1976, a number reduced during the civil war, when many emigrated. Some returned, however, when the war was over.

An official community was set up in 1944 and a synagogue was opened in 1950. El Salvador is one of the few countries to have an embassy in Jerusalem, rather than Tel Aviv.

Israelite Community of El Salvador (Conservative)
Boulevard del Hipodromo 626 # 1, Colonia San Benito, San Salvador
Telefax +503 2263 8074
Email cisraelita@integra.com.sv *Website* www.comunidadisraelitadeelsalvador.org/

ERITREA

There is one last native Jew left in Eritrea, Sami Cohen, who attends to the Asmara Synagogue and cemetery.

ASMARA
Asmara Jewish Community
P.O. Box 1475, 34 Serae Street
Tel +291 (1) 120 084/480 *Fax* +291 (1) 120 340
Email samico@gemel.com.er

ESTONIA

Despite being the only country officially declared 'Judenrein' (free of Jews) at the Wannsee conference in 1942, there is a Jewish community today. The community has always been small, and is believed to have begun in the fourteenth century. However, most Jews arrived in the nineteenth century, when Tsar Alexander II allowed certain groups of Jews into the area.

The first community was established in Tallinn in 1830. By 1939, the community had grown to 4,500 and was free from restraints. After the Soviet and Nazi occupations in the Second World War the Jews returned, mainly from the Soviet Union. Now that Estonia is independent, the Jewish community is able to practise its religion freely.

On May 16, 2007 A new Synagogue and Jewish center opened. The Jewish center has a Mikveh, Museum and Kosher restaurant, adult Education center, Yeladim (-children) center, Jewish day school.

TALLINN
Jewish Community of Estonia
16 Karu Street

Tel/Fax +372 (6) 644 370
Email office@ejc.ee Website www.ejc.ee
Community center contact *Pres.* Alla Jakobson *Email* community@jewish.ee
Rabbi Shmuel Kot *Email* rabbi@ejc.ee
Jewish Cultural Centre and Synagogue
16 Karu Street
Tel +372 (6) 662 3050

ETHIOPIA

The indigenous Jews of Ethiopia, known as Falashas, have probably lived in the country for about 2,000 years. Their origin is obscure but they are believed to be the descendants of members of the Agau tribe who accepted pre-Talmudic Judaism brought into Ethiopia (Abyssinia) from Jewish settlements in Egypt, such as that at Elephantine (Aswan). They were estimated to number half-a-million in the 17th century but by the 1970s the population had shrunk to less than 30,000. In 1975 the Israel Government recognised their right to enter under the Law of Return. Towards the end of 1984 the Israel Government undertook Operation Moses which entailed transporting about 8,000 Ethiopian Jews from refugee camps in Sudan to Israel. It is estimated that approximately 3,000 died from famine and disease before they could reach Israel. A further dramatic mass emigration to Israel was completed in 1991 and very few remain. A useful book on the subject is Emanuela Trevisan-Semi's *Jacques Faitlovitch and the Jews of Ethiopia*, obtainable from Vallentine Mitchell Publishers.
Jewish Community
P.O.B. 50 Addis Ababa

FIJI

Many Jews, mostly from Britain and some from Australia, settled in the islands in the 19th and early 20th centuries. About 12 Jewish families now live in Suva.
Correspondence K.R. Fleischman, GPO Box 905, Suva or Cherry Schneider, P.O.B 882, Suva

FINLAND

Finnish Jewry is a small minority group of 1,500, of whom about 1,100 are members of the Jewish Community of Helsinki and about 200 are members of the Jewish Community of Turku.
The Jewish settlement in Finland is relatively recent, dating back to 1825. The first Jews to settle in the country were Russian army conscripts, so-called cantonists, who served in Russian-ruled Finland and who were permitted to remain there upon completion of their military service. These Jews were later joined by others from Russia, Poland and Lithuania. Jews living in Finland were subject to many restrictions, including obligatory registration. These restrictions were abolished upon the independence of Finland in December 1917. In the late 1930s, admission was granted to about 250 Jewish refugees from Central Europe, and in recent years a number of Jews from the former Soviet Union, Poland and elsewhere in Eastern Europe have found sanctuary in the country.
The Jewish Community of Helsinki has addressed as its central priority the preservation of Jewish heritage, including stemming the tide of assimilation. In addition to attending the Jewish school and other extracurricular Jewish educational activities provided by the community, most Jewish youngsters are sent for a visit to Israel as teenagers in order to strengthen their sense of Jewish identity. The community also maintains a kindergarten for ages 3–6 with some 40 children, and a home for the aged. There are two synagogues in the country – one in Helsinki and the other in Turku, where services are conducted according to Modern Orthodox practice. In Helsinki, there is also a store selling kosher products, which is open five days a week.
Finnish Jews have been active in inter-Nordic cooperation and in reaching out to their Jewish neighbours across the Baltic, particularly in Estonia.
The Jewish communities of Finland are represented by the Central Council of the Jewish

Communities, which has been a voting member of both the World Jewish Congress and the European Jewish Congress since their inception.

For further details about the Jewish communities in Finland, please contact the Jewish Community of Helsinki.

Jewish Community of Helsinki
Malminkatu 26, 00100 Helsinki
Tel +358 (9) 586 0310
Fax +358 (9) 586 0313 0
Email srk@jchelsinki.fi
Website www.jchelsinki.fi
The offices are open Monday-Friday 8.30am–4pm (Friday 8.30am–2pm during winter).

FRANCE

France now boasts the largest Jewish community in Europe. The Jewish connection with France is a long one: it dates back over 1,000 years as there is evidence of Jewish settlement in several towns in the first few centuries of the Jewish Diaspora. The community grew in early medieval times, and contributed to the economy of the region. Two great Jewish commentators, Rashi and Rabenu Tam, both lived in France. However, French Jewry suffered both from the Crusaders and from other antisemitic outbursts in the medieval period.

Napoleon's reign heralded the emancipation of French Jewry and, as his armies conquered Europe, the emancipation of other communities began. Despite this, later incidents, such as the Dreyfus Affair, highlighted the fact that anti-semitism was not yet dead. The worst case of antisemitism in France occurred under the German occupation, when some 70,000 Jews were deported from the community of 300,000. After the war, France became a centre for Jewish immigration, beginning with 80,000 from eastern Europe, and then many thousands from North Africa, which eventually swelled the Jewish population to nearly 700,000.

The community is well served with organisations. Paris alone has 380,000 Jews, more than in the whole of the UK. There are many kosher restaurants, synagogues in many towns throughout the country, newspapers, radio programmes and schools in several cities. In Carpentras and Cavaillon there are synagogues which are considered to be national monuments.

PARIS

Consistoire Central The principal Jewish religious organisation in France. It administers the **Union des Communautés Juives de France**
17 rue St. Georges, 75009
Tel +33 (01) 40 82 26 26
Email contact@consistoire.org *Website* www.consistoire.org
Pres. Joël Mergui; *Dir. Gen.* F. Attali

Chief Rabbi of France
Rabbi Gilles Bernheim, Consistoire Central, 19 rue Saint-Georges, 75009
Tel +33 (01) 49 70 88 00 *Fax* +33 (01) 40 16 06 11

Communauté Israélite de la Stricte Observance
10 rue Cadet, 75009
Tel +33 (01) 42 46 36 47

Conseil Représentatif du Judaisme Traditionaliste
c/o Eric Schieber 6 rue Albert Camus, le Montigny 75010 Paris 16¡.
Tel +33 (01) 45 04 94 00
Representative organisation of Orthodox Jewry.
Pres. I. Frankforter; *Sec. Gen.* E. Schieber

Jeunesse Loubavitch
8 Rue Lamartine, 75009
Tel +33 (01) 45 26 87 60 *Fax* +33 (01) 45 26 24 37

Mouvement Juif Libéral de France (MJLF)
11 Rue Gaston de Caillavet, 75015
Tel +33 (01) 44 37 48 48 *Fax* +33 (01) 44 37 48 50
Affiliated to World Union of Progressive Judaism. *Pres.* Félix Mosbacher; *Rabbis* Daniel and Gabriel Farhi

Mouvement Loubavitch
8 rue Lamartine 9°
Tel +33 (01) 45 26 87 60
Union Libérale Israélite
24 rue Copernic, 75116 Organisation of LJ.
Pres. C Bloch. *Tel* +33 (01) 47 04 37 27

SYNAGOGUES
Orthodox Synagogues
10 rue Cadet, 9°; 31 rue de Montévidéo, 16°; 10 rue Pavee, 4°; 6 rue Ambroise Thomas, 9°; 3 rue Saulnier, 9°; 32 rue Basfroi, H°; 25 rue des Rosiers, 4°; 17 rue des Rosiers, 4°; 24 rue de Bourg Tibourg, 4°; 80 rue Doudeauville, 18°; 5 rue Duc, 18°; 18 rue des Ecouffes, 4°
Conservative Synagogue
Adath Shalom, 22 bis, rue des Belles Feuilles, 75116 Paris
Tel +33 (01) 45 53 84 09
Liberal Synagogues
24 rue Copernic, 16°; 11 rue Gaston de Caillavet 15°
There are also many synagogues in the Paris suburbs and in the Provinces.

AVIGNON
Avignon Synagogue
2 Place J·rusalem, 84 000 Avignon
Tel +33 (04) 90 85 21 24

BORDEAUX
CONTACT INFORMATION
Rue du Grand-Rabbin-Joseph-choen, Bordeaux
Tel +33 (05) 56917939

LYON
Grande Synagogue
13 qui Tilsitt, Lyon
Tel +33 (04) 78 37 13 43 *Fax* +33 (04) 78 38 26 57
Email aci@9online.fr *Website* www.consistoiredelyon.fr

MARSEILLE
Consistoire Israélite de Marseille
117-119 rue breteuil, 13006 Marseille
Tel +33 (04) 91 37 49 64, +33 (04) 91 81 13 57 *Fax* +33 (04) 91 37 83 90
Email consistoiremarseille@yahoo.fr *Website* www.consistoiremarseille.com
Dayan Rabbi Shmouel Melloul *Email* grandrabbinatmarseille@yahoo.fr
Etz Haim Community
18 Bd Michelet, 13008 Marseille
Rabbi and *Dayan*, Rav Hai Amram *Email* ravamram@yahoo.fr

NICE
Bet Yossef Synagogue (Sephardic, Orthodox)
16 rue alexis Mossa, 06000 Nice
Tel +33 (04) 97 07 18 89
Email betyossef@hotmail.fr

GEORGIA

The Jews of Georgia are divided into two groups; the native Georgian-speaking Jews, who have a history going back 1,500 years (some claim much longer) and the Ashkenazi Jews who came to Georgia following its annexation by Russia at the beginning of the nineteenth century. The Jewish population of Georgia has declined over the last 35 years due to emigration, mostly to Israel. Once numbering as many as 100,000, today the Georgian Jewish population is approximately 13,000. Tiblisi has the largest Jewish population at 11,000. Jewish communities are also located in Kutaisi, Batumi, Oni, Achaltische,

Ahalkalaki, Surami, Kareli, and Gori, and synagogues are located in most of these cities.

The Georgian Synagogue
45-47 Leselidze Street, Tbilisi
Tbilisi Hillel
c/o JDC Office, Galaktion Tabidze st. 5/3 Rm. 48, Tbilisi
Tel +995 (32) 517 7185

GERMANY

It may be a surprise to many that Germany comes immediately after France and the UK in the population table of Western European Jews. German Jews have contributed much to the culture of European Jews in general since their arrival, in what is now Germany, in the fourth century. The massive Jewish presence in Poland and other eastern European states stemmed from German Jews escaping persecution in the late Middle Ages. They took the early Medieval German language with them, which formed Yiddish, the old *lingua franca* of European Jews.

The Jews who stayed behind in Germany contributed much towards Jewish and German culture, with the Reform movement starting in nineteenth-century Germany, and Heine and Mendelssohn contributing to German poetry and music respectively. The Enlightenment Torah Im Derech Eretz and the Masorti also began in Germany.

The rise of Nazism destroyed the belief that the German Jews were more German than Jewish. Most managed to escape before 1939, but 180,000 were killed in the Holocaust (of the 503,000 who lived in Germany when Hitler came to power). Following the events of 1933–45, it seems incredible that any Jew should want to live in Germany again. However, the community began to re-form, mainly with immigrants from Eastern Europe, especially Russia. Now there are again Jewish shops in Berlin, and kosher food is once more available. There are many old synagogues which have been restored, and several concentration camps have been kept as monuments. There is also a great interest in Jewish matters among some of the non-Jewish younger generation.

Visitors to Berlin should try to visit the new Jewish Museum (officially opened in September 2001). It covers the history of German Jewry through the Middle Ages and up to the present. It revives the tradition of an earlier museum opened in 1933 before the Nazis came to power.

Allgemeine Rabbinerkonferenz
Rabbiner Dr. Henry G. Brandt. c/o IsraelitischeKultusgemeinde Schwaben-Augsburg, Hunoldsgraben 28, 86150 Augsburg

B'nai B'rith Lodges
Berlin, Cologne, Düsseldorf, Frankfurt a.Main, Hamburg, Munich and Saarbrücken

Bundesverband Jüd. Studenten
Oranienburger Str. 29-31, D-10117 Berlin
Tel +39 (30) 885 5304
Email info@bjsd.de
Also at Jewish Student Organisations at Aachen, Cologne, Frankfurt, Stuttgart, Hanover, Hamburg, Heidelberg and Munich

Chabad Berlin
Tel +49 (30) 2128 0830
Email service@jg-berlin.org *Website* www.jg-berlin.org
Rabbi Tiechtel

Israelitische Kultusgemeinde München und Oberbayern
Tel +49 (89) 2024 0021
Email rabbinate@ikg-m.de *Website* www.ikg-m.de
Rabbi Steven Langnas

Jewish Agency for Israel
Hebelstr. 6,D- 60318 Frankfurt
Tel +49 (69) 943 3340 *Fax* +49 (69) 9433 3420

INFORMATION REGARDING SYNAGOGUES, SERVICES AND KASHRUT
Orthodoxe Rabbinerkonferenz in Deutschland
c/o Synagogen-Gemeinde köln, Roonstr., 50674 Koln
Email info@ordonline.de *Website* www.ordonline.de
The Union of Progressive Jews in Germany, Austria & Switzerland
Herman-Hummel-Str. 18, D-82166 Graäfelfing
Tel +49 8980 9373
Email info@liberale-juden.de
Zentralarchiv zur Erforschung der Geschichte der Juden in Deutschland
Bienenstr. 5, D-69117 Heidelberg
Tel +49 (62) 2116 4141 *Fax* +49 (62) 2118 1049
Website www.zentralarchiv.uni-hd.de
Zentralrat der Juden in Deutschland (Central Council of Jews in Germany)
Tucholskystr. 9, D-10117 Berlin
Tel +49 (30) 284 4560 *Fax* +49 (30) 2844 5613
Email info@zentraltatdjuden.de *Website* www.zentraltatdjuden.de

GIBRALTAR

In 1473 there was a suggestion that the promontory should be reserved for Marranos (*See* D. Lamelas, *The Sale of Gibraltar in 1474*, 1992). The present Jewish community was formed of immigrants from north Africa shortly after the British annexation in 1704, but Jews had no legal right to settle in the north territory until 1749, by which year however, the Jewish residents numbered about 600, a third of the total number of residents, and had two synagogues.

During the siege of 1779 to 1783 the size of the Jewish population was reduced, a large proportion removing to England. After the siege the numbers rose again, being at their highest in the middle of the nineteenth century, when they rose above two thousand. (For the history of the Jews of Gibraltar, *See* A. B. M. Serfaty, *The Jews of Gibraltar under British Rule*, 1933.)

Following the period of decline, the last ten to fifteen years has seen a marked increase in the Jewish numbers, with a large number of Gibraltarians returning from study and residence abroad. This has created a young and vibrant community.

Managing Board of the Jewish Community
91 Irish Town
Tel +350 (200) 72606 *Fax* +350 (200) 40487
Pres. H. J. M. Levy *Fax* +350 (200) 40487 *Admin.* S. Levy *Email* mbjc@gibtelecom.net
Gibraltar Jewish Community
10 Bomb House Lane, Gibraltar; *Tel* +350 (200) 72606

For more information on Jewish life in Gibraltar including kosher restaurants, visit www.haruth.com/jw/JewsGibraltar.html

GREECE

After the Hellenistic occupation of Israel (the Jewish revolt during this occupation is commemorated in the festival of Hanukah), some Jews were led into slavery in Greece, beginning the first recorded Jewish presence in the country. The next significant Jewish immigration occurred after the Inquisition, when many Spanish Jews moved to Salonika, which was a flourishing Jewish centre until the German occupation in the Second World War. In 1832 Jews were granted the same equal rights as all other Greek citizens.

By the early 1940s, the Jewish population had grown to over 70,000, with 45,000 living in Salonika. The country was occupied in July 1941 and split among the Axis (German, Italian and Bulgarian) forces. During the occupation a relatively large number of Jews joined the Partisans. Many local Christians protected their Jewish neighbours in Athens. After the war many of the survivors emigrated to Israel.

Today there are Sephardi synagogues in Greece and, in Athens, a community centre and a Jewish museum. There are Jewish publications and a library in the community centre. In Aegina, Corfu and other Greek islands, ancient synagogues may be visited.

ATHENS
B'nai B'rith
15 Paparigopoulou Street, 105 61
Tel +30 (210) 323 0405
Central Board of Jewish Communities
36 Voulis Street, GR 105 57
Email hhkis@ath.forthnet.gr *Website* www.kis.gr
Pres. Moissis Constantinis *Tel* +30 (210) 324 4315 *Fax* +30 (210) 331 3852
Beth Shalom Synagogue
5 Melidoni Street, 105 53
M. Rabbi Jakob Arar *Tel* +30 (210) 325 2773
THESSALONIKI
Jewish Community Office
26 Vasileos Irakliou Street, 54624
Tel +30 (2310) 275 701 *Fax* +30 (2310) 229 063
Monastirioton Synagogue
35 Sigrou Street, 54630
Tel +30 (2310) 524 968

OTHER COMMUNITIES
Corfu Jewish Community
25 Agias Sofias Street, GR-491 00, Corfu
Pres. Moisis Velelis *Tel/Fax* +30 (2661) 037 713
Halkis Jewish Community
5 Papingi Street, 34100
Pres. M. Maissis *Tel* +30 (2221) 060 111 *Fax* +30 (2221) 083 781
Ioannina Jewish Community
18 Joseph Eliyia Str. GR 452 21
Pres. M. Elisaf *Tel* +30 (2651) 025 195
Larissa Jewish Community
Platia Evreon Martiron, 29 Kentavron Street, GR 412 22
Pres. M. Magrizos *Tel* +30 (2410) 532 965
Rodos Jewish Community
5 Polidorou Str. GR 85100
Tel +30 (2241) 022 364 *Fax* +30 (2241) 073 039
Email jcrhodes@otenet.gr
Pres. Bella Angel-Restis
Trikala Jewish Community
11 Sokratous Street, GR-421 00
Pres. Ovadias Sabas *Tel* +30 (2431) 021 623/025 834
Volos Jewish Community
51 Hatziargyuri Street, GR 383 33
Email jcvol@otenet.gr *Website* www.atlantis.gr/kis/volos.html
Pres. M. Solomon *Tel/Fax* +30 (2421) 025 302

GUADELOUPE
GOSIER
Gosier Synagogue
Bas du Fort, Lot 1
Tel +590 909 909
The community centre and restaurant/kosher store are also located here.

GUATEMALA
Conversos were the first recorded Jews in the country, but a few centuries later, the next Jewish immigration occurred with the arrival of German Jews in 1848. Later, some eastern European Jews arrived but Guatemala was not keen to accept refugees from Nazism, and, as

a result, passed some laws which, although not mentioning Jews directly, were aimed against Jewish refugees.

Even though these laws were in place, in 1939 there were 800 Jews in Guatemala. An Ashkenazi community centre was built in 1965, but despite accepting some Jewish Cuban refugees, the community is shrinking due to assimilation and intermarriage.

Most Jews live in Guatemala City, and others in Quetzaltenango and San Marcos. There is a Jewish school and kindergarten.

GUATEMALA CITY
Centro Hebreo (East European Jews)
7a. Av. 13-51 Zona 9
Tel +502 (2) 331 1975
Pres. Boris Barac
Comunidad Judia Guatemalteca
7a. Av. 13-51 Zona 9, Guatemala City, C.A.
Tel +502 (2) 560 1509 *Fax* +502 (2) 560 1589
Pres. T. Rybar
Consejo Central Sionista de la Comunidad Judia de Guatemala
Apto. Postal 502, Guatemala, C.A.
Pres. Mano Permuth
Maguen David (Sephardi)
7a. Avenida 3-80 Zona 2
Tel +502 (2) 232 0932 *Fax* +502 (2) 360 1589
Pres. Moises Beer

HAITI

Christopher Columbus brought the first Jew to Haiti–his interpreter, Luis de Torres, a *Converso* who had been baptised before the voyage. Thereafter more Jews settled, but the community was destroyed in an anti-European revolt by Toussaint L'Ouverture in 1804. A hundred or so years later, Jews from the Middle East and some refugees from the Nazis settled in Haiti, but many subsequently emigrated to Israel.

The remaining community has benefitted from the help of the Israeli embassy, and services are held in the embassy or in private homes. The community is too small to support other Jewish facilities.

The Jewish Community Of Haiti
The Honorary Consul, Gilbert Bigio, P.O. Box 687, Port-au-Prince
Tel 509 1 20 638

HONDURAS

During the Spanish colonial period, some *Conversos* did live in Honduras, but it was only in the nineteenth century that any significant Jewish immigration occurred. In the early twentieth century refugees from Nazism followed a handful of immigrants from eastern Europe. Honduras was one of the small number of countries to aid refugees from Nazism, and many Jews owe their lives to the help of Honduran consulates which issued visas in wartime Europe. The capital Tegucigalpa contains the largest Jewish population, but the only synagogue in the country is in San Pedro Sula (services are held in private homes in Tegucigalpa).

San Pedro Sula Synagogue and Community Centre
Sec. M. Weizenblut *Tel* +504 552 8136 *Fax* +504 557 5244
Comunidad hebrea de Tegucigalpa
P.O. Box U 8914, Tegucigalpa
Tel 504 238 5114 *Fax* 504 236 7776

HUNGARY

There were Jews living in Hungary in Roman times, even before the arrival of the Magyars (ancestors of the present-day Hungarians). The Jews suffered during the Middle Ages when there was a good deal of antisemitism, but conditions improved under Austro-Hungarian rule, and Judaism was recognised as being on a legal par with Christianity in 1896. Hungary lost a considerable amount of territory after the First World War and, as a result, many of its original Jewish communities (such as Szatmar) found themselves within other countries. Anti-semitism reached a peak in March 1944, when, during the German occupation, most Jewish communities began to be transported to Auschwitz. A number of those who were deported survived when Auschwitz was liberated by the Red Army in January 1945. After the war Hungary had the largest Jewish community in central Europe. Inevitably the community dwindled through emigration (especially after the 1956 uprising) and assimilation. Communism in Hungary was far more lenient than in other Warsaw Pact countries, and synagogues were allowed to operate. Since 1989, religious interest has increased, and the government has recently renovated the Dohany Synagogue, the second biggest synagogue in the world and the largest in Europe. The Jewish population is still the largest in the region, although most Jews are not very observant. The Hungarian national tourist office has published 'Shalom', an excellent guide to Jewish Hungary.

BUDAPEST
Central Rabbinate
Budapest VII Sip utca 12
Dir. Robert Deutsch, Chief Rabbi
The Budapest Jewish Community
1075 Budapest VII Sip utca 12
Tel +36 (1) 413 5569 *Fax* +36 (1) 342 1790
Man. Dir. Gusztav Zoltai; *Dir. Foreign Rel.* Ernö Lazarovits
Main Synagogue (Conservative)
The Dohány Street Synagogue (Dohány utcai zsinagóga)
Pest, VII. district, Budapest, Dohány utca 2
Tel +36 (1) 342 8949
Website www.bpjewmus.hu
There are 20 other synagogues and prayer houses in Budapest. The main provincial communities are at Debrecen, Miskolc, Szeged, Pécs, Györ

INDIA

The Jewish population of India can be divided into three components: the Cochin Jews, the Bene Israel and the Baghdadi Jews. The Cochin Jews are based in the south of India in Kerala. This community can be further divided into Black (believing themselves to be the original settlers) and White (of European or Middle Eastern origin), and the Paradesi. Most of the community has emigrated, but there is still a synagogue in Cochin that is a major tourist attraction.

The Bene Israel believe they are descended from Jewish survivors of a ship wrecked on its voyage from ancient Israel during the period of King Solomon. No reliable documentary evidence, however, exists to support this claim. More reliable evidence dates settlement to around the tenth century. The Bene Israel follow only certain Jewish practices, such as kosher food and Shabbat, and also adhere to certain Muslim and Hindu beliefs; for example, they abstain from eating beef. In the eighteenth century, they settled in Bombay and now form the largest group of Indian Jews.

Baghdadi Jews, immigrants from Iraq and the other Middle Eastern countries, arrived in India in the late eighteenth century, and followed British Colonial rather than local custom. Many emigrated to Israel in the 1950s and 1960s.

During the Indo-Pakistan war of 1972, the leading Indian military figure was General Samuels. In 1999 Lt-Gen J.F.R. Jacob was appointed Governor of Punjab State.

There is a central Council of Indian Jewry, based in Mumbai, where most of the Indian Jews live. Kosher food is available, and there are three Jewish schools in the city. Relations with Israel have recently improved and it is now a major trading partner.

Council of Indian Jewry
c/o The Jewish Club, Jeroo Building, 2ⁿᵈ Floor, 137 Mahatma Gandhi Road, Bombay, 400023
Tel +91 271 628

Pres. N. Talkar *Tel* +91 515 195/861 941; *V. Pres.* A. Talegawkar, A. Samson; *Sec.* J. Bhattacharya *Tel* +91 632 0589

Ohel David Synagogue
9 Dr. Ambedkar Road, Pune 411 001, Maharashtra
Tel +91 (20) 261 32 048
Email dsoloman2002@yahoo.com

INDONESIA

After World War II, many Jews left Indonesia because they had lost their homes and possessions during the war, but several families remained. By the 1950s, the Jewish communities were beginning to thrive again, especially in Surabaya. In the early 1960s, with the rise of nationalist and anti-Dutch sentiments among the people of Indonesia, many Jews emigrated to the United States, Australia, and Israel. By 1970, most of the thriving Jewish communities of Indonesia had almost vanished, leaving only a scattering of Jews behind. Today, about 20 Jews live in Indonesia, and Judaism is not recognized as a religion.

The local Jewish cemetery is frequently vandalized. Of the seventy graves with marble tablets, many are illegible.

Synagogue Kajoon (Orthodox)
Rivka Sayers, Jalan Kajoon #6, Surbaya, Jawa Timur
Tel +62 (315) 777 770 or +62 (315) 455 2815

IRAN

Jews have lived in the country at least since the time of the Persian King Cyrus in the sixth century BCE. Many of the tombs of Jewish biblical figures, such as Daniel, Habakkuk, Esther and Mordechai, are located in the cities of Iran. These holy places are respected by both Jews and Muslims. From the beginning of the twentieth century, the Iranian Jewish population has been under 70,000. Today it is in the region of 20,000. There are some legal differences between the majority and minority religions in Iran. Jews have been free to maintain their religious affairs and ceremonies, and culture training of Jewish students since the Islamic Revolution of 1979. There has been a Jewish representative in every Islamic parliament in the modern period. Iranian Jews live in Tehran, Shiraz, Isfahan, Kerman, and Kermanshah.

TEHRAN

Synagogues
Yousef-abad, 15th Street, Seyed Jama-leddin Assad-abadi Avenue; Abrishami, 4th Street, North Felestin Avenue *Chief Rabbi* Rabbi Yousef Haim Hamedani Cohen.

Tehran Jewish Committee
223 Sheikh-Hadi Street, Jomhuri Avenue, 11397 3 3317
Tel +98 6670 2556 *Fax* +98 6671 6429
Email iranjewish@iranjewish.com

IRAQ

From 1949 to 1951, 104,000 Jews were evacuated from Iraq. In 2004, approximately 35 Jews were living in Baghdad, but by 2008, the once-thriving community of Jews living in the capital dwindled to below 10, not enough to hold a minyan (the requisite 10 men needed for most religious rituals), and a handful more in the Kurdish-controlled northern parts of Iraq. The community still lives in fear, scared even to publicize the exact numbers of Jews remaining in Baghdad, but the Jewish Agency estimates it at about seven.

The one synagogue, the Meir Taweig Synagogue, was closed in 2003, after it became too dangerous to gather out in the open.

IRELAND, REPUBLIC OF

Jews lived in Ireland in the Middle Ages, and a Sephardi community was established in Dublin in 1660, four years after the Resettlement in England. In the eighteenth century there was also a community founded in Cork. The Dublin congregation declined in the reign of George III, and was dissolved in 1791, but was revived in 1822. The community received its largest influx of members around 1900, the immigrants coming from Eastern Europe, Lithuania in particular. There are now nearly 2,000 Jews in the country (per the 2011 Irish Census). Organised communities exist in Dublin and Cork, and there are clusters of nascent Jewish settlements in counties Kildare and Limerick.

Chief Rabbi
Office Herzog House, 1 Zion Road, Dublin 6
Tel +353 (1) 492 37 51 *Fax* +353 (1) 492 08 88
Email irishcom@iol.ie
Irish Jewish Community Office
Herzog House, 1 Zion Road, Dublin 6
Tel +353 (1) 492 3751 *Fax* +353 (1) 492 0888
Email office@jewishireland.org *Website* www.jewishireland.org
Sec. Nora Tillman
    Also located at **Herzog House**
Chief Rabbi's Office
Tel +353 (1) 492 3751
Community Rabbi, Zalman S. Lent; *Cantor*, Alwyn Shulman
Irish-Jewish Museum (Est. 1984).
3-4 Walworth Road, Portobello, Dublin 8
Tel +353 (1) 453 1797
The museum contains memorabilia of the Irish-Jewish Community and houses a former synagogue.
Jewish Representative Council of Ireland
Ch. Leonard Abrahamson; *Pres.* Stephen Molins

CORK
Hebrew Congregation
10 South Terrace
Website www.jewishcork.com
(Est. 1880). *Ch. of Tru.* F. Rosehill 7 Beverly, Ovens, Co. Cork *Tel* +353 (021) 487 0413
Email rosehill@iol.ie

DUBLIN
Dublin Hebrew Congregation
(Merged with Terenure Hebrew Congregation in 2004)
Rathfarnham Road, Terenure, Dublin 6
Email dhebc@eircom.net
Tel +353 (1) 490 59 69
Dublin Jewish Progressive Congregation
Pres. Malcolm Lewis
Tel +353 872 303 435
Email djpc@liberaljudaism.org
For further information please contact the secretary.

SYNAGOGUES
Knesset Orach Chayim (Dublin Jewish Progressive Congregation)
7 Leicester Avenue, Rathgar, Dublin 6 *Correspondence* P.O. Box 3059, Rathgar, Dublin 6
Tel +353 (1) 285 6241 *Email* djpc@liberaljudaism.org
(Est. 1946). *M.* Rabbi C. Middleburgh; *Hon. S.* J. Solomon *Tel* +353 (1) 285 6241

ISRAEL

Palestine was administered until May 14, 1948, by Great Britain under a Mandate approved by the Council of the League of Nations, the preamble to which incorporated the Balfour Declaration. On November 29, 1947, the Assembly of the United Nations recommended that Palestine should be reorganised as two States, one Jewish, the other Arab, together with an internationalised Jerusalem and district, combined in an economic union. On the surrender of the Mandate by Britain on May 14, 1948, the Jewish territory, with a Jewish pop. of 655,000, took the name of Israel and set up a Provisional Government, with Dr. Chaim Weizmann as President and David Ben-Gurion as PM. On July 5, 1950, the 'Law of Return' was proclaimed, conferring on every Jew the right to live in Israel.

The signing of a declaration of a set of principles by Israel and the PLO under the leadership of Yasser Arafat on September 13, 1993, concluded an era of forty-five years of strife between Israel and her Arab neighbours and recognised the aspirations of Palestinian Arabs for territory proposed for them by the UN in 1947. A peace treaty with Jordan was agreed in 1994. PM Rabin was assassinated in November 1995.

Key events in this history include:

The invasion of the Jewish state by the Arab armies in 1948 concluded by a series of armistices in 1949 and the recognition of Israel by the UN on May 11, 1949; the annexation of Arab Palestine by Jordan in 1950; the absorption by Israel of Jews from Arab lands. The establishment of Palestinian refugee camps in the Arab states; seizure by Egypt of the Suez Canal Zone and the (Franco-British and Israeli) Sinai-Suez campaign of 1956; Egypt's closure of the Straits of Tiran in May 1967 which provoked the Six-Day War of June 1967 and saw the Israeli capture of Jerusalem and occupation of Gaza, Sinai, the Golan and the West Bank and the first Nat. Unity Coalition (1967–70); the Yom Kippur War of October 1973 and the ensuing negotiations leading to partial Israeli withdrawals in Sinai and the Golan; the Likud election victory of 1977 and the visit to Israel by Egyptian President Anwar Sadat in November 1977 which led to the Camp David Agreement of March 26, 1979, the establishment of diplomatic relations between Egypt and Israel, and the Israeli withdrawal from the whole of Sinai in April 1982; Israel's 'Operation Peace for Galilee' in Lebanon in June 1982 and withdrawal in 1985, a war which caused great divisions in Israel; the *Intifada* of the Palestinians in Gaza and the West Bank starting in 1988; the US-inspired five-point peace plan of 1989 and its failure in 1990; the Gulf War (January 1991) following the Iraqi invasion of Kuwait, when the PLO supported Iraq and Israel sustained scud missile attacks without retaliation; the launching of negotiations for a comprehensive Middle East 'peace settlement' between Israel, the Arabs, and representatives of the Palestinians at a meeting in Madrid in October 1991.

It is these negotiations that came to fruition on the eve of the New Year 5754. The continuing 'Peace Process' was repeatedly put in jeopardy through the actions of terrorists intent on destabilizing any progress towards détente and under protest at the consolidation of Israeli settlements. President Clinton endeavoured to broker a new agreement between PM Barak and the PLO, but this failed and Mr. Barak resigned. Nonetheless Mr. Barak's achievement in securing withdrawal of Israeli forces from southern Lebanon indicated positive efforts to reconcile neighbourly relations. The new *Intifada* broke out in 2000 and Israel's predicament has been exacerbated by the aftermath of the terror of September 2001, the American war against the Taliban of Afghanistan and the Anglo-American war of 2003 against Saddam Hussein's Iraq. Interventions by President George W. Bush and the promulgation of a 'Road Map' for reviving the peace process have faltered. Ariel Sharon saw through the construction of a barrier-wall to deflect continuing bombing raids from Gaza into Israel but broke with his Likud government in 2005 when he also forced through the withdrawal from Gaza. With the establishment of his Kadima Party he indicated some prospect of withdrawals also from parts of the West Bank.

The death of Yasser Arafat and the election of Mahmoud Abbas as PLO President were followed by Palestinian elections at the beginning of 2006. These were won by Hamas who, in government, have not rescinded their policy towards the destruction of Israel. Ariel Sharon suffered a stroke ahead of the scheduled elections in Israel and, while Kadima secured power at these elections, the new government found itself at increased risk from continuing militancy in Gaza and a new embroilment in Lebanon, which was provoked by the rise and belligerency of the Hizbollah, turning northern Israel into a war-zone. Following UN Resolution 1701 on the cease-fire in southern Lebanon, and the monitoring of the withdrawal of Hizbollah under UN control, a tentative measure of peace has been restored. Against this, the increasing stridency of Iranian rhetoric and her unabashed pursuit of nuclear power leave Israel exposed to untold dangers.

Government

The Provisional Government of Israel was replaced by a permanent one after the election of the First **Knesset** (Parl.) in January, 1949.

Israel's Basic Law provides that elections must be 'universal, nationwide, equal, secret and proportional'. A general election must be held at least every four years. The Knesset is elected by a form of proportional representation in which members are selected in strict proportion to the votes cast for each party. Any candidate who obtains one per cent of the total votes cast is assured of a Knesset seat.

Mainly as a result of the voting system, no single party has so far been able to form a government on the basis of its own Knesset majority. Until the election in 1977, the dominant political force was a coalition of the Left, which formed governments with the help of various smaller parties, usually those with a religious programme. In the elections of 1977 and 1981 an alliance of the Right was able to form an administration with the help of religious parties. One feature of the political situation has been that the religious parties, in particular, have been able to exercise an influence out of proportion to their members.

Within recent years, however, there has been a marked polarisation of attitudes among sections of Israeli society and this was reflected by the proliferation of small parties which contested the 1984 election. The 1984 election produced an inconclusive result, with only three seats separating the two big party blocs. The two big parties formed Israel's second Nat. Unity Government to cope with the urgent economic and other problems. The office of PM was held in rotation, first by Shimon Peres, the Labour Alignment leader, and then by Yitzhak Shamir, the Likud leader. The 1988 election was also inconclusive and was followed by another Coalition Government, with Mr. Shamir continuing as PM and Mr. Peres as V. Premier. The Nat. unity government broke up in March 1990 when the Likud declined to go along with a U.S. plan to promote peace talks. Mr. Shamir constructed a centre-right religious government, supported by 66% of the 120 members of the Knesset. The elections of 1992 produced a Labour coalition led by Yitzhak Rabin. Demographic changes brought about by the influx of settlers from Eastern Europe and political and economic pressures, contributed in large part to this outcome. The Knesset elections of 1996 were the first at which there was also direct voting for the position of PM. Following the resignation of Mr. Barak in 2001, Ariel Sharon was elected PM while the 15th Knesset remained in session. While political power rests constitutionally in the Knesset, the President of Israel, essentially a symbolic and representational figure, can in certain circumstances exercise a degree of de facto power based on his prestige. In particular, he can emerge as the voice of the nation's conscience.

The President is elected for a five-year period, renewable only once. Moshe Katsav was elected President in 2000, but was obliged to stand down in 2007.

The results of the March 2006 election gave Mr. Olmert the opportunity to form a Centrist government with Labour support in a coalition of 73 seats. He resigned in August 2008 and Foreign Secretary, Tzipi Livni won the Kadima vote to succeed him in negotiations for a new coalition. This failed to materialise and new elections were held in February 2009.

Elections to the 19th Knesset were held in January 2013. Public debate over the Tal Law nearly led to elections in 2012, but they were aborted after Kadima briefly joined the government. Elections were later called in October 2012 after failure to agree on the budget for the 2013 fiscal year. The elections saw the emergence of Likud Yisrael Beiteinu alliance, the largest faction in the Knesset, winning 31 of the 120 seats. Likud leader Benjamin Netanyahu formed the country's thirty-third government after establishing a coalition with Yesh Atid, the Jewish Home and Hatnuah.

Party votes were as follows:

Likud Yisrael Beitenu	31	(-11)	Hatnuah	6	(+6)
Yesh Atid	19	(+19)	Meretz	6	(+3)
Labour Party	15	(+7)	United Arab List-Ta-al	4	(-)
The Jewish Home*	12	(+9)	Hadash	4	(-)
Shas	11	(+1)	Balad	3	(-)
United Torah Judaism	7	(+2)	Kadima	2	(-26)

* formerly the National Religious Party.

The Presidents of Israel Chaim Weizmann 1949–52; Yitzhak Ben Zvi 1952–63; Zalman Shazar 1963–73; Prof. Ephraim Katzir 1973–78; Yitzhak Navon 1978–83; Chaim Herzog 1983–93; Ezer Weizman 1993–2000; Moshe Katsav 2000–07; **Shimon Peres** 2007–2014; Reuven Rivlin 2014-

The Prime Ministers of Israel David Ben-Gurion 1948–53 and Nov. 1955–63; Moshe Sharett Dec. 1953–55; Levi Eshkol 1963–69; Golda Meir 1969–74; Yitzhak Rabin 1974–77 and 1992–95; Menachem Begin 1977–83, Yitzhak Shamir Oct. 1983–Sept. 1984, Oct. 1986–June 1992; Shimon Peres Sept. 1984–Oct. 1986, Nov. 1995–May 1996; Benjamin Netanyahu, May 1996–99; Ehud Barak, May 1999–Feb. 2001; Ariel Sharon, Feb. 2001–06; Ehud Olmert (Apr. 2006–09); Benjamin Netanyahu (2009-)

Judiciary The *Pres.* appoints judges on the recommendation of an independent committee.

Defence Forces Unified command of Army, Navy and Air Force. Small regular force; compulsory military service for men and women aged between 18 and 29 followed by annual service in the Reserve.

Area Following 1949 armistice agreements – approx. 20,750 sq. km. Following withdrawal from Sinai in April 1982, approx. 28,161 sq. km. (including Golan Heights, West Bank and Gaza).

Neighbouring countries Egypt, Jordan, Syria, Lebanon.

Population Sept. 1998: 4,850,000. These figures include 17,000 Druse on the Golan Heights but not the other territories occupied in the Six-Day War (Est. at 1,381,000).

Main Towns Jerusalem (the capital), Tel Aviv, Haifa, Ramat Gan, Petach Tikvah, Netanya, Holon, Bnei Brak, Rehovot, Hadera, Nazareth, Rishon le-Zion, Beersheba, Ashkelon, Ashdod, Bat Yam, Tiberias, Eilat.

Industry Main products: Cement, fertilisers, metal products, polished diamonds, ceramics, tyres and tubes, plywood, textiles, clothing and footwear, citrus by-products, electrical and electronic applicances, micro-electronics, chemicals, canned fruit, military equipment.

Agricultural Products Citrus, fruit, vegetables, eggs, milk, wheat, barley, tobacco, groundnuts, cotton, sugarbeet, beef, fish, flowers, wine.

Minerals Potash and bromine, magnesium, phosphate, petroleum, salt, glass, sand, clay, gypsum, granite, copper, iron, oil, natural gas.

With the exception of Jerusalem and Haifa, the country's largest port, the main centres of population are concentrated in the flat and fertile western coastal plain. Tel Aviv, the centre of Israel's largest metropolitan area, is the chief commercial and industrial centre. Beersheba is the capital of the arid northern Negev, while Eilat, the country's southernmost port, has become a bustling Red Sea township linked to the northern centres by a modern highway and giving access now to Jordan as well. In the north lies the largely Arab centre of Nazareth, the popular health resort of Tiberias, and Safad. Round Tel Aviv are clustered a number of towns, including Ramat Gan, Holon and Bnei Brak.

Pres. of State Reuven Rivlin; Knesset Speaker Yuli-Yoel Edelstein

ISRAELI EMBASSIES AND LEGATIONS

Israel now enjoys diplomatic relations with 160 countries and many of these ties have come into being or have been renewed following the peace agreements of 1993. For more information and a full list of Israeli embassies around the world, please visit www.mfa.gov.il/MFA/

Main Political Parties

ISRAEL LABOUR PARTY

Established 1968 by the merger of Mapai, Achdut Avoda and Rafi. Its programme: 'To attain nat., social and pioneering aims, in the spirit of the heritage of the Jewish People, the vision of socialist Zionism and the values of the Labour movement'.

Ch. Amir Peretz 1 Urim Street, Tel Aviv *Tel* +972 689 9444

KADIMA ('Forward')

Website www.kadimahsharon.co.il

A new party that defines itself as a broad popular movement which works to ensure the future of Israel as a Jewish democratic state. The party, formed by Ariel Sharon in November

2005 following the Israeli withdrawal from Gaza which split the Likud alliance, has adopted a 'centrist and liberal' platform designed to uphold a moderate political agenda.
Ch. Tsipi Livni, Petah Tikva *Tel* +972 (3) 978 8000 ext.157 *Fax* +972 (3) 978 8009

LIKUD PARTY
Email webmaster@likud.org.il
Conservative Political Party. Dedicated to the principles of a free-market economy and the attainment of peace with security while preserving Israel's national interests.
Ch. B. Netanyahu Metsudat Ze'ev, 38 King George Street, Tel Aviv *Tel* +972 (03) 621 0666

MERETZ-YACHAD
Website www.meretz.org.il
Meretz-Yachad was formed in 1992 by a merger of 'Ratz', 'Mapam' and the then 'Shinui'. It was led by Shulamit Aloni. The party disbanded in 2003 and joined Yossi Belin's 'Shahar' party which renamed itself 'Yachad' but the original name re-emerged in 2005 under Belin's chairmanship. Meretz-Yachad defines itself as a Zionist Green left wing social democratic party. It has inherited Meretz's membership in the Socialist International.
Ch. Yossi Belin

GIL (Pensioners' Party)
Founded 2005, by Rafi Eitan to fight the Knesset Elections, committed to support for pensioners.

NATIONAL RELIGIOUS PARTY
Tel +972 (02) 537 727
Created through the merger of Mizrachi and Hapoel Hamizrachi in 1956. Its motto 'The People of Israel in the Land of Israel, according to the Torah of Israel'. *Ch.* Binyamin Elon

SHINUI ('Change' in English)
Established 1971. A reformist and liberal party. Maintains that the rights of the individual are supreme and that all legislation must be measured against that principle. A democratic, secular, liberal, Zionist, peace-seeking party.
Ch. R. Levinthal 100 Hashmona'im Street, P.O. Box 20533, Tel Aviv 61200 *Tel* +972 (03) 562 0118

AGUDAT ISRAEL
Founded in 1912 in Katowice, Poland. Its principle is that only the Torah unites the Jewish people. *Political Sec.* M. Porush *Central Office* Haherut Sq., Jerusalem *Tel* +972 (02) 384 357 and 5 Bardechefsky Street, Tel Aviv *Tel* +972 (02) 561 7844

SHAS
Founded in 1984 as representing Haredi Sephardi Judaism. The party was formed under the leadership of Rabbi Ovadia Yosef (former Israeli Chief Rabbi), who remains its spiritual leader today. *Ch.* Eli Yishai

YISRAEL BEYTENU
Website www.beytenu.org.il
A right-wing party formed by Avigdor Lieberman in 1997 to create a platform for Russian immigrants who support a hard line in negotiations with the Palestinian Authority.

HISTADRUT – GENERAL FEDERATION OF LABOUR IN ISRAEL
93 Arlozoroff Street, Tel Aviv. 62098
Tel +972 (03) 692 1511 *Fax* +972 (03) 692 1512
Dir. Intl. Dept. Avital Shapira-Shabirow *Email* avital@histadrut.org.il; *Ch.* Avi Nissenkorn; Histadrut, the largest labour organisation in Israel, is a democratic organisation. It strives to ensure the welfare, social security and rights of working people, to protect them and act for their professional advancement. It endeavours to reduce the gaps in society to achieve a more just society. The executive body of Histadrut is separate from the elected body and the legislative body. The legislative and regulatory body, the Histadrut Assembly, represents the

relative strengths of the different political groups of Israel.

Membership is voluntary, and open to all men and women of 18 years of age and above who live on the earnings of their own labour without exploiting the work of others. Membership totals over 700,000, including workers from all spheres, housewives, self-employed and professionals as well as the unemployed, students and pensioners. Workers' interests are protected through a number of occupational and professional unions affiliated to the Histadrut. The Histadrut operates courses for trade unionists and new immigrants and apprenticeship classes. It maintains an Institute for Social and Economic Issues and the International Institute, one of the largest centres of leadership training in Israel, for students from Africa, Asia, Latin America and Eastern Europe. The institute includes the Levinson Centre for Adult Education and the Jewish–Arab Institute for Regional Cooperation. Attached to the Histadrut is a women's organisation, 'Na'amat'. This promotes changes in legislation, operates a network of legal service bureaux and vocational training courses, and runs counselling centres for the treatment and prevention of domestic violence, etc.

Selected Educational and Research Institutions

BAR-ILAN UNIVERSITY

Correspondence BIU, Ramat Gan, Israel 52900

Tel +972 (03) 531 8111 *Student information Tel* +972 (03) 531 8274 *Fax* +972 (03) 535 1522
Website www.biu.ac.il

Since its founding in 1955, Bar-Ilan has grown to become Israel's second-largest university, with a modern 70-acre campus in Ramat Gan, outside Tel Aviv and five regional colleges across Israel. Over 6,000 courses are taught in the faculties of Exact Sciences, Life and Social Sciences, Humanities, Jewish Studies and Law, by 1,300 academic faculty to 25,000 students. Today, Israel's largest schools of educational and social work and the premier Jewish studies faculty operate at Bar-Ilan. Additionally, the university is home to world-class scientific research institutes in Physics, Med. Chemistry, Mathematics, Brain Research, Economics, Strategic Studies, Developmental Psychology, Musicology, Archaeology, Bible, Jewish Law and Philosophy, and more. Some 40 prominent universities around the world maintain academic cooperation agreements with Bar-Ilan. Every day, Israelis of widely varying backgrounds and religious beliefs work and study together in harmony at Bar-Ilan. *Chancellor* Rabbi Prof. Emanuel Rackman; *Pres.* Prof. Moshe Kaveh; *Rector* Prof. J. Menis

BEN GURION UNIVERSITY OF THE NEGEV, BEERSHEVA

Founded 1969, the university includes the following faculties: Humanities and Social Sciences, Natural Sciences, Engineering Sciences, Health Sciences, School of Management, the Kreitman School of Advanced Graduate Studies and the Jacob Blaustein Institute for Desert Research. *Pres.* Prof. R. Carmi P.O. Box 653, BeerSheva, 84105 *Tel* +972 (08) 646 1279

CENTER FOR JEWISH ART

Hebrew University of Jerusalem, Mount Scopus, Humanities Building, Jerusalem 91905
Tel +972 (02) 588 2281 *Fax* +972 (02) 540 0105
Email cja@vms.huji.ac.il *Website* www.lcja.huji.ac.il
Dir. Dr. R. Talgam; *Acad. Ch.* Prof. R. Elior

HAIFA UNIVERSITY

Mount Carmel, Haifa 31905
Tel +972 (04) 824 011 *Fax* +972 (04) 828 8110
Website www.haifa.ac.il

Established in 1963, Haifa is one of the seven accredited research universities in Israel. Academic instruction is conducted in the framework of the six Faculties (Humanities, Social Science, Law, Social Welfare and Health, Education, Sciences). Most of the 59 departments and schools offer bachelor, master and Ph.D. degrees. Research activity is carried out in the framework of research institute and centres. The Research Authority encourages and coordinates research at the University. *Pres.* A. Ben-Ze'ev; *Rector* Y. Ben-Artzi

HEBREW UNIVERSITY OF JERUSALEM
Mount Scopus, Jerusalem, 91905
Tel +972 (02) 588 2811 *Fax* +972 (02) 588 0058
Website www.huji.ac.il
Founded in 1918 and opened in 1925 on Mount Scopus. When, contrary to the provisions of the Armistice Agreement after the War of Independence in 1949, access to Mount Scopus was denied by Jordan, the University functioned in scattered temporary quarters until a new campus was built on Givat Ram, and a med campus in Ein Kerem, both in Jerusalem. After the Six-Day War of June 1967, the Mount Scopus campus was rebuilt and expanded. Today the University serves some 24,000 students in its seven faculties: Humanities, Social Sciences, Science, Law, Med, Dental Med and Agricultural, Food and Environmental Quality Sciences (the latter located in Rehovot). There are 11 Schools: Education, Business Administration, Nutritional Sciences, Nursing, Occupational Therapy, Pharmacy, Public Health, Social Work, Veterinary Medicine, Library, Archive and Information Studies, and the Rothberg International School. The Jewish National and University Library is on the Givat Ram campus and there are about 100 research centres. The Magnes Press/Hebrew University publishes scientific and academic works. Five graduates and faculty have received Nobel prizes since 2001. *Ch. Bd. of Govs.* Charles H. Goodman; *Pres.* Prof. Menachem Magidor; *Rector* Prof. Haim Rabinowitch

ISRAEL NATURE AND PARKS AUTHORITY
3 Am Ve'Olamo Stret, Givat Shaul, Jerusalem 95463
Tel 972 (02) 500 5444 *Fax* +972 (02) 652 9232 *Website* www.parks.org.il
The Authority is the result of a merger in 1968 of two bodies, one of which was in charge of the Israeli nature reserves and the other of national parks and heritage sites in Israel.

ISRAEL OCEANOGRAPHIC AND LIMNOLOGICAL RESEARCH
(Est. 1967) To develop knowledge and technology for sustainable use of marine and fresh water resources. *Dir. Gen.* Prof. Barak Herut, Tel Shikmona, P.O.B. 8030, Haifa 31080 *Tel* +972 (04) 856 5200 *Fax* +972 (04) 851 1911 *Email* barak@ocean.org.il

JERUSALEM ACADEMY OF JEWISH STUDIES - Yeshivat Dvar Yerushalayim
53 Katzenellenbogen Street, Har Nof, P.O.B. 34580, Jerusalem 91344 *Tel* +972 (02) 652 2817 *Fax* +972 (02) 652 287 *Email* dvar@dvar.org.il *Website* www.dvar.org.il
Courses for students without a background in Jewish Learning and more advanced courses. The student body comes from many countries. Students can take part in the Academy's community educational projects. Special features include: Classes in English, Hebrew, Russian, German, French, part-time and summer courses; Kollel and research department; recognised Ulpan; tours of historic sites; and college credits. A special one-year programme, accredited by Touro and other U.S. colleges, for post high school graduates and post 6th formers. *Dean* Rabbi B. Horovitz, MA; UK office (Reg. Charity No. 262716), 1007 Finchley Road, London NW11 7HB *Ch.* A. Maslo *Tel/Fax* 020 8458 8563 *Student Off.* Rabbi Taubman *Tel* 020 8203 0333/07957 650 325 (*See* p. 99).

JERUSALEM COLLEGE OF TECHNOLOGY
Established in 1969 to train engineers and applied scientists within a religious framework. The College has a men's campus in Jerusalem-Machon Lev and Machon Naveh, and 2 campuses for women Machon Tal in Jerusalem and Machon Lustig in Ramat Gan. These have departments in Electro-Optics and Applied Physics, Medical Engineering, Electronic Engineering, Computer Sciences, Technology Management and Marketing, Software Engineering, Teacher Training and Registered Nursing. The men's Jerusalem complex and a Bet Midrash for Jewish studies; a one year yeshiva academic programme for English-speaking students. The women's programmes also include religious studies.
Pres. Prof. J. Bodenheimer; *Rector* Prof. M. Steiner 21 Havaad Haleumi Street, Jerusalem *Tel* +972 (02) 675 1111 *Fax* +972 (02) 642 2075

THE LOUIS GUTTMAN ISRAEL INSTITUTE OF APPLIED SOCIAL RESEARCH
Founded in 1946 to advise governmental, public and private bodies on research in social psychology, sociology, psychology and related disciplines. *Scientific Dir.* Professor S. Kugelmass *Tel* +972 (02) 231 421

MIKVEH ISRAEL AGRICULTURAL SCHOOL
Mikveh Israel, Doar Holon, 58910
Tel +972 (03) 842 050
The first agricultural school in Israel, it was founded by Charles Netter of the Alliance Israelite Universelle in 1870. The curriculum, in addition to training in agriculture, comprises instruction in the humanities, Jewish subjects, science, etc.

ORT ISRAEL NETWORK
Head office, 39 King David Boulevard, Tel Aviv 61160 *Tel* +972 (03) 520 3275
Email zvikap@admin.ort.org.il *Website* www.ort.org.il
(Est. 1949) ORT Israel manages Scientific and Tech. Colleges and schools for around 100,000 young and adult students yearly. *Dir. Gen.* Z. Peleg

TECHNION-ISRAEL INSTITUTE OF TECHNOLOGY
Tel +972 (04) 829 4986 *Fax* +972 (04) 823 5195
Website www.technion.ac.il
Established in 1924 as a small technology institute, it now has more than 12,500 students, making it the largest full-service university wholly dedicated to science and technology in Israel. The institute has 19 faculties and department including: Aerospace, Biomedical, Chemical, Civil, Electrical and Industrial Engineering and Architecture, Chemistry, Computer Science and Management, Medicine and Physics. The Technion is located on Mount Carmel. The main buildings include the Winston Churchill Auditorium and the Shine Student Union. It also has a graduate school, a school for continuing education and a Research & Development Foundation. *Pres.* Prof. Y. Apeloig, Technion City, Mount Carmel, Haifa 32000

TEL AVIV UNIVERSITY
Ramat Aviv, Tel Aviv
Tel +972 (03) 545 0111
The university sponsors studies and research in all the arts and sciences and includes, among its faculties, a department of space and planetary sciences. Its observatory, at Mitzpe Ramon in the Negev, was the first in Israel. A science based industry utilising the university's manpower and equipment has been established. Its Graduate School of Business Administration was the first established in the country. There is a one year course which prepares new immigrants for entry into Israeli universities. *Pres.* Prof. Joseph Klafter; *Rector* Prof. Aron Shai

WEITZ CENTER FOR DEVELOPMENT STUDIES
P.O.B. 12 Rehovot, 76100
Tel +972 (08) 947 4111 *Fax* +972 (08) 947 5884
Website www.ort.org.il
Founded in Rehovot in 1963, its main object is interdisciplinary research & training activities related to regional development in Israel and the developing world.

WEIZMANN INSTITUTE OF SCIENCE
P.O.B. 26, Rehovot 76100
Tel +972 (08) 934 3111 *Fax* +972 (08) 934 107
Website www.weizmann.ac.il
The Institute engages in research in Mathematical Sciences, Chemistry, Physics, Biology, Biochemistry and Science Teaching. *Pres.* Prof. D. Zajfman; *V. Pres.* Prof. H. Garty

THE ZINMAN COLLEGE OF PHYSICAL EDUCATION AND SPORTS SCIENCES AT THE WINGATE INSTITUTE
P.E. College at Wingate Institute, Netanya, Israel 42902
Tel +972 (09) 863 922 *Fax* +972 (09) 865 0960

Website www.zin.macam98.ac.il
(Est. 1944) Teachers College for Physical Educators. Offers a four-year Bachelor of Education course, including Teachers' Diploma. Specializes in early childhood, special education, sports for the disabled, posture cultivation, cardiac rehabilitation, physical activity for the elderly, public health, behaviour analysis, dance and movement, leisure and recreation education, nautical education, scouting education and sports media. Joint M.A. programme with Haifa University. Faculty of 200, student body of 900 full-time students, 1,500 in part-time in-service courses.

Selected Commercial Organisations
BANK OF ISRAEL
Email webmaster@bankisrael.gov.il
Set up by the Knesset in 1954. Its functions include those usually discharged by central banks. It issues the currency and acts as Government banker, and manages the official gold and foreign reserves. The governor is chief economic advisor to the Government, Rechov Eliezer Kaplan, Kiryat Ben-Gurion, Jerusalem, 9100 *Tel* +972 (02) 655 2211 *Fax* +972 (02) 652 8805

ISRAEL-AMERICA CHAMBER OF COMMERCE AND INDUSTRY
35 Shaul Hamelech Boulevard, Tel Aviv
Tel +972 (03) 695 2341 *Fax* +972 (03) 695 1272
Email amcham@amcham.co.il *Website* www.amcham.co.il
Exec. Dir. Tamar Guy
ISRAEL-BRITISH CHAMBER OF COMMERCE
29 Hamered Street, P.O. Box 50321, Tel Aviv 61502
Tel +972 (03) 510 9424 *Fax* +972 (03) 510 9540
Website www.ibcc.co.il
(Est. 1951). *Ch.* L. Judes, *Exec. Dir.* F. Kipper

MANUFACTURERS' ASSOCIATION OF ISRAEL
29 Hamered Street, Tel Aviv 68125
Tel +972 (03) 519 8787 *Fax* +972 (03) 510 3154
Email trade@industry.org.il
Pres. S. Brosh

Other Selected Organisations
ASSOCIATION FOR THE WELLBEING OF ISRAEL'S SOLDIERS
Head Office P.O. Box 21707, Tel Aviv 61217
Overseas Dept 60 Weizman Street, Tel Aviv 62155
Tel +972 (03) 546 5135 *Fax* +972 (03) 546 5145
(Ha'aguda Lemaan Hechayal. Charity No. 580004307) The Association for the Wellbeing of Israel's Soldiers was founded in 1942, during the Second World War, at a time when the young men of pre-state Israel were being drafted into the allied armies and the Jewish Brigade. The slogan back then was 'The Heart of the People is with its Soldiers', and this sentiment continues to guide the Association's activity today.

BETH HATEFUTSOTH
Tel Aviv University Campus, Ramat-Aviv, P.O.B. 39359, Tel Aviv 61392
Tel +972 (03) 745 7800 *Fax* +972 (03) 745 7891
Website www.bh.org.il
The Nahum Goldmann Museum of the Jewish Diaspora, which opened in Tel Aviv in 1978, tells the story of the Jewish people from the time of their expulsion from the Land of Israel 2,500 years ago to the present. History, tradition and the heritage of Jewish life in all parts of the world are brought to life in murals, reconstructions, dioramas, audio-visual displays, documentary films and interactive multi-media presentation. *Dir.* Hasia Israeli

CHIEF RABBINATE
Beit Yahav, 80 Yirmiyahu Street, P.O.B. 36016, Jerusalem 91360
Tel +972 (02) 5313191/531 3190 *Fax* +972 (02) 537 7872

The Chief Rabbinate consists of two joint Chief Rabbis and the Chief Rabbinical Council of 16. *Chief Rabbis* Rabbi Israel Yona Metzger (Ashkenazi) and Rabbi Shlomo Amar (Rishon Lezion, Sephardi). There are District Rabbinical Courts (Batei Din) in Jerusalem, Haifa, Petach Tikvah, Rehovot, Tiberias-Safad, Beersheba and Ashkelon.

ISRAEL MOVEMENT FOR PROGRESSIVE JUDAISM (IMPJ)
13 King David Street, Jerusalem 94101
Tel +972 (02) 620 3448
Email info@reform.org.il *Website* www.reform.org.il
The Israel Movement for Progressive Judaism (IMPJ) is Israels liberal Jewish religious movement, and a constituent member of the World Union for Progressive Judaism.

THE ISRAEL MUSEUM
Ruppin Boulevard, Jerusalem, P.O. Box 71117, Jerusalem 91710
Tel +972 (02) 670 8811 *Fax* +972 (02) 563 1833
Website www.imj.org.il
Israel's leading cultural institute and a museum of world-class status. Its 20-acre campus houses an encyclopaedic collection of art and archaeology, with special emphasis on the culture of the Land of Israel and the Jewish people. The Museum has the world's most extensive collections of the archaeology of the Holy Land, Judaica and the ethnography of the Jewish world. It also has significant and extensive holdings in the Fine Arts, ranging from Old Masters to Contemporary Art. There are separate departments for Asian Art, the Arts of Africa and Oceania, Prints and Drawings, Photography, and Architecture and Design. The campus also includes the Shrine of the Book, which houses the Dead Sea Scrolls, the Billy Rose Art Garden and a Youth Wing. *Dir.* James Snyder

JEWISH AGENCY FOR ISRAEL
Website www.Jewishagency.org
Founded 1929; Reconstituted 1971. Constituents are the World Zionist Organisation, United Israel Appeal, Inc. (USA), and Keren Hayesod. By reasons of its record and world-wide organisation, the Jewish Agency has come to be widely regarded as the representative organisation of Jews the world over, particularly in regard to the development of Israel and immigration to it. The governing bodies of the Jewish Agency are: the Assembly, which lays down basic policy, the Board of Governors, which manages its affairs between annual Assembly meetings, and the Executive, responsible for day-to-day operations. *Ch. Exec.* Natan Sharansky; *Ch. Bd.* James S. Tisch; *Dir. Gen.* Alan Hoffmann

KEREN KAYEMETH LEISRAEL (Jewish National Fund)
P.O. Box 283, Jerusalem 91002 *World Ch.* Yehiel Leket; *Dir. Division of Resource and Dev.* Avi Dickstein. (Est. 1901) A non-profit organisation dedicated to the development of Israel through improvement of the quality of life, through afforestation, water conservation, ecology and educational activities.

SHAMIR - ASSOCIATION OF JEWISH RELIGIOUS PROFESSIONALS FROM THE FORMER SOVIET UNION AND EASTERN EUROPE
6 David Yellin Street, P.O.B. 5749, Jerusalem
Tel +972 (02) 538 5384 *Fax* +972 (02) 538 5118
Email shamirbooks@bezeqint.net *Website* www.shamirbooks.org.il
Sec. Bayla Granovsky

STANDWITHUS ISRAEL
King George 58, Jerusalem, Israel 91073
Tel +972 (02) 636 0200 *Fax* +972 (02) 624 0558
Email israel@standwithus.com *Website* www.standwithus.co.il
The international office of StandWithUs. A leader in Israel advocacy with offices and chapters in the United States, Canada, Israel, the UK and Australia. StandWithUs hosts speakers and conferences, offers website resources and creates brochures and materials about Israel that are distributed globally. *Dir.* Michael Dickson

WOMEN'S INTERNATIONAL ZIONIST ORGANISATION (Wizo)
38 David Hamelech Boulevard, Tel Aviv 64237
Tel +972 (03) 692 3717 *Fax* +972 (03) 695 8267
(Reg. Charity No. 580057321). 250,000 women, 100,000 of them in Israel, are members of
this organisation which maintains 800 institutions and services in Israel. *World Wizo Pres.*
Helena Glaser; *Ch. World Wizo Exec.* Tova Ben-Dov

WORLD ZIONIST ORGANISATION
P.O. Box 92, Jerusalem 91000
Tel +972 (02) 602 2080 *Fax* +972 (02) 625 2352
Founded by Theodor Herzl at the First Zionist Congress in Basle in 1897, it was the moving
spirit in the events leading up to the establishment of the State of Israel in 1948. The
'Jerusalem Programme', adopted by the 27th Zionist Congress in Jerusalem in 1968,
reformulated the aims of the Zionist Movement as: the unity of the Jewish people and the
centrality of the State of Israel in its life. The ingathering of the exiles in the historic Jewish
homeland by aliya. The strengthening of the State of Israel, which is founded on the
prophetic ideals of justice and peace. Preserving the uniqueness of the Jewish people by
promoting Jewish and Hebrew education and upholding Jewish spiritual and cultural values.
Defending the rights of Jews wherever they live. The supreme body of the WZO is the
Zionist Congress, to which delegates are elected by members of Zionist Federations abroad
and by the Zionist parties in Israel. The two gov. bodies elected by the Congress are: the
Executive, and the Zionist General Council to which the Executive is responsible and which
decides Zionist policy between Congresses. *Ch. of Exec.* S. Meridor

YAD VASHEM
Har Hazikaron (Mount of Remembrance), Jerusalem
Tel +972 (02) 644 3400 *Fax* +972 (02) 644 3443
P.O.B. 3477, Jerusalem 91034
Email general.information@yadvashem.org.il *Website* www.yadvashem.org
The Holocaust Martyrs' and Heroes' Authority, Archives, Library, International School for
Holocaust Studies, International Institute for Holocaust Research, Holocaust Museum, Art
Museum, Hall of Remembrance, Hall of Names, Children's Memorial, Memorial to the
Deportees, Avenue and Garden of the Righteous Among the Nations, Valley of the
Communities, Visual Centre, Synagogue.

UJIA Israel (incorporating the British Olim Society)
Head Office 76 Ibn Gvirol Street, P.O.B. 16266, Tel Aviv 61162
Tel +972 (03) 696 5244 *Fax* +972 (03) 696 8696
Email israel@ujia.org.il
There are branches in Jerusalem and Karmiel. UJIA Israel is the official representative of
the United Jewish Israel Appeal of Great Britain & Northern Ireland, form. known as the
British Olim Society (Est. 1949 in order to assist and support new immigrants from the UK
settling in Israel).
UJIA Israel represents UJIA UK on all campaign and renewal-related activities and aims
at strengthening the ties between British Jewry and Israel, through projects, guests, missions
and Israel Experience youth programmes.
UJIA Israel provides comprehensive absorption services to immigrants from the UK,
Australia and Scandinavia and promotes the absorption needs of new immigrants in Israel.
During 1990, the BOS Charitable Trust was established as a funding conduit for new
immigrant activities and programmes in Israel, essentially aimed at helping the disadvantaged and less fortunate.

Israel English Speaking Legal Experts
P.O. Box 2828, Jerusalem
Tel +972 (02) 582 0126 *Fax* +972 (02) 623 2742
Provides legal advice and representation.

Israel, Britain and the Commonwealth Association (IBCA)
Industry House, 29 Hamored Street, Tel Aviv 68125

Fax +972 (03) 510 4646
Branches in Haifa and Jerusalem. The main aims of the Association are to encourage, develop, and extend social, cultural and economic relations between Israel and the British Commonwealth. *Ch.* L. Harris; *V. Ch.* Dr. A. Lerner; *Hon. S.* Madelaine Mordecai; *Contact* Freida Peled

ITALY

Italy has an ancient connection with the Jews, and was home to one of the earliest Diaspora communities. Before the Roman invasion of ancient Israel, Judah Maccabee had a representative in Rome, and one of the reasons for the invasion was the Romans' desire to access the salt supply from the Dead Sea. There were Jewish communities in Italy after the destruction of the Second Temple, as Italy was the trading hub of the Roman empire. After Christianity became the official religion in 313CE, restrictions began to be placed on the Jewish population, forcing the community to migrate from town to town across the country.

In the medieval period there was a brief flourishing of learning, but the Spanish conquered southern Italy in the fifteenth century, expelling the Jews from Sicily, Sardinia and, eventually, Naples. The first ever ghetto was established in Venice in 1516. Later in the century descendants of those expelled from Spain and Portugal arrived. Conquest by Napoleon led to the emancipation of Italian Jewry, and full equal rights were granted in 1870.

Ironically, the Italian Fascist party contained some Jewish members, as Mussolini was not antisemitic. The situation changed after Germany's occupation of the north in 1943. Eventually almost 8,000 Italian Jews were killed in Auschwitz, although Italians hid many of those who survived.

Today there is a central organisation which provides services for Italian Jews. There are kosher restaurants in Rome, Milan and other towns. There are also Jewish schools.

ROME
Central organisation
Unione delle Comunità Ebraiche Italiane, 00153 Roma, Lungotevere Sanzio 9
Tel +39 (06) 4554 2200 *Fax* +39 (06) 589 9569 *Pres.* R. Gattegna
Chief Rabbinate of Rome
Comunita Ebraica di Roma, Lungotevere Cenci, Tempio, 00186
Tel +39 (06) 687 5051/2/3 *Fax* +39 (06) 684 00684
Email segretaria@romacer.org *Website* www.romacer.org
Chief Rabbi Dr. Riccardo Shmuel Di Segni

MILAN
Comunita Ebraica di Milano
Chief Rabbi Alfonso Arbib
Tel +39 (02) 4831 10225
Email direttore@mosaico-cem.it *Website* www.mosaico-cem.it
For more info on synagogues and Jewish travel around Italy, please visit the website www.jewisheurope.org/city.asp?City=Milan

JAMAICA

During the time of Spanish colonisation, Jamaica witnessed many *Conversos* arriving from Portugal. After the British took over in 1655 many of these could again practise Judaism openly. Soon other Jews, mainly Sephardim, followed from Brazil and other nearby countries. The community received full equality in 1831 (before a similar step was taken in England).

The Jews played an important role in Jamaican life, and in 1849 the House of Assembly did not meet on Yom Kippur! However, assimilation and intermarriage took their toll and in 1921 the Ashkenazi and Sephardi synagogues combined. There is now only one synagogue on the island, but there are remains of old synagogues in Kingston, Port Royal and other towns.

Community life includes WIZO, B'nai B'rith and a school (the Hillel Academy). The community lost members after the Cuban revolution, because many feared a similar revolution in Jamaica.

United Congregation of Israelites
92 Duke Street, Kingston (walk-in entrance on Charles Street or drive in from John's Lane)
Tel +876 922 5931
Email ChabadOfJamaica@gmail.com *Website* www.ucija.org
United Congregation of Israelites, Synagogue Shaare Shalom
Duke Street (Synagogue built 1885, rebuilt 1911)
Acting Spiritual Leader Stephen C. Henriques *Tel* +1 (809) 924 2451

JAPAN

After Japan became open to Western ideas and Westerners in the mid-nineteenth century, a trickle of Jewish immigrants from the Russian Empire, the UK and the USA began to make their homes there. The first Jewish community at Yokohama was founded in 1860. Many were escaping antisemitism and by 1918 there were several thousand in the country.

Individual Japanese, despite being allied to Nazi Germany, did not adopt the antisemitic attitude of the Nazis, and Chiune Sagihara, the Japanese consul in Kovno, Lithuania, even helped the Mir Yeshivah escape from occupied Europe in 1940.

The post-war American occupation of the country brought many Jewish servicemen, and the community was also augmented by Jews escaping unrest in China. In recent years, there have been some Jewish 'gaijin' (foreign workers).

In Tokyo, there is a synagogue which provides meals on Shabbat, a Sunday school, and offices for the Executive Board of the Jewish Community of Japan, which is the central body.

Jewish Community of Japan
8-8 Hiroo 3-chome, Shibuya-Ku, Tokyo 150-0012
Tel +81 (03) 3400 2559 *Fax* +81 (03) 3400 1827
Email office@jccjapan.or.jp
M. Rabbi Henri Noach; Kosher meals available on Shabbat and during the week. Please say in advance if you would like to come.

KAZAKHSTAN

The Jews of Kazakhstan are predominately Russian-speaking Ashkenazim and identify with Russian culture. Many arrived only in the 1940s, fleeing the Nazis or 'exiled' by Stalin. There are a number of Bukharian Jews and Tat (Caucasian Mountain Jews). Some 7,000 Jews now remain in the country. Almaty is the main Jewish centre. Smaller Jewish communities are spread out across this large country, in Karaganda, Chimkent, Astana, Semipalatinsk, Kokchetav, Jambyl Region, Uralsk, Aktyubinsk, Petropavlovsk, Shymkent and several villages.

Association of Jewish Communities of Kazakhstan
66/120 Buhar-zhirau Street, Almaty 480057
Tel/Fax +7 (3272) 45 00 43

KENYA

Jewish settlement in East Africa dating from 1903, when the British Government offered the Zionist Organisation a territory in the present Kenya for an autonomous Jewish settlement. The offer was refused but not unanimously and shortly afterwards a few Jews settled in the colony. Later, a number of Central European Jewish refugees settled here. The Jewish population today is about 100 families, most of whom are Israelis, together with others employed in the diplomatic services and NGOs. *See Jews of Nairobi 1903–1962*, by Julius Carlebach. The community marked its centenary with a new history by Cynthia Salvadori 'Glimpses of the Jews of Kenya: the Centennial History of the Nairobi Hebrew Congregation 1904–2004, 5664–5764.

Nairobi Hebrew Congregation
P.O. Box 40990, 00100

Tel +254 (20) 222-770 and 219-703,
Email info@nhc.co.ke *Website* www.nhc.co.ke
(Est. 1904) *Rosh Kehilla* Dr. D. Silverstein; *Hon. T.* M. Abbema; *Hon. S.* Ms A. Zola

KYRGYZSTAN

This central Asian ex-Soviet republic has only a short history of Jewish settlement. The community originated from migrants after the Russian Revolution and evacuees from the German advance into the Soviet Union in the Second World War. As a result, community members are almost all Russian speakers and are assimilated into the Russian minority of the country. Before the collapse of the Soviet Union there was no organised community. There has been a synagogue in the capital Bishkek since 1991, where there is also a Jewish library and an Aish Ha Torah centre. The main umbrella group is the Menorah Society of Jewish Culture.

Jewish Community of Bishkek
Karpinskogo str. 193, Bishkek, Kyrgyzstan 720000
Tel +99 (312) 681 966

LATVIA

The Jews in the medieval principalities of Courland and Livonia represent the earliest Jewish settlement in Latvia. Tombstones from the fourteenth century have been found. After the Russian take-over Jews were only allowed to live in the area if they were considered 'useful', or had lived there before the Russians took control, because the area was outside the 'Pale of Settlement' that the Russian Empire had designated for the Jews.

The Jews contributed much to Latvia's development, but this was never recognised by the government, which tried to restrict their influence in business matters. Religious Jewish life, however, was strong. When the Nazis invaded Latvia, 90 per cent of the 85,000 Jews were systematically murdered by them and their Latvian collaborators.

The bulk of today's community originates from immigration into Latvia after the war, although 3,000 Holocaust survivors did return to the country. Before the collapse of communism there was much Jewish dissident activity. There is a Jewish school and a Jewish hospital. There are some Holocaust memorial sites in the capital Riga, and also in the Bierkernieki Forest, where 46,000 Holocaust victims were shot.

Chabad Lubavitch Community of Latvia
Lachplesha str. 141, Riga, Latvia LV1003
Tel +371 720 4022
www.chabadcenters.com/riga
Jewish Community Centre, Museum and Library (LOEK)
6 Skolas Street 226050
Tel +371 6728 9580
Com. Leader A, Suharenko
The Riga Synagogue
Lachplesha str. 141, Riga, Latvia LV1003
Tel +371 720 5313

LEBANON

During the civil war, which broke out in 1975, most of the 2,000 Jews left the country. About 100 remain in Beirut.

LIBYA

About the time that Libya became an independent State in 1951 there was a mass emigration of most of its 37,000 Jews to Israel, and only very few remain in Tripoli.

LITHUANIA

The history of Lithuanian Jewry is as old as the state of Lithuania itself. There were Jews in the country in the fourteenth century, when Grand Duke Gedeyminus founded the state. The community eventually grew, and produced many famous yeshivas and great commentators, such as the Vilna Gaon. The community began to emigrate (particularly to South Africa) at the beginning of the nineteenth century; even so, in 1941 there were still 160,000 Jews in the country. Ninety-five per cent of these were murdered in the Holocaust by the local population as well as the Nazis.

The remaining post-war community included some who had hidden or had managed to survive by other means, and some Jews from other parts of the Soviet Union. Interestingly, the Lithuanian Soviet Socialist Republic was more tolerant of Jewish activity than some of the neighbouring republics, such as Latvia. Now that Lithuania is independent, Jewish life is free once again.

The Lubavitch movement is present, and there are synagogues in the capital Vilnius (known to many as Vilna) and Kaunas. There is also a school and it is possible to study Yiddish. There are tours available to show the old Jewish life in Lithuania. The grave of the Vilna Gaon can be visited, as well as Paneriai, otherwise known as Ponary, where thousands of Jews were shot during the Holocaust.

Jewish Community of Lithuania
Pylimo Street 4, 01117 Vilnius
Tel +370 (521) 613 003
Email office@litjews.org or jewishcom@post.5ci.lt
There are also communities in Druskininkai, Klaipeda, Panevezys and Shiauliai.

LUXEMBOURG

The small community in Luxembourg faced massacres and expulsions during medieval times, and Jews only began to resettle here several hundred years later. Napoleon heralded the rebirth of the community when he annexed Luxembourg, and by 1823 a synagogue had been built but the community remained small, although in 1899 another synagogue was built. Later, many refugees from the Nazis arrived in the country, bringing the number of Jews to nearly 4,000. After the Nazi take-over 750 Luxembourg Jews were killed, but many others were saved by the local population.

The present community is generally prosperous and assimilated. The Consistoire Israelite, established by Napoleon, is recognised by the government as the representative of the community, and is also financed by the government. The Orthodox synagogue is situated fairly centrally in Luxembourg City.

Chief Rabbi
Joseph Sayagh, 45, Ave Montery
Ch. M. Bulz Tel +352 452 314
Or Chadash Liberal Jewish Community (affiliated to LJ)
Correspondence 29 rue Leandre Lacoix, 1-1913
Tel +352 316 594
Email lljc@liberaljudaism.org
Ch. Erica Peresman
Chabad Lubavitch of Luxembourg
Rabbi Mendel Edelman
10 Boulevard Royal, L-2449 Luxembourg
Tel +352 28 770 770
Email info@lubavitch.lu *Website* www.lubavitch.lu

MACEDONIA (Republic)

The Jewish presence in Macedonia (form. Yugoslavia) dates back to the 6th century B.C.E. with a considerable influx during the Roman Second-Temple period. The largest migration of Jews to Macedonia took place in the early Ottoman period following the expulsions from Spain and Portugal. In such cities as Bitola, Shtip and Skopje, Jews came to prosper in medicine, law and trade, as well as more traditionally in agriculture. By 1910 there were more than 90,000 Jews in Macedonia, mostly in Salonika (now Greek Thessaloniki, qv.), by which time Ladino was widely spoken in that city, and the Shabbat was widely observed throughout all sectors. When Greece took over the city in 1912, prohibitions on residence were brought in and a mass emigration to other parts of Europe and to North America began. Nonetheless, even in 1941 there were over 100,000 living in Macedonia when the effects of the Nazi-domination of Europe and the pressures of the Holocaust took their toll. Those who survived Auschwitz and Treblinka mostly settled in Israel and few returned to Macedonia. Today's community is mainly based in the capital Skopje, but there is little access to Jewish life. However, the community does have contact with Jews in Serbia and Greece.

The Macedonian Jewish Community, after a long period of 60 years, has a new Rabbi, Macedonia-born, Avi M. Kozma, a student of the Chief Rabbi of the Jewish Community in Serbia Isak Asiel, who was also Rabbi of Macedonia. Rabbi Kozma, was inaugurated on 5 May 2008 at the Macedonian Synagogue 'Beth Yaakov'.

SKOPJE
Jewish Community of the Republic of Macedonia
Borka Talevski Street, No. 24, 1000
Tel +389 (2) 321 4799 *Fax* +389 (2) 321 4880
ezrm *Pres.* Z. Sami; *Gen. Sec.* Z. Mucheva

Synagogue "Beth Ya'akov"
Borka Talevski Street, No. 24, 1000
Tel +389 (2) 323 7543
Chief Rabbi Rabbi A.M. Kozma (2008-)

MALTA
There have been Jews in Malta since pre-Roman times and, just before the Spanish-directed expulsion in 1492, one-third of the population of the then capital city, Mdina, was Jewish. After the coming of the Knights of St John, the only Jews in Malta became their captives and slaves, held for ransom. This situation persisted until Napoleon overthrew the Knights and released all their prisoners. Following the defeat of the French by the British, a small Jewish community was established early in the nineteenth century which has survived until the present day. There were never more than about 20 families, under 100 people, and the community was financially unable to build a synagogue. However, following a successful appeal, launched in 1998, local and international donations enabled the acquisition and conversion of premises into a Jewish Centre and Synagogue. The Malta Jewish Community now, once again, owns its own property, after a gap of over 500 years.

Jewish Community of Malta
182/2 St. Ursula Street, Valletta, P.O. Box 42, Birkirkara
Tel +356 676 926 *Fax* +356 676 926

MARTINIQUE
SCHOELCHER
Kenafe Haarets A.C.I.M.
12 rue de l'Ecole Hoteliere 97233
Tel +596 616 672
There is a Community, which supplies kosher food, plus a kosher meat restaurant.

MAURITIUS
There is no permanent Jewish community. The Jewish cemetery contains the graves of 125 refugees from Europe. They were part of a group of 1,700 Jews denied entry to Palestine and interned on the island during 1940-1945.
Corr. P. M. Birger P.O. Box 209, Port Louis, Mauritius *Tel* +230 202 0200 *Fax* +230 208 3391

MEXICO
Conversos were the first Jews in the country, and some achieved high positions in early Spanish colonial Mexico. As the Inquisition was still functioning there some 200 years after

the sixteenth century, the number of Jewish immigrants was small. When Mexico became independent Jews gradually began to enter the country, coming from Germany and other European communities.

It was during the twentieth century that most Jewish immigrants entered Mexico. There were both Ashkenazim and Sephardim, and they settled throughout the country. The communities grew parallel, rather than together, with two languages, Yiddish and Ladino. The current community is largely middle class, and all the various factions come under the Comite Central Israelita. There are numerous synagogues and there are also kosher restaurants. The community is well equipped with Jewish schools and yeshivas.

MEXICO CITY
Central Committee of the Jewish Community in Mexico
Cofre de Perote 115, Col. Lomas Barrilaco, 11010 Mexico DF
Tel +52 (55) 209 393 *Fax* +52 (55) 403 050
Exec. Dir. Mauricio Lulka

CANCUN
Chabad-Lubavitch of Cancun
Cancun, 77500 Mexico
Co-Dir. Rabbi Mendel Druk
Tel +51 (998) 219 5601

MOLDOVA
Chisinau, the capital of the republic of Moldova, was part of the former Soviet Union. It became a flourishing Jewish centre in the 18th century when a growing economy presented new commercial and industrial opportunities.

By the turn of the twentieth century, there were 16 Jewish schools with 2,100 students and 70 synagogues.

In 1903, 49 Jews were massacred by frenzied mobs. Hundreds were seriously injured; thousands were left homeless and property damage was measured in millions of gold rubles. In 1905 a second pogrom claimed the lives of another 19 Jews. A flood of emigration began, which continued through the inter-war years.

The devastation of the Jewish community of Chisinau was completed by the Nazis who killed 53,000 of the 65,000 Jewish inhabitants of the city. Communism brought more restrictions to the remaining Jews. In 1964, all synagogues were closed, except one - the one which is used today.

Towns with Jewish populations include: Baltsy, Bendery, Dubossary, Chisinau, Orxey, Rybnitsa, Rezina, Soroky and Tiraspol.

CHISINAU
Federation of the Jewish Communities
Str. Alecsandri, 125 apt. 2, Chisinau, Moldova 2012
Tel +373 (22) 541 023 *Fax* +373 (22) 541 020
Website www.moldova.org
Chief Rabbi of Kishinev and Moldova Rabbi Zalman Abelsky *Email* Rabbiabelsky@kishinev.org

MONACO
Some French Jews lived in Monaco before 1939. The government issued them with false papers during the war, thus saving them from the Nazis. This tiny country has also attracted retired people from France, north Africa and the UK.

There is an official Jewish body, the Association Culturelle Israelite de Monaco, and there is a synagogue, a school and a kosher food shop. Half of the total Jewish population are Ashkenazi and the other half are Sephardi. 60 per cent of the community is retired.

The Jewish Community of Monte Carlo
Association Culturelle Israelite de Monaco
15 Avenue de la Costa, 98000 Monte Carlo

MOROCCO

There were Jews in Morocco before it became a Roman province (they first arrived after the destruction of the Temple in 587 BCE). Since the first century, the Jewish population settled in Morocco has increased steadily, owing to several waves of immigration from Spain and Portugal following the expulsion of Jews by the Inquisition in 1492.

Under Moslem rule, the Jews experienced a general climate of tolerance, although they did suffer some persecution. During the Vichy period in the Second World War, Sultan Mohammed V protected the community. Almost 250,000 Jews have emigrated to Israel, Canada, France, Spain and Latin America, but they maintain strong links with the Kingdom. Since ancient times the Jewish community has succeeded in cohabiting harmoniously with the Berber and then with the Arab community. Today the present Jewish population is an active community, playing a significant role in Moroccan society, although they have declined in number.

CASABLANCA
Community Offices
12 rue Abou Abdallah Al Mahassibi
Tel +212 (2) 222 2861 *Fax* +212 (2) 226 6953
There are also communities in Fez, Kenitra, Marrakech, Meknès, Rabat, Tangier, Tetuan, and Agadir.
Chabad Lubavitch au Maroc
10 Rue Washington
Tel +212 (2) 269 037 Fax +212 (2) 201 233

MOZAMBIQUE

The small community in Mozambique originally consisted of South African Jews who were forced out of South Africa by President Kruger for supporting the British at the beginning of the twentieth century. The synagogue was opened in 1926, and there is a cemetery in Alto Maha. The biggest Jewish community is in Maputo.

NAMIBIA

Namibian Jewry began at the time when the country was a German colony before the First World War. The cemetery at Swakopmund dates from that settlement. Keetmanschoop also had a congregation, but this no longer exists. The Windhoek synagogue is still in use, and was founded in 1924. Services are held on Shabbat and festivals.

South Africa provides some help for the community, such as a cantor on festivals. The Cape Board of Jewish Education assists with Hebrew education. From approximately 100 Jewish families in the 1920s and 1930s, the number has dwindled.

WINDHOEK
Windhoek Hebrew Congregation
P.O. Box 140, Windhoek
Tel +266 (61) 221 990 *Fax* +264 (62) 226 444

NEPAL

Nepal has no Jewish history. It is however well visited by Israeli and other young Jewish tourists. Each year a large Seder is organised by the Lubavitch movement. In 2000 approximately 1,000 attended at the Radisson Hotel.

KATHMANDU
Chabad House Synagogue
GHA 2-516-4 Thamel 3
Tel +977 (1) 470 0492

NETHERLANDS

Although some historians believe that the first Jews in Holland lived there during Roman times, documentary evidence goes back only to the twelfth century. The contemporary settlement occurred when Portuguese *Marranos* found refuge from the Inquisition in Holland. Religious freedom was advocated in the early seventeenth century and Jews contributed much to the Netherlands' 'golden age' of prosperity and power. The Sephardi community in London was closely associated with Amsterdam.

By the time of Napoleon, the community had grown to 10,000 (the largest in Western Europe), mainly by incoming Jewish traders from Eastern Europe. The Jews were emancipated in 1796, but the community began to decline slowly during the nineteenth century. Of the 140,000 Jews (including 30,000 German Jewish refugees) in Holland in 1939, the Nazis transported 100,000 to various death camps in Poland, but the local Dutch population tended to behave sympathetically towards their Jewish neighbours, hiding many. Anne Frank and her family are the most famous of the hidden Jews from Holland. Amsterdam witnessed a strike in February 1941, called as a protest against the Jewish deportations.

Today there are four Jewish councils in the Netherlands representing the Ashkenazi, Sephardi, Reform and Orthodox communities. There are many synagogues in Amsterdam, as well as synagogues in other towns. Amsterdam also has many historical sites: Anne Frank House, the Portuguese Synagogue, still lit by candlelight, and the Resistance Museum.

Rabbinate Ashkenazi Community: Amsterdam Chief Rabbi Aryeh L. Ralbag, Dayan Eliezer Wolff, Rabbi Shmuel Katz (secr) Rabbi Zvi Spiero **The Hague** Rabbi Shmuel Katzman, **Rotterdam** Rabbi Raphael Evers, **Other communities** Chief Rabbi Binyomin Jacobs
Rabbinate Sephardic Community Rabbi Dr. P. Toledano.
Rabbinate Liberal Jewish Congregations Rabbi D. Lilienthal (Amsterdam); Rabbi A. Soetendorp (The Hague); Rabbi Dr E. van Voolen (Arnhem)

AMSTERDAM

Anne Frank House Prinsengracht 267 **Judith Drake Library** at the Liberal Community Centre. There are other small communities are in Amersfoort, Arnhem, Bussum, Eindhoven, Groningen, Haarlem, The Hague, Rotterdam, Utrecht and Zwolle.

Ashkenazi Community Centre and Offices
Van der Boechorststraat 26, 1081 BT
Tel +31 (20) 646 0046 *Fax* +31 (20) 646 4357
Email info@nihs.nl

Liberal Community Centre and Synagogue
J. Soetendorpstraat 8, 1079 *Tel* +31 (20) 642 3562 *Fax* +31 (20) 642 8135
Amsterdam and Dutch Liberal Rabbinate *Tel* +31 (20) 644 2619 *Fax* +31 (20) 642 8135

Sephardi Communal Centre
Visserplein 3, 1011 RD
Tel +31 (20) 624 5351 *Fax* +31 (20) 625 4680
Email info@esnoga.com

NETHERLANDS ANTILLES (West Indies)

CURAÇAO

A Sephardi Jewish settlement was established in 1651, making it the oldest community in the New World. The Mikve Israel-Emanuel Synagogue building, which dates from 1732, is the oldest in continuous use in the Western Hemisphere; there is a small Jewish museum in the synagogue compound. About 350 Jews live in Curaçao. The cemetery (Bet Hayim) at Blenheim (Est. 1659) is the oldest in the Americas.

Synagogue Mikvé Israel-Emanuel
P.O. Box 322, Curaçao
Tel +599 (9) 461 1067
Email information@snoa.com *Bd. of Dir.* directiva@snoa.com *Rabbi* rabbi@snoa.com

NEW CALEDONIA

The Jewish community in New Caledonia is predominately located in Noumea. The Jewish community was established in 1987. This relatively new community is composed of 50 Sephardi immigrants from France. Most of the Jews work in commercial businesses or in the state government. There is one synagogue in Noumea and one Jewish community center, Association Culturelle Israelite de Nouvelle Caledonie. Kosher food is imported from Australia.

NEW ZEALAND

The settlement of Jews in New Zealand dates from the establishment of British sovereignty in 1840. In the first emigrant ships were a number of Jews from England. But still earlier a few Jewish wayfarers had settled in the northern part of New Zealand, including John Israel Montefiore, a cousin of Sir Moses Montefiore, who settled at the Bay of Islands in 1831, Joel Samuel Polack, one of the earliest writers on the country, in which he travelled in 1831-37, and David Nathan, who laid the foundations of the Jewish community in Auckland in the early 1840s.

The Wellington Jewish community was founded by Abraham Hort, under the authority of the Chief Rabbi, on January 7, 1843, when the first Jewish service was held. Communities were later established in Christchurch and Dunedin and other parts of the South Island. From the earliest times Jewish settlers have helped to lay the foundation of the commercial and industrial prosperity of the country.

The number of Jews in New Zealand at the census of 2001 was over 8,000. Most live in Auckland and Wellington. There has been recent settlement from the former Soviet Union, South Africa and Israel.

Today the community has six synagogues, four on the North Island and two on the South Island. Auckland and Wellington have Jewish day schools, and the 'Kosher Kiwi Guide' is published in Auckland. There has been recent Jewish immigration from South Africa.

WELLINGTON
Hebrew Congregration
80 Webb Street *Pres.* G. Stone *Tel* +64 (4) 384 5081
Jewish Community Centre
80 Webb Street Moriah Kindergarten open daily.
Progressive Jewish Congregation (Temple Sinai)
P.O. Box 27 176
Tel +64 (04) 385 0720

AUCKLAND
Beth Israel Synagogue
108 Greys Avenue P.O. Box 68 224 *Tel* +64 (9) 373 2908
(Est. 1841).
Beth Shalom
The Auckland Congregation for Progressive Judaism, 180 Manukau Road Epsom
Website www.bethshalom.org.nz
Pres. L. Lipman
Hebrew Congregation
Pres. J. Barnett P.O. Box 68 224 *Tel* +64 (9) 373 2908

NORWAY

The only way Jews could enter Norway before the nineteenth century was with a 'Letter of Protection', as Danish control limited the amount of Jewish entry. The situation changed in 1851 when a Norwegian liberal poet, Henrik Wergeland, argued for the admission of Jews into the country, and the parliament eventually agreed. There were only some 650 Jews in the country after emancipation in 1891, mainly in Oslo and Trondheim. By 1920 the community numbered 1,457, and by the time of the Nazi invasion there were 1,800. Despite attempts by the Norwegian resistance to smuggle Jews to Sweden, 767 Jews were transported to Auschwitz, although 930 were able to reach Sweden. The Jewish survivors were joined after the war by Displaced Persons, especially invited by the Norwegian government.

The current situation forbids shechita, but there are no other restrictions on Jewish life. There is a synagogue in Oslo, and a kosher food shop. There is also a Jewish magazine. An old-age home was built in 1988. Trondheim, in the north of the country, has the northernmost synagogue in the world

Chief Rabbi Michael Melchior (Honorary position since he left in 1986 and lives in Israel now.)

Det Mosaiske Trossamfund (Jewish Community)
Bergstien 13 0172 Oslo
Tel +47 (2) 320 5750 *Fax* +47 (2) 320 5781
Website www.dmt.oslo.no
Pres. A. Sender
Synagogue and Community Centre
Bergstien 13, Oslo 0172 Postbooks 2722, St Hanshaugen, 0131
Synagogue and Community Centre
Ark. Cristiesgt. 1, Trondheim
Tel +47 (7) 352 6568
Pres. R. Abrahamsen

PANAMA

Some Jews, most of them pretending to be Christians, came to Panama during colonial times. Panama was an important crossroads for trade and, as a result, many Jews passed through the country on their journeys in the region.

In 1849 immigrant Sephardi Jews in Panama founded the Hebrew Benevolent Society, the first Jewish congregation in the Isthmus. They came from the pious congregation of the Netherlands Antilles (Curaçao) to settle in Panama.

Jews from Saint-Thomas (Virgin Islands) and Curaçao founded in 1876 the Kol Shearith Israel Synagogue in Panama City, and in 1890 the Kahal Hakadosh Yangacob in Colon.

By the end of the First World War a number of Middle Eastern Jews had settled in the country and founded the Israelite Benevolent Society Shevet Ahim. During the Second World War immigrants from Europe arrived in Panama, establishing Beth-El, the only Ashkenazi community in the country. The majority of the Jewish community is Sephardi (around 80%). There have been two Jewish presidents in Panama, the only country – apart from Israel – where this has happened.

Beth El (Conservative)
Apartado 3087, Panama 3, Panama City
Consejo Central Comunitario Hebreo de Panama
Apartado 55-0882-Paitilla, Panama City
Tel +507 (2) 638 411 *Fax* +507 (2) 647 936
Contact Pres. Sion Harari *Email* sion@plazareg.com
Kol Shearith Israel (Reform)
Apartado 4120, Panama City
Tel +507 (2) 254 100 *Fax* +507 (2) 256 512
There are smaller communities in Colon and David.

PARAGUAY

Jewish settlement in this land-locked country came late for this area of South America. The few who came over from Western Europe at the end of the nineteenth century rapidly assimilated into the general population. The first synagogue was founded early in the twentieth century by Sephardim from Palestine, Turkey and Greece. Ashkenazim arrived in the 1920s and 1930s from Eastern Europe, and some 15,000 came to the country to escape Nazism, intending to move on into Argentina. Some of these settled in Paraguay.

Paraguay, in more recent times, has accepted Jews from Argentina who were fleeing from the military regime.

Today there are three synagogues, a Jewish school and a Jewish museum in Asuncion. There is a high rate of intermarriage, but children of mixed marriages may receive a Jewish education.

Consejo Representativo Israelita del Paraguay (CRIP)
General Diaz 657. Asuncion, P.O.B. 756
Tel +595 (21) 41744

PERU

The first Jews in Peru arrived with the first Europeans, as many *Conversos* were officers in the Spanish army which invaded the country in 1532. After the Inquisition was set up in 1570 the Jews were persecuted, and many were burned alive. From 1870 groups of Jews came over from Europe, but tended to disappear into the general population. In 1880, a group of North African Jews settled in Iquitos and worked in the rubber industry. More Jewish immigration occurred after the First World War and, later, refugees from the Nazis entered the country. By the end of the Second World War the Jewish population had reached 6,000, but this subsequently declined.

Almost all of the present Jewish population are Ashkenazi. There are two Jewish newspapers and most Jewish children go to the Colegio Leon Pinelo school, which is well known for its high standards. There is a cemetery at Iquitos built by the nineteenth-century community. The community is shrinking owing to intermarriage and assimilation.

LIMA

Chabad Lubavitch de Peru
Avenue Salaverry 3075, Lima, 27 Peru
Tel +51 (1) 264 6060
Fax +51 (1) 264 5499
Gan Chabad
Ave. Salavemy 3095
Lima, 27 Peru
Tel +51 (1) 422 0082
Fax +51 (1) 221 1628
Synagogue and Communal Centre
Húsares de Junin 163 (Jesus Maria), Lima *Tel* +51 (1) 241 412/312 410

KASHRUT INFORMATION
Chief Rabbi Abraham Benhamu *Email* abenhamu@gmail.com
Union Israelita del Peru (Orthodox Ashkenazi)
210 Carlos Porras Osores, San Isidro
Tel +51 (1) 421 3684
Email unionisraelita@gmail.com *Website* www.kosherperu.com
Kosher Peru
Manuel de la Fuente 676, Barranco, Lima - 04
Tel +51 (1) 251 9628
Website www.kosher.pe

CEMETERY
Bena Vista Cemeterio
Av. O.R. Benavides 2215, Callao
Tel +51 (1) 429 0731
Monday - Thursday 8.30am to 4pm, Friday 8.30am to 12pm, Sunday 8.30am to 1pm

PHILIPPINES

Conversos who came with the Spanish in the sixteenth century were the first Jewish presence in the region. In the late nineteenth century, western European Jews came to trade in the area, and after the Americans occupied the country in 1898 more Jews arrived from a variety of places, including the USA and the Middle East. The first synagogue was built in 1924. The Philippines accepted refugees from Nazism, but the Japanese occupied the islands during the war and the Jewish population was interned. After the war many of the community emigrated. However, a new synagogue opened in 1983, and services are also held in the US Air Force bases around the country.

Jewish Association of the Philippines (Beth Yaakov Synagogue)
110 H.V. de la Costa, crn. Tordesillas West, Salcedo Village, Makati City, Metro Manila 1227 *Tel* Office +63 (2) 815 0265 Rabbi Eliyhau Azaria *Tel* +63 (2) 815 0263 *Fax* +63 (2) 840 2566 *Email* jap.manila@gmail.com
Services on Monday and Thursday mornings, Shabbat and all holidays. *Pres.* Paul Rosenberg

POLAND

After just five years of German occupation in the Second World War the thousand-year-old Jewish settlement in Poland, one of the largest Jewish communities in the world, had been almost totally eradicated. Jews came to Poland in order to escape antisemitism in Germany in the early Middle Ages. They were initially welcomed by the rulers, and Jews became greatly involved in the economy of the country.

Until 1918 most Jews lived in the east and south of the country, under Russian and Austrian domination, respectively. After 1918 Poland became an independent country once more, with over 3,000,000 Jews (300,000 in Warsaw.) The community continued to flourish before 1939, with Yiddish being the main language of the Jews. The community was destroyed in stages during the war, as Poland became the centre for the Nazi's destruction of European Jewry. After the war, the borders shifted again, and the 100,000 or so survivors mostly tried to emigrate. The few who remained endured several pogroms even after the events of the Holocaust.

Today the community is comparatively small and most of the members are elderly, but there is a functioning synagogue in Warsaw and many Jewish historical sites are scattered throughout the country. The Polish Tourist Board publishes information about the Jewish heritage in Poland.

WARSAW
Secular Organisation
Towarzystwo Spoleczno-Kulturalne Zydów w Polsce (Social and Cultural Association of Jews in Poland), Zarzad Glowny (Central Board), Warsaw, 00-104, Plac. Grzybowski 12/16 *Tel* +48 (22) 20 05 57/20 05 54
Synagogue and Religious Organisation
Zwiazek Religijny Wyznania Mojzeszowego (Religious Union of Mosaic Faith)
Warsaw 00-105. ul. Twarda 6
Tel +48 (22) 20 43 24/20 06 76

PORTUGAL

Portuguese Jewry had a parallel history to Spanish Jewry until the twelfth century, when the country emerged from Spain's shadow. Jews worked with the Portuguese kings in developing the country. However, they were heavily taxed and had to live in special areas, although they were free to practise their religion as they pleased. As a result the community flourished. Persecution began during the period of the Black Death, and the Church was a key instigator of the riots which broke out against the Jews. After the Inquisition in neighbouring Spain many Jews fled to Portugal, but were expelled in 1497. Many Jews converted in order to remain in the country and help with the economy. These became the Portuguese 'Conversos' and some of their descendants are converting back to Judaism today.

Over the last century and a half Jews have begun to re-enter the country, and many others used it as an escape route to America during the last war. Most of the community are Sephardi, and there is a Sephardi synagogue in Lisbon. There is also a central Jewish organisation which is a unifying force for Jews in the country.

LISBON
Communal Offices
Rua do Monte Olivete, 16 r/c 1200-280 Lisbon

Tel +351 (21) 393 1130 *Fax* +351 (21) 393 1139
Email secretaria@cilisboa.org *Website* www.cilisboa.org
Jewish Centre
Rua Rosa Araujo 10
Tel +351 (21) 357 2041

PUERTO RICO

The Jewish community in Puerto Rico is just over 100 years old, with the first Jews arriving from Cuba in 1898 after the beginning of American rule. During the Second World War, many Jewish American servicemen went to the island, along with refugees from Nazism. The Jewish Community Centre dates from the early war years. After the war the community grew with an influx of Cuban and American Jews.

The capital, San Juan, has the largest Jewish population, and there are two synagogues. There is also a Hebrew school held in the Community Centre. The first Chief Justice of Puerto Rico was Jewish.

Shaare Zedeck Synagogue (Conservative) and **Community Centre**
903 Ponce de León Avenue Santurce, P.R. 00907-3390
Tel +1 (787) 809 724 4110 *Fax* +1 (787) 722 4157
Temple Beth Shalom (Reform)
101 San Jorge & Loiza Street, Santurce, P.R. 00911
Tel +1 (787) 721 6333

ROMANIA

Jews have been resident in the territory that now forms Romania since Roman times. Today they number 10,000, of whom some 4,000 live in Bucharest, and the rest in 160 communities. There are 42 synagogues, three of them in Bucharest, 11 Talmud Torahs and 8 kosher restaurants. A newspaper in Hebrew, Romanian and English, *Realitatea*, with a circulation of 4,500, is published fortnightly. There is a Yiddish theatre in Bucharest, the publishing house Hasefer, a Museum of Jewish History and a Holocaust Exhibit.

BUCHAREST
Federation of Jewish Communities
Centre of Romanian Jewish History Research Mamulari Str., 4, Etaj 1, Apt. 1, Sectorul 3,
Tel/Fax +40 (21) 315 1045
Dir. D. Hîncu

RUSSIA (Russian Federation)

In early Russian history Jews were not allowed to settle, and the few who did were later expelled by various Tsars. After 1772, however, Russia acquired a large area of Poland, where lived a significant number of Jews. There were still restrictions against the Jews, but eventually they were allowed to settle in the 'Pale of Settlement', an area in the west of the Russian Empire. Between 1881 and 1914, 2,000,000 Jews emigrated from the Empire, fleeing from antisemitism.

Jews were only allowed into Russia itself in the mid-nineteenth century, and by 1890 there were 35,000 Jews in Moscow. Most were expelled the following year. The community grew after the Second World War, drawing Jewish immigration from Belarus and Ukraine to cities such as Moscow and Leningrad. Birobidzhan was a failed experiment to give the Jews their own 'Autonomous District', and those who moved there (in the far east, near China) soon moved away. Under communism both religious practices and emigration were restricted, but since 1991 there has been a revival in Jewish learning. There are synagogues functioning in many cities, and there are now 100 Jewish schools. The major threat is still from antisemitic right-wing groups, who are unfortunately increasing their activity.

MOSCOW
Rabbinical Alliance of the CiS
Central Office 5A 2nd Vysheslavtzev Pereulok, Moscow, Russia, 127055

Tel +7 (495) 737 8275 *Fax* +7 (495) 783 8471 Rabbi Berel Lazar
Email lazar@jewish.ru *Website* www.fjc.ru
Rabbinical Court of Moscow
Chief Rabbi Pinchas Goldschmidt
Tel +7 (095) 923 4788
Email kasher@post.ru *Website* www.kasher.ru
World Union for Progressive Judaism - Orosir
2 Usevolovsky Pereulot, Entrance 1, Moscow 119034
Email wupj-orosir@yandex.ru
Rabbi Gregory Kotlyar

ST PETERSBURG
Jewish Association 'LEA'
Ryleeva 29-31, 191123
Tel +7 (812) 275 6104 *Fax* +7 (812) 275 6103
Other centres of Jewish population include those of Astrakhan, Berdichev, Berehovo, Birobidzhan, Irkutsk, Krasnoyarsk, Kuybyshev, Kursk, Malakhavka, Nalchik, Novosibirsk, Ordzhonikidze, Penza, Perm, Rostov, Saratov, Sverdlovsk, Tula.

SERBIA (Republic)

Jews have lived in this territory since Roman times. In 1941 there were about 34,000 Jews in the territory of the former Yugoslavia and some 29,000 perished in the Holocaust.

BELGRADE (BEOGRAD)
Federation of Jewish Communities of Serbia
Ulica Kralja Petra 71a, III, 11000 Belgrade P.O.B. 512 Belgrade
Tel +381 262 1837/291 0363 *Fax* +381 262 6674
Email office@savezscg.org
Pres. A. Nećak; *Sec.* D. Danon
Jewish Community of Belgrade
Ulica Kralja Petra 71a/II
Tel +381 262 2449 *Fax* +381 262 4289
Email jcb@ikomline.net
Pres. Miroslav Herzog *Tel* +381 262 3535/328 1468
Communities also in Kikinda, Novi Sad, Niš, Pančevo, Sombor, Subotica, Zemun and Zrenjanin.

SINGAPORE

As Singapore developed into an important south-east Asian trading centre in the mid-nineteenth century, some Jewish traders from India and Iraq set up a community there in 1841. A synagogue was built in 1878, and another in 1904. By the time of the Japanese occupation in the Second World War the community had grown to 5,000, and included some Eastern European Jews. The Japanese imprisoned the community and took their property. After the war emigration to Australia and the USA reduced numbers, but in recent years Israelis who work in the country and other Jews have moved in. Ninety per cent of the community are Sephardi. David Marshall, who was a POW in Japan, returned to Singapore and in 1955 became Chief Minister.
One of the two synagogues is used regularly, and there is a mikveh and a newsletter. The Sir Manasseh Meyer Community Centre is the hub of Jewish life. The Jewish community today is small and mainly composed of professionals.
Jewish Welfare Board
24/26 Waterloo Street, 187950
Tel +65 (9) 337 2189 *Fax* +65 (9) 336 2127
Tel +65 (9) 731 2181 Rabbi Mordechai Abergel
Pres. Jacob Ballas. *Hon. S.* M. Whelan
Email enquiries@jwb.org.sg *Website* www.singaporejews.com

Synagogue Maghain Aboth
24 Waterloo Street, 187950
Tel +65 337 2189 *Fax* +65 336 2127
Email jewishwb@singnet.com.sg
Open daily except Monday mornings. Mikveh available.
Com. Rabbi Mordechai Abergel *Tel* +65 737 9112 *Email* mordehai@singnet.com.sg
United Hebrew Congregation (Reform)
65 Chulia Street, OCBC Centre #31-00 East Lobby, 049513
Pres. K. Lewis *Tel* +65 536 8300

SLOVAKIA

Slovakia has passed through the control of various countries over the centuries, finally gaining independence after the peaceful splitting of Czechoslovakia in January 1993. Before 1918 the region was part of Hungary, and many in southern Slovakia, near the Hungarian border still speak Hungarian.

In 1939 the Jewish population in the Slovak area of Czechoslovakia numbered 150,000, but the Hungarians occupied the south of the country and assisted the Germans in deporting Jews to Auschwitz and other camps. Many survivors emigrated after the war, but some remained and are now rediscovering their Jewish heritage. Since independence, B'nai B'rith and Maccabi have been established, but antisemitism has re-emerged. There are kosher restaurants in Bratislava and Kosice, and Jewish education is available once more.

BRATISLAVA
Bratislava Jewish Community
Kozia 18, 81103 Bratislava
Tel +421 (2) 5441 6949
Email noba@znoba.sk
Central Union of Jewish Religious Communities (UZZNO)
Hon. Ch. Prof Pavel Traubner, PhD.; *Exec. Ch.* Fero Alexander Kozia 21/II, 81447 Bratislava
Tel +421 (2) 5441 2167 *Fax* +421 (2) 5441 1106

KOSICE
Jewish Religious Community
Zvonárska 5, 04001 Kosice
Kosher restaurant, Mikveh. *Pres.* Dr P. Sitar *Tel/Fax* +421 (5) 5622 1272

There are Jewish communities in Galanta, Dunajska Streda, Presov, Banska Bystrica, Nove Zamky, Komarno, Zilina, Nitra.

SLOVENIA

Maribor was the centre for medieval Jewish life in what is now Slovenia. Expulsion followed after the Austrian occupation in the late Middle Ages, but in 1867 the Jews in the Austrian empire were emancipated and some returned to Slovenia. The community was never large. During the Second World War the members of the small Jewish community either escaped to Italy, fought with the Yugoslav partisans, or were deported.

After WWII, the Jewish Community of Slovenia was formed and was attached to the Federation of Yugoslav Jewish Communities until Slovenia's secession in 1991. In 1997, the first official Jewish Community office since WWII was bought and the community activities increased. In 1999 Rabbi Ariel Haddad was inaugurated as the first Chief Rabbi of Slovenia in history.

Today, Slovenian Jews gather for the major Jewish Holidays and Festivals, and there are lectures and dancing classes. A cultural and educational bulletin is published monthly and there is a Youth group, which organises Shabbatot, educational events and outings.

Traces of Jewish history are to be found in Lendava, and there is a restored (but non-functioning) synagogue in Maribor.

Jewish Community of Slovenia
Tržaška, 1000 Ljubljana

Tel/Fax +386 61 221 836
Website www.jewishcommunity.si

SOUTH AFRICA

Although some believe that Jews were present in the country at around the time of the first European settlement in the area in the seventeenth century, the community only really began in the nineteenth century when religious freedom was granted. In 1836 the explorer Nathaniel Isaacs published 'Travels and Adventures in Eastern Africa', an important contemporary account of Zulu life and customs.

The year 1841 saw the first Hebrew Congregation in Cape Town, and the discovery of diamonds in the Transvaal later in the century prompted a wave of Jewish immigration.

The main immigration of Jews into South Africa occurred at the end of the nineteenth century, when many thousands left Eastern Europe, the majority from Lithuania (40,000 had arrived by 1910). Although the country did not officially accept refugees from the Nazis, about 8,000 Jews managed to enter the country after their escape from Europe.

Today the community is affluent and has good relations with the government. There is a South African Board of Deputies, and many international Jewish associations are present in the country. There are kosher hotels and restaurants, and Jewish museums. Kosher wine is produced at the Zaandwijk Winery.

COMMUNAL INSTITUTIONS
Lubavitch Foundation of S.A.
55 Oaklands Road, Orchards 2192 Johannesburg
Tel +27 (11) 640 7561
Mizrachi Organisation of S.A.
P.O. Box 29189, Sandringham 2131
Tel +27 (11) 640 4420
S.A. Jewish Board of Deputies
2 Elray Street, Raedene, 2192, P.O. Box 87557, Houghton 2041
Tel +27 645 2523 *Fax* +27 645 2559
Email sajbod@beyachad.co.za *Website* www.jewishsa.co.za *Nat. Dir.* W. Kahn
S.A. Union for Progressive Judaism
P.O.B. 1190, Houghton 2041
Tel +27 (11) 646 7903 *Fax* +27 (11) 646 7904
Email saupj@worldonline.co.za
Union of Orthodox Synagogues of South Africa
P.O. Box 46559, Orange Grove 2119, Johannesburg
Tel +27 (10) 214 2600 *Fax* +27 (11) 640 7528
Email info@uos.co.za *Website* www.uos.co.za
Incorporating the Johannesburg Beth Din, Kashrut Division, Office of the Chief Rabbi, Jews for Judaism and Jewish Tradition. Rabbi Dr. W. Goldstein, Chief Rabbi of South Africa

CAPE TOWN
Union of Orthodox Synagogues of S.A. and Beth Din
191 Buitenkant Street
Tel +27 (21) 461 6310 *Fax* +27 (21) 461 8320
Exec. Dir. M. Glass

SOUTH KOREA

About 25 Jewish families live in Seoul, the capital.
Religious services are held on Friday evenings at the 8th U.S. Army Religious Retreat Centre. *Tel* +82 7904 4113

SPAIN

Spain has an ancient connection with the Jews, and the term 'Sephardi' originates from the Hebrew word for Spain. Beginning in Roman times the Jews have suffered the usual cycle of acceptance and persecution, with a 'golden age' under the Islamic Moorish occupation which began in 711. Great Jewish figures arose from the Spanish community, such as Ibn Ezra and the Rambam. However, the situation changed when the Christians gained the upper hand, and blood libels began. In 1492, almost 100 years after a particularly violent period of persecution, the Jews were expelled from Spain. Many thousands were baptised but practised Judaism in secret *(the Conversos)*, and thousands were caught doing so and burnt at the stake.

Jewish life began again in the nineteenth century. The Inquisition ended in 1834 and by 1868 Spain had promulgated religious tolerance. Synagogues could be built after 1909, and Spain accepted many thousands of Jewish refugees before and during the Second World War. Angel Sanz-Briz alone helped to save thousands of Hungarian Jews by issuing 'letters of protection' and entry visas.

There has been a recent immigration from North Africa, and the community today has a central body and synagogues in several towns (including Torremolinos and Malaga). Rambam's ruined synagogue in Cordoba can be visited, and there are several other old synagogues throughout the country.

BARCELONA
Barcelona: Comunidad Israelita de Barcelona
Avenir, 24 08001
Tel +34 (93) 200 8513
Email info@cibonline.org *Website* www.cibonline.org
Chabad Lubavitch de Barcelona
Calle Joan Gamper 27, Barcelona, 08014 Spain
Tel +34 (93) 410 0685 *Fax* + 34 (93) 419 9151
Website www.jabadbarcelona.org
Rabbi Libersohn

MADRID
Comunidad Judía de Madrid
Balmes, 3-28010
Tel +34 (91) 591 3131 *Fax* +34 (91) 594 1517
Website www.comjudiamadrid.org
Federación de Comunidades Judias de España
Calle Miguel Ángel 7, 1°C 28010 Madrid
Tel +34 (91) 700 1208 *Fax* +34 (91) 391 5717
Email fcje@fcje.org *Website* www.fcje.org
Benidorm Comunidad Judía de Alicante
C/ Berlín Edificio Parque Loix 3500 Benidorm *Contact* Harvey Bourne
Las Palmas de Gran Canaria
Pres. Bendahan, Ap. Correos 2142, Las Palmas 35080
Mallorca: Comunidad Judía de Baleares
Monsenyor Palmer 3 – 07014 – Palma de Mallorca *Contact* Abraham Barchilón
Malaga: Comunidad Israelita de Malaga
Duquesa de Parcent, 8, 3° 29001 Alameda Principal, 47, 2°B. *Pres.* Mr Hayon
Marbella: Comunidad Judía de Marbella
Jazmines 21 (Urb. El Real) – 29600 – Marbella *Tel* +34 (952) 859 395 *Fax* +34 (952) 765 783
Email cimarbella@yahoo.es *Pres.* Mr. Cohen
Melilla: Comunidad Israelita de Melilla
Duquesa de la Victoria, No19, 52001 *Tel* +34 (952) 674 057
Seville: Comunidad Israelita de Sevilla
41003-Bustos Tavera, 8 *Tel* +34 (95) 427 5517
Valencia: Comunidad Israelita de Valencia
Ingeniero Joaquin Benlloch 29 2ª 46006- Valencia
Tenerife
38001-Jewish Community, P. Abecasis, Ap. de Correos 939, Villalba Hervas, Santa Cruz de Tenerife

Torremolinos: Comunidad Israelita de Torremolinos
Av. Palma de Mallorca 55, 29620 *Tel* +34 (952) 602 583
Pres. Mr Stern *Email* rs@yonah-by.info

SRI LANKA

Solid evidence for Jewish settlement was recorded about 1.000 years ago by Muslim travellers. There was a small Jewish community when the Dutch took the island as a colony. This attracted Jews from southern India to the island because of the possibility of trade.

There was a plan put forward when the island came under British rule for mass Jewish immigration. The Chief Justice, Sir Alexander Johnston appeared to consider the idea a serious one, but the British government did not act on it. A coffee estate was founded in 1841 near Kandy by European Jews.

There is no communal organization on the island. The Sri Lankans appear supportive of Israel, despite the government's official pro-Arab stance. Diplomatic relations with Israel were resumed in May 2000.

Correspondence A. Ranasinghe, 82 Rosmead Place, Colombo 7 *Tel* +94 (11) 269 5642

SURINAME

Suriname is one of the oldest permanent Jewish settlements in the Western Hemisphere. The Sephardi Congregation was established about 1661, but earlier settlements in 1632, 1639 and 1652 have been reported. Some 225 Jews are members of the two synagogues, where Sephardi services are conducted.

Synagogue and Office
Keizerstraat 82 - 84, Paramaribo
Tel +597 472 817
Email isrgem@cq-link.sr

SWEDEN

Sweden was under the influence of the Lutheran church until the late eighteenth century, and was opposed to Jewish settlement. Aaron Isaac from Mecklenburg in Germany, a seal engraver, was the first Jew admitted into the country in 1774. The emancipation of Jews in Sweden was a slow process; Jews had limited rights, as they were designated a 'foreign colony'. After a gradual lifting of restrictions in the nineteenth century Jews were fully emancipated in 1870, although the right to hold ministerial office was closed to them until 1951. The emancipation heralded the growth of the community, and many Eastern European Jews found refuge in Sweden at the beginning of the twentieth century. The initial refusal to accept Jews fleeing the Nazis changed to sympathy as evidence for the Holocaust mounted, and in 1942 many Jews and other refugees were allowed into the country, followed, in 1943, by almost all of Danish Jewry. Sweden also accepted Hungarian, Czechoslovakian and Polish Jews after the war.

There is an Official Council of Jewish Communities in Sweden, and many international Jewish groups are represented. There are three synagogues in Stockholm, including the imposing Great Synagogue built in 1870. There are synagogues in other large towns. Although shechita is forbidden, kosher food is imported, and there are some kosher shops.

Official Council of Jewish Communities in Sweden
Wahrendorffsgatan 3b, 10391 Stockholm
Tel +46 (8) 5878 5800

GÖTEBORG
Judiska Församlingen (Jewish Community)
Östra Larmgatan 12, 411 07
Tel +46 (31) 109 400 *Fax* +46 (31) 711 9360
Email kansli@judiskaforsamlingen.se *Website* www.judiskaforsamlingen.se

MALMÖ
Judiska Församlingen (Jewish Community)
Box 4198,203 13
Tel +46 (40) 611 8460 *Fax* +46 (40) 23 4469

STOCKHOLM
Judiska Församlingen (Jewish Community)
Wahrendorffsgatan 3, Box 7427, 103 91 Stockholm
Tel +46 (8) 5878 5800 *Fax* +46 (8) 5878 5858
Email kansli@jfst.se *Website* wwwjfst.se

SWITZERLAND

Swiss Jewry originated in medieval times and their history followed the standard course of medieval European Jewry: working as money-lenders and pedlars, attacked by the local population, who accused them of causing the Black Death, then resettling a few years afterwards, only to be subsequently expelled.

By the late eighteenth century, when the Helvetic Confederation was formed, there were three small communities. Freedom of movement was allowed, and full emancipation was granted in 1866. Theodor Herzl held the first World Zionist Conference in Basle in 1897. Although Switzerland accepted some refugees from Nazism, many were refused, and most of the new refugee Jewish population emigrated soon after the war. The community today has a central body and is made up of various factions, from ultra-Orthodox to Reform. The major towns have synagogues and kosher meat is imported. There are several hotels with kosher facilities. Over half of the community live in the German-speaking area, the French-speaking area has the second largest number, and a small population is found in the southern Italian-speaking area.

Switzerland elected its first Jewish (and first female) president, Ruth Dreifuss in1998. In 2001 it was reported that evidence had been found of an early Jewish presence in the country; a ring bearing images of a menorah and a ram's horn dating from 200CE.

Swiss Federation of Jewish Communities
PO Box 2105, 8027 Zurich
Tel +41 (43) 305 0777 *Fax* +41 (43) 305 0766
Website www.swissjews.org

BASEL
Basel Community Centre
Leimenstrasse 24
Tel +41 (61) 279 9850
Email igb@igb.ch *Website* www.igb.ch

BERNE
Berne Communal Centre and Synagogue
Kapellenstrasse 2
Tel +41 (31) 381 4992
Email info@jgb.ch *Website* wwwjgb.ch
M. Rabbi D. Polaner

GENEVA
Geneva Communal Centre
21av. Dumas 1206
Tel +41 (22) 317 8900
Email secretgen@comisra.ch

LAUSANNE
Lausanne Communal Centre
3 Avenue Georgette Case Postale 336, 1001 Lausanne
Tel +41 (21) 341 7240

Email secretariat@cilv.ch *Website* www.cilv.ch
Synagogue
1 Avenue Juste-Oliver (corner Avenue Florimont) *Tel* +41 (21) 311 7168

ZURICH
Zürich Communal Centre
Lavaterstrasse 33, 8002
Tel +41 (44) 283 2299
Website www.icz.org

SYRIA

The remnants of this historic Jewish community, living in Damascus, Aleppo and Kamishli, have been estimated at 100, following recent aliyah.

DAMASCUS
Pres. of Rabbinical Court Rabbi Ibrahim Hamura, Ecole Ben-Maymoun, Kattatib. Al-Ittihad Al-Ahlieh School (Alliance Israélite), rue El Amine

TAHITI (FRENCH POLYNESIA)

The first known Jew in Tahiti was Alexander Salmon, the son of a Rabbi from Hastings (England), who arrived in 1841 and later married the Queen's sister. No community developed however until the 1960s when refugees came from Algeria.

Tahiti Synagogue
121196 Temple Dorette Assael, Rue Morenhout, Quartier Fariipiti, Papeete
Tel +689 437 156 *Fax* +689 433 086

TAIWAN

The US Army brought the first Jews to Taiwan in the 1950s, when an American base was set up in the country. In the 1970s some Jewish businessmen began to work on the island, serving two- or three-year contracts with their companies. Most are Americans, although there are some Israelis and other nationalities. Services are held on Shabbat in a hotel, and there is a Jewish community centre.

Taiwan Jewish Community Centre
Information F. Chitayat *Tel* +886 (2) 861 6303 c/o Donald Shapiro, Trade Winds Company, P.O. Box 7-179, Taipei 10602, Taiwan *Tel* +886 (2) 396 0159 *Fax* +886 (2) 396 4022
Services are held at Landis Hotel, 41 Min Chuan East Road, Sec. 2 Taipei. For details contact Rabbi Dr E. Einhorn at *Tel* +886 (2) 597 1234 *Fax* +886 (2) 596 9223

TAJIKISTAN

One of the former Soviet Republics, Tajikistan has a small Jewish population. After the fall of the Soviet Union, many Jews emigrated to Israel. The community is a mix of 40 per cent Bokharans and 60 per cent Soviet Jews from other parts of the former USSR who migrated to Tajikistan during the Second World War. The Bokharan Jews are believed to be descendants of Persian Jewish exiles. Dushanbe, the capital, and Shakhrisabz are provided with synagogues, and Dushanbe also has a library.

Jewish Community of Dushanbe
Nazima Khikmata Street, 26 Dushanbe 7340001
Tel +7 (372) 217 658

THAILAND

Although the first confirmed presence of Jews in Thailand was in 1890, Thai Jewry really began with Jews escaping Russia and Eastern Europe in the 1920s and 1930s, although most of them emigrated after 1945.

The present community arrived in the post-war period of the 1950s and 1960s. They came from Syria and Lebanon, and also from Europe and America. Some Israelis also came, and jewellery is an important source of trade with Israel. Another relatively large influx came in 1979, as Jews left Iran after the fall of the Shah.

Bangkok has Ashkenazi, Sephardi and Lubavitch synagogues. The community centre is based in the Ashkenazi synagogue. The Lubavitch synagogue offers several communual activities, including Seders at Passover, which have a large attendance.

Jewish Association of Thailand
Beth Elisheva Synagogue, Mikveh and Jewish Centre
121 Soi Sai Nam Thip 2, Sukhumvit 22, Bangkok
Tel +66 (2) 663 0244 *Fax* +66 (2) 663 0245
Email rabbi@jewishthailand.com
Jewish Community of Thailand
121 Soi Sai Nam Thip 2, Sukhumvit Soi 22 Bangkok, Thailand
Tel +66 (2) 663 0244 *Fax* + 66 (2) 663 0245
Email rabbi@jewishthailand.com *Website* www.jewishthailand.com
Rabbi Yosef C Kantor
Ohr Menachem-Chabad
96 Ram Buttri Road, Kaosarn Road, Banglampoo
Tel +66 (2) 629 2770 *Fax* +66 (2) 629 1153
Website www.jewishthailand.com
Daily services. *M.* Rabbi Y. Kantor

TRINIDAD AND TOBAGO

Jewish links go back to 1658 when Portuguese Jews from Livorno and Amsterdam settled there. Most of them left by the end of the 17th century. Portuguese Jews from Venezuela and Curaçao settled in Trinidad in the 19th century. The names of many Catholic families are traceable to 'conversos' of the earlier period. In the mid-1930s some 800 Jews sought temporary refuge in Trinidad and Tobago from Nazi persecution in Germany and Austria and later from other parts of Nazi - occupied Europe. Those with German and Austrian passports were subject to internment between 1940 and 1943. Numbers have dropped since with only a few Jews living there now.

Correspondence Hans Stecher, c/o The Tackle Shop, 176A Western Main Road, Carenago, Trinidad, W.I. (Caribbean) *Tel/Fax* +1 (868) 637 3870

TUNISIA

There is written proof of ancient Jewish settlement in Carthage in the year 200CE, when the region was under Roman control. The community was successful and was left in peace. Under the Byzantine Empire conditions for the Jews worsened, but after the Islamic conquest the 'golden age' of Tunisian Jewry occurred. There was prosperity and many centres of learning were established. This did not continue into the Middle Ages, as successive Arab and Spanish invasions led to discrimination. Emancipation came from the French, but the community suffered under the Nazi-influenced Vichy government. After the war many emigrated to Israel or to France and the community is currently shrinking.

There are synagogues in the country, together with kindergartens and schools. Tunisia is not as extreme in its attitude towards Israel as some Arab states, and there has been communication between the two countries at a high level. An Israeli Interest Bureau in Tunis acts as an unofficial embassy. The Bardo Museum in Tunis has an exhibition of Jewish ritual objects.

TUNIS
Chabad Lubavitch of Tunisia
73 Rue de Palestine, Tunis
Tel +216 (71) 782 536 *Fax* +216 (71) 344 099
Grand Rabbinat de Tunisie
26 Rue Palestine, Tunis
Community Offices, 15 Rue du Cap Vert

TURKEY

There have been Jews in Turkey since at least the fourth century BCE, making Turkey one of the earliest Jewish communities. The fifteenth and sixteenth centuries were periods of major prosperity for the Jews of Turkey.
After the expulsion of the Jews from Spain in 1492, at a time when Jews were not tolerated in most of the Christian countries of Western Europe, what was then the Ottoman (Turkish) Empire was their principal land of refuge. The Sultan was reported to have said of the Spanish King: 'By expelling the Jews, he has impoverished his country and enriched mine'. During the Second World War Turkey was neutral and accepted those Jews able to enter it.

ISTANBUL
Chief Rabbinate
Yemenici Sok. No. 23 Tünel, Beyoglu
Tel +90 (212) 293 8794/5 *Fax* +90 (212) 244 1980
Chief Rabbi Isak Haleva
Communal Centre
Büyük Hendek Sokak No. 61, Galata
Tel +90 (212) 244 1576 *Fax* +90 (212) 292 0385
There are ten charitable and social institutions, six youth clubs, a high school and an elementary school in Istanbul. Synagogues also in Izmir, Ankara, Bursa and Adane.

TURKMENISTAN

Although some 2,500 Jews lived in Turkmenistan in 1989, many have now emigrated and less than 1,000 remain today, mostly in the capital city, Ashkhabad.

UKRAINE

Federation of Jewish Communities of the CIS Central Office
5A 2nd Vysheslavtzev Pereulok, Moscow, Russia, 127055
Tel +7 (495) 737 8275 *Fax* +7 (495) 783 8471
Website www.fjc.ru/communities/communities.asp?aid=80062

KIEV
Association of Jewish Organisations
Kurskaya ul. 6, r. 42 03049
Tel +38 (044) 248 3670
Email vaad-ua@ukr.net
Association of Progressive Jewish Congregations in Ukraine
01023 Kiev-23, P.O.B. 517
Tel +38 (044) 234 2215, *Tel/Fax* +38 (044) 234 8482
'Hatikva' Congregation, M. Rabbi A. Dukhovny

Other towns with Jewish centres include Bershad, Chernigov, Chernivtsi, Kharkov, Kremenchug, Lviv, Odessa, Simferopol, Uzhgorod and Zhitomir.

ODESSA
Jewish Community of Odessa
Osipova str. 21, 651125, Odessa
Tel +38 (048) 728 0770
Email odessachabad@gmail.com

UNITED STATES OF AMERICA

The first Jews came to what is now the United States of America in 1654. The ship had come from the West Indies and included 23 Jews from Brazil, attempting to escape the arrival of the Inquisition, following Portugal's recapture of Brazil from the Dutch earlier that year. It is believed they thought they were travelling to Amsterdam in the Netherlands, rather than to New Amsterdam (as New York was then called). Within ten years, however, the community was moribund. The surrender of New Amsterdam to the British in 1664 brought substantial changes to the Jewish settlement, as some restrictions to both civil and religious rights were lifted. In a few colonies they were even granted the right to vote.

Following the English takeover, communities were established along the eastern coast, and by 1700 there were between 200 and 300 Jews in the country. At the time of the Revolution there were between 1,500 and 2,000 Jews and they served both in the Militia (which was compulsory) and as officers and soldiers. In the decades immediately before the Civil War, the Jewish population rose from 15,000 to 150,000 as a result of emigration, mainly from German areas. During that war Jews served on both sides with their respective communities.

Immigration was at its peak between 1880 and 1925 (when free emigration ended) and during this period the Jewish population grew from 280,000 to 4,500,000. Unfortunately, during the 1930s, only a small number of the Jewish refugees trying to escape from Germany were able to enter the USA. America's numerical position in world Jewry has declined, with its population being in 1948 as much as ten times the population of Israel, to its current approaching parity. The largest concentration by far has always been in New York.

Each of the main religious groups has its own association of synagogues and rabbis and, unlike many other countries, there is no central religious organisation. There is therefore no central supervision of kashrut. Instead there are many hashgachot issued by both individual local communal organisations and rabbis, as well as by companies who issue such certificates on a commercial basis. Travellers may always check with a local rabbi to ascertain the appropriate supervisory body in a relevant location.

For general information about the American Jewish Community write to the UJA
UJA - Federation Resource Line 130E 59th Street, New York 10022
Tel +1 (800) 852 3337 *Email* resourceline@ujafedny.org *Website* www.ujafedny.org

REPRESENTATIVE ORGANISATIONS
American Jewish Committee
165 E. 56th Street, New York City, 10022
Email bandlerk@ajc.org
American Jewish Congress
National Headquarters 825 Third Avenue, Suite 18, New York, NY 10022
Tel +1 (212) 879 4500 *Fax* +1 (212) 758 1633
Email contact@ajcongress.org
Conference of Presidents of Major Jewish Organizations
633 Third Avenue, New York, NY 10017
Tel +1 (212) 318 6111
Email info@conferenceofpresidents.org
Consultative Council of Jewish Organizations
15W 16th Street, 6th Floor, New York, NY 10011
Tel +1 (917) 606 8260
Co-ordinating Board of Jewish Organizations
1640 Rhode Island Avenue, N.W. Washington, DC 20036
United Jewish Communities Federations of North America
P.O. Box 30, Old Chelsea Station, New York City, NY 10113
World Confederation of Jewish Community Centers
15 E. 26th Street New York City, NY 10010
World Jewish Congress
501 Madison Avenue, 17th Floor, New York City, NY 10022
Tel +1 (212) 755 5770

RELIGIOUS ORGANISATIONS
Agudath Israel of America
84 William Street, New York City, 10038
Central Conference of American Rabbis
355 Lexington Avenue, New York City, 10017-6603

Tel +1 (212) 972 3636 (Reform)
Lubavitcher Headquarters
770 Eastem Parkway, Brooklyn, NY 11213 New York
Board of Rabbis, 10 E. 73rd Street, New York City, 10021
Rabbinical Alliance of America (Orthodox)
305 Church Avenue, Brooklyn, NY 11218
Tel +1 (718) 871 4534
Email info@rabbinicalalliance.org
Rabbinical Assembly (Conservative)
3080 Broadway, New York City, 10027
Tel +1 (212) 280 6000
Rabbinical Council of America (Modern Orthodox)
305 Seventh Avenue, 12th Floor, New York, NY 10001
Tel +1 (212) 807 9000
Email office@rabbis.org
Reconstructionist Rabbinical Association
1299 Church Road, Wyncote, PA 19095
Tel +1 (215) 576 5210 *Fax* +1 (215) 782 8805
Email info@therra.org
Union of American Hebrew Congregations
633 Third Ave, New York City, NY 10017
Tel +1 (212) 650 4000
Union of Orthodox Jewish Congregations
Eleven Broadway, New York, NY 10004
Tel +1 (212) 563 4000
Email info@ou.org
Union of Orthodox Rabbis
235 E. Broadway, New York City, NY 10002
Union of Sephardic Congregations
8 W 70th Street, New York City, NY 10023
United Synagogue of America (Conservative)
820 Second Avenue, New York, NY 10017
Tel +1 (212) 533 7800
Email info@uscj.org
World Union for Progressive Judaism
633 Third Avenue, 6th Floor, New York, NY 10017
Tel +1 (212) 452 6530
Email wupj@urj.org
Jewish National Fund
42 E. 69th Street, New York City, NY 10021
Tel +1 (888) 563 0099
Email communications@jnf.org
World Zionist Organization
American Section, 515 Park Avenue, New York City, NY 10022

EDUCATIONAL AND CULTURAL ORGANISATIONS
Center for Cultural Judaism
80 Eighth Avenue, Suite 206, New York, NY 10011
Tel +1 (212) 564 6711
Website www.culturaljudaism.org
Center for Holocaust Studies
Documentation & Research, 1610 Avenue J., Brooklyn, NY 11230
Center for Jewish History
15 West 16th Street, New York City, NY 10011
Tel +1 (212) 294 6160 *Fax* +1 (212) 294 8302

Website www.cjh.org

The Center has brought together American Jewish Historical Society, American Sephardi Federation, Leo Baeck Institute, Yeshiva University Museum and YIVO Institute for Jewish Research to create the largest single repository for Jewish history in the Diaspora. It has over 500,000 volumes and over 100 million documents. Tours are available.

Holocaust Museum and Learning Center
12 Milestone Campus Drive 63146, St Louis
Tel +1 (314) 432 0020 *Fax* +1 (314) 432 1277
Website www.hmlc.org
Open 10am to 5.30pm.

URUGUAY

After the *Conversos* in the sixteenth century, there was no known Jewish community in Uruguay until the late nineteenth century when the country served as a stop-over on the way to Argentina. The Jewish population rose in the twentieth century, with immigration from the Middle East and eastern Europe. A synagogue was opened by 1917. Despite restrictive immigration laws imposed against European Jews fleeing Nazism, 2,500 Jews managed to enter the country between 1939 and 1940. Further Jewish immigration followed from Hungary and the Middle East in the post-war period.

There are many Jewish organisations functioning in Uruguay, including Zionist and women's organisations. Kosher restaurants exist in Jewish institutions, and there are a number of synagogues.

There is a Museum of the Holocaust (Museo del Holocausto, Uruguay) which was the first one in South America and the only one until the year 2000. It is situated in the Comunidad Israelita del Uruguay, Canelones 1084 Ground Floor and on its 3rd floor, there is an institution which involves mainly survivors of the Shoa. It is the Centro Recordatorio del Holocausto. There is also a Memorial of the Holocaust in the promenade in Montevideo. There are also communities at Maldonado and Paysandu.

The Jewish Community is vibrant and active in Uruguay. Each community maintains its own synagogues. There are two Jewish schools and an ORT University.

MONTEVIDEO
Comite Central Israelita Del Uruguay (CCIU)
Rio Negro 1308 P5 Esc. 9, 11100 Montevideo
Tel +598 (2) 901 6057/902 9195 *Fax* +598 (2) 900 6562
Email cciu@cciu.org.uy *Website* www.cciu.org.uy

UZBEKISTAN

The ancient Jewish community in this central Asian republic is believed to have originated from Persian exiles in the fifth century. The Jews were subject to harsh treatment under the various rulers of the region, but still managed to become important traders in this area, which straddled the route between Europe and China and the Far East. In the late Middle Ages Jewish weavers and dyers were asked to help in the local cloth industry, and Buhara became a key Jewish city after it became the capital of the country in the 1500s. Once the area had been incorporated into the Russian Empire in 1868, many Jews from the west of the Empire moved into Uzbekistan. A further influx occurred when Uzbekistan was used to shelter Jews during the Nazi invasion of the Soviet Union, and many subsequently set up home there.

The original Bukharan Jews are generally more religious than the Ashkenazim who entered the area in the nineteenth and twentieth centuries. There are Jewish schools in the area, and although there is no central Jewish organisation, there are many Jewish bodies operating on separate levels for the Ashkenazim and the Buharans.

BUHARA
Jewish Community of Buhara
Tcentralnaya str. 20, Buhara, Uzbekistan

Tel +998 (365) 224 2380
Website www.fjc.ru/buhara
Buharian Jewish Community
9 Chkalova Street, Tashkent, 100031 Uzbekistan
Tel +998 (71) 256 6336
Website www.fjc.ru/tashkent

SAMARKAND
3,000 Jews live in Samarkand. Many are Bukharan and live in the special mahala, the quarter designated for Jews.
Synagogue Gumbaz
Gumbaz 2-i Ilyazarov proezd 1, Samarkand, Uzbekistan
Tel +998 (66) 223 6516
Website www.fjc.ru/samarkand
Jewish Community of Samarkand
Respublikanskaya str. 45, Samarkand, 703000 Uzbekistan
Tel +998 (66) 233 1145/236 8392
Website www.fjc.ru/samarkand

TASHKENT
Jewish Community of Tashkent
15/17 2-ya Kunaeva Street, Tashkent, 700015 Uzbekistan
Tel +998 (71) 152 5978 *Fax* +998 (71) 120 6431
Website www.fjc.ru/tashkent
Dir. Rabbi Abba D. Gurevitch
Lubavitch in Uzbekistan & Asia
30 Balakiereva Street (Shohjahon tor –kuchasi), 15 Second Mirobad Street 100100
Tel +998 (71) 253 9640/252 5978 *Fax* +998 (71) 120 6431
Website www.jewishhuz.com
Central organisation: Lubavitch
Lubavitch in Uzbekistan & Central Asia
30 Shokhzhakhon Street, Tashkent, 100100 Uzbekistan
Tel +998 (71) 152 5978 *Fax* +998 (71) 120 6431
Website www.fjc.ru/tashkent

VENEZUELA

Settlement in Venezuela began in the early nineteenth century from the Caribbean. The Jews were granted freedom early (between 1819 and 1821), which encouraged more settlement. The community at that time was not religious. At the beginning of the twentieth century some Middle Eastern Jewish immigrants organised a central committee for the first time. The powerful influence of the Catholic Church meant few Jews were accepted as immigrants in the pre-war rush to escape Nazi Europe.

After the war however, the community began to expand, with arrivals from Hungary and the Middle East. The successful oil industry and the excellent Jewish education system attracted immigrants from other South American countries.

Today most Jews live in Caracas, the capital. Fifteen synagogues serve the country. The Lubavitch movement is present and maintains a yeshivah. Caracas has a Jewish bookshop and a weekly Jewish newspaper. Venezuela has an expanding Jewish community, in contrast to many of its South American neighbours. The oldest Jewish cemetery in South America, in Coro, with tombstones dating from 1832, is still in use today.

CARACAS
Confederación de Asociaciones Israelitas de Venezuela (CAIV)
Representative organisation of Venezuelan Jewry, Av. Washington (al lado del Hotel Avila), San Bernardino
Tel +58 (2) 551 0368/+58 (2) 550 2454 *Fax* +58 (2) 551 0377/550 1721

Ashkenazi Synagogue and Centre: Unión Israelita de Caracas
Av. Washington, San Bernardino
Tel +58 (2) 551 5253 *Fax* +58 (2) 552 7956 *M.* Rabbi Pynchas Brener
Sephardic Synagogue and Centre: Asociación Israelita de Venezuela
Tiferet Yisrael, Av. Maripérez, Frente al Paseo Colón, Los Caobos
Tel +58 (2) 574 4975/574 8297 *Fax* +58 (2) 577 0259 *M.* Rabbi Isaac Cohén
Chabad Lubavitch
9na. Trans. Altamira final de Ae Luis Roche Altamira
Tel +58 (2) 264 0711 *Fax* +58 (2) 264 7011
Website www.jabadve.com
Chabad Lubavitch
Avenue J Washington QTA Lore No. 8
Tel +58 (2) 552 0044 *Fax* +58 (2) 552 2184
Great Synagogue of Caracas (Ashkenazi)
Avenida Francisco Javier Ustariz, San Bernardino
Tel +58 (2) 511 869
Union Israelita de Caracas Synagogue & Community Centre (Ashkenazi)
Avenida Marques del Toro 9, San Bernardino
Tel +58 (2) 552 8222 *Fax* +58 (2) 552 7628
If notified in advance, kosher lunches can be arranged, a meat snack bar is also open in the evening.

VIETNAM
HO CHI MINH CITY
Chabad House Synagogue
121/137 Le Loi Street, Ben Nghe District 1
Tel +84 (8) 821 8055/+84 090 916 770
Email chabadvietnam@gmail.com

VIRGIN ISLANDS
Jews first began to settle on the island in 1655, taking advantage of liberal Danish rule. They were mainly traders in sugar cane, rum and molasses, and by 1796 a synagogue had been founded. The Jewish population of 400 made up half of the islands' white community in 1850. There have been three Jewish governors. One was Gabriel Milan, the first governor who was appointed by King Christian of Denmark.
The community began to shrink after the Panama Canal was opened in 1914, and by 1942 only 50 Jews remained. Since 1945 the community has expanded again, with families arriving from the U.S. mainland.

Hebrew Congretation of St Thomas (Reform)
P.O.B. 266, St Thomas, 00804-0266
Tel +1 (340) 774 4312 *Fax* +1 (340) 774 3249
Email hebrewcong@islands.vi *Website* www.onepaper.com/synagogue
Jewish Community
Crystal Gade, Charlotte Amalie. *M.* Rabbi A. F. Starr

YEMEN
Since 1948 the vast majority of Yemeni Jews (who then numbered about 50,000) have emigrated to Israel. It is estimated about 1,200 remain in Sa'ana. The bulk of the Jews of Aden, situated in the south of the country in what was known as South Yemen until 1990, left the country prior to Aden attaining independence from Britain in 1967.

ZAMBIA
The Jewish community began in the early twentieth century, with cattle ranching being the main attraction for Jewish immigrants. The community grew, and the copper industry was

developed largely by Jewish entrepreneurs. With refugees from Nazism and a post-war economic boom, the Jewish community in the mid-1950s totalled 1,200. The community declined after independence in 1964.

Today the Council for Zambian Jewry (founded in 1978) fulfils the role of the community's central body.

The Council for Zambia Jewry Ltd
P.O. Box 30020, Lusaka 10101
Tel +260 (211) 229 190 *Fax* +260 (211) 221 428
Ch. M. C. Galaun *Email* ceo@galaunia.co.zm

ZIMBABWE

Jews were among the earliest pioneers in Zimbabwe. The first white child born there (April 1894) was Jewish. The first synagogue in Zimbabwe (formerly Rhodesia) was set up in 1894, in a tent in Bulawayo. In 1897 a Jew was elected as the first mayor of Bulawayo. The first Jews came from Europe (especially Lithuania), and they became involved in trade and managing hotels. They were joined in the 1920s and 1930s by Sephardim from Rhodes. Some senior politicians in the country were Jewish, including one prime minister.

The 1970s saw the turbulent transition to Zimbabwe, and many Jews emigrated to escape the unrest. The community is now mainly Ashkenazi, with an important Sephardi component. Harare has both an Ashkenazi and a Sephardi synagogue; Bulawayo has a Ashkenazi synagogue. There are community centres and schools, in both the towns, although the latter have many local, non-Jewish pupils.

Central African Zionist Organisation
(Head Office) P.O. Box AC 783, Ascot, Bulawayo
Tel +263 (9) 250 443
Email cazobyo@gatorzw.com
Pres. C. Bernstein (Southern Region)

JEWISH STATISTICS

The Jewish population statistics for the United States and rest of the world have been reproduced with kind permission by Ira M. Sheskin and Arnold Dashefsky. Dashefsky, Arnold and Sheskin, Ira M. (Eds), *The American Jewish Year Book 2012*, chapters 5 and 6 (Dordrecht: Springer, 2012). The statistics for England, Wales and Scotland, are from the 2011 Census, Office for National Statistics and the National Records of Scotland.

JEWISH POPULATION BY COUNTRY

Country	Jewish Population [a]
WORLD TOTAL	13,746,100
AMERICA TOTAL	6,183,200
Canada	375,000
United States	5,425,000
Total North America [b]	5,800,000
Bahamas	300
Costa Rica	2,500
Cuba	500
Dominican Republic	100
El Salvador	100
Guatemala	900
Jamaica	200
Mexico	39,200
Netherland Antilles	200
Panama	8,000
Puerto Rico	1,500
Virgin Islands	500
Other	200
Total Central America	54,200
Argentina	181,800
Bolivia	500
Brazil	95,300
Chile	18,500

Table 1 continued

Country	Jewish Population [a]
Colombia	2,500
Ecuador	600
Paraguay	900
Peru	1,900
Suriname	200
Uruguay	17,300
Venezuela	9,500
Total South America [b]	**329,000**
EUROPE TOTAL	**1,426,900**
Austria	9,000
Belgium	30,000
Bulgaria	2,000
Czech Republic	3,900
Denmark	6,400
Estonia	1,700
Finland	1,300
France [c]	480,000
Germany	119,000
Greece	4,500
Hungary	48,200
Ireland	1,200
Italy	28,200
Latvia	6,200
Lithuania	3,200
Luxembourg	600
Netherlands	29,900
Poland	3,200
Portugal	600
Romania	9,500
Slovakia	2,600
Slovenia	100
Spain	12,000

Table 1 continued

Country	Jewish Population [a]
Sweden	15,000
United Kingdom [d]	291,000
Other European Union [e]	100
Total European Union	**1,109,400**
Belarus	12,000
Moldova	3,900
Russian Federation [f]	194,000
Ukraine	67,000
Total FSU Republics	**276,900**
[Total FSU in Europe] [g]	**288,000**
Gibraltar	600
Norway	1,300
Switzerland	17,500
Total Other West Europe [b]	**19,400**
Bosnia-Herzegovina	500
Croatia	1,700
Macedonia	100
Serbia	1,400
Turkey [f]	17,400
Other Balkans	100
Total Balkans	**21,200**
ASIA TOTAL	**5,941,100**
Israel [h]	5,582,100
West Bank and Gaza [i]	319,000
Total Israel and Palestine	**5,901,100**
Azerbaijan	8,800
Georgia	3,000

Table 1 continued

Country	Jewish Population [a]
Kazakhstan	3,300
Kyrgyzstan	500
Turkmenistan	200
Uzbekistan	4,200
Total FSU in Asia [j]	**20,000**
China [k]	2,500
India	5,000
Iran	10,200
Japan	1,000
Korea, South	100
Philippines	100
Singapore	300
Syria	100
Taiwan	100
Thailand	200
Yemen	200
Other Asia	200
Total Other Asia	**20,000**
AFRICA TOTAL	**75,300**
Egypt	100
Ethiopia	100
Morocco	2,500
Tunisia	900
Total North Africa [b]	**3,600**
Botswana	100
Congo D.R.	100
Kenya	400
Namibia	100
Nigeria	100

Table 1 continued

Country	Jewish Population [a]
South Africa	70,200
Zimbabwe	400
Other Sub-Saharan Africa	300
Total Sub-Saharan Africa [l]	**71,700**
OCEANIA TOTAL	**119,600**
Australia	112,000
New Zealand	7,500
Other Oceania	100

[a] Includes all persons, who, when asked, identify themselves as Jews or who are identified as Jews by a respondent in the same household, and do not have another monotheistic religion. It also includes persons of Jewish parentage who claim no current religious or ethnic identity.
[b] Including countries not listed separately.
[c] Including Monaco.
[d] Including Channel Islands and Isle of Man.
[e] Cyprus and Malta.
[f] Including Asian regions.
[g] Including Baltic republics.
[h] Total legal population of Israel, including Jews and non-Jews in East Jerusalem and the Golan Heights and Jews (enlarged definition) in the West Bank, but excluding the Palestinian population in the West Bank and Gaza. 1/1/2012: 7,837,500.
[i] Total Palestinian population on 1/1/2012 in the West Bank (without East Jerusalem): 2,238,500; Gaza: 1,600,000; Total 3,838,500 (our revised estimate).
[j] Including Armenia and Tajikistan with less than 100 Jews each. Not including Asian regions of the Russian Federation.
[k] Including Hong Kong and Macao.
[l] Sudan and Ethiopia included in Northern Africa.

JEWISH POPULATION IN ENGLAND, WALES AND SCOTLAND

Country	Jewish Population
ENGLAND	261,282
North East	4,503
North West	30,417
Yorkshire and the Humber	9,929
East Midlands	4,254
West Midlands	4,621
East	34,830
London	148,602
South East	17,761
South West	6,365
WALES	2,064
SCOTLAND	5,887

Taken from the 2011 Census, Office for National Statistics and the National Records of Scotland.

There were probably individual Jews in England in Roman and (though less likely) in Anglo-Saxon times, but the historical records of any organised settlement here start after the Norman Conquest of 1066. Jewish immigrants arrived early in the reign of William the Conqueror and important settlements came to be established in London (at a site still known as Old Jewry), Lincoln and many other centres. In 1190 the massacres of Jews occurred in many cities, most notably in York. The medieval settlement was ended by Edward I's expulsion of the Jews in 1290, after which date, with rare and temporary exceptions, only converts to Christianity or secret adherents to Judaism lived here for the next 350 years. The Domus Conversorum, the House for Converted Jews (on the site of the former Public Record Office in Chancery Lane, London) had been established in 1232. Perhaps the most notable Jews in medieval England were the financier, Aaron of Lincoln (d.c. 1186), and Elijah Menahem of London (d. 1284), financier, physician and Talmudist.

After the expulsion of the Jews from Spain in 1492 a secret Marrano community became established in London, but the present Anglo-Jewish community dates in practice from the period of the Commonwealth. In 1650 Menasseh ben Israel, of Amsterdam, began to champion the cause of Jewish readmission to England, and in 1655 he led a mission to London for this purpose. A conference was convened at Whitehall and a petition was presented to Oliver Cromwell. Though no formal decision was then recorded, the conference was advised that there was nothing to stop Jews living in England; the expulsion had been on the personal edict of Edward I and it was not renewed by Edward II. In 1656 the Spanish and Portuguese Congregation in London was organised. Charles II confirmed the resettlement in 1661. The Sephardim were followed towards the end of the seventeenth century by the establishment of an Ashkenazi community, which increased rapidly inside London as well as throwing out offshoots to a number of provincial centres and seaports. The London community, has, however, always been the largest part of British Jewry.

Britain has the distinction of being one of the few countries in Europe where during the course of the past three centuries there have been no serious outbreaks of violence against Jews and in which there has been no ghetto system. In 1753, though, the passage through Parliament of a Bill to facilitate the naturalisation of some foreign-born Jews caused such an outcry that it was soon repealed. A short-lived outbreak of antisemitism in 1772, associated with the so-called 'Chelsea murders' is equally notable for its rarity.

Although Jews in Britain had achieved virtual economic and social emancipation by the early nineteenth century, they had not yet gained 'political emancipation'. Minor Jewish disabilities were then, however, progressively removed and Jews were admitted to municipal rights and began to win distinction in the professions. The movement for the removal of Jewish political disabilities became an issue after the final removal of political disabilities from Protestant dissenters and then Roman Catholics (1829), and a Bill with that object was first introduced into the House of Commons in 1830. Among the advocates of Jewish emancipation were Macaulay, Lord John Russell, Gladstone (from 1847) and Disraeli. The latter, who was a Christian of Jewish birth, entered Parliament in 1837. Jewish MPs were repeatedly elected from 1847 onwards, but were prevented from taking their seats by the wording of the various oaths required from all new members. Owing to the opposition in the House of Lords it was not until 1858 that a Jew (Lionel de Rothschild) was formally admitted to Parliament, this being followed in 1885 by the elevation of his son (Sir Nathaniel de Rothschild) to the Peerage. Meanwhile, in 1835, David Salomons was the first Jew to become Sheriff of London, and in 1855 Lord Mayor of London. The first to be a member of the government was Sir George Jessel, who became Solicitor-General in 1871, and the first Jewish Cabinet Minister was Herbert Samuel in 1909.

During the 19th century British Jews spread out from those callings which had hitherto been regarded as characteristic of the community. A further mark of their organisational consolidation can be seen in the growth and strength of many of the communal institutions mentioned elsewhere in this book, such as the Board of Deputies (founded 1760), the Board of Guardians (founded 1859), and the United Synagogue (founded 1870), as well as the development of the office of Chief Rabbi and the longevity of the Jewish Chronicle, which marked its 170th anniversary in 2011. Equally significant, by the middle of the century, was the appearance of a number of newer Jewish communities which had been formed in many of the new industrial centres in the North of England and the Midlands.

There has always been a steady stream of immigration into Britain from Jewish communities in Europe, originally from the Iberian Peninsula and Northern Italy, later from Western and Central Europe. The community was radically transformed by the large influx of refugees which occurred between 1881 and 1914, the result of the intensified persecution of Jews in the Russian Empire. The Jewish population rose from about 25,000 in the middle of the 19th century to nearly 350,000 by 1914. It also became far more dispersed geographically. The last two decades of the nineteenth century saw a substantial growth in the number of communities both in England and in Scotland and, in consequence, the 'provinces' became more significant both in numbers and in their influence upon the community as a whole. The impact of this immigration on the Anglo-Jewish community was intensified because very many of the Jews who left Eastern Europe on their way to North America or South Africa passed through Britain. From 1933 a new emigration of Jews commenced, this time from Nazi persecution, and again many settled in this country. Since the end of the Second World War, and notably since 1956, smaller numbers of refugees have come from Egypt, Iran, Iraq and Hungary. There is, also, a large Israeli 'diaspora' in certain areas.

One of the main features of the years after 1914 was the gradual transfer of the leadership of the community from the representatives of the older established families of Anglo-Jewry to the children and grandchildren of the newer wave of immigrants. Another feature was the growth of Zionist movements, firstly the Chovevei Zion (Lovers of Zion) in the 19th century and later, from the inspiration provided by Theodor Herzl, the English Zionist Federation. The government took soundings from the community and as a result of the comments of the Chief Rabbi and Lord Rothschild issued the historic Balfour Declaration in November 1917. In 1920 the first British High Commissioner in Mandate Palestine was Sir Herbert Samuel. It was after the withdrawal of the British Government from the Mandate that the State of Israel was proclaimed in 1948.

A mark of British Jewry's full participation in public life is reflected in the number of Jewish signatories to the proclamation of accession of Queen Elizabeth II in 1952, which included seven Jewish Privy Counsellors. At the Jubilee there were 21 and in 2012 there were 36 in the highest offices of the State, in Parliamentary and municipal life, in the Civil and Armed Services, in the judiciary and the universities. In all professions and occupations, the Jewish subjects of the Crown – both at home and overseas – play their full part as inheritors of the political and civic emancipation that was achieved in the mid-nineteenth century. There were 23 Jewish Members in the House of Commons elected in May, 2010. There are no Jewish members of the Scottish Parliament.

In recent years the religious affiliation of the members of the community has seen substantial change. While the numbers of Reform and Liberal Jews have remained almost unchanged as a proportion of the total community, the ultra-Orthodox Chareidi community has grown substantially. The community remains over 70% Orthodox.

The events marking the celebration of the 350th anniversary of Readmission (1656-2006) culminated in public festivities in Trafalgar Square, a royal reception at St James's Palace and an address by the Prime Minister at Bevis Marks.

In its internal life and organisation, British Jewry has constructed the complex fabric of religious, social and philanthropic institutions enumerated in this book. The Jews in Britain are now estimated to number about 267,000 (see the relevant note in the statistical tables) of whom some 168,000 reside in Greater London and the remainder are spread in some 90 regional communities. The census returns of 2001 disclose the fact that there are Jews who live in all but one (the Scilly Isles) of Britain's areas of registration.

UNITED KINGDOM LEGISLATION CONCERNING JEWS

HISTORICAL BACKGROUND

In the Middle Ages, hostility towards Jews was a common feature in many European countries. In England, during the reign of Edward I (1272–1307), the *Statutum de Judeismo* was passed in 1275. This statute forbade usury and included an order continuing to oblige Jews to wear a distinguishing badge and imposing upon them an annual poll tax.

In 1290, Edward personally decreed the expulsion of Jews from England. During the reign of Charles I (1625–49) the number of Jews in England steadily increased. Menasseh ben Israel (1604–57) of Amsterdam made a direct appeal to Cromwell to authorize readmission. His 'Humble Addresses' presented to the Lord Protector in October 1655 urged the revocation of the edict of 1290 and entreated that the Jews be accorded the right of public worship and the right to trade freely. No formal announcement was ever made of the Jews' 're-admission' but Charles II gave instructions they were to be allowed to live in the country. It also transpired that, as Edward II had not extended the expulsion with his own decree, there had been nothing to stop them living in England since the death of Edward I.

The Religious Disabilities Act 1846 extended to Jews the provisions of the Toleration Act 1688. Under the 1846 Act, British subjects professing the Jewish religion were to be subject to the same laws, in respect of their schools, places for religious worship, education and charitable purposes, and the property held with them, as Protestant dissenters from the Church of England.

UPDATING THE LEGISLATION SECTION OF THE JEWISH YEAR BOOK

(Prepared by His Honour Judge Aron Owen and updated by His Honour Judge Martyn Zeidman QC and further by Jonathan Arkush and Eleanor F. Platt QC)

This part of the Year Book, summarising legislation, has in the past been prepared by His Honour Judge Aron Owen z'l who sadly died on 23rd September 2009 - three days after Rosh Hashanah. His elegant explanations are still applicable and there has been very little to report since the last edition. We are very grateful to Judge Owen's son in law, His Honour Judge Martyn Zeidman QC. for taking over responsibility and for Eleanor F. Platt QC who has undertaken the responsibility now.

On 13th January 2010 **The Holocaust (Return of Cultural Objects) Act 2009** came into force and its title summarises the effect of the change. In the past, museums which held items seized by the Nazis were in a legal dilemma: could and should they return the articles to their true Jewish owners, or must the museum hold onto to them as the law seemed to require. A change was necessary. Andrew Dismore proposed the Bill and he explained its purpose:- "the Bill will right a long-standing injustice by giving powers to museums and galleries to return pieces of art and cultural objects taken from their rightful owners during the period of the Nazi regime. Whilst I do not envisage the Act having to be used very frequently, this is an important moral step, to ensure that we can close yet a further chapter on the appalling crimes of the Holocaust." In a rare display of unity, the Bill received cross-party support and the then Culture Minister, Margaret Hodge, observed "For too long, families who had heirlooms stolen from them by the Nazis were unable to reclaim them, although they were the rightful owners. This new Act will restore this possibility for families who suffered so terribly during the Nazi era, to get some justice by getting back their heirlooms.".

Not strictly legislation, but the new Supreme Court (which has replaced the Judicial Committee of the House of Lords) in one of its first decisions considered the admissions policy of JFS. The full and profound ruling which has had a drastic effect upon all Jewish schools is reported as **R (on the application of E) (Respondent) v The Governing Body of JFS and the Admissions Appeal Panel of JFS and others (Appellants) [2009] UKSC 15** and it can be read in full on line at www.supremecourt.gov.uk/decided-cases/docs/UKSC_2009_0136_Judgment.pdf

In short, it comes to this:- If over-subscribed, faith schools are permitted to discriminate (select) on grounds of religion but not on the basis of race. It follows that a school may require an entrant to have a certain level of Jewish observance (e.g. attendance at synagogue, observance of Kashrut, or Shabbat) but a school may not require the child to satisfy the Halachic (Jewish legal) definition of a Jew. It follows that a school may not require the child to have a Jewish mother or to have gone through a valid conversion – in the eyes of the court such a requirement amounts to an unlawful racial (rather than a permitted religious) selection. The court emphasised that in reaching its decision no personal criticism was intended. The court's own summary provides that "the judgments of the Court should not be read as criticising the admissions policy of JFS on moral grounds or suggesting that any party to the case could be considered 'racist' in the commonly understood, pejorative, sense. The simple legal question to be determined by the Court was whether, in being denied admission to JFS, M was disadvantaged on grounds of his ethnic origins (or his lack thereof) (paras [9], [54], [124] and [156])." It is argued by some that legislation should be introduced to over-turn the effect of this decision and Parliament most certainly would have the authority to do so, but as yet there is no change. In practice, schools have amended their admission requirements to satisfy the new understanding of the law.

ENGLAND, WALES AND NORTHERN IRELAND

PRESENT POSITION

Today, English Law does not regard Jews as a separate nationality or as different from any other British citizen. They have no special status except in so far as they constitute a dissenting religious denomination.

Provision for that special religious position of Jews has, from time to time, been made in legislation (see, for example, the 1846 Act mentioned above). Various sections of the current edition of Halsbury's Laws contain relevant information on the position of Jews in the 21st Century in the UK.

Some of the various statutory provisions in force today are set out briefly below. Further information and details can be obtained from the Board of Deputies, 6 Bloomsbury Square, London, WC1A 2LP Tel 020 7543 5400). Legal advice should be sought by those wishing to know the impact of specific legislation upon their own particular circumstances.

1. The *Representation of the People Act 1983* (which is a consolidation of several previous Acts) enables a voter in a parliamentary or local election, 'who declares that he is a Jew' and objects on religious grounds to marking the ballot paper on the Jewish Sabbath, to have, if the poll is taken on a Saturday, his vote recorded by the presiding officer. This right does not apply to Jewish Holy-days other than the Sabbath. A person unable by reason of 'religious observance' to go in person to the polling station may apply to be treated as an absent voter and be given a postal vote for a particular parliamentary or local election.

2. The *Education Act 1994* permits Jewish parents to have their children, if they are attending state or state-aided voluntary schools, withdrawn from any period of religious instruction and/or worship where such instruction or worship is not in the Jewish faith. In order to take advantage of these provisions of the Act, a written request must be submitted to the head teacher of the school.

3. The *Oaths Act 1978*. A Jew may take an oath (in England, Wales or Northern Ireland) by holding the Old Testament in his uplifted hand, and saying or repeating after the officer administering the oath, the words: 'I swear by Almighty God that ...' followed by the words of the oath prescribed by law. The officer will administer the oath in that form and manner without question, unless the person about to take the oath voluntarily objects thereto or is physically incapable of so taking the oath.

Any person who objects to being sworn (whether in that way or in the form and manner usually administered in Scotland) is at liberty instead to make a *solemn affirmation* which will have the same force and effect as an oath. The form of the affirmation is as follows: 'I ... do solemnly, sincerely and truly declare and affirm that ...' followed by the words of the oath prescribed by law. The form of affirmation omits any words of imprecation or calling to witness.

4. *Marriage Act 1949*. English law expressly recognizes the validity of marriages by Jews in England if the ceremonies of the Jewish religion have been complied with.

The Secretary of a synagogue has statutory powers and duties in regard to keeping the marriage register books, and the due registration of marriages between persons professing the Jewish religion under the provisions of the Marriage Act 1949. He has no authority unless and until he has been certified, in writing, to be the Secretary of a synagogue in England of persons professing the Jewish religion, by the President of the Board of Deputies. In addition when the West London Synagogue was established, acting on the advice of the Chief Rabbi and other recognized Jewish ecclesiastical authorities, the President of the Board of Deputies refused to certify the secretary of the new congregation. Accordingly, by the Marriage Act 1949, it is enacted that the Secretary of the West London Synagogue of British Jews, if certified in writing to the Registrar-General by twenty householders being members of that synagogue, shall be entitled to the same privileges as if he had been certified by the President of the Board of Deputies. These privileges are also accorded to a person whom the Secretary of the West London Synagogue certifies in writing to be the secretary of some other synagogue of not less than twenty householders professing the Jewish religion, if it is connected with the West London Synagogue and has been established for not less than one year.

The Marriages (Secretaries of Synagogues) Act 1959 gives similar rights to Liberal Jewish synagogues.

5. *Divorce (Religious Marriages) Act 2002*. This Act, which was passed on 24 February 2002, came into operation on 24 January 2003. It is not retrospective. It amends the Matrimonial Causes Act 1973 by the insertion of a new clause, 10A which enacts important provisions for orthodox Jewish couples seeking a divorce, where a *Get* (Jewish Religious Divorce) is essential.

The relevant wording of the new section 10A reads as follows:

10A Proceedings after decree nisi: religious marriage
(1) This section applies if the decree of divorce has been granted but not made absolute and the parties to the marriage concerned –
    (a) were married in accordance with
        (i) the usage of the Jews ... And
    (b) must co-operate if the marriage is to be dissolved in accordance with those usages.
(2) On the application of either party, the court may order that a decree of divorce is not to be made absolute until a declaration, made by both parties that they have taken such steps as are required to dissolve the marriage, in accordance with those usages, is produced to the court.
(3) An order made under subsection (2) –
    (a) may be made only if the court is satisfied that in all the circumstances of the case it is just and reasonable to do so; and
    (b) may be revoked at any time ...

The effect of the statutory provisions, now in operation, is that where the parties, who have been married in accordance with the usages of Jewish Law (that is *Chuppah* and *Kiddushin*), seek a divorce then, before a Jewish husband and wife would be granted a civil decree absolute of divorce by the English court, they could be required to declare that there had been a *Get*, that is, the Jewish religious divorce. There would thus be a barrier to such a Jewish husband or wife obtaining a civil divorce and being able to remarry, unless and until there has been a prior *Get*.

It is hoped that these new statutory provisions will go some way towards alleviating the plight of an *Agunah*. The usual case of an *Agunah* (literally 'a chained woman') is that of a wife whose husband refuses to give her a *Get*, so that she is unable to remarry in accordance with orthodox Jewish law. Under the above provisions of the Divorce (Religious Marriages) Act 2002, such a husband would himself be unable to obtain a civil divorce and remarry.

To invoke the provisions of section 10A, an application, by either wife or husband, has to be made to the Court. This application must be made in accordance with the Family Proceedings (Amendment) Rules 2003. It is advisable to consult a solicitor (practising, *inter alia*, in Family Law) to ensure that the necessary legal proceedings are carried out correctly.

6. The Marriage (Same Sex Couples) Act 2013 came into force, in part only, on receiving Royal Assent in July 2013. Most of the Act's provisions had been brought into force by 14 June 2014. In so far as such marriages between Jews are concerned there has to be an opt-in by the relevant group before such marriages may be performed. Both Reform and Liberal Judaism have opted in.

7. *Shechita*. Animals and birds slaughtered by the Jewish method (*shechita*) for the food of Jews, by a Jew duly licensed by the Rabbinical Commission, constituted for the purpose, do not come within the provision of the Slaughterhouses Act 1974 or the Slaughter of Poultry Act 1967, relating to the methods of slaughter of animals and birds. The right to practice *shechita* is thus preserved.

In March 1995 both Acts (the Slaughterhouses Act 1974 and the Slaughter of Poultry Act 1967) were repealed and replaced by secondary legislation in the form of a Statutory Instrument. This implements the European Community's Directive (93/119/EC) on the protection of animals at the time of slaughter. In 2013 the government repealed the Welfare of Animals (Slaughter or Killing) Regulations (WASK) 1995 and replaced them with Welfare of Animals at the Time of Killing Regulations (WATOK) following EU Council Regulation 1099/2009. In keeping with the previous legislation, the requirement for animals and poultry to be stunned before slaughter does not apply in the case of animals subject to methods of slaughter required by certain religious rites. *Shechita* is accordingly safeguarded.

Shechita UK was established in 2003 to promote clarity and understanding of Shechita, the Jewish religious humane method of animal slaughter for food and to counter misinformation and popular misconceptions. It continues to lobby on behalf of the Jewish community in the UK and across Europe for the protection of Shechita.

In addition, The Rabbinical Commission for the Licensing of Shochtim has been retained as the only statutory body with authority for licensing slaughter-men for the purposes of Shechita.

8. The *Sunday Trading Act*, which came into operation on 26 August 1994, has removed many of the difficulties caused by the Shops Act 1950. All shops with a selling and display area of less than 280 square metres may be open at any time on Sundays. Shops with a selling and display area of 280 square metres or more are still subject to some restriction, with an opening time limited to a continuous period of six hours between 10am and 6pm.

There is, however, a special exemption for 'persons observing the Jewish Sabbath' who are occupiers of these 'large' shops. Provided such an individual (and there are parallel conditions for partnerships and companies) gives a signed notice to the Local Authority that he is a person of the Jewish religion and intends to keep the shop closed for the serving of customers on the Jewish Sabbath, he may open it as and when he wishes on a Sunday.

The notice given to the Local Authority must be accompanied by a statement from the minister of the shopkeeper's synagogue, or the secretary for marriages of that synagogue, or a person designated by the President of the Board of Deputies, that the shopkeeper is a person of the Jewish religion. There are severe penalties for any false statements made in connection with this intention to trade.

Large shops which were previously registered under Section 53 of the Shops Act 1950, may continue to trade on Sundays without new notification. But occupiers of food stores and kosher meat shops over 280 square metres who, even if closed on Shabbat, did not previously require exemption, may well have formally to notify their Local Authority that their premises will be closed on Shabbat to enable them to open on Sunday.

Jewish shopkeepers who close their premises for the 25 hours of Shabbat may open after Shabbat.

9. Discrimination against a person on account of his being a Jew is unlawful under the *Equality Act 2010*.

10. *Friendly Societies Act 1974* (which consolidates the Friendly Societies Acts 1896 to 1971 and certain other enactments). A Friendly Society may be registered for the purpose, *inter alia*, of ensuring that money is paid to Jews during *Shiva* (referred to in the Act as 'the period of confined mourning'). Friendly Societies have, since January 2010, become part of the Association of Financial Mutuals. The Jewish Friendly Societies, so useful for help for poor Jews in the C19 and early C20, have been largely superseded.

11. By the *Places of Worship Registration Act 1855*, as amended by the *Charities Act 1960*, the Registrar-General may certify a synagogue. The effect of Certification is freedom from uninvited interference by the Charity Commissioners and, if exclusively appropriate to public worship, from general and special rates.

12. By the *Juries Act 1870*, the minister of a synagogue who has been certified, was free from liability to serve on a jury, provided he follows no secular occupation except that of a schoolmaster. This provision was retained in the consolidating Act of 1974 but removed by Schedule 33 of the Criminal Justice Act 2003. It follows that any minister, like Judges, are liable for jury service.

THE LAW IN SCOTLAND

(Prepared by Sheriff Sir G. H. Gordon, CBE, QC, LL.D)

There are no records relating to Jews in Scotland prior to the creation of the United Kingdom in 1707, and accordingly no legislation regarding either their expulsion or their re-admission. Jews do not appear in Scots legislation as a unique group, except in relation to United Kingdom statutes which treat them as such, of which the only one still in force is the Representation of the People Act 1983.

European Regulations apply in Scotland as they do in England.

The Education (Scotland) Act 1980 provides by section 9 that every public and grant-aided and self-governing school shall be open to all denominations, and that any pupil may be withdrawn by his parents from instruction in religious subjects and from any religious observance in any such school. It provides further that no pupil shall be placed at any disadvantage with respect to secular instruction by reason of his or his parents denomination or his withdrawal from religious instruction.

Section 10 of that Act provides that where the parents of a boarder in any such school requests permission for the pupil to attend worship on any day exclusively set apart for religious observance by the religious body to which the parent belongs, or to receive religious instruction or practise religious observance in accordance with such tenets, the school shall afford facilities for such observance etc on its premises, provided that does not involve expenditure by the school.

The oath is administered by the judge in Scots courts, and the witness repeats the words (which begin 'I swear by Almighty God') after him with his right hand upraised. No books are used. A Jewish witness is in practice allowed to cover his head if he wishes to do so. Anyone who indicates a wish to affirm is allowed to do so.

Section 8 of the Marriages (Scotland) Act 1977 provides that a religious marriage may be solemnized by the minister or clergyman of any religious body prescribed by Regulations, or by any person recognized by such a body as entitled to solemnize marriages. The bodies prescribed by the Marriage (Prescription of Religious Bodies) (Scotland) (Regulations) 1977 (S.I.No. 1670) include 'The Hebrew Congregation', whatever that denotes. In practice all Rabbis appointed to an established Synagogue or Community (i.e. not necessarily owning premises, e.g. Edinburgh Liberal Jewish Community) are automatically recognised by the Registrar General for Scotland (RG) as being "recognised by the Hebrew Congregation". The RG requires explicit confirmation that all other Rabbis of any persuasion are so recognised before it will recognise a religious marriage "solemnised" by them as also constituting a civil marriage. In practice, the RG contacts the Scottish Council of Jewish Communities (SCoJeC) to ask whether a Rabbi is recognised. SCoJeC enquires of the head office of the relevant brand of Judaism in the relevant country, and, on the basis of information received, informs the RG whether or not the said Rabbi is recognised.

Section 15 of the Family Law (Scotland) Act 2006, which inserted a new clause 3A into the Divorce (Scotland) Act, was included at the specific request of the Jewish community. It comes into effect when

"(2)(a) the applicant is prevented from entering into a religious marriage by virtue of a requirement of the religion of that marriage; and

(2)(b) the other party can act so as to remove, or enable or contribute to the removal of, the impediment which prevents that marriage."

The Scottish legislation looks forward to a situation in which a party to a divorce may be "prevented from entering into a religious marriage by virtue of a requirement of the religion of that marriage" whereas the English legislation looks back to a situation in which the parties to the existing marriage "were married in accordance with the usage of the Jews". The Scottish legislation therefore covers more bases, since, unlike the English legislation, it could be used by a Jewish couple who were married only in a civil ceremony but who would, nonetheless, require a get in order for either party to be able to contract a subsequent religious marriage.

The Law Reform (Miscellaneous Provisions) (Scotland) Act 1980 includes regular ministers of any religious denomination among those persons who, although eligible for jury service, are entitled to be excused therefrom as of right.

The Race Relations Act 1976 (Equalities Act 2010) applies to Scotland, but the Sunday Trading Act 1994 does not, nor does the Places of Worship Registration Act 1855.

'Section 96 of the Crime and Disorder Act 1998 obliges sentencers to take account, as an aggravation, of the fact that any offence has been motivated by ill-will towards members of a group, defined by reference to colour, nationality, or ethnic or national origins ('a racial group'), and section 74 of the Criminal Justice (Scotland) Act 2003 makes similar provision in respect of members of a religious group.'

MARRIAGE REGULATIONS IN ENGLAND AND WALES

Marriages registered for civil purposes may be contracted according to the usages of the Jews between persons *both* professing the Jewish religion. This is provided that due notice has been given to the Superintendent Registrar of the local authority register office where the bride and groom live and that certificates for this purpose have been obtained. There is no restriction regarding the hours within which the marriage may be solemnised, nor the place of marriage, which may be a synagogue, private house, or any other building.

The date and place of the intended marriage having been decided, the parties should consult the Minister or Secretary for Marriages of the synagogue through which the marriage is to be solemnised. S/he will explain the necessary preliminary steps and the suitability of the proposed date.

The Registrar's certificates must be handed to the Synagogue Marriage Secretary in advance of the date decided. In the case of a marriage in a building other than a synagogue, care should be taken that these documents contain the words *"both* parties professing the Jewish Religion" following the description of the building.

If the marriage is to be solemnised at or through a synagogue under the jurisdiction of the Chief Rabbi, his Authorisation of Marriage must also be obtained. Enquiries relating to this should be directed to the Marriage Authorisation Office at the Office of the Chief Rabbi (*Tel* 020 8343 6314).

No marriage is valid if solemnised between persons who are within the degrees of kindred of affinity (e.g., between uncle and niece) prohibited by English law, even though such a marriage is permissible by Jewish law.

A marriage between Jews must be registered immediately after the ceremony by the Secretary of Marriages of the synagogue of which either the bride or the groom must be a member. If he or she is not already a member, membership may be established by signing a membership form and paying a membership fee in addition to the marriage charges.

No marriage between Jews should take place without due notice being given to the Superintendent Registrar, and without being registered in the Marriage Register of a synagogue. Marriages in such circumstances may not be valid in English law. (Outside England and Wales e.g. in Scotland, other regulations apply and the Minister of the synagogue should be consulted.)

For information on dates when marriages may not be placed, please see page 468.

LISTED SYNAGOGUES, FORMER SYNAGOGUES AND OTHER JEWISH SITES IN THE UK

This list is compiled by **Jewish Heritage UK** (*see* p. 98).
Room 204, Ducie House, 37 Ducie Street, Manchester, M1 2JW
Tel 0161 238 8621 *Email* director@jewish-heritage-uk.org
For regular updates see website www.jewish-heritage-uk.org/
See also *Jewish Heritage in England: An Architectural Guide* (2006, 2nd Edn. 2015) and *The Synagogues of Britain and Ireland* (2011) both by Sharman Kadish.

SYNAGOGUES

LONDON
Grade I
Bevis Marks, EC3 (Joseph Avis 1699–1701)
New West End, St Petersburgh Place, W2 (George Audsley in association with N.S. Joseph 1877–79)

Grade II*
In use as synagogue
Hampstead, Dennington Park Road, NW6 (Delissa Joseph 1892–1901)

Former synagogues
Princelet Street, E1 (Former synagogue 1870 behind Huguenot house 1719. Hudson 1869-70. Remodelled by Lewis Solomon 1893)
Spitalfields Great Synagogue, 59 Brick Lane/Fournier Street, E1 (Former French church 1743. Converted into synagogue 1897-98. Now London Jamia Mosque)

Grade II
In use as synagogues
Golders Green, 41 Dunstan Road, London NW11 (Lewis Solomon & Son [Digby] 1921-22. Enlarged by Messrs. Joseph 1927)
New London, 33 Abbey Road, NW8 (H.H. Collins 1882. Formerly St John's Wood United Synagogue)
New Synagogue, Egerton Road, N16 (Joseph & Smithem 1915. Interior reconstructed from Great St Helen's, Bishopsgate, by John Davies 1837-38)
Sandys Row, E1 (Former chapel 1766. Converted into synagogue 1867. Remodelled by N.S. Joseph 1870)
Spanish & Portuguese, Lauderdale Road, W9 (Davis & Emanuel 1895-96)
West London (Reform), Upper Berkeley Street, W1 (Davis & Emanuel 1869-70)
Western & Marble Arch, 32 Great Cumberland Place, W1 (T. P. Bennett & Son 1960-61)

Former synagogues
Dollis Hill, Parkside, NW2 (Sir Owen Williams 1936-38. Torah Temimah Primary School)
East London, Rectory Square, E1 (Davis & Emanuel 1876-77. Flats)
Hackney, Brenthouse Road, E9 (Delissa Joseph 1897. Enlarged by Cecil J. Eprile 1936. Church)

ENGLISH REGIONS
Grade I
Liverpool, Old Hebrew Congregation, Princes Road, L8 (W. & G. Audsley 1872-74)

Grade II*
In use as synagogues
Birmingham, Singers Hill, Blucher Street, B1 (Henry R. Yeoville Thomason 1855-56)
Bradford Synagogue (Reform), Bowland Street, BD1 (T.H. & F. Healey 1880-81)
Brighton, Middle Street, BN1 (Thomas Lainson 1874-75)
Chatham Memorial Synagogue, High Street, Rochester, ME1 (H.H. Collins 1865-70)

Cheltenham, St James's Square, GL50 (W.H. Knight 1837-39)
Exeter, Mary Arches Street, EX4. (1763-64. Refronted 1835)
Plymouth, Catherine Street, PL1 (1761-62)
Ramsgate, Montefiore Synagogue, Honeysuckle Road, CT11 (David Mocatta 1831-33)

Former synagogues
Liverpool, Greenbank Drive, L17 (E. Alfred Shennan 1936-37)
Manchester, Spanish & Portuguese, 190 Cheetham Hill Road, M8 (Edward Salomons 1873-74. Manchester Jewish Museum)

Grade II
In use as synagogues
Bristol, Park Row, BS1 (H.H. Collins with S. C. Fripp 1870-71)
Coventry, Barras Lane, CV1 (Thomas Naden 1870)
Grimsby, Sir Moses Montefiore Synagogue, Heneage Road, DN32 (B.S. Jacobs 1885-88 and *Mikveh* 1915-16)
Leicester, Highfield Street, LE2 (Arthur Wakerley 1897-98)
Manchester, Withington Spanish & Portuguese, 8 Queenston Road, West Didsbury, M20 (Delissa Joseph 1925-27)
Manchester, Higher Crumpsall, Bury Old Road, Salford, M7 (Pendleton & Dickinson 1928-29)
Manchester, South Manchester, Wilbraham Road, M14 (Joseph Sunlight 1912-13)
Reading, Goldsmid Road, RG1 (W.G. Lewton 1900-01)

Former synagogues
Grade I
Brighton, 26 Brunswick Terrace, Hove, BN3 (Rooftop private synagogue of Philip Salomons *ca.* 1850s)

Grade II
Birmingham, Severn Street, The Athol Masonic Hall, Severn Street, B1 (Richard Tutin 1825-27)
Blackpool, Leamington Road, FY1 (R.B. Mather 1914-16)
Brighton, 38 Devonshire Place, BN2 (Remodelled by David Mocatta 1837-38. Flats)
Canterbury, King Street, CT1 (Hezekiah Marshall 1847-48. King's School Recital Room)
Carmel College Synagogue, Mongewell Park, Crowmarsh, Wallingford, Oxfordshire, OX10 (Thomas Hancock 1961-63)
Falmouth, Smithick Hill, TR11 (1808. Studio)
Hull, The Western Synagogue, Linnaeus Street, HU3 (B.S. Jacobs 1902-03)
Leeds, New Synagogue, Louis Street/Chapeltown Road, LS7 (J. Stanley Wright 1929-32. Northern School of Contemporary Dance)
Newcastle upon Tyne, Leazes Park Road, NE1 (John Johnstone 1879-80. Flats)
Sheffield, Wilson Road, S11 (Rawcliffe & Ogden 1929-30. Church)
Sunderland, Ryhope Road, SR2 (Marcus K. Glass 1928)

WALES
Grade II
Former synagogues
Cardiff, Cathedral Road, CF11 (Delissa Joseph 1896-97. Demolished behind façade)
Merthyr Tydfil, Bryntirion Road, Thomastown, CF47 (1872-77)

SCOTLAND
Scottish A List
Glasgow, Garnethill, 129 Hill Street, G3 (John McLeod in association with N.S. Joseph 1877-79)

Scottish B List
In use as synagogue
Edinburgh, Salisbury Road, Newington, EH16 (James Miller 1929-32)

Former synagogue
Glasgow, Queen's Park, 4 Falloch Road, G42 (Ninian MacWhannel 1925-27. Flats)

NORTHERN IRELAND
Former synagogue
Belfast, Hebrew Congregation, 4 Annesley Street, BT14 (Young and Mackenzie with B.S. Jacobs 1904)

OTHER LISTED JEWISH BUILDINGS

Grade II
London, Beth Holim, 253 Mile End Road, E1 (Manuel Nunes Costello 1912-13. Flats)
London, Soup Kitchen for the Jewish Poor, Brune Street, E1 (Lewis Solomon 1902. Flats)
London, Stepney Jewish Schools, Stepney Green, E1 (Davis & Emanuel 1906-07)
London, No. 88, Whitechapel High Street, E1: former offices of the *Jewish Daily Post*, with shop signs by Arthur Szyk (*ca.*1935)
London, Whitechapel Drinking Fountain, (King Edward VII Jewish Memorial Drinking Fountain), Whitechapel Road, E1 (opposite Royal London Hospital), (W.S. Frith 1911)
Carmel College, Mongewell Park, Crowmarsh, Wallingford, Oxfordshire, OX10; Julius Gottlieb Gallery & Boathouse (Sir Basil Spence, Bonnington & Collins 1968-70, Grade II*); Amphitheatre (Thomas Hancock 1965)
Belfast, Jaffe Memorial Fountain, Victoria Square, BT1 (1877)

Post-war synagogues currently housed in listed buildings
Grade II*
London, Sukkat Shalom Reform Synagogue, 1 Victory Road, Hermon Hill, E11 (Merchant Seaman's Orphan Asylum at Wanstead Hospital, chapel by George Somers Clarke 1861-63. Contains fixtures and fittings from the synagogue at the former Tottenham Jewish Home & Hospital 1913-18)

Grade II
Elstree Liberal Synagogue, Elstree High Street, Hertfordshire, WD6 (Church of England school house 1882–83. Synagogue 1979)
Nottingham Hebrew Congregation, Shakespeare Street, NG1 (Wesleyan Methodist Chapel by Thomas Simpson 1854. Synagogue 1954. Contains Ark from former Chaucer Street Synagogue 1890)

Medieval sites with possible Jewish associations
Grade I
Bury St Edmunds, Moyses Hall, Cornhill, IP33 (*ca.*1180)
Lincoln: Jews' Court, 2-3 Steep Hill, LN2 (*ca.*1170); Jews' House, 15 The Strait, LN2 (*ca.*1170); Aaron the Jew's House (the Norman House), 47 Steep Hill, LN2 (*ca.*1170)
Norwich, the Music House or Jurnet's House, Wensum Lodge, 167-169 King Street, NR1 (*ca.*1175)

Scheduled Ancient Monuments
Bristol, Jacob's Well, 33 Jacob's Well Road, Bristol BS8 (Possible Medieval *Mikveh* *ca.*1140)
York, Clifford's Tower, YO1 (Rebuilt)

JEWISH BURIAL GROUNDS, MAUSOLEA AND MEMORIALS

Sites (or parts of sites, e.g. boundary walls, screens and gates, buildings or memorials). Listed Buildings, Scheduled Ancient Monuments or on the English Heritage Parks and Garden Register (P&G).

LONDON
Grade II
Alderney Road, E1 (Ashkenazi) (1696-97)
Mile End Velho (Sephardi), 253 Mile End Road, E1 (1657)
Mile End Nuevo (Sephardi), Queen Mary University of London Campus, New section (1874), P&G, Listed boundary walls and tablet)
Rothschild Mausoleum (Matthew Digby Wyatt 1866), West Ham Jewish Cemetery, Buckingham Road, E15

ENGLISH REGIONS
Grade II*
Ramsgate, Montefiore Mausoleum, Honeysuckle Road, CT11 (1862)

Grade II
Bath, Greendown Place and 174 Bradford Road, Combe Hill, BA2 (1812)
Birmingham, Granville Street Cemetery Memorial (1876), whole cemetery (1869-71) P&G II
Birmingham, *Ohel*, Witton New Jewish Cemetery, Warren Road, B44 (Essex & Goodman 1937)
Brighton, Florence Place, Ditchling Road, BN1 (1826, *Ohel* by Lainson & Son 1893)
Brighton, Sassoon Mausoleum, Paston Place, Kemp Town, BN2 (1892)
Bristol, St Philip's Cemetery, Barton Road, BS2 (oldest tombstone 1762)
Manchester, Philips Park Cemetery, M40, Jewish Section, (1875) whole cemetery (1866-67) P&G II
Coventry, London Road Cemetery, CV1, Jewish Section, (1864) whole cemetery (1845) P&G II*
Exeter, Magdalen Street, Bull Meadow, EX2 (1757)
Ipswich, Salthouse Lane, off Star Lane, IP4 (1796)
Ipswich, Old Cemetery, Cemetery Lane, IP4, Jewish Section (1855), whole cemetery, (1855) P&G II
King's Lynn, Millfleet, Stonegate Street, PE30 (Before 1811)
Liverpool, Deane Road, Fairfield, L7 (1836)
Penzance, Lestinnick Terrace, TR18 (oldest tombstone 1791)
Ramsgate Jewish Cemetery, *Ohel* and section of boundary wall, Upper Dumpton Park Road, CT11 (1872)
Southampton, *Ohel*, Southampton Old/Common Cemetery, Cemetery Road, SO15 (1854), whole cemetery (1846) P&G II*
Wolverhampton, Old Jewish Cemetery, Cockshutt Lane, Thomson Avenue, WV2 (1851)

Scheduled Ancient Monument
Falmouth Jews' Burial Ground, Penryn Road, Ponsharden, TR11 (*ca.* 1780)

SCOTLAND
Scottish A List
Glasgow, Jews' Enclosure, Glasgow Necropolis, Cathedral Square, G4 (1836)

Scottish B List
Edinburgh, Sciennes House Place (Braid Place), Causewayside, EH9 (1820)
Edinburgh, Newington Cemetery, Echobank, EH16, Jewish Section (1867)
Glasgow, Janefield Jewish Cemetery, Eastern Necropolis, Gallowgate, G31 (1856)
Glasgow, Western Necropolis, Tresta Road, G23, Jewish Section (1882/3, including the *Ohel* 1898)
Greenock Cemetery, Bow Road, PA16, Jewish Section (1911)

HONOURS LIST 2014

The following members of the Jewish community received honours in 2014.

CMG

Matthew Gould, For promoting relations between Britain and Israel.

Knight Bachelor

Michael Codron, For services to the theatre.
Daniel Day-Lewis, For services to drama.
Andras Schiff, For services to music.
Anthony Seldon, For services to Education and to Modern Political History.

CBE

Dr. Ros Altmann, For services to pensioners and pension provision.
David Bernstein, For services to sport.
Lady Ruth Morris, For services to the community.
Mark Pears, For services to business and charity.
James Smith, For services to Holocaust Education.
Robert Voss, For services to British industry and voluntary services to the UK.

OBE

Zeev Aram, For services to design and architecture.
Anthony Horowitz, For services to literature.
David Landau, For services to advancing British-Israel understanding and peace in the Middle East.
Martin Lewis, For services to consumer rights and charitable services.
Maurice Ostro, For services to charity and interfaith relations.
Isaac Jehuda Schapira, For services to British interests and charitable work in Israel.
Jonathan Shalit, For services to the entertainment industry.
Susan Terpilowski, For services to small businesses in London.

MBE

Judith Dimant, For services to theatre.
Shelley Gilberty, For services to bereaved children.
Martin Kolton, For services to the hairdressing industry.
Herman Martyn, For services to Education.
Harry Shindler, For services to British veterans and to the community in Italy.
Rev. Reuben Turner, For services to the Anglo-Jewish community, especially to Jewish Music.
Alan Weinberg, For services to education and the Redbridge community.
Barry Welck, For services to education and learning for disabled people.
Mark Winer, For services to interfaith dialogue and social cohesion in the UK.

BEM

Philip Brandeis, For services to children and young people.
Dr. Claire Lemer, For services to children's health.
Ruth Myers, For services to improving telecommunications access for deaf people.

PRIVY COUNSELLORS, PEERS, MPs, etc

PRIVY COUNSELLORS

John Bercow, MP
Lord Brittan of Spennithorne, QC
Lord Brown of Eaton-under-Heywood
Sir Stanley Burnton, QC
Lord Clinton-Davis
Lord Collins of Mapesbury
Lady Cosgrove, CBE
Lord Dyson, Master of the Rolls
Sir Terence Etherton, Chancellor of the
    High Court
Sir Lawrence Freedman
Sir Martin Gilbert, CBE
Lord Goldsmith, QC
Sir Peter Henry Gross
Baroness Hayman, GBE
Margaret Hodge, MP
Lord Hoffman
Lord Howard of Lympne, CH, QC
Sir Francis Jacobs, KCMG, QC
Sir Gerald Kaufman, MP
Lord Lawson of Blaby
Oliver Letwin, MP
Sir Brian Leveson, President of the
    Queen's Bench Division
Sir Kim Lewison, Lord Justice of Appeal
David Miliband
Edward Miliband, MP
Lord Millett
Lord Neuberger of Abbotsbury
Baroness Oppenheim-Barnes
Lord Phillips of Worth Matravers, KG
Sir Malcolm Rifkind
Sir Brian Rix, QC
Sir Stephen Sedley, QC
Grant Shapps, MP
Lord Sheldon
Lord Woolf
Lord Young of Graffham, DL

LIFE PEERS

Lord Alliance, CBE
Lord Beecham
Rt. Hon. Lord Brittan of Spennithorne, QC
Rt. Hon. Lord Brown of Eaton-under-Heywood
Lord Browne of Madingley
Lord Carlile of Berriew, QC, CBE
Rt. Hon. Lord Clinton-Davis
Rt. Hon. Lord Collins of Mapesbury
Baroness Deech, DBE
Lord Dubs
Lord Ezra, MBE
Lord Feldman
Lord Feldman of Elstree
Lord Fink

Lord Finkelstein, OBE
Lord Gavron, CBE [I have added]
Lord Glasman
Lord Gold
Rt. Hon. Lord Goldsmith, QC
Lord Grabiner, QC
Lord Grade of Yarmouth, CBE
Baroness Greengross, OBE
Baroness Hamwee [I have added]
Lord Haskel
Rt. Hon. Baroness Hayman, GBE
Baroness Henig, CBE
Rt. Hon. Lord Hoffman
Rt. Hon. Lord Howard of Lympne, CH, QC
Lord Janner of Braunstone, QC
Lord Joffe, CBE
Lord Kalms
Lord Kestenbaum
Baroness King of Bow
Baroness Kramer
Rt. Hon. Lord Lawson of Blaby
Lord Leigh of Hurley
Lord Lester of Herne Hill, QC
Lord Levene of Portsoken, KBE
Lord Levy
Lord Livingston of Parkhead
Lord Mendelsohn
Rt. Hon. Lord Millett
Lord Moser, KCB, CBE
Rt. Hon. Lord Neuberger of Abbotsbury
Baroness Neuberger, DBE
Rt. Hon. Baroness Oppenheim-Barnes
Lord Palmer of Childs Hill, OBE
Lord Pannick
Lord Peston
Rt. Hon. Lord Phillips of Worth Matravers, KG
Lord Puttnam, CBE
Baroness Rebuck, DBE
Lord Saatchi
Lord Sacks
Lord Sassoon
Rt. Hon. Lord Sheldon
Lord Sherbourne of Didsbury, CBE
Lord Sterling of Plaistow, CBE, GCVO
Baroness Stern, CBE
Lord Stern of Brentford
Lord Stone of Blackheath
Lord Strasburger
Lord Sugar
Lord Triesman
Lord Turnberg
Lord Wasserman
Lord Weidenfeld
Lord Winston
Lord Wolfson of Aspley Guise
Lord Wolfson of Sunningdale

Rt. Hon. Lord Woolf
Rt. Hon. Lord Young of Graffham, DL

MEMBERS OF PARLIAMENT

Abrahams, Debbie, (Lab.), Oldham East and Saddleworth.
Bercow, Rt. Hon John, PC, (Mr Speaker), Buckingham
Berger, Luciana, (Lab.), Liverpool Wavertree
Djanogly, Jonathan S. (C.), Huntingdon
Ellis, Michael (C), Northampton North
Ellman, Louise (Lab.), Liverpool Riverside
Fabrikant, Michael (C.), Lichfield
Featherstone, Lynne (Lib.), Hornsey & Wood Green
Halfon, Robert, (C), Harlow
Hamilton, Fabian (Lab.), Leeds North East
Harrington, Richard, (C), Watford
Hodge, Rt. Hon Margaret, PC (Lab.), Barking
Huppert, Julian, (Lib.), Cambridge
Kaufman, Rt. Hon. Sir Gerald, PC (Lab.), Manchester, Gorton
Letwin, Rt Hon. Oliver, PC (C.), Dorset West
Lewis, Ivan (Lab.), Bury South
Lewis, Dr Julian (C.), New Forest East
Miliband, Rt. Hon Edward, PC, (Lab.) Doncaster North
Rifkind, Rt. Hon. Sir Malcolm, PC, (C.), Kensington & Chelsea
Scott, Lee (C.), Ilford North
Shapps, Rt. Hon. Grant, PC (C.), Welwyn and Hatfield
Winnick, David (Lab.), Walsall North

KNIGHTS

Sir Martyn Arbib, Kt, DL
Hon. Sir David Bean, Kt, QC
Sir Franklin Berman, KCMG
Sir Howard Bernstein, Kt
Sir Michael Berry, Kt, FRS
Sir Geoffrey Bindman, Kt, Hon QC
Sir Victor Blank, Kt
Sir Louis Blom-Cooper, Kt, QC
Sir Walter Bodmer, Kt, FRS
Sir Arnold Burgen, Kt, FRS
Rt. Hon. Sir Stanley Burnton, Kt, PC, QC
Hon. Sir Michael Burton, Kt, QC
His Honour Sir Clive Callman, Kt
Sir Roy Calne, Kt, FRS
Sir Trevor Chinn, Kt, CVO
Sir Michael Codron, Kt, CBE
Sir Ivor Harold Cohen, Kt, CBE, TD
Sir Philip Cohen, Kt, FRS
Sir Ronald Cohen, Kt
Hon. Sir Anthony Colman, Kt, QC
Sir Alcon Copisarow, Kt
Sir Ivor Crewe, Kt, DL

Sir Jonathan Cunliffe, Kt, CB
Sir Harry Djanogly, Kt, CBE
Hon. Sir Bernard Eder. Kt, QC
Sir Arnold Elton, Kt, CBE
Sir Anthony Epstein, Kt, CBE, FRS
Rt. Hon. Sir Terence Etherton, Kt, PC, QC
Sir Marc Feldmann, Kt, FRS
Sir Alan Fersht, Kt, FRS
Sir Paul Fox, Kt, CBE
Rt. Hon. Sir Lawrence Freedman, KCMG, CBE, PC,
Sir Ian Gainsford, Kt
Sir Peter Gershon, Kt, CBE, FREng
Rt. Hon. Sir Martin Gilbert, Kt, CBE, PC
Sir Clive Gillinson, Kt, CBE
Hon. Sir Henry Globe, Kt
Sir David Paul Goldberg, Kt
Sir Roy Goode, Kt, CBE, QC, FBA
Sir Donald Gordon, Kt
Sir Gerald Henry Gordon, Kt, CBE, QC (Scot)
Sir Allan Green, KCB, QC
Sir Philip Green, Kt
Sir Alan Greengross, Kt, DL
Sir Ronald Grierson, Kt
Sir Ralph Halpern, Kt
Sir Ronald Harwood, Kt, CBE
Sir Maurice Hatter, Kt
Sir Michael Heller, Kt
Hon. Sir Richard Henriques, Kt, QC
Sir Peter Hirsch, Kt, FRS
Sir Nicholas Hytner, Kt
Sir Jeremy Isaacs, Kt
Rt. Hon. Sir Francis Jacobs, KCMG, PC, QC
Sir Anish Kapoor, Kt
Rt. Hon. Sir Gerald Kaufman, Kt, PC, MP
Sol Kerzner, KCMG
Sir Aaron Klug, OM, Kt, FRS
Sir Ralph Kohn, Kt, FRS
Sir Hans Kornberg, Kt, FRS
Sir Peter Lachmann, Kt, FRS
Sir Dennis Landau, Kt
Sir Elihu Lauterpacht, Kt, CBE, QC
Sir Ivan Lawrence, Kt, QC
Sir Geoffrey Leigh, Kt
Rt. Hon. Sir Brian Leveson, Kt, PC, QC
Sir Leigh Lewis, KCB
Rt. Hon. Sir Kim Lewison, Kt, PC, QC
Sir Gavin Lightman, Kt, QC
Sir Stuart Anthony Lipton, Kt
Sir Sydney Lipworth, Kt, Hon. QC
Sir Michael Marmot, Kt,
Sir David Michels, Kt
Sir Jonathan Miller, Kt, CBE
Sir Michael Moritz, KBE
Sir Harry Ognall, Kt, DL
Sir Michael Pepper, Kt, FRS
Sir Mark Pepys, Kt, FRS

Sir Brian Pomeroy, Kt, CBE
Sir Erich Reich, Kt
Rt. Hon. Sir Malcolm Rifkind, KCMG, PC, QC, MP
Sir John Ritblat, Kt
Rt. Hon. Sir Bernard Rix, Kt, PC, QC
Sir Nigel Rodley, KBE
Sir Norman Rosenthal, Kt
Sir Evelyn de Rothschild, Kt
Sir Peter Rubin, Kt
Sir Sydney Samuelson, Kt, CBE
Rt. Hon. Sir Stephen Sedley, Kt, PC, QC
Sir Nicholas Serota, CH, Kt
Sir Peter Shaffer, Kt, CBE
Sir Nigel Sheinwald, GCMG
Sir Antony Sher, KBE
Sir Maurice Shock, Kt
Hon. Sir David Sieff, Kt
Hon. Sir Stephen Silber, Kt, QC
Sir David Iser Smith, KCVO, AO
Sir Harry Solomon, Kt
Sir Martin Sorrell, Kt
Sir Sigmund Sternberg, Kt
Sir Tom Stoppard, OM, Kt, CBE
Sir Michael Stratton, Kt, FRS
Hon. Sir Michael Supperstone, Kt, QC
Sir Guenter Treitel, Kt, QC
Sir Nicholas Wald, Kt, FRS
Sir Mark Walport, Kt
Sir Mark Weinberg, Kt
Sir Arnold Wesker, Kt
Sir Bernard Zissman, Kt
Sir Jack Zunz, Kt, FREng

DAMES

Abramsky, Dame Jennifer
Blume, Dame Hilary
Duffield, Dame Vivien
Genn, Dame Hazel, QC (Hon.)
Higgins, Dame Rosalyn, (QC)
Hyde, Dame Helen
Porter, Dame Shirley
Rebuck, Dame Gail
Robins, Dame Ruth, BA
Ronson, Dame Gail
Rose, Dame Vivien, (Hon. Mrs Justice)
Suzman, Dame Janet
Waterman, Dame Fanny
Wolfson de Botton, Dame Janet

HEREDITARY PEERS

5th Viscount Bearsted
3rd Viscount Samuel
3rd Baron Greenhill
3rd Baron Marks of Broughton
3rd Baron Morris of Kenwood

3rd Baron Nathan
4th Baron Rothschild
5th Baron Swaythling

BARONETS

Cahn, Sir Albert Jonas
Jessel, Sir Charles John
Richardson, Sir Anthony Lewis
Tuck, Sir Bruce A. R.
Waley-Cohen, Sir Stephen

FELLOWS OF THE ROYAL SOCIETY

Abramsky, Samson
Berry, Sir Michael
Bodmer, Sir Walter
Born, Prof. Gustav Victor Rudolf
Brenner, Prof. Sydney, CH
Burgen, Sir Arnold
Calne, Sir Roy
Cohen, Prof. Sydney, CBE
Dunitz, Prof. Jack David
Dwek, Raymond
Epstein, Sir Michael Anthony, (Vice-President, 1986–91)
Fersht, Prof. Sir Alan
Glynn, Prof. Ian Michael
Goldstone, Prof. Jeffrey
Grant, Ian Philip
Halpern, Jack
Hirsch, Prof. Sir Peter Bernhard
Huppert, Dr Herbert
Ish-Horowicz, David
Josephson, Prof. Brian David
Kalmus, George Ernest
Kennard, Dr Olga, OBE
Klug, Sir Aaron, OM, (President 1995–2000)
Kohn, Sir Ralph, FRS
Kornberg, Prof. Sir Hans Leo
Lachmann, Sir Peter Julius
Levitt, Prof. Malcolm
Levitt, Prof. Michael
Mandelstam, Prof. Stanley
Mestel, Prof. Leon
Neumann, Prof. Bernard H.
Pepper, Dr Sir Michael
Pepys, Prof. Sir Mark
Roitt, Prof. Ivan
Sanders, Prof. Jeremy
Segal, Prof. Dr Anthony Walter
Stratton, Sir. Michael
Wald, Prof. Nicholas
Waldmann, Prof. Herman
Weinberg, Prof. Felix
Weiskrantz, Prof. Lawrence
Woolfson, Prof. Michael Mark

FELLOWS OF THE BRITISH ACADEMY

Abulafia, Prof. David Samuel
Bogdanor, Prof. Vernon, CBE
Caspi, Prof. Avshalom
Collins, of Mapesbury, Lord
de Lange, Rabbi Nicholas
Feldman, Prof. David, QC (Hon)
Fredman, Prof. Sandra
Freeman, Prof. Michael
Gershuny, Prof. Jonathan
Genn, Prof. Dame Hazel, CBE
Glucksmann, Prof. Miriam
Goode, Sir Roy
Goodman, Prof. Martin
Gordon, Prof. Robert
Hajnal, Prof. John
Hamilton, Prof. Alastair
Israel, Prof. Jonathan Irvine
Josipovici, Prof. Gabriel David
Lappin, Prof. Shalom
Lewis, Prof. Bernard
Lowenthal, Professor David
Lukes, Prof. Steven
Marks, Prof. Shula
Moser, Lord, KCB, CBE
Steiner, Prof. George
Stern, of Brentford, Lord
Supple, Prof. Barry, CBE
Treitel, Sir Guenter
Yamey, Prof. Basil Selig, CBE

Corresponding Fellows

Aumann, Prof. Robert J.
Bar-Yosef, Prof. Ofer
Blau, Prof. Joshua
Chomsky, Prof. Noam
Cohen, Prof. Ralph
Wasserstein, Prof. Bernard

Honorary Fellows

Marmot, Sir Michael
Rothschild, Lord, OM, GBE
Woolf, Lord Harry

VICTORIA CROSS

Lieutenant Frank Alexander De Pass
Captain Robert Gee, M.C.
Lance Corporal Leonard Keysor
Acting Corporal Issy Smith
Private Jack White
Lieut.-Cmdr. Thomas William Gould, RNVR
Flt Sgt Arthur Louis Aarons
Co Sgt Major John Kenneally

GEORGE CROSS

Errington, Harry
Lewin, Sgt. Raymond M., RAF
Latutin, Capt. Simmon
Newgass, Lieutenant-Commander Harold
Reginald, RNVR

ORDER OF MERIT

Howard, Sir Michael Eliot
Klug, Sir Aaron, FRS
Rothschild, Lord
Stoppard, Sir Tom

COMPANIONS OF HONOUR

Joseph Herman Hertz (1943)
Leopold Amery (1945)
Arthur David Waley (1956)
Lewis Silkin (1965)
Emanuel Shinwell (1965)
Arnold Abraham Goodman (1972)
Robert Mayer (1973)
Henry Cohen (1974)
Max Perutz (1975)
Lucian Freud (1983)
Keith Joseph (1986)
Sydney Brenner (1987)
Cesar Milstein (1995)
Denys Lasdun (1995)
Eric Hobsbawm (1998)
Harold Pinter (2002)
Michael Eliot Howard, (2002)
Michael Howard, QC (2011)
Nicholas Serota (2013)

NOBEL PRIZE WINNERS

Between 1901 and 2014, Nobel Prizes have been awarded to more than 800 individuals, of whom at least 20% were Jews.

Peace

Tobias Asser; Menachem Begin; Rene Cassin; Alfred Fried; Henry Kissinger; Shimon Peres; Yitzhak Rabin; Sir Joseph Rotblat; Elie Wiesel.

Physics

Alexi Abrikosov; Zhores Alferov; Hans Bethe; Felix Bloch; Aage Bohr; Niels Bohr; Max Born; Georges Charpak; Claude Cohen-Tannoudji; Leon Cooper; Albert Einstein; Francois Englert; Richard Feynman; James Franck; Ilya Frank; Jerome Friedman; Dennis Gabor; Murray Gell-Mann; Vitaly Ginzburg; Donald Glaser;

Sheldon Glashow; Roy Glauber; David Gross; Serge Haroche; Gustav Hertz; Robert Hofstadter; Brian Josephson; Lev Landau; Leon Lederman; David Lee; Gabriel Lippmann; Albert Michelson; Ben Mottelson; Douglas D. Osheroff; Wolfgang Pauli; Saul Perlmutter; Arno Penzias; Martin Perl; H. David Politzer; Isidor Isaac Rabi; Frederick Reines; Burton Richter; Adam Riess; Melvin Schwartz; Julian Schwinger; Emilio Segre; Jack Steinberger; Otto Stern; Igor Tamm; Steven Weinberg; Eugene Wigner.

Chemistry

Sidney Altman; Adolph von Baeyer; Paul Berg; Herbert Brown; Melvin Calvin; Martin Chalfie; Aaron Ciechanover, Walter Gilbert; Fritz Haber; Herbert Hauptman; Dudley Herschebach; Gerhard Herzberg; George de Hevesy; Avraham Hershko; Roald Hoffmann; Jerome Karle; Martin Karplus; Aaron Klug; Walter Kohn; Roger Kornberg; Robert Lefkowitz; Michael Levitt; Rudolf Marcus; Henri Moissan; Max Perutz; Ilya Prigogine; Irwin Rose; Daniel Shechtman; William Stein; Otto Wallach; Arieh Warshel; Richard Willstatter; Ada Yonath.

Physiology and Medicine

Richard Axel; Julius Axelrod; David Baltimore; Robert Barany; Gary Becker; Baruj Benacerraf; Bruce Beutler; Gunter Blobel; Konrad Bloch; Baruch Blumberg; Sydney Brenner; Michael Brown; Sir Ernst Chain; Stanley Cohen; Gerald Maurice Edelman; Gertrude Eilon; Paul Ehrlich; Joseph Erlanger; Andrew Z. Fire; Edmund H. Fischer; Robert Furchgott; Herbert Gasser; Alfred Gilman; Joseph Goldstein; Paul Greengard; H. Robert Horvitz; Francois Jacob; Eric Kandel; Sir Bernard Katz; Arthur Kornberg; Sir Hans Krebs; Karl Landsteiner; Joshua Lederberg; Rita Levi-Montalcini; Fritz Lipmann; Otto Loewi; Salvador Luria; Andre Lwoff; Elias Metchnikoff; Otto Meyerhoff; Cesar Milstein; Hermann Joseph Muller; David Nathans; Marshall Nirenberg; Andrew Schally; Stanley Prusiner; Tadeus Reichstein; Martin Rodbell; James E. Rothman; Randy W. Schekman; Ralph Steinman; Howard Martin Temin; John Robert Vane; Harold Varmus; Selman Abraham Waksman; George Wald; Otto Warburg; Rosalyn Yalow.

Literature

Shmuel Agnon; Saul Bellow; Henri Bergson; Joseph Brodsky; Elias Canetti; Nadine Gordimer; Paul von Heyse; Imre Kertész; Elfriede Jelinek; Boris Pasternak; Harold Pinter; Nelly Sachs; Jaroslav Seifert; Isaac Bashevis Singer.

Economics

George Akerlof; Kenneth Arrow; Robert Aumann; Gary Becker; Peter Diamond; Robert Fogel; Milton Friedman; John Harsanyi; Leonid Hurwicz; Daniel Kahneman; Leonid Kantorovich; Lawrence Klein; Paul Krugman; Simon Kuznets; Wassily Leontief; Harry Markowitz; Eric Maskin; Merton Miller; Franco Modigliani; Roger Myerson; Alvin E. Roth; Paul Samuelson; Myron Scholes; Reinhard Selten; Herbert Simon; Robert Solow; Joseph Stiglitz.

Who's Who

AARON, Martin, MBA, FAIA, FRSM, FRSA.
b. London, Jan. 25, 1937; m. Jean née Joseph; Vis. Prof. Staffordshire University; Life Fel. Royal Society Medicine; Life Fel. Royal Society of Arts; Hon. T. British Association for the Study of Spirituality (2010-); Pres. B'nai B'rith First-lodge of England (2009-11); M. Advisory Cttee. Chizuk for Mental Health (2006-); Fdr. Ch. National Spirituality and Mental Health (interfaith) Forum (2003–); Adv. M. All-Party Parliamentary Group on Mental Health (2001-); Mem. Advisory Council, Three Faiths Forum (1998-); Fdr. and H. Pres. Jewish Association for the Mental Illness (1989-); Mentor, The Prince's Trust (1995–2006); form. Mem. Concern for the Mentally Ill (1992-98); T. Ravenswood Foundation (1986-90); Mem. Board of Deputies (1979-86); Fdr. Ch. Jewish Society for the Mentally Handicapped (1977-86); form. Mem. Adv. Council, MIND (1976-83); form. Mem. Adv. Council, MENCAP (1975-83); Fdr. Ch. Ravenswood Aid Cttee. (1955-63).
Add c/o JAMI, Olympia House, Armitage Road, London NW11 7RQ
Tel 020 8458 2223 Mob 07973 375 170
Email mentalitygb@aol.com

ABRAHAM, Dayan Yonason,
Rabbi, New Hendon Minyan (2006-); Dayan, London Beth Din (2001-); Dayan, Melbourne Beth Din (1997-2001); Rabbi, Caulfield Hebrew Congregation (1995-2001); Rabbinical Consultant, Jewish Association for Business Ethics.
Add The London Beth Din, 305 Ballards Lane, North Finchley, London N12 8GB
Tel 020 8343 6270 *Fax* 020 8343 6257
Email info@bethdin.org.uk *Website* www.theus.org.uk

ABRAMS, Hester,
Dir. Jewish Book Week (2012-); Board of Deputies, Deputy, United Synagogue (2012-); Mem. Commission on Women in Jewish Leadership (2011-12); Board of Deputies Deputy, Brondesbury Park United Synagogue (2009-12); Advisor and Tru. Project Mosaic (2009-12); Mediator, Communications consultant, TV researcher, Facilitator (2004-12); Ed. Reuters Magazine (2000-04); Foreign and Financial correspondent and Ed. Reuters (1988-2004).
Add Jewish Book Week, ORT House, 126 Albert Street, London NW1 7NE
Tel 020 7446 8772
Email hester@jewishbookweek.com *Website* www.jewishbookweek.com

ABRAMSON, Glenda (née Melzer), BA, MA, PhD (Rand), H. D.Litt (HUC).
b. Johannesburg, Nov. 16, 1940; m. David; Academic; Prof. Hebrew and Jewish Studies, University Oxford (2006-); Leverhulme Emer. Fellowship (2009-10); form. Cowley Lecturer Post-Biblical Hebrew, Oxford (1989-2006); Dr. of Humane Letters Honoris Causa HUC-JIR (1998); Ed. Journal of Modern Jewish Studies. Among recent publications: Soldiers' Tales: Two Palestinian Jewish Soldiers in the Ottoman Army during the First World War (2013); Hebrew Writing of the First World War (2008); Ed. with H. Kilpatrick, Religious Perspectives in Modern Hebrew and Islamic Literatures (2006); Ed. Encyclopaedia of Modern Jewish Culture (2005); Modern Jewish Mythologies (2000); The Experienced Soul: Studies in Amichai (1997); The Oxford Book of Hebrew Short Stories (1996); Tradition and Trauma (1995, with D. Patterson); Jewish Education and Learning (1994, with T. Parfitt); Journal of Modern Jewish Studies (Ed.).
Add Clarendon Institute Building, Walton Street, Oxford OX1 2HG
Email glenda.abramson@stx.ox.ac.uk

ABULAFIA, David Samuel Harvard, MA, PhD, Litt.D, FBA, FRHistS.
b. Twickenham, Dec. 12, 1949; m. Anna née Sapir; Historian; Prof. Mediterranean History, Cambridge; Fel. Gonville and Caius College (1974-); Commendatore dellí Ordine della Stella della Solidarietà Italiana (2003). Among recent publications: The Great Sea (2011); The Discovery of Mankind (2008); Italy in the Central Middle Ages (Ed. 2004); The Mediterranean in History (2003); Medieval Frontiers (Ed. 2002); Mediterranean Encounters (2000); Cambridge Medieval History, vol. 5, 1198-1300 (Ed. 1999); The Western

Mediterranean Kingdoms (1997).
Add Gonville & Caius College, Cambridge CB2 1TA
Tel 01233 332 473
Email dsa1000@hermes.cam.ac.uk

ALBERTI, Sir (Kurt) George Matthew Mayer, MA, BM, BCh, Kt, DPhil, FRCP, FRCPE, FRCPath.
b. Sept. 27, 1937; m. Prof. Stephanie A. Amiel; Ch. Kings College Hospital NHS Foundation Trust, London (2011-15); Ch. Diabetes UK (2009-12); Snr. Research Fel. Investigator, Imperial College, London (2002-); Pres. Royal College of Physicians (1997–2002); Prof. of Medicine, University of Newcastle upon Tyne (1985–2002), Dean of Medicine (1995–97); H. DSc: Warwick, Cranfield (2005). Publ.: Author and Ed. of many medical publications.
Add 57 Lancaster Avenue, West Norwood, London SE27 9EL
Tel 020 8670 8770
Email george.alberti@ncl.ac.uk

ALDERMAN, Geoffrey, D. Litt (Oxon), MA, D.Phil (Oxon), FRHistS, FRSA, FICPD, MIQA, MCMI.
b. Hampton Court, Feb. 10, 1944; m. Marion née Freed; Prof. Politics Contemporary History University Buckingham (2007-); Guest Prof. Ariel University, Israel (2010-16); V. Pres. American Intercontinental University, London (2002-06); V. Pres. Touro College, N.Y. (1999-2002); Pro. V. Ch. and Prof. Middlesex University (1994-99); Visiting Fel. Oxford Centre for Higher Education Policy Studies; form. Prof. of Politics and Contemporary History, Royal Holloway College (London University). Among recent publications: Modern British Jewry; Controversy and Crisis: Studies in the History of the Jews in Modern Britain (2008); The Federation of Synagogues 1887-1987, London Jewry and London Politics, 1889-1986; British Jewry Since Emancipation.
Add 172 Colindeep Lane, London NW9 6EA
Email geoffreyalderman@gmail.com *Website* www.geoffreyalderman.com

ALEXANDER-PASSE, Anita,
b. London, July 23, 1931; Speaker; Fundraiser; Initiated exchange of nurses and medical personnel between Homerton Hospital in Hackney and Rambam Medical Centre in Haifa, Israel (2001-); Dir. British Friends of Rambam Medical Centre (1993-); Ch. Operation Wheelchairs Cttee. (1991-); Past Ch. Na'amat/Pioneer Women and WIZO; Correspondent, Jewish Chronicle (1980-90); Volunteer, Miyad (1993-97); Mem. Board of Deputies; JIA; Achdut and Friends of Ben Gurion University. Publ.: A Celebration of Life in Poetry and Prose (2001).
Add 1 Opal Court, 120 Regents Park Road, London N3 3HY
Tel 020 8371 1500
Email anita@rambamuk.co.uk *Website* www.rambamuk.co.uk

ALONY, Rabbi Dr Dayan Michel Asher, B.A. PhD.
b. Dublin; Mar. 29, 1946; Dayan in Europe, based in Gateshead UK (2005-); Dayan, USA Federation Kashrus Board (1999-2005); Chief Rabbi and Av Beth Din, Helsinki, The Jewish Community of Finland (1996-98); Chief Rabbi and Av Beth Din, The Jewish Community of Estonia (1996-98); Snr. Rabbi, Concord Hotel, New York (1990-96); Dayan, USA The Federation Kashrus Board (1990-96); Rabbi and Dayan Long Island Iggud Harabonim (1988-90); Snr. Lecturer, Ida Crown College, Chicago (1985-88); Rabbinical Advisor to Lord Bishop Cremin of the Catholic Community, Sydney (1982-84); Fdr. Hineni Movement of Australia (1975 -); Chief Min. Central Synagogue Sydney Australia (1975-84); Dayan, the Sydney Beth Din (1975-84); Supervising Rabbi, Liverpool Kashrut Board (1973-75); Rabbi Southport Hebrew Congregation (1968-75); Ch. Council of Christians and Jews (1968-75); Chaplain the Jewish Home for the Blind (1969-75); Co-Fdr. Counterpoint Programmes; Board mem. Shalom College, University of New South Wales; Presenter N.S.W. Yiddish Programs; Chaplain Merseyside J.L. & G. Brigade, Major.
Add 46 Windermere Street West, Gateshead, Tyne & Wear NE8 1TX
Tel 0191 442 0576/07949 613 613
Email rebmichel@live.co.uk

ALPERT, Michael, MA, PhD.

b. London, Dec. 24, 1935; m. Marie Pradillo Gomez de Acosta; Pres. JHSE (2009-10); Emeritus Prof. of Modern and Contemporary History of Spain, University Westminster (1996-2001), Snr. Lecturer, Reader, (1966-96). Publ.: The Republican Army in the Spanish Civil War (2013); The Chaste Wife, translated from Elia Karmona's Ladino Novel La Muz'er Onesta, (2009); Secret Judaism and the Spanish Inquisition (2nd Edition 2008); A New International History of the Spanish Civil War (1994, 2nd Edition 2004); London 1849 (2004); Two Spanish Picaresque Novels (2nd Edition 2003).

Add 3 Donaldson Road, London NW6 6NA

Tel 020 7624 9116

Email malpert@onetel.com

ANGIER, Carole (née Brainin), MA (Oxon), MLitt (Cantab), FRSL.

b. London, Oct. 30, 1943; Writer; Associate Lecturer, Creative Writing MA, Oxford Brookes University (2011-12); Tutor in Life Writing, Birkbeck College, London (2005-11); Royal Literary Fund Fel. Oxford Brookes University (2010-11), University Warwick (2008-09, 1999-2003); Fdr. and Tutor, Practice of Biography, University Warwick (2002-03); Tutor, Open University (1975-85). Among recent publications: Jean Rhys: Life and Work and the Double Bond: Primo Levi, A Biography (both reissued, 2011); Life Writing: A Writers' and Artists' Companion (Co-author Sally Cline 2010); See How I Land: Oxford poets and exiled writers (Co-Ed. 2009); Lyla and Majnon by Hasan Bamyani (T. and Ed. 2008); The Story of My Life: Refugees Writing in Oxford (Ed. 2005); The Double Bond: Primo Levi, a Biography (2002); Tongue Pie by Fred Russell (Ed.).

Add 13 High Street, Ascott-under-Wychwood, Oxon OX7 6AW

Tel 01993 830 414

Email carole@cangier.co.uk

ANTICONI, Paul,

Chief Exec. World Jewish Relief (2006-); T. Tree Aid (2006-); Head of International Aid, British Red Cross Society (1999–2006); Leader of Disaster Response Operations, Red Cross (1994-2006).

Add World Jewish Relief, Oscar Joseph House, 54 Crewys Road, London NW2 2AD

Tel 020 8736 1250 *Fax* 020 8736 1259

Email info@wjr.org.uk *Website* www.wjr.org.uk

APPLE, Rabbi Dr Raymond, AO, RFD, MLitt, BA, LLB, Hon LLD, Hon DUniv.

b. Melbourne, Dec. 27, 1935; Jt. Pres. Australian Council of Christians and Jews (1996-); Snr. Rabbi, Australian Defence Force (1988-2006); Dayan and Reg. Sydney Beth Din (1975-2005); Emer. Rabbi, Great Synagogue, Sydney, Snr. Rabbi (1972-2005); Life Rabbinic Gov.; Pres. Association of Rabbis and Ministers of Australia and New Zealand (1988-1992, 1980-4); Pres. Australian Jewish Historical Society (1985-9); M. Bayswater Synagogue (1960-5), Hampstead Synagogue (1965-1972); H. V. Pres. New South Wales Bd. of Jewish Education; Tru. and Emer. Master Mandelbaum House, Sydney University; form. Lecturer, Judaic Studies, Sydney University; Lecturer, Jewish Law, NSW University; Religious Dir. AJY (1959-63). Publ.: Cast and Characters: Jewish Notes on New Testament People (2014); 80 Days and 80 Nights: Wise Words for Everyday (2012); Education by Degrees: Masonic Notes (2012); Oz Torah: Weekly emails since 1995; Episodes and Eccentrics (2010); Freemasonry: Studies, Speeches and Sensibilities (2009); 'Let's Ask the Rabbi' (2009); To Be Continued: Memoirs and Musings (2009); The Big Shule: A History of the Great Synagogue, Sydney (2008); The Jewish Way: Jews and Judaism in Australia (3rd edition 2002); Francis Lyon Cohen: The Passionate Patriot (1995); The Hampstead Synagogue, 1892-1967 (1967).

Add 20/6 Hatekufah, Jerusalem 92628 Israel

Tel +972 (2) 6794 180

Email rabbiapple@oztorah.com *Website* www.oztorah.com

ARIEL, David, PhD, MA, BA.

b. New York, USA, June 30, 1949; Pres. Oxford Centre for Hebrew and Jewish Studies (2011-); Pres. Siegal College of Judaic Studies, Cleveland, Ohio, USA (1982-2007). Publ.: Kabbalah: The Mystic Quest in Judaism (2006); Spiritual Judaism (1998); What do Jews Believe? (1995).

Add Oxford Centre for Hebrew And Jewish Studies, Yarnton Manor, Yarnton Oxford OX5 1PY

ARKUSH, Jonathan,

b. London, 1954; Barrister and Mediator, 11 Stone Buildings; Deputy Master Chancery Division; V. Pres. Board of Deputies of British Jews (2009-); ADRg Award for services to Mediation (2006); Called to Bar, Middle Temple (1977); Mem. Lincoln's Inn.

Add 6 Bloomsbury Square, London WC1A 2LP

Email arkush@11sb.com *Website* www.bod.org.uk www.11sb.com

ARKUSH, Rabbi Shmuel,

b. May 5, 1951; Rabbi, Birmingham Jewish Community Care (2000-); Chaplain of the Midlands Region Chaplaincy Bd. (1980-85); Dir. Lubavitch in the Midlands; Dir. Operation Judaism; Hd. B.J.E.B. Talmud Torah.

Add 95 Willows Road, Birmingham B12 9QF

Tel 0121 440 6673

Email sarkush@lubavitchuk.com

AUERBACH, Geraldine Yvonne (née Kretzmar), MBE, BA (rand), STC (UCT).

b. Kimberley, South Africa, to UK 1962; m. Ronnie; Fdr. Dir. Jewish Music Institute, SOAS, University London (1999-2011); Dir. 'Klezimer in the Park', Regents Park (2009-10), 'Simcha on the Square', Trafalgar Square (2006-8); Hon. Fel. SOAS (2008); presented a Day of Jewish Culture, Millennium Dome (2000), many premières including Kaddish for Terezin, Canterbury Cathedral (1986); Sacred Service, St Paul's Cathedral (1995) and York Minster (1990); Fdr. Dir. London Jewish Music Festival (1984-2000); established first full-time Jewish music lectureship at City University (With Professor Malcolm Troup, 1991); initiated a record label for historic or unrecorded Jewish music (1985) and established Jewish Music Distribution.

Add P.O. Box 232, Harrow, Middlesex HA1 2NN

Tel 020 8909 2445 *Fax* 020 8909 1030

AVIDAN, Rabbi Hillel, MA .

b. London, July 16, 1933, m. Ruth; M. Durban Progressive Jewish Congregation (2005-); First Ch. South African Faith Communities Environment Institute (SAFCEI 2007-8); Ch. Southern African Association Progressive Rabbis (2004-8); M. Bet David Reform Congregation, Johannesburg (1992-2003); Ch. Southern African Association Progressive Rabbis (1995-9); M. Ealing Liberal Synagogue (1986-92); and Ch. ULPS Rabbinic Conference (1990-2); form. M. West Central Liberal Synagogue (1985-92); form. M. Wimbledon and District Reform Synagogue (1974-81), Ch. RSGB Assembly of Rabbis, (1978-80), Teacher Reali High School, Haifa; Libr. Haifa University. Publ.: Feasts and Fasts of Israel, (Contr.) Judaism and Ecology; Renewing the vision.

Add 28 O'Connor Road, Durban 3629 RSA

Tel +27 31 266 2792 *Fax* +27 31 209 2429

Email dpjc@sbsa.com

AZIZ, Alan, BSc., ACCA.

b. London, Aug. 1, 1968; Chartered Accountant; Dir. Zionist Council Europe (1998-); Exec. Dir. ZF Great Britain and Ireland; Dir. Israel Connect European Training Programme.

Add Zionist Federation, Box 1948, 116 Ballards Lane, Finchley, London N3 2DN

Tel 020 8202 0202

Email alan@zfuk.org

BAKER, Adrienne, PhD, BSc.

b. Manchester, Feb. 15, 1936; UKCP Regd. Psychotherapist; Family Therapist and University Lecturer; Hon. Visiting Fel. School of Psychotherapy, Regent's College, London; Private Clinical Practice. Publ.: The Jewish Woman in Contemporary Society: Transitions and Traditions (1993).

Add 16 Sheldon Avenue, Highgate, London N6 4JT

Tel 020 8340 5970 (home)

Email adriennebaker@hotmail.co.uk *Website* www.highgate-psychotherapy.co.uk

BALFOUR-LYNN, Dr Lionel Peter, MA, MD (Cantab), FRCPCH, DCH.

b. London, May, 4, 1928; m. June Anne née Herbert; Retired Paediatrician; Hon Paediatric Consultant, Hammersmith Hospital. Publ: numerous articles on Paediatric Asthma.

Add 69 Hampstead Way, London NW11 7LG

Tel 020 8455 9063

Email lbl@120harley.co.uk

BANNISTER, Sharon,

Pres. Jewish Representative Council of Greater Manchester and Region.

Add JRC, Jewish Community Centre, Bury Old Road, Manchester M7 4QY

Tel 0161 720 8721

Email office@jewishmanchester.org *Website* www.jewishmanchester.org

BARNETT, Rt. Hon. Joel Barnett, Baron of Heywood & Royton, PC, JP.

b. Manchester, Oct. 14, 1923, m. Lilian née Goldstone; Accountant and Ch. and Dirs. of Companies; form. V. Ch. BBC Govs.; Mem. European Union Select Cttee.; Ch. European Union Sub. Cttee. on Finance, Trade and Industry; T. Victoria and Albert Museum; Ch. Education Broadcasting Society Trust; Ch. Public Accounts Cttee. House of Commons (1979-83); MP (Lab.) for Heywood and Royton (1964-83); Mem. of Cabinet (1977-79); Chief Sec. to H.M. Treasury (1974-79); form. Ch. Mem. Public Exp. Cttee.; Hon. Fel. Birkbeck College, London University; H. Doctorate, Strathclyde; Mem. Halle Cttee. Publ.: Inside the Treasury (1982).

Add 7 Hillingdon Road, Whitefield, Manchester M45 7QQ

BARNETT, Sara M., BA (Hons), RGN, RM, PGCE.

b. London, June 22, 1967; m. Dr Benjamin Jacobs; Research Midwife, Imperial College London (2010); Lecturer in Midwifery, City University London (2001); Antenatal and Resuscitation Midwife, The Portland Hospital (1993).

Add 32 Wykeham Road, London NW4 2SU

Tel 020 8203 2241 Mobile 07932 730 944

Email sara@smbarnett.com

BARON-COHEN, Gerald, BA, FCA.

b. London, July 13, 1932, m. Daniella née Weiser; Chartered Acct.; Pres. First Lodge of England, B'nai B'rith; National T. B'nai B'rith, District 15; V. Pres. Hillel Foundation; V. Ch. U.J.S.; Ed. Mosaic; Dep. Ed. New Middle East; Ch. Bamah-Forum for Jewish Dialogue (Jewish Unity Working Group).

Add 70 Wildwood Road NW11 6UJ

Email office2gbc@gmail.com

BAUM, Prof. Michael, MB, ChB, ChM, FRCS, FRCR (Hon), MD (Hon).

b. May 31, 1937; m. Judith née Marcus; Prof. Emer. Surgery and Visiting Prof. Medical Humanities, University College London; Prof. Surgery, University College London (1996-2002), Prof. Surgery, Royal Marsden Hospital and Institute of Cancer Research (1990-96), Prof. Surgery, Kings College London (1980-90). Publ.: The Third Tablet of the Holy Covenant (2013); Breast Beating: One man's odyssey in the search for an understanding of breast cancer, the meaning of life and other easy questions (2010); Classic Papers in Breast Disease (2003); Breast Cancer—The Facts (1981, 3rd edition 1994); multiple publications on breast cancer, cancer therapy, cancer biology and the philosophy of science; Karl

Popper Memorial Lecture, LSE 2009. Prizes: Gold Medal, Worshipful Company Apothecaries for Innovation in Therapeutics (2009); Swiss, St. Gallen Award, Breast Cancer Research (2007); Gold medal, International College of Surgeons (1994).

Add 4 Corringway, London NW11 7ED

Tel 020 8905 5069

Email michael@mbaum.freeserve.co.uk *Website* www.michaelbaum.co.uk/home.html

BAYFIELD, Rabbi Prof. Anthony Michael, CBE, MA (Cantab) DD (Cantaur).

b. Ilford, July 4, 1946; Pres. Movement for Reform Judaism; Prof. Jewish Theology and Thought, Leo Baeck College; Hd. Movement for Reform Judaism (2005-10); Chief Exec. Reform Synagogues of Great Britain (1995-2004); Dir. Sternberg Centre for Judaism (1983-2004); Rabbi, North-West Surrey Synagogue (1972-82); Ch. Assembly of Rabbis, RSGB (1980-1). Publ.: Beyond the Dysfunctional Family: Jews, Christians and Muslims in Dialogue (2012); He Kissed Him and They Wept (Ed. with Sidney Brichto and Eugene Fisher) (2001); Sinai, Law and Responsible Autonomy (1993); Dialogue with a Difference (Ed. with Marcus Braybrooke) (1992); Churban, The Murder of the Jews of Europe (1981).

Add c/o The Sternberg Centre for Judaism, 80 East End Road N3 2SY

BEECHAM, Lord Jeremy Hugh, MA, DCL, DL, H. Fellow, Northumbria University.

b. Leicester, Nov. 11, 1944; m. Brenda Elizabeth née Woolf (dec'd); Solicitor; Opposition Justice Spokesman, House of Lords (2012-); V. Ch. Members Adv. Bd. Harold Hartog School of Government, Tel Aviv University (2009-); Mem. Bd. New Israel Fund (2007-); Newcastle City Councillor (1967-); Ch. Local Govt. Association (1997-04), V. Ch. (2004-10); Ch. Labour Party NEC (2005-06); Ch. Association Metropolitan Authorities (1991-97); Leader Newcastle City Council (1977-94); Com. English Heritage (1983-87).

Add 39 The Drive, Newcastle upon Tyne NE3 4AJ

Email beechamj@parliament.uk

BELLOS, Vivienne, LRAM, ARCM.

b. Southend-on-Sea, Apr. 3, 1951; Musician; Dir. of Music, North Western Reform Synagogue; Musical Dir. Alyth Youth Singers; Artisitic Dir. Alyth Centre for Jewish Music.

Tel 020 8457 8795

Email viv@alyth.org.uk

BENARROCH, Rev. Halfon, BA.

b. Tangiers, Apr. 12, 1939; m. Delia née Sabah; Retired M. Bevis Marks; Emer. Hazan, Spanish and Portuguese Jews' Congregation.

Add 23 Lauderdale Tower, Barbican, London EC2Y 8BY

Tel 020 7638 5100

Email d.h@broch.org.uk

BENEDICTUS, David Henry, BA (Oxon).

b. London, Sept. 16, 1938; author; playwright; theatre Dir.; Hd. Drama, Putney High School; Royal Literary Fund Fel. (2007-08); Ed. Readings BBC Radio (1989-94) plus Radio 3 Drama from 1992; Commissioning Ed. Channel 4 (1984-86); Judith E. Wilson Vis. Fel. Cambridge University (1981-82); Producer 'Something Understood' (with Mark Tully); Berkoff's Macbeth for BBC Radio 4. Among recent publications: The Fourth of June (1962, 2013); Return to the Hundred Acre Wood (2009); Dropping Names (Memoirs) (2005); Floating Down to Camelot (1985); The Stamp Collector (1984); Local Hero (1983); Who Killed the Prince Consort? (1983); Whose Life is it Anyway? (1981); Lloyd George (1981); A Twentieth Century Man (1978); The Rabbi's Wife (1976); A World of Windows (1971); The Guru and the Golf Club (1969); Hump, or Bone by Bone Alive (1967); This Animal is Mischievous (1965); You're a Big Boy Now (1963).

Add Flat 1, 39 Sackville Gardens, Hove, East Sussex BN3 4GJ

Tel 07986 041386

Email davidbenedictus@hotmail.com

BENJAMIN, Bill,

Ch. UJIA (2012-); Mem. Jewish Leadership Council; form. Co-Ch. Assembly of Masorti Synagogues; form. Tru. JCoSS, Snr. Partner, Ares Management.

Email wbenjamin@aresmgmt.com

BENJAMIN, Marc Jonathan (Jon), LLB (Hons) (Manchester).

b. Croydon, Oct. 31, 1964; m. Suzanne née Taylor; Solicitor; Chief Exec. Board of Deputies of British Jews (2005-); form. Chief Exec. British ORT (1999-2004); Ch, Chief Executives' Forum for Jewish Charities; Bd. Mem. World Council of Jewish Communal Service; Mem, Charity Commission's Faiths Advisory Council; Mem. Policy Research Advisory Group, Institute for Jewish Policy Research.

Add Board of Deputies of British Jews, 6 Bloomsbury Square, London WC1A 2LP

Email info@bod.org.uk *Website* www.bod.org.uk

BERCOW, John, BA, MP.

b. Edgware, Jan. 19, 1963; m. Sally née Illman; Public Affairs Consultant; Speaker, House of Commons (2009-); Mem. International Development Select Committee (2004-); MP for Buckingham (1997-); Shadow Sec. of State, International Development (2003-4); Shadow M. Work and Pensions (2002); Shadow Chief Sec. to Treasury (2001-2); Special Adv. to Treasury M. (1995), to National Heritage Secretary (1995-96); Lambeth Councillor (1986-90).

Add House of Commons, London SW1A 0AA

Tel 020 7219 5300

Email bercowj@parliament.uk

BERKOVITCH, Rev. Mordechai, BA (Ed), Dip. Counselling, FIBA.

b. Sunderland, Feb. 15, 1934; H. Vis. M. Nightingale House (1974-2002); Dir. Jewish Studies, Carmel College (1984-92); H. Dir. Welfare Chief Rabbi's Cabinet (1980-1985); M. Kingston, Surbiton and District Synagogue (1972-84), Penylan Synagogue, Cardiff (1968-72), Central Synagogue, Birmingham (1956-68); Jewish Chaplain, Heathrow Airport (1976).

Add POB 2207, 45/3 King David Boulevard, Efrat 90435, Israel

Tel +972 (02) 676 4341 *Fax* +972 (02) 1532 676 4341

Email motisali@012.net.il

BERLINER, Martin,

CEO, Maccabi GB.

Add Shield House, Harmony Way, London NW4 2BZ

Email enquiries@maccabigb.org *Website* www.maccabigb.org

BERNSTEIN, Sir Howard, Kt.

b. Apr. 9, 1953; m. Vanessa; Chief Exec. Manchester City Council (1998-); Ch. ReBlackpool, (2008–10); Mem. Bd. Olympic Delivery Authority (2006–8); Sec. Commonwealth Games Organising Cttee. (1996–2002); Chief Exec. Manchester City Centre Task Force (1996–9).

Add Manchester City Council, Town Hall, Manchester M60 2LA

Tel 0161 234 3006

BINSTOCK, Dayan Ivan Alan, BSc.

b. London, Oct. 27, 1950; Dayan London Beth Din; Rabbi, St. Johns Wood Synagogue (1996-); M. Golders Green Synagogue (1980-1996), New Synagogue (1978-80), Finsbury Park Synagogue (1974-78), R. South-East London District Synagogue (1972-74); Principal, North West London Jewish Day School.

Add 2 Vale Close, Maida Vale, London W9 1RR

Tel 020 7289 6229

BLACK, Gerald David, LLB, PhD, FRHistS.

b. Montreal, Jan 9, 1928; m. Anita née Abrahams; Mem. of Council of JHSE (1992-), Pres. (1998-2000), Hon. S. (2000-05); T. London Museum of Jewish Life and Jewish Museum (1983-); Ch. Balfour Society for Children (1964-). Among recent publications: The Right School in the Right Place: The History of the Stepney Jewish School, 1864-2013; Service with a Smile: A History of The League of Jewish Women (2010); Frank's Way: Frank Cass and 50 Years of Publishing (2008); The Joys of Friendship: A History of the Association of Jewish Friendship (2008); Jewish London: an Illustrated History (2003); Lord Rothschild and the Barber (2000); JFS: The History of the Jews' Free School (1997); Living Up West: The Jews of West End (1994).

Add 54 St. Johns Court, Finchley Road, London NW3 6LE

Tel 020 7624 8320 *Fax* 020 7372 9015

Email gblack4455@aol.com

BLACK, Keith,

b. 1959; KB & JB Properties LLP (2009-); T. UJIA National (2005-); Managing Dir. Regatta Ltd (1982-); T. Manchester CST.

Add Regatta Ltd, Risol House, Mercury Way, Urmston, Manchester M41 7RR

BLANK, Sir (Maurice) Victor, MA (Oxon), Hon FRCOG, CIMgt.

b. Manchester, 1942; m. Sylvia Helen née Richford; H. V. Pres. Jewish Leadership Council; form. Ch. Trinity Mirror Plc, Gus Plc and Lloyds Banking; T. Said Business School, Oxford; Adv. Texas Pacific Group; Ch. Rothschild Foundation Europe; Ch. Wellbeing of Women (RCOG Health Research Charity); H. Pres. UK/Israel Britain Business; Gov. Tel Aviv University; Ch. UJS/Hillel; Mem. Advisory Bd. UJIA; Ch. Social Mobility Foundation; Ch. European Adv. Bd. Cheung Kong graduate School of Business; form. British Business Ambassador; form. Council Mem. Oxford University; form. Mem. Financial Reporting Council. Publ.: Weinberg and Blank on Takeovers and Mergers.

Add P.O. Box 57793, London NW11 1HJ

Tel 07747 555 555

Email personalassistant@victorblank.com

BLUE, Rabbi Lionel, OBE, BA, MA, Dr. Div. (Durham) Dr Univ (Open U.).

b. London, Feb. 6, 1930; Broadcaster; Lecturer, Leo Baeck College (1967-); form. Convener Beth Din, RSGB; H. V. Pres. RSGB; V. Ch. Standing Conference Jews, Christians, Moslems in Europe; form. Rel. Dir. (Europe) World Union for Progressive Judaism; Ch. Assembly of Rabbis RSGB; form. M. St George's Settlement Synagogue, Middlesex New Synagogue. Templeton Prize 1993. Among recent publications: The Godseeker's Guide (2010); Best of Blue (2006); Hitchhiking to Heaven (2004); The Little Book of Lionel Blue Thoughts (2001); My Affair with Christianity (1999); Tales of Body and Soul (1995); How to get up when life gets you down (co-author, 1991).

Add 28 Cornwall Avenue, London N3 1LG

BLUMENFELD, Jeffery, OBE, BA (Hons), MA.

b. London, Dec. 1949; m. Judith née Freimark. Ch. Greater Manchester Jewish Mental Health Alliance (2009-); CEO, 'Chizuk' mental health organisation (2003-); Ch. Chief Rabbi's Steering Group on Social and Moral Education (1994-2002); Hd. Jewish Studies, Deputy Hd. Rosh Pinah Primary School (2002-3); Mem. Govt. Adv. Group, Marriage and Relationship Support (1997-2002); Act-Ch. JMC Legal Group (1993-2002); Dir. Jewish Marriage Council (1987-2002); Ed. Resources Bulletin, School Assemblies Council (1978-80); form. Dir. US Youth and Com Services Dept.

Add 41 Holders Hill Crescent, London NW4 1NE

Tel 020 8203 1458

Email jeffery@flowersfield.co.uk

BOGDANOR, Vernon, MA, FBA, CBE, FRSA.

b. London, July 16, 1943; Academic; Emer. Prof. of Government, Oxford University; Research Prof. King's College, London; Gresham Prof. of Law, Gresham College; Hon. Fel. Society for Advanced Legal Studies; Fel. Royal Academy of Social Sciences; Chevalier de la Legion d'Honneur; H. DLitt. University of Kent; Sir Isaiah Berlin Prize, 2008. Publ.: The Coalition and the Constitution (2011); The New British Constitution (2009); Joined-Up Government (2005); Devolution in the UK (1999); The Monarchy and the Constitution (1995); People and the Party System (1981); The British Constitution in the 20th Century.

Add 21 Edmunds Walk, London N2 0HU

Email virginia.preston@kcl.ac.uk

BOLCHOVER, Richard Louis, BA (Hons.), Mlitt. (Oxon).

b. Manchester, Aug. 15, 1960; m. Josephine née Rosenfelder; Fund Manager; Partner, Nimrod Capital LLP; V. Ch. Anglo-Israel Association; Fdr. form. Dir. Close Fund Management Ltd; form. Dir. Jewish Chronicle. Publ.: British Jewry and the Holocaust (1993, 2nd. Edition Littman Library 2004).

Add Nimrod Capital LLP, 3 St Helen's Place, London EC3A 6AB

Email info@nimrodcapital.com *Website* www.nimrodcapital.com

BOROWSKI, Ephraim, MA (Hons)(Glasgow), BPhil (Oxon), MBE.

b. Glasgow, Nov. 19, 1949; m. Margalit; Regional Ch. Board of Deputies (2009-, 2000-06); Dir. Scottish Council of Jewish Communities (1999-); V. Convenor, BEMIS (2004-11); Convenor (2011-14); General Teaching Council (M. nominee (2001-11), appointed Lay Mem. (2012); Scottish Qualifications Authority: Principal Assessor for Advanced Higher Philosophy (2000-08); Equal Opportunities Commission, Scottish Com. (2005-07); Commission for Racial Equality, Scottish Bd. (2005-07); V. Ch. and Acting Ch. Forum on Scottish Education (2003-07); Glasgow Jewish Representative Council: V. Pres. (2001-04, 1998-2000); Hon. T. Scottish Interfaith Council (2001-03); Pres. Royal Philosophical Society of Glasgow (2000-03), H. Mem. (2013); Race Equality Adv. Forum, Scottish executive (1999-2001); Tru. AUT (1993-96); University Glasgow: Snr. Lecturer in Philosophy (1976-91); Hd. Dept. (1993-95); Pres. Glasgow AUT (1985-90). Publ.: Scotland's Jews (with Kenneth Collins and Leah Granat, 2008); Collins Dictionary of Mathematics (UK: 1989; 2nd Edition, 2002, rev. Edition 2005, US: 1991, 2nd 2006).

Add 19 Norwood Drive, Glasgow G46 7LS

Tel 07831 121 300

Email ephraim@scojec.org *Website* www.scojec.org

BRAIER, Amy,

Dir. The Pears Foundation (2012-), Deputy Dir. (2007-12).

Add The Pears Foundation, Clive House, 2 Old Brewery Mews, Hampstead, London NW3 1PZ

Tel 020 7433 3333 *Fax* 020 7433 3343

Email contact@pearsfoundation.org.uk *Website* www.pearsfoundation.org.uk

BRASS, Laurence Stephen, LL.B.

b. London, July 26, 1947; m. Hilary née Stone; Tribunal Judge; Asylum Appeals Adjudicator (2000-); Mem. Board of Deputies, (1974-), Nat. T. (2009-); Ch. NHS Doctors Disciplinary Appeals Panel; Adviser, Liberal Democrats on Middle-East Affairs; form. V. Ch. Lib Dem Friends of Israel; Ch. Bushey Interfaith Forum; Ch. Board of Deputies 250th Anniversary Cttee.

Add 22 Grange Road, Bushey, Hertfordshire WD23 2LE

Tel 01923 223528 *Fax* 01923 490324

Email l.brass@ntlworld.com

BRAWER, Rabbi Naftali, PhD.

m. Dina; Chief Exec. Spiritual Capital Foundation (2011-); Co-V. Ch. Rabbinical Council of the United Synagogue (2008-11); Rabbi, Borehamwood and Elstree Synagogue (2007-11); Rabbi, Northwood Synagogue (1996-2007); Adv. Rene Cassin Education; Chief Rabbi's Cabinet; Adv. Children of Abraham; Columnist, Jewish Chronicle; Broadcaster, BBC; Honorary research Fel. and Lecturer, LSJS; Author.

Add 7 Welbeck Street, London W1G 9YE

Tel 020 7487 0466

Email nbrawer@spiritual-capital.org *Website* www.spiritual-capital.org

BRICKMAN, Rev. Stanley Ivan,

b. London, Mar. 29, 1939; London Regional V. Pres. Cantorial Council of America (1994-); Cantor, Hampstead Synagogue (1987-2004); Assistant Grand Chaplain, United Grand Lodge of England (2003); Freeman, City of London (2002); Ch. Association of M. (Chazanim); Cantor: Great Synagogue, Cape Town (1983-86), Singers Hill Synagogue, Birmingham (1971-83), New London Synagogue (1969-71), Ilford Synagogue (1966-69), Great Synagogue, Sheffield (1960-65). Publ.: Friday Evening Service with Zemirot for Children (Birmingham, 1976); Recording: Synagogue Liturgy Music with Singers Hill Choir (1981).

Add 3 Chatsworth Close, Borehamwood, Hertfordshire WD6 1UE

Tel 020 8387 9962

Email sib3432@googlemail.com

BRIER, Norma, OBE, BA (Hons), MSc, CQSW, JP.

b. London, Dec. 23, 1949; OBE for services to children and people with learning disabilities (2013); Co-Ch. Women in Leadership (May 2013); Interim Exec. Dir. Services, Scope (May-Dec 2012); Independent Consultant (Social Care Sector) Cross-Sector Consultancy (2011-); Tru. JC Trust (2011); Chief Exec. Norwood (1997-2011); Exec. Dir. Ravenswood Foundation (1989-96); Dir. of Com. Services, Ravenswood and Jewish Society for Mental Handicap (1985); Lecturer in Sociology and Social Work/Counselling, Harrow College (1982); Psychiatric Social Worker (1972), Social Worker, Camden (1968).

Add c/o Norwood, Broadway House, 80-82 The Broadway Stanmore, Middlesex HA7 4HB

Tel 020 8809 8809 *Fax* 020 8420 6800

Email normabrier@hotmail.com

BRIER, Sam, PhD, MA.

b. London, July 19, 1946; Dir./Management Consultant, Cross-Sector Consulting Ltd; Snr. Research Associate, Institute for Voluntary Action Research, University of London; form. Chief Exec. KIDS (1999-2005); form. Exec. Dir. (Resources), Norwood Ravenswood (1996-99); form. Exec. Dir. Norwood Childcare (1984-96).

Add IVAR, 25-31 Tavistock Place, London WC1H 9UT

Tel 07939 542 461

Email sambrier@hotmail.com *Website* www.cross-sectorconsulting.co.uk

BRITTAN, Lord Leon, of Spennithorne, PC, QC, MA (Cantab), H. DCL, Newcastle, Durham, H. LLD, Hull, Edinburgh, Bradford, Bath, D.Econ., Korea.

b. London, Sept. 25, 1939; Government trade adviser (2010-11); V. Pres. Commissioner of the European Communities (1989-99); MP (Con) for Richmond, North Yorkshire (1983-88); Sec. of State for Trade and Industry (1985-86); Home Sec. (1983-85); Bencher of the Inner Temple (1983); Chief Sec. to the Treasury (1981-83); MP (Con) for Cleveland and Whitby (1974-83); M. of State, Home Office (1979-81); V. Ch. Employment Cttee. of Parl. Conservative Party (1974-76); Ch. Bow Group (1964-65); Pres. Cambridge Union (1960). Among recent publications: A Diet of Brussels (2000); The 1997 Rede Lecture; European Competition Policy (1992); Europe: the Europe we need (1990); Hersch Lauterpacht Memorial Lectures, University of Cambridge (1990); Discussions on Policy (1989); Europe: Our Sort of Community (1989 Granada Guildhall Lecture); Monetary Union: the issues and the impact (1989).

Add House of Lords, London SW1A 0PW

BRODER, Rabbi Gavin, BA (Hons), MA (London).

b. Uitenhage, South Africa, Apr. 17, 1963; London Region's Jewish University Chaplain; Chief Rabbi of Ireland (1996-2000); form. M. Newbury Park Synagogue (1990-96), Staines Hebrew Congregation (1988-90); form. Governor, Avigdor Primary School.

Tel 07811 286 664

Email rabbibroder@mychaplaincy.co.uk *Website* www.mychaplaincy.co.uk

BRODIE, Rev. Gabriel,

b. Bratislava, July 7, 1924; Snr. M. Emer. Manchester Great New and Central Synagogue; Sec. Manchester Yeshiva; Ch. Jerusalem Academy Study Groups; H. Chaplain, Jewish Meals on Wheels, 45 Aid Society.

Add 43 Stanley Road, Salford M7 4FR

Tel 0161 740 2506

BRODIE, Rabbi Yehuda, BA (Hons).

b. Manchester, Oct. 3, 1950; CEO, MBD Shechita Services Ltd; MBD Kosher Certification Services Ltd; MBD Community Mikveh Ltd; Registrar, Manchester Beth Din; T. Keren L'David Education Trust.

Add Manchester Jewish Community Centre, Jubilee School, Bury Old Road M7 4QY

Tel 0161 740 9711

Email yb@mbd.org.uk *Website* www.mbd.org.uk

BROWN, Malcolm Denis, FSA, MA.

b. Fulwood, Mar. 24, 1936; m. Barbara née Langford; Research historian; V. Pres. JHSE (1999-), Pres. (1996-98); Lecturer, Extra-Mural Dept. University of London (1969-81); Archivist, Anglo-Jewish Archives (1965-66); Assistant Ed. Journal of Warburg and Courtauld Institutes (1962-64); form. Assistant Keeper of Manuscripts, British Museum. Publ.: David Salomons House: Catalogues of Mementos, Commemorative Medals and Ballooniana (1968, 1969 and 1970).

Add c/o The Jewish Historical Society of England, 33 Seymour Place, London W1H 5AP

Tel 020 7723 5852

BRUMMER, Alexander, BSc (Econ), MSc (Business Administration).

b. Brighton, May 25, 1949; m. Patricia Lyndsey née Magrill; City Office; City Ed. Daily Mail (2000-), Consultant Ed. (1999-2000); V. Pres. and Ch. International Division, Board of Deputies, (2012-), Tru. Holocaust Memorial Day Trust (2013-), V. Ch International Division (2006-12); Guardian (1973-99); Associate Ed. (1998-99); Financial Ed. (1990-8); Foreign Ed. (1989-90); Washington Bureau Chief (1979-89); Financial Correspondent (1973-9); Publ: Bad Banks (2014); Britain for Sale (2012); Great Pensions Robbery (2010); The Crunch (2008); Weinstock: Life and Times (1999); Hanson: A Biography (1994); Awards: Overseas Journalist of the Year 1988; Financial Journalist of the Year (1998); Wincott Award (2001); Columnist of the Year (2007); Financial Columnist of the Year (2009); Business Journalist of the Year (2010); Financial Journalist of the Year (2013).

Add Northcliffe House, 2 Derry Street, London W8 5TT

Tel 020 3615 1906

Email alex.brummer@dailymail.co.uk

BURGER, Daniel Richard, BA (Hons).

b. London, Sept. 19, 1975; m. Natalie née Burns; Exec. Dir. Jewish Child's Day (2006-11); Hd. Community Fundraising, Norwood (2003-06); Chief Exec. Magen David Adom UK; Ch. Fundraising Cttee. Young Norwood, Sue Harris Bone Marrow Trust.

Add c/o MDA, Shield House, Harmony Way, London NW4 2BZ

Tel 020 201 5900

Email info@mdauk.org *Website* www.mdauk.org

BURMAN, Michael Alfred, BSc (Hons), PGCE, FRGS.

b. Southport, Sept. 20, 1944; m. Barbara née Schiltzer; form. Dir. Admin. Liberal Jewish Synagogue (2007-11); form. Ch. and T. Masorti; Sec. Masorti Europe; form. Ch. European Masorti Beth Din Man. Cttee.; form. Ch. Gov. Clore Shalom School; T. Akiva School; T. Jewish Community Day School Advisory Board.

Add 71 Longfield Avenue, Mill Hill, London NW7 2SA

Tel 020 8201 7522

Email michael.burman@virgin.net

BURMAN, Rickie Amanda, FRSA, MA (Cantab), MPhil.

b. Liverpool, July 5, 1955, m. Prof. Daniel Miller; Dir. Jewish Museum, London (1995-); Curator, London Museum of Jewish Life (1984-95); Museum Co-ord. Manchester Jewish Museum (1981-84); Res. Fel. in Jewish History; Manchester Polytechnic (1979-84); form. Pres. Assoc. of European Jewish Museum and Bd. Mem. London Jewish Museums Libraries and Archives Council; Visitor (Tru) of Pitt Rivers Museum, University of Oxford. Publ.: on history of Jewish women in England and museum studies; Treasures of Jewish Heritage (Ed. 2006).

Add The Jewish Museum, Raymond Burton House, 129-131 Albert Street, London NW1 7NB

Tel 020 7284 7384

Email rickie.burman@jewishmuseum.org.uk

CALLMAN, His Honour Sir Clive Vernon, Kt. BSc (Econ).

b. June 21, 1927; Gov. Hebrew University of Jerusalem (1992-); Mem. Adv. Cttee. for Magistrates' Courses (1979-); Gov. LSE (1990-2008), Council, AJA (1956); Board of Deputies (1998); Mediator, Court of Appeal (2004); Child and Family Law Q. (1995-2002); Court City University (1991-2001); Mem. Careers Advisory Board (1979-92), Gov. Birkbeck College (1982-2001); Senator, London University (1978-94), Gov. Council (1994-2001); Dep. High Court Judge, Royal Courts of Justice (1975-2000); Circuit Judge, South-Eastern Circuit (1973-2000); Dep. Circuit Judge (2000-04); Ed. Bd. Media Law and Practice (1980-95); Journal of Child Law (1988-94); Council, West London Synagogue (1981-87); Professional Negligence (1985); Ch. St Marylebone Labour Party (1960-62); Exec. Society of Labour Lawyers (1958); Dir. Vallentine Mitchell and Co. Ltd.; T. Jewish Studies Foundation; Knight for services to law, education and charity (2012).

Add 11 Constable Close NW11 6UA

Tel 020 8458 3010

CARLOWE, Melvyn, OBE, B.Soc. Sci. (Hons).

b. Abingdon, Oxon., Apr. 13, 1941; Jewish Community Ombudsman Service (1999-2008); T. Third Sector Trust, North London Hospice (1975-2006); Institute of Jewish Policy Research (2000-05); Mem. Beacon Selection Panel for the office of Deputy PM (2000-04); Mem. King's Fund Inquiry on Care Workers (2000-02); form. Chief Exec. Jewish Care (1990-2000); form. Hon. S. Central Council for Jewish Communal Service (1972-2000); form. Chief Exec. Jewish Welfare Board (1972-89); Jewish Chronicle Trust (2000-11).

Tel 020 8364 6686 *Fax* 020 8364 6686

Email karlatsky@aol.com

CESARANI, David, OBE, D.Phil.

b. London, Nov. 13, 1956; Research Prof. in History, Royal Holloway, University London (2004-); form. Prof. Jewish History and Dir. AHRB Parkes Centre for the Study of Jewish/non-Jewish Relations, University of Southampton (2000-04); Parkes-Wiener Prof. of 20th Century Jewish History and Culture (1996-2000); Dir. Institute of Contemporary History and Wiener Library (1996-2000, 1993-95); Alliance Prof. of Modern Jewish Studies, University Manchester (1995-96); Barnett Shine Snr. Res. Fel. Queen Mary College, University of London, (1986-89). Among recent publications: After the Holocaust: Challenging the Myth of Silence (Co-Ed. 2012); Major Farran's Hat: Murder, Scandal and Britain's War against Jewish Terrorism 1945-1948 (2008); Place and Displacement in Jewish History and Memory (Co-Ed. 2009); Jews in Port Cities, 1650-1990, (Co-Ed. 2006); After Eichmann, Collective Memory and the Holocaust Since 1960 (Ed. 2005); Critical Concepts: the Holocaust, (6 volumes, Ed. 2004); Eichmann: His Life and Crimes (2004); Port Jews: Jewish Communities in Cosmopolitan Maritime Trading Centres, 1650-1950 (Ed. 2003); Bystanders to the Holocaust (Co-Ed. 2002).

Add History Dept., Royal Holloway, University of London, Egham, Surrey TW20 0EX

Tel 01784 443 308

Email david.cesarani@rhul.ac.uk

CHARING, Rabbi Douglas Stephen,

b. London, Nov. 16, 1945; Vis. Rabbi, Southport Reform Synagogue and Bradford Synagogue; Dir. Jewish Education Bureau (1974-), Leeds; Tutor, Geneva Theological College, Adv. Theology and Religious Studies Board; Dir. Concord Multi-Faith/Multi-Cultural Res. Centre (Leeds); Inter-Euro. Com. on Church and School, form. Gov. Centre for Study of Rel. and Education (Salford); M. Sinai Synagogue, Leeds; Lecturer, Leeds University, Manchester Police College Mem. Bd. of Dir. British Friends of the Anne Frank Centre; Exec. M. Council for Religious Freedom. Publ.: Glimpses of Jewish Leeds; Comparative Religions (co-author), The Jewish World Visiting a Synagogue; Modern Judaism (audio-visual); Jewish Contributor, The Junior R.E. Handbook; World Faiths in Education; Praying Their Faith (contributor); Religion in Leeds (Contr.); A Dictionary of Religious Education In the Beginning (Audio-visual); The Torah; Eyewitness Judaism; Encyclopaedia of Religion (co-author), etc.

Add 8 Westcombe Avenue, Leeds LS8 2BS

Tel 0345 567 4070 *Fax* 0845 003 5370

Email rabbi@jewisheducationbureau.co.uk *Website* wwwjewisheducationbureau.co.uk

CHERNETT, Jaclyn, ALCM, MPhil.

b. St. Neots, June 16, 1941; m. Brian Chernett; Exec. Council Cantors Assembly (2011-); Chazan (2006, Academy for Jewish religion, NY); Co Ch. Assembly of Masorti Synagogues (1992-95); Dir. Masorti Association (1984-86); H. Life Pres. Edgware Masorti Synagogue; V. Pres. Assembly of Masorti Synagogues; Past V. Pres. World Council of Synagogues; Fdr. Dir. European Academy for Jewish Liturgy. Publ.: Conference papers.

Add Flat 17, Peter's Lodge, 2 Stonegrove, Edgware, Middlesex HA8 7TY

Tel 020 8958 5090 *Fax* 020 8958 7651

Email jaclyn@eajl.org *Website* www.eajl.org

CHEYETTE, Bryan, PhD.

b. Leicester, Jan. 15, 1959; m. Susan Cooklin; Prof. English Language and Literature University of Reading (2005-); Prof. Twentieth Century Literature, University of Southampton (1999-2005); form. Reader in English & Judaic Studies, Queen Mary College, University of London (1992-99); British Academy Postdoctoral Fel. School of English, University of Leeds (1989-92); Editorial board Jewish Quarterly and Patterns of Prejudice. Publ.: (Ed.), H. G. Wells, 'Tono-Bungay' (1997); Between 'Race' and Culture: Representations of 'the Jew' in English and American Literature (Ed. 1996); Constructions of 'the Jew' in English Literature and Society: Racial Representations, 1875-1945 (1993); published widely on British-Jewish Literature.

Add University of Reading, Whiteknights Campus, Reading RG6 6UR

Tel 0118 378 6500

Email b.h.cheyette@reading.ac.uk

CHINN, Sir Trevor, CVO.

b. London, July 24, 1935; m. Susan née Speelman; Pres. UJIA; Mem. Jewish Leadership Council; Mem. BICOM Exec. Board; H. V. Pres. Zionist Federation; Pres. Norwood (1996-2006); Snr Adv. CVC Capital Partners; Ch. Lex Service / RAC plc (1973-2003), Man. Dir. (1968-1973); Ch. Tusker.

Add 14 Basil Street, London SW3 1AJ

CLINTON-DAVIS, Stanley, Baron of Hackney, PC, LLB, FRSA.

b. London, Dec. 6, 1928; Solicitor; Hon. Mem. of the Council of Justice (1989-); Min. State for Trade (1997-98); Pres. UK Pilots (Marine) (1991-98); H. D. Polytechnical University of Bucharest (1993); Pres. Association of the Metropolitan Authorities (1992); Order of Leopold II for Services to EC, 1990; Mem. European Commission (1985-89); Pres. British Airline Pilots' Association (BALPA) (1980-2012), H. Life Pres. (2012-); MP (Lab.), Hackney Central (1970-83); Parl. Under Sec. for Companies, Aviation and Shipping, Dept. of Trade (1974-79); Councillor, Hackney Borough (1959-71), Mayor (1968-69); Fel. of Queen Mary and Westfield College and King's College, London University; Fel. Budapest University. Publ.: Good Neighbours? Nicaragua, Central America and the United States (Jt. author).

Add House of Lords, London SW1A 1AA

Tel 020 7219 6203

COCKS, Lady Valerie (née Davis),

b. London, July 10, 1932; m. Michael; Dir. Labour Friends of Israel and Trade Union Friends of Israel (1978-88); Exec. Com. Zionist Federation.

Add 162 South Block, County Hall, London SE1 7GE

Tel 020 7787 2539

COHEN, Adrian,

Fdr. and Ch. London Jewish Forum (2006-); Co-Hd. Partner, Clifford Chance (1998-); Co-ordinator, Canary Wharf Kehilla (2003-08); Ch. UJS (1985-86).

Add London Jewish Forum, 32-36 Loman Street, London SE1 0EH

Email adrian.cohen@cliffordchance.com

COHEN, Daniel, BA Hons (Oxon).

b. London, Jan. 15, 1974; Dir. BBC Television (2013); Controller, BBC One (2010-13), BBC Three, (2007-10); Hd. of Factual Entertainment and of E4 (2006–07); Hd. of Documentaries, Channel 4 (2004–06); Commissioning Ed. Documentaries, Channel 4 (2001–04).

Email danny.cohen@bbc.co.uk

COHEN, Harry Michael, MP.

b. Dec. 10, 1949; m. Ellen née Hussain; MP (Lab) Leyton and Wanstead (1997-2010) (Leyton, 1983–97); Mem. NATO Parly Assembly (1999-2005) (N Atlantic Assembly, 1992–99) (Rapporteur; Ch. Sub-cttee. for Economic Co-operation and Convergence with Central and Eastern Europe, 1996–2000); Mem. Select Cttee. on Defence (1997–2001); Sec. All-Party Parly Group on Race and Community; Mem. UNISON; V. Pres. Royal College of Midwives.

Add House of Commons, London SW1A 0AA

COHEN, Rabbi Jeffrey M, BA, MPhil, AJC, PhD.

b. Manchester, Feb. 19, 1940; m. Gloria née Goldberg; Scholar-in-Residence, USA (1998); Chaplain to Mayor of Harrow (1994-95); Lecturer, Liturg. Studies, Jews' College (1980-1992); Chief Examiner, Modern Hebrew, Jt. Matric Board (1973-1987); Rabbinical Adv. and Gov. Immanuel College (1990-2012); form. M. Kenton Synagogue; Snr. M. Newton Mearns Synagogue, Glasgow; Lecturer in Hebrew, Glasgow University, Principal Glasgow Hebrew College; Dir. Glasgow Bd. of Jewish Education; Dir. Jew Education, King David Schools, Manchester; Mem. Rev. Cttee. Singers Prayer Book. Among recent publications: Dear Chief Rabbi (Ed.); 1001 Questions and Answers on Pesach; Following the Synagogue Service; 1001 Questions and Answers on Rosh Hashanah and Yom Kippur; Issues of the Day; Abridged Haggadah for Rusty Readers; Let My People Go: Insights into Pesach and the Haggadah; The Bedside Companion for Jewish Patients; 500 Questions and Answers on Chanukah; Torah for Teens: Growing up Spiritually with the weekly Sidrah; Genesis in Poetry; The Siddur in Poetry; the High Holydays Machzor in Poetry; The Haggadah in Poetry.

Add 26 Belvedere Court, 115 Lyttelton Road, London N2 0AH

Tel 020 8457 5849

Email jeffreyandgloria@yahoo.co.uk *Website* www.rabbijeffrey.co.uk

COHEN, Michael, BA, MPhil, PGCE.

b. Oxford, Nov. 3, 1941; Teacher Training Co-ord. (London Borough of Hackney); Principal, MST College; Education Consultant, Stratford College, Dublin, Tiferes Shlomo School, London, American Endowment School (Budapest), Prague Jewish Community; Consultant to Broughton Jewish Cassel Fox Primary School, Manchester (1996-98); Principal of Leibler Yavneh College, Melbourne (1993-95); form. Exec. Dir. US Board of Religious Education,

London (1980-92); form. HM Mount Scopus Memorial College, Melbourne (1975-80); form. Dir. Jewish Studies, North-West London Jewish Day School (1969-75).

Add 50 Princes Park Avenue NW11 0JT

Tel 020 8458 4537 *Fax* 020 8201 9396

COHEN, Lieut-Colonel Mordaunt, TD, DL, FRSA.

b. Sunderland, Aug. 6, 1916; Solicitor (1938); Admitted Nigerian Bar (Military Advocate) (1942); Pres. Friends of Jewish Servicemen & Women (2009-); H. Life Pres. Sunderland Hebrew Congregation (1988-); Reg. Ch. Industrial Tribunals (1976-89), Ch. (1974-76); Board of Deputies, (1964-2006); H. Dir. Central Enquiry Desk (1990-2000); Ch. Edgware School (1991-96); form. Mem. Chief Rabbinate Council; T. AJEX; T. AJEX Charitable Foundation; V. Pres. and Nat. Ch. AJEX (1993-95); Dep. Lieut. Tyne & Wear; Ch. Provincial Cttee. Board of Deputies (1985-91); Ch. Mental Health Review Tribunal (1967-76); Cllr. Tyne & Wear County C. (1973-74); Dep. Ch. Northern Traffic Coms. (1972-74); Alderman Sunderland County Borough Council (1967-74); Ch. Sunderland Education Cttee. (1970-72); Ch. Govs. Sunderland Polytechnic (1969-72); Court, Newcastle upon Tyne University (1968-72); Pres. Sunderland Law Society (1970); War service, RA (1940-46) (dispatches, Burma campaign), TA (1947-55), CO 463 (M) HAA Regt. (1954-55); Territorial Decoration (1954); H. Life Pres. Sunderland AJEX.

Add 1 Peters Lodge, 2 Stonegrove, Edgware, Middlesex HA8 7TY

COHEN, Sir Philip, FRS, FRSE, FFMed.Sci, FAA, BSc, PhD.

b. Edgware, Middlesex; m. Patricia née Townsend Wade; Biochemist; Dir. Scottish Inst. for Cell Signalling (2008-12); Dir. MRC Protein Phosphorylation Unit (1990-2012); Royal Society Research Professor (1984-2010). Publ.: Control of Enzyme Activity (1976, 2nd Edition 1993); over 500 research papers and reviews in scientific journals; Honorary DSc Degrees from Abertay, Strathclyde, Linköping, Debrecen and St Andrew's; LLD from Dundee.

Add Inverbay Bramblings, Waterside, Invergowrie, Dundee DD2 5DQ

Tel 01382 562 328 *Fax* 01382 233 778

Email p.cohen@dundee.ac.uk

COHEN, Sir Ronald, MA (Oxon), MBA (Harvard).

b. London, Aug. 1, 1945; m. Sharon Ruth Harel; Businessman; Ch. Commission on Unclaimed Assets (2005-07) and Dir. Social Finance (2008-); Harvard Board of Overseers (2007-); T. British Museum (2005-); Chancellor's Court of Benefactors, Oxford University (2003-); Co-Fdr. and Ch. The Portland Trust (2003-); Ch. Bridges Ventures (2002-); V. Ch. Ben Gurion University (2002-); Hon. Fel. Exeter College, Oxford (2000-); T. International Institute of Strategic Studies (2005-10); Ch. Social Investment Task Force HM Treasury (2000-10); Jewish Leadership Council (2006-09); Mem. Dean's Board of Advisors, Harvard Business School (2003-08); Dir. NASDAQ Europe (2001-05); Co-Fdr. and form. Ch. Apax Partners Worldwide LLP (1972-05). Publ.: The Second Bounce of the Ball: Turning Risk into Opportunity.

Add 42 Portland Place, London W1B 1NB

Tel 020 7182 7801 *Fax* 020 7182 7897

Email ronald.cohen@portlandcap.com

COHEN, Shimon David, FRSA.

b. Cardiff, May 24, 1960; Ch. The PR Office Ltd.; Mem. CIPR; Mem. BAFTA; Mem. Board of Deputies; form. Dir. Bell Pottinger Consultants (1990-2003); form. Exec. Dir. Office of the Chief Rabbi (1983-90).

Email enquiries@theproffice.com *Website* www.theproffice.com

COHN-SHERBOK, Dan, BA, BHL, MA, MLitt, PhD (Cantab), DD.

b. Denver, CO, Feb. 1, 1945; Emer. Prof. University of Wales (2012-); Vis. Prof. York St John University (2011-), St Mary's University (2008-), University Middlesex (1994-), Charles University Prague (2007), Vilnius (2000), Lampeter (1994-6); Emer. Prof. Judaism, University Wales (Lampeter) (1997-); University Lecturer in Theology, University of Kent

(1975-); Vis. Prof. University of Essex (1993-4); H. Research Fel. Heythrop College, University of London (2011-); Ch. Dept. of Theology, University of Kent (1980-2); form. Rabbi in synagogues in the USA, England, S. Africa, Australia (1971-5); H. Prof. Aberystwyth University; H. Fel. Centre of Religions for Peace and Reconciliation, University of Winchester. Among recent publications: Debating Palestine and Israel (2014); The Illustrated History of Judaism (2013); Love, Sex and Marriage (2013); The Palestinian State: A Jewish Justification (2012); Introduction to Zionism and Israel (2011); Judaism Today (2010); The Dictionary of Kabbalah and Kabbalists (2009); The Dictionary of Jewish Biography (2008); Christian Zionism (2006); Kabbalah (2006); The Paradox of Antisemitism (2006); The Politics of Apocalypse (2006); Pursuing the Dream (2005); The Vision of Judaism (2004); Judaism: History, Belief and Practice (2003); Antisemitism (2002); Holocaust Theology: A Reader (2001); Interfaith Theology (2001); The Palestine–Israeli Conflict (2001); Wisdom of Judaism (2000); Jews, Christians and Religious Pluralism (1999); The Future of Jewish-Christian Dialogue (Ed. 1999); Understanding the Holocaust (1999); The Jewish Messiah (1997); Fifty Key Jewish Thinkers (1996); The Hebrew Bible (1996); Modern Judaism (1996); Medieval Jewish Philosophy (1996).

Add 89 Winchester Court, Vicarage Gate, London W8 4AF

Email cohnsherbok@googlemail.com *Website* www.dancohnsherbok.com

COLLINS, John Morris, MA (Oxon).

b. Leeds, June 25, 1931; Barrister; Doyen, North Eastern Circuit; Hd. of Chambers (1966-2002); Crown Courts Recorder (1980-98); Pres. Beth Hamidrash Hagadol Synagogue, Leeds (1992-95); past Pres. Leeds Lodge, B'nai B'rith; Board of Deputies (1971-93); Dep. Circuit Judge (1970-80); Called to the Bar, Middle Temple (1956); H. Life V. Pres. Leeds Jewish Representative Council (form. Pres. 1986-89); V. Ch. Leeds Kashrut Authority. Publ.: Summary Justice (1963).

Add 14 Sandhill Oval, Leeds LS17 8EA

Tel 0113 268 6008

Email johnmorriscollins@btinternet.com

COLLINS, Dr Kenneth Edward, MBChB, FRCGP, MPhil, PhD.

b. Glasgow, Dec. 23, 1947; Ch. Scottish Council of Jewish Communities (2007-08, 1999-2003); Pres. Glasgow Jewish Representative Council (2004-07, 1995-98); Ch. Scottish Jewish Archives Cttee. Glasgow Board of Jewish Education (1989-93); Vis Prof. Faculty of Medicine, Hebrew University; Ch. Glasgow Yeshiva. Publ.: Moses Maimonides and his Practice of Medicine (Ed. 2013); Scotland's Jews (1999, 2nd edition 2008); Be Well: Jewish Immigrant Health and Welfare in Glasgow (2001); Glasgow Jewry (1994); Second City Jewry (1990); Go and Learn (1988); Aspects of Scottish Jewry (Ed. 1987).

Add 2/2 11 Braidholm Crescent, Giffnock, Glasgow G46 6HH

Tel 0141 404 7488

Email drkcollins@gmail.com

CONWAY, Penelope Lesley (née Lennard), D.O, PGDip, PGCap, FHEA.

b. London; m. Peter; Osteopath; Ch. Status of Women Cttee. ICJW (2014-); Ch. Association of Jewish Women's Organisations (2010-14); UK V. Pres. International Council of Jewish Women (2010-14); V. Ch. Ruth Winston Centre (2009-); Pres. League of Jewish Women (2003-07).

Add ICJW, c/o League of Jewish Women, 6 Bloomsbury Square, London WC1A 2LP

Tel 020 7242 8300

Website www.icjw.org

COPISAROW, Sir Alcon Charles,

b. St. Annes-on-Sea Lancs., June 25, 1920; m. Diana Elissa Castello OBE; form. Ch. Humanitarian Trust, Hebrew University of Jerusalem, Council IJA and AJA; Lieut. Royal Navy (1943-47); Min. of Defence (1947-54), British Embassy, Paris (1954-60); Chief Scientific Officer, Min. of Technology (1964-66), Snr Partner McKinsey and Co Inc. (1966-76); Subsequently: Chairman Tr. The Prince's Youth Business Trust; Tr., Duke of Edinburgh's

Award; C. Royal Jubilee Trusts; British National Oil Corporation; Press Council; Gov., Benenden School; Dep. Chairman Gov. English Speaking Union; Ch. APAX Funds, Council of Lloyds; Patron, Conseil National des Ingénieurs et des Scientifiques de France; Association of MBA's; Ch. and Tru. The Athenaeum; By-Fellow, Churchill College, Cambridge.

Add 7 Southwell Gardens, London SW7 4SB

CORREN, Asher, MCMI.

b. Warsaw, Nov. 2, 1932; form. Dir. Central Council Jewish Community Services; form. Exec. Dir. Nightingale House; form. Mem. of Wandsworth Health Authority; form. Mem. of Exec. Cttee. Alzheimer's Society; Mem. of Adv. Cttee. St Wilfrid's Home for Aged, Chelsea; form. Co-T. and form. Mem. Exec. Cttee. Council of Christians and Jews.

Email patricia.corren@virgin.net

COSGROVE, Rt. Hon. Lady Hazel Josephine (née Aronson), CBE, LL.D.

b. Glasgow, Jan. 12, 1946; m. John A. Cosgrove; Senator of the College of Justice, Scotland (1996-2006); Dep. Ch. Boundary Commission for Scotland (1996-2006); Ch. Expert Panel on Sex Offending (1998-2001); Ch. Mental Welfare Commission for Scotland (1991-96); Sheriff of Lothian and Borders at Edinburgh (1983-96); Mem. Parole Bd.; Sheriff of Glasgow and Strathkelvin at Glasgow (1979-83); Privy Counsellor (2001), Queens Counsel (1991), Advocate (1968-79); Pres. Scottish Friends of Alyn Hospital; H. Fel. Harris Manchester College, Oxford; D. University Stirling (2004); H. LLD, St Andrews University (2003); Glasgow University (2002); Strathclyde University (2002); Napier University (1997).

Add 4 Avenue Mansions, Finchley Road, London NW3 7AU

Tel 020 7435 1236

Email hazelcosgrove@uk2.net

COSGROVE, John Allan, BDS (Glasgow).

b. Carmarthen, S. Wales, Dec. 5, 1943; m. The Rt. Honourable Lady Cosgrove (née Aronson); Dental Surgeon; Warden, St John's Wood Synagogue (2013); Pres. Edinburgh Hebrew Congregation (1986-90), Ch. Scottish Council of Jewish Communities; (2003-07); Scottish representative Chief Rabbinate selection cttee. (1989-91).

Add 4 Avenue Mansions, Finchley Road, London NW3 7AU

Tel 079 7065 7157 *Fax* 0333 344 1236

Email jacosgrove@uk2.net

CREWE, Sir Ivor Martin, Kt., D.Litt (Salford) DU (Essex).

b. Manchester, Dec. 15, 1945; University teacher; Master, University College, Oxford (2008-); V. Chancellor (1995–2007), Pro V. Chancellor (Academic) (1992-95), University of Essex; Pres. Universities UK (2003-5); Ed./Co-Ed. British Journal of Political Science (1984-92, 1977-82); Ch. Dept. of Government (1985-89); Dir. SSRC Data Archive (1974-82); Mem. High Council, European University Institute, Florence; Mem. Council SOAS; University of the Arts, London; Prof. of Government, University of Essex; Hon. Fel. Exeter College, Oxford; Nuffield College, Oxford. Publ.: SDP: The Birth, Life and Death of the Social Democratic Party (1995); Decade of Dealignment (CUP 1983) (1995, with Bo Sarlvik); Survey of Higher Civil Service (HMSO 1969) (with A. H. Halsey), etc.

Add The Master's Lodge, University College, Oxford OX1 4BH

Tel 01865 276 600

Email marion.hawtree@univ.ox.ac.uk

DANGOOR, David Alan Ezra, BSc, ARCS, DL.

b. 1948; Dep. Lieutenant of Greater London; Mem. Jewish Leadership Council (2010-); Pres. Board, Spanish & Portuguese Jews' Congregation (2011-); V. Pres. World Organisation of Jews from Iraq (2008-); Sponsor Gov. Westminster Academy (2006-); T. Jewish Association of Business Ethics (2005-12); Ch. LST Investment Committee (2004-); T. Simon Wiesenthal Centre (UK) (1996-); T. London Sephardi Tru. (1984-); Sephardi Kashrut Authority (1982-); T. The Exilarch's Foundation (1978-); Dir. Carmel College (1997-2010); S&P Mahamad & Gabay (1997-2001).

Add 4 Carlos Place, Mayfair, London W1K 3AW

Email david@dangoor.com *Website* www.dangoor.com

DANGOOR, Dr Naim E, CBE, FRAH.

b. Baghdad, 1914; m. Renée; Company Ch. Property Developer; Editor and Publisher – The Scribe, Journal of Babylonian Jewry; Fdr. and Tru. Exilarch's Foundation; Sponsor, Westminster Academy; Donor, Eliahou Dangoor Scholarships; awarded Professorship by Nanjing University; Fel. Royal Albert Hall; Fel. Birkbeck, University of London.

Add 4 Carlos Place, London W1K 3AW

Email office@dangoor.com *Website* www.dangoor.com

DAVIS, Baruch, BA (Hons) Econ, Semicha, Chief Rabbinate of Israel.

b. London, Feb. 28, 1958; m. Nechama née Lipman; Ch. Rabbinical Council, United Synagogue; Snr. Rabbi, Chigwell & Hainault United Synagogue (1997-); Chief Min. Adelaide Hebrew Congregation, South Australia (1988-97); Economist Dept of Intl. Affairs; Ministry of Finance, Jerusalem.

Add 5 Mount Pleasant Road, Chigwell, Essex IG7 5EP

Tel 020 8281 9878 Mobile 07711 231 560

Email baruch.davis@gmail.com

DAVIS, Mick,

b. Port Elizabeth, South Africa, February 15, 1958; m. Barbara née Hyman; Ch. UJIA (2006-12); Chief Exec. Xstrata plc (2002-14); Ch. Euro Chai of South Africa Trust (2002-); T. Kew Foundation (2009); Chief Exec. Xstrata AG (2001-02); Exec. Ch. Ingwe Coal Corporation (1995-2001); Chief Financial Officer and Exec. Dir. Billiton plc (prev. Gencor) (1994-2001); Exec. Dir. Eskom (1991-94); Mem. Jewish Leadership Council.

Add 6 Bloomsbury Square, London WC1A 2LP

Tel 020 7424 6400 *Fax* 020 7424 6401

Email info@thejlc.org *Website* www.thejlc.org

DE LANGE, Rabbi Nicholas R.M., FBA, MA, DPhil, DD.

b. Nottingham, Aug. 7, 1944; Emer. Prof. of Hebrew and Jewish Studies, Cambridge University; Fel. Wolfson College, Cambridge. Publ.: Penguin Dictionary of Judaism (2008); An Introduction to Judaism (2000); Illustrated History of the Jewish People (1997); Judaism (1986); Atlas of the Jewish World (1984); Apocrypha: Jewish Literature of the Hellenistic Age (1978); various specialised works and literary translations.

Add Wolfson College, Cambridge CB3 9BB

Tel 01223 740 561

Email nrml1@cam.ac.uk

DEECH, Baroness Ruth Lynn (née Fraenkel), DBE, MA (Oxon), MA (Brandeis), H. LLD (Strathclyde, Richmond); H. PhD (Ben Gurion), Barrister, QC (Hon).

b. London, Apr. 29, 1943, m. Dr John Deech; Ch. Bar Standards Board (2009-14); Gresham Prof. of Law (2008-12); Ch. Stuart Young Foundation Academic Panel (1991-); Independent Adjudicator for Higher Education (2004-08); Gov. BBC (2002-6); Rhodes Trust (1996-2006); Pro-V. Chancellor, Oxford University (2001-4); Principal, St Anne's College, Oxford (1991-2004); Freeman, Drapers' Co. (2003); Ch. UK Human Fertilisation and Embryology Authority (1994-2002); Governor, Oxford Centre for Hebrew and Jewish Studies (1994-2000); H. Bencher, Inner Temple (1996); Non-executive Dir. Oxon Health Authority (1993-94); V. Principal, St Anne's College (1988-91); Lecturer in Law, Oxford University (1970–91); Governor, Carmel College (1980-90); Snr. Proctor, Oxford University (1985-6). Publ.: From IVF to Immortality (2007).

Add House of Lords, London SW1A 0PW

Tel 020 7219 3000 *Fax* 020 7831 9217

Email deechr@parliament.uk

DESMOND, Richard Clive,

b. Dec. 8, 1951; Pres. Norwood (2006–); Proprietor, Express Newspapers (2000-); Ch. Northern and Shell Network (1974-).

Add Northern & Shell Building, Number 10 Lower Thames Street EC3R 6EN

Tel 020 8612 7000

DJANOGLY, Jonathan Simon MP,

b. London, June 3, 1965; m. Rebecca née Silk; Solicitor, SJ Berwin LLP (1990-2009); Parliamentary Under Secretary of State, Ministry of Justice (2010-12); MP Huntingdon (2001-); Shadow M. for Business (2005-10); Shadow Solicitor General (2004-10); form. Councillor, Westminster LBC (1994-2001).

Add House of Commons, London SW1A 0AA

Email jonathan.djanogly.mp@parliament.uk *Website* www.jonathandjanogly.com

DUFFIELD, Dame Vivien, DBE, CBE, MA (Oxon) H. DLitt, H. DPhil, H. RCM.

b. Mar. 26, 1946; Mem. Bd. Clore Leadership Programme (2004–); T. Jewish Community Centre for London (2004–); Dir. South Bank Bd (2002–); Gov. Royal Ballet (2002–); Ch. The Royal Opera House Endowment Fund; Ch. Clore Duffield Foundation; Bd. Weizmann Institute.

Add c/o Clore Duffield Foundation, 3 Chelsea Manor Studios, Flood Street SW3 5SR

Tel 020 7351 6061

Email info@cloreduffield.org.uk

DWEK, Joseph Claude (Joe), CBE, BSc, BA, AMCT, FTI, H. DSc UMIST.

b. Brussels, May 1, 1940; Mem. North West Development Agency (2004-12) (Ch. Environmental Cttee., V. Ch. Business and Innovations Cttee.); Mem. and Dir. Regional Advisory Cttee. of Forestry Commission; form. Mem. General Assembly, New University Manchester; form. Ch. Environlink; form. Mem. DTI/DEFRA Env. Innovation Adv. Group; Ch. Penmarric Ltd; Dir., form. Ch. and CEO, Bodycode International plc (1972-99); form. Ch. CBI North West; Gov. Manchester High School for Girls.

Add Penmarric Ltd, Suite One, Courthill House, 66 Water Lane, Wilmslow SK9 5AP

Tel 01625 549 081

Email penjcdwek@aol.com

DWEK, Raymond Allen, CBE.

b. Manchester, Nov. 10, 1941; m. Sandra; H. & Dir. Oxford Glycobiology Institute; Hon. FRCP (2007); Fel. Royal Society (1998); Fdr. Mem. Scientific Governing Bd., Shanghai Tech-University (2013-); Co-Ch. Birax Regenerative Medicine Initiative, UK/Israel (2012-); Mem. UK/Israel Science Council (2010); Ch. Scientific Cttee. (2010-) and Bd. Dir. United Therapeutics USA (2002-); Advisory Bd. Mem. Oxford University Museum of Natural History; Bd. Mem. The Scripps Korea Antibody Institute (2009-); Emer. Fel. Exeter College, Oxford (2009-); Oxford University Representative – Oxford Philomusica (2009-); Strategic Advisory Bd. Mem. National Institute for Bioprocesssing Research and Training (NIBRT) Dublin (2009-); Institute Prof. The Scripps Research Institute, La Jolla, USA (2008-); Bd. of Govs. Exec. Cttee. & Special Advisor to the President, Ben Gurion University, Israel (2005-); Bd. Scientific Govs. Scripps Research Institute, La Jolla (2003-); Dir. United Therapeutics (2002-), Prof. Glycobiology (1988-); Scientific Advisory Bd. Mem. United Therapeutics (2001-); International Advisory Bd. National Institute for Biotechnology in the Negev (NIBN), Israel (2005); Dir. Penmarric plc (1985).

Add Glycobiology Institute, Department of Biochemistry, University of Oxford, South Parks Road, Oxford OX1 3QU

Tel 01865 275 344 *Fax* 01865 275 771

Email raymond.dwek@exeter.ox.ac.uk *Website* www.bioch.ox.ac.uk/gylcob

EDER, Prof. Andrew, BDS, MSc, LDS, MFGDP, MRD, FDS, FHEA.

b. London, Apr. 21, 1964, m. Rosina née Saideman; Assoc. V. Provost (Enterprise) and Dir. of Life Learning, UCL (2013); Prof. of Restorative Dentistry and Dental Education, UCL Eastman Dental Institute; H. Consultant, Restorative Dentistry, UCLHT Eastman Dental

Hospital; Specialist, Restorative Dentistry and Prosthodontics; Exec. and Warden (2010-), Bd. of Management (1997-2010), Stanmore & Canons Park United Synagogue; Medical Advisory Panel, Chai Cancer Care, (2008-); Ch. Alpha Omega London Charitable Trust (2003-); Pres. The British Society for Restorative Dentistry (2005-06); Pres. Odontological Section, The Royal Society of Medicine (2001-02). Publ.: 923 (combination of papers, edited articles, posters, abstracts and press releases); Tooth Surface Loss (A. Eder & R. Ibbetson, 2000).

Add 2nd Floor, 57a Wimpole Street, London W1G 8YP

Tel 020 7486 7180

Email andreweder@restorative-dentistry.co.uk *Website* www.restorative-dentistry.co.uk

EDLIN, Paul Alan,

b. Glasgow, Apr. 25, 1949; Dental Surgeon; V. Pres. Board of Deputies of British Jews (2006-).

Add c/o Board of Deputies, 6 Bloomsbury Square, London WC1A 2LP

EHRENTREU, Dayan Chanoch,

b. Frankfurt-am-Main, Dec. 27, 1932; Av Beth Din, European Beth Din (2008); form. Rosh Beth Din, London Beth Din (1984-2008); Av Beth Din, Manchester Beth Din (1979-84); Principal, Sunderland Kolel (1960-79); Rav, Beth Yisroel Synagogue.

Add 55 Shirehall Park, London NW4 2QN

Tel 020 8202 2364

EIMER, Rabbi Colin, BSc (Econ), MA.

b. London, Mar. 8, 1945; Lecturer, Modern Jewish History, Leo Baeck College (2012-); Lecturer, Rabbinic Decision-Making, Leo Baeck College (2008-); Progressive Rabbinic Decision-Making (2008-); M. Sha'arei Tsedek North London Reform Synagogue (1977-); M. Finchley Reform Synagogue (2001-05); Ch. Assembly of Rabbis, RSGB (1999-2001, 1981-83); Lecturer, Hebrew, Leo Baeck College (1976-2007); form. M. Bushey Reform Synagogue (1975-77); Union Liberale Israelite Synagogue, Paris (1971-74).

Add Sha'arei Tsedek, North London Reform Synagogue, 120 Oakleigh Road North, London N20 9EZ

Tel 020 8445 3400

Email colineimer@aol.com

EISENBERG, Neville, BCom, LLB (Wits), LLM (LSE).

b. Cape Town, Apr. 12, 1962; Solicitor; Board Mem. Joint Distribution Cttee. (2014-); London Council, Confederation of British Industry (2012-); Tru. Tel Aviv Foundation (UK) (2012-); Associate Gov. Hebrew University (2004-); Man. Partner, Berwin Leighton Paisner LLP (1999-); Ch. British Israel Law Association (1996-); Freeman, City of London Solicitors Company; Ch. South African Union of Jewish Students (1982-84); Comptroller, World Union of Jewish Students (1986-89).

Add Adelaide House, London Bridge, London EC4R 9HA

Tel 020 3400 4473

Email neville.eisenberg@blplaw.com *Website* www.blplaw.com

EKER, Rita (née Shapiro), MBE.

b. London, Oct. 15, 1938; Co-Ch. Women's Campaign for Soviet Jewry (the 35s); Tru. of One to One and One to One Treks in Israel.

Add Carradine House, 237 Regents Park Road, London N3 3LF

Tel 020 8343 4156 *Fax* 020 8343 2119

Email rita@one-to-one.org *Website* www.one-to-one.org

ELLMAN, Louise Joyce, BA Hons, MPhil.

b. Nov. 14, 1945; m. Geoffrey David; Ch. Transport Select Cttee (2008–) (Mem. since 2002); Mem. Board of Deputies of British Jews (2008-); Ch. Jewish Labour Movement (2004-); V. Ch. Labour Friends of Israel (2004–); MP (Lab and Co-op), Liverpool Riverside (1997-); Leader, Lancashire County Council (1981-97); Lancs CC (1970–97); V. Pres. All

Party Parliamentary Cttee. against Antisemitism; Council Mem. Holocaust Educational Trust; Mem. Holocaust Memorial Day Trust; T. All Party Baha'i Group; V. Ch. All Party Britain-Israel Group.

Add House of Commons, London SW1A 0AA

Email louise.ellman.mp@parliament.uk *Website* www.louiseellman.co.uk

ELTON, Ben, BA.

b. May 3, 1959; m. Sophia Gare; author and performer; Royal Television Society Writers' Award (1989). Publ.: Love Never Dies (musical) (2010); Meltdown (2010); Blind Faith (2007); Chart Throb (2006); The First Casualty (2005); Past Mortem (2004); High Society (2002); We Will Rock You (musical) (2002); Dead Famous (2001); Inconceivable (1999).

Add c/o Phil McIntyre, 2nd Floor, 35 Soho Square W1D 3QX

Tel 020 7439 2270

EMANUEL, Rabbi Dr Charles, BA, MHL, DD (HUC).

b. New York, Dec. 15, 1944; m. Peduth; Rabbi Emer. North Western Reform Synagogue (2005-), M. (1983-2005); form. Ch. Assembly of Rabbis of the Reform Synagogues of Great Britain (1986-88); form M. Sinai Synagogue, Leeds (1979-83), Temple Beth-El, Huntsville, Alabama (1973-79).

Add North Western Reform Synagogue, Alyth Gardens NW11 7EN

Tel 020 8455 6763 *Fax* 020 8731 8175

Email charles@alyth.org

FABRICANT, Michael Louis David, MP, BA, MSc Systems, CEng.

b. June 12, 1950; Government Whip (2010-); Ch. Royal Marines All Party Parliamentary Group (2005–10) (Jt Ch. 1999–2005); All Party Anglo-German Group (1997–2010); All Party Group on Film Industry (1997–2010); MP (C) Lichfield (1997-2012) (Mid-Staffordshire, 1992–97); V. Ch. All Party Group on Smoking and Health (1997–); Opposition Whip (2005–10); Opposition front-bench spokesman, Trade and Industry (2003–05); Co-Fdr. and Dir. International Broadcast Electronics and Investment Group (1979–91).

Add House of Commons, London SW1A 0AA

Tel 020 7219 5022

Email michael.fabricant.mp@parliament.uk *Website* www.michaelfabricant.mp.co.uk

FARHI, Musa Moris, MBE, FRSL, FRGS.

b. Ankara, July 5, 1935; m. Nina Ruth née Gould (d. 2009); Writer; V. Pres. International PEN (2001-); Ch. International PEN Writers in Prison Cttee. (1997-2000); Ch. English PEN Writers in Prison Cttee. (1994-97); M. Ed. Bd. Jewish Quarterly. Publ.: Songs from Two Continents (2011); A Designated Man (2009); Young Turk (2004); Children of the Rainbow (1999); Journey Through the Wilderness (1989); The Last of Days (1983); The Pleasure of Your Death (1972).

Add 17 Courtenay Gate, Courtenay Terrace, Hove, East Sussex BN3 2WJ

Tel 01273 729 011

Email farhi@clara.net

FARHI, Rabbi Shlomo,

b. Jerusalem, Israel, Mar. 7, 1978; m. Chana née Abihkzer; Rabbi and Dir. Schools Department Aish Hatorah UK; form. Dir and Fdr. Chazak.

Add 379 Hendon Way, London NW4 3LP

FEATHERSTONE, Lynne (née Ryness), MP.

b. London, Dec. 20, 1951; Minister, International Development Department (2012-); Parliamentary Under Secretary of State, (Equalities Minister) for the Home Office (2010-12); MP (Lib Dem) for Hornsey and Wood Green (2005-); Councillor, Haringey (1998-2006); London Assembly (2000-05). Publ.: Marketing and Communication Techniques for Architects (1992).

Add House of Commons, London SW1A 0AA

Tel 020 8340 5459

Email lynne@lynnefeatherstone.org *Website* www.lynnefeatherstone.org

FEINSTEIN, Elaine (née Cooklin), MA (Cantab), HonD.Litt (Leic.), FRSL.

b. Bootle, Oct. 24, 1930; m. Dr Arnold Feinstein; Writer; Cholmondeley Award for Poetry (1990). Among recent publications: Bride of Ice (2009); The Russian Jerusalem (2008); Talking to the Dead (poems, 2007); Anna of All the Russias: a biography of Anna Akhmatova (2005); Collected Poems and Translations (2002); Ted Hughes: The Life of a Poet (2001); Gold (poems, 2000); Pushkin (biog. 1998); Daylight (poems, 1997); Dreamers (novel, 1996); Lawrence's Women (biog. 1993); Loving Brecht (novel, 1993); All You Need (1991); Survivors (1991); Mother's Girl (1988); A Captive Lion: The Life of Marina Tsvetayeva (1987); Badlands (poems, 1987); Bessie Smith (biog. 1985); The Border (1985); Selected poems.

Add c/o Rogers, Coleridge & White, 20 Powis Mews W11 1JN

Tel 020 8221 3717

FELSENSTEIN, Frank, BA (Hons), PhD.

b. Westminster, July 28, 1944; m. Carole; Prof. Humanities, Ball State University (2002-); Dir. Honors Program, Yeshiva College, NY (1998-2002); form. Reader in English, University of Leeds; Vis. Prof. Vanderbilt University, USA (1989-90). Publ.: Tobias Smollett, Travels through France and Italy (Ed. 2011); John Thelwall: Two Plays (Co-Ed. 2006); English Trader, Indian Maid: Representing Gender, Race and Slavery in the New World (1999); Hebraica and Judaica from the Cecil Roth Collection, exhibition catalogue (Brotherton Library, 1997); Anti-Semitic Stereotypes: A Paradigm of Otherness in English Popular Culture, 1660-1830 (1995); The Jew as Other: A Century of English Caricature, 1730-1830, exhibition catalogue (Jewish Theological Seminary, New York, 1995); Co-Dir. 'What Middleton Read' Project (www.bsu.edu/libraries/wmr); review work for 'The Jewish Quarterly Review', Journal of Modern Jewish Studies'.

Add 8 Manor Drive, Morristown, NJ 07960-2611, USA

Tel +1 (973) 889 1323

Email felsenstein@bsu.edu

FENTON, Stephen, BSc (Econ), FCA.

b. London, Mar. 26, 1952; m. Susan née Firman; Chartered Accountant; V. Pres. United Synagogue (2011-); T. US (2005-2011); Fin. Representative, Bushey Synagogue (1999-2005).

Add Palladium House, 1-4 Argyll Street, London W1F 7LD

Tel 020 7437 7666

Email Stephenfenton@hazlemsfenton.com *Website* www.theus.org.uk

FERSHT, Sir Alan Roy, MA, PhD, FRS.

b. London, Apr. 21, 1943; m. Marilyn née Persell; Master, Gonville and Caius College (2012-); Group Leader, MRC Laboratory of Molecular Biology; Emer. Herchel Smith Prof. Organic Chemistry, Cambridge; Dir. Cambridge Council for Protein Engineering; Prof. Biological Chemistry, Imperial College, London; Wolfson Res. Prof. Royal Society (1978-88); Scientific Staff, MRC Lab. Molecular Biology, Cambridge (1969-77). Publ.: Enzyme Structure and Mechanism; Structure and Mechanism in Protein Science.

Add Gonville and Caius College, Cambridge CB2 1TA

Tel 01223 332 431

Email arf25@cam.ac.uk

FINKELSTEIN, Daniel, Baron of Pinner, OBE.

b. London, Aug. 30, 1962; m. Nicola Connor; Journalist; Executive Editor, The Times, form. Associate Ed. and Chief Leader Writer (2008-), Comment Ed. (2004-8), Leader Writer (2001-); Fink Tank column (2002-); form. Conservative Party candidate, Harrow West (2001); Chief Policy Adv. to William Hague (1997-2001); form. Dir. Conservative Party Res. Dept. (1995-97). Awarded the PSA Journalist of the Year Award (2011); Chaim Bermant

Journalism Prize (2008).

Add The Times, 1 Pennington Street, London E98 1TT

Email daniel.finkelstein@thetimes.co.uk

FINLAY, Alan Stanley, LL.B.

b. London, Apr. 2, 1950; m. Kathryn née Fine; Solicitor; Pres. Federation of Synagogues (form. Treasurer); Ch. AJY (1984-88); V. Pres. World Confederation of Jewish Community Centres (1984-88); Ch. Jewish Youth Voluntary Service (1974-78).

Add 4 Orchard Close, Edgware, Middlesex HA8 7RE

Tel 020 8952 7517

Email asf@federationofsynagogues.com

FISCHER, John Joseph, BA (Hons).

b. Antwerp, Belgium, Feb. 11, 1937; Banking and Financial Services; Compiler, Calendar entry for The JC (1986-), Calendar section of the Jewish Year Book (1965-); Governor, Henrietta Barnet School, London (1968-1987); Councillor, London Borough of Barnet (Cons) (1968-1974).

Add Flat 2, 39 The Grove, London N3 1QT

Tel 020 8346 7980

FITZSIMONS, Lorna, BA Hons.

b. Aug. 6, 1967; m. Stephen Cooney; Dir. Lorna Fitzsimons Consulting LTD (2012-); CEO, BICOM (2006-12); Lorna Fitzsimons Consulting (2005–06); Snr. Associate Fel. UK Defence Acad. Advanced Res. and Assessment Group (2005); MP (Lab), Rochdale (1997–2005); contested (Lab) same seat (2005); V. Pres. Women's Cttee. Parliamentary Labour Party (2001–05), Ch. (1997–2001); Supporter, Labour Friends of Israel (1997–2005); Parliamentary Private Secretary to Leader of House of Commons (2001–03), to M. of State, FCO (2000–01); Pres. National Union of Students (1992-4).

Add Lorna Fitzsimons Consulting LTD, 200 Drake Street, Rochdale OL16 1PJ

FIXMAN, Sydney,

b. Manchester, Apr. 5, 1935; Music Lecturer, London University Institute of Education; Fdr. Conductor, Ben Uri Chamber Orchestra, Jewish Youth Orchestra; Music Dir. West London Synagogue; form. Guest Conductor, leading orchestras in Britain and abroad (seasons in Israel: 1976-89); Conductor, BBC (TV and Radio). Publ.: (Ed.) Psaume Tehillim (Markevitch); Recordings, CDs.

Add 5 Bradby House, Hamilton Terrace NW8 9XE

FRANKLIN, Andrew Cecil,

b. London, Mar. 6, 1957; m. Caroline Sarah née Elton; Dir. And Publisher Profile Books Ltd (1996-); Dir. And Publisher Pevsner Books Trust (1996-); Dir. and Publisher Jewish Community Centre UK (2004-10); Dir. And Publisher JCC Ventures Ltd (2010-2012); Dir. Jewish Literary Trust (1991-2010).

Add Profile Books, 3A, Exmouth House, Pine Street, Exmouth Market, London EC1R 0JH

Tel 020 7841 6300 *Fax* 020 7833 3969

Email andrew.franklin@profilebooks.com

FRASER, Dr Ronnie, PhD. PGCE, B.Sc..

b. London, Mar. 18, 1947; m. Lola Fraser née Jacobs; Lecturer and pro-Israel activist; Exec. Dir. Academic Friends of Israel. Publ.: The British Trade Union Movement, Israel, and Boycotts (2011), Trade Union and Other Boycotts of Israel in Great Britain and Ireland (2009), The Academic Boycott of Israel: A Review of the Five-Year UK Campaign to Defeat It (2008), The Academic Boycott of Israel: Why Britain (2005), Understanding Trades Union Hostility towards Israel and Its Consequences for Anglo-Jewry (Ed. by Paul Iganski and Barry Kosmin, 2003).

Add 1 Colman Court, Rosedale Close, Stanmore, Middlesex HA7 3QF

Tel 07973 723289

Email mail@academics-for-israel.org

FREEDLAND, Jonathan,

b. London, Feb. 25, 1967; m. Sarah née Peters; Journalist; Monthly Columnist, The Jewish Chronicle (1998-); Columnist, The Guardian (1997-); Washington Correspondent, The Guardian (1993-97); Presenter, The Long View (BBC Radio 4). Awards: David Watt Prize for Journalism (2008); Columnist of the Year, What the Papers Say Awards (2002). Publ.: (Fiction, under pseudonym Sam Bourne): Pantheon (2012); The Chosen One (2010); The Final Reckoning (2008); The Last Testament (2007); The Righteous Men (2006); (Nonfiction, under own name): Jacob's Gift (2005); Bring Home the Revolution: The Case for a British Republic (1998).

Add The Guardian, Kings Place, 90 York Way, London N1 9GU

Tel 020 7278 2332

Website www.jonathanfreedland.com

FREEDLAND, Michael Rodney,

b. London, Dec. 18, 1934; Journalist and Broadcaster; contributor to national press; Exec. Ed. and Presenter (BBC and LBC), 'You Don't Have to be Jewish' (1971-94). Among recent publications: Jolson; Andre Previn; Leonard Bernstein: Music Man; Sean Connery: A Biography; All the Way: A Biography of Frank Sinatra; Bob Hope; Bing Crosby; Michael Caine; Doris Day; Some Like it Cool; King of the Road; (with Morecambe and Wise) There's No Answer To That; (with Walter Scharf) Composed and Conducted by Walter Scharf; Confessions of a Serial Biographer; Hollywood on Trial; Witch Hunt in Hollywood; The Men Who Made Hollywood; Judy Garland: The Other Side of the Rainbow; Elvis Memories; Man on the Rock.

Add 152 Albany, Manor Road, Bournemouth BH1 3EW

Tel 01202 801 787

Email michael.freedland1@talktalk.net

FREEDMAN, Harry, PhD, MA (London), BA.

b. London, 1950; Ch. Exec. The Career Advice Centre; Lecturer, London Jewish Cultural Centre; Lecturer, JW3; form. Dir. and Lecturer Masorti Academy (1994-2001); form. Chief Exec. Assembly of Masorti Synagogues (1994-2000); European Representative, Masorti; Lay M. Exeter Synagogue (1981-87); Editorial Adv. Cttee. Jewish Bible Quarterly, Judaism Today. Publ.: The Talmud: A Biography (2014); Jerusalem Imperilled (2011); How to get a Job in a Recession (2009); The Gospels' Veiled Agenda (2009); The Halacha in Targum Pseudo-Jonathan (1999).

Add North Gate, Prince Albert Road, London NW8 7EL

Tel 084 5467 4167

Email harry.freedman@btopenworld.com *Website* www.thecareeradvicecentre.com

FREEDMAN, Jeromé David, FCA.

b. Brighton, 1935; m. Louise née Hershman; Chartered Accountant; T. Chartered Accountants' Benevolent Association (CABA 1973-2008, Pres. 2003-05); V. Pres. LJ, form. Ch. (1995-2001); form. Hon. T. (1990-95); Past Pres. South London Liberal Synagogue.

Add 5 Thanescroft Gardens, Croydon, Surrey CR0 5JR

Tel 020 8688 2250 *Fax* 020 8680 4631

Email jerome@freedman.org

FREEDMAN, Prof. Sir Lawrence, PC, KCMG, CBE, FBA, FKC.

b. Tynemouth, Dec. 7, 1948; m. Prof. Judith Anne née Hill; Prof. War Studies, King's College London (1982-); V. Principal, (2003-); H. Dir. Centre for Defence Studies (1990–); T. Imperial War Museum (2001–10); Chesney Gold Medal, RUSI (2006). Among recent publications: Strategy: A History (2013); A Choice of Enemies (2008, Lionel Gelber Prize, 2009); The Official History of the Falklands Campaign, Vols. I and II (2005); Deterrence (2004); Superterrorism (Ed. 2002); The Cold War (2001); Kennedy's Wars (2000); The Politics of British Defence (1999).

Add King's College London, James Clerk Maxwell Building, 57 Waterloo Road, London SE1 8WA

Tel 020 7848 3984 *Fax* 020 7848 3668

FREEDMAN, Vanessa Rosalind (née Gale), MA.

b. Birmingham, July 18, 1969; m. Rabbi Paul; Convenor, Hebraica Libraries Group (2012-); Librarian, Hebrew and Jewish Studies, University College London (2007-); Assistant Librarian, Leo Baeck College (2000-07).

Add UCL Library Services, University College London, Gower Street, London WC1E 6BT

Tel 020 7679 2598 *Fax* 020 7679 7373

Email v.freedman@ucl.ac.uk *Website* www.ucl.ac.uk/library

FREER, Mike,

b. May 29, 1960; Leader, Barnet Council (2006-09, 1990-94); Conservative Member of Parliament, Finchley and Golders Green; Mem. Conservative Friends of Israel; V. Pres. All Party Group Against Anti-Semitism.

Add House of Commons, London SW1A 0AA

Tel 020 7219 7071

Email mike.freer.mp@parliament.uk *Website* www.mikefreer.com

FREI, Saul David, LLB (Hons).

b. Hendon, 1954; m. Aviva Graus; Solicitor; Mem. Board of Deputies Family Law Cttee. (2000-); Gov. Hasmonean High School (1994-2009); United Synagogue Company Sec. and Dir. of External & Legal Services (2008-); Registrar, London Beth Din (1999-); Solicitor specialising in property litigation (1980-99).

Add 305 Ballards Lane, London N12 8GB

Tel 020 8343 6270 *Fax* 020 8343 6257

Email dfrei@theus.org.uk

FRESHWATER, Benzion,

b. 1948; Ch. and Managing Dir. Daejan Holdings Plc (1980-); T. Mayfair Charities Ltd.

Add Freshwater House 158-162 Shaftesbury Avenue, London WC2H 8HR

FRESHWATER, Rabbi Shlomo,

Rabbi, Sassover Beit Midrash (2003-); Managing Dir. Freshwater Group.

Add Freshwater House 158-162 Shaftesbury Avenue, London WC2H 8HR

FRIEDLANDER, Evelyn (née Philipp), ARCM, Order of Merit (Germany).

b. London, June 22, 1940; Executive Dir. Hidden Legacy Foundation; T. and Ch. Czech Memorial Scrolls Trust. Publ.: Westminster Synagogue: the First 50 Years (2007); The Jews of Devon and Cornwall (2000); Mappot ... The Band of Jewish Tradition (1997, Co-Ed.); Ich Will nach Hause, aber ich war noch nie da (1996).

Add Kent House, Rutland Gardens, London SW7 1BX

Tel 020 7584 2754 *Fax* 020 7581 8012

Email epfriedlander@gmail.com

FRIEDMAN, (Eve) Rosemary (Robert Tibber, Rosemary Tibber, Rosemary Friedman),

b. London, Feb. 5, 1929; Writer. m. Dennis Friedman; Membership: Royal Society of Literature; Society of Authors; Writers Guild of Great Britain; British Academy of Film and Television Arts; Fel. English PEN. Among recent publications: The Man Who Understood Women and other stories (2013); Life is a Joke (2010); A Writer's Commonplace Book (2006); Paris Summer (2004); Intensive Care (2001); The Writing game (1999); Vintage (1996); Golden Boy (1994). Other: An Eligible Man (Stage Play, 2008); Change of Heart (Stage Play, 2004); Home Truths (Stage Play, 1997).

Add Apt. 5, 3 Cambridge Gate, London NW1 4JX

Tel 020 7935 6252 *Fax* 020 7486 2398

Email rosemaryfriedman@hotmail.com *Website* www.rosemary.friedman.co.uk

FRIEND, John, BSc, PhD (Liv), PhD (Cantab), FIBiol, FRSA.

b. Liverpool, May 31, 1931; m. Carol née Loofe; Pres. Hull Jewish Representative Council (1999-2003); Emer. Prof. of Plant Biology, Hull University (Prof. 1969-97); Vis. Fel. Wolfson College, Cambridge (1988); Pro-V. Chancellor, Hull University (1983-87); Vis. Prof. Hebrew

University of Jerusalem (1974). Publ.: Recent Advances in the Biochemistry of Fruit and Vegetables (with MJC Rhodes, 1983); Biochemical Aspects of Plant-Parasite Relations (with D. R. Threlfall, 1976).

Add 9 Allanhall Way, Kirkella, Hull HU10 7QU

Tel 01482 658 930

Email j.friend@cj2f.karoo.co.uk

FRY, Dr Helen (née Doney), PhD, Theology (University of Exeter).

b. Ilfracombe, July 22, 1967; m. Dr Martin Fry; Historian and Biographer; Resident Scholar, JW3 (2015-); H. Research Fel. UCL (1999-). Among recent publications: The Jews of Plymouth (2015), Spymaster: The Secret Life of Kendrick (2014), The M Room: Secret Listeners Who Bugged the Nazi's (2013), The Jews of Exeter (2013), Churchill's Secret Soldiers (2013), Jewish Cemeteries of Devon (2012), Inside Nuremberg Prison (2011), Denazification (2010), German Schoolboy, British Commando (2010), From Dachau to D-Day (2009), Freud's War (2009), Music and Men: The Life and Loves of Harriet Cohen (2008), Jews in N. Devon in WW2 (2005), Christian-Jewish Dialogue: A Reader (1996).

Add 38 Temple Gardens, London NW11 0LL

Tel 07796 213 217

Email hpfry@btinternet.com

GAFFIN, Jean (née Silver), OBE, JP, HonFRCPCH, MSc, BSc (Econ).

b. London, Aug. 1, 1936; m. Alexander (dec'd); T. St. Luke's Hospice (2007-13); V. Ch. Chronic Pain Policy Coalition (2005-11); Ch. Brent Primary Care NHS Trust (2002-07); Magistrate, Harrow Bench (1981-2006); Mem. Consumer Panel Financial Services Author (1999-2003); Hon. S. Royal Society of Medicine (1997-2001); Exec. Dir. National Hospice Council (1991-98); Chief Exec. Arthritis Care (1988-91); Exec. Sec. British Paediatric Association (1982-87); Organising Sec. Child Accident Prevention Cttee. (1979-82); Lecturer II/Snr. Lecturer, Social Policy and Admin. Polytechnic of the South Bank (1973-79). Publ.: with D. Thoms, Caring and Sharing: the Centenary History of the Co-operative Women's Guild (1983, 2nd edition 1993); The Nurse and the Welfare State (Ed. 1981).

Add 79 Chalet Estate, Hammers Lane, London NW7 4DL

Tel 020 8959 9509

Email jean.gaffin@btopenworld.com

GAINSFORD, Sir Ian, BDS, DDS, FDSRCS Eng, FDSRCS Edin., FRCSEd.H., FICD, FACD, FKC, DDS (Hons) Toronto, FRSA.

b. Twickenham, June 24, 1930; m. Carmel née Liebster; Dental Surgeon; V. Pres. Jerusalem Great Synagogue; H. Pres. British Friends of Magen David Adom (1995-); Regent, Royal College of Surgeons, Edinburgh (2002-9), now Regent Emer.; Pres. Maccabaeans (2000-07); Pres. Western Marble Arch Synagogue (1998-2000); V. Principal, King's College, London (1994-97), now V. Principal Emer.; Dean, King's College School of Medicine and Dentistry (1988-97).

Add Flat 1, 12a Dor Vedorshav, Jerusalem 93117, Israel

Email iandgainsford@aol.com

GALASKO, Prof. Charles Samuel Bernard, MB, BCh. (First Class Hon), MSc (Hon), FRCSEng, FRCSEd, ChM, FMed.Sci, FCMSA (Hon), FFSEM (Ireland), FFSEM (UK).

b. Johannesburg, South Africa, June 29, 1939; m. Carol; Consultant Orthopaedic Surgeon; Emer. Prof. Orthopaedic Surgery, University of Manchester; Hunterian Prof. Royal College of Surgeons; Inaugural Pres. Intercollegiate Faculty of Sport and Exercise Medicine (UK) (2006-09); Ch. Intercollegiate Academic Board for Sport and Exercise Medicine (2002-05); Member Medical Cttee. British Olympic Association (1988-2003); Pres. British Orthopaedic Association (2000-01), Ch. Academic Board (1998-2002), V. Pres. (1999-2000); V. Pres. Royal College of Surgeons of England (1999-2001), Ch. Hospital Recognition Cttee. (1992-95), Ch. Training Board (1995-99); V. Pres. British Amateur Wrestling Association (1996-2001), Ch. (1989-96); V. Ch. English Olympic Wrestling Association (1988-2001); Ch. Jt. Cttee. of Higher Surgical Training (GB & Ireland) (1997-2000); Sir

Arthur Sims Commonwealth Prof. (1998); Pres. International Orthopaedic Research Society (1990-93); Ch. Awards Cttee., International Orthopaedic and Trauma Association (1990-93, 1984-87); V. Pres. Section of Oncology, Royal Society of Medicine (1987); H. Fel. British Orthopaedic Association; H. Fel. South African Orthopaedic Association. Publ.: Imaging Techniques in Orthopaedics (1989); Current Trends in Orthopaedic Surgery (1988); Neuromuscular Problems in Orthopaedics (1987); Recent Developments in Orthopaedic Surgery (1987); Skeletal Metastases (1986); Principles of Fracture Management (1984); Radionuclide Scintigraphy and Orthopaedics (1984); over 250 learned articles in refereed journals or book chapters.

Add 72 Gatley Road, Gatley, Cheshire SK8 4AA

Tel 0161 428 3582 *Fax* 0161 428 4558

Email carolgalasko@aol.com

GELLER, Markham Judah,

b. Corpus Christi, Texas, Jan. 2, 1949; Jewish Chronicle Prof. Dept. of Hebrew and Jewish Studies, University College London; Dir. Institute of Jewish Studies, University College London; on secondment, Gastprofessor für Wissengeschichte, at Freie Universität Berlin until 2015.

Add Dept of Hebrew and Jewish Studies, UCL, Gower Street, London WC1E 6BT

Fax 020 7209 1026

Email m.geller@ucl.ac.uk *Website* www.ucl.ac.uk/hebrew-jewish/ijs

GELLEY, Dayan Menachem,

b. Aug. 23, 1958, Newcastle; m. Devorah Silber; Snr. Dayan, London Beth Din (2007-), Dayan (1993-2006); Rabbi, Ohr Chodosh Community (2004-).

Add London Beth Din, 305 Ballards Lane N12 8GB

Tel 020 8343 6270 *Fax* 020 8343 6257

Email info@bethdin.org.uk

GILBERT, Andrew, BSc.

b. London, May 31, 1959; Managing Dir. Henry Bertrand Silk Fabrics; Ch. UJIA UK Programme Cttee. (2011-); Ch. UJIA Youth Movements Allocations Board (2010-); Tru. London Jewish Forum (2006-); Mem. UJIA UK Programme Cttee. (1997-); HW Fisher Special Award at the Jewish Volunteering Network Awards for Limmud (2010); Mem. MASA Cttee. Bd. Gov. JAFI (2009-10); Fdr. Ch. Limmud International (2006-10); V. Ch. World Reform Zionist Movement (2006-10); Mem. Education Cttee. Bd. Gov. Jewish Agency for Israel (2001-10); Fdr. Mem. Jewish Leadership Council (2003-05); Ch. RSGB (2002-05); Ch. Israel Experience Policy Group, UJIA (1997-2002); Ch. Jewish Youth Service Partners Group (1994-1998); Ch. Board of Deputies, Education, Youth and Information Cttee. (1994-1997); Exec. Mem. Board of Deputies (1994-97); Ch. Limmud (1990-97); Ch. European Hanhallah, Coalition for the Advancement of Jewish Education of North America (1996).

Add 52 Holmes Road, London NW5 3AB

Tel 020 7424 7000 *Fax* 020 7424 7001

Email alphasilk@gmail.com

GILBERT, Rt. Hon. Sir Martin, CBE, D.Litt, PC.

b. London, Oct. 25, 1936; historian; Official Biographer of Winston Churchill (since 1968); Fel. Merton College, Oxford (1962-99); Vis. Prof. Hebrew University (1995-98, 1980); Vis. Prof. UCL (1995-96); Vis. Prof. Tel Aviv University (1979). Among recent publications: Winston S. Churchill (official biographer of 6 vols., with 11 vols. documents); 85 historical works including 9 Atlases; 9 on Churchill (inc. Churchill, A Life and Churchill, Power of Words); 13 on Twentieth Century History (inc. History of both World Wars); 10 on Holocaust themes (inc. An Atlas of the Holocaust, The Holocaust, The Jewish Tragedy); 7 on Israel (inc. The Story of Israel; Israel, A History); 4 on Jewish themes (inc. Churchill and the Jews and In Ishmael's House: A History of the Jews of the Arab Lands).

Add Merton College, Oxford, Merton Street, Oxford OX1 4JD

Email esthergilbert36@gmail.com *Website* www.martingilbert.com

GINSBURY, Rabbi Mordechai Shlomo,

b. London, May 10, 1960; m. Judy née Burns; Dir. P'eir (Promoting Excellence in Rabbi's), The United Synagogue's In-Service training, Professional development and support facility for its Rabbis and Rebbetzens (2009-); Principal Hasmonean Primary School (2003-); M. Hendon US (1999-); Ch. (2005-08); V. Ch. (2002-05) Rabbinical Council, US; M. Prestwich Hebrew Congregation, Manchester (1985-99); Ch. Rabbinical Council of the Provinces (1997-98).

Add Hendon United Synagogue, 18 Raleigh Close, London NW4 2TA

Tel 020 8202 6924 *Fax* 020 8202 1720

Email rabbiginsbury@hendonus.org.uk

GINSBURY, Rabbi Philip Norman, M.A.

b. London, Mar. 26, 1936; form. M. South London Synagogue; M. Streatham District Synagogue, Brixton Synagogue; Ch. South London Rabbinical Council. Publ.: The Phases of Jewish History (2005); Jewish Faith in Action (1995).

Add 146 Downton Avenue, London SW2 3TT

Tel 020 8674 7451

Email rabbi@ginsburyp.co.uk

GLASSER, David,

b. Glasgow, Sept. 10, 1952; m. Susan née DeRose; Freeman, The Company of Arts Scholars (2013-); University Court of the London South Bank University (2012-); Ch. and Chief Exec. (pro bono) of Ben Uri, The London Jewish Museum of Art. (2000-); Northgate Consulting (1990-); Various privately owned companies (1989–1999); Ward White Group plc. (1985-1988); Company Dir. Marks and Spencer plc. (1970-1985). Publ.: Israel and Art: 60 Years through the eyes of Teddy Kollek (2008); contributed to various books on British and European artists of Jewish descent.

Add Ben Uri, 108a Boundary Road, St John's Wood, London NW8 0RH

Tel 020 7604 3991

Email davidg@benuri.org.uk

GLATTER, Robert, FCA.

b. Antwerp, Belgium, Mar. 14, 1937; Chartered Accountant, Non-Exec. Dir. Bank Leumi (UK) plc; Ch. Bank Leumi Pension Fund; Non-Exec. Dir. CP Holdings Ltd; V. Pres. Bnai Brith Hillel Foundation; H. Life Pres. Maccabi Union GB; form. T. Arbib Lucas Charity; form. V. Pres. Akiva School; Mem. Maccabi World Union; form. Ch. Maccabi Union GB; T. Woolf Institute, Cambridge; form. Council Mem. Weizmann Institute Foundation; T. Maccabi Fd.; form. T. Volcani Fund; form. Gov. T. Carmel College; Ch. NW Reform Synagogue; Ch. RSGB Cttee. for Ed. and Youth; form. Ch. RSGB Israel Action Ct.; form. T. Bd. for Jewish Sport; form. T. Manor House Trustees.

Add 12 York Gate, London NW1 4QS

Email rg@rgconsultancy.co.uk

GLAZER, Ella, MBE.

b. London; m. Stanley; Journalist; H. Exec. Dir. The Celebrities Guild of GB (founded 1977).

Add The Studio, 16 Covert Way EN4 0LT

Tel 020 8449 1234

Email info@celebritiesguild.org.uk

GLINERT, Lewis H, BA (Oxon), PhD.

b. London, June 17, 1950; m. Joan née Abraham; University Lecturer; Prof. of Hebraic Studies and Linguistics, Dartmouth College; form. Prof. of Hebrew, University of London (School of Oriental and African Studies, 1979-97); Dir. Centre for Jewish Studies, SOAS; Vis. Prof. of Hebrew Studies, Chicago University (1987/8); Assistant Prof. of Hebrew Linguistics, Haifa University (1974-77). Publ.: Mamma Dear (1997); Modern Hebrew: An

Essential Grammar (1994); Hebrew in Ashkenaz (1993); The Joys of Hebrew (1992); The Grammar of Modern Hebrew (1989).
Add Dartmouth College, 6191 Bartlett Hall, Hanover, N.H 03755, USA
Tel +1 (603) 646 8238 *Fax* +1 (603) 646 3115
Email Lewis.Glinert@Dartmouth.edu *Website* www.dartmouth.edu/~glinert/

GLOBE, Gordon Sherr,
b. Liverpool, Jan. 9, 1950; m. Maxine née Bellman; Property Management Surveyor; Dep. Merseyside Jewish Representative Council (MRJC) Board of Deputies (2011-); Pres. MJRC (2008-12); Ch. MJRC (2008-11); Dir. MJRC Charitable Ltd Company (2010-); Pres. Merseyside Jewish Community Care (MJCC) (2003-6); Dir. MJCC Charitable Ltd Company (2007-); Ch. Wardens of Orthodox Synagogues, Liverpool (1995-98); Pres. and Snr. Warden, Liverpool Greenbank Drive, Hebrew Congregation (1992-4).
Fax 0151 737 1052
Email globe.gordon@gmail.com

GOLD, Trudy,
Chief Exec. London Jewish Cultural Centre; Snr. Lecturer, Jewish History. Publ.: Lessons of the Holocaust (Ed-in-Chief, 1996).
Add LJCC, Ivy House, 94-96 North End Road, London NW11 7SX
Tel 020 8457 5000
Email admin@ljcc.org.uk

GOLDBERG, Rabbi David J, MA (Oxon), DD (Hons), OBE.
b. London, Feb. 25, 1939; Rabbi Emer. Liberal Jewish Synagogue; Co-Pres. London Society of Jews and Christians (2004-); Snr. Rabbi, L.J.S. (1986-2004), Associate Rabbi (1975-86); Interfaith Gold Medallion (1999); Premio Iglesias (1999); Ch. ULPS Rabbinic Conference (1996-98, 1981-83); M. Wembley and District Liberal Synagogue (1971-75). Publ.: The Story of the Jews (2014); This is not the Way: Jews, Judaism and Israel (2012); The Jewish People: Their History and their Religion (with John D. Rayner); To the Promised Land: A History of Zionist Thought; On the Vistula Facing East (Ed.); Progressive Judaism Today (Gen. Ed.); Aspects of LJ (Co-Ed.); The Divided Self: Israel and the Jewish Psyche Today.
Add Liberal Jewish Synagogue, 28 St. John's Wood Road NW8 7HA
Tel 020 7286 5181
Email djg@bartvillas.org.uk *Website* rabbidavidjgoldberg.com

GOLDBERG, David Jonathan, MA (Jewish Communal Service) Brandeis; Cert. Youth and Community Studies, London.
b. London, June 27, 1961; Dir. Fundraising, UJIA (2006-); Dir. UJIA Israel Experience (1998-2006); Exec. Dir. Zionist Federation of Great Britain and Ireland (1992-98); H. Ch. Association of Jewish Communal Professionals (1992-98); Snr. Youth and Community Work, Redbridge JYCC (1983-90).
Add 18 Chiltern Avenue, Bushey, Hertfordshire WD23 4QA
Tel 020 8950 0080
Email davidj.goldberg@btinternet.com

GOLDMAN, Alan,
Ch. Crest Nicholson Holdings (2009-11); form. Dir. Heron International Ltd; V. Ch. The Jewish Community Secondary School Trust; form. T. and Jt. Hon. T. Jewish Care.
Add The Jewish Community Secondary School Trust, Palladium House, 1-4 Argyll Street, London W1F 7LD

GOLDMAN, Lawrence Neil, MA, PhD (Cantab), FRHistS.
b. London June 17 1957; m. Madeleine Jean McDonald; University lecturer; Ed. Oxford Dictionary of National Biography (2004-); Fel. and Tutor in Modern History, St. Peter's College, Oxford (1990-). Publ.: Oxford Dictionary of National Biography 2001-04 (1st supplement 2009); Politics and Culture in Victorian Britain: Essays in Memory of Colin Matthew (2006, Ed. with P. Ghosh); Science, Reform and Politics in Victorian Britain

(2002); Dons and Workers: Oxford and Adult Education since 1850 (1995); The Blind Victorian: Henry Fawcett and British Liberalism (Ed. 1989).

Add Oxford DNB, OUP, Great Clarendon Street, Oxford OX2 6DP

Tel 01865 278 899

Email lawrence.goldman@spc.ox.ac.uk

GOLDMEIER, Michael,

b. London, Nov. 27, 1946; m. Philippa née Yantian; Solicitor, partner Berwin Leighton Paisner; Immigration Judge (Asylum and Immigration Tribunal) (2001-); Ch. Jewish Care (2002-06); Mem. Bd. Claims Conference (1998-2002); V. Pres. Jewish Care; V. Ch. European Council Jewish Communities (1996-2002).

Add High Liuden, 104 Marsh Lane, Mill Hill, London NW7 4PA

Tel 020 3400 4358

Email michael.goldmeier@blplaw.com

GOLDREIN, Neville Clive, CBE, MA (Cantab.).

b. Hull; m. Dr. Sonia née Sumner; Solicitor; Mem. International Association Jewish Lawyers and Jurists; Mem. BAJS; H. Life Mem. (2008-), Ch. Environment and Energy Cttee. (1993-2006); T. LIPA (2008-); Mem. Port of Liverpool Police Cttee (2000-); Ch. Liverpool Chamber of Commerce (1986-); V. Pres. Crosby MENCAP (1966-); Snr. W. Liverpool Old Hebrew Congregation (2009-10, 1968-71); V. Pres. Southport Jewish Representative Council (2003-09); Mem. Council Liverpool Institute of Performing Arts (LIPA) (2005-08); T. Southport Jewish Representative Council (1999-2006); Ch. Liverpool Royal Court Theatre Foundation (1994-2005); Ch. (Appeals), Crosby Hall Education Trust (1989-91); Board of Deputies (1992-2001, 1965-85); British Association of Chambers of Commerce, Mem. Local and Regional Affiliated Cttee. (1994-97); Leader, Conservative Group (1980-86); form. Dep. Circuit Judge; form. Mem. (Leader, 1980-81, V. Ch. 1977-80) Merseyside County Council (1973-86); Council, Liverpool University (1977-81). Publ.: Life is Too Serious to be Taken Seriously (2010).

Add Torreno, St Andrew's Road, Blundellsands, Liverpool L23 7UR / Rehov Hapalmach 20/7 Jerusalem, Israel

Tel 0151 924 2065 / +972 (02) 563 3085 *Fax* 0151 924 2065

Email goldrein@aol.com

GOLDSMITH, Rabbi Mark, MA (Leo Baeck College).

b. London, July 5, 1963; m. Nicola née Angel; Rabbi, North Western Reform Synagogue (2006-); Ch. Assembly of Reform Rabbis UK (2011-13); Rabbi, Finchley Progressive Synagogue (1999-2006); Ch. Rabbinic Conference, Liberal Judaism (2004-06); Mem. Exec. Cttee. International Interfaith Investment Group (3iG) (2004-); Rabbi, Woodford Progressive Synagogue (1996-99). Publ.: A Passion for Judaism (chapter, 2011); Great Reform lives (chapter, 2009); Aspects of Liberal Judaism (chapter, 2004); My Israel (Michael Goulston Educational Foundation, 1995); My Israel Teacher's Guide (Michael Goulston Educational Foundation, 1995).

Add North Western Reform Synagogue, Alyth Gardens, London NW11 7EN

Tel 020 8457 8791

Email mark@alyth.org.uk *Website* www.alyth.org.uk

GOLDSMITH, Lord Peter Henry, PC, QC, MA (Cantab), LLM (London).

b. Liverpool, Jan. 5, 1950; m. Joy née Elterman; Pres. (2001-), Ch. Bar Pro Bono Unit (1996-2000); European Ch. of Litigation, Devoise and Plimpton LLP; form. H.M. Attorney-General (2001-07); Co-Ch. Human Rights Institute of International Bar Association (1998-2001); Ch. Financial Reporting Review Panel (1997-2000); Ch. Bar of England and Wales (1995). Publ.: contributor to Common Values, Common Law, Common Bond (2000).

Add House of Lords London SW1A

Email phgoldsmith@devoise.com

GOLDSMITH, Walter Kenneth, FCA CiMgt, FRSA.

b. London, Jan. 19, 1938; M. Development Cttee. SOAS (2010-); V. Pres. (2008-), Ch. Jewish Music Institute (2003-08); M. London Jewish Forum (2006-10); V. Pres. (1992-), Ch. (1987-91) British Overseas Trade Group for Israel; Dir. Bank Leumi (UK) plc (1984-2013); Ch. Estates and Management Ltd. (2006-); Ch. ULPS Centenary Cttee. 2002 (1999-02); Co-Fdr. and T. Israel Diaspora Trust (1982-92); Treasurer Leo Baeck College (1987-89); Dir. Gen. Institute of Dirs. (1979-84).

Add 35 Park Lane, London W1K 1RB

Email wg@waltergoldsmith.com

GOLDSTEIN, Rabbi Aaron, BSc, BA, MA.

Snr. Rabbi, Northwood and Pinner Liberal Synagogue (2008-); Mem. JCP Panel (2007-); Hd, Community Dev. for LJ (2002-09); British Steel Strip Products (1993-97)

Add NPLS, Oaklands Gate, Green Lane, Northwood, Middlesex HA6 3AA

Tel 01923 822 592 *Fax* 01923 824 454

Email rabbiaaron@npls.org.uk *Website* www.npls.org.uk

Twitter @rabbiaaron *Blog* www.thejc.com/users/rabbi-aaron.goldstein

GOLDSTEIN, Rabbi Andrew, PhD.

b. Warwick, Aug. 12, 1943; Pres. Liberal Judaism (2013-); Rabbinic Adv. EUPJ (2012-); M. Northwood and Pinner Liberal Synagogue (1970-2008), Emer. Rabbi (2008-); Ch. LJ Rabbinic Board (Bet Din) (2008-); Liberal Rabbi, Bratislava (2008-); Ch. European Union for Progressive Judaism (2007-); Exec. Bd. ICCJ (2003-11); Ch. ULPS Prayerbook Editorial Cttee. (1990-95); Dir. Kadimah Holiday School, (1970-89); Ch. ULPS Education Cttee. (1970-88); Ch. ULPS Rabbinic Conf. (1979-81). Publ.: Haggadah B'chol Dor Va-Dor (Co-Ed. 2010); High & Holy Days: A Book of Jewish Wisdom (Co-Ed. 2010); Machzor Ruach Chadashah (Co-Ed. 2003).

Add 10 Hallowell Road, Northwood, Middlesex HA6 1DW

Tel 01923 822 818 *Fax* 01923 824 454

Email agoldstein@f2s.com

GOLDSTEIN, Michael Howard, FCA.

b. London, July 7, 1963; m. Lara née Stanton; Chartered Accountant; Partner, BDO LLP (2003-); T. JCC for London (2007-); Ch. Israel Desk (2005-); Ch. Office for Small Communities (2005-); T. UJS Hillel (2003-); V. Ch. UJIA (2003-); Gov. King Solomon High School (1992-2003); form. Partner, Blick Rothenberg (1990-2003); Chartered Accountant, BDO Stoy Hayward (1988-90).

Add 55 Baker Street, London W1U 7EU

Tel 020 7486 5888 *Fax* 020 7487 3686

Email michael.goldstein@bdo.co.uk

GOLDSTEIN, Rabbi Dr Warren, BA, LL.B., PhD, Dayanut-Kollel; Eretz Hemdah.

b. Pretoria, 1971; Chief Rabbi of South Africa, Graduate of the Yeshiva of Johannesburg (1996). Publ.: The Legacy: Teachings for Life from the Great Lithuanian Rabbis (co-author 2012); Sefer Mishpat Tzedek - Halachic work on competition and other Monetary Laws (2011); Defending the Human Spirit: Jewish Law's Vision for a Moral Society (2006); African Soul Talk - When Politics is not Enough (co-author, 2003).

Add Union of Orthodox Synagogues of South Africa, 58 Oaklands Road, Orchards 2192, Johannesburg South Africa

Tel +27 10 214 2603 *Fax* +27 11 485 1497

Email office@chiefrabbi.co.za *Website* www.chiefrabbi.co.za

GOLDSTONE, Barbara D, ALCM, LLAM, Gold Medal LAM, TC, BA (Eng)., M.Ed.

b. Salford, June 24, 1938; Schoolteacher, Tutor of Public Speaking and Drama; Pres. Manchester Bnai Brith (2011-12, 2005, 2003, 2001), Whitefield Bnai Brith (1985); Pres. Jewish Representative Council of Greater Manchester (2007-10); Ch. Prestwich Emunah (1967, 1958); Higher Broughton, Higher Crumpsall Ladies Guild; Ch. Jewish Representative Council Education Cttee.; Ch. Salford Interfaith Network; Ch. Salford Healthy

Collaborative; Mem. I.A.G

Add 1 Tower Grange, New Hall Road, Salford M7 4EL

Tel 0161 792 1305

Email barbaradgold@gmail.com *Website* www.jewishmanchester.org

GOODMAN, Martin David, MA, D.Phil, D. Litt (Oxon) FBA.

b. Aug. 1, 1953; m. Sarah Jane née Lock; Prof. of Jewish Studies, University of Oxford; Fel. of the Oxford Centre for Hebrew and Jewish Studies and Wolfson College; Jt. Ed. of Journal of Jewish Studies (1995-99); Sec. European Association for Jewish Studies (1995-98); Reader in Jewish Studies, University of Oxford (1991-96); Pres. British Association for Jewish Studies (1995). Among recent publications: Rabbinic Texts and the History of Late-Roman Palestine (Jt. Ed. 2010); Judaism in the Roman World: Collected Essays (2007); Rome and Jerusalem (2007); Representations of Empire: Rome and the Mediterranean World (Jt. Ed. 2002); The Oxford Handbook of Jewish Studies (Ed. 2002); Apologetics in the Roman Empire (Jt. Ed. 1999); Jews in a Graeco-Roman World (Ed. 1998); The Roman World 44BC-AD180 (1997).

Add Oriental Institute, Pusey Lane, Oxford OX1 2LE

Tel 01865 278 208 *Fax* 01865 278 190

Email martin.goodman@orinst.ox.ac.uk

GOODMAN, Vera (née Appleberg),

b. London; Life V. Pres. Richmond Park Conservative Assoc. (2010); Life V. Pres. (Ch. 1976-9) Richmond Park Conservative Women's Constituent Cttee.; Ch. Richmond Park Women's Conservatives (2005-8); Volunteer Royal Star and Garter Home, Richmond; Volunteer Award for Distinguished Service (2004); Board of Deputies (1973-94), Exec. Cttee. (1985-91), form. Ch. Public Relations Cttee.; Bd. of Elders, Spanish and Portuguese Jews' Congregation (1990-4, 1977-80); Greater London Conservative Women's Gen. Purposes Cttee. (1979-85); V. Ch. Govs. Russell School, Petersham (1974-82); National Council for Soviet Jewry (1977-80); Conservative Representative, National Council of Women (1974-79); form. Central London Council, Conservative Friends of Israel; Representative, Union of Jewish Women at U.N.A.; Central Council, Conservative Party; Conservative Women's National Cttee. Exec.; European Union of Women (British Section); Ch. Sephardi Women's Guild; British Council, World Sephardi Federation.

Add 87 Ashburnham Road, Ham, Richmond, Surrey TW10 7NN

Tel 020 8948 1060

GORDON, Rabbi Jeremy, MA (Hons) Cam Rabbinic Ordination, a Masters in Midrash (Rabbinic Exegesis).

m. Josephine; Rabbi, New London Synagogue (2008-); Rabbi, St Albans Masorti Synagogue (2004-08); Chaplain with the Red Cross in the aftermath of September 11th; active in a number of social action campaigns – relating to refugee issues and international development, convenor of a major interfaith dialogue forum in New York; Teacher, Midrash and contemporary Jewish legal responsa; worked for BBC and a number of independent production companies.

Add 33 Abbey Road, London NW8 0AT

Tel 020 7328 1026

Email rabbi@newlondon.org.uk

GORDON, Lionel Lawrence, BSc (Econ).

b. London, Aug. 31, 1933; form. Market Research Director.; form. Ch. Jewish Chronicle Ltd.; Ch. Jewish Renaissance.

Add The Hyde, 5 Orchard Gate, Esher, Surrey KT10 8HY

Tel 020 8398 5774

Email lionelandjillgordon@talktalk.net

GOULD, MATTHEW, MBE.

b. Aug. 20, 1971; m. Celia née Leaberry; British Ambassador to Israel.

Add 192 Hayarkon Street, Tel Aviv 63405, Tel Aviv, Israel

GOULD, Prof. Samuel Julius, MA (Oxon).

b. Liverpool, Oct. 13, 1924; Bd. of Dir. Centre for Policy Studies (1985-97); Res. Bd. & Policy Planning Group, IJA; BoD (1984-90); Res. Dir. Instit. Policy Research (1983-85); Ch. and T. Social Affairs Unit, London (1981-2007); Prof. of Sociology, Nottingham Univ. (1964-82); Reader, Social Inst. London School of Economics and Political Science. Publ.: Dictionary of the Social Sciences (Jt. Ed.); Jewish Life in Modern Britain (Jt. Ed.); The Attack on Higher Education (1977); Jewish Commitment: A study in London (1984).

Add c/o The Reform Club, Pall Mall London SW1

GOULDEN, Simon Charles, BSc (Eng), DMS, CEng, MCMI, MICE.

b. London, Mar. 1, 1949; Education and Management Consultant; Consultant, Jewish Leadership Council (2011-); Consultant, Inst. Professional Development for Jewish Studies (2009-); Principal, Simon Goulden Consultancy (2009-); Education Consultant, United Synagogue (2009-); Mem. Singer's Prayer Book Publication Cttee.; Chief Exec. Agency for Jewish Education (1995-2009); Principal Engineer, London Borough Haringey (1976-1986); form. Exec. Dir. Jews' College (1986-95); Publ.: Medinatenu: the Israel History Book (with M. Binstock, 2002).

Tel 020 8441 0475

Email simongoulden@gmail.com

GRABINER, Michael, CBE, MA (Cantab).

b. St. Albans, Aug. 21, 1950; m. Jane Olivia née Harris; Ch. World Union for Progressive Judaism (2011-); Ch. of Governors, Jewish Community Secondary School (2009-); Ch. Partnership for Schools (2005-12); Bd. Mem. UK Jewish Film Festival (2004-12); Partner, Apax Partners LLP (2002-09); Ch. Movement for Reform Judaism (2005-08); Governor Leo Baeck College (2005-08); Mem. Jewish Leadership Council (2005-08).

Email mike@grabiner.net

GRAHAM, Prof. (Stewart) David, QC, MA, BCL (Oxon), FRSA.

b. Leeds, Feb. 27, 1934; Barrister; form. Ch. Law, Parl. and Gen. Purposes Cttee. Board of Deputies; Vis. Prof. Faculty of Business, Kingston University (2004-); form. Mem. Insolvency Rules Adv. Cttee.; form. Mem. Ch. and Exec. Cttee. of Justice; Snr. Vis. Fel. Centre for Commercial Law Studies, QMW College; form. Mem. Council Insurance Ombudsman Bureau; Associate Mem. British and Irish Ombudsman Association. Publ.: Works on bankruptcy and insolvency.

Add 6 Grosvenor Lodge, Dennis Lane, Stanmore, Middlesex HA7 4JE

Tel 020 8954 3783

GRANT, Linda, BA, MA.

b. Liverpool, Feb. 15, 1951; Writer. Publ.: (fiction) Still Here (2002); When I Lived in Modern Times (2000); The Cast Iron Shore (1996); (non-fiction) We Had It So Good (2011); The Thoughtful Dresser (2009); The Clothes on Their Backs (2008); The People on the Street: A Writer's View of Israel (2006); Remind Me Who I Am Again (1998); Sexing the Millenium: A Political History of the Sexual Revolution (1993).

Add c/o A.P. Watt, Literary Agents, 20 John Street, London WC1N 2DR

Email linda@lindagrant.co.uk *Website* www.lindagrant.co.uk

GREEN, Dr Abigail Frances Floretta, B.A. Oxon 1993 1st class; Certificat en Etudes Européennes, ULB, 1994 Distinction; D.Phil. Cantab 1999.

b. Stoke Newington, May 12, 1971; m. Boaz Brosh; Tutorial Fel. History, Brasenose College, Oxford; CUF Lecturer, University of Oxford (2000-); Research Fel. St John's College, Cambridge (1998-2000). Publ.: Moses Montefiore: Jewish Liberator, Imperial Hero (2010); Fatherlands: State-building and Nationhood in Nineteenth Century Germany (2001).

Add Brasenose College, Oxford OX1 4AJ

Tel 01865 277868

Email abigail.green@bnc.ox.ac.uk

GREEN, Sir Philip, Kt.

b. London, Mar. 15, 1952; m. Tina Green; Retail Exec. Arcadia Group (2002); Bhs (2000); Sears (1999); Shoe Express (1997-98); Mark One (1996); Ch. and Chief Exec. Amber Day (1988–92).

Add Bhs Ltd, Marylebone House, 129–137 Marylebone Road NW1 5QD

GREENBAT, Alan, OBE, JP.

b. London, Apr. 1929; H. Consultant, Office of the Chief Rabbi (1995-2012); Sec. Rabbinical Commission for the Licensing of Shochetim; Pres. Norwood Old Scholars Association; Mem. Inner London Youth Courts (1964-99); V. Pres. AJY (1989-96); V. Pres. London Union of Youth Clubs (1984-94); Exec. Dir. Office of the Chief Rabbi (1990-91); Exec. and V. Ch. National Council of Voluntary Youth Services (1981-91); Dir. Association for Jewish Youth (1980-89); Dir. Victoria Community Centre (1961-80); V. Principal Norwood Home for Jewish Children (1955-61).

Email info@chiefrabbi.org

GREENBERG, Rabbi Philip T, BA, MPhil, FJC.

b. Liverpool, June 28, 1937; Emer. Rabbi, Giffnock and Newlands Synagogue, Glasgow; Ch. Va'ad HaRabbonim, Glasgow; H. Chaplain, Calderwood Lodge Jewish School, Glasgow; Rav, Glasgow Shechita Board (1993-99); Hd. Mishna Stream, Hasmonean Boys' School (1972-81); M. Nottingham Synagogue (1968-72), Highams Park and Chingford Synagogue (1959-68).

Add 72 Bridge Lane, Golders Green, London NW11 0EJ

Tel 020 8455 5685 *Fax* 020 8455 5685

Email phillip_anna@yahoo.co.uk

GREENGROSS, Dr Wendy, MB, BS (Lond), LRCP, MRCS, DObst, RCOG; Dip. Med. Law & Ethics.

b. London, Apr. 29, 1925; Medical Practitioner; Broadcaster; Medical Consultant; Marriage Guidance Council; V. Pres. AJY Fel. Leo Baeck College; T. Leonard Cheshire Foundation; Pres. Ranulf Association; Mem. Govt. Enquiry into human fertilisation and embryology; Ch. Ethics Cttee. Wellington Humana Hospital. Publ.: Living, Loving and Ageing (1989); Jewish and Homosexual (1982); Entitled to Love (1976); The Health of Women (1974); Sex in Early Marriage (1970); Sex in the Middle Years (1969); Marriage, Sex and Arthritis.

Add 35 Regency House, 269 Regent's Park Road, London N3 3JZ

Tel 020 8455 1153

GREENWOOD, Jeffrey Michael, MA, LLM.

b. London, Apr. 21, 1935; Dep. Ch. Jewish Chronicle Ltd (1995-2005); Dir. Bank Leumi (UK) plc (1988-2005); Ch. Jewish Literary Trust (2001-3); Ch. Central Council for Education and Training in Social Work (1993-98); Snr. Partner Nabarro Nathanson (1987-95); Ch. Jewish Welfare Bd. (1985-1990), Jewish Care (1990). V. Pres. Jewish Care; Council, Anglo-Israel Association; M. Council JHSE.

Add 5 Spencer Walk, Hampstead High Street, London NW3 1QZ

Tel 020 7794 5281 *Fax* 020 7794 0094

Email jeff@thegreenwoods.org

GRUNEWALD, Rabbi Jacob Ezekiel, BA.

b. Tel Aviv, Oct. 26, 1945; M. Pinner Synagogue (1976-2010); Youth Rabbi, St John's Wood Synagogue (1971-76); T. Rabbinical Council, US; Mem. Chief Rabbi's Cabinet.

Add 1 Cecil Park, Pinner, Middlesex HA5 5HJ

Tel 020 8868 7204

GRUNFELD, Rabbi Joey,

b. London. Adult education pioneer; Fdr. and Exec. Dir. Project SEED (1980-).

Add 2530 San Pablo Avenue, Suite K, Berkeley, CA 94702-2000 USA

Tel +1 (510) 644 3422 *Fax* +1 (510) 644 0566

Email jgrunfeld@seed.uk.net

GRUNWALD, Henry Cyril, OBE LLB (Hons).

b. London, Aug. 8, 1949; m. Alison née Appleton; Barrister, Queen's Counsel; Pres. National Council of Shechita Boards; Pres. World Jewish Relief (2009-); V. Pres. Council of Christians and Jews (2009-); Adv. Bd. Mem. Community Security Trust (2006-); V. Ch. National Holocaust Memorial Day Trust (2005-); Ch. Shechita UK (2003-); Bencher, H. Society of Gray's Inn (2002-); Mem. Hillel Bd. Dir. (2000-); Tru. The Holocaust Centre (Beth Shalom) (2010); Jt. Ch. Jewish Human Rights Cttee. UK (2008-10); Pres. North London Relate (2007-09); Pres. Board of Deputies (2003-09), Snr. V. Pres. (2000-03), V. Pres. (1997-2000); Ch. Jewish Leadership Council (2003-09); V. Ch. European Jewish Congress (2003-09); Ch. Pikuach Bd. Gov. (2000-09); Warden, Hampstead Synagogue (1997-07); Fel.: UCL (2006); H. Patron, Yad Vashem UK; Patron, Youth Interfaith Trust; Patron, Drugsline.

Add Charter Chambers, 33 John Street WC1N 2AT

Tel 020 7618 4400 *Fax* 020 7618 4401

Email h.grunwald@btinternet.com *Website* www.charterchambers.com

GRUNWALD-SPIER, Agnes (née Grunwald), JP, BScEcon. (Hons, Lond), MA.

b. Budapest July 1944; Magistrate Bromsgrove Bench (1948-91), Sheffield (1992-2012), Highbury (2012-14); Dep. World Jewish Relief (2009-12); Lay M. Architects' Registration Bd. (2008-13); Ch. Women in the Jewish Community Regional Co-ord. Council (1997-2003, Acting Ch. 2006-); T. Holocaust Memorial Day Trust (2004-12); Board of Deputies; Ch. Regional Assembly (2006-09), M. Defence Bd. (2003-12), Deputy for Sheffield (1997-2009); Diversity in Public Appointments Ambassador (2009-11); Lay M. Conduct and Registration Cttee. Gen. Social Care Council (2003-11); Lay M. Herbal Medicines Adv. Cttee. (2005-09); Mem. Yorkshire and Humber Faiths Forum (2005-08); Pres. Sheffield and District Jewish Representative Council (1999-2002); M. National Council, World Jewish Relief (1998-2001). Publ.:The Other Schindlers: Why Some People Chose to Save Jews in the Holocaust (2010).

Add 28 Dolphin Court, Woodlands, London NW11 9QY

Tel 07816 196 517

Email agnesgrunwaldspier@gmail.com *Website* www.agnesgrunwaldspier.com

GUBBAY, Lucien Ezra, MA (Oxon), MICE, C.Eng.

b. Buenos Aires, 1931, m. Joyce née Shammah; Consulting Engineer; Ch. Montefiore Endowment; T. and Dir. LSJS; form. Mem. Exec. Jewish Memorial Council; form. Warden Spanish and Portuguese Synagogue; form. Dir. Industrial Dwellings Society (1885) Ltd; Pres. of the Bd. of Elders, Spanish and Portuguese Jews' Congregation London (1996-2000); Flg. Off. RAF (1952-54). Publ.: A Bath of Wine for the Sabbath (2013); Encyclopaedia of Jews in the Islamic World (contr. 2010); Two Worlds Supplement (2009); Our Glorious Tradition (2007); Two Worlds (2004); Sunlight and Shadow: Jewish Experience of Islam (1999); The Sephardim (1992); You Can Beat Arthritis (1992); Quest for the Messiah (1990); Origins (1989); The Jewish Book of Why and What (1987); Ages of Man (1985).

Add 26 Linden Lea, London N2 0RG

Tel 020 8458 3385

Email lucien@gubbay.co.uk

GUTTENTAG, Rabbi Jonathan, BA (Hons).

b. Newcastle, Nov. 12, 1959, m. Deborah Halle; Jt. Pres. Manchester CCJ (2008-); Mem. Schools Strategic Implementation Group Jewish Leadership Council (2008-); Fdr. National Association Orthodox Jewish Schools (2007-); Mem. Standing Cttee. Conference European Rabbis (2000-); T. Jewish Memorial Council (2006-); Mem. Greater Manchester Faith and Communities Leaders Forum (2001-); Fdr. and T. Whitefield Community Kollel / The Forum (1990-); Rabbi, Whitefield Synagogue Manchester (1987-); Jewish Faith Representative to Metropolitan Borough of Bury Education Cttee. (1990-2003); Rabbi, Southport Hebrew Congregation (1984-87).

Add 1 Park Hill Drive, Whitefield, Manchester M45 7PD

Tel 07980 262 767 *Fax* 0161 280 5452

Email rjg@theforumwck.org *Website* www.theforumwck.org

HALBAN, Martine (née Mizrahi), BA (Hons) Sussex.

b. Alexandria, Dec. 29, 1953; m. Peter Francis Halban; Book Publisher; Dir. Halban Publishers (1992-).

Add Halban Publishers, 22 Golden Square, London W1F 9JW

Tel 020 7437 9300 *Fax* 020 7437 9512

Email books@halbanpublishers.com *Website* www.halbanpublishers.com

HALBAN, Peter Francis, BA (Princeton).

b. New York, June 1 1946; m. Martine neé Mizrahi; Book Publisher; M. Exec. UK Bd. Jerusalem Foundation (2006-), Ch. (2010); T. Woolf Centre for Study of Abrahamic Faiths, Cambridge, (2003-); T. The Humanitarian Trust (1998-); Council European Jewish Publication Society (1994-); Co-Dir. Halban Publishers Ltd. (1986-); T. Jewish Heritage UK (2007-11); Mem. Exec. Institute for Jewish Policy Research (1994-2010).

Add Halban Publishers, 22 Golden Square, London W1F 9JW

Tel 020 7437 9300 *Fax* 020 7437 9512

Email books@halbanpublishers.com *Website* www.halbanpublishers.com

HALPERN, Rabbi Elchonon,

b. Kashau, Slovakia, 1922. Life Pres. Union of Orthodox Hebrew Congregations; Principal, Pardes House School; Rabbi, Beis Medrash Beis Shmuel, Golders Green.

Add 140 Stamford Hill, London N16 6QT

Tel 020 8802 6226

HAMILTON, Fabian, BA, MP.

b. Apr. 12, 1955; m. Rosemary née Ratcliffe; MP, Leeds North-East (1997-); Mem. Foreign Affairs Select Cttee. (2001-10); Leeds City Councillor (1987-98); Ch. Education Cttee. (1996-97); Ch. Economic Development Cttee. (1994-96); Ch. Race Equality Cttee. (1988-94).

Add House of Commons, London SW1A 0AA

Tel 0113 249 6600 (Constituency Office)

Email fabian@leedsne.co.uk *Website* www.leedsne.co.uk

HARRIS, Dr Evan, MP, BA, BM, BS.

b. Sheffield, Oct. 21, 1965; Hon. Assoc. National Secular Society (2000-); Front Bench Science Spokesman (2005-10); MP (Lib. Dem.), Oxford West and Abingdon (1997-2010); Registrar in Public Health Medicine (1994-97).

Add House of Commons, London SW1A 0AA

Tel 020 7219 5128

HARRIS, Rabbi Michael Jacob, MA (Cantab), MA (Jerusalem), PhD (London).

b. London, Feb. 17, 1964; Rabbi, Hampstead Synagogue (1995-), Southend and Westcliff Hebrew Congregation (1992-95); Lecturer in Jewish Law, Jews' College, London (1995-97); Res. Fel. London School of Jewish Studies; Affiliated Lecturer, Faculty of Divinity, University of Cambridge. Publ.: Radical Responsibility: Celebrating the thought of Chief Rabbi Lord Jonathan Sacks (Co-Ed. 2012); Divine Command Ethics: Jewish and Christian Perspectives (2003).

Add The Hampstead Synagogue, Dennington Park Road, London NW6 1AX

Tel 020 7435 1518 *Fax* 020 7431 8368

Email rabbi.michael@talk21.com

HARTOG, Melvyn Allan,

b. London, Dec. 30, 1947; m. Marilyn née Green; Hd. Burial, United Synagogue; Prison Chaplain (1997-); Royal Navy (1963-71); Mem. Home Office Advisory Board on Burial and Cemeteries.

Add 305 Ballards Lane, London N12 8GB

Tel 020 8343 6283 Mobile 07939 110 508 *Fax* 020 8343 6262

HASKEL, Lord Simon,
b. Kaunas, Oct. 9, 1934; m. Carole Lewis; Life Peer; Deputy Speaker, House of Lords (2002-); Pres. Institute for Jewish Policy Research (2002-).
Add House of Lords, London SW1A 0PW
Tel 020 7219 4076
Email haskels@parliament.uk

HASSAN, Judith, OBE, BSc (Hons), Postgrad. Diploma Applied Social Sciences, CQSW.
b. London, Mar. 27, 1946; Special Advisor, Therapeutic Services for Survivors of War Trauma, Jewish Care; Ed. Bd. Kavod (2012-); Dir. of Services for Holocaust Survivors and Refugees, Jewish Care (1990-2011); Fdr. Holocaust Survivors Centre (1993). Awards: Lifetime Achievement in Care, National Care Awards (2007). Publ.: Good Practice in Promoting Recovery and Healing for Abused Adults (chapter, Recovery and Healing in Survivors of the Holocaust); A House Next Door to Trauma: Learning from Holocaust Survivors How to Respond to Atrocity (2003); The Handbook of Psychotherapy: Therapy with Survivors of the Nazi Holocaust (chapter, 1994); Witness and Vision of the Therapist: Counselling with Holocaust Survivors (chapter, 1998); Past Trauma in Later Life: From Victim to Survivor - The Possibility of Healing Aging Survivors of the Nazi Holocaust (chapter, 1997); A Global Perspective on Working with Holocaust Survivors and the Second Generation: Individual Counselling Techniques with Holocaust Survivors and Helping Elderly Survivors cope with Aging (chapters, 1995).
Add Jewish Care, Amelie House, The Wohl Campus, 221 Golders Green Road, London NW11 9DQ
Tel 07769 235 106
Email jhassan@jcare.org

HAYEK, Samuel, LLB.
b. Israel, 1953; Ch. JNF UK (2008-); Fdr. S. Hayek Holding Company (2004); Prop. Arlen Properties plc. (1984); Fdr. The Hayek Contemporary Art Centre, Old Jaffa, Israel.
Add Spring Villa Park, Middlesex HA8 7ED
Tel 020 8732 6100 *Fax* 020 8732 6148
Email info@jnf.co.uk *Website* www.jnf.co.uk

HAYMAN, Baroness Helene (née Middleweek), GBE, PC, MA (Cantab).
b. Wolverhampton, Mar. 26, 1949; m. Martin Hayman. Lord Speaker (2006-11); Ch. Human Tissue Authority (2005-06); Ch. Cancer Research UK (2001-04); Min. State, Agriculture (1999-2001); PPS Dept. of Health (1998-99); Parl. Under Sec. of State, Dept. of Environment, Transport and the Regions (1997-98); Ch. Whittington Hospital (1992-97); Labour Mem. of Parl. (1974-79).
Add House of Lords, London SW1A 0PW
Email haymanh@parliament.uk

HELFGOTT, Ben, MBE, D. Univ (Southampton), D.Litt Inst. Education, University of London.
b. Pabianice, Poland, Nov. 22, 1929; Pres. Holocaust Memorial Day Trust (2012-); Pres. Yad Vashem - UK Foundation (2005-); V. Pres. Claims Conference (2000-); Mem. Holocaust Memorial Day Home Office Steering and Education (1999-); Mem. of Exec. World Confederation of Holocaust Survivor Organisations (1998-); Founding Patron, Mem. Advisory Group of the Permanent Holocaust Exhibition at the Imperial War Museum (1995-); Ch. Polin Institute for Polish Jewish Studies (1994-); Tru. Board of Management, Holocaust Education Trust (1993-); Deputy, Board of Deputies (1982-); Mem. of Exec. Wiener Library (1982-); Ch. '45 Aid Society (1963–); V. Pres. Bnei Brith First Lodge of England (1992-93); Jt. T. Central British Fund - World Jewish Relief (1978-84); Ch. Cttee. Promotion of Yiddish and Yiddish Culture; Council, Jewish Youth Fund. Awards - Jewish News Lifetime Achievement Award (2011); Commander's Cross, Order of Merit, Poland (2005); Knight's Cross, Order of Merit, Poland (1994); British Weightlifting Champion and Record Holder; competed in Olympic Games (1960, 1956); Bronze Medal, Commonwealth Games (1958); Gold Medals, Maccabiah (1957, 1953, 1950); Lifetime Achievement Award, Jewish News.

Add 46 Amery Road, Harrow, Middlesex HA1 3UG
Tel 020 8422 1512
Email benhelfgott@talktalk.net

HELLER, Sir Michael Aron, MA, FCA.

b. London, m. Morven née Livingstone; Company Chairman; Ch. London & Associated Properties plc; Ch. Bisichi Mining plc; Ch. Electronic Data Processing plc; Dep. Ch. Centre for Policy Studies; Fel. Commoner of St. Catharine's College, Cambridge; H. Doctor, Technion, Haifa, Israel; H. Doctor, Sheffield Hallam University; H. Fel. UCL, London.

Add 24 Bruton Place, London W1J 6NE
Tel 020 7415 5000
Email m.heller@lap.co.uk

HELLNER, Rabbi Frank, BA, BHL, MA, DD (Hon).

b. Philadelphia, PA, Jan. 1, 1935; Emer. Rabbi Finchley Progressive Synagogue; Exec. Barnet Com. Rel. Council; form. Gov. Akiva School; Mem. Jewish Community Day School Adv. Bd.; T. Jewish Community Schools Adv. Bd.; V. Pres. Finchley CCJ; Mem. Leo Baeck College Co.; Extra-Mural Lecturer Birkbeck College (Pt.-time); Chaplain to Mayor of L. B. Barnet (1993-94); Ed. ULPS News (1978-86); Ch. ULPS Rabbinic Conference (1970-71). Publ.: I Promise I Will Try not to Kick My Sister and Other Sermons (1987).

Add Finchley Progressive Synagogue, 54 Hutton Grove N12 8DR
Tel 020 8446 4063
Email f.hellner@dsl.pipex.com

HENIG, Baroness Ruth,

b. Leicester, Nov. 10, 1943; m. Jack Johnstone (dcs'd 2013); Life Peer; Historian and Lecturer; Ch. Security Industry Authority (2007-13); Ch. and Pres. Association of Police Authorities (1997-2012). Publ.: A History of the League of Nations (2010); Women and Political Power (with Simon Henig, 2000); The Weimar Republic (1998); Europe 1870-1945 (with Chris Culpin, 1997); Origins of the First World War (1987); Origins of the Second World War (1985); Versailles and After (1984); The League of Nations (Ed. 1973).

Add House of Lords, London SW1A 0PW
Tel 020 7219 5133
Email ruthhenig@gmail.com

HILL, Brad Sabin, AB, FRAS.

b. New York, Nov. 2, 1953; Curator, Kiev Judaica Collection, George Washington University, Washington DC; Snr. Assoc. Oxford Centre for Hebrew and Jewish Studies; form. Dean of the Library, Snr. Res. Librarian, Yivo Institute for Jewish Research, NY (2002-07); form. Librarian and Fel. in Hebrew Bibliography, Oxford Centre for Hebrew and Jewish Studies (1996-2001); form. Hd. Hebrew Section, The British Library (1989-96); Curator of Rare Hebraica, National Library of Canada, Ottawa (1979-89). Publ.: Miscellanea Hebraica Bibliographica (Ed. 1995); Hebraica from the Valmadonna Trust (1989); Incunabula, Hebraica and Judaica (1981).

Add 35 Thackley End, 119 Banbury Road, Oxford OX2 6LB
Email hebraica@gwu.edu

HILTON, Rabbi Michael, MA(Oxon), MA (London), D.Phil (Oxon), PGCE (London).

b. London, Feb. 27, 1951; M. Kol Chai Hatch End Jewish Community (2001-); Lecturer, Leo Baeck College (2008); Hon. Res. Fel. Centre for Jewish Studies, University of Manchester (1998-); Lecturer, Three Faiths Summer School, Ammerdown Centre (1991-); M. North London Progressive Synagogue (1999-2001); M. Cheshire Reform Congregation (1987-98). Publ.: Bar Mitzvah: A History (2014); The Christian Effect on Jewish Life (1994); The Gospels and Rabbinic Judaism (with G. Marshall, 1988).

Add Hatch End Jewish Community, 434 Uxbridge Road, Pinner, Middlesex HA5 4RG
Tel 020 8906 8241
Email rabbiM@kolchai.org *Website* www.rabbim.co.uk

HIRSH, David, BSc, MA, PhD.

b. Sep. 29, 1967; Lecturer, Goldsmiths, University of London; Founding Ed. Engage website (2005-); Sociological Review Fel. (2001-02). Many publications, including: Anti-Zionism and Antisemitism (2007); Law against Genocide (2003).

Add Goldsmiths, University of London, New Cross, London SE14 6NW

Tel 020 7919 7730

Email d.hirsh@gold.ac.uk

HOCHHAUSER, Prof. Daniel, MA, D.Phil, FRCP.

b. London, July 18, 1957; m. Joanne née Garland; Kathleen Ferrier Prof. and Consultant in Medical Oncology, University College London and UCLH Trust. Publ.: articles on treatment of gastrointestinal cancer and new agents for treating cancer.

Add UCL Cancer Institute, 72 Huntley Street, London WC1E 6BT

Tel 020 7679 6006

Email d.hochhauser@ucl.ac.uk

HOCHHAUSER, Victor, CBE.

b. Kosice, Czechoslovakia, Mar. 27, 1923; m. Lillian; Impresario for international artists, orchestras, ballet companies, etc; arrived in London, 1939 as a refugee.

Add 4 Oak Hill Way NW3 7LR

Tel 020 7794 0987 *Fax* 020 7431 2531

Email admin@victorhochhauser.co.uk *Website* www.victorhochhauser.co.uk

HODGE, Rt. Hon. Margaret (Eve) (née Oppenheimer), BSc, MBE, PC.

b. Sept. 8, 1944; m. Henry Egar Garfield Hodge; MP (Lab), Barking (1994-); Ch. Public Accounts Cttee. of the House of Commons (2010-); Min. of State, DCMS (2007–08); DTI (2006-07); DWP (2005–06); M. for Children (2003-05); Higher Education M. (2001-03). Publ.: Elected Mayors and Democracy (1997); Beyond the Town Hall (1994); Quality, Equality and Democracy (1991).

Add c/o House of Commons, London SW1A 0AA

Email hodgem@parliament.uk *Website* margaret-hodge.co.uk

HOFFMAN, Eva Alfreda (née Wydra), PhD, FRSL.

b. Cracow, July 1, 1945; Writer; Distinguished Writer, Kingston University (2010-); Vis. Prof. Hunter College, CUNY (2006-), MIT (1990-05); Ed. New York Times (1980-90). Publ.: Time: Big Ideas, Small Books (2010); Illuminations (2008); After such Knowledge (2004); The Secret (2001); Shtetl (1997); Exit into History (1994); Lost in Translation (1989).

Add 18 Goldhurst Terrace, London NW6 3HU

Tel 020 7625 8771 *Fax* 020 7625 8771

HOROVITZ, Michael, OBE, MA (Oxon).

b. Frankfurt am Main, Apr. 4, 1935; Writer, Artist, Singer, Musician, Publisher; Ed. New Departures, Dir. Poetry Olympics (www.poetryolympics.com); H. C. Creative Britons Award (2000); Poetry Book Society V. C. Recommendation (1986); Arts Council Translator's Award (1983); Arts Council Writer's Award (1976). Publ.: A New Waste-Land (2007); Lost Office Campaign Poem (2005); The POT! Anthology (2005); Jeff Nuttall's Wake on Paper (2004); The Pom! Anthology (2001); The POP! Anthology (2000); The POW! Anthology (1996); Wordsounds and Sightlines: New and Selected Poems (1994); Midsummer Morning Jog Log (1986); A Celebration for Frances Horovitz (1984); Growing Up: Selected Poems and Pictures, 1951-1979 (1979); A Contemplation (1978); Love Poems (1971).

Add New Departures/Poetry Olympics, P.O. Box 9819, London W11 2GQ

Tel 020 7229 7850 *Fax* 020 7229 7850

Email michael.horovitz@btinternet.com

HOWARD, Alan,

Fdr. Alan Howard Charitable Foundation (1982-); Fdr. Brevan Howard; form. Hd. of Proprietary Training, Credit Suisse First Boston.

Add Brevan Howard, Ground and First Floor, 55 Baker Street, London W1U 8EW
Tel 020 7022 6200

HOWARD, Michael, Baron of Lympne, CH, PC, QC.

b. Gorseinon, Wales, July 7, 1941; MP (Con.) for Folkestone and Hythe (1983-2010); Leader of the Opposition (2003-05); Shadow Chancellor (2001-03); form. Home Sec. (1993-97); Sec. of State for the Environment (1992-93); Sec. of State for Employment (1990-92); Ch. Conservative Bow Group (1970-71); form. Pres. Cambridge Union.

Add House of Lords, London SW1A 0PW

HUDSON, Lucian J.,

Mem. Jewish Leadership Council; Ch. Liberal Judaism; Gov. Leo Baeck College.

Add Liberal Judaism, The Montagu Centre, 21 Maple Street, London N1T 4BE
Tel 020 7580 1663
Email montagu@liberaljudaism.org *Website* www.liberaljudaism.org

HYMAN, Barry S,

b. Scotland, June 24, 1941, m. Judith; Broadcaster, Writer; Radlett and Bushey Reform Synagogue, Pres. (2011-), H. V. Pres. (2000-11); PR consultant and newsletter Ed. to Movement for Reform Judaism (1995-2002); Mem. of the Institute of Public Relations (1987-2002); Board of Deputies Public Relations Cttee. (1988-97); Hd. of Corporate Affairs, Media Relations, Community Affairs and Company Archive, Marks and Spencer (1984-94). Publ.: Reform Judaism News (Ed. 1996-2002); A Job for a Jewish Girl ... or Boy? The Rabbinate as a Career (2000); Young in Herts (1996), a history of the Radlett and Bushey Reform Synagogue; Retail Revolutionary - The Story of Lord Marks of Broughton, Ch. of Marks and Spencer 1916-64 (co-author).

Add Radlett Reform Synagogue, 118 Watling Street, Radlett, Hertfordshire WD7 7AA
Tel 01923 856 110 *Fax* 01923 818 444
Email bsh@hypeople.co.uk

IRONSIDE, Judy (neé Mazzier),

b. Brighton, Mar. 1946; Fdr. and Dir. UK Jewish Film Festival (1997-); T. The Forgiveness Project; form. Mem. British Association of Drama Therapists.

Add UK JFF 5.09 Clerkenwell Workshops, 27-31 Clerkenwell Close, London EC1R 0AT
Tel 020 3176 0048
Email judy.ironside@ukjewishfilm.org *Website* www.ukjff.org.uk

ISAACS, Sir Jeremy (Israel), MA, Kt.

b. Sept. 28, 1932; m. Gillian Mary Widdicombe; Ch. Sky Arts; Chief Exec. Jeremy Isaacs Productions (1998–2008); General Dir. Royal Opera House (1988-97); Chief Exec. Channel Four TV Co. (1981–87).

Add 8 Shelton Street, London WC2H 9SR
Tel 020 7253 8898
Email jlp@jlp.co.uk

JACKSON, Bernard Stuart, LLB (Hons), D.Phil, LLD, DHL (h.c.).

b. Liverpool, Nov. 16, 1944; Barrister; (part-time) Professor of Law and Jewish Studies, Liverpool Hope University (2009-); Ch. The Jewish Law Association, (2008-14); Sec. Jewish Law Publ. Fund (1980-2012); Alliance Prof. of Modern Jewish Studies, Co-Dir. Centre for Jewish Studies, University Manchester (1997-2009); Ed. Jewish Law Annual (1978-97); Pres. BAJS (1993); Hd. of Academic Research; TAG Institute for Jewish Social Values (2010-11). Among major publications: Theft in Early Jewish Law; Essays in Jewish and Comparative Legal History; Semiotics and Legal Theory; Law, Fact and Narrative Coherence; Making Sense in Law; Making Sense in Jurisprudence; Studies in the Semiotics of Biblical Law; Wisdom-Laws: a study of the Mishpatim of Exodus 21:1-22:16; Essays in Halakhah in the New Testament; Agunah, The Manchester Analysis; (Ed.) Studies in Jewish Legal History in Honour of David Daube; Modern Research in Jewish Law, Jewish Law in

Legal History and the Modern World; An Introduction to the History and Sources of Jewish Law. Full list: www.legaltheory.demon.co.uk/lib-bibliobsj1.html

Add Department of Theology, Liverpool Hope University, Hope Park, Taggart Avenue, Liverpool L16 9JD

JACOBS, David,

b. Manchester, 1951; m. Hannah Rose née Noorden; synagogue Consultant, Anglo-Jewish Historian and Genealogist; Dir. of Synagogue Partnership, Movement for Reform Judaism (1992-2014); Dir. Victoria Community Centre (1988-91); Co-Fdr. London Museum of Jewish Life (1983); RSGB Youth Development Officer (1975-79); Co-Fdr. Jewish East End Project (1977); V. Pres. Jewish Genealogical Society of GB (1996-); Ch. JHSE (2009-); Ch. WP on Jewish Monuments. Publ.: A History of Our Time; Rabbi and Teachers Buried at Hoop Lane Cemetery (2006, with J. Epstein).

Add 97 Bow Lane, London N12 0JL

Tel 020 8922 5808

Email david.jacobs40@ntlworld.com

JACOBS, David Michael,

b. Bristol, June 4, 1930, m. Marion née Davis; Exec. (form. Gen. Sec.), AJA; form. Exec. Dir. Likud-Herut GB; Ch. Jewish Affiliates of the United Nations Association; form. Ch. Guild of Jewish Journalists; form. Ch. Beds.-Herts. Progressive Jewish Congregation; form. Board of Deputies, Press Officer; British Zionist Federation. Publ.: Research and writing for Jewish Communities of the World (Ed. A. Lerman, 1989); Israel (World in Colour series) 1968.

Add 56 Normandy Road, St. Albans, Hertfordshire AL3 5PW

Tel 01727 858 454

Email davidmjacobs@waitrose.com

JACOBS, Jeremy,

Chief Exec. US (2008-); Ch. Tribe (2002-8); V. Ch. University Chaplaincy Bd. (2002-06); Treasurer, US (1996-2002); Bd. of Man. Financial Representative and Warden, Belmont Synagogue (1980s and 1990s).

Add 305 Ballards Lane N12 8GB

Tel 020 8343 8989 *Fax* 020 343 6236

Email info@theus.org.uk *Website* www.theus.org.uk

JACOBS, June Ruth (née Caller),

b. London, June 1, 1930; Professional Volunteer; V. Ch. NAWO UK (National Council of Women's Organisations); Past Pres. International Council of Jewish Women; Patron, Jewish Council for Racial Equality and Jewish Black Asian Forum; Life Mem. League of Jewish Women; Life Pres. Jewish Child's Day; Mem. International Council of the New Israel Fund and their grants cttee.; Exec Mem. Memorial Foundation for Jewish Culture; Ch. Nahum Goldmann Fel.; Mem. Bd. Paideia, European Institute of Jewish Studies in Sweden; Found. Mem. Jewish Forum for Justice and Human Rights.

Add 13 Modbury Gardens, London NW5 3QE

Tel 020 7485 6027

Email juneruth@tiscali.co.uk

JACOBSON, Howard, MA (Cantab).

b. Manchester, Aug. 25, 1942; Novelist and critic; JQ/Wingate Prize for Fiction, 2001, 2007; Snr. Lecturer, Wolverhampton Polytechnic (1974-80); Supervisor in English Studies, Selwyn College (1968-72); Lecturer, English Literature, University of Sydney (1965-67); Fel. Royal Society of Lit.; H. Fel. Downing College, Cambridge; Vis. Prof. English Lit, New College of the Humanities. Among recent publications: J (2014); Zoo Time (2012); Whatever It Is, I Don't Like It (2011); The Finkler Question (2010) - Winner of the Man Booker Prize; The Act of Love (2008); Kalooki Nights (2006); The Making of Henry (2004); Who's Sorry Now? (2002); The Mighty Walzer (1999); No More Mister Nice Guy (1998); Seriously Funny: An Argument for Comedy (1996); Roots Schmoots (1993). Recent films:

Rebels of Oz (2014); Creation (Ch. 4, 2010) - Winner, The Sandford St. Martin Award; Jesus the Jew (Ch. 4, 2009).

Add c/o Curtis Brown, Haymarket House, 28-29 Haymarket, London SW17 4SP

Tel 020 7393 4400

JANNER, Greville, Baron of Braunstone, MA Hons. (Cantab), H. PhD (Haifa), H. LLD (De Montfort), QC.

b. Cardiff, July 11, 1928; Barrister-at-law; Pres. Association Jewish Ex-Servicemen and Women (2009-); Jt. Fdr and Pres. Coexistence Trust (2006-); Ch. All-Party Parl. Industrial Safety Group (1975-97); form. MP (Lab.) for Leicester West (1970-97); Ch. Select Cttee. on Employment (1993-96); Exec. Lab. Friends of Israel; Pres. Board of Deputies (1979-85); Pres. Commonwealth Jewish Council; Ch. Holocaust Educational Trust; Ch. British Israel Parl. Group; Hon. S. All-Party Parl. War Crimes Group; Cttee Against Antisemitism; V. Ch. All-Party Parl. Morocco Group; Pres. All-Party Parliament India Group; V. Ch. All-Party Parl. Jordan Group; V. Pres. AJY; Bd. Dirs. UJIA; Mem. NUJ; form. Pres. WJC (Europe); form. Dir. Jewish Chronicle; form. Pres. National Council for Soviet Jewry; H. V. Pres. WJC; Fdr. and V. Ch. All-Party Parl. Cttee. for Jews from the FSU; form. Pres. Jewish Museum; form. Pres. Maimonides Foundation; Pres. ret. Execs. Action Group (REACH); T. Elsie and Barnett Janner Trust; H. Mem. National Union Mineworkers (Leicester BR); Mem. Magic Circle and International Brotherhood of Magicians; form. Pres. Cambridge Union, Fdr. and Ch. The Bridge in Britain; Ch. Cambridge University Lab. Club; form. Ch. Brady Boys, Club. Lecturer, contributor and author of 70 books.

Add House of Lords, London SW1A 0PW

JANNER-KLAUSNER, Rabbi Laura (née Janner), BA, MA.

b. London, Aug. 1, 1963; m. Dr David Janner-Klausner; Snr. Rabbi, Reform Judaism (2012-); Rabbi, Alyth Synagogue (2004-2012). Publ.: Great Refom Lives (chapter on Leopald Zunz, 2010); DIY Rituals - A Guide to Creating Your Own Jewish Rituals; God, Doubt and Dawkins (chapter); Woodland burial (Teshuvot with Rabbi Paul Freedman); Status of second night sedarim (Teshuvot with Rabbi Paul Freedman); European Judaism. 'Education Within Our Faith Communities (Keynote, Bendorf JCM, 2001); Neshama Hadasha (A New Life) - An Anthology of New Jewish Birth Celebrations; Sources of Jerusalem history of Jerusalem (used as a text book for the 1996 international Bible Quiz).

Add Sternberg Centre, 80 East End Road, London N2 0AD

Tel 020 8349 5658

Email rabbilaura@reformjudaism.org.uk *Website* www.reformjudaism.org.uk

Twitter @LauraJanklaus

JEUDA, Basil Simon,

b. Manchester, Sept. 17, 1938; m. Laura née Madden; Chartered Accountant; Ch. NHS Pensions Agency Special Health Authority (2004-06); Ch. Macclesfield Museums Trust (2002-05); T. Manchester Jewish Museum (1998-2004); Ch. Mersey Regional Ambulance Service, NHS Trust (1999-2003); form. Leader, Cheshire County Council (1981-85). Publ.: History of Churnet Valley Railway, 1849-1999; History of Rudyard Lake, 1797-1997; The Knotty: An Illustrated History of the North Staffordshire Railway; North Staffordshire Railway in LMS Days, Vols I, II and III; History of Sha'are Sedek Synagogue, South Manchester; World War One and the Manchester Sephardim.

Add 47 Sandringham Road, Macclesfield SK10 1QB

Tel 01625 426 740

JOFFE, Joel Goodman, Baron of Liddington, CBE, BCom, LLB (Witwatersrand).

b. May 12, 1932; m. Vanetta; Lawyer; T. and Patron of various voluntary organisations including Ch. OXFAM (T. 1997-01); Ch. Thamesdown Voluntary Services Council (1974-00); Ch. Swindon and Marlborough NHT (1993-95); Ch. Swindon Health Authority (1988-93); Fdr. T. Action on Disability and Dev.; Fdr. T. Ch. Allied Dunbar Charitable Trust (1974-93); Dep. Ch. Allied Dunbar Assurance (1971-91); Ch. Swindon Private

Hospital plc (1982-87); Solicitor in Johannesburg appearing for the defence in a number of trials including that of Nelson Mandela (1952-65).

Add House of Lords, London SW1A 0PW

Email joel@lidmanor.co.uk

JOLLES, Michael Adam, MB BS MRCGP FRHistS.

b. Northampton, Apr. 4, 1951; General Practitioner; Council Mem. Jewish Historical Society of England (1999-); form. Ed. JHSE Newsletter. The Rabbi Dr Bernard Susser Annual Award (Jewish Genealogical Society of Great Britain), 2001. Publ.: The Palgrave Dictionary of Anglo-Jewish History (with W.D. Rubinstein & H.L. Rubinstein, 2011); Jews and the Carlton Club, with notes on Benjamin Disraeli, Henri Louis Bischoffsheim and Saul Isaac, M.P. (2002); A Directory of Distinguished British Jews, 1830-1930, with selected compilations from 1830 to 2000 (1999; 2002); The Chatham Hebrew Society Synagogue Ledger 1836-1865 (2000); Samuel Isaac, Saul Isaac and Nathaniel Isaacs (1998); A Short History of the Jews of Northampton 1159-1996 (1996); The Northampton Jewish Cemetery (1994).

Add 78 Greenfield Gardens, London NW2 1HY

Tel 020 8458 3193

JOSEPH, Dr Anthony Peter, MBBChir (Cantab), MRCGP, FSG.

b. Birmingham, Apr. 23, 1937; form. GP; Pres. Jewish Genealogical Society of Great Britain (1997-2013), Emer. Pres. (2013-); Ch. Birmingham Branch of JHSE (1969-); Corresponding Mem. for Great Britain, Australian Jewish Historical Society (1965-); Dir. International Association Jewish Genealogical Societies (2000-04); form. Pres. JHSE (1994-96); UK representative of Society of Australian Genealogists (1965-95); Post-graduate tutor in paediatrics, University of Birmingham (1986-91); Mem. Bd. Governors Institute for Jewish Genealogy. Contributor on Jewish Genealogy to Blackwell Companion to Jewish Culture; Author of papers in many different genealogical publications, including JHSE.

Add 3 Edgbaston Road, Smethwick, West Midlands B66 4LA

Tel 0121 555 6165 Mobile 07710 448 897 *Fax* 0121 555 5975

Email anthony.joseph@nhs.net

JOSEPH, John Michael,

b. London, Feb. 11, 1939; voluntary Ch. Jewish Blind and Disabled (1994-); Ch. GET Group (1995-2006).

Add 35 Langstone Way, Mill Hill East, London NW7 1GT

Email info@jbd.org *Website* www.jbd.org

JOSIPOVICI, Prof. Gabriel David, FRSL, FBA.

b. Nice, France, Oct. 8, 1940; Writer; University Teacher; Res. Prof. Graduate School of Humanities, University of Sussex; Prof. (1985-98), Reader in English (1973-85), Lecturer in English (1965-73), Assistant Lecturer in English (1963-65) School of European Studies, University of Sussex; Lord Weidenfeld Vis. Prof. Oxford (1996-97), FRL, FBA. Among recent publications: Infinity: The Story of Movement; The Big Glass; In a Hotel Garden; Moo Pak; Now; The Book of God; Touch; On Trust; A Life; Only Joking; The Singer on the Shore; Everything Passes; Goldberg: Variations; After; Making Mistakes; What Ever Happened to Modernism?; Hotel Andromeda.

Add 60 Prince Edward's Road, Lewes, Sussex BN7 1BH

Email gabriel@josipovici.plus.com *Website* www.gabrieljosipovici.org

JULIUS, Brigadier (Retd.) Allan Aubrey,

b. June 30, 1928; Brigadier, British Embassy (Rome) (1979-83); Most Senior Jewish Officer, British Armed Forces (1947-1983); Dep. Chief Engineer HQ BAOR, Colonel (1975-78); Commander Waterloo Company, Royal Military Academy, Sandhurst (1969-70); 9 Parachute Squadron RE, UK (1959-61); 22 Special Air Service Regiment, serving in Malaysia (1956-59); Royal Engineers (1948); Duke of Cornwall's Light Infantry (1947); Staff Off. NATO, Naples, Special Force Planning; Defence (attaché).

Add c/o 7 Grasmere Court, Holders Hill Road London NW4
Tel 020 8346 1992

JULIUS, Anthony Robert, MA (Cantab), PhD (London), PhD (H., Haifa).

b. London, July 16, 1956; Solicitor; Ch. Jewish Chronicle (2011-14); Partner, Mishcon de Reya (1984-98), Hd. Litigation (1988-98); Dep. Ch. (2009-); Ch. Oxera LLP (2014-); Ch. City and Guilds Group (2013-); Vis. Prof. Birkbeck College (2005-); V. Pres. Diana, Princess of Wales Mem. Fund (2002-13), T. (1997-2002), Ch. (1997-99); Ch. Law Panel, IJPR (1997-), reporting on Holocaust Denial Legislation; Ch. London Consortium (2005-10); Ch. Management Bd. Centre for Cultural Analysis, Theory and History, University of Leeds (2001-05); Mem. Appeals Cttee. Dermatrust (1999-2004). Publ.: Trials of the Diaspora (2010); T.S. Eliot, Antisemitism and Literary Form (1995, 2nd Edition 2003); Transgressions: The Offences of Art (2002); Idolizing Pictures (2001).

Add Mishcon de Reya, Summit House, 12 Red Lion Square London WC1R
Tel 020 7440 7000
Email anthony.julius@mishcon.com

KADISH, Sharman, BA (London), D.Phil. (Oxon), FSA, FRHist.S.

b. London, Sept. 21, 1959; m. Sydney Greenberg. Dir. Jewish Heritage UK; has lectured and held research fellowships at the universities of London and Manchester. Publ.: The Synagogues of Britain and Ireland (2011); Jewish Heritage in Gibraltar: An Architectural Guide (2007); Jewish Heritage in England: An Architectural Guide (2006); Bevis Marks Synagogue 1701-2001 (2001); Synagogues (in the Heinemann Library Places of Worship series for children 1998); Building Jerusalem: Jewish Architecture in Britain (1996 Ed.); A Good Jew and A Good Englishman: The Jewish Lads' and Girls' Brigade 1895-1995 (1995); Bolsheviks and British Jews (1992).

Add Jewish Heritage UK, Room 204, Ducie House, 37 Ducie Street, Manchester M1 2JW
Tel 0161 238 8621
Email director@jewish-heritage-uk.org *Website* www.jewish-heritage-uk.org

KAHN-HARRIS, Rabbi Dr Deborah (née Myers-Weinstein),

b. Oklahoma, USA, May 28, 1968; m. Dr Keith; Princ. Leo Baeck College, London (2011-); PhD, University of Sheffield Department of Biblical studies (completed 2011); Co-V. Ch. Assembly of Reform Rabbis (2009-2010); Lecturer, Leo Baeck College (2005-); Teaching Fel. in Judaism, SOAS, University of London (2008-2009); Associate Rabbi, Sha'arei Tsedek North London Reform Synagogue (2005-2011); Dir. Student and Young Adult Work, RSGB (2000-2001). Among recent publications: The Other Eden: Personal Reflections on Sexuality in the UK and Weaning: Personal and Biblical Reflections (chapters in book The Sacred Encounter: Jewish Perspectives on Sexuality, Ed Rabbi Lisa J. Grushcow, 2014); A Hammer for Shattering Rock: Employing Classical Rabbinic Hermeneutics to Fashion Contemporary Feminist Commentary on the Bible (PhD, completed 2011); Who Are We: An Exploration of Voice in Lam 5:19-22 (Keynote Lecture at 40th International Jewish-Christian Bible Week at Haus Ohrbeck, Osnabruck, Germany, published on line).

Add Leo Baeck College, Sternberg Centre for Judaism, 80 East End Road, London N3 2SY
Tel 020 8349 5600
Email deborah.kahn-harris@lbc.ac.uk *Website* www.lbc.ac.uk

KAHN-HARRIS, Dr Keith, MA, PhD.

b. London, Dec. 2, 1971; Rabbi Dr Deborah Kahn-Harris (née Myers-Weinstein); Sociologist; writer; Ed. The Jewish Quarterly (2013-); Ed. The Jewish Journal of Sociology; Associate Fel. Institute for Jewish Policy Research; Lecturer, Leo Baeck College; Associate Lecturer, Birkbeck College. Publ.: Uncivil War: The Israel Conflict in the Jewish Community (2014); Judaism: All That Matters, (2012); Turbulent Times: The British Jewish Community Today, (with Ben Gidley, 2010); Extreme Metal: Music and Culture on the Edge (2007).

Tel 07739 137 903
Email keith@kahn-harris.org

KALMS, Lady Pamela, MBE.

b. London, July 29, 1931; T. Chai Cancer Care (current); form. Vol. Services Co-ordinator, Edgware General Hospital; form. Deputy Ch. form. NHS Wellhouse Trust (Barnet and Edgware General Hospitals); form. Mem. Exec. Jewish Marriage Council; T. and Dir. Ravenswood Foundation.

Add 39-40 St James's Place, London SW1A 1NS

Tel 020 7491 1301 *Fax* 020 7499 3436

Email pkalms@o2.co.uk

KALMS, Lord Stanley, H. FCGI (1991), H. D.Litt CNAA/ University of London (1991), H. D. University North London (1994), H. Fellow London Business School (1995), H. D. Econ. Richmond (1996), H. D.Litt, Sheffield (2002), H. Degree, Buckingham (2002).

b. London, Nov. 21, 1931; m. Pamela née Jimack; Life Pres. Dixons Group (2002-); Vis. Prof. Business School, University of North London (1991-); Ch. Henry Jackson Society (2011-14); Hon. Fel. Shalom Hartman Institute (2005); T. Conservative Party (2001-03); Dir. Business for Sterling (1998-2002); Dir. Centre for Policy Studies (1991-2002); Ch. Dixons Group plc (1948-2002); Non-Exec. Dir. British Gas (1987-97); Ch. King's Healthcare NHS Trust (1993-96); T. The Economic Education Trust (1993); form. Ch. Jewish Education Dev. Trust (1978-89) and Jews' College (1983-89); Fdr. and Sponsor of Centre for Applied Jewish Ethics in Business and the Professions, Jerusalem; Fdr. of Stanley Kalms Foundation; Co-Fdr. and Sponsor of Immanuel College. Publ.: A Time for Change (1992).

Add House of Lords, Westminster, London SW1A 0PW

Tel 020 7629 1427

Email stanley.kalms@btinternet.com

KAPLAN, David, MA LLB.

b. Edinburgh, 1971; Dir. University Jewish Chaplaincy (2009-); Dir. US Community Services (2006-); Man. Dir. Tribe (2000-); form. Exec. Dir. British Friends of Laniado (2000-03); form. Exec. Dir. UJIA Renewal Scotland (1996-99); form. Ch. UJS (1994-95). Publ.: 60 Days for 60 Years - Israel (2008); 60 Days for 60 Years (2005); 50 Days for 50 Years (1995).

Add 305 Ballards Lane, London N12 8GB

Tel 020 8343 8989

Email dkaplan@theus.org.uk

KAPLAN, Harvey, MA.

b. Glasgow, Dec. 6, 1955; Civil Servant; Dir. Scottish Jewish Archives Centre (1987-). Publ.: The Gorbals Jewish Community in 1901 (2006).

Add Scottish Jewish Archives Centre, Garnethill Synagogue, 129 Hill Street, Glasgow G3 6UB

Tel 0141 332 4911

Email rvlkaplan@googlemail.com

KATTEN, Brenda (née Rosenblit),

b. London, Sept. 8, 1936; Co-Ch. Europeans for Israel (Israel) (2010-); Ch. World WIZO Pub. Rel. Dept. (2008-); Exec Mem. Israel, Britain and Commonwealth Association (2009); form. Ch. Israel, Britain and Commonwealth Association (2006-09); form. Ch. Public Affairs and NGO Dept. World WIZO [Israel] (2000-08); form. Ch. Bnai Brith Hillel Fd; (1994-98); Ch. UK National Cttee. Jerusalem 3000 (1995-96); form. Mem. JC Trust Ltd; H. V. Pres. Zionist Federation of Great Britain and Ireland (Ch. 1990-94); Jt. H. Pres. WIZO.uk (Ch. 1981-87).

Add c/o World WIZO, 38 David Hamelech Blvd, Tel Aviv 64237, Israel

Tel +972 (03) 692 3729 *Fax* +972 (03) 695 8267

Email brendak@wizo.org *Website* www.wizo.org

KATZ, Dovid, BA (Columbia), PhD (London).

b. New York, May 9, 1956; Yiddish linguist, author, educator, cultural historian, Holocaust scholar and activist; Awards including Guggenheim Fel. (2001-02); Leverhulme Trust

Research Award (1999-2001); British Academy Research Award (1998). Yiddish culture awards include: Leyb Rubinlicht (Tel Aviv, 2006); Y.Y. Sigal (Montreal, 1999); Manger Prize (Tel Aviv, 1997); Hirsh Rosenfeld (Montreal, 1994). Co-Fdr. Research Dir. Vilnius Yiddish Institute (2001-10); Prof. Yiddish Language, Literature and Culture, Vilnius University (1999-2010); Fdr. Dir. Center for Stateless Cultures, Vilnius University (1999-2001); Vis. Prof. Yale University (1998-9); Fel. St Antony's College Oxford (1986-97); Fdr. Yiddish Studies at Oxford University (taught 1978-1996). Among recent publications: Lithuanian Jewish Culture (2004, 2010); Seven Kingdoms of the Litvaks (2009); Windows to a Lost Jewish Past: Vilna Jewish Book Stamps (2008); Words on Fire: The Unfinished Story of Yiddish (2004, 2007). Columnist, Algemeyner Zhurnal (1997-); Yiddish Forward (1991-2002). Yiddish fiction under the name Heershadovid Menkes includes Eldra Don (1992); The Flat Peak (1993); Tales of the Misnagdim of Vilna Province (1996). From 2008, leader in campaign against Holocaust obfuscation and the 'Prague Declaration'; Seventy Years Declaration (co-author, 2012); articles in the Jewish Chronicle, Jewish Currents, Jewish News, Guardian, Irish Times, Times of Israel, Washington Jewish Week, Tablet etc.; Fdr-Ed. defendinghistory.com (form. holocaustinthebaltics.com).

Add c/o Jewish Community of Lithuania, Pylimo 4 Vilnius, Lithuania
Email dovidkatz7@yahoo.com *Website* www.dovidkatz.net

KATZ, Rabbi Steven Anthony, BA (Hons).

b. London, Dec. 18, 1948; M. Hendon Reform Synagogue; Hon. S. RSGB Assembly of Rabbis; Chaplain, University College Hospital, London.

Add Hendon Reform Synagogue, Danescroft Avenue NW4 2NA
Tel 020 8203 4168

KAUFMAN, Rt. Hon. Sir Gerald Bernard, KB, PC, MA, MP.

b. Leeds, June 21, 1930; Journalist; Ch. House of Commons Culture, Media and Sport Cttee. (1997-2005); Ch. House of Commons National Heritage Cttee. (1992-97); Mem. National Exec. Cttee. of the Labour Party (1991-1992); Opposition Spokesman for Foreign Affairs (1987-92); Labour Party Parl. Cttee. (1980-92); Opposition Spokesman for Home Affairs (1983-87); Opposition Spokesman for Environment (1980-83); MP (Lab.) for Gorton, Manchester (since 1983), Ardwick (1970-83); form. Min. of State, Dept of Industry; Parl. Under-Sec. Industry; Parl. Under-Sec. Environment. Publ.: How to be a Minister; To Build the Promised Land; How to live under Labour (co-author); My Life in the Silver Screen; Inside the Promised Land; Meet me in St Louis; The Left (Ed.); Renewal (Ed.).

Add 87 Charlbert Ct., Eamont St., London NW8 7DA
Tel 020 7219 5145 *Fax* 020 7219 6825

KAUFMANN, Flo (née Israel), JP, BA.

b. Berkhamsted, Aug. 3, 1942, m. Aubrey Kaufmann; Rotary Club of London Council (2010-); Ch. Commonwealth Jewish Council and Trust (2009-); Ch. Haifa Foundation UK (2009-); V. Pres. World Jewish Congress (2009-); V. Pres. (2007-); Ch. Council, European Jewish Congress (2007-); Ch. Valuation Tribunal of England (1996-2010); H. Officer, Board of Deputies British Jews (1979-2009); Ch. International Div. (2003-09), Ch. Organisation Div. (1997-03), T. H. Off. (1997-2009), Ch. (1994-97), V. Ch. (1989-94); Magistrate (1992-2012); Ch. Barnet Liquor Licensing Cttee. (1996-2002); Hon. T. Magistrates' Association (2001-06).

Email flokaufmann@btinternet.com *Website* www.gowiththeflo.co.uk

KEDOURIE, Sylvia (née Haim), MA, PhD (Edin).

b. Baghdad, Iraq; Independent scholar; Ed. Middle Eastern Studies. Publ.: Elie Kedourie's Approach to History and Political Thought (2006); Elie Kedourie CBE, FBA (1926-1992): History, Philosophy, Politics (1998); Arab Nationalism: An Anthology (1962, 1967, 1975).

Add 75 Lawn Road, London NW3 2XB

KEMPNER GLASMAN, Sheila (née Goldstein),

UK V. Pres. International Council of Jewish Women (2001-); Business Advisor Young Enterprise (2007); Ch. Board of Deputies Women's Issues Action Group (1995-99); Mem.

Thames Customer Service Cttee. OFWAT (1993-96); Mem. Women's National Commission (1990-94); Mem. Hillingdon District Health Authority (1983-87); V. Ch. Hillingdon Community Health Council (1974-82); form. Pres. League of Jewish Women.

Add 10 Ashurst Close, Northwood, Middlesex HA6 1EL

KENDLER, Maureen (nee Rose), BA Dip.Ed, MA.

b. London, 1956; m. Dr Hayden Kendler; Teaching Fel. London School of Jewish Studies; form. Hd. Educational Programming, London School of Jewish Studies; Hd. Jewish Literacy, UJIA (2004-07); Educational Officer, JCORE (2002-4); Teacher, North London Collegiate School (1995-02).

Add Schaller House, London School of Jewish Studies, Wohl Campus for Jewish Education, 44a Albert Road, London NW4 2SJ

Tel 020 8203 6427 *Fax* 020 8203 6420

Email maureen.Kendler@lsjs.ac.uk *Website* www.lsjs.ac.uk

KERNER, Brian Philip, MRPharms.

b. London, Nov. 21, 1934; m. Sylvia Evelyne née Goldstein; Bd. Mem. JLC (2007-); V. Ch. Britain, Israel Communications and Research Centre (BICOM, 2001-); Pres. UJIA (2000-); form. Gov. Jewish Agency for Israel; form. Co-Ch. priority Regions Sub Cttee. of Jewish Agency; form. Exec. Mem. and T. Keren Hayesod; Co-Ch. Cross Community Co-ordinating Group (CCG); Co-Ch. Fair Play Campaign Group (FPCG).

Add 4 Greenaway Gardens, London NW3 7DJ

Tel 020 7435 2494 *Fax* 020 7435 2180

Email bpkerner@googlemail.com

KERSHEN, Anne Jacqueline (née Rothenberg), BA, MPhil, PhD, FRHistS, FRSA.

b. London, June 8, 1942; Historian; H. Snr. Res. Associate, Bartlett School of Graduate Studies, UCL (2012-); H. Snr. Res. Fel. QMUL (2011-); Series Ed. Migration and Diaspora. Among recent publications: Afterword - In Fear and Loathing: Victorian Xenophobia (2013); There was a Priest, A Rabbi and an Imam: Material Religion (with Laura Vaughan, Vol. 9, Issue 1 2013); Strangers, Aliens and Asians: Huguenots, Jews and Bangladeshis in Spitalfields, 1660-2000 (2005); Food in the Migrant Experience (2002); Language, Labour and Migration (2000); A Question of Identity (1998); London, the Promised Land? (1997); (with Jonathan Romain) Tradition and Change: The History of Reform Judaism in Britain, 1840-1995 (1995); Uniting the Tailors.

Add c/o School of International Relations and Politics, QMUL, Mile End Road E1 4NS

Tel 020 7882 8600

Email a.kershen@qmul.ac.uk *Website* www.QMUL.ac.uk/politics/staff

KESSLER, Dr Edward, BA Hons. (Leeds), MTS (Harvard), MBA (Stirling), PhD (Cantab), MBE.

b. London, May 3, 1963; m. Tricia née Oakley; Exec. Dir. The Woolf Institute; Fel. St Edmunds College, Cambridge. Publ.: Jews, Christians and Muslims, In Encounter (2013); An Introduction to Jewish Christian Relations (2010); What Do Jews Believe? (2006); A Dictionary of Jewish-Christian Relations (2005); A Reader of LJ: Israel Abrahams, Claude Montefiore, Israel Mattuck and Lily Montagu (2004); Aspects of LJ: Essays in Honour of John D Rayner on the occasion of his 80th Birthday (2004, Eds. E Kessler and D J Goldberg); Bound by the Bible: Jews and the Sacrifice of Isaac (2004); An English Jew: The Life and Writings of Claude Montefiore (1989, 2nd edition 2002); Jews and Christians in Conversation: crossing cultures and generations (2002, Eds. E. Kessler, JT Pawlikowski and J Banki).

Tel 01223 741 834

Email edk21@cam.ac.uk *Website* www.woolf.cam.ac.uk

KESTENBAUM, Lord Jonathan Andrew, BA, MA, MBA.

b. Tokyo, Japan, Aug. 5, 1959; m. Deborah Jane; COO, RIT Capital Partners PLC (2011-); Ch. Five Arrows Ltd (2010-); Non-Exec. Mem. Profero Ltd. (2008-); Chief Exec. Nesta (2005-10); (Ch. Apax Partners Ltd) and Chief Exec. The Portland Trust (-2005); Chief Exec. Office of the Chief Rabbi (1991-96); Dir. Bd TSB; Tru. Rowley Lane Recreational

Trust, RSC; Chief of Staff to Sir Ronald Cohen; Chief Exec. UJIA; Tru. Yoni Jesner Foundation.

Add RIT Capital Partners PLC, 27 St James Place, London SW1A 1NR

Tel 020 7647 8565

KETT, Russell, FIH, FHOSPA.

b. Workington, May 24, 1953; m. Melinda née Sackheim; Hotel Consultant; Ch. HVS London (2012-); V. Pres. and T. United Synagogue (2011-); T. British Friends of Reuth (2009-); Man. Dir. HVS (global hotel consultancy) (1995-); Gov. JFS School (1995-2011), Ch. of Gov. (2003-09); T. JFS Charitable Trust, Development Trust, School Fund (2003-9); Warden, Belmont United Synagogue (1992-5).

Add 7-10 Chandos Street, London W1G 9DQ

Tel 020 7878 7701 *Fax* 020 7878 7799

Email rkett@hvs.com *Website* www.hvs.com

KHALILI, Nasser David,

b. Iran, Dec. 18, 1945; m. Marion née Easton; Prof. and Businessman; Fdr. The Khalili Collections; Co-Fdr. The Maimonides Foundation. Publ.: The Nasser D. Khalili Collection of Islamic Art. Awards: Goodwill Ambassador, UNESCO (2012); High Sheriff of London Award for cultural contribution to London (2007); Tru. City of Jerusalem; Knight Commander, Royal Order of St Francis I (KCFO); Knight of the Pontifical Equestrian Order of St Sylvester (KSS) (honoured by Pope John Paul II); Knight Commander in the said order (KCSS) for his work in the pursuit of peace, education and culture amongst nations (honoured by Pope Benedict XVI).

Add c/o Sue Bond Public Relations, Hollow Lane Farmhouse, Hollow Lane, Thurston, Bury St. Edmunds, Suffolk IP31 3RQ

Website www.khalili.org

KIENWALD, Dr Eli,

b. Rome, Italy, Sept. 28, 1947; m. Denise née Wassing; Architect; Chief Exec. Federation of Synagogues (2008-).

Add Federation of Synagogues, 65 Watford Way, London NW4 3AQ

Tel 020 8202 2263 *Fax* 020 8203 0610

Email eli.kienwald@federationofsynagogues.com

KIRSCH, Rabbi Danny, Dip F.M.

b. Letchworth, May 28, 1959; m. Jacqueline née Goschalk; Dir. JLE; form. Jt Ch. National Jewish Youth Council (1979); Mem. Board of Deputies (1979); form. London Student Chaplain; form. Organiser, National Jewish Youth Study Groups.

Add JLE, 152-154 Golders Green Road, London NW11 8HE

Tel 020 8458 4588 *Fax* 020 8458 4587

Email rabbikirsch@jle.org.uk *Website* www.jle.org.uk

KLASS, Melanie,

b. Aug. 31, 1969; Exec. Dir. Jewish Child's Day (2011-); Exec Dir. Hazon Yeshaya UK (2010-11); Fundraiser JNF (2009); Man. Dir. Loot Ltd (2007), Commercial Dir. (2002-07); Associated Newspapers (1990-2002).

Add Jewish Child's Day, 707 High Road, London N12 0BT

Tel 020 8446 8804

Email melanie.klass@jcd.uk.com *Website* www.jcd.uk.com

KLINER, Stephen Ivor, MA, LLB, NP.

b. Glasgow, Apr. 15, 1953; m. Barbara née Mitchell; Solicitor (Partner), Vallance Kliner and Associates, Glasgow; V. Ch. Cosgrove Care (2006-); Ch. National Habonim-Dror (2003-09); Ch. Scottish Council Jewish Communities (2007-08); Pres. Glasgow Jewish Representative Council (2001-04); V. Pres. National Executive Habonim-Dror (1993-2003); Ch. Habonim-Dror Glasgow (1990-2002); Hon. S. Giffnock and Newlands Hebrew Congregation (1995-98).

Add 1d Whitecraigs Court, Whitecraigs, Glasgow G46 6SY
Tel 0141 258 6873

KLUG, Sir Aaron, OM, ScD, FRS.

b. Aug. 11, 1926, m. Liebe née Bobrow; Pres. Royal Society (1995-2000); Dir. Laboratory of Molecular Biology, Cambridge (1986-96); Nobel Prize in Chemistry (1982); Hon. Fel. Peterhouse, Cambridge; form. Nuffield Fel. Birkbeck Col. London; Lecturer, Cambridge University, Cape Town University. Publ.: Papers in scientific journals.

Add MRC Laboratory of Molecular Biology Cambridge CB2 2QH

KLUG, Brian, MA (London), PhD (Chicago).

b. London, Jan. 15, 1949; University Teacher; Mem. Faculty of Philosophy, University of Oxford (2003-); Hon. Fel. Parkes Institute, University Southampton (2002-); Snr. Res. Fel. St Benet's Hall, Oxford (2001-); Assoc. Ed. Patterns of Prejudice. Publ.: Being Jewish and Doing Justice: Bringing Argument to Life (2010); Offence: The Jewish Case (2009); A Time to Speak Out: Independent Jewish Voices on Israel, Zionism and Jewish Identity (2008, Co-Ed. with A. Karpf, J. Rose, B. Rosebaum); Children as Equals: Exploring the Rights of the Child (2002, Co-Ed. with K. Alaimo); Ethics, Value and Reality: Selected Papers of Aurel Kolnai (1977, Co-Ed. with F. Dunlop).

Add St. Benet's Hall, 38 St. Giles, Oxford OX1 3LN

Email brian.klug@stb.ox.ac.uk *Website* www.philosophy.ox.ac.uk/members/brian_klug

KNAPP, Alexander Victor, MA, MusB, PhD (Cantab); Hon ARAM, LRAM, ARCM.

b. London, May 13, 1945; sometime Joe Loss Lecturer in Jewish Music, SOAS (1999-2006); City University (1992-99); Vis. Scholar Wolfson College, Cambridge (1983-86); Assistant Dir. of Studies, Royal College of Music, London (1977-83). Publ.: Anthology of Essays on Jewish Music (in Chinese) (1998); Four Sephardi Songs (1993). CDs: Di Sheyne Milnerin (Nimbus 2012); Yiddish Winterreise (Naxos 2010).

Add 234 Rayners Lane, Harrow, Middlesex HA2 9TZ

Tel 020 8429 9374

Email alexknapp@waitrose.com *Website* www.yiddishwinterreise.com

KNOBIL, Henry Eric, FTI, Hon. Doctorate, Bar Ilan University.

b. Vienna, Nov. 27, 1932; form. Ch. UK Friends Bar Ilan University; form. Ch. Jewish Marriage Council; form. Pres. British-Israel Chamber of Commerce; form. Bd. Gov. Immanuel College; form. Pres. Western Marble Arch Synagogue; form. Bd. Govs. Carmel College (1980-87).

Add Garden Flat, 31 Belsize Park, London NW3 4DX

Tel 020 7691 0934

Email henry@knobil.freeserve.co.uk

KOHN, Sir Ralph, FRS, FMedSci, DSc, FRCP (Hon), MAE, FRAM, DMus, Hon. DMus University of London, Hon. Medal City of Leipzig, Merit Award of the Federal Republic of Germany, Hon. DSC University of Buckingham.

b. Leipzig, Germany, Dec. 9, 1927; m. Zahava née Kanarek; Ch. Harley Street Holdings (1998-); H. DMus (Manchester 2010); Hon. Fel. British Pharmacological Society (2008); H. Fel. Royal Society (2006); Man. Dir. UK subsidiary of Robapharm AG (1965-71); T. The Kohn Foundation; Snr. Exec. Research and Development Division, Smith Kline & French of Philadelphia, USA; H. Mem. European Academy of Sciences; Fel. Royal Society of Medicine; H. Fel. Academy of Medical Sciences; H. Fel. Royal College of Physicians; Hon. T. Monteverdi Choir and Orchestra; H. Fel. Royal Academy of Music; International Governor, Israel Philharmonic Orchestra; Knighthood citation of Services to Science, Music and Charity. Numerous recitals and performances in the UK and abroad; numerous recordings; lectures on medical, scientific and musical topics.

Add 14 Harley Street, London W1G 9PQ

Tel 020 7436 6001 *Fax* 020 7255 1168

Email rkohn@harleystreetholdings.com *Website* www.ralphkohn.com

KOPELOWITZ, Lionel, MA (Cantab), MRCS, LRCP, MRCGP, J.P.

b. Newcastle upon Tyne, Dec. 9, 1926; V. Pres. Council of Christians and Jews (2009-); Council Initiation Society (1993-); Ch. St Marylebone Division BMA (1992-); Exec. Cttee. British Friends of Hebrew University (1998-2008); Ch. London Regional Council, BMA (2001-04); Council, Royal College of General Practitioners (1995-99); Council, United Synagogue (1991-96); Mem. General Medical Council (1984-94); Council, BMA (1982-94), Fel. (1980); Mem. General Optical Council (1979-1994); Pres. Old Cliftonian Society (1991-93); V. Pres. Conference on Jewish Material Claims against Germany (1985-92); Pres. EJC (1988-91); World Exec. WJC (1988-91); Pres. Board of Deputies (1985-91), now 'Father' of the Board (first elected June 1951); Pres. National Council for Soviet Jewry (1985-91); First Pres. United Hebrew Congregation Newcastle (1973-76); Life Pres. (Pres. 1964-74), Newcastle Jewish Welfare Board; Pres. Rep. Council, Newcastle Jewry (1967-73); Pres. Jesmond Hebrew Congregation, Newcastle (1963-67); V. Pres. Trades Advisory Council; Council, AJA; V. Pres. British Friends Shaare Zedek Hospital Medical Centre; Mem. Bd. of Governors, Clifton College, Bristol; V. Pres. Association of Baltic Jews.

Add 10 Cumberland House, Clifton Gardens, London W9 1DX

Tel 020 7289 6375

KOSMIN, Barry A, BA, MA, PhD.

b. London, 1946; m. Helen; Res. in Public Policy; Prof.; Exec. Dir. JPR (2000-05); Dir. of Research, Council of Jewish Federations, NY (1986-96); Founding Dir. North American Jewish Data Bank, The Graduate School and University Center of The City University of New York (1986-96); Dir. CJF 1990 US National Jewish Population Survey (1990); Exec. Dir. Research Unit, Board of Deputies of British Jews (1974-86); Fel. Institute for Advanced Studies, Hebrew University (1980-81).

Add Trinity College, 300 Summit Street, Hartford, Conn 06106-3100, USA

Tel +1 (860) 297 2388

Email isssc@trincoll.edu

KRAIS, Anthony, J.P.

b. London, May 3, 1938; General Commissioner of Taxes (1997-2008); Mem. The Appeals Service (1998-2006); Dep. Ch. Resources for Autism (1997-2004); Associate Ch. Exec. Jewish Care (1990-97); Exec. Dir. Jewish Blind Society (1980-89); Pres. British Friends of Israel Guide Dog Centre for the Blind.

Add 14 Mayflower Lodge, Regents Park Road, London N3 3HU

Tel 020 8349 0337

Email ajkrais@gmail.com

KRAMER, Baroness Susan Veronica, BA PPE, MA, MBA.

b. July. 22, 1950; m. John Davis Kramer; Dir. Infrastructure Capital Partners Ltd (1999-); MP (Lib Dem) Richmond Park (2005-10); Mem. Bd. Transport for London (2000–05); Dir. Speciality Scanners plc (2001); London Mayoral candidate (2000); V. Pres. Corporate Finance, Citibank/Citicorp, USA (1988–92).

Add 53 Riverview Gardens, London SW13 8QZ

KRAUSZ, Ernest, MSc, PhD.

b. Romania, Aug. 13, 1931; Prof. School of Behavioural Science, Netanya (2000-); Prof. Bar-Ilan University (1973-), Rector (1985-89), Prof. Emer. (1999-); Ed. Studies of Israeli Society (1979-2000); Visiting Prof. LSE (1981-82). Publ.: Exploring Reality and its Uncertainties (2010); The Limits of Science (2000), Starting the XXIst Century (2002).

Add Dept. of Sociology Bar-Ilan University, Ramat Gan 52900, Israel

Tel +972 (03) 531 7892 *Fax* +972 (03) 635 0422

Email krauszm@netvision.net.il

KRIKLER, Douglas Henry, MA.

b. London, Nov. 3, 1965; m. Tali née Zetuni; Ch. Jewish Association for Mental Illness (JAMI) (2013-); Tru. Jewish Care (2013-); Tru. London Jewish Forum (2012-); Hd. High Net

Worth Business Development, Investec; Fdr. Co-Ch. UK Task Force on issues relating to Arab Citizens of Israel (2010-12); School Gov. Campsbourne School (2003-08); Fdr. Dir. Jewish Leadership Council (2003-05); Exec. Dir. CST (2000-04); Fdr. Dir. Maimonides Foundation (1994-2000); Fdr. Dir. British Jewish Yemeni Cultural Society (1991-94); Mem. New Leadership Network; National Olympic Cttee. (NOC) Assistant for London (2004-12); Chief Exec. UJIA.

Add Investec, 2 Gresham Street, London EC2V 7QP

Tel 020 7424 6400 *Fax* 020 7424 6401

Email doug.krikler@investec.co.uk

KUSHNER, Tony, PhD.

b. Manchester, May 30, 1960; Marcus Sieff Prof. Dept of History; Dir. Parkes Institute for the Study of Jewish/Non-Jewish Relations, University of Southampton; T. Jewish Heritage UK (2007-); Pres. BAJS (2002); Historian at Manchester Jewish Museum (1985-86). Among recent publications: The Battle of Britishness, Migrant Journeys 1685 to the Present (2012); Anglo-Jewry Since 1066 (2009); Remembering Refugees: Then and Now (2006); The Holocaust: Critical Historical Approaches (2005); Philosemitism, Antisemitism and the Jews (Jt. Ed. 2004); We Europeans (2004); Disraeli's Jewishness (Jt. Ed. 2002); Refugees in an Age of Genocide (1999); Remembering Cable Street (Jt. Ed. 1999); Cultures of Ambivalence and Contempt (Jt. Ed. 1998); Belsen in History and Memory (1997).

Add Dept. of History, University of Southampton, Southampton SO17 1BJ

Tel 0238 059 2233 *Fax* 0238 059 2211

KYTE, David,

Co-Fdr. London Maccabi Recreational Trust; Fdr. and Dir. The Kyte Group Ltd (1985); Tru. Maccabi London Brady Recreational Trust; Tru. Maccabi Foundation; Bd. Mem. Maccabi World Union; Fdr. Partner, Hamilton Court FX.

Add Business Design Centre, 52 Upper Street, London N1 0QH

Tel 020 7390 7777 *Fax* 020 7390 7778

Email david.kyte@kyteinvestments.com

LASSERSON, Rachel, BA (Hons).

b. London, Dec. 11, 1968; m. James Rossiter; Ed. Jewish Quarterly (2007-); Dir. Contraband Productions Ltd. (1993-2003). Publ.: Adam International Review (Ed. 2005).

Tel 020 7267 9442

Email editor@jewishquarterly.org *Website* www.jewishquarterly.org

LATCHMAN, David Seymour, CBE, MA (Cantab.), PhD, DSc (London), FRCPath, FRSA, FKC.

b. London, Jan. 22, 1956; m. Hannah née Garson; Master of Birkbeck College (2003-); Prof. of Genetics, University of London (1999-); Dean, Institute Child Health, UCL (1999-2002); Prof. of Molecular Biology, UCL (1991-99); Pres. The Maccabaeans; Ch. T. Maurice Wohl Charitable Foundation; form. Mem. Council, US; Bd. Man. Golders Green Synagogue; form. Mem. Board of Deputies, Council JHSE. Publ.: Gene Control (6th edition Gene Regulation, 2010); Eukaryotic Transcription Factors (1991, 5th edition, 2008); Gene Regulation (1990, 5th edition 2005); Viral Vectors for Treating Diseases of the Nervous System (2003, Ed.); Stress Proteins (1999, Ed.); Landmarks in Gene Regulation (1997, Ed.).

Add Master, Birkbeck University of London, Professor of Genetics, Birkbeck & University College London, Malet Street, London WC1E 7HX

Tel 020 7631 6274 *Fax* 020 7631 6259

Email master@bbk.ac.uk *Website* www.bbk.ac.uk

LAWRENCE, Sir Ivan, MA (Oxon), Dr of Laws (Honoris Causa) (LLD) (Hon); University of Buckingham (2013), QC.

b. Brighton, Dec. 24, 1936; Barrister; Mem. of Board of Deputies (1979-), representing NW Surrey Reform Synagogue; Recorder of the Crown Courts (1983-2002); form. MP (C.) for Burton (1974-97); Bencher, Inner Temple (1990); T. Holocaust Educational Trust;

Mem. of Commonwealth Jewish Council; Vis. Prof. of Law, University Buckingham; Exec. Mem. Society of Conservative Lawyers; form. Ch. and V. Ch. Conservative Friends of Israel; form. Mem. of Policy Planning Group of IJA; form. V. Ch. Inter-Parl. Cttee. for the Release of Soviet Jewry; Knighted for Political Service (1992); Freeman of City of London. Publ.: My Life of Crime.

Add Dunally Cottage, Walton Lane, Shepperton, Middlesex TW17 8LH

Email sirilawrenceqc@aol.com

LAWSON, Arthur Abraham, MBE.

b. Glasgow, April 19, 1922; m. Toby Green née Sagman; Ret. Consulting Engineer; Ch. City of Westminster Branch AJEX (2011-13);V. Pres. AJEX (National Ch. 2002-04); Hon. S. AJEX Housing Association Ltd (1997-2006); Hon. S. Monash Branch, Royal British Legion (1998- 2006); V. Pres. Glasgow Jewish Representative Council (Pres. 1964-68); form. Ch. Glasgow Branch, AJEX and Glasgow Jewish Branch, Royal British Legion Scotland; form. Hon. T. Glasgow Maccabi; form. V. Ch. Giffnock and Newlands Hebrew Congregation; form. Ch. Newton Mearns Hebrew Congregation; Co-opted Mem. University of Strathclyde Gen. Convocation; Mem. Children's Panel for Glasgow and Strathclyde (1971-82); Jt. Ch. Scottish Committee for Jewish Christian Relations (1964-68); form. National Ch. Combined Heat & Power Association.

Add 21 Woronzow Road, London NW8 6BA

Tel 020 7722 5405

Email arthurlawson422@btintemet.com

LAWTON, Clive Allen, JP, BA, MA, MEd, MSc, Cert. Ed., ADB (Ed).

b. London, July 14, 1951; Education and organisational consultant; form. UJIA Fel. in Jewish Education, SOAS (2001-5); form. Ch. Exec. Jewish Continuity (1993-96); Snr. Consultant Limmud; Scholar-in-Residence, London Jewish Cultural Centre; Independent Mem. Metropolitan Police Authority; form. Ch. North Middlesex University Hospital NHS Trust; T. Jewish Community Centre for London; form. Ch. Tzedek; Patron, Jewish AIDS Trust; form Mem. Home Office Racial Equality Adv. Panel; form. V. Ch. Anne Frank Educational Trust; form. Ch. Shap Working Party on World Religions in Education; Ed. Shap Calendar of World Rel. Festivals; Fdr. Limmud Conference; form. HM, King David High School, Liverpool; Exec. Dir. Central Jewish Lecturer and Information Cttee. and Education Off, Board of Deputies; Co-ordinator, Vietnam Working Party; Educational Off. Yad Vashem Cttee. Exec. Council CCJ; form. V. Ch. IUJF. Publ.: Passport to Israel; Religion Through Festivals; Celebrating Cultures: Islam; Ethics in Six Traditions; The Story of the Holocaust; The Web of Insights; Auschwitz; Hiroshima.

Add 363 Alexandra Road, London N10 2ET

Email clive@clivelawton.co.uk

LAYTON, Nigel Graham, BSc (Hons).

b. London, Mar. 23, 1963; m. Sarah née Nelson; Managing Dir. Quest Ltd.; Ch. Leadership Excellence And Development Centre (LEAD), Jewish Leadership Council (2011-), Mem. (2005-); Ch. World Jewish Relief (2002-11).

Add World Jewish Relief, Oscar Joseph House, 54 Crewys Road, London NW2 2AD

Tel 020 8736 1250 *Fax* 020 8736 1259

Email nlayton@quest.co.uk

LEBRECHT, Norman,

b. London, July 11, 1948; m. Elbie née Spivack; Writer; assistant Ed. Evening Standard (2002-09); Whitbread First Novel Award 2003 (Song of Names); Presenter of Lebrecht Interview, BBC Radio3; The Record Doctor, WNYC. Publ.: Why Mahler? (2010); The Game of Opposites (2009); Maestros, Masterpieces and Madness (2007); Covent Garden: the Untold Story : Dispatches from the English Culture War, 1945-2000 (2000); When the Music Stops (1996); The Maestro Myth (1991).

Email norman@normanlebrecht.com *Website* www.norman.lebrecht.com

LEIBLER, Isi Joseph, AO, CBE, BA (Hons); D.Litt (Hon), Deakin University.
b. Antwerp, Belgium, Oct. 9, 1934; m. Naomi née Porush; Ch. Columnist, Jerusalem Post, Israel Hayom (2005-); Diaspora-Israel Relations Cttee. Jerusalem Centre for Public Affairs (2005-); Ch. and Chief Exec. Leibler Investments Ltd. (1997-); Bd. of Gov. Tel Aviv University (1990-); Snr. V. Pres. World Jewish Congress (2001-04), Ch. Gov. Bd. (1997-2001); Ch. Australian Institute of Jewish Affairs (1983-2003); Pres. Asia Pacific Region, World Jewish Congress (1981-2001); Fdr. Ch. and Chief Exec. Jetset Tours Pty Ltd. (1965-2000); Bd. of Gov. Memorial Foundation for Jewish Culture (1979-95); Dir. and Mem. Exec. Cttee. Conference on Jewish Claims Against Germany (1979-95). Among recent publications: Is the Dream Ending? Post Zionism and Its Discontents (2001); The Israel-Diaspora Identity Crisis: A Looming Disaster (1994); Jewish Religious Extremism: A Threat to the Future of the Jewish People (1991).
Add 8 Ahad Ha'am Street, 92151 Jerusalem, Israel
Tel +972 (02) 561 2241 *Fax* +972 (02) 561 2243
Email ileibler@leibler.com *Website* www.wordfromjerusalem.com

LEIGH, Howard D, BSc., FCA, ACTI.
b. London, Apr. 3, 1959; m. Jennifer née Peach; Investment Banker; Jewish Leadership Council (2010-); Pres. Westminster Synagogue (2010-), Ch. (2000-10); Exec. Board, Conservative Friends of Israel (2004-); Snr. T. Conservative Party (2001-); Ch. Jewish Care Breakfast Group (1998-); T. Jerusalem Foundation (1995-); Mem. Exec. Board Jewish Care (2004-06).
Add 40 Portland Place, London W1B 1NB
Tel 020 7908 6000 *Fax* 020 7908 6008
Email hleigh@cavendish.com

LENGA, Paul Oliver,
b. London, May 22, 1953; m. Sharon née Miller; Solicitor (England & Wales); Advocate, (Israel); Partner, Epstein Chomsky Osnat & Co & Gilat Knoller & Co Law Offices, Tel Aviv (2009–); Exec. Bd. Mem. Israel-British Chamber of Commerce (2007-); Dir. Confederation House Cultural Centre, Jerusalem (2005-); Fdr and Exec. Bd. Mem. ATID - International Partnership of Pluralistic Youth Movements (1996–); V. Pres. World Confederation of United Zionists (1995–) ; Notary Public (1989–); Life Pres. Federation of Zionist Youth of Great Britain (1984–); Mem. Israel Bar Association (1984-); Exec. Mem. Zionist General Council, World Zionist Organization (1984-2000); Mem. Law Society (1978-); Asst. Hon. S. Zionist Federation of Great Britain & Ireland (1978-1980); Solicitor of the Supreme Court of England & Wales (1977–); V.-Ch. Federation of Zionist Youth (1977), (Co-Ch. 1975). Publ.: Privatization of the Beersheva Prison: Impingement on the Freedom of the Individual or a Restriction on BOT Projects in Israel? (2010).
Add Rubinstein House, 9th Floor, 20 Lincoln Street, Tel Aviv 67134, Israel
Tel +972 (3) 561 4777 *Fax* +972 (3) 561 4776
Email lenga@ecglaw.com *Website* www.egclaw.com

LERMAN, Antony, BA Hons.
b. London, Mar. 11, 1946; Writer, Tru. The Humanitarian Trust; Mem. Bd. Directors, Paideia, European Institute for Jewish Studies, Stockholm; Hon. Fel. Parkes Inst. for Study of Jewish/Non-Jewish Relations, University of Southampton; Mem. Steering Group, Independent Jewish Voices; Exec Dir. Institute for Jewish Policy Research (2006-09; previously 1991-99); Chief Exec. Hanadiv Charitable Foundation (2000-06); Dir. European Programmes, Yad Hanadiv (1999-2000); Mem. Runnymede Trust Commission on the Future of Multi-Ethnic Britain (1998-2000); Mem. Jewish Memorial Foundation Think-Tank on the Holocaust (1996-99); Ch. Jewish Council for Community Relations (1992-94); Mem. Imperial War Museum Holocaust Exhibition Adv. Cttee. Publ.: The Making and Unmaking of a Zionist: A Personal and Political Journey (2012); Patterns of Prejudice (Ed. 1983-95, Jt. Ed. 1995-99); Antisemitism World Report (Jt. Gen. Ed. 1992-98); The Jewish Communities of the World (Ed. 1989), Survey of Jewish Affairs 1982-92 (Asst. Ed.); Jewish Quarterly (Ed. 1985-6).

Add 29 St. George's Avenue, London N7 0HB
Tel 07968 162 579
Email tonylerman@gmail.com *Website* www.antonylerman.com

LETWIN, Rt. Hon. Dr Oliver, PC.
b. London, May 19, 1956; m. Isabel Grace née Davidson; Minister for Government Policy (2010-); Ch. Conservative Party Policy Forum (2006-); MP (Dorset West 1997-); Shadow Sec. State for Environment (2005-06); Shadow Chancellor (2003-05); Shadow Home Sec. (2001-03); Shadow Chief Sec. to the Treasury (1999-2001); Shadow Financial Sec. (1998-99). Publ.: The Purpose of Politics (1999); Privatising the World (1989); Ethics, Emotion and the Unity of Self (1987).
Add House of Commons, London SW1A 0AA
Email letwino@parliament.uk *Website* www.oliver.letwinmp.com

LEVENBERG, Fayge (née Schwab), BA (Hons), MA.
b. Gateshead, Dec. 10, 1949; m. Rabbi Yechiel Levenberg; Teacher; Additional Inspector, Independent and Faith Schools (2004-); External assessor, GTP and RTP Students (2001-10); Hd. of Jewish Studies, Dep. Hd. Naima Jewish Preparatory School (1997-); Pikuach Inspector (1997-); OFSTED Inspector (1996-); form. Lecturer, Jews' college (1984-95); Inspector/Adv. US Bd. Rel. Education (1990-93), Education Off. (1988-93).
Add 76 Princes Park Avenue, London NW11 0JX
Tel 020 8381 4227 *Fax* 020 8455 0769
Email faygelevenberg@gmail.com

LEVIN, Rabbi Shlomo,
Rabbi, South Hampstead Synagogue; Rabbi, US (1983-).
Add 21/22 Eton Villas, Eton Road, London NW3 4SG
Tel 020 7722 1807 *Fax* 020 7586 3459
Email shlomo.levin@southhampstead.org

LEVY, Rabbi Abraham, Knight Commander (Encomienda) Order of Civil Merit (Spain), OBE, BA, PhD, FJC.
b. Gibraltar, July 16, 1939; m. Estelle née Nahum; Chaplain, Lord Mayor of London, Michael Bear (2010); Jewish Faith Advisor to Ministry of Defence (2010); H. Chaplain, Lord Mayor of London (1998-9); Pres. Union Anglo-Jewish Preachers (1973-75); Com. Rabbi, Spiritual Head, Spanish and Portuguese Jews Congregation, London (1980-2012), Emer. Spiritual Hd. (2012-); M. Lauderdale Road Synagogue; Jt. Ecclesiastical Authority (with the Chief Rabbi) of Board of Deputies; Dep. Pres. LSJS; V. Ch. Rabbinical Commission for the Licensing of Shochtim; Fdr. and Dir. The Sephardi Centre; form. Dir. Young Jewish Leadership Institute; Fdr. and H. Principal, Naima Jewish Preparatory School; H. Chaplain, Jewish Lads' and Girls' Brigade; Patron, Jewish Medical Association (UK); Mem. Standing Cttee. Conference of European Rabbis; V. Pres. British Friends Hebrew University; Hospital Kosher Meals Service, Jewish Care, Norwood; Pres. Jewish Child's Day; V. Pres. AJA, JHSE; Pres. Council of Christians and Jews; H. Principal Montefiore College and T. Montefiore Endowment; H. Fel. Queen Mary University London (2012-). Publ.: The Sephardim – A Problem of Survival; Ages of Man (Jt. author); The Sephardim (Jt. author).
Add 2 Ashworth Road, London W9 1JY
Tel 020 7289 2573 *Fax* 020 7289 5957
Email scadmin@spsyn.org.uk

LEVY, Dan,
Ed. Jewish Tribune; M. Enfield Synagogue. Presenter: Spectrum Radio; LBC.
Add Jewish Tribune, 97 Stamford Hill, London N16 5DN
Tel 020 8800 6688
Email info@jewishtribune.com

LEVY, Daniel, BA.

b. Feb. 8, 1962; Ch. Tottenham Hotspur (2001-); Managing Dir. ENIC International Ltd.
Add c/o Tottenham Hotspur, Bill Nicholson Way, 748 High Road, Tottenham N17 OAP

LEVY, Elkan David, BA (Hons), MHL.

b. Preston, Lancs, Mar. 29, 1943; m. Celia née Fisher (d. 2012); Solicitor; Ed. Jewish Year
Book (2010-); M. Radlett United Synagogue (2010-11, 2005); Dir. Office of Small
Communities (2004-10); Pres. United Synagogue and Ch. Chief Rabbinate Council (1996-
99); Ch. US Burial Society (1992-96); Warden, Stanmore Synagogue (1988-90); M. Belmont
Synagogue (1969-73, 1991-92); Ch. Singers Prayer Book Publication Cttee.; form. Jt. Ch.
Working Party on Monuments in the UK; form. Mem. Religious Advisory Committee to the
Armed Forces; Freemason.
Add 14/14 Rechov Hamapilim, Netanya 42264, Israel
Tel 020 8150 6117
Email elkan.levy@gmail.com

LEVY, Rabbi Emanuel, BA (Hons).

b. Manchester, July 31, 1948; m. Myriam née Blum; Ch. Rabbinical Council of the Provinces
(1986-8); F.P. Southend Community Relations Council, (1986-8); form. Chaplain to Mayor of
Southend (1981-2, 1983-4); M. Palmers Green and Southgate Synagogue; form. V. Ch.
Rabbinical Council of the US; Mem. Borough of Enfield Education Cttee.; Chaplain to
Whittington Hospital; form. H. Principal, Herzlia Jewish Day School, Westcliff-on-Sea;
form. Rabbi, Southend and Westcliff Hebrew Congregation; Chief Rabbi's Cabinet,
Regional Affairs, to Chief Rabbi's Cabinet Education Portfolio; Jewish Representative to
Standing Adv. Council for Religious Education (SACRE) for Borough of Enfield; form. Rabbi,
Langside Hebrew Congregation, Glasgow; Rabbi, South Broughton Synagogue,
Manchester. Publ.: Pninei Kahal (2005).
Add 11 Morton Crescent, Southgate, London N14 7AH
Tel 020 8882 2943
Email rabbilevy@rabbilevy.org

LEVY, Rabbi Joel Gideon, M.A. (Cantab).

b. Birmingham, 1965; m. Susanna Cohen; Rabbi, Kol Nefesh Masorti Synagogue, Edgware
(2001-); Dir. NOAM (1991-94). Rabbinic ordination - The Shalom Hartman Institute;
Congregational Rabbi and Talmud teacher; Dir. Conservative Yeshiva, Jerusalem; Mem.
European Masorti Bet Din.
Add c/o Cohen, 18 Barnet Gate Lane, Arkley, Barnet, Hertfordshire EN5 2AB
Tel 07762 901 197
Email joelglevy@gmail.com

LEVY, John David Ashley, BA (Hon) Sociology.

b. London, Sept. 10, 1947; Dir. Friends of Israel Education Fund; Exec. Dir. Academic
Study Group on Israel and Middle East; Tru. UK Society for the Protection of Nature in
Israel; form. Information Dir. Zionist Federation; Social Worker, London Borough of
Lambeth.
Add POB 42763, London N2 0YJ
Tel 020 8444 0777 *Fax* 020 8444 0681
Email john.levy@foi-asg.org *Website* www.foi-asg.org

LEVY, Rabbi Joshua Benjamin Israel, BA (Oxon), MA, MSc.

b. Manchester, 1974; m. Judith née Green; Rabbi, North Western Reform Synagogue
(Alyth) (2008-).
Add North Western Reform Synagogue, Alyth Gardens, London NW11 7EN
Tel 020 8457 8799
Email josh@alyth.org.uk

LEVY, Michael Abraham, Baron of Mill Hill, FCA, HonD (Middx).

b. London, July 11, 1944; Patron, Etz Chaim Jewish Primary School (2011-); Patron, Mathilda Marks-Kennedy Jewish Primary School (2011-); Tru. Jewish Leadership Council (2006-10); Pres. Jewish Lads' and Girls' Brigade (2006); Pres. Specialist Schools and Academies Trust (2005-08); Israel Policy Forum Recognition Award (2003); H. Patron, Cambridge University Jewish Society (2002-); Patron, Simon Marks Jewish Primary School Trust (2002-); Pres. JFS School (2001-); Mem. Exec. Cttee. Chai-Lifeline (2001-02); Mem. H. Cttee. Israel, Britain and the Commonwealth Association (2000-); Patron, Save a Child's Heart Foundation (2000-); Ch. Bd. Trustees of New Policy Network Fund (2000-07); Mem. Community Legal Service Champions Panel (1999-2010); Patron, Friends of Israel Education Trust (1998-); Pres. Community Service Volunteers (1998-); Pres. Jewish Care (1998-); T. Holocaust Educational Trust (1998-2007); Scopus Award Friends of the Hebrew University (1998); Mem. National Council for Voluntary Organisations Adv. Cttee. (1998-2011); Patron, Prostate Cancer Charitable Trust (1997-); Mem. of World Commission on Israel-Diaspora Relations (1995-); Patron, British Music Industry Awards (1995-); V. Ch. Central Council for Jewish Social Services (1994-2006); B'nai B'rith First Lodge Award (1994); Ch. Fdr. for Education (1993-2006); Ch. Chief Rabbinate Awards for Excellence (1992-2007); H. Pres. UJIA.

Add House of Lords, London SW1A 0PW

Email ml@lordlevy.com

LEVY, Peter Lawrence, OBE, BSc, FRICS.

b. London, Nov. 10, 1939; Chartered Surveyor; V. Ch. JIA (1979-81); Professional Div. JIA (1977-79); Ch. Young Leadership JIA (1973-77); V. Pres. IJPR; H. V. Pres. Reform Judaism; form. Tru. Dementia UK; Tru. Akiva School; V. Pres. Cystic Fibrosis Trust; V. Pres. London Youth.

Add 52 Springfield Road NW8 0QN

Tel 020 7328 6109 *Fax* 020 7372 7424

Email peterllevy@btinternet.com

LEWIN, Sylvia Rose (née Goldschmidt), BA (Log), (Rand), RSA Dip.Sp.L.D.

b. Johannesburg; Speech and Dyslexia Therapist; H. Life Pres. (National Pres. 1988, 1982-86) Bnai Brith UK; Ch. Leadership Training and Dev. B'nai B'rith, UK; V. Pres. Jewish Music Institute; past Ch. Jewish Music Heritage Trust.

Add White Gables, 156 Totteridge Lane N20 8JJ

Tel 020 8446 0404

Email sylvialewin@btinternet.com

LEWIS, D. Jerry, BA (Econ) (Hons, Manchester).

b. Surrey, June 12, 1949; Parl. Lobby Journalist and Broadcaster; V. Pres. Board of Deputies (2009, 2000-3), Snr. V. Pres. (2003-6), Ch. Community Issues Div. (2009–, 2000-06); Mem. Board of Deputies Exec. (2009-, 1985-2006); form. Mem. Defence Div. (2006-9) and Intl. Div. (1997-2000); Exec. (1985-2006), V. Ch. Law, Parl. and General Purposes Cttee. and Board of Deputies Constitution Standing Cttee. (1994-97), Constitution Standing Cttee. (1981-97) etc.; Mem. Exec. Cttee. ZF, National Council for Soviet Jewry; Mem. Foreign Press Association; London correspondent Israel Radio, Yediot Ahronot; Political and diplomatic Correspondence: Jewish Telegraph; contributor BBC World TV, BBC News 24, BBC World Service, BBC Radio 5 Live, Sky News, etc.

Add 9 Weech Hall, Fortune Green Road, London NW6 1DJ

Tel 020 7794 0044 Mobile 07956 968 265

Email attnjerrylewis@aol.com

LEWIS, Ivan,

b. Manchester, Mar. 4, 1967; Shadow Sec. State, International Development; Shadow Sec. State for Culture, Media and Sport (2010-11); T. Minister of State - Foreign Office (2009-10); Parl. Under Sec. for Health (2006-07); T. Holocaust Educational Trust (1998-); DFID (2008-09); Adult Skills (2001-05), Young People Learning (2001-2), Adult Learning and

Skills (2002), Young People and Adult Skills (2002-03), Skills and Vocational Education (2003-5); Economic Sec. to Treasury (2005-06); PPS Sec. State of Trade and Industry (1999-2001); Mem. Exec. Cttee. of the Commonwealth Jewish Council (1998-2001); V. Ch. Inter-Parliamentary Council Against Antisemitism (1998-2001); V. Ch. Labour Friends of Israel (1998-2001); Ch. All-Party Parliamentary Group for Parenting (1999); Mem. Health Select Cttee. (1998-99); MP (Lab.), Bury South (1997); Chief Exec. Jewish Social Services, Greater Manchester (1992-97); Co-ordinator, Contact Community Care Group (1986-89).

Add House of Commons, London SW1A 0AA

Tel 0161 773 5500

Email ivanlewis@burysouth.fsnet.co.uk *Website* www.ivanlewis.co.uk

LEWIS, Jonathan Malcolm, MA (Law) (Cantab).

b. London, Mar. 27, 1946; m. Rosemary Anne née Mays; Solicitor; Freeman of the City of London; Designated Immigration Judge, Deputy District Judge; Mem. Board of Deputies (Pinner, 1995-2009), Ch. Constitution Cttee. Exec. Cttee. (1997-03); Ch. UK Association of Jewish Lawyers and Jurists (2002-07); Authorised insolvency practitioner (1986-2000). Publ.: Insolvency in Jewish Law (1996).

Add Taylor House, 88 Rosebery Avenue, London EC1R 4QU

Tel 0845 6000 877

Email lewisjandr2004@yahoo.co.uk

LEWIS, Dr Julian Murray,

b. Swansea, Sept. 26, 1951; Historian, researcher and campaigner; MP (Con.), New Forest East (1997-); Dir. Policy Research Associates (1985-); Shadow Defence M. (2005-10, 2002-04), Shadow Min. for the Cabinet Office (2004-05), Opposition Whip (2001-2); Mem. Intelligence and Security Cttee. (2010-); Mem. Select Cttee. on Defence (2000-1); V. Ch. Cons. Parl. Foreign Affairs and Europe Committees (2000-1); Mem. Select Cttee. on Welsh Affairs (1998-2001); Jt. Sec. Cons Parl. Defence Cttee. (1997-2001); Dep. Dir. Conservative Research Dept. (1990-96); Research Dir. and Dir. Coalition for Peace Through Security (1981-85). Publ.: Racing Ace: The Fights and Flights of 'Kink' Kinkead DSO DSC* DFC* (2011); Changing Direction: British Military Planning for Post-War Strategic Defence, 1942-1947 (1988, 2nd edition, 2003, University pbk. edition, 2008); What's Liberal? Liberal Democrat Quotations and Facts (1996); Who's Left? An Index of Labour MPs and Left-wing Causes, 1985-1992 (1992).

Add House of Commons, London SW1A 0AA

Tel 020 7219 4179

Website www.julianlewis.net

LEWIS, Leonie Rachelle (née Merkel), BA (Hons), MSc, MBA, FRSA.

b. London, Dec. 1955; m. Howard Lewis; Dir. Jewish Volunteering Network (2008-); Co-Ch. Faith Forum for London (2012-); Co.-Ch. United Synagogue Women (USW) (2012-); Exec. Mem. London Jewish Forum (2006-); Exec. Mem. JLC Women's Commission (2012-); Tru. Faith Based Regeneration Network (2000-); Adv. Children's Aid Cttee. (2003-); Project Dir. Office of the Chief Rabbi (2007-08); Dir. Communities, US (1995-2007). Publ.: Ten out of Ten: Perspectives on Community Development.

Add 659 Uxbridge Road, Pinner, Middlesex HA5 3LW

Tel 020 8866 9239

Email leonie@jun.org.uk

LEWIS, Steven,

Mem. Jewish Leadership Council; New Leadership Network; Ch. Jewish Care.

Add JLC, 6 Bloomsbury Square, London WC1A 2LP

Email stevenlewisandpartners.com *Website* www.lewisandpartners.com

LIBESKIND, Daniel, B.Arch, MA, BDA.

b. Lodz, May 12, 1946; m. Nina née Lewis; Architect; Principal, Studio Daniel Libeskind (1989-); Prof. Hochschule fur Gestaltung, Karlsruhe; Cret Ch. of Architecture, University of Pennsylvania; Frank O. Grety Ch. University of Toronto. Recent architectural projects include: Danish Jewish Museum (Copenhagen, 2003); Maurice Wohl Convention Centre (Bar Ilan University, 2003); University of North London Graduate School (2003); Imperial War Museum North (Manchester, 2002); Jewish Museum (Berlin, 2001). Among recent publications: The Space of Encounter (2001); Fishing from the Pavement (1997); Radix: Matrix: Works and Writings (1997).

Add Studio Daniel Libeskind, Windscheidstr. 18, 10627 Berlin, Germany

Tel +49 (30) 327 7820 *Fax* +49 (30) 3277 8299

Email info@daniel-libeskind.com

LIBSON, James,
Ch. World Jewish Relief; Tru. Jewish Leadership Council; New Leadership Network; Exec. Partner, Mischon de Reya Solicitors, London.

Add Mischon De Reya, 12 Red Lion Square, London WC1R 4QD

Email james.libson@mishcon.com *Website* www.mishcon.com

LIGHTMAN, Sir Gavin Anthony,
b. London, Dec. 20, 1939; Patron, UK LFI (2012-), The Hammerson Home (1995-2012) and British Fulbright Scholars Association (2009-); Ch. Commonwealth Jewish Association (1999-2006); Ch. Sainer Legal Fund (1999-); Association of Jewish Lawyers and Jurists (2011-); V. Pres. Hillel (1994-), Ch. Education Cttee. (1992-94); V. Pres. AJA (1994-), Ch. Education Cttee. (1988-94), Deputy Pres. (1986-92); Pres. Gemme (European Assoc. of Judges for Mediation) (2009-12); Ch. Investment Cttee. Harbour Litigation Funding (2010-); T. Lincolns Inn (2008); Justice of the High Court, Chancery Division (1994-08); Fel. University College London (2002); Ch. Legal Friends of University Haifa (1986-2002); QC (1980-94); Bencher of Lincolns Inn (1987). Publ.: (with G. Moss) Law of Admin. and Receivers of Companies (5th edition 2011); (with G. Battersby) Cases and Statutes on the Law of Real Property (1965).

Add Serle Chambers, 6 New Square, Lincoln Inn London WC2

Tel 020 7242 6105

Email gavinlightman@yahoo.co.uk

LIGHTMAN, Sidney, FCIL.
b. London, Apr. 5, 1924; journalist, translator; Foreign News Dept. Jewish Chronicle (1963-96); Asst. Foreign Ed. Jewish Chronicle (1981-89); form. Ed. Jewish Travel Guide (1966-89); Ed. Dept. Jewish Observer and Middle East Review (1959-63); Asst. Ed. Israel and Middle East (Tel Aviv) (1951-4); Sec. British and European Machal Association.

Add 5 West Heath Court, North End Road, London NW11 7RE

Tel 020 8455 1673 *Fax* 020 8455 1673

Email lightmantranslations@talktalk.net

LIND, Eleanor Frances (née Platt), QC, LLB (London).
b. May 6, 1938; m. Frederick (Freddy) M. Lind; Barrister, Gray's Inn 1960, Q.C. (1982); Mem. Panel Jewish Genealogy and Ethics (2011-); Legal Assessor, GDC (2010-); V. Ch. Defence Division BoD (2012-15); Ch. 'Get' Cttee./FamLaw Working group BoD (1999-); Legal assessor GMC (1995-); V. Pres. and Ch. Defence and Group Relations, Board of Deputies (2003-6), Mem. (1984-); Jt. H. 1 Garden Court Family Law Chambers (1990-2007); Pres. Medico-Legal Society. (2002-04); Deputy High Court Judge, Family Division (1987-2004); Recorder Crown Court (1982-2004); Ch. New London Synagogue (1994-99); Act. Ch. Family Law Bar Association (1995), T. (1990-5); Ch. Law, Parliamentary Gen. Purposes Cttee. (1988-94).

Add 1 Garden Court, Temple, London EC4Y 9BJ

Tel 020 7797 7900

Email platt@1gc.com

LIPMAN, Maureen Diane, CBE, H. D.Litt.
b. Hull, May 10, 1946; Actress/Writer. Theatre: Re:Joyce; Lost in Yonkers; The Cabinet M.; See How they Run (Olivier Award for Best Comedy Performance, 1985); Peggy For You;

Oklahoma; Aladdin; Glorious. TV: Agony; About Face; The Knowledge: Eskimo Day; In Search of Style - Art Deco; Dr Who; Sensitive Skin; He Kills Coppers; Casualty; Skins. Film: The Pianist. Publ.: 7 books of anecdotes published by Robson Books. Regular column in Guardian; Good Housekeeping.

Add c/o Conway Van Gelder, 18/21 Jermyn Street SW1Y 6HP

Tel 020 7287 0077

LIPTON, Sir Stuart (Anthony), Kt.

b. Nov. 9, 1942; m. Ruth Kathryn neé Marks; Deputy Ch. Chelsfield LLP (2006-); Mem. Royal Opera House (1998–2006); Ch. (2003–06), Chief Exec. (1995–2003), Stanhope PLC; Ch. CABE (1999–2004).

Add 53 Grosvenor Street W1K 3HU

Email slipton@chelsfield.com

LIPWORTH, Sir (Maurice) Sydney, BCom, LLD, Kt, QC.

b. May 13, 1931; m. Rosa neé Liwarek; T. Philharmonic Orchestra (1982–); T. International Accounting Standards Cttee. Foundation (2000–06); Ch. Financial Reporting Council (1993–2001); Ch. Monopolies and Mergers Commn (1988–93); Dir. Allied Dunbar Assurance plc (form. Hambro Life Assurance) (1971–88).

Add International Accounting Standards Board, 30 Cannon Street EC4M 6XH

LIVINGSTON, Edward Colin, MBE, MB, BS (London), JP.

b. London, Mar. 22, 1925; Med. Practitioner; Barrister; Ch. Austrian Fund Com. AJR Agudas; Ch. Emergency Fund; Ch. H.S.C. Adv. Cttee. form. Ombudsman, Central Council for Jewish Community Services; Medical Examiner, Medical Fund for Care of Victims of Torture; P/T Ch. Social Sec. Appeal Tribunal, Harrow; V. Pres. Harrow Community Trust; Liveryman. Society of Apothecaries; Freeman, City of London; form. P/T Ch. Disability Appeal Tribunal, South East Region; Flt./Lieut (Med. Br.) RAFVR (1948-50).

Add Wyck Cottage, Barrow Point Lane, Pinner, Middlesex HA5 3DJ

LOBENSTEIN, Josef H, MBE.

b. Hanover, Apr. 27, 1927; m. Bella neé Mosbacher; Mayor, London Borough of Hackney (1997-2001); Conservative Opposition Leader, London Borough of Hackney (1974-97); Councillor, Metropolitan Borough of Stoke Newington (1962-65); H. Freeman, London Borough of Hackney; Pres. Adath Yisroel Synagogue and Burial Society; Ch. North London Jewish Liaison Cttee.; V. Pres. Union of Orthodox Hebrew Congregations and Ch. External Affairs Cttee.; V. Ch. Agudath Israel of Great Britain; Mem. Editorial Bd. Jewish Tribune; V. Pres. National Shechita Council; Exec. Shechita UK; Ch. and Bd. Gov. Yesode Hatorah Snr. Girls' School; Bd. Gov. Homerton University Hospital; Pres. Hackney Conservative Association; form. Gen. Sec. Agudath Israel of Great Britain; Mem. Board of Deputies; T. Jewish Secondary School Movement; H. Pres. Hackney and Tower Hamlets Chamber of Commerce; Gov. Avigdor Primary School, Craven Park Primary School.

Add 27 Fairholt Road, London N16 5EW

Tel 020 8800 4746 Mobile 07976 724 081 *Fax* 020 7502 0985

LUCAS, Stella, MBE, JP.

b. London, July 30, 1916; née Waldman; Pres. First Women's Lodge B'nai B'rith (1975-77); V. Pres. (Ch. 1978-84), Frs. of Hebrew University (Women's Group); Pres. Dollis Hill Ladies' Guild; Ch. Union of Jewish Women (1966-72); Exec. Off. International Council of Jewish Women (1963-66); Ch. Women Frs. of Jews' Coll. (1957-66); V. Pres. Jewish Care; Ch. Stepney Girls' Club and Settlement; V. Pres. Assn. of US Women; Central Council for Jewish Social Services; Board of Deputies; Ch. Brodie Institute; Convenor, Board of Deputies Central Enquiry Desk; Fdr. 'All Aboard Shops'.

Add 51 Wellington Court, Wellington Road NW8 9TB

Tel 020 7586 3030

LUSTIGMAN, Stuart,
Pres. European Maccabi Confederation; V. Pres. Maccabi GB; Pres. Faithfold FC; Exec. Mem. Maccabi World Union; International Co-Ch. Maccabi World Union Sports Dept.; Pres. Maccabi Junior Football League; Ch. Maccabi Masters Football League.
Tel 020 8958 8767
Email stuartlustigman@aol.com

LYONS, Anne Rebecca (née Goldman), J.P; Ll.B; Barrister at Law.
b. Seascale, Cumbria; m. Alan; Legal indexer; Ch. Association of Jewish Women's Organisations in the UK (2014-); Ch. Kingston Wizo (1981–2010); Rebecca Sieff Award 2006; Wimbledon Magistrates Court (1984-2011); Ch. S. W London Probation Cttee. (1998-2000).
Add Association of Jewish Women's Organisations in UK, 108-110, Finchley Road, London NW3 5JJ
Tel 020 7319 9169 *Fax* 020 7431 3671
Email contact@ajwo.org *Website* www.ajwo.org

MAGONET, Rabbi Prof. Dr Jonathan David, MB, BS, PhD (Heid.), FRSA.
b. London, Aug. 2, 1942; Research Prof. Seinan Gakuin University, Fukuoka, Japan (2010-14); Theologische Hochschule Wuppertal (2004-10); Schalom Ben Chorim Prof. Jewish Studies, University Würzburg and Augsburg (2008); Principal, Leo Baeck College (1985-2005), form. Emer. Prof. of Bible; Guest Prof. University Lucerne (2004), University Oldenberg (1999); V. Pres. Movement for Reform Judaism. Among recent publications: Netsuke Nation: Tales from Another Japan (2013); A Rabbi Reads the Torah (2013); Seder Ha-t'fillot Forms of Prayer: Daily and Sabbath (Ed. 8th edition 2008); Einführung in Judentum (2004); Talking to the Other: Interfaith Dialogue with Christians and Muslims (2003); Abraham-Jesus-Mohammed: Interreligioser Dialog aus Jüdischer Perspektiv (2000); Rabbino Seishokaishak: Yudaiyakkuo to Kiristokuo No Taiwa (Japanese: Rabbinic Bible Commentary, Jewish Christian Dialogue) (2012); Ed. European Judaism (2005-), Co-Ed. (1992-2005).
Add 22 Avenue Mansion, Finchley Road, London NW3 7AX
Tel 020 7209 0911
Email jonathan.magonet@gmail.com *Website* www.jonathanmagonet.co.uk

MANN, John, BA.
b. Jan. 10, 1960; m. Joanna White; MP (Lab) Bassetlaw (2001-); Mem. Editorial Advisory Panel, People Management (2005–9); Liaison Officer, National Trade Union and Lab Party (1995–2000); Hd of Res. and Education, AEU (1988–90); Mem. (Lab), Lambeth BC (1986–90); Ch. Parliamentary Cttee. against Antisemitism; commissioned the All-Party Parliamentary Inquiry into Antisemitism.
Add Stanley Street, Worksop, Notts S81 7HX
Tel 020 7219 8345
Email mannj@parliament.uk *Website* www.johnmannmp.com

MARANTZ, Jason,
Chief Exec. London School of Jewish Studies.
Add Schaller House, Wohl Campus for Jewish Education, 44a Albert Road, London NW4 2SJ
Tel 020 8203 6427 *Fax* 020 8203 6420
Email info@lsjs.ac.uk *Website* www.lsjs.ac.uk

MARCUS, Rabbi Barry, BA (Hons), PGCE.
b. Cape Town, Oct. 28, 1949; Patron, Yad Vashem UK (2005-); T. Holocaust Memorial Day Trust (2004-); Rabbi, Central Synagogue (1995-); Pioneer of the one-day educational visits to Auschwitz-Birkenau. Publ.: You Are Witnesses (1999); Father and son (1986).
Add 40 Hallam Street, London W1W 6NW
Tel 020 7580 1355 *Fax* 020 7636 3831
Email administrator@centralsynagogue.org.uk *Website* www.centralsynagogue.org.uk

MARCUS, Mark Hyman, BA (Com).

b. Manchester, Feb. 22, 1933; form. Exec. Dir. B'nai B'rith UK (1984-98); form. Ch. B'nai B'rith London Bureau of International Affairs; Dir. Provincial and London Divisions, UJIA.

Add B'nai B'rith UK, ORT House, 126 Albert Street, London NW1 7NE

MARGOLYES, Miriam, BA (Cantab), LGSM&D.

b. Oxford, May 18, 1941; Actress. BAFTA Best Supporting Actress (1993); Sony Radio Award, Best Actress on Radio (1993); Best Supporting Actress, LA Critics Circle Awards (1989). Major film credits include: Cold Comfort Farm; Magnolia; The Life and Death of Peter Sellers; Modigliani; Professor Sprout in the Harry Potter films and many more. TV credits include: Blackadder; The Girls of Slender Means; Oliver Twist; The History Man; Vanity Fair; Supply & Demand. Frannie's Turn; BBC TV documentary series about Charles Dickens. Stage credits include: Dickens' Women (world tour 2012); Endgame; WICKED (London and Broadway), Blithe Spirit (Melbourne Theatre Company); The Vagina Monologues; Romeo & Juliet (Los Angeles production), She Stoops to Conquer; Orpheus Descending (London). Many audio book recordings, including: Oliver Twist; Great Expectations; Matilda; Pinnocchio; The Worst Witch series; The Queen & I; The Little White Horse; The Sea; Troy; Wise Child.

Add c/o Lindy King, United Agents, 12-26 Lexington Street, London W1F 0LE

Tel 020 3214 0800 *Fax* 020 3214 0803

Email lking@unitedagents.co.uk *Website* www.miriammargolyes.com

MARINER, Rabbi Rodney John, BA (Hons), Dip. Ed.

b. Melbourne, Australia, May 29, 1941; m. Susan; Emer. Rabbi, Belsize Square Synagogue; Convener, Beth Din, Reform Judaism (Ret. 2013); Associate M. Edgware and District Reform Synagogue (1979-82); Assistant M. North Western Reform Synagogue (1976-79). Publ.: Prayers For All The Year: Part 1, Shabbat; Part 2, Festivals; Part 3, New Year; Part 4, Atonement; Part 5, Evening Prayers.

Add 92 North Road, London N6 4AA

Tel 020 8347 5306

Email rodmariner@aol.com

MARKS, Laura,

Snr. V. Pres. Board of Deputies.

Add Board Of Deputies, 6 Bloomsbury Square, London WC1A 2LP

Tel 020 7543 5400 *Fax* 020 7543 0010

Email info@bod.org.uk *Website* www.bod.org.uk

MARKS, Shula Eta (née Winokur), Emer. Prof, SOAS, OBE, FBA, BA (UCT), PhD (London), H. DLitt (UCT), H. D.Soc.Sci. (Natal), H. DLitt (University of Johannesburg; Distinguished Africanist Award, African Studies Assoc. (UK) (2002); Distinguished Res. Fel. SAS, London; H. Fel., SOAS (2005-); H. Prof., UCT (2005-10).

b. Cape Town, Oct. 14, 1936; m. Isaac Meyer Marks; Historian; Emer. Prof. History of Southern Africa, SOAS (2001-), Prof. (1993-2001); Ch. International Records Management Trust (1995-2004); Ch. Council for Assisting Refugee Academics, (CARA) (1993-2004); Mem. Council (1983-2013); Mem. Canon Collins Education and Legal Assistance Trust (2004-14); Mem. Arts and Humanities Research Bd. (1998-2000); Dir. Institute of Commonwealth Studies, University of London (1983-93). Publ.: Divided Sisterhood: Class, Race and Gender in the South African Nursing Profession (1994); Not Either an Experimental Doll: The Separate Lives of Three South African Women (1987); In Defence of Learning: The Plight, Persecution and Placement of Academic Refugees, 1933-80 (with Paul Weindling and Laura Wintour).

Add 43 Dulwich Common, London SE21 7EU

Email shula.e.marks@gmail.com

MARKS-WOLDMAN, Olivia,
Chief Exec. Holocaust Memorial Day Trust.
Add PO Box 61074, London SE1P 5BX
Tel 020 7785 7029
Email enquiries@hmd.org.uk *Website* www.hmd.org.uk

MARMUR, Rabbi Dow,
b. Sosnowiec, Poland, Feb. 24, 1935; Rabbi Emer. Holy Blossom Temple, Toronto; form. Pres. Toronto Board of Rabbis; form. Ch. Council of Reform and Lib. Rabbis; M. North Western Reform Synagogue (1969-83); South-West Essex Reform Synagogue (1962-69). Publ.: Beyond Survival; The Star of Return; Walking Toward Elijah; On being a Jew; Six Lives: a Memoir; Reform Judaism (Ed.); A Genuine Search (Ed.); Choose Life.
Add 1950 Bathurst Street, Toronto, Ontario, M5P 3K9, Canada
Tel 416 789 3291 *Fax* 416 789 9697
Email dmarmur@hotmail.com

MASSIL, Stephen W, BA, Dip. Lib, FLA, FSA, FRAS.
b. Eynsham, Oxon, Sept. 21, 1941; m. Brenda Goldstein; Librarian; posts at the Garrick Club (2006-); National Trust (2006-); Sir John Soane's Museum (2002-6); University College London (2002-3); Warburg Institute (1999/2002); Cambridge (1996-2000); London University (1977-96); University of Birmingham (1966-77); consultant for Unesco, the British Council and other international organisations; V. Pres. JHSE (2006-), Pres. (2004-6); T. Jewish Literary Trust, Ed. Jewish Book News and Reviews (1986-); Ed. Jewish Year Book (Vallentine Mitchell, 1994-2009, JC 1989-93); Convenor, Hebraica Libraries Group (1991-2007); Ed. Jewish Travel Guide (1991-4). Publ.: Anglo-Jewish Bibliography, 1971-90 (Co-Ed. 1992); Facsimile edition of 'Jewish Year Book, 1896' (Ed.); articles and conference papers on library history, bibliography; consultancy reports for Unesco and the British Council.
Add JHSE, 33 Seymour Place, London W1H 5AP

MICHAELS, Rabbi Maurice Arnold, MA.
b. Woolmer's Park, Herts., Aug. 31, 1941; Rabbi, North Western Reform Synagogue; Hd. Vocational Studies and Lecturer, Leo Baeck College; Lecturer, Gregorian University, Rome; V. Pres. Movement for Reform Judaism; H. Life V. Pres. Leo Baeck College; T. Interfaith Network UK; Gov. Chlore Tikva School; Patron, Haven House Children's Hospice; Patron, Waging Peace; form. Ch. and V. Pres. RSGB; Ch. Leo Baeck College; Ch. Assembly of Reform Rabbis; Ch. SW Essex Reform Synagogue; Ch. of Govs. Clore Tikva School; Ch. Redbridge Business Education Partnership; Ch. and T. Ahada Bereavement Counselling; T. Empathy Counselling; Gov. Redbridge College; Gov. Akiva School; Gov. Jewish Jt. Burial Society; T. Redbridge Racial Equality Council; T. Limmud; Council Mem. Redbridge Campaign Against Racism and Fascism; Dir. Harlow Enterprise Agency; V. Ch. Harlow and District Employers' Group; Dir. Refugee and Migrant Forum of East London; Man. Cttee. Redbridge Faith Forum; Patron, St Francis Hospice; Chaplain London 2012.
Add 19 Moray Close, Rise Park, Essex RM1 4YJ
Tel 020 8554 2812
Email ramaby@ntlworld.com

MIDDLEBURGH, Rabbi Charles H, BA Hons, PhD, FZS.
b. Hove, Oct. 2, 1956; Rabbi, Cardiff Reform Synagogue (2005-14), Dublin Jewish Progressive Congregation (2002-11), Shir HaTzaphon, Copenhagen (2002-05), Harrow and Wembley Progressive Synagogue (1983-97); Dir. Jewish Studies, Leo Baeck College (2011-), Snr. Lecturer Rabbinics (2004-), Lecturer Aramaic, Practical Rabbinics (2002); Co-Ed. Mahzor Ruach Chadashah (1996-2003); Exec. Dir. Union of Liberal and Progressive Synagogues (1997-2002); Fel. Zoological Society, London; Publ.: A Jewish Book of Comfort (with Rabbi Dr. A. Goldstein, 2014); High and Holy Days: A Book of Jewish Wisdom (with Rabbi Dr. A. Goldstein, 2010); Tefillot ve-Tachanunim (with A. Goldstein, 2006).
Add Leo Baeck College, 80 East End Road, London N3 2SY

Tel 020 8349 5615 *Fax* 020 8349 5619
Email charles.middleburgh@lbc.ac.uk

MILIBAND, Rt. Hon. David (Wright), BA, MSC.

b. July. 15, 1965; m. Louise neé Shackelton; MP (Lab) South Shields (2001-13); Shadow Foreign Sec. (2010); Sec. of State for Foreign and Commonwealth Affairs (2007-10); Sec. of State for Environment, Food and Rural Affairs (2006–07); Cabinet Office (2004–05); M. of State: DfES (2002–04); Hd. PM's Policy Unit (1998–2001).

Add 122 East 42nd Street, New York 10168-1289, USA
Email mcgeeb@parliament.uk *Website* www.davidmiliband.net

MILIBAND, Rt. Hon. Edward, BA, MSc.

b. Dec. 24, 1969; m. Justine née Thornton; Leader of Labour Party (2010-); MP (Lab) Doncaster North (2005-); Sec. of State for Energy and Climate Change (2008-10); Chancellor of the Duchy of Lancaster and M. for the Cabinet Office (2007–08); Parly Sec. Cabinet Office (2006–07); Council of Econ. Advs. HM Treasury (2004–05); Special Adv. to Chancellor of the Exchequer (1997–2002).

Add House of Commons, London SW1A 0AA

MILLER, Helena, Cert Ed., Adv. Dip. Ed., MA, PhD Jewish Education (London).

b. London, Oct. 27, 1955; m. Steve Miller; Research Dir. UJIA; Dir. of Research and Education, Dir. Community Israel Engagement, UJIA (2007-); Ch. Pikuach Schools Inspection Service (2006-); Dir. of Education, Leo Baeck College (2001-07); Awarded Max Fisher Prize for Contribution to Jewish Education in the Diaspora (2012). Publ.: Four Years On: A Review of Inspections of Jewish Schools 2007-11 (2012); The International Handbook of Jewish Education (2011); Beyond the Community: Jewish Day School Education in Britain (2009); Meeting the Challenge: the Jewish Schooling Phenomenon in the UK (2001); The Magic Box (1995); Craft in Action (1981).

Add 37 Kentish Town Road, London NW1 8NX
Tel 020 7424 6400 *Fax* 020 7424 6401
Email helena.miller@ujia.org *Website* www.ujia.org

MILLER, Jonathan Moss, BSc (Hons), ARCS, PGCE, MA, NPQH.

m. Hannah née Babad; Hd. JFS (2008-).

Add JFS, The Mall, Kenton, Harrow, Middlesex HA3 9TE
Tel 020 8206 3100 *Fax* 020 8206 3101
Email admin@jfs.brent.sch.uk *Website* www.jfs.brent.sch.uk

MILLETT, Rt. Hon. Lord Peter, Baron of St. Marylebone, PC, MA (Cantab), H. DLL (University London).

b. London, June 23, 1932; m. Anne Mireille Harris; Hon. Fel. Queen Mary College, London (2013); Hon. LLD London University (2008); Non-Permanent Judge, Court of Final Appeal, Hong Kong (2000-); T. Lincoln's Inn (2004); Lord of Appeal in Ordinary (1998-2004); Mem. Court of Appeal (1994-8); Pres. West London Synagogue (1991-5); Hon. Fel. Trinity Hall (1994); Judge of the High Court Chancery Div. (1986-94); form. Ch. Lewis Hammerson Home (1981-91); QC (1973-86), Mem. Insolvency Law Review Cttee. (1976-82); Standing Jnr. Counsel, Trade and Industry Dept. (1967-73); Bencher, Lincoln's Inn; Called to Bar, Middle Temple. Publ.: (Contr.) Halsbury's Law of England; Editor-in-Chief: Encyclopaedia of Forms and Precedents.

Add 18 Portman Close, London W1H 6BR
Tel 020 7935 1152

MILSTON, Michael, BA (London).

b. June 7, 1949; m. Helen Esther née Moss; Freelance journalist; Radio Producer, Tikkun Spectrum; Lecturer, English as a Foreign Language; Lecturer, Magen Ohel Avraham Shiur; Lay Preacher, Fieldgate Street Great Synagogue; Ch. Friends of East London Orthodox Association of Synagogues (2001-). Publ.: A Critical Review (2nd Edition 2003).

Add 6 Elmfield House, 77 Carlton Hill, London NW8 9XB

Tel 020 7624 8183 *Fax* 020 7624 8183

Email francamil@talk21.com

MIRVIS, Chief Rabbi Ephraim Yitzchak, BA.

b. Johannesburg, Sept. 7, 1956; m. Valerie née Kaplan; Chief Rabbi of the United Hebrew Congregations of the Commonwealth (2013-); Associate Pres. Conference of European Rabbis (2013-); Pres. London School of Jewish Studies (2013-); Rabbi, Finchley Synagogue (1996-2013); Chaplain to the Mayor, London Borough of Barnet (2006-07); Chaplain to the Mayor, London Borough of Redbridge (2004-05); Mem. Chief Rabbi's Cabinet; Ed. Daf Hashavua (2001-06); Ch. Rabbinical Council of the US (1999-2002); M. Western Marble Arch Synagogue (1992-96); form. Chief Rabbi, Jewish Communities of Ireland (1984-92); M. Dublin Hebrew Congregation (1982-84); Lecturer Machon Meir, Jerusalem (1980-82); Mem. Standing Cttee. of Conference of European Rabbis; Religious Adv. to the Jewish Marriage Council; Dir. Kinloss Learning Centre; Dir. Kinloss Kollel; H. Princ. Morasha Jewish Primary School.

Add Office of the Chief Rabbi, 305 Ballards Lane, London N12 8GB

Tel 020 8343 6301 *Fax* 020 8343 6310

Email info@chiefrabbi.org *Website* www.chiefrabbi.org

MITCHELL, Lord Parry Andrew, (Baron Mitchell of Hampstead), B.Sc. (London), MBA (Columbia).

b. London, May 6, 1943; m. Hannah née Lowy; Ch. Coexistence Trust (2008-); Ch. eLearning Foundation (2006-); Ch. Weizmann UK (2006-); Mem. House of Lords Select Cttee. for Science and Technology; T. Genesis Research Trust; T. Lowy Mitchell Foundation.

Add House of Lords, London SW1A 0PW

Tel 020 7433 3238

Email parrym@mac.com

MOONMAN, Eric, OBE, FRSA, M.Sc.

b. Liverpool, Apr. 29, 1929; m. Gillian Louise née Mayer; Adv. IRN Counter-Terrorism; Snr. Fel. Inter-University Centre for Terrorism, Washington, USA; Pres. Zionist Federation (2001-); Ch. Academic Response to Racism and Antisemitism (1994-2005); Ch. Friends Natural History Museum (2007-11); Ch. ERG Group of Radio Stations (1991-2002); (seconded) Ch. WJC Europe Branch Cttee. on Antisemitism (1998-2002, 1985-92); V. Pres. Board of Deputies (1994-2000), Snr. V. Pres. (1985-91); Ch. National Aliyah and Volunteers Council (1975-99); CRE Award for Multi-Racial Service (1996); Ch. Community Research Unit, (1985-96); Hon. Pres. Friends of Union of Jewish Students (1990-95); Dir. Natural History Museum Dev. Trust (1989-91); MP (Lab.) for Basildon (1974-9), for Billericay (1966-70); Ch. Media Network; Prof. Health Management, City University, London (2000-13); T. Balfour Trust; Tru. Everton Former Players Foundation; Exec. Mem. Association of Former MPs, responsible for Outreach programme. Publ.: Learning to Live with the Violent Society (2004); The Alternative Government; The Manager and the Organisation; Reluctant Partnership; European Science and Technology, etc.

Add 1 Beacon Hill N7 9LY

MORGENSTERN, Philip Louis, BA.

b. London, Jan. 15, 1932; m. Estelle Pamela née Erenberg; Solicitor; Ch. Institute of Jewish Studies (1999-2013, Emer. Pres. 2013-); Dir. Jewish Law Publication Fund (1990-2012); Dir. Kessler Foundation 1993-2011); Partner, Nicholson Graham & Jones (1962-95); Freeman, City of London.

Add 7 Princes Close, Edgware, Middlesex HA8 7QB

Tel 020 3271 0035

Email plmorgen@gmail.com

MORRIS, Henry,

b. London, Mar. 5, 1921; Pres. Jewish Military Museum; form. Ch. Jewish Defence and Group Relations Cttee. Jewish Board of Deputies; V. Pres. (National. Ch. 1979-81), AJEX. Publ.: We Will Remember Them (1989, Addendum 1994, 2nd Edition 2011); The AJEX

Chronicles: A History of the Association (2000).
Add 4 Ashbrook, Stonegrove, Edgware, Middlesex HA8 7SU
Tel 020 8958 7154

MORRIS, Simon, CQSW (Certificate of qualification in Social Work), BA Hons Sociology and Applied Social Studies (Keele University), MBA (Henley/Brunel).
b. June 4, 1960; m. Lucille née Balcombe; Chief Exec. Jewish Care; form. Dir. of Community Services, Jewish Care (1999-2003); Assistant Dir. Community Services, Jewish Care (1996-99); London Borough of Hounslow, Commissions Manager Adult Services (1994-96), Team Manager Community (1988-94).
Add Jewish Care, Amélie House, Maurice and Vivienne Wohl Campus, 221 Golders Green Road, London NW11 9DQ
Tel 020 8922 2000 *Fax* 020 8458 7802
Email smorris@jcare.org

MOSES, Jennifer,
Est. ARK children's charity (2002); form. Special Adv. British PM; form. Chief Exec. Centreforum (think tank); Gov. King Solomon Academy; Acland Burghley School; JCC.
Add ARK, 15 Adam Street, London WC2N 6AH
Tel 020 7395 2050
Email info@arkonline.org

MOSS, Stephen David, CBE, LLB, MBA.
b. London, September 13, 1952; m. Joy Rochelle née Berger; read Law at King's College, London, Gray's Inn and MBA at London Business School; Ch. Grosvenor Securities; Ch. Bibendum Wine Holdings Ltd.; Ch. Bonasystems Europe; Fdr. and Ch. Springboard Charity; Tru. Institute of Jewish Policy Research; T. Jewish Child's Day; Tru. JCOSS; Ch. (2002-05); Pres. West London Synagogue (2011-); Ch. (2008-11), Jt. T. (2005-), Reform Judaism.
Add 28 Bolton Street, London W1J 8BP
Email stephen@stephenmoss.co.uk *Website* www.stephenmoss.co.uk

MYERS, Bernie,
b. Apr. 2, 1944; m. Sandra; Dir. Industrial Dwellings Society (1885) Ltd; T. Grief Encounter; Dir. Rothschild Group companies; form. Ch. Norwood; form. V. Ch. British Friends of the Hebrew University; form. Ch. Harrow Citizens Advice Bureau.
Add New Court, St. Swithin's Lane, London EC4N 8AL
Email bernie.myers@rothschild.com

NAGLER, Neville Anthony, OBE, MA (Cantab).
b. London, Jan. 2, 1945; m. Judy née Mordant; Exec. Dir. Taxation Disciplinary Bd. (2007-); form. Dir. Gen. Board of Deputies (1991-2005); Certificate in Public Services Management (2000); form. Assistant Sec. Home Office (1980-91); Fin. Representative and Warden, Pinner Synagogue (1979-91); Ch. Council of Europe Drug Co-op Group (1984-88); UK Representative to UN Narcotics Commission, (1983-88); Haldane Essay Prize (1979); Pte. Sec. Chancellor of Exchequer (1971); Lord Chancellor's Adv. Cttee. for Justices of the Peace for West London; form. V. Ch. Investigation Cttee. CIMA (Chartered Inst. of Management Accountants); form. Dir. Sternberg Fund; form. V. Ch. Inter-Faith Network; Principal H.M. Treasury.
Add 24 Dawlish Drive, Pinner HA5 5LN
Tel 020 8868 3103
Email n.nagler@btinternet.com

NATHAN, Clemens Neumann, CTexFTI, FRAI, Officers' Cross, Austria; Cavalieri, al Merito della Repub. Italiana.
b. Hamburg, Aug. 24, 1933; Company Dir.; Society of Heshaim, Spanish and Portuguese Jews Congregation, London (1979-), Bd. of Elders (1977-83); Companionship of the Textile Institute (2007); form. Ch. Centre for Christian–Jewish Studies, Cambridge (1998-2004); V. Pres. Anglo-Jewish Association (Pres. 1983-9, T. 1965-71); CCJ, Fdr. Mem. International

Cttee. for Human Rights in Soviet Union (1966); Jt. Ch. Consultant Council of Jewish Organisations (Non-Govt. Organisation at United Nations); Hon. Fel. Shenkar College, Israel; Pres. Centre for German-Jewish Studies, Sussex; Hon. Fel. SSEES, University London; Dir. Sephardi Centre; Textile Institute Medal for services to the Industry and Institute. Publ.: The Changing Face of Religion and Human Rights (2009); Technological, Marketing and Human Rights Works.

Add Flat 10, 3 Cambridge Terrace, London NW1 4JL

Tel 020 7034 1980

NEUBERGER, Lord David Edmund, Baron of Abbotsbury,, P.C. MA.

b. January 10, 1948, m. Angela Holdsworth; Lawyer; Pres. Supreme Court (2012-); Master of the Rolls (2009-12); Ch. Schizophrenia Trust (2003-14); Tru. MHRUK (2014-); Ch. Adv. Cttee. on Spoliation of Art during the Holocaust (1999-); Gov. University of the Arts London (2000-10); Lord of Appeal in Ordinary (2007-09); Lord Justice of Appeal (2004-07); Supervisory Chancery Judge, Midland Wales and Chester (2001-04); High Court Judge, Chancery Division (1996); Recorder (1990-96); Queen's Counsel (1987); Called to Bar, Lincolns Inn (1974); Mem. Privy Council.

Add Supreme Court of the United Kingdom, Parliament Square, London SW1P 3BD

Email jackie.sears@supremecourt.uk *Website* www.supremecourt.gov.uk

NEUBERGER, Rabbi Dame Julia Babette Sarah (née Schwab), Baroness, DBE, MA (Cantab), H. Doctorates University Humberside, Ulster, City, Stirling, Oxford Brookes, Teesside, Nottingham, Open University, Queens Belfast, Sheffield Hallam, Aberdeen, Liverpool, London, Southampton.

b. London, Feb. 27, 1950; m. Anthony; Ch. Camden and Islington Community Health Services NHS Trust (1993-97); Ch. Review of the Liverpool Care Pathway (2013-); Tru. Van Leer Foundation (2012-); Snr. Rabbi, West London Synagogue (2011-); Ch. One Housing Group (2009-12); Ch. Responsible Gambling Strategy Bd. (2009-11); T. Booker Prize Foundation (2003-10); T. New Philanthropy Capital (2007-11); T. Jewish Care (2009-11, 2005-07); Ch. Adv. Panel on Judicial Diversity (2009-10); Vis. Prof. Bloomberg Ch. Harvard (2006); T. Imperial War Museum (1999-2006); Chief Exec. The King's Fund (1997-2004); Civil Service Commissioner (2001-2); Chancellor, University Ulster (1994-2000); Prime Minister Gordon Brown's Champion for Volunteering (2007-09); Rabbi, S. London Liberal Synagogue (1977-89); Lecturer, Leo Baeck College; Hon. Fel. Royal College Physicians; Hon. Fel. Royal College GPs, Royal College Psychiatrists; Hon. Fel. Royal College of Obstetricians and Gynaecologists. Among recent publications: Is That All There Is? (2011); Not Dead Yet: a Manifesto for Old Age (2008); The Moral State We're In (2005); Caring for Dying Patients of Different Faiths (3rd edition 2004); Dying Well: A Guide to Enabling a Good Death (2nd ed., 2004); Hidden Assets: Decision Making in the NHS (Jt. Ed., 2002); On Being Jewish (Co-Ed, Canon John White, 1995).

Add West London Synagogue, 33 Seymour Place, London

Tel 020 7535 0255

Email julia.neuberger@wls.org.uk *Website* www.wls.org.uk

NEUFELD, Edgar, OBE, BSc, PhD, CPhys, FBCS, CEng, FRSA.

b. Vienna, Apr. 18, 1933; m. Sue Robinson; Ch. Governing Body, Park View Academy (1999-2006); H. Doctorate, Middlesex University (2003), Pro. Chancellor (2000), Ch. Bd. of Governors (1991-96); Ch. Haringey Employment Commission Report (1997); Group Dir. IBM Europe (1987-89), IBM UK (1961-89); Ch. Governors, Haringey Sixth Form Centre; T. and V. Ch. Shelter; Founding Ch. North London Cultural Diversity Forum; T. Finsbury Park Community Trust.

Add 32 Bancroft Avenue, London N2 0AS

Email neufeld@blueyonder.co.uk

NEWMAN, Aubrey Norris, MA (Glasgow), MA, D.Phil (Oxon), FRHistS.

b. London, Dec. 14, 1927; m. Bernice Freda née Gould; Prof. (Emer.) of History, Leicester University; Pres. Jewish Historical Society (1977-79, 1992-93); form. Pres. Leicester Hebrew Congregation. Publ.: Jewish Migration to South Africa (Jt. Ed. 2006); The

Holocaust (2002); Patterns of Migration, 1850-1914 (Jt Ed. 1996); The History of the Board of Deputies (1985); The Jewish East End, 1840-1939 (Ed. 1981); The US, 1870-1970 (1977); Provincial Jewry in Victorian Britain (Ed. 1975); Migration and Settlement (Ed. 1970); The Stanhopes of Chevening (1970).

Add 33 Stanley Road, Stoneygate, Leicester LE2 1RF

Tel 0116 270 4065 (home) *Fax* 0116 252 3986

Email new@le.ac.uk

NEWMAN, Eddy,
b. Liverpool, May 14, 1953. Councillor Woodhouse Park (Lab); Manchester City Councillor (1979-85, 2002-); Mem. of the European Parliament's Delegation for Relations with Israel and the Knesset (1994-99); Labour MEP for Greater Manchester Central (1984-99); Ch. European Parliament Cttee. on Petitions (1994-97); V. Ch. Cttee. on Petitions (1997-99); V. Ch. European Parliament Regional Policy and Regional Planning Cttee (1984-87); Ch. Wythenshaw Community Housing Group; Ch. Manchester City Council's Health Scrutiny Cttee. Publ.: Contributor to 'The European Ombudsmen' (2005).

Add 234 Ryebank Road, Manchester M21 9LU

Tel 0161 881 8147

Email cllr.e.newman@manchester.gov.uk

NEWMAN, Rabbi Jeffrey, MA (Oxon.).
b. Reading, Dec. 26, 1941; m. Bracha; Emer. form Rabbi, Finchley Reform Synagogue (1973-2001); Ed. Living Judaism (1969-73); Dir. Earth Charter UK; form. Ch. Rabbinic In-service training, Leo Baeck Rabbinical College (LBC); form. Ch. Pastoral Skills and Counselling Department LBC; form. Ch. of Tru. Israel Palestine Centre for Research and Information; Lecturer in Heimler Training; contributor to various journals on Judaism, psychology, spirituality and Earthcharter.

Add 46 Torrington Park, London N12 9TP

Email jeffrey@jnewman.org.uk

NEWMAN, Dr Joanna Frances, BA (hons), MA in Jewish History (UCL), PhD (Southampton).
b. London; m. Uwe Westphal; Dir. UK Higher Education International and Europe Unit, Universities UK (2011-); Civil Servant; Hon. S. JHSE (2007-); Hd. Higher Education, British Library (2007-11); Exec. Dir. Arts and Education, London Jewish Cultural Centre (2002-2006); Bd. Mem. Artsdepot; V. Ch. Centre for German-Jewish Studies, University Sussex; Hon. Fel. University Southampton; Postdoctoral Fel. Institute of Commonwealth Studies; Mem. Council, Wiener Library; Parkes Fel. (Southampton). Publ.: (Ed. with Toby Haggith) Holocaust and the Moving Image: Representation in Film and Television Since 1993 (2005).

Add The British Library, 96 Euston Road, London NW1 2DB

Email info@Universitiesuk.ac.uk

NEWMAN, Lotte Therese, CBE, MB, BS, LRCP, MRCS, FRCGP FRNZCGP.
b. Frankfurt am Main, Jan. 22, 1929; m. Norman Aronsohn, 1959; form. posts held General Practitioner; Ch. of Circumcision Working Group (1999-2005); Mem. Board of Deputies (1999-2005); Mem. Hampstead Synagogue Board of Management (1999-2005); Medical Adv. St John Ambulance (1999-2003); Pres. London Jewish Medical Society (1998-99); Gov. PPP Medical Trust (1996-99); Ch. Registration Cttee. General Medical Council (1997-98); Mem. GMC (1984-98); Pres. Royal College General Practitioners (1994-97); Freeman, City of London; Mem. Defence Group Relations Cttee. Publ.: Papers on Medicine, health and medical training issues especially relating to women doctors, and 'medicine and the Jews'.

Add The White House, 1 Ardwick Road, London NW2 2BX

Tel 020 7436 6630 *Fax* 020 7435 6672

NEWMAN, Colonel Martin, DL, FCIPR.
b. Prestbury, Sept. 26, 1947; m. Lisa Chernin; Public relations consultant; Pres. United Synagogue, Manchester, Mead Hill Shul (2012-); Colonel Cmdt Gibraltar Cadet Force (2012-); Dept. Lieutenant of Greater Manchester (2009); Mem. Management and Trustees

Cttee. Fusiliers Museum Lancashire (2007-); Tru. and V. Pres. Friends of Jewish Servicemen and Women (2006-); Ch. Jewish Committee, HM Forces (2007-); Colonel Special Advisor MOD Youth Policy Unit (2002-09); Lt. Col. CO ACF PR Unit (1994-2002); NW Regional Ch. Inst. of Public Relations (1994-96); Major TA Pool of Public Information Officers (1986-2004); Commissioned TA Gen List (ACF) 1975; Editor, Menorah magazine and Easy Resettlement magazine. PR Officer, AJEX.

Add 12 Conisborough Place, Whitefield, Manchester M45 6EJ

Email martin.newman@armymail.mod.uk

NEWMARK, Brooks Philip Victor, MP.

b. Norwalk, Connecticut, May 8, 1958; m. Lucy née Keegan; Businessman; Govt. Whip (Office of the Deputy Prime Minister and Dept. for International Development (2011-12)); Dir. Fdr. 'A Partner in Education' (2010-); Business, Innovation and Skills, Wales Office (2010-11); Opposition Whip (Foreign Affairs 2009-10, Treasury 2007-09); Co-Ch. Conservative Party 'Women2Win' (2006-); Dir. Harvard University Alumni Association (2005-); MP (Cons.), for Braintree (2005-); Mem. Treasury Sect Cttee. (2006-07, 2012-); Mem. Science and Technology Sect Cttee. (2005-07); Partner, Apollo LP (1998-05); Ch. Southwark and Bermondsey Conservative Association (1990-93). Publ.: The Price of Irresponsibility (CPS, 2008); Simply Red: The True State of the Public Finances (CPS, 2006); Direct Democracy: an Agenda for a New Model Party (2005).

Add House of Commons, London SW1A 0AA

Tel 020 7219 3464

Website www.brooksnewmark.com

NEWMARK, Jeremy, MCIPR.

b. Hertfordshire, Sept. 19, 1972; m. Hilary née Cawson; Mem. Steering Group and Ch. Global Coalition for Israel (2010-); Tru. Ebor Eruv Trust (2010-); Ch. 'Salute to Israel' Group (2008-); Mem. JLC School's Strategy Implementation Group (2008-); Mem. Bd. Directors, European Institute for the Study of Antisemitism (2007-); Mem. Government Interdepartmental Task Force on Antisemitism (2007-); Chief Exec. Jewish Leadership Council (2006-13); Mem. BBC Standing Conference on Religions and Faith (2010); Dir. Antisemitism Co-ordination Unit (2004-06); Mem. Gov. Review Panel - 'Working with Faith Communities' (2003-04); Director of Communications, Office of the Chief Rabbi (1999-2004); Chief Media Officer, Israel 50 (UK) (1999); International Affairs Officer, Board of Deputies (1997-99); Campaigns Organiser, UJS (1995-96); Man. Council Fair Play Campaign Group; Jt. Hd. Stop the Boycott; form. T. Anglo-Israel Association; form. Man. Council, Searchlight Education Trust.

NOE, Leo,

T. Kisharon; T. Seed; Ch. F&C; REIT Asset Management; V. Pres. and Tru. Jewish Leadership Council; Ch. Board of Deputies; Jt. Ch. Joint Liaison Group; Fdr. Lee Baron Commercial Limited, property consultants; Chief Exec. Bourne End Properties PLC 1989-97).

Add c/o 6 Bloomsbury Square, London WC1A 2LP

Tel 020 7242 9734 *Fax* 020 7099 5897

Email info@thejlc.org

OPPENHEIM-BARNES, Sally, Baroness of Gloucester, PC.

b. Dublin, July 26, 1930; Non-Exec. Dir. HFC Bank (1989-98); Dir. (non-exec.) Robert Fleming (1989-97); Non-Exec. Dir. Boots (1983-94); Ch. National Consumer Council (1987-89); MP (Conservative) for Gloucester (1970-87); M. of State, Consumer Affairs (1979-83); Mem. Shadow Cabinet (1974-79); form. Ch. Conservative Party Parl. Prices and Consumer Protection Cttee.; form. National V. Pres. National Union of Townswomen's Guilds; form. National V. Pres. ROSPA.

Add House of Lords, London SW1 0AA

OPPENHEIMER, Peter Morris, MA.

b. London, Apr. 16, 1938; Pres. Oxford Centre for Hebrew and Jewish Studies (2000-8); Dir. Jewish Chronicle Ltd (1986-2006), Ch. (2001-04); Delbanco, Meyer and Co. Ltd. (1987-

2001); Dir. Dixons plc (1987-93); Chief Economist, Shell International Petroleum Co. (1985-86); Student (Fel.) Emer. Christ Church Oxford.

Add Christ Church, Oxford OX1 1DP

Tel 01865 558 226 *Fax* 01865 516 834

Email peter.oppenheimer@chch.ox.ac.uk

OZIN, Malcolm John, MBE.

b. London, Nov. 14, 1934; Pres. Jewish Blind and Disabled; T. Cecil Rosen Foundation; Hon. S. Cavendish Housing Trust Ltd.

Add 35 Langstone Way, London NW7 1GT

Tel 020 8371 6611 *Fax* 020 8371 4225

Email mjo@manninggroup.co.uk

PACK, Stephen Howard John, MA, BA, FCA.

b. London, Apr. 26, 1950; m. Cheryl née Klyne; Chartered Accountant; Pres. United Synagogue (July 2011-); Tru. United Synagogue (2002-); Tru. JLC Board; Ch. Chief Rabbinate Trust; Life Pres. Hadley Wood Jewish Community; form. Partner, Price Waterhouse (1984-2010), Dir. I/C operations for the audit practice and London office, Hd. Risk and Quality for the UK firm; form. Ch. Cockfosters Synagogue; form. Pres. Hadley Wood Association.

Add United Synagogue, 305 Ballard's Lane, London N12 8GB

Tel 020 343 8989

Email president@theus.org.uk *Website* www.theus.org.uk

PADWA, Rabbi Ephraim,

Hd. Beth Din of the Union of Orthodox Hebrew Congregations.

Add Union of Orthodox Hebrew Congregations, 140 Stamford Hill, London N16 6QT

Tel 020 8802 6226

PADWA, Joseph,

Dayan, Beth Din of the Union of Orthodox Hebrew Congregations (2000-).

Add UOHC, 140 Stamford Hill N16 6QT

Tel 020 8802 6226

PAISNER, Harold Michael, BA (Oxon).

b. London, June 4, 1939; m. Judith née Rechtman; Solicitor; Snr. Partner of Berwin Leighton Paisner LLP; Mem. of the Paris Bar pursuant to European Directive 98/5/CE; H. Mem. of the Lithuanian Bar; form. UK National Pres. Union Internationale des Avocats; Ch. International Issues Cttee. the Law Society; Mem. the International Bar Association, the British Baltic Lawyers Association and the American Bar Association; Directorships, Interface, Inc.; Puma High Income VCT plc.; Ch. The Institute of Jewish Policy Research and Ben Gurion University Foundation; Gov. Ben Gurion University of the Negev.

Add 16 Ilchester Place, London W14 8AA

Email Harold.paisner@blplaw.com

PAISNER, Martin David, CBE, MA (Oxon), LLM (Ann Arbor, Michigan).

b. Windsor, Berks., Sept. 1, 1943; m. Susan Sarah née Spence; Solicitor; Partner, Berwin Leighton Paisner Solicitors; Ch. The Jerusalem Foundation (1997-2010); Ch. Weizmann UK; Ch. Myers JDC Brookdale Institute; Bd. Mem. – The American Jewish Joint Distribution Cttee. Inc; Oxford Centre for Hebrew and Jewish Studies, Shaare Zedek UK; Holocaust Educational Trust; Ovarian Cancer Action; The Royal Free Cancerkin Breast Cancer Trust, British Library Trust; Governor, Weizmann Institute of Science; Hon. Fel. Queen Mary, University of London; Worcester College; Oxford; King's College, London and IDC Herzliya; H. Doctorate, University of Glasgow; Hon. PhD Weizmann (2011).

Add 4 Heath Drive, Hampstead, London NW3 7SY

PANNICK, Lord David, QC, MA, BCL.

b. London, Mar. 7, 1956; m. Nathalie née Trager-Lewis; Barrister; Mem. House of Lords (2008-); QC 1992; Deputy High Court Judge (1998); Recorder, South Eastern Circuit

(1995); Queen's Counsel (1992); Junior Counsel to the Crown in Common Law (1988-92); called to the Bar, Gray's Inn (1979). Publ.: Human Rights Law and Practice (3rd edition, 2009).

Add Blackstone Chambers, Blackstone House, Temple, London EC4Y 9BW

Tel 020 7583 1770

Email davidpannick@blackstonechambers.com

PASCAL, Julia, BA (Hons) (London), M.Phil (University of York).

m. Alain Carpentier; Playwright/Theatre Director; Dir. Pascal Theatre Co.; Leverhulme writer-in-Residence, Wiener Library (2007-); Artistic Dir. Pascal Theatre Co. (1983-2009); Nesta Dream Time Fellowship (2006); Theatre Dir. National Theatre (1978); Prima Ballerina Assoluta in Virago's 'Truth, Dare or Promise' and Boxtree's 'Memoirs of a Jewish Childhood'. Plays include: Nineveh (2013); Honeypot (2011); The Merchant of Venice (2007); Crossing Jerusalem (2003); The Golem (2002); Woman in the Moon (2001); 20/20 for Amici Dance Theatre (2000); London Continental (2000); The Yiddish Queen Lear (1999); Elegy for Amici Dance Theatre Co. Other publ. include: Political Plays (2013); The Shylock Play (2007); Crossing Jerusalem (2002); The Holocaust Trilogy (2000).

Add c/o United Agents, 120 Lexington Street, London W1F 0LE

Tel 020 3214 0800 *Fax* 020 3214 0801

Email juliapascal7@gmail.com *Website* www.juliapascal.org

PAUL, Geoffrey D, OBE, FRSA.

b. Liverpool, Mar. 26, 1929; Dir. Anglo-Israel Association (2001-3); American Affairs Ed. Jewish Chronicle (1991-96), Ed. (1977-90).

Add 1 Carlton Close, West Heath Road NW3 7UA

Tel 020 8458 6948

Email infoman@btinternet.com

PEPPER, Sir Michael, Kt., BSc, MA, PhD, ScD, Hon D.Sc, FREng, FRS.

b. London, Aug. 10, 1942, m. Jeannette; Prof. Nanoelectronics, University College London; Emer. Physics Prof. Cambridge University; Fel. Trinity College; Warren Research Fel. Royal Society (1978-86); Vis. Prof. Bar-Ilan University (1984).

Email michael.pepper@ucl.ac.uk

PEPYS, Prof., Sir Mark Brian, Kt, MD, PhD, FRCP, FRCPath, FRS, FMedSci.

b. Sept. 18, 1944; m. Dr Elizabeth Olga Winternitz; Fdr. National Health Service National Amyloidosis Centre; Emer. Prof. of Medicine, University College London; Dir. Wolfson Drug Discovery Unit; H. Consultant Physician, Royal Free Hospital, London; form. Hd. Division of Medicine, Royal Free Campus, UCL (1999-2011); International Society for Amyloidosis: Mandema Memorial Lecturer (2012); UCL Business Award (2011); Dundee University: Adam Neville Lecture (2010); Medical Research Society: Gordon Cumming Memorial Lecturer (2010); Michael Feiwel Lecturer (2010); Academy of Medical Sciences: Keynote Lecturer (2009); Royal Society of Medicine: Richard Kovacs Lecturer (2009); Imperial College: Ernst Chain Prize and Lecture (2008); Royal Society of London: GlaxoSmithKline Prize and Lecture (2007); Royal College of Physicians: Harveian Orator (2007); Israel Society for Rheumatology: Gerald Loewi Memorial Lecturer (2004); Fel. Imperial College Faculty of Medicine (2004), UCL (2003); American Society of Nephrology: State of the Art Lecturer (2003); British Society for Rheumatology: Heberden Medallist and Orator (2002); Renal Association: Chandos Lecturer (2000); Prof. of Immunological Medicine, Royal Postgraduate School (1984-99).

Add 22 Wildwood Road, London NW11 6TE

Tel 020 8455 9387

Email mbpepys@aol.com *Website* www.ucl.ac.uk/medicine/amyloidosis

PERL, Benjamin, MBE.

b. Jan. 27, 1945; m. Dr. Shoshana Perl; Ch. The Huntingdon Foundation (2008-); H. Pres. Yavneh College, Borehamwood; Morasha Primary School, Finchley; Beis Yaakov Primary

School, Colindale; BNOS Primary School, Kingsbury; T. JNF; Founding Mem. Beth Jacob Primary School, Colindale; Moriah Primary School, Pinner; Nancy Rubin Primary School, Hendon; Torah Vodaath Primary School, Golders Green; Morasha Primary School, Finchley; Noam Primary School, Wembley; Hertsmere Primary School, Borehamwood.

Add 35-37 Brent Street, Hendon, London NW4 2EF

Email bperl@sixtrees.co.uk

PERLMAN, Suzanne,

Prize winning artist; Officer of the Royal Order of Oranje Nassau; Hon. Fel. Israel Museum; Patron, Hebrew University, Jerusalem; Ch. Women's Group; British Friends of Hebrew University; WIZO International Rebecca Sieff Prize, Israel; Freeman of the City of London. Numerous art exhibitions worldwide. Most recent exhibition, Suzanne Perlman Painting London at Ben Uri Gallery and Museum, London (2014). Works of Art - Permanent Collections: London, England, Museum of London; House of Lords; Ben Uri Gallery; House of Orange Nassau, The Netherlands; Mikve Israel Jewish Cultural Historical Museum, Curacao; Museum of Fine Arts, Willemstad, Netherlands Antilles; Galleria Bellas Artes and Instituto Bolkivariana, Caracas, Venezuela; Joods Historisch Museum, Amsterdam, The Netherlands; Jewish Museum, Budapest, Hungary.

Add Chancery House, 53-64 Chancery Lane, London WC2A 1QS

PERSOFF, Dr Meir, JP, MA, PhD, FRHistS, FRSA.

b. Letchworth, Aug. 25, 1941; Jewish Chronicle, Judaism Ed. Saleroom Editor (1981-2000), Features Ed. (1976-90), Arts Ed. (1980-85), News Ed. (1974-76); Pres. Israel-Judaica Philatelic Society; form. Publ. Cttee. Jewish Marriage Council; Silver Medallist, international philatelic exhibitions, Jerusalem, London, Stockholm, Pretoria, Paris, Madrid. Among recent publications: Hats in the Ring: Choosing Britain's Chief Rabbis from Adler to Sacks (2013); Another Way, Another Time: Religious Inclusivism and the Sacks Chief Rabbinate (2010); Faith Against Reason: Religious Reform and the British Chief Rabbinate, 1840-1990 (2008); Immanuel Jakobovits: a Prophet in Israel (2002), etc.

Add 14 Hanasi Str., P.O. Box 4130, Jerusalem 91041, Israel

Tel +972 (02) 623 5834

Email meir-per@013.net

PESTON, Robert,

b. Apr. 25, 1960; m. Sian Busby (dec'd 2012); BBC's Economic Editor; Business Ed. BBC News (2006-); Fdr. Speakers for Schools (2011); City Ed. The Sunday Telegraph (2002-05); Political, Financial Ed. Financial Times (1991-2000); Journalist, The Independent (1986-90); Investors Chronicle (1983-86). Awards: Harold Wincott Snr. Financial Journalist of the Year Award (2005); Royal Television Society Scoop of the Year (2007); Broadcasting Press Guild, Best Performer in Non-Acting Role (2008); Royal Television Society Journalist of the Year, Specialist Journalist of the Year, Scoop of the Year (2008); London Press Club: Business Journalist of the Year (2008). Publ.: How Do We Fix This Mess (2012); Who Runs Britain? (2008); Brown's Britain (2005).

Add New Broadcasting House, London W1A 1AA

Tel 020 3614 0823

Email peston@gmail.com *Website* www.bbc.co.uk/robertpeston

PHILLIPS, Karen, MBE, DL.

b. Aug. 15, 1951; Chief Exec. The Fed (The Federation of Jewish Services) (2009-); Manchester Jewish Federation (1997-2009); Dir. Manchester Jewish Social Services (1995-97), Social Services Manager (1993-95); Probation Off. Salford Probation Service (1987-93); Area Manager, Trafford and South Manchester, Chest, Heart and Stroke Association (1980-87).

Add The Fed, Heathlands Village, Heathlands Drive, Prestwich, Manchester M25 9SB

Tel 0161 772 4800 *Fax* 0161 772 4934

Email info@thefed.org.uk *Website* www.thefed.org.uk

PHILLIPS, Melanie, BA.

b. June 4, 1951; m. Joshua Rufus Rozenberg; Columnist, the Times (2014-), Daily Mail (2001-14), Sunday Times (1998–2001), Observer (1993–98); News Ed. Guardian (1984–87), Leader Writer (1980–84), Social Services Corres. (1978–80), Reporter (1977). Publ.: Guardian Angel: My Story, My Britain (2013); The World Turned Upside Down: The Global Battle Over God, Truth and Power (2010); Londonistan (2007); The Ascent of Woman (2003); All Must Have Prizes (1996).

Add c/o Daily Mail, Northcliffe House, 2 Derry Street W8 5TT

Tel 020 3002 0068

Email melanie@melaniephillips.com

Twitter @MelanieLatest

PINNICK, Jeffrey, FCA.

b. London, Dec. 6, 1935; H. V. Pres. All Aboard Shops (2014-), H. Tru. (1987-2013), H. Ch. (2008-12), Hon. T. (1987-2008); H. Ch. Yad Vashem UK Foundation (2004-09); H. Ch. British Friends of Boys Town, Jerusalem (2000-08); Hon. T. Board of Deputies (1985-91).

Add Stella Lucas House, 105 High Street, Edgware HA8 7DB

Tel 020 8381 1717

Email community@allaboardshops.com *Website* www.allaboardshops.com

PINTER, Rabbi Abraham (Avraham),

b. Jan. 21, 1949; m. Rachel; Dean, Beer Miriam Seminary (2008-); Ch. Chizuk (1996-); Principal, Yesodey Hatorah Schools (1994-); T. Union of Orthodox Hebrew Congregations (1990-); Mem. (Lab) Hackney BC (1982–90); V. Ch. Ezer Leyoldos (Children and Families).

Add 6 Northdene Gardens N15 6LX

Tel 020 8826 5500 *Fax* 020 8826 5505

Email yeshatorah@aol.com

PLANCEY, Rabbi Alan,

b. Edinburgh, Oct. 30, 1941; Herts County Councillor (2009-); Associate Jewish Chaplain, London Luton Airport; M. Northwood US (2007-9); Borehamwood and Elstree Synagogue (1976-2007); Ch. Rabbinical Council US (1987-94); Youth M. Hampstead Garden Suburb Synagogue (1970-6); M. Luton Synagogue (1965-9); Mem. Chief Rabbi's Cabinet; H. V. Pres. and Rel. Adv. Jewish Care; Area Chaplain Herts. Police; H. Chaplain JLGB; H. Chaplain Jewish Scouting Adv. Cttee.; Freeman of the City of London.

Add 98 Anthony Road, Borehamwood, Hertfordshire WD6 4NB

Tel 020 8207 3759 *Mobile* 07768 906 627 *Fax* 020 8207 0568

Email alan.plancey@lineone.net

PLASKOW, Rev. Michael Lionel, MBE, LTSC, ALCM.

b. Israel, July 8, 1936; form. Chaplain, Jewish Deaf Association, England; Emer. Chazan, Woodside Park Synagogue; Life Pres. Central Foundation School, Jewish Old Boys Group; Chaplain to the Mayor of Barnet (1999-2000); Freeman City of London (1994); Norman B. Spencer Award for research into Freemasonry (1992). Publ.: The Story of a Community: Woodside Park 1937-1987.

Add 4/4 Nitza Boulevard, 42262 Netanya, Israel

Tel +972 (09) 832 9592

Email michaelplaskow@hotmail.com

PLEN, Matt,

b. London, July 17, 1972; m. Atira Winchester; Chief Exec. Masorti Judaism (2012-), Dir. (2008-12); Founding Gov. Alma Primary School (2012-); Tru. London Citizens (2011-12); Teacher/Lecturer, Conservative Yeshiva and Masorti High School, Jerusalem (2004-8); Snr Educator, Melitz (2000-04).

Add Alexander House, 3 Shakespeare Road, London N3 1XE

Tel 020 8349 6656

Email matt@masorti.org.uk *Website* www.mattplen.blogspot.org.uk

POLAK, Stuart,
Dir. Conservative Friends of Israel (1989-); Education Dir. Board of Deputies (1985); Youth and Community Worker, Edgware (1984); Fdr. Ch. European Friends of Israel; T. Langdon Foundation; T. Yavneh College; Bd. Mem. Europe Near East Forum.
Tel 020 7262 2493 *Fax* 020 7224 8941

POLLOCK, Karen,
Mem. JC Power 100 Panel (2007-); Chief Exec. Holocaust Educational Trust (2002-); Mem. Jewish Human Rights Coalition UK.
Add BCM Box 7892, London WC1N 3XX
Fax 020 7233 0161
Website www.het.org.uk

POLONSKY, Antony, BA (Rand), MA, D.Phil (Oxon), Doc h.c. (Vars), Officer's Cross of the Order of Merit, Poland, Officer's Cross of the Order of Merit of Independent Lithuania.
b. Johannesburg, Sept. 23, 1940, m. Arlene née Glickman; Albert Abramson Prof. of Holocaust Studies at the United States Holocaust Memorial Museum and Brandeis University; V. Pres. Institute for Polish-Jewish Studies, Oxford; V. Pres. American Association for Polish-Jewish Studies, Cambridge, MA. Among recent publications: The Jews in Poland and Russia, Vol III: 1914-2008 (2012), Vol. II: 1881-1914 (2010), Vol. I: 1350-1881 (2010); The Neighbours Respond: the Controversy Over the Jedwabne Massacre (2004); Contemporary Jewish Writing in Poland (Ed. 2001); The Jews in Old Poland (Ed. 1992); The Jews of Warsaw (Ed. 1991); Polish Paradoxes (Ed. 1990); Recent Polish Debates about the Holocaust (1990).
Add 322 Harvard Street, Cambridge, MA 02139 USA
Tel +1 (617) 492 9788 *Fax* +1 (617) 736 2070
Email polonsky@brandeis.edu

POSEN, Felix, BA (John Hopkins University), D.Phil. (H., Hebrew University, Tel Aviv University), H. Fel. (Hebrew University).
b. Berlin, Oct. 24, 1928; m. Jane née Levy; Gov. Emer. and Hon. Fel. Oxford Centre for Hebrew and Jewish Studies; Gov. Hebrew University; T. Institute of Archaeo-metallurgical Studies, University of London; Fdr. Posen Foundation.
Add Flat 6, 7 Sheffield Terrace, London W8 7NG
Tel 020 7313 9521
Email felix@nesop.co.uk *Website* www.posenfoundation.com

POSEN, Michael,
Mem. JC Power 100 Panel (2007); Man. Agudas Israel Community Services; Cttee. and T. Interlink Foundation and Chizuk.
Add 46 Riverside Road, London N15 6DA
Tel 020 8800 6688 *Fax* 020 3240 0110
Email mposen@agudas.org.uk

PRESTON, Rosalind (née Morris), OBE.
b. London, Dec. 29, 1935; Professional Volunteer; Ch. Jewish Human Rights Coalition UK (2010-); Adv. Bd. Olive Tree Trust (2009-); Pres. Jewish Volunteering Network (2009-); T. Jewish Chronicle (2000-); Ch. Nightingale House (1999-07, T. 1999-); H. V. Pres. WIZO UK (1993-); Jt. Hon. S. CCJ (1997-05); form. Pres. The National Council of Women of Great Britain (1988-90); form. Co-Ch. Interfaith Network, UK; form. V. Pres. Board of Deputies.
Add 7 Woodside Close, Stanmore, Middlesex HA7 3AJ
Tel 020 8954 1411 *Fax* 020 8954 6898
Email rpreston@f2s.com

PROSOR, Ron, MA.
b. 1958; m. Hadas; Israeli Ambassador to the United Nations (2011-); Ambassador of Israel to the Court of St. James's (2007-11); Dir. Gen. Israeli Foreign Ministry (2004-2007); Snr.

Deputy Dir. Gen. Foreign Ministry (2004), Chief of Staff to the Foreign Minister (2003-04); Deputy Dir. Gen. for Strategic Affairs, Counter-Terrorism and Nuclear Disarmament (2003); M. Counsellor, Political Affairs, Israeli Embassy, Washington DC (1998-2002); Spokesman, Israeli Embassy, London (1995-98); Dir. Operations Center, Foreign Ministry (1993-95); Deputy Dir. European Division, Foreign Ministry (1992-93); Spokesman, Israeli Embassy, Bonn (1988-92).

Add c/o Embassy of Israel, 2 Palace Green, Kensington, London W8 4QB

Email club-sec@london.mfa.gov.il

PULZER, Peter George Julius, MA, B.Sc.(Econ.), PhD.

b. Vienna, May 20, 1929; Grosses Silbernes Ehrenzeichen, Republic Austria (2008); Bundesverdienst Kreuz, Rep. of Germany (2004); Gladstone Prof. Government and Publ. Admin. Fel. All Souls, Oxford (1985-96); Official Student (Fel.) in Politics, Christ Church, Oxford (1962-84). Publ.: The Rise of Political Antisemitism in Germany and Austria; Political Representation and Elections in Britain; Jews and the German State: The Political History of a Minority (1848-1933); German Politics 1945-1995; Germany 1870-1945: Politics, State Formation and War; contributor German Jewish History in Modern Times (Ed. M. Meyer).

Add All Souls College, Oxford OX1 4AL

Tel 01865 559 347 *Fax* 01865 279299

Email peter.pulzer@ntlworld.com

RABINOWITZ, Rabbi Lippa,

b. Manchester, Nov. 15, 1930; Rav, Vine St Synagogue, Manchester; Principal, Manchester Jewish Grammar School; form. Principal, Judith Lady Montefiore College, Ramsgate; Lecturer, Etz Haim Yeshiva, Tangier. Publ.: Eleph Lamateh Chidushim on Sugioth (Israel).

Add 57 Waterpark Road, Salford

RAJAK, Tessa (née Goldsmith), MA, D.Phil(Oxon).

b. London, Aug. 2, 1946, m. Harry Rajak; Classicist and Jewish Historian; Emer. Prof. Ancient History, University Reading; Res. Fel. Somerville College, Oxford. Publ.: Translation and Survival: The Greek Bible and the Ancient Jewish Diaspora; The Jewish Dialogue with Greece and Rome; Josephus: the Historian and His Society; Jewish Perspectives on Hellenistic Rulers; Philosophy and Power; The Jews among Pagans and Christians in the Roman Empire.

Add 64 Talbot Road, London N6 4RA

Email tessa.rajak@orinst.ox.ac.uk

RAPHAEL, Frederic Michael, MA (Cantab), FRSL.

b. Chicago, Aug. 14, 1931; Writer. Among recent publications: Non-fiction: Byron; Somerset Maugham; Cracks in the Ice; Of Gods and Men; France: the Four Seasons; The Necessity of Antisemitism; Popper: Historicism and its Poverty; Eyes Wide Open; The Benefits of Doubt (essays), A Spoilt Boy (autobiography); Some Talk of Alexander; Josephus and his Kind; Distant Intimacy (with Joseph Epstein); J. Robert Oppenheimer, For example. Published Screenplays and Drama: Two for the Road; Darling, Oxbridge Blues; Eyes Wide Shut (with Stanley Kubrick). Novels: The Limits of Love; Lindmann; The Glittering Prizes; Fame and Fortune; Final Demands: Short Stories; Sleeps Six; Uxbridge Blues; Think of England. Notebooks: Personal Terms, Rough Copy, Cuts and Bruises; Ifs and Buts; There and Then. Translations: The Satyrica of Petronius; The Poems of Catullus (with Kenneth McLeish); The Plays of Aeschylus; Sophocles' Aias; Euripides' Medea; Bacchae and Hippolytus.

Add Ed Victor Ltd., 6 Bayley Street, London WC1B 3HE

RECHTSCHAFFEN, Shlomo, LLB, LLM, MBA.

b. Israel, Aug. 10, 1975; Solicitor; Co-Fdr. Pantheon India and Pantheon Bond (2010); Bd. Mem. Ramat-Gan Foundation in the UK (2010-); Chief Exec. British Friends of Bar Ilan (2009-); Lectures, Corporate and Commercial Law, University of London (2004-); leading Israeli law firm S. Horowitz & Co. (2001-03) and GKH Law (2001-02); Mem. Israeli Bar and

the Law Society of England & Wales (2000-).
Add 109 Baker Street, London W1U 6RP
Tel 020 7486 7394 *Fax* 020 7935 1192
Email shlomo@bfbiu.org

REIF, Stefan, BA, PhD (London), LittD (Cantab), PhD (Hon) (Haifa).
b. Edinburgh, Jan. 21, 1944; m. Shulamit, d. 2010; Pres. Cambridge Theological Society
(2002-04); Pres. British Association for Jewish Studies (1992); Pres. JHSE (1991-92);
Fdr. Dir. Taylor-Schechter Genizah Research Unit, Cambridge University Library; Emer.
Prof. of Medieval Hebrew Studies Cambridge University; Fel. St John's College,
Cambridge; Hon. Fel. Mekize Nirdamim Society, Jerusalem; Adv. Panel, International
Society for the Study of Deuteronomical and Cognate Literature; T. Cambridge
Traditional Jewish Congregation. Among recent publications: The History and Religious
Heritage of Old Cairo (2013); Death in Jewish Life: Burial and Mourning Customs among
the Jews in Europe (2014); A Jewish Archive from Old Cairo; Why Medieval Hebrew
Studies?; Problems with Prayers; (Ed.) Interpreting the Hebrew Bible; Genizah Research
after Ninety Years; The Cambridge Genizah Collections; Cambridge University Library
Genizah Series; Charles Taylor and the Genizah.
Add Genizah Research Unit, University Library, Cambridge CB3 9DR
Tel 01223 766 370 *Fax* 01223 333 160
Email scr3@cam.ac.uk

REUBEN, David,
b. Sept. 14, 1938; m. Debra; T. Reuben Brothers Foundation (2002-); Jt. Chief Exec. Officer,
Reuben Brothers Ltd (1988-); Ch. Trans World Metals Group (1977–2000).
Add Millbank Tower, 21-24 Millbank, London SW1P 4PQ
Website www.reubenfoundation.com

REUBEN, Simon,
m. Joyce Nounou; T. Reuben Foundation (2002-); Jt. Chief Exec. Officer, Reuben Brothers
Ltd (1988-); Dir. and Jt. Principal, Trans-World Metals Group (1977–2000).
Add c/o Reuben Foundation, Millbank Tower, 21-24 Millbank, London SW1P 4PQ
Website www.reubenbrothers.com

RICH, Ben,
b. London, Mar. 29, 1966; m. Rachael Reeves; Communications Consultant for Jewish and
other faith organisations; Gov. Avanti House School Harrow.
Add 69 Cecil Park, Pinner, Middlesex HA5 5HL
Twitter @BenRichMRJ

RICH, Rabbi Danny, BA (Hons) Dip. Crim.
b. London, Mar. 7, 1961; Emer. Rabbi, Kingston Liberal Synagogue (2005-), Rabbi (1989-
2005); Founding Ch. Royal Borough of Kingston Interfaith Forum (2005-); Chief Exec. LJ
(2005); Dir. Kadimah Summer Camp (1990-2005); Jewish Chaplain to HMP Highdown,
Coldingley, Kingston Hospital and Surrey and Borders NHS Trust; Founding Ch. Dittons
Council of Christians and Jews. Publ.: Co-author, Zionism: A Jewish Communal Response
from the UK (2010); LJ and Mixed Marriage (2004).
Add The Montagu Centre, 21 Maple Street, London W1T 4BE
Tel 020 7631 9830 *Fax* 020 7631 9838
Email d.rich@liberaljudaism.org *Website* www.liberaljudaism.org

RIFKIND, Rt. Hon. Sir Malcolm, MP, QC, PC.
b. Edinburgh, June 21, 1946; MP, Kensington (2010-); Ch. Intelligence and Security Cttee.
(2010-); Ch. Standards and Privileges Cttée. (2009-10); MP, Kensington and Chelsea (Con.)
(2005-10); form. MP for Edinburgh, Pentlands (Con.) (1974-97); Foreign Secretary (1995-
97), Min. of Defence (1992-95), Min. of Transport (1990-92); Sec. of State for Scotland
(1986-90), Min. of State Foreign and Commonwealth Office (1983-86); Parl. Under-Sec. of
State, FCO (1982-83); Select Cttee. on Overseas Dev. (1978-79); Hon. S. Conservative

Friends of Israel Parl. Group (1974-79); Opposition Spokesman on Scottish Affairs (1975-76); Edinburgh Town Council (1970-74).

Add House of Commons, London SW1 0AA

Tel 020 7219 5683 *Fax* 020 7219 4213

RIGAL, Margaret H. (née Lazarus),

b. London, Nov. 28, 1932; Co-Ch. Women's Campaign for Soviet Jewry (the 35s); Pres. Jewish Aged Needy Pension Society; Ch. Jewish Aid Cttee.; Hon. S. London Society of Jews and Christians.

Add 31 St. John's Wood Ct., St. John's Wood Road, London NW8 8QR

Tel 020 7286 4404

Email Margaret.Rigal@gmail.com

RITBLAT, Sir John (Henry), Kt, FRICS, Hon. DLitt London Metropolitan, Hon. DLitt University of Buckingham.

b. Oct. 3, 1935; m. Jillian Rosemary Zilkha; Colliers International (UK) Ltd (2010-12); V. Pres. Seafarers UK (2010), (Hon. Surveyor, 1979-); H. Pres. The British Land Company PLC (2007, Ch. 1970-2006, Man. Dir. 1970–2004); Tru. Tate Gallery (2006–); Ch. and Tru. Wallace Collection (2005–); Colliers Conrad Ritblat Erdman (2000–); Ch. Conrad Ritblat Group plc (1993–97); Prince of Wales' Royal Parks Tree Appeal Cttee. (1987–); Mem. Council, Business in the Community (1987–); Olympic Appeal Cttee. 1984, 1988, 1996 and 2000; British Olympic Assoc. (1979); Commander, Crown Estate Paving Commission (1969–), now Commander Emeritus; Fdr. Partner, Conrad Ritblat & Co., Consultant Surveyors and Valuers (1958); Articles with West End firm of Surveyors and Valuers (1952–58).

Add Lansdowne House, Berkeley Square, London W1J 6ER

ROBERG, Rabbi Meir, BA (Hons), MPhil, DipEd.

b. Wurzburg, Germany, June 25, 1937; Dean, Lauder Midrasha, Berlin; Education Consultant to Jewish Schools and Colleges in the CIS and England; Reporting Inspector of Schools in Pikuach; Pres. Association of Head Teachers of Orthodox Schools; form. HM, Hasmonean; Ch. Academic Cttee. Massoret Institute; Dep. HM, Yavneh Grammar School.

Add 19 Sorotzkin Street Jerusalem, Israel

Tel 020 538 6020

Email hineni@zahav.net.il

ROBSON, Jeremy,

b. Llandudno, Sept. 5, 1939; Publisher, J. R. Books Ltd. Publ.: 33 Poems, In Focus (poetry); Poetry anthologies, incl. The Young British Poets (Ed.); Poems from Poetry and Jazz in Concert (Ed.).

Add J.R. Books, 10 Greenland Street, London NW1 0NO

RODEN, Claudia,

Cookery writer; Contributor, The Jewish Princess; Patron, The Food Chain Charity. Publ.: Arabesque—Sumptuous Food from Morocco, Turkey and Lebanon (2005); The New Book of Middle Eastern Food (2000); The Book of Jewish Food (1997); A Book of Middle Eastern Food (1968).

Add The Food Chain, New North House, 202–208 New North Road, London N1 7BJ

Website www.foodchain.org.uk

RODRIGUES-PEREIRA, Miriam, BA.

b. Manchester, July 4, 1922; Retired Civil Servant; Hon. Archivist, Spanish & Portuguese Jews Congregation, London (1985-). Publ.: Bevis Marks Records (on Genealogy and History) (parts iv 1991, v 1993, vi 1997, co-author/ed.).

Add 22 Latymer Court, Hammersmith Road, London W6 7JD

Tel 020 8748 6298

ROMAIN, Rabbi Jonathan Anidjar, MBE, BA; PhD.

b. London, Aug. 24, 1954; m. Sybil Sheridan; M. Maidenhead Synagogue; Ch. Assembly of Rabbis (2007-09); Ch. Youth Association of Synagogues in Great Britain (1972-74); Dir. Jewish Information and Media Service; Chaplain, Jewish Police Association; form. M. Barkingside Progressive Synagogue. Among recent publications: Assisted Dying: Rabbinic Responses; Tradition and Change, Till Faith Us Do Part, Renewing the Vision, Your God Shall Be My God, Reform Judaism and Modernity; God, Doubt, and Dawkins; Really Useful Prayers; Great Reform Lives; A Passion for Judaism; Signs and Wonders; Royal Jews; The Jews of England.

Add Grenfell Lodge, Ray Park Road, Maidenhead, Berks SL6 8QX

Tel 01628 671 058

RONSON, Dame Gail (née Cohen), DBE.

b. July. 3, 1946; m. Gerald Maurice Ronson; Ambassador, Royal Opera House (2014-), Dir. (2001-14); Pres. RNIB (2012-); H. Pres. Jewish Care (2011-), Dep. Pres. (2010-), Dep. Ch (2002-), Bd. Mem. (1992-); Dep. Ch. Gerald Ronson Foundation (2005–); Co-Ch. Association for Research into Stammering in Childhood (1991–); T. Royal Opera House Trust (1985–); St Mary's Hospital Save the Baby Fund (1985–96); T. Ronson Foundations (1980–95); T. Home Farm Develt Trust (1991–94); Jt Ch. Council for a Beautiful Israel (1987–94).

Add 4 Bentinck Street, London W1U 2EF

Email gailronson@heron.co.uk

RONSON, Gerald Maurice, CBE, Hon. DcL (Northumbria University, Hon. PhD (Hebrew University).

b. London, May 27, 1939; m. Dame Gail née Cohen; H. Fel. College of Estate (2012); Pres. JCOSS; Fdr. Mem. JLC (2004); Fdr. Mem. Cancer Research Campaign/Imperial Cancer Research Fund, Appeal Cabinet Mem. (2001-); Ch. Liaison Cttee. Office of the Chief Rabbi (2001-); Fdr. Ch. Community Security Trust (1995-); Mem. Major Gift Board Prince's Trust (1986-); Patron, Philip Green Memorial Trust (1985-); Fdr. Ch. Group Relations Educational Trust (1978-); Ch. Trustees, Gerald Ronson Foundation (2005); Gov. London Academy (2004); Patron, Princess Royal Trust for Carers (2003); Ch. Development Council of the Roundhouse (2000); V. Pres. Joint Israel Appeal (1984); V. Pres. NSPCC (1984). Previous positions: Fdr. Ch. of Trustees, The Ronson Foundation; Co-Ch. Chindit Memorial Appeal; V. Pres. Jewish Educational Trust (1976-); Co-Ch. Israel Bonds in the UK (1988-93); Mem. Councils of British Olympic Appeals (1992, 1988); T. Natural History Museum (1987-91); Fdr. Mem. One Per cent Club (1986); Ch. SNAX 24 Corporation Ltd (1996); Fdr. Heron Group (1956). Awards: City AM Personality of the Year Award (2011); Variety Club 'Props' Lifetime Achievement Award (2011); Property Week - Lifetime Achievement Award (2010); Encomienda de Numero, Order of Civil Merit for services to Spain (2009); H. Doctorate, Northumbria University (2009); Norwood Lifetime Achievement Award (2008); Property Industry Award (2007); Property awards, personality of the Year (2002/2001 and 2000); Variety Club of Great Britain, Entrepreneur of the Year (2000); Hambros Businessman of the Year (1984); "The Director" Award for Excellence (1984); The Inaugural estates Gazette Architecture Award.

Add 4 Bentinck Street, London W1U 2EF

RONSON, Mark Daniel,

b. Sept. 4, 1975; British music producer, artist; Co-Fdr. Allido Records (2004-); BRIT Award Winner (2008); Grammy Award Winner (2008).

Add 19 Mercer Street, 5th Floor New York, NY 10013, USA

Tel +1 (212) 226 7320? *Fax* +1 (212) 226 7346

Website www.markronson.co.uk

ROSE, Aubrey, OBE, CBE, D. University (Hon), FRSA.

b. London, Nov. 1, 1926; Solicitor; Snr. V. Pres. Board of Deputies (1994, 1991); Pres. Indian Jewish Association UK; Pres. Royal British Nurses Assoc.; Commissioner and Dep. Ch.

Commission for Racial Equality (CRE); Dep. Ch. British Caribbean Association; T. Project Fullemploy; T. Commonwealth Human Rights Initiative; Mem. Working Group Commonwealth Jewish Council; form. Ch. Defence and Group Rel. Cttee. Board of Deputies; Ch. Working Group on Environment Board of Deputies. Publ.: Sea Olympics (2012); Arieh Handler: Modest Jewish Hero (2010); Jewish Communities in the Commonwealth (CJT); Letters to my Wife (2007); The Rainbow Never Ends (2005); From Bitter Came Sweet (2004, Ed.); The Story of Vera (2001, Ed.); Brief Encounters of a Legal Kind (1997); Journey into Immortality, the Story of David Rose (1997); Judaism and Ecology (1992).

Add 14 Pagitts Grove, Hadley Wood, Hertfordshire EN4 0NT

Tel 020 8449 2166 *Fax* 020 8449 1469

Email as.rose@virgin.net *Website* www.aubreyrose.org.uk

ROSE, Dinah, QC, BA (Hons) Oxon, Diploma in Law with distinction.

Barrister of the Year, The Lawyer Awards (2009); City University Barrister of the Year (2009); Human Rights Lawyer of the Year, Liberty and Justice Human Rights Awards (2009); Appointed to Silk (2006); Called to Bar, Gray's Inn (1989); Mem. Treasury "A" Panel; Mem. New North London Synagogue; T. Responsibility; Regular lecturer on public law, human rights and employment law.

Add Blackstone Chambers, Blackstone House, Temple, London EC4Y 9BW

Tel 020 7583 1770 *Fax* 020 7822 7350

ROSE, Harvey John,

b. London, June 10, 1946; m. Sandra née Dudack; Chartered Accountant; Ch. Zionist Federation of Great Britain and Ireland (2010-); Tru. Save a Child's Heart UK (2007-).

Add 7 Arkenside Road, London NW3 5RA

Tel 020 7794 5636

ROSEN, Clive H, FCOptom., FSMC, Dip. Sports Vision.

b. London, Apr. 15, 1938; Ed. PG&SS Pages Magazine (2012-13); Ch. Palmers Green and Southgate Synagogue (2011-13), Mem. Bd. of Management (2008-); H. Pres. Broomfield House-owners and Residents Association (2002-); Hon. Officer. ZF (2002-08, 1994-98); Cttee. Mem. Sports Vision Association (1997-2006); Consultant to Leyton Orient FC (1997-2003); Hon. T. East London and City Health Authority L.O.C. (1994-2002); Ch. Israel-Judaica Stamp Club (1990-2010); Ed. The Israel-Judaica Stamp Club Journal (1990-2010); Zionist Federation National Council (1989-2010); H. Off. JNF (1983-90, 1979-81); Dir. David Elliott (Opticians) Ltd. (1965-2003); Freeman, City of London (1964).

Add 152 Morton Way, London N14 7AL

Tel 020 8886 9331 *Fax* 020 8886 5116

Email clive@cliverosen.co.uk *Website* www.israeljudaica.co.uk

ROSEN, Rabbi Jeremy, MA (Cantab), PhD.

b. Sept. 11, 1942; Rabbi, Persian Jewish Community, New York (2009-); Prof. Jewish Studies F.V.G. Antwerp. (1991-); Dir. Yakar Foundation (1999-2009); Rabbi, Western Marble Arch Synagogue (1991-92); Rabbi, Western Synagogue (1985-91); Chief Rabbi's Cabinet adv. Interfaith (1987-90); T. Yakar Foundation; Principal, Carmel College (1971-84); Rabbi, Giffnock and Newlands Synagogue Glasgow (1968-71). Publ.: Right or Right: How to Reconcile Religion with Rationality (2014); Deborah (2010); Mad Messiah (2010); Wallingford (2009); Kabbalah Inspirations (2005); Understanding Judaism (2003); Exploding Myths that Jews Believe (2001).

Add 1965 Broadway, New York, NY 10023, USA

Email jeremyrosen@msn.com *Website* www.jeremyrosen.com

ROSENBERG, Rosita (née Gould),

b. London, Sept. 2, 1933; V. Pres. form. Exec. Dir. Liberal Judaism. Publ.: Liberal Judaism: the First Hundred Years (Jt. author, 2004).

Add The Montagu Centre, 21 Maple Street W1T 4BE

Tel 020 7580 1663 *Fax* 020 7631 9838

ROSENBLATT, Harvey,
Ch. Nightingale Hammerson; Mem. Jewish Leadership Council.
Add Nightingale Hammerson, Nightingale House, 105 Nightingale Lane, London
SW12 8NB
Tel 020 8673 3495
Email info@nightingalehammerson.org *Website* www.nightingalehammerson.org

ROTHSCHILD, Sir Evelyn de,
b. Aug. 29, 1931; Merchant Banker; Ch. EL Rothschild Ltd; Ch. ERANDA Foundation; Gov.
Emer. London School of Economics and Political Science; Fel. Imperial College London; H.
Life Pres. Norwood and Ravenswood Children's Charity; Ch. and CEO, NM Rothschild and
Sons Ltd (1976-2003); Ch. Economist Newspaper (1972-89); Ch. United Racecourse Ltd
(1977-94); British Merchant Banking and Securities Houses Assoc. (form. Accepting
Houses Cttee.) (1985-89); Bd. Dir. De Beers and IBM UK; Dep. Ch. Milton Keynes
Development Corporation; Ch. St Mary's Hospital Medical School; Mem. Council of
Shakespeare Globe Trust; Pres. The Evelina Children's Hospital Appeal.
Add 31 Tite Street, London SW3 4JP
Tel 020 7376 5271

ROTHSCHILD, Lord Nathaniel Charles Jacob,
b. Cambridge, Apr. 29, 1936; Ch. RIT Capital Partners plc, J. Rothschild Capital
Management plc and Five Arrows Ltd; Sir Winston Churchill Award, Technion (2004); Pres.
IJPR (1992-2002); Commonwealth Council Award (2001); Ch. Trustees of the National
Heritage Memorial Fund (1992-98); Ch. Trustees of the National Gallery (1985-91);
Weizmann Award (1977); Ch. Yad Hanadiv; Ch. Rothschild Foundation; T. Weizmann
Institute; Hon. Fel. City of Jerusalem; Hon Fel. Israel Museum.
Add 14 St James's Place SW1A 1NP
Tel 020 7493 8111 *Fax* 020 7647 8585

ROTHSCHILD, Rabbi Sylvia Helen Fay, BSc.
b. Bradford, West Yorkshire, Nov. 21, 1957; m. Martin Fischer; M. Wimbledon Synagogue
(2002-15); Ch. Assembly of Rabbis (2000-2003), Co-Ch. (1998-2000); M. Bromley and
District Reform Synagogue (1987-2002). Publ.: Co-Ed. Taking up the Timbrel (2000).

ROWE, Joshua, MBE, LLB Hons Bar.
Ch. of Governors, Manchester King David School; Jt. Pres. Manchester UJIA.
Add KDHS, Eaton Road, Manchester M8 5DY

ROZENBERG, Joshua Rufus, MA (Oxon).
b. London, May 30, 1950; m. Melanie Phillips; Freelance legal commentator (2009-); Legal
Ed. Daily Telegraph (2000-08); H. Bencher, Gray's Inn (2003); BBC News (1975-2000)
(Legal and Constitutional Affairs Corr. 1997-2000, Legal Affairs Corr. 1985-97); Solicitor
(1976). Publ.: Privacy and the Press (2004); Trial of Strength (1997); The Search for Justice
(1994); The Case for the Crown (1987); Your Rights and the Law (with N. Watkins, 1986).
Add BCM Rozenberg, London WC1N 3XX
Email joshua@rozenberg.net *Website* www.rozenberg.net

RUBEN, David-Hillel, BA, PhD.
b. Chicago, July 25, 1943; Emer. Prof. Philosophy, University of London; Dir. Arcadia
University, London (2012-13); Prof. Philosophy, Birkbeck College (2004-11); Dir. New York
University in London (2000-11); form. Dir. London School of Jewish Studies (1998-99);
Prof. of Philosophy, London School of Economics (1984-97); The City University, London,
Snr. Lecturer in Philosophy (1979-84); University of Essex, Lecturer in Philosophy (1975-
79); University of Glasgow, Lecturer in Philosophy (1970-75). Publ.: Action and Its
Explanation (2003); Explaining Explanation (1990); The Metaphysics of the Social World
(1985); Marxism and Materialism (1979).
Add 29 Sunny Gardens Road, London NW4 1SL

Tel 07799 694 103 *Fax* 020 8922 7410
Email d.ruben@bbk.ac.uk david.ruben1.yahoo.co.uk
Website http://www.bbc.ac.uk/philosophy/our-staff/visiting-professors/ruben

RUBENS, Kenneth David, OBE, FRICS, FRSA.

b. London, Oct. 10, 1929; Chartered Surveyor; V. Pres. Jewish Museum, London; L. Elder, Spanish and Portuguese Jews Congregation; Past Ch. Council World Jewish Relief; Past Master, Worshipful Company, Painter-Stainers.; H. Life Mem. British Property Federation.

Add Flat 20, Westfield, 15 Kidderpore Avenue, London NW3 7SF

Tel 020 7794 7259

Email kenneth@rubens.org

RUBINSTEIN, William David, BA, PhD, FAHA, FASSA, FRHistS.

b. New York, Aug. 12, 1946; m. Hilary L. Rubinstein; Adjunct Prof. Monash University, Melbourne, Australia (2013-); Pres. JHSE (2002-04), Mem. Council (1996-); ret. Prof. of History, The University of Wales, Aberystwyth, now Emer.; Ed. Journal of the Australian Jewish Historical Society (1988-95); Prof. of Social and Economic History, Deakin University, Australia (1987-95); Mem. Cttee. of Management, Executive Council of Australian Jewry (1983-95); Pres. Australian Association for Jewish Studies (1989-91). Among recent publications: Shadow Pasts (2008); Genocide: a History (2004); Twentieth Century Britain: A Political History (2003); The Jews in the Modern World: A History since 1750 (co-author, 2002); Philosemitism: Admiration and Support in the English-speaking World for Jews 1840-1939 (with Hilary L. Rubinstein, 1999); Britain's Century: A Political and Social History 1815-1905 (1998); The Myth of Rescue (1997); A History of the Jews in the English-Speaking World: Great Britain (1996).

Add 4/1 Frederick Street, Caulfield South, Victoria 3162, Australia

Email wdr@aber.ac.uk

RUDMAN, Michael Edward, MA (Oxon), BA (Oberlin College).

b. Tyler, Texas, USA, Feb. 14, 1939; Artistic Director, Sheffield Theatres (1992-94); Dir. Chichester Festival Theatre (1989-90); Associate Dir. National Theatre, (1979-88); Dir. Lyttelton Theatre (1979-81), Bd. Dirs. Art. Director, Hampstead Theatre (1973-78); Art. Dir. Traverse Theatre Club (1970-73).

Add c/o Peter Murphy, Curtis Brown Group, 4th Floor, 28/29 Haymarket SW1Y 4SP

Tel 020 7396 6600 *Fax* 020 7396 0110

RUDOLF, Anthony, BA (Cantab), Chevalier de l'Ordre des Arts et des Lettres, FRSL, FEA.

b. London, Sept. 6, 1942; Writer, Publisher, Translator. Royal Literary Fund Fel. University Hertfordshire and Westminster (2002-8); Publ.: Journey Round My Apartment (2015); Silent Conversations: A Readers Life (2013); A Vanished Hand (2013); ZigZag (2010); Claude Vigée's Songs of Absence (2007); Piotr Rawicz and Blood from the Sky (2007, 1996); Kitaj (2001); The Arithmetic of Memory (1999); The Diary of Jerzy Urman (1991, rev. ed. forthcoming); Primo Levi's War against Oblivion (1990); After the Dream (1979).

Add 8 The Oaks, Woodside Avenue N12 8AR

Email anthony.rudolf@virgin.net

SACERDOTI, Cesare David Salomone,

b. Florence, Feb. 24, 1938; m. Judith née Margulies; Publisher, Company Director; Dir. Sephardi Centre Ltd (1997-); T. Winnicott Clinic of Psychotherapy Charitable Trust (1999-2009); Publications Dir. International Psychoanalytical Association (2002-08); Pres. Bd. of Elders, Spanish and Portuguese Jews' Congregation (2000-04), Thesoureiro (2000-03), V. Pres. (1996-2000), Parnas Heshaim (1995-2000); Man. Dir. H. Karnac (Books) Ltd (1984-99); 'Associate of the British Psychoanalytical Society' awarded 2011; 'Premio Cesare Musatti' awarded 2003 by the Societa' Psicoanalitica Italiana.

Add 25 Manor House Drive, London NW6 7DE

Tel 020 8459 2012 *Fax* 020 8451 8829

Email cesare@sacerdoti.com

SACKS, Rabbi, Lord Jonathan Henry, MA (Cantab), PhD, DD (Lambeth), H. DD (Cambridge), H. DD (King's College, London), H. D. University (Middx.), H. D. University (Glasgow).

b. London, Mar. 8, 1948; m. Elaine née Taylor; The Ingeborg and Ira Rennert Global Distinguished Prof. Judaic Thought, New York University, USA (2013-); The Kressel and Ephrat Family University Prof. Jewish Thought, Yeshiva University, USA (2013-); Prof. Law, Ethics and the Bible at King's College, London (2013-); Associate Pres. Conference European Rabbis (1999-2013); Hon. Fel. Gonville and Caius College Cambridge (1993-); Ch. Rabbi of the United Hebrew Congregations of the Commonwealth (1991-2013); BBC Reith Lecturer (1990); Vis. Prof. Philosophy, University Essex (1989-90); Ed. L'Eylah (1984-1990); form. Principal, Jews College and holder of the Lord Jakobovits Ch. (1984-90); M. Marble Arch Synagogue (1983-90); M. Golders Green Synagogue (1978-82); Vis. Prof. Philosophy Hebrew University; Vis. Prof. Theology and Religious Studies, King's College, London. Publ.: Koren Sacks Pesah Mahzor (2013); Koren Sacks Yom Kippur Mahzor (2012); Koren Sacks Rosh Hashanah Mahzor (2011); The Great Partnership (2011); Future tense (2009); The KorenSacks Siddur (2009); Authorised Daily Prayer Book (4th edition New translation and commentary, 2007); The Home We Will Build Together (2007); To Heal a Fractured World (2005); From Optimism to Hope (2004); The Passover Haggadah (2003); The Dignity of Difference (2002); A Letter in the Scroll (2000); Celebrating Life (2000); Radical Then, Radical Now (2000); Morals and Markets (1999); The Politics of Hope (1997); Community of Faith (1995); Faith in the Future (1995); Will We Have Jewish Grandchildren? (1994); One People: Tradition Modernity and Jewish Unity (1993); Crisis and Covenant (1992); Arguments for the Sake of Heaven (1991); Orthodoxy Confronts Modernity (1991); The Persistence of Faith (1991); Tradition in an Untraditional Age (1990); Traditional Alternatives (1989); Torah Studies (1986); Tradition and Transition (1986).

Email joanna@rabbisacks.org

SAIDEMAN, Seymour Geoffrey, FCA.

b. London, Apr. 5, 1939; m. Shirley née Lewis; Elder, Stanmore and Canons Park Synagogue; H. Life Pres. B'nai B'rith Europe; Mem. B'nai B'rith International Advisory Council and Delegate, 36th Zionist Congress of the World Zionist Organisation; form. Snr. V. Pres. B'nai B'rith International (2006-09); form. Pres. B'nai B'rith Europe (1999-2003); form. National Pres. B'nai B'rith District 15 of Great Britain and Ireland (1997-9); form. Ch. Chief Rabbinate Council (1992-6); form. Pres. US (1992-6); form. Ch. Governors JFS Comprehensive School (1984-7); form. Ch. London Bd. of Jewish Rel. Education (1984-7).

Add 10 Oak Lodge Close, Stanmore HA7 4QB

SALAMON, Rabbi Thomas, PhD.

b. Kosice, May 10, 1948; m. Renée née Heffes; Rabbi/Solicitor; M. Westminster Synagogue (1997-); M. Hampstead Reform Jewish Com. (1988-90); M. Hertsmere Progressive Synagogue (1980-88); Exec. Dir. Norwood Child Care (1975-80); Associate M. West London Synagogue (1972-75).

Add Westminster Synagogue, Kent House, Rutland Gardens London SW7

Tel 020 7584 3953 *Fax* 020 7581 8012

Email thomas@westminstersynagogue.org *Website* www.westminstersynagogue.org

SALASNIK, Rabbi Eli,

b. Old City of Jerusalem; Rav in London since 1950; District Rav, London Bd. for Shechita.

Add 8 The Lindens, Prospect Hill, Waltham Forest, London E17 3EJ

SALASNIK, Rabbi Zorach Meir, BA, FJC.

b. London, July 29, 1951; M. Bushey and District Synagogue (1979-); Ch. Rabbinical Council, US (2002-05); Snr. Jewish Hospital Chaplain; Cttee. Health Care Chaplaincy Faith and Belief Group; Rabbinic representative, Jewish Emergency Support Service; Hertfordshire SACRE; Hertsmere Forum of Faiths; form. Sec. Chief Rabbi's Cabinet; form. Chaplain, Rishon Multiple Sclerosis Aid Group; form. Gov. Agency for Jewish Education; form. M. Notting Hill Synagogue, Leytonstone and Wanstead Synagogue.

Add 8 Richfield Road, Bushey Heath, Hertfordshire WD23 4LQ
Tel 07961 366 689
Email zm@salasnik.net

SAMUELSON, Sir Sydney Wylie, CBE, H. D. Sheffield Hallam Uni.

b. Paddington, London, Dec. 7, 1925, m. Doris née Magen; first recipient, The Friese-Greene Award for Outstanding Career in Cinema (2011); Pres. (2002-) Projected Picture Trust; F. T. (1977-2008), British Academy of Film and Television Arts, T. (1973-2008), Fel. (1993), Ch. of Council (1973-76); Fel. British Film Institute (1997); First British Film Commissioner (1991-97); Patron (1997), Fdr. Ch. and Chief Exec. Samuelson Group PLC (1954-1990); Mem. Council/Tru., Cinema and Television Benevolent Fund, Pres. (1983-86); Pres. (1980-81), Cinema and Television Veterans, Mem. (1970); British Kinematograph Sound and Television Society, Hon. Fel. (1970); Pres. (1985-), Israel Association for the Mentally Handicapped (AKIM); Guild of British Camera Technicians; Mem. Beth Hatefutsoth Museum, Tel Aviv; Founding Pres. Hon. Life Patron, UK Jewish Film.

Add 31 West Heath Avenue NW11 7QJ
Tel 020 8455 6696 *Fax* 020 8458 1957
Email sydney.samuelson@zen.co.uk

SANDERS, Jeremy Keith Morris, CBE, ScD., FRS, FRSC, CChem.

b. London, May 3, 1948; m. Louise Sanders née Applebaum; Research Chemist and Academic; University of Cambridge: Pro-V. Chancellor for Institutional Affairs (2011-), Prof. (1996-), Hd. of School of Physical Sciences (2009-11), Deputy V. Chancellor (2006-10), Hd. of Dept. (2000-06), Reader (1992-96), Lecturer in chemistry (1973-92). Publ.: Modern NMR Spectroscopy (with B.K. Hunter, 1987, 2nd edition 1993).

Add University Chemical Laboratory, Lensfield Road, Cambridge CB2 1EW
Tel 01223 336 411 *Fax* 01223 336 017
Email jkms@cam.ac.uk *Website* www.ch.cam.ac.uk/person/jkms

SAPERSTEIN, Prof. Marc Eli, AB (Harvard), MA (H.U.), MA (Hebrew Union C.), PhD (Harvard).

b. Brooklyn, NY, Sept. 5, 1944; m. Tamar de Vries Winter; Academic; Council, JHSE (2008–); Vis. Prof. Harvard (Spring 2012); Prof. Jewish Studies, Kings College London (2008-); Principal, Leo Baeck College, London (2006-11); Prof. Jewish History, George Washington University (1997-2006); Prof. Jewish History and Thought, Washington University, St. Louis (1986-97); Associate Prof. Jewish Studies, Harvard Divinity School (1983-86). Among recent publications: Edited volumes and contributed articles in Jewish history, literature and thought. Books: Jewish Preaching in Times of War 1800-2001 (2008); Exile in Amsterdam: Saul Levi Morteira's Sermons to a Congregation of 'New Jews' (2005); 'Your Voice Like a Ram's Horn': Themes and Texts in Traditional Jewish Preaching (1996); Jewish Preaching 1200-1800 (1989); Moments of Crisis in Jewish-Christian Relations (1989); Decoding the Rabbis (1980).

Add 21 Owlstone Road, Cambridge CB3 9JH
Tel 01223 312 082
Email msaper@gwu.edu

SARAH, Rabbi Elizabeth Tikvah, BSc (Soc.).

b. 1955; Semichah Leo Baeck College (1989); Associate Jewish Chaplain, University Sussex (2008-), Brighton University (2003-); Rabbi, Brighton and Hove Progressive Synagogue (2001-); Mem. Editorial Bd. MANNA (1994-); Ch. Rabbinic In-Service Training, Leo Baeck College (1996-2002); Rabbi, Leicester Progressive Jewish Congregation (1998-2000); Pt. time Lecturer Leo Baeck College (1997); Dep. Dir. Sternberg Centre (1994-97); Rabbi, Buckhurst Hill Reform Synagogue (1989-94); Dir. Programmes RSGB. Among recent publications: Trouble-Making Judaism (2011); Compelling Commitments (2007); Aspects of LJ (2004); Machzor Ruach Chadashah (2003); Lesbian Rabbis - the First Generation (2001); Taking up the Timbrel (2000); Renewing the Vision (1996); Contributions to Jewish Explorations of Sexuality (1995).

Add Brighton & Hove Progressive Synagogue, 6 Lansdowne Road BN3 1FF

Tel 01273 737 223
Email bhps@freenetname.co.uk

SAXTON, Robert Louis Alfred, MA (Cantab), BMus (Oxon), DMus (Oxon), FGSM.
b. London, Oct. 10, 1953; Composer and University Lecturer; Prof. of Composition, Oxford (2008-); Fel. and Tutor in Music, Worcester College, Oxford (1999-); Hd. Composition, RAM (1998-99); Hd. Composition, GSMD (1991-97). Publ.: Over 50 compositions; 20 commercial recordings; articles.
Add Worcester College, Oxford OX1 2HB
Email robert.saxton@music.ox.ac.uk

SCHAMA, Simon Michael, CBE, PhD.
b. London, Feb. 13, 1945; m. Virginia Papaioannou; Writer and Broadcaster; University Prof. Columbia University. Presented BBC TV series: A History of Britain. Publ.: Patriots and Liberators: Revolution in the Netherlands, 1780-1813 (1977); Two Rothschilds and the Land of Israel (1978); The Embarrassment of Riches: An Interpretation of Dutch Culture in the Golden Age (1987); Citizens: A Chronicle of the French Revolution (1989); Dead Certainties: Unwarranted Speculations (1991); Landscape and Memory (1995); Rembrandt's Eyes (1999); A History of Britain (3 vols, 2000-2).
Add Columbia University, 1180 Amsterdam Avenue, MC 2533, New York NY 10027

SCHIFF, Rabbi Naftali,
Exec. Dir. Aish UK (1999-); Fdr. GIFT (Give It Forward Today); Fdr. Dir. JRoots; Dir. Forum for Jewish Leadership; Dir. Chazon UK; Dir. JLink; Common Denominator; Chazak; The Danny Frei Jerusalem Fellowship.
Add Aish, 79 Hendon Way, London NW4 3LP
Tel 020 8457 4444 *Fax* 020 8457 4445

SCHMOOL, Marlena (née Lee), BSoc. Sc.
b. Leeds, 1941; Social Res. Consultant; Dir. Community Issues Divison, Board of Deputies (1999-2003); Tru. Jewish Journal of Sociology; Action for Childrens Arts. Publ.: Reflections on the 2011 Census of England and Wales (2011); Jews in Britain: a Snapshot from the 2001 Census (with D. Graham and S. Waterman, 2007); The Relaxation of Community? (2003); A Profile of British Jewry (with F. Cohen) (1998); Women in the British Jewish Community (with S.H. Miller) (1994); various statistical publications.

SCHNEIDER, Prof. Michael,
Hd. National Heart and Lung Institute (2009-11), Hd. Cardiovascular Science (2007-); Prof. of Medicine, Molecular and Cellular Biology, Molecular Physiology and Biophysics, Dir. Center for Cardiovascular Dev. Baylor College of Medicine, Texas (1984-2007); Dir. British Heart Foundation Centre at Imperial College London; Mem. MRC Council. Recipient, Medical Futures Cardiovascular Innovation Award (2008).
Add BHF Centre, Imperial College London, South Kensington Campus, London SW7 2AZ
Tel 020 7589 5111
Email m.d.schneider@imperial.ac.uk

SCHOCHET, Rabbi Yitzchak, MA.
b. Canada; Rabbi, Mill Hill Synagogue (1993-), Richmond Synagogue (1991-93); Principal, Rosh Pinah Primary School, Edgware; Columnist, Jewish News; Diary Rabbi, Guardian; Mem. Chief Rabbi's Cabinet.
Add 305 Ballards Lane, London N12 8GB

SCHONFIELD, Jeremy Joseph, BA (East Anglia), PhD (Cantab).
b. London, July 11, 1951; m. Tamar née Rahmani; Research Fel. Oxford Centre for Hebrew and Jewish Studies (2011-), Mason Lecturer (1989-); Thesoureiro do Heshaim (2004-); Lecturer, Leo Baeck College (1995-); John Rayner Reader in Liturgy (2014-); Ed. Jewish Historical Society of England (1981-2012), Contributing Ed. (2013): Transactions, Vols 27-35; Jewish Historical Studies, Vols. 36-45; Assistant Dir. Israel Diaspora Trust (1988-2002);

Editorial team (1982-99), Bulletin of the Anglo-Israel Archaeological Society, Jt. Founding Ed. (1982). Among recent publications: Sabbath and Morning Prayers of the Spanish and Portuguese Jews' Congregation (Ed. 2011); Megillat Esther (Ed. 2007); Undercurrents of Jewish Prayer (2006); The North French Miscellany (Ed. 2003); The Rothschild Haggadah (Ed. 2000); Perek Shirah (Ed. 1996); Me'ah Berakhot (Ed. 1994).

Add 71 Woodland Rise, London N10 3UN

Tel 020 8365 3226

Email jeremy.schonfield@blueyonder.co.uk

SCOTT, Lee, M.P.

b. London, Apr. 6, 1956; m. Estelle née Dombey; Consultant; MP (Con.) for Ilford North (2005-); Council Redbridge (1998-2006); Scott Associates Consultancy on Regeneration.

Add House of Commons, London SW1A 0AA

Tel 020 7219 8326

Email scottle@parliament.uk *Website* www.leescott.co.uk

SEAL, Gail (née Lew),

b. London, Oct. 29, 1948; m. Michael Seal; form. Mem. Jewish Leadership Council; Adv. Bd. LJCC; T. Tel Aviv Found.; Bd. Latrun, Israel; T. UK Friends of OR; Fdr. Mem. and Co-Ch. Communal Liaison Group; V. Pres. Zionist Federation; Bd. Mem. BICOM; JNF (Pres. 1995-2007, Deputy Pres. 1993, Education Officer, 1987).

Add c/o Zionist Federation of GB and Ireland, BM Box 1948, London WC1N 3XX

SECHER, Paul, LLB, Chartered MCIPD.

b. Whitehaven, Mar. 1, 1951; Ch. JSB Group (Management Development,Training and Consulting); Mem. Employment Tribunal; V. Pres. Commonwealth Jewish Council. Author/contributor, books and articles on employment law, communication and management; Ed. Employment Lawletter.

Add Dove House, Arcadia Avenue, London N3 2JU

Tel 020 8371 7000 *Fax* 020 8371 7001

Email paul.secher@jsbonline.com *Website* www.jsbonline.com

SEFTON, Kevin,

T. Moishe House, Ch. Limmud (2012-); Ch. Limmud Conference (2007), Tru. (2012-); Mem. JC Power 100 Panel (2007); Fdr. NuMa - Creative space for new Jewish ideas including the Jewish Bee Project hosted by the JCC for London.

Tel 020 8816 7895

Email kevin.sefton@4000rpm.co.uk

SEGAL, Anthony Walter, MB, ChB, MD, MSc, PhD, DSc, FRCP, FMedSci, FRS.

b. Johannesburg, Feb. 24, 1944; Charles Dent Prof. of Med. London University; attached University College and Middlesex Hospital Medical School.

Add The Rayne Institute, Centre for Molecular Medicine, 5 University Street, London WC1E 6JF

Tel 020 7679 6175

Email t.segal@ucl.ac.uk

SEROTA, Sir Nicholas (Andrew), CH, Kt, BA, MA.

b. Apr. 27, 1946; m. Teresa neé Gleadowe; Mem. Olympic Delivery Authority (2006-12); Dir. Tate Gallery (1988-); Dir. Whitechapel Gallery (1976-88); Dir. Museum of Modern Art, Oxford (1973-6). Publ.: Experience or Interpretation: The Dilemma of Museums of Modern Art (1996).

Add Tate Gallery, Millbank SW1P 4RG

Tel 020 7887 8003

SHAERF, Paul Simon, MA (Cantab).

b. London, Mar. 4, 1950; m. Judith née Tunkel; Judicial officeholder; Ombudsman (2001-).

Add Board of Deputies, 6 Bloomsbury Square, London WC1A 2LP

Tel 020 7543 0105 *Fax* 020 7543 0010

Email ombudsman@bod.org.uk

SHAPPS, Grant,

b. Watford, Sept. 14, 1968; m. Belinda neé Goldstone; M. of State for Housing & Local Government (2010-); Shadow Housing M. (2007–10); MP (Cons), Welwyn Hatfield (2005-); Fdr. and Ch. Printhouse Corporation (1990-2007); V. Ch. (Campaigning), Conservative Party (2005–07).

Add House of Commons, London SW1A 0AA

Tel 020 7219 8497 *Fax* 020 7219 0659

Email grant@shapps.com

SHAW, Rabbi Andrew Clive, BEng. (Hons), MA.

b. London, Sept. 18, 1971; m. Gila née Zamir; United Synagogue Dir. Living and Learning; Community Development Rabbi, Stanmore and Canons Park Synagogue; Exec. Dir. Tribe (2003-13); Consultant, Facilitator, Jewish Association for Business Ethics (2000-12); Chaplain, Mayor of Harrow (2006-07); Dir. Youth New Hempstead Synagogue, NY (1998-2000); form. National Education Co-ordinator, UJS (1994-95). Publ.: 60 Days for 60 Years: Israel (gen. Ed. 2008); 60 Days for 60 Years (Ed. 2005); 50 Days for 50 Years (Ed. 1995).

Tel 020 8343 5693

Email rabbishaw@theus.org.uk *Website* www.theus.org.uk

SHAW, Martin, BA.

b. London, Aug. 16, 1949; Fundraising and Management Consultant (2002-), Gen. Man. Variety Club, GB (2001-2); Ch. Haringey Shed (2001-); Ch. Jubilee Waterside Centre (1998-2008); Snr. Consultant, Charity Recruitment (1999-2001); Independent Consultant, Action Planning (1995-99); Exec. Dir. Association for Jewish Youth (1989-95); Snr. Youth Off. London Borough of Ealing (1986-89). Publ.: Young People and Decision; Putting the Fun into Fundraising.

Add 64 The Grove, Edgware, Middlesex HA8 9QB

Tel 020 8958 6885

Email mshaw@dircon.co.uk

SHEFF, Sylvia Claire (née Glickman), MBE, JP, BA.

b. Manchester, Nov. 9, 1935; Ret. Teacher (1958-77); Exec. Cttee. Mem. Jewish Representative Council of Greater Manchester and Region (2009-); Fdr. Dir. Organisation of Jewish Lawyers (2009-); Concert and events promoter (2002-); Mem. UK Assoc. Jewish Lawyers & Jurists (2001-); Del. Board of Deputies (1987-); Pres. (1980-), Manchester 35 Group Women's Campaign for Soviet Jewry, Fdr. Ch. (1972-80); Associate Dir. Jewish Cultural and Leisure Centre (1990-93); International Co-ord. Yeled Yafeh Fel. of Children of Chernobyl (1990-94); Fdr. and Dir. Friendship with Israel, Group (European Parl.) (1979-90); Hon. S. National Council for Soviet Jewry (1987-89); Asst. Nat. Dir. Conservative Friends of Israel (1985-89); Fdr. Mem. Bury Family Conciliation Service Management Cttee. (1985-87); Nat. Projects Dir. Conservative Friends of Israel (1974-85); Magistrate (1976).

Add 6 The Meadows, Old Hall Lane, Whitefield, Manchester M45 7RZ

Tel 0161 766 4391 *Fax* 0161 766 4391

Email sylvia@sheff.fsbusiness.co.uk

SHELDON, Peter, OBE, JP, FCA.

b. Chesterfield, June 11, 1941; m. Judith Marion née Grunberger; International Business Consultant; Ch. Kardan N.V. (2012-); Ch. Chief Rabbinate Trust (2010-13, 2003-05), T. (2005-10); T. The Jerusalem Foundation UK (2010-); T. Finchley Jewish Primary School Trust (2007-); T. TrainE TraidE (2012-); Dep. Board of Deputies (2006-13); Ch. North West London Eruv Cttee. (2001-12); Ch. BATM Advanced Communications Ltd (1999-); T. Hadassah Medical Relief Association UK (2006-11); British Israel Chamber of Commerce (2006-10); Pres. United Synagogue (1999-2005), H. Officer (1996-99); Ch. Kashrut Division London Beth Din (1996-99); Ch. Kerem Schools (1976-88).

Add 8 Denver Court, 132 Hendon Lane, Finchley N3 3RH

Tel 020 8346 5155

Email sheldp@btinternet.com

SHELLEY, Ronald Charles, MBE.

b. London, Mar. 27, 1929; V. Pres. AJEX; form. National Ch. AJEX (2004-06, 1975-77); T. Board of Deputies (1991-97); Ch. AJEX Housing Association (1987-91); Ch. Jewish Military Museum; Ch. AJEX Charitable Foundation; Winner, LB of Barnet Civic Award 2010.

Add AJEX Charitable Foundation, Shield House, Harmony Way, Hendon NW4 2BZ

Tel 020 7323 6626 *Fax* 020 7255 1203

SHERIDAN, Rabbi Sybil Ann, MA (Cantab).

b. Bolton, Lancs., Sept. 27, 1953; m. Rabbi Dr Jonathan Romain; M. Wimbledon and District Reform Synagogue (2003-14); form. M. Thames Valley Jewish Community (1994-2003), Ealing Liberal Synagogue; Chaplain, Roehampton University. Publ.: Shirei Hatefilla (Ed. 2012); Abraham's Children: Jews, Christians and Muslims in Conversation (Contr. 2006); Feminist Perspectives on History and Religion (Contr. 2001); Taking up the Timbrel (Ed. 2000); Stories from the Jewish World (1987, 1998); Renewing the Vision (Contr. 1996); Creating the Old Testament (Contr. 1994); Hear Our Voice (Ed. 1994).

Add 1 Queensmere Road, Wimbledon, London SW19 5QD

Tel 020 8946 4836 *Fax* 020 8944 7790

SHINDLER, Colin, BSc, MSc DipEd (Further Education), PhD.

b. Hackney, London, Sept. 3, 1946; Founding Ch. European Association of Israeli Studies (2009-13); Emer. Prof. SOAS (2011-), Prof. Israeli Studies (2008-11); Centre for Jewish Studies, (2006-10); Dir. European Jewish Publication Society (1995-2010); Ed. Judaism Today (1994-2000); Ed. Jewish Quarterly (1985-94); Associate Lecturer in Chemistry, Open University. Among recent publications: Israel and the World Powers (Ed. 2014); Israel and the European Left (2012); History of Modern Israel (2008, 2013); What do Zionists Believe? (2007); The Triumph of Military Zionism (2005, 2009); The Land Beyond Promise (2002); Israel, Likud and the Zionist Dream (1995).

Add SOAS, Thornhaugh Street, Russell Square, London WC1H 0XG

Tel 020 7898 4358

Email cs52@soas.ac.uk

SHINDLER, Rabbi Julian, MSc, PhD.

b. London, Jan 9, 1950; m. Rosalyn née Brysh; Programmes Dir. PEIR (2010-); Exec. Dir. Rabbinical Council of the US (1999-); Dir. Marriage Authorisation Office, Office of the Chief Rabbi (1987-); Rabbi, Muswell Hill Synagogue (1987-99); UJS London Region Student Chaplain (1986-7); Kalms Fel. (1983-86); Hd. Science, Menorah Grammar School (1980-84); Chief Rabbi's Cabinet (Rabbinic Liaison).

Add 305 Ballards Lane, London N12 8GB

Email rabbi.shindler@chiefrabbi.org

SHIRE, Rabbi Dr Michael, BA (Hons) UCL, MA, PhD (Hebrew Union College LA); MA, Hon Doctorate, Jewish Religious Education (2008), Jewish Religious Education; Hon Fel. Leo Baeck College (2012); Rabbinic Ordination at Leo Baeck College (1996).

b. 1957; Dean and Prof. of Jewish Education, Hebrew College Boston (2011-); V. Principal, Leo Baeck College (2001-2011); Dir. Centre for Jewish Education (1988-2001); Dir. of Education, Temple Beth Hillel, Hollywood (1983-88). Publ.: Mazal Tov (2003); The Jewish Prophet (2002); L'Chaim! (2000); The Illuminated Haggadah (1998); Ed. Cons. Illustrated Atlas of Jewish Civilization.

Add Hebrew College, 160 Herrick Road, Newton Centre, MA 12459, USA

Tel +1 (617) 559 8617

Email mshire@hebrewcollege.edu

SILKIN, Yitzchok, MA (Cantab), MSc (London).

b. London, Feb. 26, 1947; m. Sylvia née Wieselberg BA; CEO, Agudas Israel Great Britain

(2009-); Seminars Dir. Seed (1984-2009).

Add 97-99 Stamford Hill, London N16 5DN

Tel 020 8800 6688

Email ysilkin@agudas.org.uk

SILVERMAN, Rabbi Robert (Reuven), BA, PhD, DD, FLBC, MBACP, Adv. Dip. Counselling.

b. Oxford, July 26, 1947; m. Prof. Isobel Braidman; Ch. Assembly of Rabbis, RSGB (1991-93); M. Manchester Reform Synagogue; Hon. Fel. Middle Eastern Studies Dept. and Centre for Jewish Studies, University Manchester; Anglo-Israel Friendship League, Manchester; Chaplain, Progressive Jewish Students, Manchester; form. Second M. Edgware Reform Synagogue; M. Mikve Israel Emanuel, Curacao. Publ.: Baruch Spinoza.

Add 26 Daylesford Road, Cheadle, Cheshire SK8 1LF

Tel 0161 834 0514 *Fax* 0161 834 0415

Email rabbi@jacksonsrow.org

SIMONS, Dayan Shmuel,

b. London, Jun 3, 1963; m. Miriam née Zucker; Dayan, London Beth Din; Principal (Rosh Kolel), London Academy Jewish Studies (1998-06). Publ.: Sefer Meil Shmuel (Jerusalem 1994).

Add 15 Elmcroft Crescent, London NW11 9TB

Tel 07974 837 456

SINCLAIR, Clive John, BA, PhD (East Anglia University), FRSL.

b. London, Feb 19, 1948; British Library Penguin Writers Fel. (1996); Writer-in-Residence, Uppsala University (1988); form. Lit. Ed. Jewish Chronicle. Prizes: Jewish Quarterly Award for Fiction (1997); PEN Silver Pen for Fiction (1997); Somerset Maugham Award (1981). Publ.: Death and Texas; The Brothers Singer; Bedbugs; Hearts of Gold; Bibliosexuality; Blood Libels; Diaspora Blues; Cosmetic Effects; Augustus Rex; The Lady with the Laptop; A Soap Opera from Hell; Meet the Wife; Clive Sinclair's True Tales of the Wild West.

Add 16 Canonbury Grove, London N1 2HR

SINCLAIR, Rabbi Dr Daniel Bernard, LLB, LLM, LLD.

b. London, June 30, 1950; Prof. Jewish Law and Comparative Biomedical Law, Striks Law School, CMAS, Israel; Prof. in Jewish Law, Fordham University, NY; Lecturer in Jewish Law and Comparative Biomedical Law, Tel Aviv University (1988-); Snr. Research Fel. Institute for Research in Jewish Law, Jerusalem (1987-); Principal, Jews' College (1994-97); Lecturer in Jewish and Comparative Bioethics, Hebrew University, Jerusalem (1991); Assistant Ed. Jewish Law Annual (1990); Lecturer in Jewish Law and Philosophy of Halakhah, Pardes Institute, Jerusalem (1988-90); Jacob Herzog Memorial Prize (1980). Publ.: End of Life: Oxford Handbook of Jewish Ethics (2012); Jewish Biomedical Law: Legal and Extra-Legal Dimensions (2003); Law, Judicial Policy and Jewish Identity in the State of Israel (2000); Selected Topics in Jewish Law, vols. 4-5 (1994); Tradition and the Biological Revolution (1989).

Add 3/21 Ben Tabbai Street, Jerusalem 93591, Israel

Tel +972 (02) 678 4268

Email dsinclair@law.fordham.edu

SINCLAIR, Dr Michael J,

b. London, Dec. 20, 1942, m. Penny; Ch. Sinclair Montrose Trust Ltd.; Ch. Laniado UK; Ch. and Exec. Bd. World Council of Torah Educ.; Ch. of Management Cttee. Sidney and Ruza Last Foundation Home; V. Ch. JNF; Bd. Mem. British Friends of Arad; T. Jewish Outreach Network; Exec. Ch. Care Capital.

Add 6th Floor, 54 Baker Street, London W14 7BU

Tel 020 7034 1949 *Fax* 020 7034 1941

SINGER, Malcolm John,

b. London, July 13, 1953; m. Sara née Nathan; Composer and Conductor; Director of Music, Yehudi Menuhin School (1998-).

Add Yehudi Menuhin School, Stoke D'Abernon, Cobham, Surrey KT11 3QQ

Tel 01932 584 402

Email malcolmsinger@yehudimenuhinschool.co.uk

SINGER, Norbert, CBE, BSc, PhD, H. DSc (Greenwich), C.Chem., FRSC.

b. Vienna, May 3, 1931; Physical Chemist; Fel. Queen Mary and Westfield College; Fel. Nene College; Ch. Gov. St. Peter's CE Primary School (2004-11); Vis. Prof. University Westminster (1996-2001); Ch. Oxleas NHS Trust (1994-2001); Ch. Rose Bruford College Gov. Body (1994-9); Ch. Bexley District Health Authority (1993-4); Mem. of C.N.A.A. and Cttees. (1982-93); V. Chancellor, University Greenwich [form. Thames Polytechnic] (1978-92); Assistant then Dep. Dir. Polytechnic of North London (1974-8); Res. Chemist, Morgan Crucibles Co. Ltd. (1954-7).

Add Croft Lodge, Bayhall Road, Tunbridge Wells, Kent TN2 4TP

Tel 01892 523 821

Email n.singer@greenwich.ac.uk

SKEAPING, Lucie (née Finch),

b. London, Dec. 30, 1951; m. Rodrick Mursell Skeaping; Musician; Dir. The Burning Bush, Klezmer/Sephardi Music (1990-); Writer on early and traditional music; Columnist for BBC Music Magazine (2005-); BBC Broadcaster; Presenter 'The Early Music Show' BBC Radio 3 (1999-). Publ.: Broadside Ballads (Faber Music 2005); Let's Make Tudor Music (Stainer and Bell, 2000); Singing Simplan and other Bawdy Jigs (UEP, 2014). CDs include: Music of the Old Jewish World (2003); Best of Yiddish, Klezmer and Sephardic Music (1996); Raisins and Almonds (1990).

Add 19 Patshull Road, London NW5 2JX

Email lucieskeaping@hotmail.com *Website* www.lucieskeaping.co.uk and www.theburningbush.co.uk

SKELKER, Philip David, MA (Oxon).

b. Sept. 7, 1946; HM, Immanuel College (2000-12); Educ. Leadership Dir. UJIA (1998-2000); English Master, Eton College (1997-98); HM, Carmel College (1984-97); HM, King David High School, Liverpool (1981-84).

Add 4 Broadhurst Avenue, Edgware, Middlesex HA8 8TR

Tel 020 8950 0604 *Fax* 020 8950 8687

Email pdskelker@gmail.com

SKLAN, Alexander, BSc, Soc. Sci, MSc Econ, CQSW.

b. London Jan. 13, 1947; Dir. of Clinical Services, Medical Foundation for Care of Victims of Torture (1997-); Jt. Ch. Assembly of Masorti Synagogues (1996-2000); Dir. of Social Services, Jewish Care (1990-96); Dir. of Quality Assurance; Dir. of Social Services, Jewish Welfare Bd. (1979-90).

Add 111 Isledon Road, London N7 7JW

Tel 020 7697 7777 *Fax* 020 7697 7799

Email asklan@torturecare.org.uk

SMITH, Rabbi Amnon Daniel, MA.

b. Hadera, Israel, Oct. 10, 1949; Snr. M. Edgware and District Reform Synagogue; form. Ch. RSGB Assembly of Rabbis; form. M. Wimbledon and District Synagogue; form. Associate M. West London Synagogue; Fdr. Ch. Raphael Centre – a Jewish counselling service.

Add 118 Stonegrove, Edgware, Middlesex HA8 8AB

SMITH, Leon Adrian,

b. Bristol, July 17, 1950; m. Claude née Cohen; Charity Director; Exec. V. Pres. Nightingale Hammerson, Chief Exec. (1998-2013); various management roles, Nightingale House

(1973-1997); Dir. English Community Care Association; Mem. Board of Deputies.

Add Nightingale Hammerson, Nightingale House, 105 Nightingale Lane, London SW12 8NB

Tel 020 8673 3495

Email info@nightingalehammerson.org *Website* www.nightingalehammerson.org

SMITH, Stephen, MBE.

b. April 15, 1967; Exec. Dir. USC Shoah Foundation Institute (2009-); Ch. Holocaust Memorial Day Trust (2004-); Executive Dir. Shoah Foundation (2009); Co-Fdr. Aegis Trust (2000); Co-Fdr. Beth Shalom Holocaust Centre (1995). Publ.: Forgotten Places: The Holocaust and the Remnants of Destruction (2001); The Holocaust and the Christian World (Co-Ed.) (2000); Making Memory: Creating Britain's First Holocaust Centre (1999).

Add The Holocaust Centre, Beth Shalom, Laxton, Newark, Notts NG22 0PA

Tel 01623 836 627 *Fax* 01623 836 647

Email office@holocaustcentre.net *Website* www.holocaustcentre.net

SOBER, Phillip, FCA, FRSA.

b. London, Apr. 1, 1931; m. Vivien; Chartered Accountant; form. Dir. Capital Shopping Centres plc (Ch. Audit Cttee.) (1994-2006); form. Dir. Capital and Counties plc (1993-2002); Mem. Finance Cttee, University of London (1999); Mem. Council, University of London (1998); form. Mem. Council, University of Arts, London (1997); form Gov. and Ch. of Audit Cttee. London Institute of Higher Education Corporation (1994); Pres. Norwood Child Care (1989-94); Crown Estate Commissioner (1983-94); T. Royal Opera House Trust (1985-91); Consultant, BDO Stoy Hayward, Chartered Accountants (1990); Partner, Stoy Hayward, Chartered Accountants (1958-90); form. Dir. Liberty International plc; form. T. Jewish Association of Business Ethics; form. Ch. Central Council for Jewish Community Services; form. Jt. T. Ravenswood. Publ.: Articles in professional press on various subjects but primarily on property company accounting.

Add 5 Sheffield Terrace, London W8 7NG

Tel 020 3220 0165

Email viviphil@aol.com

SOLOMON, Sir Harry, KB, FRCP (Hon).

b. Middlesbrough, Mar. 20, 1937; m. Judy; Non-Exec. Dir. Hillsdown Holdings plc (1993-97), Fdr. Ch. (1975-1993); Fel. Royal College of Physicians (H.).

Add Hillsdown House, 32 Hampstead High Street, London NW3 1QD

Tel 020 7431 7739

SOLOMON, Rabbi Norman, PhD (Manc), MA (Cantab.), BMus (London).

b. Cardiff, May 31, 1933; Fel. Oxford Centre for Hebrew and Jewish Studies (1995-2001); Pres. BAJS (1994); Ed. Christian Jewish Relations (1986-91); form. Lecturer, Faculty of Theology, University Oxford; form. Dir. Centre for Study of Judaism and Jewish Christian Relations, Selly Oak College; form. M. Birmingham Central Synagogue, Hampstead Synagogue, London, Greenbank Drive Synagogue, Liverpool, Whitefield Hebrew Congregation, Manchester. Publ.: Torah From Heaven (2012); The Talmud: Selections (2009); Ed. Abraham's Children (2006); Historical Dictionary of Judaism (1998); A Very Short Introduction to Judaism (1996); The Analytic Movement (1993); Judaism and World Religion (1991).

Add Clarendon Institute, Walton Street, Pusey Lane, Oxford OX1 2HG

Tel 01865 278 200

Website www.normansolomon.info

SPIRO, Nitza (née Lieberman), M.Phil. (Oxon).

b. Jerusalem, Nov., 1937; m. Robin; Recipient of Hebrew University Jerusalem Katz Prize for examining Adult Education throughout Scandinavia (1959-1968); Dep. Dir. Ulpan Akiva, Netanya, Israel; Co-Dir. Women's Centre in Arab Village of Tibe; Lecturer, Hebrew & Hebrew Lit., Oxford University (1976-83); Organiser, over 50 National and International tours to places of Jewish interest and hundreds of cultural events at both the Spiro Institute and Spiro Ark; Teaching Hebrew on LBC Radio; Creator, Hebrew Correspondence course; Co-author, International programme for Suggestive Method Learning of Hebrew (created on Scholarship in Liechtenstein); Creator & Dir. of many intensive Ulpanim in London; Creator & Co-Organiser (with Husband Robin), Spiro Institute (now LJCC), Spiro Ark and the Jewish Enigma, Open University, Multimedia course on Jewish History & Culture broadcast on BBC Radio and TV for fourteen successive years; Part-time lecturer, Jewish History & Culture, Florida Atlantic University; Organiser, Remembering for the Future (Holocaust International Conference) of Film and Symposia events at the ICA; Co-Creator, the first Jewish Film Festival and the first Israeli Film Festival in London.

Add The Spiro Ark, 788-790 Finchley Road, London NW11 7TJ

Tel 020 7289 6321

Email education@spiroark.org *Website* www.spiroark.org

SPIRO, Robin Myer, MA (Oxon), M.Phil (Oxon), FCA.

b. London, Feb. 9, 1931; m. Nitza née Lieberman; Jt. Developer, Anglo-Jewish Heritage Trail (with Marcus Roberts, 2006-13); Jt. Developer and Fdr. Spiro Institute (now LJCC), Spiro Institute (1978-98), Spiro Ark (1998-); Dir. Property Companies (1961-78); Creator and developer of St Christopher's Place, off London's Oxford St. (W1); Part time lecturer to adults, Jewish History in London and Florida Atlantic University, Boca Raton, USA (1980-2013); organiser and contributor, The Jewish Enigma multimedia learning programme (Open University, BBC). organiser, Oxford and Cambridge A/O Level syllabus in Modern Jewish History; Initial Lecturer to 'All comers' in Schools Programme, Harrow, Eton, UCS, City of London, Sth Hampstead High School; responsible for fundraising at both Spiro Institute and Spiro Ark. Clubs: MCC, Cavalry and Guards.

Add 80 St. John's Wood Court, St. John's Wood Road, London NW8 8QS

Tel 020 7289 6321

Email rspiro@ukpt.co.uk *Website* www.spiroark.org

STANTON, Prof. Stuart Lawrence Richard, MB, BS, FRCS, FRCSE, FRCOG.

b. Oct. 24, 1938; m. Julia Heller; Pres. British Society of Urogynaecology (2003–); form. Ch. Hadassah UK (2010-11); Pres. Obstetric and Gynaecological Section of the Royal Society of Medicine (2003-4); Prof. of Pelvic Surgery and Urogynaecology, St George's Hospital Medical School (1997–2003), now Emer. Prof.; Consultant Gynaecologist; Dir. of tru. Boys Town Jerusalem; Urogynaecology Unit, St George's Hospital (1984–2003); H. FRANZCOG (2000); V. Ch. and T. Patron, British Friends Hebrew University; Tru. Jewish Music Institute. Publ.: Pelvic Floor Re-education and Practice (2008); Gynaecology (2003); Female Pelvic Reconstructive Surgery (2002); Urinary Tract Infection in the Female (2000); (Co-Ed.) Clinical Urogynaecology (1999).

Add Flat 10, 43 Wimpole Street W1G 8AE

Tel 020 7486 0677

Email stuartstanton@hotmail.co.uk *Website* www.stuartstanton.com

STEPHENS, His Hon. Martin, QC, MA (Oxon).

b. Swansea, June 26, 1939; Circuit Judge (1986-2012); Bencher, Middle Temple (2004); Mem. Main Board, Judicial St. Board (1997-2000); Mem. Parole Board (1995-2000, 2011-); form. Ch. Cardiff Jewish Representative Council (1986-95); Recorder (1979-86).

Add c/o Central Criminal Court, City of London, London EC4M 7EH

STERLING, Jeffrey Maurice, Baron of Plaistow, GCVO, CBE; H. DBA (Nottingham Trent University); H. DCL (Durham), Kt., Order of St John.

b. Dec. 27, 1934; m. Dorothy Ann née Smith; V. Pres. British ORT (1978-); Ch. Sterling Guarantee Trust plc (1969-) (merging with P&O 1985); Ch. P&O (1983-2005); Ch. Queen's Golden Jubilee Weekend Trust (2002); Ch. P&O Princess Cruises (2000); Gov. Royal Ballet (1986-99); Ch. Govs. Royal Ballet School (1983-99); H. Fel. Research Institute of Naval Architects (1997); Fel. of the ISVA (1995); Pres. European Community Shipowners' Associations (1992-94); Hon. Fel. Institute of Chartered Shipbrokers (1992); Elder Brother, Trinity House (1991); H. Captain, Royal Naval Reserve (1991); Hon. Fel. Institute of Marine

Engineers (1991); Spl Adv. to Sec. of State for Trade and Industry (1983-90) and to Sec. of State for Industry (1982-83); Dep. Ch. and Hon. T. London Celebrations Cttee. Queen's Silver Jubilee (1975-83); Freeman of the City of London.

Add 15 St. James's Place, London SW1A 1NP (Office

Tel 020 7409 2345

STERNBERG, Sir Sigmund, KC*SG, JP, DU: Essex; H. LLD Leicester; H. Fellow UCL; DUniv Open; Hon DHLitt Richmond American Internat; Hon DHLitt Hebrew Union College.

b. Hungary, June 2, 1921; m. Hazel née Everett Jones; Life Pres. Movement for Reform Judaism (2011-); Snr. Life V. Pres. Royal College Speech and Language Therapists (2002-); Religious Adv. World Economic Forum (2002-); Life Pres. Sternberg Centre for Judaism (1996-); Pres. Movement for Reform (1998-2011); Alawite Officer Wissam (Morocco) (2009); St. Mellitus Medal (2008); The FIRST Lifetime Achievement Award (2008); LL.D. (Leic, 2007); Order Pentru Merit (Romania, 2007); Knight Grand Cross, Royal Order of Francis I (2005); Patron, Board of Deputies (2005); Hungarian Jewry Award (2004); Miranda Award (Venezuela, 2004); Order of Merit (Hungary, 2004); Off. Legion d'Honneur (2003); Order of Merit (Portugal, 2002); Order of Ukraine for Public Services (2001); Order of Bernardo O'Higgins Gran Cruz (Chile, 1999); Order of Commandatore of the Italian Republic (Italy) (1999); The Commander's Cross with a Star of the Order of Merit (Poland) (1999); Templeton Prize for Progress in Religion (1998); Wilhelm Leuschner Medal (Wiesbaden) (1998); Commander, Royal Order of Polar Star (Sweden) (1997); Patron, International Council of Christians and Jews; Gov. Hebrew University of Jerusalem; Co-Fdr. Three Faiths Forum; Fel. Leo Baeck College; Commander Order of Honour (Greece); Commander's Cross Order of Merit (Germany).

Add Star House, 104-108 Grafton Road NW5 4BA

Tel 020 7485 2538 *Fax* 020 7485 4512

Email sternberg@sternberg-foundation.co.uk

STOBIETSKY, Yeshua,

Fdr. Hamodia Newspaper (1999-).

Add Hamodia UK, 113 Fairview Road, London N15 6TS

Tel 020 8442 7777 *Fax* 020 8442 7778

STONE, Andrew Zelig, Baron of Blackheath, H. LLD (Oxford Brookes), H. D. Design (Kingston).

b. Sept. 9, 1942; m. Vivienne née Lee; Ch. Dipex; Patron Gauchers Association; Gov. Weizmann Institute; Gov. British University of Egypt; Mem. Labour Friends of Israel; Dep. Ch. Moon Valley; Pres. DIPEX Charity; form. Jt. Man. Dir. Marks and Spencer plc (1994-2000).

Add House of Lords, London SW1A 0PW

STONE, Richard,

Fdr. and Co-Ch. Alif Aleph (2003-); Pres. Jewish Council for Racial Equality; V. Ch. Runnymede.

Add The Jewish Council for Racial Equality, P.O. Box 47863, London NW11 1AB

Tel 020 8455 0896

STOPPARD, Sir Tom, OM, Kt, FRSL, CBE.

b. July. 3, 1937; Playwright, Journalist and Novelist. Journalist: Bristol Evening World (1958–60). Plays: Rock 'n' Roll (2006); Arcadia (1993); The Real Thing (1982); Rosencrantz and Guildenstern Are Dead (1966). Publ.: Rock 'n' Roll (2006); Heroes (2005); Henry IV (2004).

Add c/o United Agents, 12–26 Lexington Street, London W1F 0LE

STROM, Alex,

Columnist; Jewish Tribune.

Add Jewish Tribune, 215 Golders Green Road, London NW11 9BY

Tel 020 8458 9988

SUGAR, Lord Alan (Michael), Kt.

b. Mar. 24, 1947; m. Ann neé Simons; Presenter, The Apprentice (BBC TV) (2005-); Exec. Ch. Viglen (1997-), Amstrad Plc (1997-2008); Chief Exec. Tottenham Hotspur (1998–2000); Fdr. Amsair (1993); Owner, Amsprop Estates; Ch. Amscreen. Publ.: The Apprentice: How to Get Hired Not Fired (2005).

Add Brentwood House, 169 King's Road, Brentwood, Essex CM14 4EF

Tel 01277 228 888

SUMBERG, David Anthony Gerald,

b. Stoke-on-Trent, June 2, 1941, m. Carolyn née Franks; Solicitor; form. MEP, North West England (1999-2009); Dir. Anglo-Israel Association (1997-2001); Mem. Foreign Affairs Select Cttee. House of Commons (1992-97); form. MP (Cons) for Bury South (1983-97); Mem. Lord Chancellor's Adv. Cttee. on Public Records (1992); Mem. Home Affairs Select Cttee. House of Commons, (1991-92); Parl. Pte. Sec. Attorney Gen. (1986-90); Jt. Hon. S. Parl. Group, Conservative Friends of Israel, V. Ch. All-Party Committee, Release of Soviet Jewry; V. Ch. All-Party War Crimes Group.

Add 42 Camden Square, London NW1 9XA

Tel 020 7267 9590

Email david@sumberg.fsnet.co.uk

TABICK, Rabbi Jacqueline Hazel (née Acker), BA (Hons.), Dip. Ed, PhD.

b. Dublin, Oct. 8, 1948; Convenor, Beit Din for Movement of Reform Judaism and European Progressive Synagogues; Patron, JCORE; Past Ch. Assembly of Rabbis, RSGB; Past Ch. Council of Reform and Liberal Rabbis; Co. Pres. World Congress of Faiths.

Add Sternberg Centre, 80 East End Road, Finchley N3 2SY

Tel 020 8349 5645

Email jackie.tabick@gmail.com

TABICK, Rabbi Larry Alan, BA, MA, FLBC.

b. Brooklyn, NY, Nov. 24, 1947; Rabbi, Hampstead Reform Jewish Com. (1990-, 1976-81); Lecturer, Kabbalah and Hasidim, Leo Baeck College (2014-); Rabbi, Leicester Progressive Jewish Community (1994-98); Associate Rabbi, Edgware and District Reform Synagogue (1986-90); Assistant Rabbi, Middlesex New Synagogue (1981-86). Publ.: The Aura of Torah (2014); Growing into your Soul (2005).

Add 1 Ashbourne Grove, Mill Hill NW7 3RS

Tel 020 8959 3129

Email rabtab@tabick.abel.co.uk *Website* www.tabick.abel.co.uk

TAHAN, Ilana Antoinette (née Mattes), OBE, BA (HU), MPhil (Aston) Dip. Lib., CILIP.

b. Bucharest, Dec. 6, 1946; m. Dr Menashe Tahan; Librarian; Lead Curator, Hebrew and Christian Orient Studies (2010-), Hd. of Hebrew Section (1997-) and Hebraica Curator (1989-), British Library; Convenor, Hebraica Libraries Group (2007-12). Publ.: The Golden Haggadah (The British Library Treasures in Focus Series, 2011); Hebrew Manuscripts: the power of script and image (2007); Memorial volumes to Jewish communities destroyed in the Holocaust: a bibliography of BL holdings (2004).

Add APAC, The British Library, 96 Euston Road, London NW1 2DB

Tel 020 7412 7646 *Fax* 020 7412 7641

Email ilana.tahan@bl.uk *Website* www.bl.uk

TAUB, Daniel,

b. London, 1962; m. Zehava; Israeli Diplomat; Ambassador of Israel to the Court of St. James's (2011-); over two decades of experience, Israel's Ministry of Foreign Affairs; expert in International law, with specializations in counter-terrorism and the laws of war; form. legal adviser, Israel's missions to the United Nations in New York and Geneva; form. Deputy Legal Counsel, Israeli Foreign Ministry; form. Education Officer, UJS; form. Pres. Oxford University Israel Soc. and Jewish Soc.; regular speaker, Limmud; lecturer on Middle

Eastern issues, international law and negotiation theory; combat medic and reserve officer in the IDF's international law division.

Add Embassy of Israel, 2 Palace Green, London W8 4QB

TAUBE, Prof. (Hirsch) David, BA, BM, BCh.

b. Oct. 4, 1948; m. Dr. Clare Allen; Dir. Imperial College AHSC (2012-); Consultant Nephrologist, Hammersmith and St Mary's Hospital's (1990-); H. Consultant Nephrologist, Royal Brompton Hospital; Prof. of Transplant Medicine, Imperial College.

Add 66 Harley Street, London W1G 7HD

Email davidtaube@msn.com

TAYLOR, Derek Albert Joseph, OBE., MA (Cantab).

b. London, 1932; m. Diane Louise née Milman; Hotel Consultant; Ed. Bd. International Journal of Hospitality Management (1990-2007); Visiting Prof. University of Bournemouth (1997-9), University of Wales (1992-7), University of Surrey (1980-92); Hon. Fel. Oxford Poly. (1983-88); Past Pres. Institute of Hospitality (1983-84); Dir. Grand Metropolitan plc. (1967-81). Author of many books on the Hotel Industry and recently, Chief Rabbi Hertz (2014), Jewish Year Book (with Elkan D. Levy, Ed. 2010-); Thank You For Your Business (2012); Sunderland Beth Hamedrash 1889 - 1999 (with Harold Davis) (2010); Solomon Schonfeld (2009); Don Pacifico (2008); Jewish Parliamentarians (with Lord Janner) (2008); British Chief Rabbis 1664-2006 (2006).

Email derekanddiane@aol.com

TAYLOR, Irving, MD ChM, FRCS, FMed Sci, FHEA.

b. Leeds, Jan. 7, 1945; m. Dr Berenice Penelope née Brunner; Prof. Surgery, V. Dean, UCL Medical School, London; V. Dean (Professional Affairs) and Dir. Medical Studies, University College London (2006-); Elected Council member, Royal College of Surgeons (2004-13); Medical Case Examiner, General Medical Council (2003-); Prof. Surgery Hd. Dept. University College London (1993-2006); Prof. Surgery Hd. Dept. University of Southampton (1981-93); Snr. Lecturer, Surgery, University of Liverpool (1977-81); Past Pres. British Association, Surgical Oncology; Past Pres. Society of Academic and Research Surgeons; Past Pres. European Society of Surgical Oncology. Publ.: Over 600 publications in peer review journal and Ed./Author of 27 books.

Add 43 Francklyn Gardens, Edgware, Middlesex HA8 8RU

Tel 020 895 8364

Email irving.taylor@ucl.ac.uk

TEACHER, Michael,

CEO. Ontex NV (2006-); Norwood Advisory Council (2008-); Ch. Norwood (2004-08), Deputy Ch. (2001-04), T. (1981-2001); Chief Exec. Hillsdown Holdings Plc (1987-1999); Mem. Jewish Leadership Council (2004-08); Ch. Ruralbridge Ltd.

Add Hillsdown House, 32 Hampstead High Street, London NW3 1QD

Email michael.teacher@ruralbridge.com

TEMERLIES, Marc Stephen, ACA, BSc, ALCM.

b. Hove; m. Idit née Herstik; Chartered Accountant and Investment Banker; Conductor, Choirmaster, Arranger and Pianist; Choirmaster, St John's Wood Synagogue (1996-); Fdr. and Conductor, Ne'imah Singers (1993-); Chazan, Hove Hebrew Congregation (1991-2).

Add 6 Sirkin Street, Raanana 43374, Israel

Tel +972 (9) 772 4857

Email marc.temerlies@citigroup.com

TERRET, Norman Harold, JP; Compagnon d'Europe, MBA.

b. Ayr, Scotland, Jan. 10, 1951; Ch. Telecom Associates Group; Ch. Leap2market Ltd.; Ch. Jewish Lads' and Girls' Brigade (JLGB); Snr. Adv. to Somaliland Govt (2008-); Pres. Equant (1984-97).

Tel 020 8866 8587

Email normanterret@btinternet.com

TOWNSLEY, Barry Stephen, CBE.

b. London, Oct. 14, 1946; m. Laura Helen née Wolfson; Stockbroker; Dir. William J. Clinton Foundation Insamlingsstiftelse (2010-); Company Dir. Caprice Holdings Ltd. (2005-); Non Exec. Dir. UTB Partners Ltd. (2004-); United Trust Bank Ltd. (2004-); V. Pres. Weizmann Institute (2004-); Wentworth Group Holdings Ltd. (2004-); Non Exec. Dir. United Trust Bank Ltd. (2004-13); Principal Sponsor, Stockley Academic, Hillingdon (2000-); Ch. Oxford Children's Hospital Campaign (2004-09); Bd. Mem. National Gallery East Wing Dev. Project (2002-07); V. Ch. Serpentine Gallery.

Add c/o The United Trust Bank, 80 Haymarket, London SW1Y 4TE

Email barry.townsley@hobartcapital.com

TRAVIS, Anthony Selwyn,

b. June 9, 1932; m. Philippa née Brostoff; Emer. Prof. of Planning, Prof. Urban Regional Studies, University of Birmingham; late Visiting Prof. in Tourism, Glasgow Caledonian University; Dir. East-West Tourism Consultancy; form. Programme Co-ordinator EEC PHARE. Tourism Programme for Poland; Prof and Dir. Centre for Urban and Regional Studies, University of Birmingham; Past Mem. Birmingham and West Midland Jewish Representative Council; Past Ch. 'Grads' ORT, FHU etc. Lecturer on synagogue design, history and Israel. Publ.: 300, including My Life in Travel (2013); Planning for Tourism, Leisure and Sustainability (CABI, 2011); Realising Tourism Potential of the S. Wales Valleys (1985); Recreation Planning for the Clyde (1970); Report on 'Synagogue Design and Siting' (for Board of Deputies).

Add 20 Mead Rise, Birmingham B15 3SD

Tel 0121 454 1215 *Fax* 0121 454 1215

Email tony.travis@btinternet.com

TURNBERG, Lord Leslie Arnold, MB, ChB, MD, Kt Hon D. Sc. Manchester; Salford; Imperial College; Keele.

b. Mar. 22, 1934; m. Edna Barme; British medical professional; T. The Joseph Interfaith Foundation (2006-08); Pres. Medical Protection Society (1997-2007); Pres. Medical Council on Alcoholism (2000-05); Ch. Bd. of the Public Health Laboratory Service (1997-2005); Ch. UK Forum for Genetics and Insurance (1998-2002); Pres. Royal College of Physicians (1992-97); Prof. of Medicine, University of Manchester (1973-97); Dean, Medical School (1983-86); Scientific Advisor, Association of Medical Research Charities; T. Wolfson Foundation; form. V. Pres. Academy of Medical Sciences; T. Foulkes Foundation; T. Weizmann UK; T. Ovarian Cancer Action; T. Daniel Turnberg Trust Fund. Publ.: Forks in the Road (biography, 2014); 150 articles and books on Medical Science.

Add House of Lords, London SW1A 0PW

TURNER, Rev. Reuben, MBE.

b. Karlsruhe; Mem. Chief Rabbis Cabinet (1986-91); Dir. JNF Education Dept. (1973-91); Gen. Sec. Mizrachi-Hapoel Hamizrachi Federation of Great Britain (1970-73); Dir. Zionist Federation Synagogue Council (1967-70); Reader, Brixton Synagogue (1950-68); Min. Finsbury Park Synagogue (1948-50). Publ.: Jewish Living, The Popular Jewish Bible Atlas; Producer, The Four Brothers Kusevitsky (CD), Selections from the Seder service (CD), The Master Chazanim Collection (20).

Add 13 St Peter's Court NW4 2HG

Tel 020 8202 7023

TYLER, Alan Joseph Lawrence,

b. London, Apr. 2, 1924; m. Jill Naomi née Woolf; Ret. Lieutenant Commander, Royal Navy; Pres. Jewish Committee, HM Forces (2009-), (Ch. 2000-09); Wimbledon Deputy, Board of Deputies (1973-94); Ch. Wimbledon Synagogue (1976-79). Publ: Cheerful and Contented (Autobiography, 2000).

Add 9 Ashcombe Avenue, Surbiton, Surrey KT6 6PX

Tel 020 8399 1542 *Fax* 020 8399 1542

Email jalans@hotmail.co.uk

UNTERMAN, Rev. Alan, BA, B.Phil, PhD.

b. Bushey, Herts., May 31, 1942; form. M. Yeshurun Synagogue, Gatley, Cheshire; form. Lecturer, Comparative Rel. and Chaplain to Jewish Students, Manchester University; Lecturer, Jerusalem Academy of Jewish Studies; Hillel Dir. Victoria, Australia. Publ.: Encyclopaedia Judaica (Contributions); Wisdom of the Jewish Mystics; The Jews: their religious beliefs and practices; Judaism; Penguin Dictionary of Religion (Contributions on Judaism and Hinduism); Penguin Handbook of Living Religions (Contr. Judaism); Dictionary of Jewish Lore and Legend; The Kabbalistic Tradition; Historical Dictionary of the Jews.

Add 5 Rechov Fichman, Jerusalem 92584, Israel

Email unterman_alan@hotmail.com

VAN DEN BERGH, Rabbi Martin, B.ED, MA.

b. Hilversum, Holland, Dec. 2, 1952; m. Anna Leon; Dir. Yiftach; Rabbi, Bevis Marks Synagogue (2010-12); Welfare Portfolio, Chief Rabbi's Cabinet (1998-); Snr. Rabbi, Ohel Leah Synagogue, Hong Kong (2006-10); Ch. Multi-Faith Group for Healthcare Chaplaincy (2005-06); Snr. Hospital Chaplain, United Synagogue Visitation Cttee. (1995-2006); Communal Rabbi, Wembley United Synagogue (1994-2006); Rabbi, Withington Congregation of Spanish & Portuguese Jews, Manchester (1983-94); Founding Ch. Spanish & Portuguese Congregation in Israel (1981-83).

Add Dolphin House, 12 Beaumont Gate, Radlett WD7 7AR

Tel 07948 916 009

Email rabbimartin@mvdbergh.com

VAN DER ZYL, Nikki, BA (Hons).

b. 1935, Berlin; m. George Rooker; Actress; Barrister; Poet; Artist; Singer/Composer; Board of Deputies of British Jews (1997-2009); Una Jewish Affiliates, Chipping Barnet Heritage Trust (2000); Presenter on SHALOM FM (1996); Fdr. Sternberg Theatre Actors Repertory Society (STARS); appeared in West End Theatre; Re-voicing Artiste on James Bond films.

Add 5 Greenview Court, 1431-1433 High Road, Whetstone, London N20 9RN

Tel 020 8446 5866 *Fax* 020 8446 5866

Email nikkivanderzyl@waitrose.com *Website* www.nikkivanderzyl.co.uk

VOGEL, Michele,

Mem. Jewish Leadership Council; Pres. WIZO UK.

Add WIZO House, 107 Gloucester Place, London W1U 6BY

Tel 020 7486 2691

Website www.wizouk.org

VOGEL, Rabbi Shraga Faivish,

b. Salford, Lancs, Apr. 22, 1936; Ch. Centre for Jewish Life; form. Dir. Lubavitch Foundation (1960-2007).

Add 11 Hallswelle Road, London NW11 0DH

Tel 020 8458 9039

Email faivish@thecjl.org

WAGERMAN, Josephine Miriam (née Barbanel), OBE, BA (Hons.), PGCE, Ac. Dip., MA (Ed).

b. London, Sept. 17, 1933, m. Peter; Ch. Legacy Division UJIA (2011-13); Cttee. Women's Interfaith Network (2004-); Independent Assessor NHS Non-Exec. Appointments Panel (1998-2000); Mem. Adv. Bd. UJIA (1997-); Gov. Naima Jewish Prep. School (1996-2012); Inner Cities Religious Council (Dept. of the Environment) (1994-2009); Mem. Academic Panel, Stuart Young Awards (1990-); Hadassah International Volunteer of Distinction (2003); form. Pres. Board of Deputies (2000-3), Snr. V. Pres. (1997-2000), V. Pres. (1994-7); Adv. to the Trustees, Pierre and Maniusia Gildesgame Trust (1996-9); Mem. Council Centre for Study of Jewish Christian Relations, Selly Oak Colleges (1995-8); Jewish Care Woman of Distinction (1996); Gov. Central Foundation Schools London (1996); Chief Exec. Lennox Lewis College (1994-6); form. Hd. JFS (1985-93); Pres. London AMMA (1982-3); form.

Mem. ILEA Standing Jt. Adv. Cttee. Working Party on Teachers Service Conditions, History and Social Studies Adv. Cttee.

Add 38 Crespigny Road, London NW4 3DX

Tel 020 8203 7471

Email wagerman@btinternet.com

WAGERMAN, Dr Peter Henry, LDS.RCS (Eng).

b. London, June 10, 1932; m. Josephine Miriam née Barbanel; retired Dental Surgeon; Mem. BLind Veterans UK (2012-); Ch. Friends of Jewish Servicemen and Women (2010-); V. Pres. Association of Jewish Ex-Servicemen & Women (2010-); Nat. Ch. AJEX (2008-10), Nat. Dep. Ch. (2006-8); Mem. Jewish Cttee. HM Forces (2005-); Board of Deputies of British Jews (2003-), Community Issues Division (2003-12); Freeman, City of London (2000); Ch. Hendon Branch, AJEX (1998-2006); Ch. London Dental Cttee. JIA (1984-6); Mem. London Jewish Male Choir (1961-81); General Dental Practitioner (1960-2007); Flt. Lt. Royal Air Force (1956-9); House Surgeon, King's College Hospital (1956).

Add 38 Crespigny Road, London NW4 3DX

Tel 020 8203 7471

Email wagerman@btinternet.com

WAGNER, Leslie, CBE, MA (Econ.) D. University Middx, D. University Leeds Metropolitan, D. Civil Laws, Huddersfield, D. University, Open, D. University Derby.

b. Manchester, Feb. 21, 1943, m. Jennifer; Ch. Commission on Jewish Schools (2008); Chancellor, University of Derby (2003-8); Ch. Education Leeds (2004-7); Ch. Higher Education Academy (2004-7); Ch. University Vocational Awards Council (2001-3); V. Chancellor, Leeds Metropolitan University (1994-2003); Dir. Leeds TEC Ltd (1997-2001); Ch. Yorkshire and Humberside Universities Association (1996-9); Ch. Higher Education for Capability (1994-8); Ch. Jewish Community Allocation Bd. (1994-6); Ch. Society for Research into Higher Education (1994-96); V. Pres. US (1992-3); V. Chancellor and Chief Exec. University of North London (1987-93); Mem. Council, US; T. Chief Rabbinate Trust; T. Jewish Chronicle. Publ.: Choosing to Learn: Mature Students in Education (with others); The Economics of Education Media; Agenda for Institutional Change in Higher Education (Ed.); Readings in Applied Microeconomics (Ed.).

Add 12 Aminadav, Jerusalem 93549 Israel

Tel +972 (2) 563 9638

Email vcwagner@hotmail.com

WALDMANN, Prof. Herman, BA, MB BChir, PhD, MRCPath, MRCP, FRS.

b. Feb. 27, 1945; m. Judith Ruth Young; Emer. Prof. Pathology, Oxford University (2013-); JDRF Excellence in Clinical Res. Award (2005); José Carreras Award, European Haematology Association (2005); Thomas Starzl Prize in Surgery (2007); Fel. Lincoln College, Oxford (1994); Fel. Royal Society (1990).

Add Sir William Dunn School of Pathology, South Parks Road, Oxford OX1 3RE

Email hermanwaldmann@path.ox.ac.uk

WALSH, David, LLB (Hons).

b. Leeds, May 21, 1937; m. Jenny, née Cronin; Solicitor; Dir. Peek Plc, Carlisle Group Plc; Mem. Bd. of UJIA; form. Ch. RSGB, now V. Pres.; Pres. West London Synagogue (1988-91), Ch. (1981-85).

Add 82 North Gate, Prince Albert Road, London NW8 7EJ

Tel 020 7586 1118 *Fax* 020 7483 2598

WARREN, Loraine,

b. London, Dec. 15, 1947; m. Paul Warren; Pres. WIZOuk, (form. Ch. of Trustees (2006-12).

Add WIZOuk, Charles House, 108/110 Finchley Road, London NW3 5JJ

Tel 020 7319 9169 *Fax* 020 7486 7521

Email lorainewarren@yahoo.co.uk

WARRENS, Anthony Nigel, BSc (Glasgow), BM, BCh, DM (Oxon), PhD (London), FRCP, FRCPath, FEBS, FHEA.

b. Glasgow, Oct. 24, 1959; m. Ruth née Burns; Dean for Education; Dir. Institute of Health Sciences Education; Prof. Renal and Transplantation Medicine, Barts and The London School of Medicine and Dentistry, Queen Mary, University of London; Consultant Physician, Royal London Hospital, Wellington Hospital, The Physicians' Clinic, BMI Garden Hospital and BMI London Independent Hospital; Ch. London School of Jewish Studies (2009-); Co-Ch. Immanuel College, Bushey (2001-); Tru. United Jewish Israel Appeal (2004-12), Ch. Educational Leadership Policy Group, Ch. UK programme; Tru. Jewish Continuity (1993-6); previously Bd. Mem. Hampstead United Synagogue and Finchley United Synagogue.

Add Office of the Dean of Education, Barts and The London School of Medicine and Dentistry, Garrod Building, Turner Street, London E1 2AD

Tel 020 7882 2261

Email a.warrens@qmul.ac.uk

WASSERSTEIN, Bernard Mano Julius, MA, DPhil, DLitt, FRHistS, FBA.

b. London, Jan. 22, 1948; Meyer Prof. Modern Jewish History Emer. University Chicago (2003-); Guggenheim Fel. (2007-08); Prof. History, University Glasgow (2000-03); Pres. JHSE (2000-02); Pres. Oxford Centre for Hebrew and Jewish Studies (1996-2000); form. Prof. of History, Brandeis University (1982-96), Dean of Graduate School of Arts and Sciences (1990-92); form. Res. Fel. Nuffield College, Oxford. Publ.: The British in Palestine; Britain and the Jews of Europe 1939-1945; The Secret Lives of Trebitsch Lincoln; Herbert Samuel; Vanishing Diaspora; Secret War in Shanghai; Divided Jerusalem; Israel and Palestine; Barbarism and Civilization; On the Eve; The Ambiguity of Virtue.

Add 167 Nassaukade, Amsterdam 1053 LL, The Netherlands

Email bmjw@uchicago.edu

WASSERSTEIN, David John, MA, DPhil, FRHistS, FRAS.

b. London, Sept. 21, 1951; Academic; Prof. History and Jewish Studies, Eugene Greener Jnr. Prof. Jewish Studies, Vanderbilt University (2004-), Dir. Program in Jewish Studies (2005-08); Fel. Davis Center, History Department, Princeton University (2008-09); Prof. (1994-2004), Associate Prof. (1990-94), Islamic History, Tel Aviv University; Fel. Institute for Advanced Studies, Jerusalem (2002-03); Fel. Wissenschaftskolleg zu Berlin (1999-2000); Assistant Lecturer (later College Lecturer), Semitic Languages Dept. University College, Dublin (1978-90). Among recent publications: From Hellenism to Islam, Cultural and Linguistic Change in the Roman Near East (Co-Ed. 2009); Language of Religion, Language of People: Medieval Judaism, Christianity and Islam (Co-Ed. 2006); Madrasa: Mamluks and Ottomans (Ed. with A. Ayalon, 2006); The Legend of the Septuagint, from Classical Antiquity to Today (with A. Wasserstein, 2006); Education, Religion and State in the Middle East (Ed. with A. Ayalon, 2004).

Add Dept. of History, Vanderbilt University, VU Station B# 351802, 2301 Vanderbilt Place, Nashville TN 37235-1802 USA

Tel +1 (615) 322 7801 *Fax* +1 (615) 343 6002

Email david.wasserstein@vanderbilt.edu

WEBBER, Alan, MSc, PhD, FRICS.

b. London, Sept. 5, 1933; m. Roseruth Freedman; Ch. Israel, Britain and Commonwealth Association; V. Ch. New Synagogue Netanya; Deputy Ch. B'nai B'rith Hillel Foundation Executive (2001-05); Ch. B'nai B'rith Hillel Foundation (1998-2001), Hon. S. (1990-98); Ch. of Governors, St. Margaret's School, Hampstead (1990-2001); Pres. First Lodge, B'nai B'rith (1995-97); Ch. Jewish Community Information (1994-97); H. Officer, St. John's Wood Synagogue (1990-91); H. Officer, Hampstead Synagogue (1970-76). Publ.: The B'nai B'rith Hillel Foundation – 1953-1993; B'nai B'rith – 150 years of service to the community; First Century: B'nai B'rith First Lodge of England 1910-2010.

Add 14/1 Ha M'Apilim, Netanya 42264, Israel

Email alanwebber@012.net.il

WEBBER, Anne, BSc (Hons), FRSA.

b. Manchester; Governor, Oxford Centre for Hebrew and Jewish Studies (2012-); Pres. Jewish Book Council (2005-), Ch. (2002-5); Dir. Central Registry of Information on Looted Cultural Property, 1933-1945 (2001-); Fdr. and Co-Ch. Commission for Looted Art in Europe (1999-); Producer and Dir. Legend Films (1994-98); Producer and Dir. BBC TV Documentaries and Features Depts (1980-94).

Add 76 Gloucester Place, London W1U 6HJ

Tel 020 7487 3401 *Fax* 020 7487 4211

Email annewebber@lootedartcommission.com

Website www.lootedartcommission.com

WEGIER, Michael, MA, BA.

Chief Exec. UJIA (2012-); Exec. Dir. Melitz educational institute in Jerusalem (2007-12); Dir. Programme and Planning, UJIA (2002-07); Mandel Jerusalem Fel. (2002-02); Dir. Jewish Education, Jewish Community Centre (JCC), Baltimore, USA (1996-99).

Add UJIA, 37 Kentish Town, London NW1 8NX

Tel 020 7424 6400

Email central@ujia.org *Website* www.ujia.org

WEIDENFELD, George, Baron of Chelsea, GBE, H. MA (Oxon), H. PhD, Ben Gurion University, D.Litt, Exeter; Holder of the Knight Commander's Cross (Badge & Star) of the German Order of Merit; Holder of the Golden Knight's Cross with Star of the Austrian Order of Merit, Austrian Cross of Honour for Arts and Science; Order of Merit of Italian Republic; Chevalier de l'Ordre National de la Légion d'Honneur, France, Charlemagne Medal for European Media, Italian Order of Merit, Teddy Kollek Life Achievement Award (2009), Italian Grand Officer of the Order of Merit (2005) Fel. King's College London, Honorary Degree, Oxford University (2010), Degree of Doctor of Letters, Honoris Causa, Oxford University 2010.

b. Vienna, Sept. 13, 1919; Publisher; Ch. Weidenfeld and Nicolson, London; Founding Pres. Institute for Strategic Dialogue, Weidenfeld Scholarships and Leadership Programme, Oxford; H. Ch. Bd. of Govs. Ben Gurion University of Negev (2005), Ch. (1995-2004); H. Senator, University Bonn (1996); Hon. Fel. St. Anne's College, Oxford (1993), St. Peter's College, Oxford (1992); Political adv. to Pres. Weizmann of Israel (1949-50); Mem. Bd. Govs. Institute of Human Science, Vienna; Gov. Weizmann Institute of Science; Gov. Tel Aviv University; T. Jerusalem Foundation; Freeman City of London, etc. Awards: Tolerance Ring of the European Academy of Science and the Arts, Frankfurt 2012); Polish Bene Merito Distinction (2011); Order of Merit, Land Baden-Württemberg, Germany (2008); London Book Fair/Trilogy Lifetime Achievement Award for International Publishing (2007). Publ.: The Goebbels Experiment; Remembering My Good Friends (auto).

Add 9 Chelsea Embankment SW3 4LE

Tel 020 7351 0042 *Fax* 020 7379 1604

Email george.weidenfeld@orionbooks.co.uk

WEIL (BREUER-WEIL), Georges,

b. Vienna, July 7, 1938; Sculptor, painter, jeweller; exhibited UK, US, Israel, Tokyo, Switzerland, South Africa etc.; portrait busts of Ben-Gurion, Churchill, General de Gaulle, etc.; Specialist in Judaica, including Bar-Ilan collection shown in Mann Auditorium, Tel Aviv; collections in British Museum, Antwerp Museum, Royal Museum of Scotland, etc.; H. Mem. Japanese Art Carvers Society.

Add 93 Ha Eshel Street, Herzlia Pituach, Israel

Email gweil@netvision.net.il

WEINBERG, Joanna, BA, PhD (London).

b. London, Nov. 11, 1949; Catherine Lewis Fel. in Rabbinics, Oxford Centre for Hebrew and Jewish Studies (2001-); James Mew Lecturer in Rabbinic Texts, University of Oxford (1999-); Reader in Rabbinics, Leo Baeck College, London (1982-2001). Publ.: Azariah de' Rossi's

Observations on the Syriac New Testament (2005); The Light of the Eyes of Azariah de' Rossi: An English translation with introduction and notes (2001).

Add The Oriental Institute, Pusey Lane, Oxford OX1 2LE

Tel 01865 288 213

Email joanna.weinberg@orinst.ox.ac.uk

WEINBERG, Sir Mark (Aubrey), BCom, Kt.

b. South Africa, Aug. 9, 1931; m. Anouska Hempel; Ch. Pension Insurance Corporation Holdings (2006-); Ch. Synergy Insurance Holdings (2005-); Pres. St James's Place Group (2004-), Ch. (1991–2004); T. Tate Gallery (1985–92); Hon. T. NSPCC (1983–91); Gov. LSE. Publ.: Weinberg and Blank on Take-overs and Mergers (1962).

Add SJP Head Office, St James's Place House, 1 Tetbury Road, Gloucester GL7 1FP

Tel 0800 0138 137

WEINER, Rabbi Chaim, BA (Hebrew University of Jerusalem), M.A. (Hebrew University of Jerusalem), Rabbinical Ordination Seminary of Judaic Studies Jerusalem (Masorti), European Masorti Bet Din. Av Bet Din.

b. Sydney, Nova Scotia, Nov. 11, 1958; m. Judy; Dir. European Masorti Bet Din (2005-); form. M. New London Synagogue (2000-05); Jerusalem Fel. (1998-2000); form. M. Edgware Masorti Synagogue (1991-98); Dir. Gesher, Masorti Teenage Centre, London (1991-96); National Dir. of Noam, Masorti Youth Movement, Israel (1987-91).

Add c/o Masorti Bet Din, 3 Shakespeare Road, London N3 1XE

Email weiner@masorti.org.uk *Website* www.masorti.org.uk

WEISMAN, Malcolm, OBE, MA (Oxon), OCM.

Barrister-at-Law; Gladstone Pupillage Awardee, Middle Temple; Hd. of Chambers Emer. 1 Grays Inn Square; Recorder, S.E. Circuit; V. Pres. Commonwealth Jewish Trust; T. International Chaplaincy, University Derby; Rel. Adv. to Small Communities; Mem. Chief Rabbi's Cabinet; Chaplain, Oxford University and new Universities; National H. Chaplain, AJEX (2000-); Special Adjudicator, Immigration Appeals (1998-); Pres. Snr. Allied Air Force Chaplains (1993-), Ch. and Sec. Gen. (1980-); Interfaith Award Peterborough (2012); Special Interfaith Award, Peterborough Interfaith Council (2011, 2013); Chaplain, London District (2009), 14 Prisons, US Bases (2010); Officiating Chaplain, Military (2009); Co-Chaplain, Basket Makers Company (2008-09); Chaplain to Mayor of Montgomery (2006-7), to Mayor of Redbridge (2005-6), to Mayor of Barnet (1994-5); US Rabbi of the Year Award (2006); Award for Outstanding Leadership, Rabbinical Council, US (2005); ICCJ Gold Medallion (2001); Chief Rabbi's Award for Excellence (1993); Patron, JNF; Patron, Davar; Snr. Jewish Chaplain to H.M. Forces; T. Jewish Music Institute; T. International Multi-Faith Centre, University Derby; Ed. Menorah; Sec. Allied Air Forces Chaplain Cttee.; Tru. Council of Christians and Jews; Ct. Lancaster, East Anglia, Kent, Warwick, Sussex and Essex Universities; Exec. United States Military Chaplains Association; form. JWB, AJEX Exec.; Jewish Youth Fund; Pres. University College Jewish Society; form. Hon. S. IUJF; form. V. Pres. Torah V'avodah Organisation; Provincial Exec. JIA; V. Pres. and Religious Adv. Commonwealth Jewish Council; Small Jewish Community Council; V. Pres. and Religious Adv. Commonwealth Jewish Council.

Add Board of Deputies, 6 Bloomsbury Square, London WC1A 2LP

Tel 020 8459 4372

Email rosalie_weisman@hotmail.com

WEISSBORT, Daniel, MA (Cantab).

b. London, Apr. 30, 1935; m. Valentina Polukhina; Prof.; Research Fel. Dept. of English, King's College, London (2001-); Fdr. Ed. (with Ted Hughes), Modern Poetry in Translation (1965-2004); H. Prof. Centre for Translation and Comparative Cultural Studies, University Warwick (2002); Emer. Prof. of English and Comparative Literature, University of Iowa (2001). Publ.: Contemporary Russian Women's Poetry (with Valentina Polukhina, 2004); From Russian with Love: A Translation Memoir of Joseph Brodsky (2003); Letters to Ted

(2003); What was all the Fuss About (2002); Selected Poems of Yehuda Amichai (2000); Selected Poems of Nikolai Zabolotsky (1999), etc.

Add 3 Powis Gardens, London NW11 8HH

WEISSER, Jacques,

b. Antwerp, Feb. 7, 1942; m. Judy née Blitz; Exec. Dir. AJEX (2007-), Gen. Sec. (1994-2007); Tru. Yad Vashem - UK Foundation (2004-); Dep. T. Zionist Federation (2004-), Ch. (2007-09), V. Ch. (2006-07); Bd. Man. Radlett US (2002-); Gen. Sec. International Council of Jewish War Veterans (1998-); Bd. Man. Wembley US (1983-2001); T. and Ch. North West London Teenage Centre (1985-94); M. and T. Jewish Lads' and Girls' Brigade.

Email Jacques@ajex.org.uk

WEITZMAN, Peter David Jacob, MA, MSc, D.Phil (Oxon), DSc (Bath), FSB, FRSC.

b. London, Sept. 22, 1935; m. Avis née Galinski; Higher Education consultant; Emer. Prof. University Wales; V. Pres. Bournemouth Hebrew Congregation (2010-12); Ch. South Wales Jewish Representative Council (1997-2003); Pres. Penylan House Jewish Retirement Home, Cardiff (1991-99); Dir. of Academic Affairs, University Wales Institute, Cardiff (1988-93); Prof. of Biochemistry, University Bath (1979-88); Ch. Bournemouth Branch, Friends Israel Sport Centre. Publ.: Scientific writings.

Add 28 Albany, Manor Road, Bournemouth BH1 3EN

Email pdjw@btinternet.com

WESKER, Sir Arnold, Kt., FRSL, D.Litt (H. UEA), DHL (Denison University), H. Fel. Queen Mary & Westfield College London, Fel. Award, Royal Central School of Speech and Drama FCSSD.

b. London, May 24, 1932, m. Dusty Bicker; CoP, International Playwrights Cttee. (1980-83); Ch. British Section, International Theatre Institute (1978-83); Dir. Centre 42 (1960-70). Among recent work - Plays: Amazed and Surprised (2006); Longitude (2002); The Kitchen Musical (2000); Break, My Heart (1997); Denial (1997); Circles of Perception (1996); Circles of Perception (1996); Bluey (1993); The Confession (1993); Wild Spring (1992); Blood Libel (1991); Men Die Women Survive (1990); Letter to a Daughter (1990). Books: Fiction - Honey (2005); The King's Daughters (1998); Non-Fiction - The Birth of Shylock and the Death of Zero Mostel (1997); As Much As I Dare (autobiography) (1994). Film scripts: Letter to Myself (2003); Maudie (1995); Homage to Catalonia (1990). Television: Barabbas (2000); Menace (1961). Radio: Groupie (2001) (later adapted for stage). Libretto: Grief (2008). Collections: Wesker's Comedies (2012); Wesker's Historical Plays (2012); Wesker's Domestic Plays (2012); Joy and Tyrany (2011); Wesker's Political Plays (2010); Wesker's Social Plays (2009) (including Rocking Horse (BBC World Service 75th Anniversary Commission, 2007)); All Things Tire of Themselves (poems) (2008); Wesker's Love Plays (2008); Wesker's Monologues (2008).

Add 14 Champions Row, Wilbury Avenue, Hove BN3 6AZ

Tel 01273 734 013

Email wesker@compuserve.com *Website* www.arnoldwesker.com

WHINE, Michael David, MBE, BA (Hons), FCIM.

b. London, Apr. 4, 1947; m. Ester née Kamenetzky; Dir. Government and Intl. Affairs, Community Security Trust; UK Mem. European Commission against Racism and Intolerance (2013-); form. Consultant, Defence and Security, European Jewish Congress; Dir. Defence and Group Relations Division, Board of Deputies (1986-2012); Hate Crime Independent Advisors Group, Ministry of Justice (2007-); London CPS Hate Crime Scrutiny Panel (2012-); Adv. Counter Terrorism Div. CPS (2009-12); Metropolitan Police Authority, Hate Crime Forum (2003-12). Publ.: Trans-European Trends in Right-Wing Extremism (2012); Terrorism Against Jewish Communities and Israeli Institution Abroad (2011); The Radicalization of Diasporas and Terrorism (2009); The Homegrown Terrorist Threat in Europe (2008); An Unholy Alliance: Nazi Links with Arab Totalitarianism (2006); Holocaust Denial in the UK (2006); Islamism and Totalitarianism: Similarities and Differences (2001).

Add P.O. Box 35501, London NW4 2FZ

Tel 020 8457 9960

Email mike.w@thecst.org.uk *Website* www.thecst.org.uk

WHITESON, Adrian Leon, OBE, MBBS (Hons.), MRCS, LRCP.

b. London, Dec. 12, 1934; m. Myrna; Med. Practitioner; V. Pres. of the British Paralympic Association; form. Ch. World Boxing Council and European Boxing Union Med. Commission; form. Chief Med. Off. British Boxing Bd. of Control; Pres. (form. Ch.), The Teenage Cancer Trust; Mem. Govt. Review Body for Sport for People with Disabilities.

Add 2 Welbeck Mansions, 35a Wellbeck Street, London W1G 8EZ

Tel 020 7842 5789

WIESEL, Elie, D.Lett (hc), D.Hum.Lett (hc), D.Hebrew.Lett. (hc), PhD (hc), DL (hc), etc.

b. Sighet, Romania, Sept. 30, 1928; m. Marion; Survivor of Auschwitz and Buchenwald; Fdr. Elie Wiesel Foundation for Humanity; Andrew W. Mellon Prof. in the Humanities, Boston University; Bd. Dirs. International Rescue Cttee. Grand-Croix, Legion of Honour; International Peace Prize Royal Belgian Acad.; Presidential Medal of Freedom (1992); Nobel Peace Prize (1986); US Congress Gold Medal (1986); Ch. US Holocaust Memorial Council (1980-86); Ch. US Pres. Com. on Holocaust (1979-80); District Prof. Judaic Studies, City University, N.Y. (1972-76). Among recent publications: The Sonderberg Case (2010); A Mad Desire to Dance (2009); Confronting Antisemitism: essays (with Kofi Annan 2006); Night (new translation 2006); Time of the Uprooted (2005); Wise Men and Their Tales (2003); Memoirs: All Rivers Run to the Sea; Vol. II: And the Sea is Never Full (1999); From the Kingdom of Memory; Reminiscences; The Forgotten, etc.

Add Boston University, 147 Bay State Road, Boston, MA 02215 USA

WINEMAN, Vivian, MA (Cantab).

b. London, Feb. 14, 1950; m. Naomi Helen née Greenberg; Solicitor; Consultant, DWFM Beckham (2010-); Ch. JLC (2009-); Pres. Board of Deputies (2009-), Snr. V. Pres. (2006-09); V. Pres. European Jewish Congress (2009-); Advisory Bd. Three Faiths Forum (2007-); V. Ch. UK Inter Faith Network (2007-); H. Legal Counsel High Premium LLoyd's of London Group (2004-); Ch. Defence and Group Relations Div. (2006-09); Partner, David Wineman (1981-2008); Ch. New Israel Fund (1992-94). Publ.: Contracts (Rights of Third Parties) Act, 1999 (2001).

Add 76 Meadway, London NW11 6QH

WINER, Rabbi Dr Mark L, PhD, DD.

b. Logan, Utah, Dec. 12, 1942; m. Suellen née Mark; V. Ch. WUPJ (2005-); Ch. International Interfaith Task Force (1998-); Snr. Rabbi, West London Synagogue (1998-2010); Chaplain to Lord Mayor of Westminster (2008-09, 2000-01); Pres. National Council of Synagogues (USA) (1995-98); Mem. International Jewish Cttee. for Interreligious Consultations (1987-98); V. Pres. Synagogue Council of America (1993-94). Publ.: articles in Manna, European Judaism, etc.

Add West London Synagogue, 33 Seymour Place, London W1H 5AU

Tel 020 7723 4404 *Fax* 020 7224 8258

Email rabbi@wls.org.uk

WINNICK, David, MP.

b. Brighton, June 26, 1933; Mem. Home Affairs Cttee. (2005-); MP (Lab.), for Walsall North (1979-), Croydon South (1966-70).

Add House of Commons, London SW1A 0AA

Tel 020 7219 5003 *Fax* 020 7219 0257

Email winnickd@parliament.uk

WINSTON, Clive Noel, BA (Cantab).

b. London, Apr. 20, 1925; m. Beatrice Jeannette née Lawton; V. Pres. (form. Ch.) LJ; form. T. European Bd. of WUPJ; form. Dep. Solicitor, Metropolitan Police.

Add 2 Bournwell Close, Cockfosters, Hertfordshire EN4 0JX

Tel 020 8449 5963

WINSTON, Robert Maurice Lipson, Baron of Hammersmith, FMed Sci, Hon. FREng, FRCSE, DSc, FRCP, FRCOG.

b. London, July 15, 1940; Prof. Science and Society and Emer. Prof. Fertility Studies, Imperial College London; Ch. Royal College of Music (2007-); Consultant Obstetrician and Gynaecologist, Hammersmith Hospital, London (-2003); Chancellor, Sheffield Hallam University (2001-); Ch. Science and Technology Select Cttee. House of Lords (1999-); Dean, Institute of Obstetrics and Gynaecology (1995-); Chief Rabbi's Open Award for Contribution to Society (1993); Prof. of Gynaecology, Texas University (1980-81); Vis. Prof. Leuven University, Belgium (1976-77). Publ.: Reversibility of Female Sterilization; Tubal Infertility; Infertility: a Sympathetic Approach; Scientific writings on aspects of reproduction; The Story of God (2005).

Add House of Lords, London SW1A 0PW

Email r.winston@imperial.ac.uk *Website* www.robertwinston.org

WISEMAN, Debbie, MBE, H. Fel. Trinity College of Music and Guildhall School of Music and Drama.

b. London, May 10, 1963. Currently one of the busiest composers and conductors in the UK; Commissioned to compose a movement of new 'Water Music' for The Queen's Diamond Jubilee Pageant (June 2012). Scores: A Poet in New York, The Whale, Father Brown; Lost Christmas; The Passion; Jekyll; Flood; Stephen Fry in America; Judge John Deed; Joanna Lumley's Nile; Tom and Viv; Freeze Frame; The Guilty; Land Girls; Before You Go; Othello; Arsene Lupin; He Knew He Was Right; Michael Palin's New Europe; Sherlock Holmes and the Baker Street Irregulars; My Uncle Silas; Tom's Midnight Garden; Wilde; WPC 56; and many more.

Tel Roz Colls Music Matters Intl. 020 8979 4580

Email wisemaninfo@aol.com *Website* www.debbiewiseman.co.uk

WISTRICH, Robert Solomon, BA, MA (Cantab, 1970), PhD (London, 1974).

b. Lenger (USSR), Apr. 7, 1945; University Professor; First Holder of the Jewish Chronicle Ch. in Jewish Studies, University College, London; Dir. Vidal Sassoon International Centre for the Study of Antisemitism (2002-); Neuberger Ch. of Modern Jewish History, Hebrew University of Jerusalem (1985-). Awards: Journal for Antisemitism Lifetime Achievement (2011); Austrian State Prize for Danubian History (1992); H.H. Wingate/Jewish Quarterly Prize for Non-Fiction (1992); James Parkes Prize (1984). Among recent publications: From Ambivalence to Betrayal: The Left, The Jews and Israel (2012); A Lethal Obsession: Antisemitism from Antiquity to the Global Jihad (2010); Laboratory of World Destruction: Germans and Jews in Central Europe (2007); Obsession: Radical Islamic War Against the West (film, 2006); Blaming the Jews (film, 2003); Nietzsche: Godfather of Fascism (2002); Hitler and the Holocaust (2001); Demonizing the Other: Antisemitism, Racism and Xenophobia (1999).

Add Aliyat Hanoar Street 6/3, Ramot Alon Jerusalem, Israel

Email sicsa@mail.huji.ac.il *Website* http://sicsa.huji.ac.il

WITTENBERG, Rabbi Jonathan, MA, PGCE.

b. Glasgow, Sept. 17, 1957; m. Nicola Solomon; Snr. Rabbi, Masorti Judaism UK (2008-); Rabbi, New North London Masorti Synagogue (1987-). Publ.: Walking with the Light: From Frankfurt to Finchley (2013); The Silence of Dark Water: An Inner Journey (2008); The Eternal Journey: Meditations on the Jewish Year (2001); A Pesach Companion (Ed. and co-author, 1997); The Laws of Life: A Guide to Traditional Jewish Practice in Times of Bereavement (1997); A High Holyday Companion (Ed. and co-author, 1996); The Three Pillars of Judaism: A Search for Faith and Values (1996).

Add 10 Amberden Avenue, London N3 3BJ

Tel 020 8343 3927 *Fax* 020 8346 1914

Email rabbi@nnls-masorti.org.uk

WOLFE, Joy Sylvia (née Gillman), MBE JP.

b. London, Jan. 4, 1938; m. Brian Wolfe; retired PR Consultant, Journalist and Newspaper

Editor; Ch. Manchester Balfour Trust (2008-); Ch. StandWithUs UK (2006-); Gov. North Cheshire Jewish Primary School (1984-); Life Pres. Manchester Zionist Central Council (2001); Life Pres. Manchester Wizo (1997); V. Ch. Langdon College Governors; UK Ch. Friends of Meir and Bracha Victims of Terror Support Centre, Jerusalem; V. Pres, Zionist Federation.

Add 24 Marchbank Drive, Cheadle, Cheshire SK8 1QY

Tel 0161 491 1350/ 07876 192 414

Email joywol@gmail.com

WOLFF, David,

Ch. JC Maccabi (Southern) Football League (1970-); V. Pres. London FA (1970-); V. Pres. MaccabiGB.

Add 36 Poplar Way, Barkingside, Essex IG6 1EN

Tel 020 8551 2384

Email dawolff@gotadsl.co.uk

WOLFSON, Dianna (née Sherry), BA, DCE.

b. Birmingham, June 29, 1938; Hd. (retd.); Mem. Scottish Inter Faith Council (2004-); H. Pres. Glasgow Jewish Representative Council (2001-), Pres. (1998-2001); Hd. Calderwood Lodge Jewish Primary School (1976-98); Ch. West of Scotland Council of Christians and Jews (1992-95).

Add 22 Park Court, Giffnock, Glasgow G46 7PB

Tel 0141 620 0650

Email d.wolfson@tinyworld.co.uk

WOOLF, Lord Harry, PC, LLB, H. FBA, DLL (H.).

b. Newcastle upon Tyne, May 2, 1933; m. Marguerite née Sassoon; UCL Laws 1954; Fellow 1981; Ch. UCL Council (2005–08); called to the Bar (1955); Judge 1979; Law Lord (1992); Master of the Rolls (1996–2000); Lord Chief Justice of England and Wales (2000–05); President of the Courts of England and Wales; Chancellor, Open University of Israel (2004-13); Ch. Bank of England Financial Markets Law Cttee. (2006-09); Ch. Judging Panel, annual FIRST Magazine Responsible Capitalism Awards; Patron, The Woolf Institute; Mem. Blackstone Chambers, accredited mediator and Chartered Arbitrator (Cairn); Ch. Prison Reform Trust (2011-); non-permanent judge, Court of Final Appeal of Hong Kong (2003-12); First Pres. Qatar Financial Centre Civil and Commercial Court (2006-12); Mem. Select Cttee. on Inquiries Act (2005); Mem. Crossbench Peers (1992); served on House of Lords Constitution Cttee; Ch. Sub-Cttee. Members' Interests; Patron, Rehabilitation for Addicted Prisoners Trust; form. Ch. Institute of Advanced Legal Studies; Ch. network of the Presidents of the Supreme Judicial Courts of the EU Working Group on mediation and the Financial Markets Law Cttee; produced The Woolf Reforms (1999), Strangeways Report into the British Prison System (1990), Access to Justice report (1996); The Woolf Committee, produced report, Ethical Business Conduct in BAE Systems plc: the way forward (2008). Ch. independent inquiry into the LSE's relationship with Libya and with Saif Gaddafi (published 2011); Lifetime Achievement Award by the IAM (International Academy of Mediators) (2009); Hon. Degrees from twelve universities; Hon Fel. British Academy, the Academy of Medical Sciences, The Royal Society of Medicine, (2012), of UCL and the US College of Trial Lawyers and is an Hon Member of the American Law Institute. Among recent publications: various editions (jointly) of De Smith's Judicial Review of Administration (7th edition); An Independent Governance Review of the International Cricket Council (2012); The Pursuit of Justice (2008).

Add House of Lords, London SW1A 0PW

WOOLFSON, Michael Mark, MA, PhD, DSc, FRS, FRAS, FInstP.

b. London, Jan. 9, 1927; Emer. Prof. Theoretical Physics, York University; form. Reader in Physics, Manchester Institute of Science and Technology. Publ.: Direct Methods in Crystallography; An Introduction to X-ray Crystallography; The Origin of the Solar System; Physical and Non-physical Methods of Solving Crystal Structures; An Introduction to Computer Simulation; The Origin and Evolution of the Solar System; Planetary Science;

Mathematics for Physics; The Formation of the Solar System; Everyday Probability and Statistics; Time, Space, Stars and Man; Materials, Matter and Particles; On the Origin of Planets; The Fundamentals of Imaging.
Add Physics Dept., University of York, York YO10 5DD
Tel 01904 432 230
Email mmw1@york.ac.uk

WOUK, Herman, BA, Columbia University, 1934; LHD (H.), Yeshiva University; LLD (H.), Clark University; DLitt (H.), American International College; PhD (H.), Bar-Ilan University, Hebrew University; DLitt (H.) Trinity College; DLitt George Washington University.
b. New York, May 27, 1915; Writer. Publ.: Non-fiction: This is My God; The Will to Live On; The Language God Talks. Novels: Aurora Dawn; Marjorie Morningstar; The Winds of War; War and Remembrance; Youngblood Hawke; Don't Stop the Carnival; The Caine Mutiny; Inside, Outside; City Boy; The Hope, The Glory; A Hole in Texas; The Lawgiver. Plays: The Caine Mutiny Court-Martial, etc. TV Screenplays: The Winds of War, War and Remembrance.
Add c/o B.S.W. Literary Agency, 303 Crestview Drive, Palm Springs CA 92264 USA
Website www.hermanwouk.com

WRIGHT, Rabbi Alexandra (née Levitt), MA, PGCE.
b. London, Dec. 10, 1956; Snr. Rabbi, The Liberal Jewish Synagogue (Associate M. 1986-9); Jewish Chaplain, North London Hospice (1997-2005); M, Radlett and Bushey Reform Synagogue (1990-2003); Lecturer in Classical Hebrew, Leo Baeck College (1987-97). Publ.: 'An approach to feminist theology' in Hear Our Voice (1994); 'Judaism' in Women in Religion (1994).
Add Liberal Jewish Synagogue, 28 St John's Wood Road, London NW8 7HA
Email a.wright@ljs.org *Website* www.ljs.org

WRIGHT, Rosalind (née Kerstein), CB, QC (Hon Causa), LLB (Hons) (London).
b. London, Nov. 2, 1942; m. Dr David J. M. Wright; Barrister; Mem. Regulatory Bd. ACCA (2012-); Mem. Cttee. UKAJLJ (2012-); Complaints Com. London Metal Exchange (2010-); form. Non-Exec. Dir. Insolvency Service Steering Bd. (2006-11); Mem. Supervisory Cttee. of OLAF (European anti-Fraud Office) (2005-12); Ch, Fraud Adv. Panel (2003-); Tru. Jewish Association for Business Ethics (2002); Non-Exec. Dir. DTI Legal Services Group (2001-09); Non-Exec. Dir. Office of Fair Trading (2003-07); Dir. Serious Fraud Office (1997-2003); Hd. Prosecutions, Exec. Dir. Securities and Futures Authority (1987-97); Assistant Dir. Hd. of Fraud Investigation Group, DPP (1985-87).
Add Fraud Advisory Panel, P.O. Box 433, Chartered accountants Hall, Moorgate Place, London EC2R 6EA
Tel 020 7920 8721
Email info@fraudadvisorypanel.org *Website* www.fraudadvisorypanel.org

YENTOB, Robert,
Delegate Ch. Spanish and Portuguese Jews' Congregation; Mem. Jewish Leadership Council; T. Maimonides Foundation.
Add 6 Bloomsbury Square, London WC1A 2LP

YOUNG, Rt. Hon. David Ivor, Baron of Graffham, PC, LLB (Hons.).
b. London, Feb. 27, 1932; Solicitor; Dir. Salomon Inc. (1990-); Exec. Ch. Cable and Wireless plc (1990-); Pres. Jewish Care (1990-); Ch. Oxford Centre for Hebrew and Jewish Studies (1989-92); Dep. Ch. Conservative Party (1989-90); Sec. of State for Trade and Industry (1987-9); Ch. National Economic Development Organisation (1982-9); Sec. of State for Employment (1985-7); Min. without Portfolio, Min. in Cabinet (1984-5); Ch. Manpower Services Com. (1982-4); Ch. Admin. Cttee. World ORT Union (1980-4); Ch. International Council, Jewish Social and Welfare Services (1982-83); Dir. Centre for Policy Studies (1979-82); Gov. Oxford Centre for Post-Graduate Heb. Studies; Pres. Chai Cancer Care; T. Coexistence Trust; Ch. Jewish Museum, London; form. Pres. British ORT. Publ.: The Enterprise Years: A Businessman in the Cabinet (1990).
Add Young Associates, Harcourt House, 19 Cavendish Square, London W1G 0PL

ZALUD, Rabbi Norman, APhS, FRSA.

b. Liverpool, Oct. 5, 1932; Rabbi Emer. Liverpool Reform Synagogue; M. Sha'arei Shalom Synagogue, Manchester; M. Blackpool Reform Jewish Congregation; Jewish Chaplain to H.M. Prisons.

Add Blackpool Reform Jewish Congregation, Raikes Parade, Blackpool FY1 4EX

Tel 01253 623 687

ZARUM, Rabbi Dr Raphael E.S., BSc, MA, PhD.

b. London, Nov. 22, 1968; m. Jacqueline Nicholls; Educator; Dean, London School of Jewish Studies. Publ.: Torah L'Am; The Jampacked Bible.

Add c/o LSJS, Wohl Campus for Jewish Education, Schaller House, 44a Albert Road, London NW4 2SJ

Tel 020 8203 6427 *Fax* 020 8203 6420

Email info@lsjs.ac.uk *Website* www.lsjs.ac.uk

Twitter @SuperSedra

ZEIDMAN, His Honour Judge Martyn, QC, LLB.

b. Cardiff May 30, 1952; m. Verity née Owen; Circuit Judge (2001-); Pres. Mental Health Tribunal (1999-); Ch. Jewish Marriage Council (2004); Recorder (1995). Publ.: Making Sense of the Leasehold Reform Housing and Urban Development Act 1993 (1994); A Short Guide to the Road Traffic Act 1991 (1991); A Short Guide to the Courts and Legal Services Act 1990 (1990); Steps to Possession (1989); A Short Guide to the Housing Act 1988 (1988); A Short guide to the Landlord and Tenant Act 1987 (1987).

Add The Crown Court at Snaresbrook, The Court House, Hollybush Hill, London E11 1QW

Tel 020 8530 0000 *Fax* 020 8530 0073

ZELLICK, Graham John, CBE, QC (Hon), MA, PhD (Cantab), H. LHD (NYU), FAcSS, H. LLD (Richmond, Birm), H. FSALS, Hon.FRAM H. FBS, H. DLit (London, QM).

b. London, Aug. 12, 1948; Barrister; Mem. Investigatory Powers Tribunal (2013-); Pres. Valuation Tribunal for England (2009-); Ch. Senate, West London Synagogue (2006-); H. Prof. of Law, University Birmingham (2004-11); Hon. Fel. Gonville and Caius College, Cambridge (2001-); Emer. Prof. of Law, University of London (1998-), Prof. (1982-98); Master, Drapers' Company (2009-10); Gov. Tel Aviv University (2000-9); Ch. Criminal Cases Review Commission (2003-08); H. Fel. Leo Baeck College (2007), Ch. Bd. Gov. (2005-06); Pres. West London Synagogue (2000-06); Electoral Commissioner (2001-04); V. Chancellor and Pres. University London (1997-2003), Dep. V. Chancellor (1994-97); V. Ch. National Adv. Council, Academic Study Group for Israel and The Middle East. (1995-2003); Master of the Bench, Middle Temple (2001, Reader 2013); Principal, Queen Mary and Westfield College, University of London (1991-98); Freeman, City of London.

Add 63 Hampstead Way, London NW11 7DN

Tel 020 7426 3916 (office) *Fax* 020 7247 6598

Email graham.zellick@gmail.com

ZERMANSKY, Victor David, LLB (H.).

b. Leeds, Dec. 28, 1931, m. Anita née Levison; Solicitor; Past Pres. Leeds Law Society (1988-9); form. Immigration Appeals Adjudicator (1970-8); H. Life. V. Pres. (Pres. 1974-7), Leeds Jewish Rep. Council; form. Assistant Recorder; Life Pres. Leeds Z.C.; form. Ch. Leeds Kashrut Authority, Beth Din Admin. Cttee.

Add 52 Alwoodley Lane, Leeds LS17 7PT

Tel 0113 267 3523 *Fax* 0113 267 3523

Email victor.zermansky@virgin.net

ZIFF, MICHAEL,

Ch. Maccabi GB.

Add Shield House, Harmony Way, London NW4 2BZ

ZIMMELS, Erla (née Broekema), Dip.Lib.

b. Amsterdam, Aug. 16, 1947; m. Judge Martin Zimmels; Librarian, London School of Jewish Studies (1999-); Librarian, Jews' College, London (1974-76); Librarian, Ets Haim

Library, Sephardi Community, Amsterdam (1969-73); Librarian, Bibliotheca Rosenthaliana, Amsterdam (1968-73).

Add London School of Jewish Studies, Schaller House, Wohl Campus for Jewish Education, 44a Albert Road, London NW4 2ST

Tel 020 8203 6427 *Fax* 020 8203 6420

Email erla.zimmels@lsjs.ac.uk

ZIMMERMAN, Stephen, BA.

Ch. Jewish Care (2006-11); Ch. NewSmith Asset Management (2003-); Ch. Royal Marsden Hospital Cancer Campaign (2001-03); V. Pres. Merrill Lynch and Co. Inc. and Mem. Executive Management Cttee. (1997-2001); Dep. Ch. Mercury Asset Management Group (1995-97); Fund Manager, SG Warburg (1971-95); Mem. Jewish Leadership Council; Chief Operating Officer, Merrill Lynch Investment Managers.

Add 6 Bloomsbury Square, London WC1A 2LP

ZISSMAN, Sir Bernard Philip, H. LLD (B'ham), H. D. (BCU).

b. Birmingham, Dec. 11, 1934; Ch. Millennium Point Trust (2006-13); Pres. Representative Council of Birmingham and Midland Jewry (2005-); T. City of Birmingham Symphony Orchestra (1992-); Pres. Council Birmingham Hebrew Congregation (1999-2004); Ch. Good Hope Hospital NHS Trust (1998-2003); Dir. BRMB radio station (1995-2000); Leader, Conservative Group, Birmingham City Council (1992-5); Mem. Birmingham City Council (1965-95); Ch. Alexandra Theatre (Birmingham) Ltd (1986-93); Freeman of the City of London (1991); Lord Mayor, City of Birmingham (1990-1); Ch. Cttee. to establish Birmingham International Convention Centre/Symphony Hall (1982-6); Council Mem. Birmingham, Chamber of Commerce and Industry; Mem. Appeal Council National Memorial Arboretum; Tru. Birmingham Jewish Community Care; Marie Curie Hospice Development Appeal. Publ.: Herzl's Journey (2008); Knight out with Chamberlain (2002).

Add 4 Petersham Place, Richmond Hill Road, Birmingham B15 3RY

Tel 0121 454 1751 *Fax* 0121 454 1751

Email sirbernardz@aol.com *Website* www.bernardzissman.com

ZNEIMER, Rabbi Saul, MA (Oxon), DipPFS.

b. Wokingham, Berkshire, Oct. 12, 1960; m. Elizabeth née Colman; Consultant, HBFS Wealth Management (2011-); Hd. of Business Dev. at Bank Hapoalim UK (2008-11); Chief Operating Officer, Lyons Presentations Group (2007-08); Chief Executive of the US (2001-07); Dir. Jewish Outreach Network (1999-2001); Rabbi, Kenton US (1994-2000); Rabbinic Liaison Officer, Office of the Chief Rabbi (1993-94); Dir. Informal Education, US Bd. of Religious Education (1992); Dir. of Youth Programme, Yakar (1984-86); form. Mem. Chief Rabbi's Cabinet.

Add HBFS Financial Services Ltd, 3 Theobald Court, Theobald Street, Borehamwood, Herts WD6 4RN

Email saul@hbfs.co.uk *Website* www.hbfs.co.uk

ZUCKER, Kenneth Harry, MA, QC.

b. London, Mar. 1935; m. Ruth Erica née Brudno; Retired; Circuit Judge (1989-2005); Recorder (1981-89).

Add 60 Gurney Drive, London N2 0DE

Email kenneth.zucker@btinternet.com

Dannie Abse, Although best known as a poet, he worked in the medical field, and was a specialist at a chest clinic for over thirty years. He received numerous literary awards and fellowships for his writing. At 91.

Lauren Bacall, Actress who appeared in dozens of films over the course of her career spanning six decades. Previously married to Humphrey Bogart. At 89.

Helen Bamber, Founder of the Medical Foundation for the Care of Victims of Torture. At 89.

Philip Berg, Founder of the Kabbalah Centre, which brought celebrities including Madonna to the mystical practice. At 84.

Sid Caesar, Great comedian who changed the face of television with his sketch classics including, 'Your Show of Shows'. At 91.

Manny Carter, Former Financial adviser to the Chief Rabbinate. At 89.

Anna Craft, Open University professor. At 52.

Felix Dennis, Publisher. At 67.

Cecil Franks, Manchester solicitor who captured the Labour stronghold of Barrow and Furness for the Conservatives in 1983. At 78.

Charles Gordon, Innovative financier who met serial reversals of fortune, whose boldest venture was Spey Investments. At 87.

Sybil Greenstein, Westcliff stalwart. At 66.

Sir Ronald Grierson, A banker and public servant who served with the wartime SAS and became an international networker par excellence. At 93.

Abraham Guz, An authority on respiratory sensation who developed one of the first ECG monitoring units. At 84.

Morris Hoffman, Served as FZY movement's education officer during a period when he also worked as a code-breaker at Bletchley Park, helping the British war effort, pinpointing the location of Nazi troops. At 98.

Ruth Hoffman, Specialised in child psychiatry, working closely with Jungian figures, corresponding with Primo Levi, and worked in several hospitals before turning to child guidance clinics. At 91.

John Ingram, Fashion style setter. Menswear designer whose refined tailoring made his clothes and shops a favourite of 1960s mods. At 83.

Lord Anthony Jacobs, Successful businessman who brought BSM driving schools and Spudulike restaurants to streets in Britain. Famous for his entrepreneurial flair combined with a political career that earned him a knighthood and a peerage. At 82.

Dan Jacobson, South African-born writer, novelist and critic who became a professor at University College London. At 85.

Elsbeth Juda, Fashion photographer who captured the drama of Fifties fashions and the twilight of Winston Churchill. At 103.

Monika Kinley, Dealer, collector and curator, championing in particular the cause of outsider artists – the self-taught and self-motivated who were not part of the mainstream. At 88.

Maria Lidka, Violinist, who took part in many National Gallery concerts, played with the London String Trio, and at the peak of her career, participated in two Proms in the 1950's. At 99.

Phil Michaels, A passionate environmental lawyer who, as head of the legal department of Friends of the Earth, made a deep impact on the way environmental law and freedom of information was utilise. At 42.

Baroness Doreen Miller, Women's rights activist. founded the International Beauty Club, offering mail-order cosmetics to the woman of the 1970s, attracting 750,000 subscribers. At 81.

Conrad Morris, Philanthropist. An investor in SodaStream and Israeli newspaper Makor Rishon, he sat on the boards of numerous charitable organizations and donated funds to Jewish schools both in Britain and Israel. At 82.

Monty Moss, Fourth-generation chairman of Moss Bros, the menswear and formal wear chain, and a strict arbiter of sartorial correctness. At 90.

Abraham Nemeth, Inventor of the Nemeth Braille Code, enabling blind people to study complex mathematics. At 94.

Wally Olins, Branding and corporate identity expert who masterminded the public face of corporate giants such as BT, Volkswagen and Renault. At 83.

Rachel Pinter, Headmistress. At 67.

Dame Julia Polak, Pathologist who did pioneering work in histochemistry and later led research into using stem-cell technology to produce artificial organs for implantation. At 75.

Sigbert Prais, Professor who was a refugee from Nazi Germany. He campaigned to raise standards of maths teaching in British schools. At 85.

Joan Rivers, Comedian known best for her cutting wit and scathing assessment of her peers, as well as her staunch support of Israel. At 81.

Henry Rollin, Enlightened psychiatrist and champion of Britain's asylums, which he helped transform from custodial institutions to therapeutic hospitals. At 102.

Harold Rose, Leeds Education guru. At 99.

Joyce Rose, Observant Jew and Chair of Magistrates Association as well as Chair of Women's Liberal Association. Involved heavily in work for many charities. At 84.

Mary, Duchess of Roxburghe, The daughter of a marquess who resisted an attempt by her husband to evict her from his 100-room ducal seat. At 99.

Merton Sandler, A pioneer in the field of psychopharmacology, the study of the effects of chemicals in the brain on mood, sensation and thought. At 88.

David Saville, Law teacher. At 72.

Sir Nicholas Scheele, A businessman who rose through the ranks of the Ford organisation and restored Jaguar as an icon of design. At 70.

Stephen Sebag-Montefiore, Distinguished Harley Street doctor, he started his own private general practice in Kensington where he gained a formidable reputation among his patients from all walks of life. At 87.

Philippa Seligman, Founding member of British Union of Social Workers. Renowned family therapist and supporter of the arts in Wales. At 85.

Ariel Sharon, Israeli politician and general, who served as the 11th Prime Minister of Israel 2001-06. At 85.

Michael Sherbourne, Hagana volunteer in the War of Independence and veteran activist on behalf of Soviet Jewry. At 97.

Cheryl Shilkin, Former CBF Executive Director. At. 69.

Robert Steiner, Professor and radiologist whose MRI breakthrough changed modern medical imaging. At 95.

Lady Hazel Sternberg, Humanitarian. Wife of Sir Sigmund Sternberg. The first Jewish woman to be appointed to the Papal Order of St Sylvester and also received the Order of St Francis. At 86.

Nachman Sudak, As Head Shliach and Principal, Sudak oversaw the growth of Chabad Lubavitch UK into a national organisation with 14 schools, 25 community houses and 11 campus houses. At 78.

Professor Gerald 'Charlie' Westbury, Was a surgeon who pioneered new procedures to remove cancers which offered hope of a return to normal life. At 86.

Camille Wolff, one of Britain's pre-eminent book dealers, from her home, in the literature of true crime. At 102.

EVENTS IN 2015

As Jews we commemorate our defeats - Yom Kippur and Tisha b'Av - as we celebrate our victories - Chanukkah and Purim. The list below marks major anniversaries and some which have been overlooked in years gone by. To all those who still carry on the traditions of their founders, we offer our congratulations and hope you will enjoy many more years of success.

Anniversaries

1275th	Archbishop of York prohibitys Christians associating with Jews on Jewish festivals.
995th	King Canute banishes the Jews from England.
945th	William the Conqueror brings Jews from Rouen
940th	Settlement of Jews in Oxford.
925th	Attacks on Jews in Eastern Counties.
880th	Birth of Rabbi Moses Maimonides.
825th	Massacre of Jews in Cliffords Tower, York.
790th	Jews of Norwich accused of ritual murder.
760th	Jews of Lincoln accused of ritual murder.
745th	Rabbis authorised to excommunicate Jews who would not contribute to the repair of their cemeteries.
740th	Statute of Jewry enacted.
735th	Jews compelled to attend conversionist services.
725th	Jews banished from England.
705th	Mission of Jews to England to petition for readmission.
360th	Menassah ben Israel comes to London.
360th	Whitehall Conference.
355th	Thomas Violet petitions King Charles II and Parliament for the expulsion of the Jews and the confiscation of their property.
355th	Establishment of first Sephardi synagogue.
330th	Legal recognition of Jewish resettlement by King James II.
290th	Foundation of Hambro Synagogue.
275th	Act of Parliament conferring citizenship on Jewish residents of American colonies.
270th	Initiation Society formed (Mohelim).
255th	Foundation of the Board of Deputies.
255th	New Synagogue in London.
250th	David Tevele Schiff made Chief Rabbi.
235th	Portsmouth Synagogue.
235th	Meshivath Nephesh, first Ashkenazi charity.
235th	Hull Synagogue.
235th	Jews settle in Manchester.
235th	Swansea Hebrew Congregation.
235th	Liverpool Old Hebrew Congregation.
230th	Original Brighton synagogue.
220th	Jews Hospital founded.
210th	First compact between three London synagogues.

185th	First Jewish Literary Society.
180th	Sir David Saloman elected Alderman for Aldgate Ward, City of London.
180th	Jacob Montefiore appointed Commissioner for the colonies of South Australia.
175th	First misson of Sir Moses Montefiore to Damascus to prevent persecution.
175th	West London Synagogue of British Jews.
170th	Act to relieve Jews elected to municipal office from taking Christian oath.
165th	Wolverhampton Synagogue.
160th	Singers Hill Synagogue, Birmingham.
160th	Opening of Jews College.
155th	Oath Act passed to enable Jews not to swear on Christian oath when elected to parliament.
155th	First Leeds synagogue.
150th	Alderman Benjamin Phillips elected Lord Mayor of London.
150th	Belfast Hebrew Congregation.
150th	Holy Law, South Broughton Hebrew Congregation.
145th	Foundation of United Synagogue.
145th	Opening of Central Synagogue.
145th	Act to allow Orthodox Jews to work on Sundays.
145th	Sir George Jessel, first Jewish cabinet minister as Solicitor General.
140th	Garnethill Synagogue, Glasgow.
140th	South Shields Hebrew Congregation.
135th	Bradford Synagogue.
135th	ORT.
130th	Dalston Synagogue.
130th	Jews Temparary Shelter.
130th	Death of Sir Moses Montefiore.
130th	Lord Rothschild ennobled as first Jewish peer.
125th	Death of Chief Rabbi Nathan Marcus Adler.
125th	Nottingham Synagogue.
125th	Hammersmith Synagogue.
125th	Sunderland Beth Hamedresh.
125th	Public meeting at Guildhall to protest Russian persecution of the Jews.
120th	Jewish Lads Brigade.
115th	B'Nai Brith.
115th	Barrow in Furness Synagogue.
115th	Notting Hill Federation Synagogue.
110th	Aliens Act passed.
110th	Bournemouth Hebrew Congregation.
110th	Llandudno & Colwyn Bay Synagogue.
105th	Liberal Synagogue.
105th	Herbert Samuel appointed Postmaster General.
105th	Edwin Montagu made Secretary of State for India.
105th	Rufus Isaacs made Attorney General.
105th	Jewish Women's Voluntary Aid Detachment.
105th	Samuel Lewis Convalescent Home at Walton-on-the-Naze.
105th	Jewish Religious Education Board.

100th	First Jewish Chaplain to the Forces - Rev. Michael Adler.
100th	Lieutenant Frank de Pass, first Jewish VC.
100th	Acting Corporal Issy Smith awarded VC.
100th	Private Leonard Kaysor awarded VC.
100th	Stamford Hill Synagogue dedication.
100th	Foundation stone laid for new Western Synagogue.
100th	Consecration of Margate Synagogue.
95th	Combined Charities Committee.
95th	Kashrut Commission.
95th	WIZO.
80th	Adath Yisroel Synagogue, Manchester.
80th	Childwall Synagogue, Liverpool.
80th	Edgware Reform Synagogue.
80th	Federation of Zionist Youth.
80th	Sinai Federation Synagogue.
80th	Finchley Synagogue.
80th	Hendon Synagogue.
80th	Parkes Library at Southampton University.
75th	Bnei Akiva.
75th	Formation of British branch of Hashomer Hatzair.
75th	Peterborough Hebrew Congregation.
70th	North West London Jewish Day School.
65th	British/Israel Chamber of Commerce.
65th	Hagdalim Charitable Organisation.
60th	Borehamwood & Elstree Synagogue.
60th	Brighton New Synagogue.
60th	Leo Baeck Institute.
55th	Inter-University Jewish Federation.
50th	Destruction of Brondesbury Synagogue by fire.
50th	Passing of Race Relations bill.
50th	Resignation of Chief Rabbi Israel Brodie.
50th	Attempted attacks on Golders Green, Clapton, Ilford and Stanmore Synagogues.
45th	Liberal Friends of Israel.
45th	Coventry Synagogue.
45th	Likud-Herut Movement of Great Britain.
40th	British/Israel Arts Foundation.
40th	National Council for Soviet Jewry.
30th	Waltham Abbey Cemetery Holocaust memorial.
25th	Jewish Care.
25th	Wanstead & Woodford Synagogue.

The following courses are available on Jewish Studies:

Centre for German-Jewish Studies, University of Sussex, Brighton
Website www.sussex.ac.uk
History (Modules include: 1938 Kristallnacht, 1942 Holocaust; Philosopher of Israel's Mission: An Intellectual Biography of David Einhorn, 1809-1879; Jewish Studies in Europe: Comparative Perspectives; The Zionists among the "Prague Circle" of German-Jewish Intellectuals and their Role in the Debates about Jewish Nationalism: The Case of Robert Weltsch, Hans Kohn and Shmuel H. Bergman)

Heythrop College, University of London, London
Website www.heythrop.ac.uk
BA Abrahamic Religions
BA Philosophy, Religion and Ethics
MA Biblical Studies
MRes Biblical Studies

King's College London, London
Website www.kcl.ac.uk
MA Jewish Studies

Leo Baeck College - Centre for Jewish Education, London
Website www.lbc.ac.uk
BA Jewish Education
Graduate Diploma Hebrew and Jewish Studies 1 and 2
MA Jewish Education
MA Applied Rabbinic Theology
MA European Jewish History (taught jointly with Queen Mary University of London)
MPhil/PhD Hebrew and Jewish Studies
Postgraduate Diploma Hebrew and Jewish Studies
Advanced Diploma Professional Development: Jewish Education

Liverpool Hope University, Liverpool
Website www.hope.ac.uk
MA Jewish Studies

London School of Jewish Studies (LSJS), London
Website www.lsjs.ac.uk
MA Jewish Studies
MA Jewish Education

Nottingham University, Nottingham
Website www.nottingham.ac.uk
BA Biblical Studies and Theology
MA Jewish History and Thought

Oxford Centre for Hebrew and Jewish Studies, Oxford
Website www.ochjs.ac.uk
MSt Jewish Studies (for course options, see website)

The Parkes Institute, University of Southampton, Southampton
Website www.southampton.ac.uk/parkes
BA History Pathways in Jewish History and Culture

MA Jewish History and Culture
MRes Jewish History and Culture
MPhil/ PhD Jewish Studies

Queen Mary University, London
Website www.qmul.ac.uk
MA European Jewish History (taught jointly with Queen Mary University of London)

Royal Holloway, London
Website www.rhul.ac.uk
MA Holocaust Studies

School of Oriental and African Studies (SOAS), London
Website www.soas.ac.uk
BA Hebrew and Israeli Studies
BA Hebrew (along with another subject)
BA Middle Eastern Studies
MA Israeli Studies

Stanley Burton Centre for Holocaust Studies, University of Leicester, Leicester
Website www2.le.ac.uk/centres/stanley-burton-centre
MA Holocaust Studies

Trinity College Dublin, Dublin
Website www.tcd.ie
BA Jewish and Islamic civilisations

University of Aberdeen, Aberdeen
Website www.abdn.ac.uk
Jewish Studies MLitt

University of Birmingham, Birmingham
Website www.birmingham.ac.uk
MA/PhD Jewish and Holocaust Studies

University College London, London
Website www.ucl.ac.uk
BA Hebrew & Jewish Studies

University of Edinburgh
Website www.ed.ac.uk
Mth/MSc Biblical Studies

University of Manchester, Manchester
Website www.manchester.ac.uk
BA Hebrew and Israel Studies
MA Biblical Studies
MA Jewish Studies

The Woolf Institute, Cambridge, Center for the study of Christian-Jewish relations
Website www.woolf.cam.ac.uk
MA Master of Arts in Jewish–Christian Relations
MSt Master of Studies in the Study of Jewish–Christian Relations

PUBLICATIONS & PUBLISHERS

The following is a list of notable books of Jewish interest published between November 2013 and October 2014.

THE ARTS
Halina Goldberg: Music in Chopin's Warsaw, Oxford University Press
Alexander Samely, Philip Alexander, Rocco Bernasconi, Robert Hayward: Profiling Jewish Literature in Antiquity: An Inventory, from Second Temple Texts to the Talmuds, Oxford University Press
Joshua S. Walden: Sounding Authentic: The Rural Miniature and Musical Modernism, Oxford University Press

BIOGRAPHY
Elaine Feinstein: It Goes with the Territory: Memoir of a Poet, Alma Books
Pam Fox: Isidor Mattuck: Architect of Liberal Judaism, Vallentine Mitchell
Denis Guenoun: A Semite: A memoir of Algeria, Columbia University Press
Irma Kertz: My life in Agony: Confessions of a Professional Agony Aunt, Alma Books
Yehuda Koren, Eilat Negev: Giants: The Dwarfs of Auschwitz, Robson Press
Joanne Lipman, Melanie Kupchynsky: Strings Attached, Hyperion Books
Frederic William Maitland, H.A.L. Fisher: The Collected Papers of Frederic William Maitland (Vol. 3), Cambridge University Press
Norman Manea: The Hooligan's Return, Yale University Press
Michal Oron: Rabbi, Mystic, or Impostor?: The Eighteenth-Century Ba'al Shem of London, The Littman Library
Robert Renwick: Helen Suzman: Bright Star In A Dark Chamber, Biteback Publishing
Anthony Rudolf: Silent Conversations: A Reader's Life, University of Chicago Press
Eva Schloss: After Auschwitz: A Story of Heartbreak and Survival by the Stepsister of Anne Frank, Hodder & Staughton
Gary Shteyngart: Little failure: A Memoir, Random House
Derek Taylor: Chief Rabbi Hertz: The Wars of the Lord, Vallentine Mitchell
Barbara Winton: If it's not impossible ...: The Life of Sir Nicholas Winton, Matador

CULTURE
Anne Karpf: How To Age (School of Life), Macmillan
Lynne Segal: Out of Time: The Pleasures and the Perils of Ageing, Verso Books
Daniel Rosenthal: The National Theatre Story, Oberon Books

CURRENT AFFAIRS
Andrew Hussey: The French Intifada: The Long War between France and its Arabs, Granta

HISTORY
James K. Aitken, James N. Carleton Paget: The Jewish-Greek Tradition in Antiquity and the Byzantine Empire, Cambridge University Press
Peter C. Appelbaum: Loyal Sons: Jewish Soldiers in the German Army in the Great War, Vallentine Mitchell
Patrick Bishop: The Reckoning: How the Killing of One Man Changed the Fate of the Promised Land, William Collins
Ian Buruma: Year Zero: A History of 1945, Atlantic Books
Anna Cichopek-Gajraj: Beyond Violence: Jewish Survivors in Poland and Slovakia, 1944–48, Cambridge University Press
Alon Confino: A world without Jews: The Nazi Imagination from Persecution to Genocide, Yale University Press
Margarete Myers Feinstein: Holocaust Survivors in Postwar Germany, 1945–1957, Cambridge University Press
Irving Frankel: The Ark Before Noah: Decoding the Story of the Flood, Hodder & Staughton
Ben-Zion Gold: The Life of Jews in Poland Before the Holocaust: A Memoir, University of Nebraska Press

Michael Goldfarb: Emancipation, Scribe
Yosef Gorny: The Jewish Press and the Holocaust, 1939–1945: Palestine, Britain, the United States, and the Soviet Union, Cambridge University Press
Moshe Halbertal: Maimonides: Life and Thought, Princeton University Press
Yaron Harel: Syrian Jewry in Transition, 1840-1880, (new in PB) Littman Library
William Horbury: Jewish War under Trajan and Hadrian, Cambridge University Press
John Doyle Klier: Russians, Jews, and the Pogroms of 1881–1882, Cambridge University Press
Daniel Lee: Pétain's Jewish Children: French Jewish Youth and the Vichy Regime, 1940-1942, Oxford University Press
Mark Levene: Devastation: Volume I: The European Rimlands 1912-1938, Oxford University Press
Mark Levene: Annihilation: Volume II: The European Rimlands 1939-1953, Oxford University Press
Michael A. Livingston: The Fascists and the Jews of Italy: Mussolini's Race Laws, 1938–1943, Cambridge University Press
Bo Lindegaard: Countrymen: The Untold Story of How Denmark's Jews Escaped the Nazis, Atlantic
Sheridan Marhsall: Forgetting to Remember: Religious Remembrance and the Literary Response to the Holocaust, Vallentine Mitchell
Esther Meir-Glitzenstein: The 'Magic Carpet' Exodus of Yemenite Jewry: An Israeli Formative Myth, Sussex University Press
Caroline Moorehead: Village of Secrets: Defying the Nazis in Vichy France, Chatto & Windus
Maren R. Niehoff: Jewish Exegesis and Homeric Scholarship in Alexandria: Cambridge University Press
Yohanan Petrovsky-Shtern: Jews in the Russian Army, 1827–1917: Drafted into Modernity, Cambridge University Press
Doreen Rappaport: Beyond Courage: The Untold Story of Jewish Resistance during the Holocaust, Random House
Marc Saperstein: Leadership and Conflict: Tensions in Medieval and Early Modern Jewish History and Culture, Littman Library
Seth Schwartz: The Ancient Jews from Alexander to Muhammad, Cambridge University Press
Anita Shapira: Israel: A History, Weidenfeld & Nicolson
Si Sheppard: The Jewish Revolt AD 66-74, Random House
Arlene Stein: Reluctant Witnesses: Survivors, Their Children, and the Rise of Holocaust Consciousness, Oxford University Press
Martin Sugarman: Under the Heel of Bushido: Last Voices of the Jewish POWs of the Japanese in the Second World War, Vallentine Mitchell
Derek Taylor: A Lesson in Tolerance: Hillel House 1904-1948, Perse School, Cambridge
Francesca Trivellato, Leor Halevi and Catia Antunes: Religion and Trade: Cross-Cultural Exchanges in World History, 1000-1900, Oxford University Press
Rosemary Wenzerul: Tracing Your Jewish Ancestors: A Guide for Family Historians, Pen & Sword
Tim Whitmarsh, Stuart Thomson: The Romance between Greece and the East, Cambridge University Press

HOLOCAUST

Rota Goldberg: Motherhood, Growing up with Holocaust, Halban Publishers
Bernard Wasserstein: The Ambiguity of Virtue: Gertrude Van Tijn and the Fate of the Dutch Jews, Harvard University Press
Ron Jones: The Auschwitz Goalkeeper: A Prisoner of War's True Story, Gomer Press
Bengt Jangfelot: The Hero of Budapest: The Triumph and Tragedy of Raoul Wallenberg, I.B.Taurus
Wechert Ten Havert: The Persecution of the Jews in the Netherlands 1940-1945, Amsterdam University Press

ISRAEL

Shlomo Aronson, Naftali Greenwood: David Ben-Gurion and the Jewish Renaissance, Cambridge University Press

Katell Berthelot, Joseph E. David, Marc Hirshman: The Gift of the Land and the Fate of the Canaanites in Jewish Thought, Oxford University Press

Keith Kahn-Harris: Uncivil War: The Israel Conflict in the Jewish Community, David Paul

Dov Lipman: To Unify a Nation: My Vision for the Future of Israel, Urim Publications

Inbari Motti: Messianic Religious Zionism Confronts Israeli Territorial Compromises, Cambridge University Press

JUDAISM

Maya Balakirsky Katz: The Visual Culture of Chabad, Cambridge University Press

Yechiel Michael Barilan: Jewish Bioethics: Rabbinic Law and Theology in their Social and Historical Contexts, Cambridge University Press

Michael Fishbane, Joanna Weinberg: Midrash Unbound: Transformations and Innovations, Littman Library

Aaron Goldscheider: The Night that Unites Passover Haggadah: Teachings, Stories and Questions from Rabbi Kook, Rabbi Soloveitchik, and Rabbi Carlebach, Urim publications

Avraham Grossman: RASHI, Littman Library

Zvi Grumet: Moses and the Path to Leadership, Urim Publications

Sarah Hermelin: Journey Together: 49 Steps to Transforming a Family: Urim Publications

Alex P. Jassen: Scripture and Law in the Dead Sea Scrolls, Cambridge University Press

Rabbi Shlomo Katz: The Torah Commentary of Rabbi Shlomo Carlebach: Genesis Part II, Urim Publications

Aaron Koller: Esther in Ancient Jewish Thought, Cambridge University Press

Herbert Edward Ryle, Montague Rhodes James: Psalms of the Pharisees: The Psalms of Solomon, Cambridge University Press

Michael Smart, Barbara Ashkenas: Kaddish, Women's Voices, Urim Publications

Norman Solomon: Judaism: A Very Short Introduction: Second Edition, Oxford University Press

Haym Soloveitchik: Collected Essays, Volume 2: Littman Library

Daniel Sperber: On the Relationship of Mitzvot between Man and His Neighbour and Man and His Maker, Urim Publications

Shaul Stampfer: Lithuanian Yeshivas of the Nineteenth Century: Creating a Tradition of Learning, Littman Library

Shaul Stampfer: Families, Rabbis, and Education: Traditional Jewish Society in Nineteenth-Century Eastern Europe, (New in PB) Littman Library

Isiah Tishby: Messianic Mysticism: Moses Hayim Luzzatto and the Padua School, Littman Library

MODERN TIMES

Julia Phillips Cohen: Becoming Ottomans: Sephardi Jews and Imperial Citizenship in the Modern Era, Oxford University Press

Jane Gerber: The Jews in the Caribbean, Littman Library

Aaron W. Hughes: Rethinking Jewish Philosophy: Beyond Particularism and Universalism, Oxford University Press

Mira Katzburg-Yungman, (translated by Tamar Berkowitz): Hadassah: American Women Zionists and the Rebirth of Israel: Littman Library

Cecile Esther Kuznitz: YIVO and the Making of Modern Jewish Culture: Scholarship for the Yiddish Nation: Cambridge University Press

Natalya Lusty: Julian Murphet: Modernism and Masculinity, Cambridge University Press

Stephen H. Norwood: Antisemitism and the American Far Left, Cambridge University Press

Rebecca Rossen: Dancing Jewish: Jewish Identity in American Modern and Postmodern Dance, Oxford University Press

Ronald Schechter, Liz Clarke: Mendoza the Jew: Boxing, Manliness, and Nationalism, A Graphic History, Oxford University Press

Margreet L. Steiner, Ann E. Killebrew: The Oxford Handbook of the Archaeology of the Levant: c. 8000-332 BCE, Oxford University Press

PHOTOGRAPHY
Gemma Levine: Just One More ... A Photographer's Memoir, Elliott & Thompson
Judah Passow: No Place Like Home, Bloomsbury

RELIGION
Edwin A. Abbott: 'The Son of Man': Or Contributions to the Study of the Thoughts of Jesus, Cambridge University Press
Reza Aslan: Zealot: The Life and Times of Jesus of Nazareth, The Westbourne Press
Mara H. Benjamin: Rosenzweig's Bible: Reinventing Scripture for Jewish Modernity, Cambridge University Press
Loriliai Biernacki, Philip Clayton: Panentheism across the World's Traditions, Oxford University Press
Arthur Carr: St Matthew: The Revised Version, Cambridge University Press
Dan Caspi, Nelly Elias: Ethnic Minorities and Media in the Holy Land, Vallentine Mitchell
Anna Collar: Religious Networks in the Roman Empire: The Spread of New Ideas, Cambridge University Press
Ann Conway-Jones: Gregory of Nyssa's Tabernacle Imagery in Its Jewish and Christian Contexts, Oxford University Press
Lewis M. Donald: The Origins of Christian Zionism: Lord Shaftesbury and Evangelical Support for a Jewish Homeland, Cambridge University Press
Dawud El-Alami, Dan Cohn-Sherbok, George D. Chryssideas: Why can't they get along?: A Conversation Between a Muslim, a Jew and a Christian, Lion Books
Anver M. Emon, Matthew Levering, David Novak: Natural Law: A Jewish, Christian, and Islamic Trialogue, Oxford University Press
David Govrin: The Journey to the Arab Spring: The Ideological Roots of the Middle East Upheaval in Arab Liberal Thought, Vallentine Mitchell
Susan Gillingham: A Journey of Two Psalms: The Reception of Psalms 1 and 2 in Jewish and Christian Tradition, Oxford University Press
Daniel R. Langton: The Apostle Paul in the Jewish Imagination: A Study in Modern Jewish-Christian Relations, Cambridge University Press
Willard G. Oxtoby, Amir Hussain, Roy C. Amore: World Religions: Western Traditions (Fourth Edition), Oxford University Press
Yitzhak Reiter: Contesting Symbolic Landscape in Jerusalem: Jewish/Islamic Conflict over the Museum of Tolerance at Mamilla Cemetery, Sussex Academic Press
Joel Yehudah Rutman: Why Evolution Matters: A Jewish View, Vallentine Mitchell
Todd H. Weir: Secularism and Religion in Nineteenth-Century Germany: The Rise of the Fourth Confession, Cambridge University Press
Edwin Williamson: The Cambridge Companion to Jorge Luis Borges, Cambridge University Press

SOCIOLOGY
Nicholas Adams: The Impact of Idealism, The Legacy of Post-Kantian German Thought: Volume 4, Religion, Cambridge University Press
Karl Ameriks Boyle: The Impact of Idealism: The Legacy of Post-Kantian German Thought, Cambridge University Press
Simon J. Bronner: Jewish Cultural Studies, Volume 4, Framing Jewish Culture: Boundaries and Representations, Littman Library
Marcia J. Bunge: Children, Adults, and Shared Responsibilities: Jewish, Christian and Muslim Perspectives, Cambridge University Press
Marcus Düwell, Jens Braarvig, Roger Brownsword: The Cambridge Handbook of Human Dignity: Interdisciplinary Perspectives, Cambridge University Press

Todd M. Endelman: Broadening Jewish History: Towards a Social History of Ordinary Jews Littman Library

Benjamin Fain: The Poverty of Secularism: An Open World Governed by the Creator Versus A Closed, Imaginary World that Develops on Its Own, Urim Publications

Tova Hartman, Charlie Buckholtz: Are You Not a Man of God?: Devotion, Betrayal, and Social Criticism in Jewish Tradition, Oxford University Press

Natan Ophir: Rabbi Shlomo Carlebach: Life, Mission, and Legacy Urim Publications

David Patterson: Genocide in Jewish Thought, Cambridge University Press

Uzi Rebhun: The Social Scientific Study of Jewry: Sources, Approaches, Debates, Oxford University Press

Isaac Sassoon: The Status of Women in Jewish Tradition, Cambridge University Press

Bernard Spolsky: The Languages of the Jews: A Sociolinguistic History, Cambridge University Press

Rabbi Dr. Shmuly Yanklowitz: The Soul of Jewish Social Justice, Urim Publications

TRAVEL

Gideo Leis Kraus: A Sense of Direction: Pilgrimage for the Restless and the Hopeful, One Books

The following list are Publishers of books of Jewish interest.

CUP (Cambridge University Press)
University Printing House, Shaftesbury Road, Cambridge, CB2 8BS
Tel 01223 358 331
Email information@cambridge.org *Website* www.cambridge.org
(Est. 1584)

FIVE LEAVES PUBLICATIONS
PO Box 8786, Nottingham NG1 9AW
Tel 0115 969 3597
Email info@fiveleaves.co.uk *Website* www.fiveleaves.co.uk
Publishes 15 or so books a year. Our main areas of interest are fiction and poetry, social history, Jewish secular culture, with side orders of Romani, young adult, Catalan and crime fiction titles.

LITTMAN LIBRARY OF JEWISH CIVILIZATION
PO Box 645, Oxford OX2 0UJ
Tel 01865 790 740
Email info@littman.co.uk *Website* www.littman.co.uk
(Est. 1965. Reg. Charity No. 1000784) Established for the purpose of publishing scholarly works aimed at disseminating an understanding of the Jewish heritage and Jewish hist., and making Jewish religious thought and literary creativity accessible to the English-speaking world. *Dirs.* Mrs C. C. Littman, R. J. Littman; *Contact* Connie Webber (Editorial); *Chief Exec. Off.* Ludo Craddock

OUP (Oxford University Press)
Great Clarendon Street, Oxford, OX2 6DP
Tel 01865 556 767 *Fax* 01865 556 646
Email WebEnquiry.UK@oup.com *Website* www.oup.com
(Est 1478) Oxford University Press is a department of the University of Oxford. It furthers the University's objective of excellence in research, scholarship, and education by publishing worldwide.

SCHOCKEN BOOKS
1745 Broadway, New York, NY 10019, USA
Tel +1 (212) 782 9000
Email pantheonpublicity@randomhouse.com
Website www.randomhouse.com/schocken
(Est. 1931) Schocken Books joined Random House Publishing in 1987. Books are on Jewish literature, non-fiction, cookbooks, and more.

SUSSEX ACADEMIC PRESS
PO Box 139, Eastbourne, East Sussex, BN24 9BP
Tel 01323 479 220
Email edit@sussex-academic.com *Website* www.sussex-academic.com
Contact Editorial Dir. Anthony V. P. Grahame

URIM PUBLICATIONS
9 HaUman Street, 2nd floor, P.O.Box 52287, Jerusalem 91521 Israel
Tel +972 (2) 679 7633 *Fax* +972 (2) 679 7634
Website www.urimpublications.com
(Est. 1997) Independent publishing house based in Jerusalem and New York. Publishes books of wide Jewish interest. Main areas of interest include: Jewish

Thought, Spiritual or Meditative Works, Women and Judaism, Jewish Law and Modernity, Bible Commentary, Israel Studies, Modern Biographies, and Children's Illustrated Books. Publisher, Tzvi Mauer *Email* Publisher@UrimPublications.com; Ed., *Email* Editor@UrimPublications.com; Children's Book *Ed.* Shari Dash Greenspan *Email* Children@UrimPublications.com

VALLENTINE MITCHELL PUBLISHERS

Middlesex House, 29/45 High Street, Edgware, Middlesex HA8 7UU
Tel 020 8952 9526 *Fax* 020 8952 9242
Email info@vmbooks.com *Website* www.vmbooks.com
(Reg. Charity No. 472549) International publisher of books of Jewish interest, both for the scholar and general reader. Subjects published include Jewish history, culture and heritage, modern Jewish thought, biography and reference. *Dir.* His Hon. Sir C.V. Callman, A.E. Cass, S.L. Cass, H.J. Osen

BOOKSELLERS

The booksellers listed below specialise in Jewish books. Many also supply religious requisites.

GREATER LONDON

Carmel Gifts
Tel 020 8958 7632 *Fax* 020 8958 6226
Email carmelgifts@aol.com

Brauns Judaica and Gifts
82 Dunsmure Road, London N16 5JY *Tel* 020 8809 9393 *Fax* 020 8809 9494
Email info@braunsjudaica.com *Website* www.braunsjudaica.com

Daunt Books
193 Haverstock Hill, NW3 4QL *Tel* 020 7224 2295
Email contact@dauntbooks.co.uk *Website* www.dauntbooks.co.uk

Divrei Kodesh
13 Edgwarebury Lane, Edgware HA8 8LH *Tel* 020 8958 1133
Email enquiries@divreikodesh.co.uk *Website* www.divreikodesh.co.uk

J. Aisenthal
11 Ashbourne Parade, Finchley Road, NW11 0AD *Tel* 020 8455 0501
Email info@aisenthal.co.uk

Jerusalem the Golden Ltd.
146-148 Golders Green Road, NW11 8HE *Tel* 020 8455 4960 *Fax* 020 8458 3593
Email yechiel@jerusalemthegolden.com *Website* www.jerusalemthegolden.com

Joseph's Bookstore and Café Also
1255-7 Finchley Road, Temple Fortune, NW11 0AD *Tel* 020 8731 7575
Fax 020 8731 6699
Email info@josephsbookstore.com *Website* www.josephsbookstore.com
   Cafe Also *Tel* 020 8455 6890

Kuperard
59 Hutton Grove, N12 8DS *Tel* 020 8446 2440 *Fax* 020 8446 2441
Email office@kuperard.co.uk *Website* www.kuperard.co.uk
publishers and distributors, mail order, educational suppliers, book fairs, book launches

Manor House Books, John Trotter Books
Sternberg Centre, 80 East End Road, London N3 2SY *Tel* 020 8349 9484
Email johntrotterbooks@gmail.com *Website* www.ukbookworld.com/members/trotter
New, used and rare Jewish and Hebrew books

Mesoirah Seforim & Books
61 Old Hill Street, N16 6LU *Tel* 020 8809 4310

M. Rogosnitzky
20 The Drive, NW11 9SR *Tel* 020 8455 7645/4112
Antique Jewish books

Muswell Hill Bookshop
72 Fortis Green Road, N10 3HN *Tel* 020 8444 7588
Website www.muswellhillbookshop.com

On Your Doorstep Jewish Books & Gifts (Sandra E. Breger)
1 Rosecroft Walk, Pinner, Middlesex HA5 1LJ *Tel* 020 8866 6236

Steimatzky Hasifria
46 Golders Green Road, NW11 8LL *Tel* 020 8458 9774 *Fax* 020 8458 3449
Email info@steimatzky.co.uk *Website* www.steimatzky.co.uk

Torah Treasures
16 Russell Parade, Golders Green Road, NW11 9NN
Tel 020 8458 8289
Email sale@torahtreasures.co.uk *Website* www.torahtreasures.co.uk
Waterstones
68 Hampstead High Street, NW3 1QP *Tel* 020 7794 1098
Email enquiries@hampstead.waterstones.com *Website* www.waterstones.com

REGIONS

GATESHEAD
Lehmann's Retail
28-30 Grasmere Street. West, NE8 1TS *Tel* 0191 477 3523
Mail order and wholesale: Unit E, Viking Industrial Park, Rolling Mill Road, Tyne & Wear
NE32 3DP *Tel* 0191 430 0333 *Fax* 0191 430 0555 *Email* info@lehmanns.co.uk

GLASGOW
J & E Levingstone
47 & 55 Sinclair Drive, G42 9PT *Tel* 0141 649 2962 *Fax* 0141 649 2962

LIVERPOOL
Jewish Book & Gift Centre
Harold House, Dunbabin Road, L15 6XL (Orders) *Tel* 0151 722 3303
Sunday only, 11am-1pm

MANCHESTER & SALFORD
B. Horwitz (wholesale & retail Judaica)
2 Kings Road, Prestwich, M25 0LE *Tel/Fax* 0161 773 4956
Hasefer
18 Merrybower Road, Salford M7 4HE *Tel* 0161 740 3013 *Fax* 0161 721 4649
J. Goldberg
11 Parkside Avenue, Salford, M7 0HB *Tel* 0161 740 0732
Jewish Book Centre (Mr. Klein)
25 Ashbourne Grove, Salford, M7 4DB *Tel* 0161 792 1253 *Fax* 0161 661 5505

OXFORD
B. H. Blackwell Ltd.
48-51 Broad Street, OX1 3BQ *Tel* 01865 792 792 *Fax* 01865 794 143
Email oxford@blackwell.co.uk *Website* www.blackwell.co.uk
Has a Jewish book section

SOUTHEND
Dorothy Young
21 Colchester Road, SS2 6HW *Tel* 01702 331 218 for appointment
Email dorothy@dorothyyoung.co.uk *Website* www.dorothyyoung.co.uk

The Jewish Calendar is a lunar one, adapted to the solar year by various expedients. The hour is divided into 1,080 portions or *minims*, and the month between one new moon and the next is reckoned as 29 days, 12 hours, 793 minims. The years are grouped in cycles of 19. The present calendar was fixed by the post-Biblical Jewish Patriarch, Hillel II, in 358 C.E. In early Talmudic times the new moons were fixed by actual observation. They were announced from Jerusalem to the surrounding districts and countries by messenger or beacon.

If the time elapsing between one new moon and another were *exactly* 29½ days, the length of the months could be fixed at alternately 29 and 30 days. But there are three corrections to make which disturb this regularity: (1) The excess of 793 minims over the half day, (2) the adjustment to the solar year (civil), (3) the requirement that the incidence of certain Jewish festivals shall not conflict with the Sabbath. To overcome these difficulties the Jewish Calendar recognises six different classes of years; three of them common and three leap. Both the common and the leap years may be either regular, "minimal", or full. The regular year has an alternation of 30 and 29 days. The "minimal" year gives Kislev only 29 days instead of 30, while in a full year Marcheshvan has 30 instead of 29 days. The leap years, which are the 3rd, 6th, 8th, 11th, 14th, 17th, and 19th of the Metonic cycle of 19 years, are composed of thirteen months, an additional month being added. It is usually stated that this leap month is inserted after the month of Adar which in the ordinary year is of 29 days, but in a leap year has 30 days. In reality though the inserted month precedes the ordinary Adar and always has 30 days.

Besides the lunar cycle of 19 years there is a solar cycle of 28 years. At the beginning of this the *Tekufah* of Nisan (the vernal equinox) returns to the same day and the same hour. There are 4 periods to the year - the Vernal Equinox, the Summer Solstice, the Autumnal Equinox and the Winter Solstice.

The chief disturbing influence in the arrangement of the Jewish Calendar is to prevent the Day of Atonement (Tishri 10th) from either immediately preceding or immediately succeeding the Sabbath, and Hoshana Rabba (Tishri 21st) from falling on the Sabbath. Consequently the New Year (Tishri 1st) cannot fall upon Sunday, Wednesday or Friday. A further complication of a purely astronomical character is introduced by the consideration that the Jewish day formally starts six hours before midnight. If the Molad (or lunar conjunction) for the month of Tishri, i.e. the exact moment of the moon's renewal, occurs at noon or later, the new moon will be seen only after 6pm and the Festival is postponed to the next day. When, after paying regard to these and certain other considerations, the days upon which two successive New Year Festivals fall are determined, the number of days in the intervening year is known and the length of Marcheshvan and Kislev is fixed accordingly.

It is customary to describe the type of Jewish year by a "Determinative" consisting of three Hebrew letters. The first of these indicates the day of the week upon which the New Year Festival falls, the second whether the year is regular, "minimal", or full, and the third the day of the week upon which Passover occurs. To this "Determinative" is added the Hebrew word for "ordinary" or "leap".

Authorities differ regarding the manner in which the figure employed for the Jewish Era (this year 5775) is arrived at; the chronology is based on biblical data. A Jewish year is normally described by the initials AM standing for Anno Mundi, the year of the world.

Secular dates are described in Jewish sources as BCE Before the Current Era or CE Current Era.

For the beginning of Sabbaths and Festivals, rules were laid down for the latitude of London by David Nieto, Haham of the Sephardi Community (1702-1728). The hours for nightfall given here are based on those fixed by Nathan Marcus Adler, Chief Rabbi, 1845-1890 in accordance with the formula of Michael Friedlander, Principal of Jews' College, but adjusted to take account of the movement of the Jewish population within the Metropolis since their day.

The times for 2015 are those fixed by the London Beth Din; the times for January and February 2016 have not yet been published by them.

THE JEWISH YEAR

The times in this calendar for the beginning and ending of Sabbaths, Festivals and Fasts in London are given in Greenwich Mean Time (from January 1 to March 28 and October 25 to the end of the calendar), and in British Summer Time (from March 29 to October 24, 2015). The times will differ according to how far you are from London (*See* p. 467 for an approximate time for the ending of the Sabbath)

5775 (25th September 2014 – 13th September 2015)

is known as **775** on the short system and is a regular common year of 12 months, 51 Sabbaths and 354 days. It is 'Kesidran – In Order', that is the month of Cheshvan has 29 days and the month of Kislev has 30 days. The 1st day of Rosh Hashanah is on a Thursday and the 1st day of Passover is on a Sabbath.

It is the 18th year of the 304th minor or lunar cycle (of 19 years each) since the Era of Creation and the seventh of the 207th major or solar cycle (of 28 years each) since the same epoch. It is the seventh year of the seven year Shemittah cycle.

5776 (14th September 2015 – 2nd October 2016)

is known as **776** on the short system and is a full leap year of 13 months 55 Sabbaths and 384 days. It is 'Shleimah – Complete', that is both the months of Cheshvan and Kislev have 30 days each. The 1st day of Rosh Hashanah is on a Monday and the 1st day of Passover is on a Sabbath.

It is the 19th year of the 304th minor or lunar cycle (of 19 years each) since the Era of Creation, and the eighth of the 207th major or solar cycle (of 28 years each) since the same epoch. It is the first year of the seven year Shemitah cycle.

PRINCIPAL FESTIVALS AND FASTS 2014–2022 (5775–5782)

Festival or Fast	Hebrew Date	5775 2014-15	5776 2015-16	5777 2016-17	5778 2017-18	5779 2018-19	5780 2019-20	5781 2020-21	5782 2021-22
New Year	Tishri 1	Sept. 25	Sept. 14	Oct. 3	Sept. 21	Sept. 10	Sept. 30	Sept. 19	Sept. 7
Day of Atonement	Tishri 10	Oct. 4	Sept. 23	Oct. 12	Sept. 30	Sept. 19	Oct. 9	Sept. 28	Sept. 16
Tabernacles, 1st Day	Tishri 15	Oct. 9	Sept. 28	Oct. 17	Oct. 5	Sept. 24	Oct. 14	Oct. 3	Sept. 21
Tabernacles, 8th Day	Tishri 22	Oct. 16	Oct. 5	Oct. 24	Oct. 12	Oct. 1	Oct. 21	Oct. 10	Sept. 28
Simchat Torah	Tishri 23	Oct. 17	Oct. 6	Oct. 25	Oct. 13	Oct. 2	Oct. 22	Oct. 11	Sept. 29
Chanucah	Kislev 25	Dec. 17	Dec. 7	Dec. 25	Dec. 13	Dec. 3	Dec. 23	Dec. 11	Nov. 29
Purim	Adar[1] 14	Mar. 5	Mar. 24	Mar. 12	Mar. 1	Mar. 21	Mar. 10	Feb. 26	Mar. 17
Passover, 1st Day	Nisan 15	Apr. 4	Apr. 23	Apr. 11	Mar. 31	Apr. 20	Apr. 9	Mar. 28	Apr. 16
Passover, 7th Day	Nisan 21	Apr. 10	Apr. 29	Apr. 17	Apr. 6	Apr. 26	Apr. 15	Apr. 3	Apr. 22
Israel Indep. Day	Iyar 5[2]	Apr. 23	May 12	May 2	Apr. 19	May 9	Apr. 29	Apr. 15	May 5
Shavuot	Sivan 6	May 24	June 12	May 31	May 20	June 9	May 29	May 17	June 5
Fast of Ab	Ab 9	July 26[3]	Aug. 14[3]	Aug. 1	July 22[3]	Aug. 11[3]	July 30	July 18	Aug. 7

1. Adar Sheni 14 in Leap Years.
2. When this date occurs on Friday or Sabbath, Israel Independence Day is observed on the previous Thursday. When it occurs on Monday, Independence Day is postponed to Tuesday (to avoid Remembrance Day beginning when Sabbath ends).
3. Ab 10 (Ab 9 being Sabbath).

ABRIDGED JEWISH/BRITISH CALENDAR 2015 (5775-5776)

Fast of Tevet, 5775/New Years Day/Bank Holiday, UK	Thursday	2015 January	1
Rosh Chodesh Shevat	Wednesday		21
Tu B'Shevat - New Year for Trees	Wednesday	February	4
Rosh Chodesh Adar, 1st day	Thursday		19
Fast of Esther	Wednesday	March	4
Purim	Thursday		5
Shushan Purim	Friday		6
Rosh Chodesh Nisan	Saturday		21
British Summer Time begins	Sunday		29
Fast of Firstborn/ Good Friday/ Bank Holiday, UK	Friday	April	3
First Day Pesach (Passover)	Saturday		4
Second Day Pesach/ Easter Day	Sunday		5
Bank Holiday, UK	Monday		6
Seventh Day Pesach	Friday		10
Eighth Day Pesach	Saturday		11
Holocaust Memorial Day	Thursday		16
Rosh Chodesh Iyar, 1st day	Sunday		19
Yom Ha'Atzmaut - Israel Independence Day	Thursday		23
Pesach Sheni - Minor Passover	Sunday	May	3
Bank Holiday, UK	Monday		4
Lag Ba'Omer - Thirty-third day of the Omer	Thursday		7
Yom Yerushalayim - Jerusalem Day	Sunday		17
Rosh Chodesh Sivan	Tuesday		19
First Day Shavuot (Pentecost/ Feast of Weeks)	Sunday		24
Second Day Shavuot/Bank Holiday, UK	Monday		25
Rosh Chodesh Tammuz, 1st day	Wednesday	June	17
Fast of Tammuz	Sunday	July	5
Rosh Chodesh Av	Friday		17
Tisha B'Av (Fast of 9th Av)	Sunday		26
15th Av (Festival)	Friday		31
Rosh Chodesh Elul, 1st day	Saturday	August	15
Bank Holiday, UK	Monday		31
First Day Rosh Hashanah (New Year), 5776	Monday	September	14
Second Day Rosh Hashanah	Tuesday		15
Fast of Gedaliah	Wednesday		16
Yom Kippur (Day of Atonement)	Wednesday		23
First Day Succot (Tabernacles)	Monday		28
Second Day Succot	Tuesday		29
Hoshana Rabba	Sunday	October	4
Shemini Atzeret (Eighth Day of Assembly)	Monday		5
Simchat Torah (Rejoicing of the Law)	Tuesday		6
Rosh Chodesh Marcheshvan, 1st day	Tuesday		13
British Summer Time ends	Sunday		25
Remembrance Sunday, UK	Sunday	November	8
Rosh Chodesh Kislev, 1st day	Thursday		12
First Day Chanucah	Monday	December	7
Rosh Chodesh Tevet, 1st day	Saturday		12
Fast of Tevet	Tuesday		22
Christmas Day	Friday		25
Boxing Day	Saturday		26
Bank Holiday, UK	Monday		28

ABRIDGED JEWISH/BRITISH CALENDAR 2016 (5776-5777)

New Years Day/ Bank Holiday, UK	Friday	2016 January 1
Rosh Chodesh Shevat 5776	Monday	11
Tu B'Shevat - New Year for Trees	Monday	25
National Holocaust Memorial Day	Wednesday	27
Rosh Chodesh Adar I, 1st day	Tuesday	February 9
Purim Katan -Minor Purim	Tuesday	23
Shushan Purim Katan - Minor Shushan Purim	Wednesday	24
Rosh Chodesh Adar II, 1st Day	Thursday	March 10
Fast of Esther	Wednesday	23
Purim	Thursday	24
Shushan Purim/ Good Friday/ Bank Holiday, UK ...	Friday	25
British Summer Time begins	Sunday	27
Easter Monday/ Bank Holiday, UK	Monday	28
Rosh Chodesh Nisan	Saturday	April 9
Fast of Firstborn	Friday	22
First Day Pesach (Passover)	Saturday	23
Second Day Pesach	Sunday	24
Seventh Day Pesach	Friday	29
Eighth Day Pesach	Saturday	30
Bank Holiday, UK	Monday	May 2
Yom Hashoah - Holocaust Memorial Day	Thursday	5
Rosh Chodesh Iyar, 1st day	Sunday	8
Yom Ha'Atzmaut - Israel Independence Day	Thursday	12
Pesach Sheni - Minor Passover	Sunday	22
Lag Ba'Omer - Thirty-third day of the Omer	Thursday	26
Bank Holiday, UK	Monday	30
Yom Yerushalayim - Jerusalem Day	Sunday	June 5
Rosh Chodesh Sivan	Tuesday	7
First Day Shavuot (Pentecost/ Feast of Weeks)	Sunday	12
Second Day Shavuot	Monday	13
Rosh Chodesh Tammuz, 1st day	Wednesday	July 6
17th Tammuz (Fast) (deferred)	Sunday	24
Rosh Chodesh Av	Friday	August 5
Tisha B'Av (Fast of 9th Av) (deferred)	Sunday	14
15th Av (Festival)	Friday	19
Bank Holiday, UK	Monday	29
Rosh Chodesh Elul, 1st day	Saturday	September 3
First Day Rosh Hashanah (New Year), 5777	Monday	October 3
Second Day Rosh Hashanah	Tuesday	4
Fast of Gedaliah	Wednesday	5
Yom Kippur (Day of Atonement)	Wednesday	12
First Day Succot (Tabernacles)	Monday	17
Second Day Succot	Tuesday	18
Hoshana Rabba	Sunday	23
Shemini Atzeret (Eighth Day of Assembly)	Monday	24
Simchat Torah (Rejoicing of the Law)	Tuesday	25
British Summer Time ends	Sunday	30
Rosh Chodesh Marcheshvan, 1st day	Tuesday	November 1
Remembrance Sunday, UK	Sunday	13
Rosh Chodesh Kislev	Thursday	December 1
First Day Chanucah/ Christmas Day	Sunday	25
Boxing Day	Monday	26
Rosh Chodesh Tevet	Friday	30

HEBREW AND ENGLISH CALENDAR

JANUARY 2015

Day			Begins previous day	Ends	
Thursday	1	Fast of 10th Tevet begins	06.17	16.50	10
Friday	2		15.48	16.58	11
Saturday	3	Vayechi			12
Sunday	4				13
Monday	5				14
Tuesday	6				15
Wednesday	7				16
Thursday	8				17
Friday	9				18
Saturday	10	Shemot	15.57	17.06	19
Sunday	11				20
Monday	12				21
Tuesday	13				22
Wednesday	14				23
Thursday	15				24
Friday	16				25
Saturday	17	Va'era - Mevarchim Shevat	16.07	17.16	26
Sunday	18				27
Monday	19				28
Tuesday	20				29
Wednesday	21	Rosh Chodesh Shevat			SHEVAT 1
Thursday	22				2
Friday	23				3
Saturday	24	Bo	16.19	17.27	4
Sunday	25				5
Monday	26				6
Tuesday	27	National Holocaust Memorial Day			7
Wednesday	28				8
Thursday	29				9
Friday	30				10
Saturday	31	Beshallach - Shabbat Shirah	16.31	17.28	11

FEBRUARY 2015

12 SHEVAT - 11 ADAR I 5775

Day		Event	Begins previous day	Ends	
Sunday	1				12
Monday	2				13
Tuesday	3				14
Wednesday	4	Tu B'Shvat - New Year for Trees			15
Thursday	5				16
Friday	6				17
Saturday	7	Yitro	16.44	17.49	18
Sunday	8				19
Monday	9				20
Tuesday	10				21
Wednesday	11				22
Thursday	12				23
Friday	13				24
Saturday	14	Mishpatim - Shabbat Shekalim - Mevarchim Adar Rishon	16.57	18.01	25
Sunday	15				26
Monday	16				27
Tuesday	17				28
Wednesday	18				29
Thursday	19	1st day Rosh Chodesh Adar I			30
Friday	20	2nd day Rosh Chodesh Adar I			ADAR RISHON 1
Saturday	21	Terumah	17.09	18.13	2
Sunday	22				3
Monday	23				4
Tuesday	24				5
Wednesday	25				6
Thursday	26				7
Friday	27				8
Saturday	28	Tetzaveh - Parshat Zachor	17.22	18.25	9

MARCH 2015

10 ADAR - 11 NISSAN 5775

Day			Begins previous day	Ends	
Sunday	1				10
Monday	2				11
Tuesday	3				12
Wednesday	4	Fast of Esther begins	05.02	18.27	13
Thursday	5	Purim			14
Friday	6	Shushan Purim			15
Saturday	7	Ki Tissa	17.35	18.38	16
Sunday	8				17
Monday	9				18
Tuesday	10				19
Wednesday	11				20
Thursday	12				21
Friday	13				22
Saturday	14	Vayakhel Pekude Parshat Parah Mevarchim Nissan	17.47	18.50	23
Sunday	15				24
Monday	16				25
Tuesday	17				26
Wednesday	18				27
Thursday	19				28
Friday	20				29
Saturday	21	Vayikra Parshat Hachodesh Shabbat Rosh Chodesh Nissan	17.59	19.02	NISSAN 1
Sunday	22				2
Monday	23				3
Tuesday	24				4
Wednesday	25				5
Thursday	26				6
Friday	27				7
Saturday	28	Tzav Shabbat Hagadol	18.11	19.14	8
Sunday	29	START OF BST			9
Monday	30				10
Tuesday	31				11

APRIL 2015

12 NISSAN-11 IYYAR 5775

Day	Date	Event	Begins previous day	Ends	OMER	
Wednesday	1					12
Thursday	2	Bedikat Chametz				13
Friday	3	Last time for eating Chametz	10.53			
		Last time for burning Chametz	11.59			
		Erev Pesach Fast of the Firstborn - 1st Seder in Evening				14
Saturday	4	1st day PESACH	19.22	20.27		15
Sunday	5	2nd day PESACH		20.49	1	16
Monday	6	1st day Chol Hamoed Pesach			2	17
Tuesday	7	2nd day Chol Hamoed Pesach			3	18
Wednesday	8	3rd day Chol Hamoed Pesach			4	19
Thursday	9	4th day Chol Hamoed Pesach			5	20
Friday	10	7th day PESACH	19.33		6	21
Saturday	11	8th day PESACH	19.34	20.4	7	22
Sunday	12				8	23
Monday	13				9	24
Tuesday	14				10	25
Wednesday	15				11	26
Thursday	16	Holocaust Memorial Day			12	27
Friday	17				13	28
Saturday	18	Shemini Mevarchim Iyyar Machar Chodesh	19.46	20.53	14	29
Sunday	19	1st day Rosh Chodesh Iyyar			15	30
Monday	20	2nd day Rosh Chodesh Iyyar			16	IYYAR 1
Tuesday	21				17	2
Wednesday	22	Yom Hazikaron - Memorial Day			18	3
Thursday	23	Yom Ha'Atzmaut - Israel Independence Day			19	4
Friday	24				20	5
Saturday	25	Tazria-Metzorah	19.58	21.06	21	6
Sunday	26				22	7
Monday	27				23	8
Tuesday	28				24	9
Wednesday	29				25	10
Thursday	30				26	11

MAY 2015

12 IYYAR - 13 SIVAN 5775

Day			Begins previous day	Ends	OMER	
Friday	1				27	12
Saturday	2	Achare Mot-Kedoshim	20.09	21.19	28	13
Sunday	3				29	14
Monday	4				30	15
Tuesday	5				31	16
Wednesday	6				32	17
Thursday	7	Lag B'Omer			33	18
Friday	8				34	19
Saturday	9	Emor	20.21	21.33	35	20
Sunday	10				36	21
Monday	11				37	22
Tuesday	12				38	23
Wednesday	13				39	24
Thursday	14				40	25
Friday	15				41	26
Saturday	16	Behar-Bechukotai Mevarchim Sivan	20.32	21.46	42	27
Sunday	17	Yom Yerushalayim - Jerusalem Day			43	28
Monday	18				44	29
Tuesday	19	Rosh Chodesh Sivan			45	SIVAN 1
Wednesday	20				46	2
Thursday	21				47	3
Friday	22				48	4
Saturday	23	Bamidbar - SHAVUOT in evening	20.42	21.58	49	5
Sunday	24	1st Day SHAVUOT	21.59			6
Monday	25	2nd Day SHAVUOT		22.01		7
Tuesday	26					8
Wednesday	27					9
Thursday	28					10
Friday	29					11
Saturday	30	Naso	20.51	22.09		12
Sunday	31					13

JUNE 2015

14 SIVAN - 13 TAMMUZ 5775

Day			Begins previous day	Ends
Monday	1	14		
Tuesday	2	15		
Wednesday	3	16		
Thursday	4	17		
Friday	5	18		
Saturday	6	19	Beha'alotecha	20.58	22.18
Sunday	7	20		
Monday	8	21		
Tuesday	9	22		
Wednesday	10	23		
Thursday	11	24		
Friday	12	25		
Saturday	13	26	Shelach Lecha Mevarchim Tammuz	21.04	22.24
Sunday	14	27		
Monday	15	28		
Tuesday	16	29		
Wednesday	17	30	1st day Rosh Chodesh Tammuz	
Thursday	18	TAMMUZ 1	2nd day Rosh Chodesh Tammuz	
Friday	19	2		
Saturday	20	3	Korach	21.07	22.28
Sunday	21	4		
Monday	22	5		
Tuesday	23	6		
Wednesday	24	7		
Thursday	25	8		
Friday	26	9		
Saturday	27	10	Chukkat	21.08	22.28
Sunday	28	11		
Monday	29	12		
Tuesday	30	13		

JULY 2015

14 TAMMUZ - 15 AV 5775

Day	Date	Event	Begins previous day	Ends	Hebrew
Wednesday	1				14
Thursday	2				15
Friday	3				16
Saturday	4	Balak	21.06	22.24	17
Sunday	5	Fast of 17th Tammuz (postponed) begins	03.05	22.18	18
Monday	6				19
Tuesday	7				20
Wednesday	8				21
Thursday	9				22
Friday	10				23
Saturday	11	Pinchas - Haftarah Mattot - Mevarchim Av	21.02	22.18	24
Sunday	12				25
Monday	13				26
Tuesday	14				27
Wednesday	15				28
Thursday	16				29
Friday	17	Rosh Chodesh Av			AV 1
Saturday	18	Mattot-Masei	20.55	22.09	2
Sunday	19				3
Monday	20				4
Tuesday	21				5
Wednesday	22				6
Thursday	23				7
Friday	24				8
Saturday	25	Devarim - Shabbat Chazon	20.47	21.58	9
Sunday	26	Fast of 9th Av (postponed)	20.59	21.50	10
Monday	27				11
Tuesday	28				12
Wednesday	29				13
Thursday	30				14
Friday	31	Tu B'Av			15

AUGUST 2015

16 AV - 16 ELLUL 5775

			Begins previous day	Ends	
Saturday	1	Vaetchanan - Shabbat Nachamu	20.36	21.45	16
Sunday	2				17
Monday	3				18
Tuesday	4				19
Wednesday	5				20
Thursday	6				21
Friday	7				22
Saturday	8	Ekev Mevarchim Ellul	20.24	21.31	23
Sunday	9				24
Monday	10				25
Tuesday	11				26
Wednesday	12				27
Thursday	13				28
Friday	14				29
Saturday	15	Re'eh - 1st day Rosh Chodesh Ellul	20.11	21.16	30
Sunday	16	2nd day Rosh Chodesh Ellul			ELLUL 1
Monday	17	Sephardim begin Selichot			2
Tuesday	18				3
Wednesday	19				4
Thursday	20				5
Friday	21				6
Saturday	22	Shoftim	19.57	21.00	7
Sunday	23				8
Monday	24				9
Tuesday	25				10
Wednesday	26				11
Thursday	27				12
Friday	28				13
Saturday	29	Ki Tetze	19.42	20.43	14
Sunday	30				15
Monday	31				16

SEPTEMBER 2015 — 17 ELLUL 5775 - 17 TISHRI 5776

Day	Date		Begins previous day	Ends	
Tuesday	1				17
Wednesday	2				18
Thursday	3				19
Friday	4				20
Saturday	5	Ki Tavo	19.26	20.27	21
Sunday	6	Ashkenazim begin Selichot			22
Monday	7				23
Tuesday	8				24
Wednesday	9				25
Thursday	10				26
Friday	11				27
Saturday	12	Nitzavim	19.10	20.10	28
Sunday	13	Erev Rosh Hashanah			29
Monday	14	1st day ROSH HASHANAH 5776	19.05	20.05	TISHRI 1 5776
Tuesday	15	2nd day ROSH HASHANAH		20.03	2
Wednesday	16	Fast of Gedaliah begins	04.55	19.54	3
Thursday	17				4
Friday	18				5
Saturday	19	Vayelech - Shabbat Shuvah	18.54	19.53	6
Sunday	20				7
Monday	21				8
Tuesday	22	Erev Yom Kippur - Kol Nidre			9
Wednesday	23	YOM KIPPUR	18.45	19.44	10
Thursday	24				11
Friday	25				12
Saturday	26	Ha'azinu	18.38	19.37	13
Sunday	27				14
Monday	28	1st day SUKKOT	18.33	19.32	15
Tuesday	29	2nd day SUKKOT		19.30	16
Wednesday	30	1st day Chol Hamoed SUKKOT			17

OCTOBER 2015

18 TISHRI - 18 CHESHVAN 5776

			Begins previous day	Ends	
Thursday	1	2nd day Chol Hamoed SUKKOT			18
Friday	2	3rd day Chol Hamoed SUKKOT			19
Saturday	3	Shabbat Chol Hamoed SUKKOT	18.22	19.21	20
Sunday	4	Hoshanah Rabbah			21
Monday	5	SHEMINI ATZERET	18.17	19.16	22
Tuesday	6	SIMCHAT TORAH		19.14	23
Wednesday	7				24
Thursday	8				25
Friday	9				26
Saturday	10	Bereshit - Shabbat Bereshit - Mevarchim Cheshvan	18.06	19.05	27
Sunday	11				28
Monday	12				29
Tuesday	13	1st day Rosh Chodesh Cheshvan			30
Wednesday	14	2nd day Rosh Chodesh Cheshvan			CHESHVAN 1 5776
Thursday	15				2
Friday	16				3
Saturday	17	Noach	17.51	18.50	4
Sunday	18				5
Monday	19				6
Tuesday	20				7
Wednesday	21				8
Thursday	22				9
Friday	23				10
Saturday	24	Lech Lecha	17.36	18.37	11
Sunday	25	END OF BST			12
Monday	26				13
Tuesday	27				14
Wednesday	28				15
Thursday	29				16
Friday	30				17
Saturday	31	Vayera	16.23	17.24	18

NOVEMBER 2015 — 19 CHESHVAN - 18 KISLEV 5776

Day	Date	Event	Begins previous day	Ends	
Sunday	1				19
Monday	2				20
Tuesday	3				21
Wednesday	4				22
Thursday	5				23
Friday	6				24
Saturday	7	Chayye Sarah Mevarchim Kislev	16.10	17.13	25
Sunday	8				26
Monday	9				27
Tuesday	10				28
Wednesday	11				29
Thursday	12	1st day Rosh Chodesh Kislev			30
Friday	13	2nd day Rosh Chodesh Kislev			KISLEV 1
Saturday	14	Toldot	15.59	17.03	2
Sunday	15				3
Monday	16				4
Tuesday	17				5
Wednesday	18				6
Thursday	19				7
Friday	20				8
Saturday	21	Vayetze	15.50	16.55	9
Sunday	22				10
Monday	23				11
Tuesday	24				12
Wednesday	25				13
Thursday	26				14
Friday	27				15
Saturday	28	Vayishlach	15.43	16.50	16
Sunday	29				17
Monday	30				18

DECEMBER 2015

19 KISLEV - 19 TEVET 5776

			Begins previous day	Ends	
Tuesday	1				19
Wednesday	2				20
Thursday	3				21
Friday	4				22
Saturday	5	Vayeshev Mevarchim Tevet	15.38	16.46	23
Sunday	6	1st Chanukah Candle and begin Tal Umatar in evening			24
Monday	7	Chanukah Day 1			25
Tuesday	8	Chanukah Day 2			26
Wednesday	9	Chanukah Day 3			27
Thursday	10	Chanukah Day 4			28
Friday	11	Chanukah Day 5			29
Saturday	12	Chanukah Day 6 Mikketz - Shabbat Chanukah - 1st day Rosh Chodesh Tevet	15.36 - 16.45		30
Sunday	13	Chanukah Day 7 - 2nd day Rosh Chodesh Tevet			TEVET 1
Monday	14	Chanukah Day 8			2
Tuesday	15				3
Wednesday	16				4
Thursday	17				5
Friday	18				6
Saturday	19	Vayigash	15.37	16.47	7
Sunday	20				8
Monday	21				9
Tuesday	22	Fast of 10th Tevet begins	06.14	16.42	10
Wednesday	23				11
Thursday	24				12
Friday	25				13
Saturday	26	Vayechi	15.41	16.51	14
Sunday	27				15
Monday	28				16
Tuesday	29				17
Wednesday	30				18
Thursday	31				19

Please note the times for January 2016 have not yet been settled by the London Beth Din.

JANUARY 2016　　　20 TEVET - 21 SHEVAT 5776

Day	Date	Event	Begins previous day	Ends	Hebrew
Friday	1				20
Saturday	2	Shemot	16.27	17.26	21
Sunday	3				22
Monday	4				23
Tuesday	5				24
Wednesday	6				25
Thursday	7				26
Friday	8				27
Saturday	9	Va'era Mevarchim Shevat	16.33	17.31	28
Sunday	10				29
Monday	11	Rosh Chodesh Shevat			SHEVAT 1
Tuesday	12				2
Wednesday	13				3
Thursday	14				4
Friday	15				5
Saturday	16	Bo	16.39	17.37	6
Sunday	17				7
Monday	18				8
Tuesday	19				9
Wednesday	20				10
Thursday	21				11
Friday	22				12
Saturday	23	Beshallach - Shabbat Shirah	16.45	17.43	13
Sunday	24				14
Monday	25	Tu B'Shvat - New Year for Trees			15
Tuesday	26				16
Wednesday	27				17
Thursday	28				18
Friday	29				19
Saturday	30	Yitro	16.51	17.49	20
Sunday	31				21

Please note the times for February 2016 have not yet been settled by the London Beth Din.

FEBRUARY 2016

22 SHEVAT - 20 ADAR I 5776

Day			Begins previous day	Ends	
Monday	1				22
Tuesday	2				23
Wednesday	3				24
Thursday	4				25
Friday	5				26
Saturday	6	Mishpatim - Mevarchim Adar Rishon	16.58	17.54	27
Sunday	7				28
Monday	8				29
Tuesday	9	1st day Rosh Chodesh Adar Rishon			30
Wednesday	10	2nd day Rosh Chodesh Adar Rishon			ADAR I 1
Thursday	11				2
Friday	12				3
Saturday	13	Terumah	17.04	18.00	4
Sunday	14				5
Monday	15				6
Tuesday	16				7
Wednesday	17				8
Thursday	18				9
Friday	19				10
Saturday	20	Tetzaveh	17.10	18.06	11
Sunday	21				12
Monday	22				13
Tuesday	23	Purim Katan			14
Wednesday	24	Shushan Purim Katan			15
Thursday	25				16
Friday	26				17
Saturday	27	Ki Tissa	17.15	18.11	18
Sunday	28				19
Monday	29				20

EVENING TWILIGHT VARIATION FOR REGIONS

This table shows the number of minutes required to be added to, or substracted from, the times for London, in order to determine the time of the termination of Sabbath, Festival, or Fast. For dates between those indicated here, an approximate calculation must be made.

Acknowledgement is made to the Royal Greenwich Observatory for valued co-operation in the compilation of this table.

		BIRMINGHAM	BOURNEMOUTH	GLASGOW	LEEDS	LIVERPOOL	MANCHESTER	NEWCASTLE
Jan.	1	+ 9	+15	0	+ 4	+11	+ 8	0
	11	+ 9	+14	+ 1	+ 4	+11	+ 8	0
	21	+ 9	+14	+ 3	+ 5	+12	+ 9	+ 2
	31	+ 9	+13	+ 6	+ 6	+12	+ 9	+ 3
Feb.	10	+ 9	+12	+ 9	+ 7	+13	+10	+ 5
	20	+ 9	+11	+12	+ 8	+14	+11	+ 7
Mar.	2	+10	+10	+16	+10	+16	+13	+10
	12	+10	+ 9	+20	+12	+18	+15	+13
	22	+10	+ 7	+22	+12	+18	+15	+14
Apr.	1	+11	+ 7	+27	+15	+20	+17	+18
	11	+12	+ 7	+31	+17	+22	+19	+22
	21	+13	+ 7	+35	+20	+24	+21	+26
May	1	+16	+ 7	+40	+23	+27	+24	+30
	11	+18	+ 7	+46	+26	+30	+27	+35
	21	+20	+ 7	+52	+30	+34	+31	+42
	31	+23	+ 7	+57	+34	+37	+34	+48
June	10	+25	+ 7	+63	+38	+40	+38	+55
	20	+26	+ 7	+64	+40	+41	+39	+58
	30	+26	+ 7	+62	+38	+40	+38	+55
July	10	+23	+ 7	+57	+35	+38	+35	+50
	20	+21	+ 7	+51	+31	+34	+31	+43
	30	+19	+ 8	+46	+27	+30	+27	+38
Aug.	9	+17	+ 8	+40	+24	+27	+24	+32
	19	+16	+ 8	+35	+20	+25	+22	+27
	29	+16	+ 8	+30	+18	+23	+20	+23
Sept.	8	+14	+ 8	+26	+15	+20	+17	+18
	18	+13	+ 8	+23	+12	+18	+15	+15
	28	+13	+10	+20	+12	+18	+15	+14
Oct.	8	+12	+10	+16	+10	+16	+13	+10
	18	+11	+12	+13	+ 9	+15	+12	+9
	28	+11	+12	+10	+ 8	+14	+11	+6
Nov.	7	+10	+13	+ 7	+ 6	+13	+10	+4
	17	+10	+14	+ 4	+ 5	+12	+ 9	+3
	27	+10	+14	+ 2	+ 4	+11	+ 8	+1
Dec.	7	+10	+15	0	+ 4	+11	+ 8	0
	17	+ 9	+15	0	+ 3	+11	+ 7	- 1
	27	+ 9	+15	0	+ 3	+11	+ 8	- 1
	31	+ 9	+15	0	+ 4	+11	+ 8	0

According to the regulations valid among Orthodox Jews in Britain, marriages may not be solemnised on the following dates (all dates inclusive):

EVENT	2015	2016
Fast of 10th Tevet	1st January	———————
Fast of Esther	4th March	23rd March
Purim	5th March	24th March
The day before Pesach and the whole of Pesach	3rd to 11th April	22nd to 30th April
From 2nd Iyyar until the day before Lag B'Omer	21st April to 6th May	10th to 25th May
From the day after Lag B'Omer until 29th Iyyar	8th to 18th May	27th May to 6th June
The day before Shavuot and Shavuot	23rd May to 25th May	11th to 13th June
The Three Weeks from the Fast of 17th Tammuz until the Fast of 9th Av	5th July to 26th July	24th July to 14th August
The day before Rosh Hashanah and Rosh Hashanah	13th to 15th September	2nd to 4th October
The Fast of Gedaliah	16th September	5th October
The day before Yom Kippur and Yom Kippur	22nd and 23rd September	11th to 12th October
The day before Sukkot until Simchat Torah	27th September to 6th October	16th to 25th October
Fast of 10th Tevet	22nd December	———————

Nor on any Sabbath

Among Reform Jews, marriages are solemnised during the Omer Period (2ND Iyyar until 29th Iyyar), during the Three Weeks from the Fast of 17th Tammuz until the Fast of 9th Av (but not on the Fast of 9th Av itself), on the days that precede festivals, on the second days of festivals, and on Purim but not on the other days mentioned above.

JEWISH CALENDAR FOR THIRTY YEARS

5759–5788 (1998–2028)

INSTRUCTIONS FOR USE

The following Table shows on one line the civil date and the day of the week on which every date of the Jewish year falls during the thirty years which it covers; those dates which occur on Sabbath are printed in *heavier* type. Thus, Tishri 10, 5773, coincides with September 26, 2012, and this is a Wednesday, since September 22 is marked as being Sabbath. The civil dates on which the festivals and fasts (or any other occasion of the Jewish Calendar) occur in any particular year may be ascertained in the same manner. The Table is arranged according to the months of the Hebrew Year, the day of the month being shown in the left-hand column.

YAHRZEIT. – This is always observed on the Jewish date on which the parent died. It has never been customary under the jurisdiction of the Chief Rabbi of the United Hebrew Congregations of the British Commonwealth to observe the Yahrzeit after the death on the anniversary of the burial as is enjoined, in certain circumstances, by some authorities. If the death took place after dark, it must be dated from the next civil day, as the day is reckoned among Jews from sunset to sunset. This date must be located in the Table, according to the month and day, and the civil date of the Yahrzeit in any particular year will be found on the same line in the column beneath the year in question. It should be noted, however, that if a parent died during Adar in an ordinary year, the Yahrzeit is observed in a leap year in the first Adar. (Some people observe it in both Adars.) If the death took place in a leap year the Yahrzeit is observed in a leap year in the same Adar (whether First or Second) during which the death happened. The Yahrzeit begins and the memorial light is kindled on the evening before the civil date thus ascertained.

BARMITZVAH. – A boy attains his Barmitzvah (religious majority) when he reaches his thirteenth birthday, i.e., on the first day of his fourteenth year, this being computed according to the Jewish date on which he was born. The date and year of birth being located in the Table, the corresponding civil date of the first day of his fourteenth year will be found on the same line in the 13th column. If this be a Sabbath, he reads his *Parsha* on that day; if a week-day, he reads it on the following Sabbath. By consulting the Calendar, the scriptural portion of the week may be ascertained. It should be noted, however, that if a boy be born in Adar of an ordinary year and become Barmitzvah in a leap year, the celebration falls in the second Adar. If he were born in a leap year and becomes Barmitzvah in a leap year it is celebrated in that Adar (whether First or Second) during which his birth occurred. If he were born in a leap year and the Barmitzvah is in an ordinary year, it is observed in Adar.

The 30 year calendar is updated every 5 years. It starts from at least 13 years ago to enable barmitvah dates to be accurately pinpointed.

TISHRI (30 days)

Tish	5759	60	61	62	63	64	65	66	67	68	69	70	71	72	73	74	75	76	77	78	79	80	81	82	83	84	85	86	87	88
	1998	99	2000	01	02	03	04	05	06	07	08	09	10	11	12	13	14	15	16	17	18	19	20	21	22	23	24	25	26	27
	Sept-Oct	Sept-Oct	Sept-Oct	Sept-Oct	Sept-Oct	Sept-Oct	Sept-Oct	Oct-Nov	Sept-Oct	Sept-Oct	Sept-Oct	Sept-Oct	Sept-Oct	Sept-Oct	Sept-Oct	Sept-Oct	Sept-Oct	Sept-Oct	Oct-Nov	Sept-Oct	Sept-Oct	Sept-Oct	Sept-Oct	Sept-Oct	Sept-Oct	Sept-Oct	Oct-Nov	Sept-Oct	Sept-Oct	October
1	21	11	30	18	7	27	16	4	23	13	30	19	9	29	17	5	25	14	3	21	10	30	19	7	26	16	3	23	12	2
2	22	12	1	19	8	28	17	5	24	14	1	20	10	30	18	6	26	15	4	22	11	1	20	8	27	17	4	24	13	3
3	23	13	2	20	9	29	18	6	25	15	2	21	11	1	19	7	27	16	5	23	12	2	21	9	28	18	5	25	14	4
4	24	14	3	21	10	30	19	7	26	16	3	22	12	2	20	8	28	17	6	24	13	3	22	10	29	19	6	26	15	5
5	25	15	4	22	11	1	20	8	27	17	4	23	13	3	21	9	29	18	7	25	14	4	23	11	30	20	7	27	16	6
6	26	16	5	23	12	2	21	9	28	18	5	24	14	4	22	10	30	19	8	26	15	5	24	12	1	21	8	28	17	7
7	27	17	6	24	13	3	22	10	29	19	6	25	15	5	23	11	1	20	9	27	16	6	25	13	2	22	9	29	18	8
8	28	18	7	25	14	4	23	11	30	20	7	26	16	6	24	12	2	21	10	28	17	7	26	14	3	23	10	30	19	9
9	29	19	8	26	15	5	24	12	1	21	8	27	17	7	25	13	3	22	11	29	18	8	27	15	4	24	11	1	20	10
10	30	20	9	27	16	6	25	13	2	22	9	28	18	8	26	14	4	23	12	30	19	9	28	16	5	25	12	2	21	11
11	1	21	10	28	17	7	26	14	3	23	10	29	19	9	27	15	5	24	13	1	20	10	29	17	6	26	13	3	22	12
12	2	22	11	29	18	8	27	15	4	24	11	30	20	10	28	16	6	25	14	2	21	11	30	18	7	27	14	4	23	13
13	3	23	12	30	19	9	28	16	5	25	12	1	21	11	29	17	7	26	15	3	22	12	1	19	8	28	15	5	24	14
14	4	24	13	1	20	10	29	17	6	26	13	2	22	12	30	18	8	27	16	4	23	13	2	20	9	29	16	6	25	15
15	5	25	14	2	21	11	30	18	7	27	14	3	23	13	1	19	9	28	17	5	24	14	3	21	10	30	17	7	26	16
16	6	26	15	3	22	12	1	19	8	28	15	4	24	14	2	20	10	29	18	6	25	15	4	22	11	1	18	8	27	17
17	7	27	16	4	23	13	2	20	9	29	16	5	25	15	3	21	11	30	19	7	26	16	5	23	12	2	19	9	28	18
18	8	28	17	5	24	14	3	21	10	30	17	6	26	16	4	22	12	1	20	8	27	17	6	24	13	3	20	10	29	19
19	9	29	18	6	25	15	4	22	11	1	18	7	27	17	5	23	13	2	21	9	28	18	7	25	14	4	21	11	30	20
20	10	30	19	7	26	16	5	23	12	2	19	8	28	18	6	24	14	3	22	10	29	19	8	26	15	5	22	12	1	21
21	11	1	20	8	27	17	6	24	13	3	20	9	29	19	7	25	15	4	23	11	30	20	9	27	16	6	23	13	2	22
22	12	2	21	9	28	18	7	25	14	4	21	10	30	20	8	26	16	5	24	12	1	21	10	28	17	7	24	14	3	23
23	13	3	22	10	29	19	8	26	15	5	22	11	1	21	9	27	17	6	25	13	2	22	11	29	18	8	25	15	4	24
24	14	4	23	11	30	20	9	27	16	6	23	12	2	22	10	28	18	7	26	14	3	23	12	30	19	9	26	16	5	25
25	15	5	24	12	1	21	10	28	17	7	24	13	3	23	11	29	19	8	27	15	4	24	13	1	20	10	27	17	6	26
26	16	6	25	13	2	22	11	29	18	8	25	14	4	24	12	30	20	9	28	16	5	25	14	2	21	11	28	18	7	27
27	17	7	26	14	3	23	12	30	19	9	26	15	5	25	13	1	21	10	29	17	6	26	15	3	22	12	29	19	8	28
28	18	8	27	15	4	24	13	31	20	10	27	16	6	26	14	2	22	11	30	18	7	27	16	4	23	13	30	20	9	29
29	19	9	28	16	5	25	14	1	21	11	28	17	7	27	15	3	23	12	31	19	8	28	17	5	24	14	31	21	10	30
30	20	10	29	17	6	26	15	2	22	12	29	18	8	28	16	4	24	13	1	20	9	29	18	6	25	15	1	22	11	31

In the left-hand margin figures in **black type** denote major Holy-days; elsewhere they denote Sabbaths.
1st and 2nd, New Year; 3rd, Fast of Gedaliah (if on Sabbath, postponed to Sunday); 10th, Day of Atonement; 15th to 23rd, Tabernacles, etc.; 30th, First day of New Moon of Marcheshvan.

CHESHVAN or MARCHESHVAN (29 or 30 days)

Chesh	5759	60	61	62	63	64	65	66	67	68	69	70	71	72	73	74	75	76	77	78	79	80	81	82	83	84	85	86	87	88
	1998	99	2000	01	02	03	04	05	06	07	08	09	10	11	12	13	14	15	16	17	18	19	20	21	22	23	24	25	26	27
	Oct-Nov	Oct-Nov	Oct-Nov	Oct-Nov	Oct-Nov	Oct-Nov	Oct-Nov	Nov-Dec	Oct-Nov	Oct-Nov	Oct-Nov	Oct-Nov	Oct-Nov	Oct-Nov	Oct-Nov	Oct-Nov	Oct-Nov	Oct-Nov	Nov	Oct-Nov	Oct-Nov	Oct-Nov	Oct-Nov	Oct-Nov	Oct-Nov	Oct-Nov	Nov-Dec	Oct-Nov	Oct-Nov	Nov
1	21	11	30	18	7	27	16	3	23	13	30	19	9	29	17	5	25	14	2	21	10	30	19	7	26	16	2	23	12	1
2	22	12	31	19	8	28	17	4	24	14	31	20	10	30	18	6	26	15	3	22	11	31	20	8	27	17	3	24	13	2
3	23	13	1	20	9	29	18	5	25	15	1	21	11	31	19	7	27	16	4	23	12	1	21	9	28	18	4	25	14	3
4	24	14	2	21	10	30	19	6	26	16	2	22	12	1	20	8	28	17	5	24	13	2	22	10	29	19	5	26	15	4
5	25	15	3	22	11	31	20	7	27	17	3	23	13	2	21	9	29	18	6	25	14	3	23	11	30	20	6	27	16	5
6	26	16	4	23	12	1	21	8	28	18	4	24	14	3	22	10	30	19	7	26	15	4	24	12	31	21	7	28	17	6
7	27	17	5	24	13	2	22	9	29	19	5	25	15	4	23	11	31	20	8	27	16	5	25	13	1	22	8	29	18	7
8	28	18	6	25	14	3	23	10	30	20	6	26	16	5	24	12	1	21	9	28	17	6	26	14	2	23	9	30	19	8
9	29	19	7	26	15	4	24	11	31	21	7	27	17	6	25	13	2	22	10	29	18	7	27	15	3	24	10	31	20	9
10	30	20	8	27	16	5	25	12	1	22	8	28	18	7	26	14	3	23	11	30	19	8	28	16	4	25	11	1	21	10
11	31	21	9	28	17	6	26	13	2	23	9	29	19	8	27	15	4	24	12	31	20	9	29	17	5	26	12	2	22	11
12	1	22	10	29	18	7	27	14	3	24	10	30	20	9	28	16	5	25	13	1	21	10	30	18	6	27	13	3	23	12
13	2	23	11	30	19	8	28	15	4	25	11	31	21	10	29	17	6	26	14	2	22	11	31	19	7	28	14	4	24	13
14	3	24	12	31	20	9	29	16	5	26	12	1	22	11	30	18	7	27	15	3	23	12	1	20	8	29	15	5	25	14
15	4	25	13	1	21	10	30	17	6	27	13	2	23	12	31	19	8	28	16	4	24	13	2	21	9	30	16	6	26	15
16	5	26	14	2	22	11	31	18	7	28	14	3	24	13	1	20	9	29	17	5	25	14	3	22	10	31	17	7	27	16
17	6	27	15	3	23	12	1	19	8	29	15	4	25	14	2	21	10	30	18	6	26	15	4	23	11	1	18	8	28	17
18	7	28	16	4	24	13	2	20	9	30	16	5	26	15	3	22	11	31	19	7	27	16	5	24	12	2	19	9	29	18
19	8	29	17	5	25	14	3	21	10	31	17	6	27	16	4	23	12	1	20	8	28	17	6	25	13	3	20	10	30	19
20	9	30	18	6	26	15	4	22	11	1	18	7	28	17	5	24	13	2	21	9	29	18	7	26	14	4	21	11	31	20
21	10	31	19	7	27	16	5	23	12	2	19	8	29	18	6	25	14	3	22	10	30	19	8	27	15	5	22	12	1	21
22	11	1	20	8	28	17	6	24	13	3	20	9	30	19	7	26	15	4	23	11	31	20	9	28	16	6	23	13	2	22
23	12	2	21	9	29	18	7	25	14	4	21	10	31	20	8	27	16	5	24	12	1	21	10	29	17	7	24	14	3	23
24	13	3	22	10	30	19	8	26	15	5	22	11	1	21	9	28	17	6	25	13	2	22	11	30	18	8	25	15	4	24
25	14	4	23	11	31	20	9	27	16	6	23	12	2	22	10	29	18	7	26	14	3	23	12	31	19	9	26	16	5	25
26	15	5	24	12	1	21	10	28	17	7	24	13	3	23	11	30	19	8	27	15	4	24	13	1	20	10	27	17	6	26
27	16	6	25	13	2	22	11	29	18	8	25	14	4	24	12	31	20	9	28	16	5	25	14	2	21	11	28	18	7	27
28	17	7	26	14	3	23	12	30	19	9	26	15	5	25	13	1	21	10	29	17	6	26	15	3	22	12	29	19	8	28
29	18	8	27	15	4	24	13	1	20	10	27	16	6	26	14	2	22	11	30	18	7	27	16	4	23	13	30	20	9	29
30	19	9	-	-	5	25	-	-	21	-	-	17	7	-	-	3	-	12	-	-	8	28	-	-	24	-	1	-	10	30

Figures in **black type** denote Sabbaths.
30th, First day of New Moon of Kislev.

KISLEV (29 or 30 days)

Kis	88	87	86	85	84	83	82	81	80	79	78	77	76	75	74	73	72	71	70	69	68	67	66	65	64	63	62	61	60	5759
	27	26	25	24	23	22	21	20	19	18	17	16	15	14	13	12	11	10	09	08	07	06	05	04	03	02	01	2000	99	1998
	Dec	Nov-Dec	Nov-Dec	Dec	Nov-Dec	Nov-Dec	Nov-Dec	Nov-Dec	Nov-Dec	Nov-Dec	Nov-Dec	Dec	Nov-Dec	Nov-Dec	Nov-Dec	Nov-Dec	Nov-Dec	Nov-Dec	Nov-Dec	Nov-Dec	Nov-Dec	Nov-Dec	Dec	Nov-Dec	Nov-Dec	Nov-Dec	Nov-Dec	Nov-Dec	Nov-Dec	Nov-Dec
1	1	11	21	2	14	25	5	17	29	9	19	1	13	23	4	15	27	8	18	28	11	22	2	14	26	6	16	28	10	20
2	2	12	**22**	3	15	**26**	**6**	18	**30**	**10**	20	2	**14**	24	5	16	28	9	19	**29**	12	23	**3**	15	27	7	**17**	29	11	**21**
3	3	13	23	4	16	27	7	19	1	11	21	**3**	15	25	6	**17**	29	10	20	30	13	24	4	16	28	8	18	30	12	22
4	**4**	**14**	24	5	17	28	8	20	2	12	22	4	16	26	7	18	30	11	**21**	1	14	**25**	5	17	**29**	**9**	19	1	**13**	23
5	5	15	25	6	**18**	29	9	**21**	3	13	23	5	17	27	8	19	1	12	22	2	15	26	6	18	30	10	20	**2**	14	24
6	6	16	26	**7**	19	30	10	22	4	14	24	6	18	28	**9**	20	2	**13**	23	3	16	27	7	19	1	11	21	3	15	25
7	7	17	27	8	20	1	11	23	5	15	**25**	7	19	**29**	10	21	**3**	14	24	4	**17**	28	8	**20**	2	12	22	4	16	26
8	8	18	28	9	21	2	12	24	6	16	26	8	20	30	11	22	4	15	25	5	18	29	9	21	3	13	23	5	17	27
9	9	19	**29**	10	22	**3**	**13**	25	**7**	**17**	27	9	**21**	1	12	23	5	16	26	**6**	19	30	10	22	4	14	24	**6**	18	**28**
10	10	20	30	11	23	4	14	26	8	18	28	**10**	22	2	13	**24**	6	17	27	7	20	1	11	23	5	15	25	7	19	29
11	**11**	**21**	1	12	24	5	15	27	9	19	29	11	23	3	14	25	7	18	**28**	8	21	**2**	12	24	**6**	**16**	26	8	**20**	30
12	12	22	2	13	**25**	6	16	**28**	10	20	30	12	24	4	15	26	8	19	29	**9**	22	3	13	25	7	17	27	**9**	21	1
13	13	23	3	**14**	26	7	17	29	11	21	1	13	25	5	**16**	27	9	**20**	30	10	23	4	14	26	8	18	28	10	22	2
14	14	24	4	15	27	8	18	30	12	22	**2**	14	26	**6**	17	28	**10**	21	1	11	**24**	5	15	**27**	9	19	29	11	23	3
15	15	25	5	16	28	9	19	1	13	23	3	15	27	7	18	29	11	22	2	12	25	6	16	28	10	20	30	12	24	4
16	16	26	**6**	17	29	**10**	**20**	2	**14**	**24**	4	16	**28**	8	19	30	12	23	3	**13**	26	7	**17**	29	11	21	1	**13**	25	**5**
17	17	27	7	18	30	11	21	3	15	25	5	**17**	29	9	20	**1**	13	24	4	14	27	8	18	30	12	22	2	14	26	6
18	**18**	**28**	8	19	1	12	22	4	16	26	6	18	30	10	21	2	14	25	**5**	15	28	**9**	19	1	**13**	**23**	3	15	**27**	7
19	19	29	9	20	**2**	13	23	**5**	17	27	7	19	1	11	22	3	15	26	6	**16**	29	10	20	2	14	24	4	**16**	28	8
20	20	30	**10**	**21**	3	14	24	6	18	28	8	20	2	12	**23**	4	16	**27**	7	17	30	11	**21**	3	15	25	5	17	29	**9**
21	**21**	1	11	22	4	15	25	7	19	29	**9**	21	3	**13**	24	5	**17**	28	8	18	**1**	12	22	**4**	16	26	6	18	30	10
22	22	2	12	23	5	16	26	8	20	30	10	22	4	14	25	6	18	29	9	19	2	13	23	5	17	27	7	19	1	11
23	23	**3**	**13**	24	6	**17**	**27**	9	**21**	**1**	11	23	**5**	15	26	**7**	19	30	10	**20**	3	14	**24**	6	18	28	8	**20**	2	**12**
24	**24**	4	14	25	7	18	28	10	22	2	**12**	**24**	6	16	27	**8**	20	1	11	21	4	15	25	**7**	19	29	9	21	3	13
25	**25**	**5**	15	26	8	19	29	11	23	3	13	25	7	17	28	9	21	2	**12**	22	5	**16**	26	8	**20**	**30**	10	22	**4**	14
26	26	6	16	27	**9**	20	30	**12**	24	4	14	26	8	18	29	10	22	3	13	23	6	17	27	9	21	1	11	**23**	5	15
27	27	7	17	**28**	10	21	1	13	25	5	15	27	9	19	**30**	11	23	**4**	14	24	7	18	28	10	22	2	12	24	6	16
28	28	8	18	29	11	22	2	14	26	6	**16**	28	10	**20**	1	12	**24**	5	15	25	**8**	19	29	**11**	23	3	13	**25**	7	17
29	29	9	19	30	12	23	3	15	27	7	17	29	11	21	2	13	25	6	16	26	9	20	30	12	24	4	14	26	8	18
30	30	10	**20**	31	—	**24**	**4**	—	**28**	**8**	18	—	**12**	22	3	—	26	7	17	**27**	—	21	**31**	—	25	5	15	—	9	**19**

Figures in **black type** denote Sabbaths.

25th to 29th or 30th, Chanucah (opening days); 30th, First day of New Moon of Tebet.

TEBET (29 days)

Teb	88	87	86	85	84	83	82	81	80	79	78	77	76	75	74	73	72	71	70	69	68	67	66	65	64	63	62	61	60	5759
	27/28	26/27	25/26	25	23/24	22/23	21/22	20/21	19/20	18/19	17/18	16/17	15/16	14/15	13/14	12/13	11/12	10/11	09/10	08/09	07/08	06/07	06	04/05	03/04	02/03	01/02	2000/01	99/2000	1998/1999
	Dec-Jan	Dec-Jan	Dec-Jan	Jan	Dec-Jan	Dec-Jan	Dec-Jan	Dec-Jan	Dec-Jan	Dec-Jan	Dec-Jan	Dec-Jan	Dec-Jan	Dec-Jan	Dec-Jan	Dec-Jan	Dec-Jan	Dec-Jan	Dec-Jan	Dec-Jan	Dec-Jan	Dec-Jan	Jan	Dec-Jan	Dec-Jan	Dec-Jan	Dec-Jan	Dec-Jan	Dec-Jan	Dec-Jan
1	31	11	21	1	13	25	5	16	29	9	19	30	13	23	4	14	27	8	18	28	10	22	1	13	26	6	16	27	10	20
2	1	12	22	2	14	26	6	17	30	10	20	31	14	24	5	15	28	9	19	29	11	23	2	14	27	7	17	28	11	21
3	2	13	23	3	15	27	7	18	31	11	21	1	15	25	6	16	29	10	20	30	12	24	3	15	28	8	18	29	12	22
4	3	14	24	4	16	28	8	19	1	12	22	2	16	26	7	17	30	11	21	31	13	25	4	16	29	9	19	30	13	23
5	4	15	25	5	17	29	9	20	2	13	23	3	17	27	8	18	31	12	22	1	14	26	5	17	30	10	20	31	14	24
6	5	16	26	6	18	30	10	21	3	14	24	4	18	28	9	19	1	13	23	2	15	27	6	18	31	11	21	1	15	25
7	6	17	27	7	19	31	11	22	4	15	25	5	19	29	10	20	2	14	24	3	16	28	7	19	1	12	22	2	16	26
8	7	18	28	8	20	1	12	23	5	16	26	6	20	30	11	21	3	15	25	4	17	29	8	20	2	13	23	3	17	27
9	8	19	29	9	21	2	13	24	6	17	27	7	21	31	12	22	4	16	26	5	18	30	9	21	3	14	24	4	18	28
10	9	20	30	10	22	3	14	25	7	18	28	8	22	1	13	23	5	17	27	6	19	31	10	22	4	15	25	5	19	29
11	10	21	31	11	23	4	15	26	8	19	29	9	23	2	14	24	6	18	28	7	20	1	11	23	5	16	26	6	20	30
12	11	22	1	12	24	5	16	27	9	20	30	10	24	3	15	25	7	19	29	8	21	2	12	24	6	17	27	7	21	31
13	12	23	2	13	25	6	17	28	10	21	31	11	25	4	16	26	8	20	30	9	22	3	13	25	7	18	28	8	22	1
14	13	24	3	14	26	7	18	29	11	22	1	12	26	5	17	27	9	21	31	10	23	4	14	26	8	19	29	9	23	2
15	14	25	4	15	27	8	19	30	12	23	2	13	27	6	18	28	10	22	1	11	24	5	15	27	9	20	30	10	24	3
16	15	26	5	16	28	9	20	31	13	24	3	14	28	7	19	29	11	23	2	12	25	6	16	28	10	21	31	11	25	4
17	16	27	6	17	29	10	21	1	14	25	4	15	29	8	20	30	12	24	3	13	26	7	17	29	11	22	1	12	26	5
18	17	28	7	18	30	11	22	2	15	26	5	16	30	9	21	31	13	25	4	14	27	8	18	30	12	23	2	13	27	6
19	18	29	8	19	31	12	23	3	16	27	6	17	31	10	22	1	14	26	5	15	28	9	19	31	13	24	3	14	28	7
20	19	30	9	20	1	13	24	4	17	28	7	18	1	11	23	2	15	27	6	16	29	10	20	1	14	25	4	15	29	8
21	20	31	10	21	2	14	25	5	18	29	8	19	2	12	24	3	16	28	7	17	30	11	21	2	15	26	5	16	30	9
22	21	1	11	22	3	15	26	6	19	30	9	20	3	13	25	4	17	29	8	18	31	12	22	3	16	27	6	17	31	10
23	22	2	12	23	4	16	27	7	20	31	10	21	4	14	26	5	18	30	9	19	1	13	23	4	17	28	7	18	1	11
24	23	3	13	24	5	17	28	8	21	1	11	22	5	15	27	6	19	31	10	20	2	14	24	5	18	29	8	19	2	12
25	24	4	14	25	6	18	29	9	22	2	12	23	6	16	28	7	20	1	11	21	3	15	25	6	19	30	9	20	3	13
26	25	5	15	26	7	19	30	10	23	3	13	24	7	17	29	8	21	2	12	22	4	16	26	7	20	31	10	21	4	14
27	26	6	16	27	8	20	31	11	24	4	14	25	8	18	30	9	22	3	13	23	5	17	27	8	21	1	11	22	5	15
28	27	7	17	28	9	21	1	12	25	5	15	26	9	19	31	10	23	4	14	24	6	18	28	9	22	2	12	23	6	16
29	28	8	18	29	10	22	2	13	26	6	16	27	10	20	1	11	24	5	15	25	7	19	29	10	23	3	13	24	7	17

Figures in **black type** denote Sabbaths.
1st to 2nd or 3rd, Chanucah (final days); 10th, Fast of Tebet.

SHEBAT (30 days)

Sheb	88	87	86	85	84	83	82	81	80	79	78	77	76	75	74	73	72	71	70	69	68	67	66	65	64	63	62	61	60	5759
	28	27	26	25	24	23	22	21	20	19	18	17	16	15	14	13	12	11	10	09	08	07	06	05	04	03	02	01	2000	1999
	Jan-Feb	Jan-Feb	Jan-Feb	Jan-Feb	Jan-Feb	Jan-Feb	Jan-Feb	Jan-Feb	Jan-Feb	Jan-Feb	Jan-Feb	Jan-Feb	Jan-Feb	Jan-Feb	January	Jan-Feb	Jan-Feb	Jan-Feb	Jan-Feb	Jan-Feb	Jan-Feb	Jan-Feb	Jan-Feb	Jan-Feb	Jan-Feb	Jan-Feb	Jan-Feb	Jan-Feb	Jan-Feb	Jan-Feb
1	**29**	**9**	19	30	11	23	3	14	27	7	17	**28**	11	21	2	**12**	25	6	**16**	26	8	**20**	30	11	**24**	**4**	14	25	**8**	18
2	30	10	20	31	12	24	4	15	28	8	18	29	12	22	3	13	26	7	17	27	9	21	31	12	25	5	15	26	9	19
3	31	11	21	**1**	**13**	25	5	**16**	29	9	19	30	13	23	**4**	14	27	**8**	18	28	10	22	1	13	26	6	16	**27**	10	20
4	1	12	22	2	14	26	6	17	30	10	**20**	31	14	**24**	5	15	**28**	9	19	29	11	23	2	14	27	7	17	28	11	21
5	2	13	23	3	15	27	7	18	31	11	21	1	15	25	6	16	29	10	20	30	**12**	24	3	**15**	28	8	18	29	12	22
6	3	14	**24**	4	16	**28**	**8**	19	**1**	**12**	22	2	**16**	26	7	17	30	11	21	**31**	13	25	**4**	16	29	9	**19**	30	13	**23**
7	4	15	25	5	17	29	9	20	2	13	23	3	17	27	8	18	31	12	22	1	14	26	5	17	30	10	20	31	14	24
8	**5**	**16**	26	6	18	30	10	21	3	14	24	**4**	18	28	9	**19**	1	13	**23**	2	15	**27**	6	18	**31**	**11**	21	1	**15**	25
9	6	17	27	7	19	31	11	22	4	15	25	5	19	29	10	20	2	14	24	3	16	28	7	19	1	12	22	2	16	26
10	7	18	28	**8**	**20**	1	12	**23**	5	16	26	6	20	30	**11**	21	3	**15**	25	4	17	29	8	20	2	13	23	**3**	17	27
11	8	19	29	9	21	2	13	24	6	17	**27**	7	21	**31**	12	22	**4**	16	26	5	18	30	9	21	3	14	24	4	18	28
12	9	20	30	10	22	3	14	25	7	18	28	8	22	1	13	23	5	17	27	6	**19**	31	10	**22**	4	15	25	5	19	29
13	10	21	**31**	11	23	**4**	**15**	26	**8**	**19**	29	9	**23**	2	14	24	6	18	28	**7**	20	1	**11**	23	5	16	**26**	6	20	**30**
14	11	22	1	12	24	5	16	27	9	20	30	10	24	3	15	25	7	19	29	8	21	2	12	24	6	17	27	7	21	31
15	**12**	**23**	2	13	25	6	17	28	10	21	31	**11**	25	4	16	**26**	8	20	**30**	9	22	**3**	13	25	**7**	**18**	28	8	**22**	1
16	13	24	3	14	26	7	18	29	11	22	1	12	26	5	17	27	9	21	31	10	23	4	14	26	8	19	29	9	23	2
17	14	25	4	**15**	**27**	8	19	**30**	12	23	2	13	27	6	**18**	28	10	**22**	1	11	24	5	15	27	9	20	30	**10**	24	3
18	15	26	5	16	28	9	20	31	13	24	**3**	14	28	**7**	19	29	**11**	23	2	12	25	6	16	28	10	21	31	11	25	4
19	16	27	6	17	29	10	21	1	14	25	4	15	29	8	20	30	12	24	3	13	**26**	7	17	**29**	11	22	1	12	26	5
20	17	28	**7**	18	30	**11**	**22**	2	**15**	**26**	5	16	**30**	9	21	31	13	25	4	**14**	27	8	**18**	30	12	23	**2**	13	27	**6**
21	18	29	8	19	31	12	23	3	16	27	6	17	31	10	22	1	14	26	5	15	28	9	19	31	13	24	3	14	28	7
22	**19**	**30**	9	20	1	13	24	4	17	28	7	**18**	1	11	23	**2**	15	27	**6**	16	29	**10**	20	1	**14**	**25**	4	15	**29**	8
23	20	31	10	21	2	14	25	5	18	29	8	19	2	12	24	3	16	28	7	17	30	11	21	2	15	26	5	16	30	9
24	21	1	11	**22**	**3**	15	26	**6**	19	30	9	20	3	13	**25**	4	17	**29**	8	18	31	12	22	3	16	27	6	**17**	31	10
25	22	2	12	23	4	16	27	7	20	31	**10**	21	4	**14**	26	5	**18**	30	9	19	1	13	23	4	17	28	7	18	1	11
26	23	3	13	24	5	17	28	8	21	1	11	22	5	15	27	6	19	31	10	20	**2**	14	24	**5**	18	29	8	19	2	12
27	24	4	**14**	25	6	**18**	**29**	9	**22**	**2**	12	23	**6**	16	28	7	20	1	11	**21**	3	15	**25**	6	19	30	**9**	20	3	**13**
28	25	5	15	26	7	19	30	10	23	3	13	24	7	17	29	8	21	2	12	22	4	16	26	7	20	31	10	21	4	14
29	**26**	**6**	16	27	8	20	31	11	24	4	14	**25**	8	18	30	**9**	22	3	**13**	23	5	**17**	27	8	**21**	**1**	11	22	**5**	15
30	27	7	17	28	9	21	1	12	25	5	15	26	9	19	31	10	23	4	14	24	6	18	28	9	22	2	12	23	6	16

Figures in **black type** denote Sabbaths.

15th, New Year for Trees; 30th, First day of New Moon of Adar.

ADAR (29 days); in Leap Year, known as ADAR RISHON — 1st ADAR (30 days)

Adar	88	87	86	85	84	83	82	81	80	79	78	77	76	75	74	73	72	71	70	69	68	67	66	65	64	63	62	61	60	5759
	28	27	26	25	24	23	22	21	20	19	18	17	16	15	14	13	12	11	10	09	08	07	06	05	04	03	02	01	2000	1999
	Feb-Mar	Feb-Mar	Feb-Mar	March	Feb-Mar	Feb-Mar	Feb-Mar	Feb-Mar	Feb-Mar	Feb-Mar	Feb-Mar	Feb-Mar	Feb-Mar	Feb-Mar	Feb-Mar	Feb-Mar	Feb-Mar	Feb-Mar	Feb-Mar	Feb-Mar	Feb-Mar	Feb-Mar	March	Feb-Mar	Feb-Mar	Feb-Mar	Feb-Mar	Feb-Mar	Feb-Mar	Feb-Mar
1	28	8	18	1	10	22	2	13	26	6	16	27	10	20	1	11	24	5	15	25	7	19	1	10	23	3	13	24	7	17
2	29	9	19	2	11	23	3	14	27	7	17	28	11	21	2	12	25	6	16	26	8	20	2	11	24	4	14	25	8	18
3	1	10	20	3	12	24	4	15	28	8	18	1	12	22	3	13	26	7	17	27	9	21	3	12	25	5	15	26	9	19
4	2	11	21	4	13	25	5	16	29	9	19	2	13	23	4	14	27	8	18	28	10	22	4	13	26	6	16	27	10	20
5	3	12	22	5	14	26	6	17	1	10	20	3	14	24	5	15	28	9	19	1	11	23	5	14	27	7	17	28	11	21
6	4	13	23	6	15	27	7	18	2	11	21	4	15	25	6	16	29	10	20	2	12	24	6	15	28	8	18	1	12	22
7	5	14	24	7	16	28	8	19	3	12	22	5	16	26	7	17	1	11	21	3	13	25	7	16	29	9	19	2	13	23
8	6	15	25	8	17	1	9	20	4	13	23	6	17	27	8	18	2	12	22	4	14	26	8	17	1	10	20	3	14	24
9	7	16	26	9	18	2	10	21	5	14	24	7	18	28	9	19	3	13	23	5	15	27	9	18	2	11	21	4	15	25
10	8	17	27	10	19	3	11	22	6	15	25	8	19	1	10	20	4	14	24	6	16	28	10	19	3	12	22	5	16	26
11	9	18	28	11	20	4	12	23	7	16	26	9	20	2	11	21	5	15	25	7	17	1	11	20	4	13	23	6	17	27
12	10	19	1	12	21	5	13	24	8	17	27	10	21	3	12	22	6	16	26	8	18	2	12	21	5	14	24	7	18	28
13	11	20	2	13	22	6	14	25	9	18	28	11	22	4	13	23	7	17	27	9	19	3	13	22	6	15	25	8	19	1
14	12	21	3	14	23	7	15	26	10	19	1	12	23	5	14	24	8	18	28	10	20	4	14	23	7	16	26	9	20	2
15	13	22	4	15	24	8	16	27	11	20	2	13	24	6	15	25	9	19	1	11	21	5	15	24	8	17	27	10	21	3
16	14	23	5	16	25	9	17	28	12	21	3	14	25	7	16	26	10	20	2	12	22	6	16	25	9	18	28	11	22	4
17	15	24	6	17	26	10	18	1	13	22	4	15	26	8	17	27	11	21	3	13	23	7	17	26	10	19	1	12	23	5
18	16	25	7	18	27	11	19	2	14	23	5	16	27	9	18	28	12	22	4	14	24	8	18	27	11	20	2	13	24	6
19	17	26	8	19	28	12	20	3	15	24	6	17	28	10	19	1	13	23	5	15	25	9	19	28	12	21	3	14	25	7
20	18	27	9	20	29	13	21	4	16	25	7	18	29	11	20	2	14	24	6	16	26	10	20	1	13	22	4	15	26	8
21	19	28	10	21	1	14	22	5	17	26	8	19	1	12	21	3	15	25	7	17	27	11	21	2	14	23	5	16	27	9
22	20	1	11	22	2	15	23	6	18	27	9	20	2	13	22	4	16	26	8	18	28	12	22	3	15	24	6	17	28	10
23	21	2	12	23	3	16	24	7	19	28	10	21	3	14	23	5	17	27	9	19	29	13	23	4	16	25	7	18	29	11
24	22	3	13	24	4	17	25	8	20	1	11	22	4	15	24	6	18	28	10	20	1	14	24	5	17	26	8	19	1	12
25	23	4	14	25	5	18	26	9	21	2	12	23	5	16	25	7	19	1	11	21	2	15	25	6	18	27	9	20	2	13
26	24	5	15	26	6	19	27	10	22	3	13	24	6	17	26	8	20	2	12	22	3	16	26	7	19	28	10	21	3	14
27	25	6	16	27	7	20	28	11	23	4	14	25	7	18	27	9	21	3	13	23	4	17	27	8	20	1	11	22	4	15
28	26	7	17	28	8	21	1	12	24	5	15	26	8	19	28	10	22	4	14	24	5	18	28	9	21	2	12	23	5	16
29	27	8	18	29	9	22	2	13	25	6	16	27	9	20	1	11	23	5	15	25	6	19	29	10	22	3	13	24	6	17
30	—	R	—	—	R	—	R	—	—	R	—	—	R	—	R	—	—	R	—	R	R	—	—	R	—	R	—	—	R	—

Figures in **black type** denote Sabbaths.

13th, Fast of Esther (if on Sabbath, observed the preceding Thursday); 14th, Purim; 15th, Shushan Purim.

NOTE. — In a Jewish leap year, indicated by the letter R (for Adar Rishon) at the foot of a column, the above days are observed in 2nd Adar.

In a leap year, 30th day is First day of New Moon of the 2nd Adar.

2nd ADAR — ADAR SHENI, also known as VE-ADAR (29 days)

2nd Adar	5759 / 1999	60 / 2000	61 / 01	62 / 02	63 / 03	64 / 04	65 / 05	66 / 06	67 / 07	68 / 08	69 / 09	70 / 10	71 / 11	72 / 12	73 / 13	74 / 14	75 / 15	76 / 16	77 / 17	78 / 18	79 / 19	80 / 20	81 / 21	82 / 22	83 / 23	84 / 24	85 / 25	86 / 26	87 / 27	88 / 28
		Mar-Apr			Mar-Apr		Mar-Apr			Mar-Apr			Mar-Apr			March		Mar-Apr			Mar-Apr			Mar-Apr		Mar-Apr			Mar-Apr	
1		8			5		**12**			**8**			7			3		11			8			4		11			10	
2		9			6		13			9			8			4		**12**			9			**5**		12			11	
3		10			7		14			10			9			5		13			10			6		13			12	
4		**11**			**8**		15			11			10			6		14			11			7		14			**13**	
5		12			9		16			12			11			7		15			12			8		15			14	
6		13			10		17			13			**12**			**8**		16			13			9		**16**			15	
7		14			11		18			14			13			9		17			14			10		17			16	
8		15			12		**19**			**15**			14			10		18			15			11		18			17	
9		16			13		20			16			15			11		**19**			**16**			**12**		19			18	
10		17			14		21			17			16			12		20			17			13		20			19	
11		**18**			**15**		22			18			17			13		21			18			14		21			**20**	
12		19			16		23			19			18			14		22			19			15		22			21	
13		20			17		24			20			**19**			**15**		23			20			16		**23**			22	
14		21			18		25			21			20			16		24			21			17		24			23	
15		22			19		**26**			**22**			21			17		25			22			18		25			24	
16		23			20		27			23			22			18		**26**			**23**			**19**		26			25	
17		24			21		28			24			23			19		27			24			20		27			26	
18		**25**			**22**		29			25			24			20		28			25			21		28			**27**	
19		26			23		30			26			25			21		29			26			22		29			28	
20		27			24		31			27			**26**			**22**		30			27			23		**30**			29	
21		28			25		1			28			27			23		31			28			24		31			30	
22		29			26		**2**			**29**			28			24		1			29			25		1			31	
23		30			27		3			30			29			25		**2**			**30**			**26**		2			1	
24		31			28		4			31			30			26		3			31			27		3			2	
25		**1**			**29**		5			1			31			27		4			1			28		4			**3**	
26		2			30		6			2			1			28		5			2			29		5			4	
27		3			31		7			3			**2**			**29**		6			3			30		**6**			5	
28		4			1		8			4			3			30		7			4			31		7			6	
29		5			2		**9**			**5**			4			31		8			5			1		8			7	

Figures in **black type** denote Sabbaths.

13th, Fast of Esther (if on Sabbath, observed on the preceding Thursday); 14th, Purim; 15th Shushan Purim.

NISAN (30 days)

Nis	88	87	86	85	84	83	82	81	80	79	78	77	76	75	74	73	72	71	70	69	68	67	66	65	64	63	62	61	60	5759
	28	27	26	25	24	23	22	21	20	19	18	17	16	15	14	13	12	11	10	09	08	07	06	05	04	03	02	01	2000	1999
	Mar-Apr	Apr-May	Mar-Apr	Mar-Apr	Apr-May	Mar-Apr	Apr-May	Mar-Apr	Mar-Apr	Apr-May	Mar-Apr	Mar-Apr	Apr-May	Mar-Apr	April	Mar-Apr	Mar-Apr	Apr-May	Mar-Apr	Mar-Apr	Apr-May	Mar-Apr	Mar-Apr	Apr-May	Mar-Apr	Apr-May	Mar-Apr	Mar-Apr	Apr-May	Mar-Apr
1	28	8	19	30	9	23	2	14	26	6	17	28	9	21	1	12	24	5	16	26	6	20	30	10	23	3	14	25	6	18
2	29	9	20	31	10	24	3	15	27	7	18	29	10	22	2	13	25	6	17	27	7	21	31	11	24	4	15	26	7	19
3	30	10	21	1	11	25	4	16	28	8	19	30	11	23	3	14	26	7	18	28	8	22	1	12	25	5	16	27	8	20
4	31	11	22	2	12	26	5	17	29	9	20	31	12	24	4	15	27	8	19	29	9	23	2	13	26	6	17	28	9	21
5	1	12	23	3	13	27	6	18	30	10	21	1	13	25	5	16	28	9	20	30	10	24	3	14	27	7	18	29	10	22
6	2	13	24	4	14	28	7	19	31	11	22	2	14	26	6	17	29	10	21	31	11	25	4	15	28	8	19	30	11	23
7	3	14	25	5	15	29	8	20	1	12	23	3	15	27	7	18	30	11	22	1	12	26	5	16	29	9	20	31	12	24
8	4	15	26	6	16	30	9	21	2	13	24	4	16	28	8	19	31	12	23	2	13	27	6	17	30	10	21	1	13	25
9	5	16	27	7	17	31	10	22	3	14	25	5	17	29	9	20	1	13	24	3	14	28	7	18	31	11	22	2	14	26
10	6	17	28	8	18	1	11	23	4	15	26	6	18	30	10	21	2	14	25	4	15	29	8	19	1	12	23	3	15	27
11	7	18	29	9	19	2	12	24	5	16	27	7	19	31	11	22	3	15	26	5	16	30	9	20	2	13	24	4	16	28
12	8	19	30	10	20	3	13	25	6	17	28	8	20	1	12	23	4	16	27	6	17	31	10	21	3	14	25	5	17	29
13	9	20	31	11	21	4	14	26	7	18	29	9	21	2	13	24	5	17	28	7	18	1	11	22	4	15	26	6	18	30
14	10	21	1	12	22	5	15	27	8	19	30	10	22	3	14	25	6	18	29	8	19	2	12	23	5	16	27	7	19	31
15	11	22	2	13	23	6	16	28	9	20	31	11	23	4	15	26	7	19	30	9	20	3	13	24	6	17	28	8	20	1
16	12	23	3	14	24	7	17	29	10	21	1	12	24	5	16	27	8	20	31	10	21	4	14	25	7	18	29	9	21	2
17	13	24	4	15	25	8	18	30	11	22	2	13	25	6	17	28	9	21	1	11	22	5	15	26	8	19	30	10	22	3
18	14	25	5	16	26	9	19	31	12	23	3	14	26	7	18	29	10	22	2	12	23	6	16	27	9	20	31	11	23	4
19	15	26	6	17	27	10	20	1	13	24	4	15	27	8	19	30	11	23	3	13	24	7	17	28	10	21	1	12	24	5
20	16	27	7	18	28	11	21	2	14	25	5	16	28	9	20	31	12	24	4	14	25	8	18	29	11	22	2	13	25	6
21	17	28	8	19	29	12	22	3	15	26	6	17	29	10	21	1	13	25	5	15	26	9	19	30	12	23	3	14	26	7
22	18	29	9	20	30	13	23	4	16	27	7	18	30	11	22	2	14	26	6	16	27	10	20	1	13	24	4	15	27	8
23	19	30	10	21	1	14	24	5	17	28	8	19	1	12	23	3	15	27	7	17	28	11	21	2	14	25	5	16	28	9
24	20	31	11	22	2	15	25	6	18	29	9	20	2	13	24	4	16	28	8	18	29	12	22	3	15	26	6	17	29	10
25	21	1	12	23	3	16	26	7	19	30	10	21	3	14	25	5	17	29	9	19	30	13	23	4	16	27	7	18	30	11
26	22	2	13	24	4	17	27	8	20	1	11	22	4	15	26	6	18	30	10	20	31	14	24	5	17	28	8	19	1	12
27	23	3	14	25	5	18	28	9	21	2	12	23	5	16	27	7	19	1	11	21	1	15	25	6	18	29	9	20	2	13
28	24	4	15	26	6	19	29	10	22	3	13	24	6	17	28	8	20	2	12	22	2	16	26	7	19	30	10	21	3	14
29	25	5	16	27	7	20	30	11	23	4	14	25	7	18	29	9	21	3	13	23	3	17	27	8	20	1	11	22	4	15
30	26	6	17	28	8	21	1	12	24	5	15	26	8	19	30	10	22	4	14	24	4	18	28	9	21	2	12	23	5	16

In the left-hand margin figures in **black type** denote major Holy-days; elsewhere they denote Sabbaths.
14th, Fast of the Firstborn (if on Sabbath, observed on the preceding Thursday; 15th to 22nd, Passover; 30th, First day of New Moon of Iyar.

IYAR (29 days)

Iyar	88	87	86	85	84	83	82	81	80	79	78	77	76	75	74	73	72	71	70	69	68	67	66	65	64	63	62	61	60	5759
	28	27	26	25	24	23	22	21	20	19	18	17	16	15	14	13	12	11	10	09	08	07	06	05	04	03	02	01	2000	1999
	Apr-May	May-Jn	Apr-May	Apr-May	May-Jn	Apr-May	May	Apr-May	Apr-May	May-Jn	Apr-May	Apr-May	May-Jn	Apr-May	May	Apr-May	Apr-May	May-Jn	Apr-May	Apr-May	May-Jn	Apr-May	Apr-May	May-Jn	Apr-May	May	Apr-May	Apr-May	May-Jn	Apr-May
1	27	**8**	**18**	29	9	**22**	2	13	**25**	6	16	27	9	20	1	11	23	5	15	**25**	6	19	**29**	10	22	**3**	**13**	24	6	**17**
2	28	9	19	30	10	23	3	14	26	7	17	28	10	21	2	12	24	6	16	26	7	20	30	11	23	4	14	25	7	18
3	**29**	10	20	1	**11**	24	4	15	27	8	18	**29**	11	22	**3**	**13**	25	**7**	**17**	27	8	**21**	1	12	**24**	5	15	26	8	19
4	30	11	21	2	12	25	5	16	28	9	19	30	12	23	4	14	26	8	18	28	9	22	2	13	25	6	16	27	9	20
5	1	12	22	**3**	13	26	6	**17**	29	10	20	1	13	24	5	15	27	9	19	29	**10**	23	3	**14**	26	7	17	**28**	10	21
6	2	13	23	4	14	27	**7**	18	30	**11**	**21**	2	**14**	**25**	6	16	**28**	10	20	30	11	24	4	15	27	8	18	29	11	22
7	3	14	24	5	15	28	8	19	1	12	22	3	15	26	7	17	29	11	21	1	12	25	5	16	28	9	19	30	12	23
8	4	**15**	**25**	6	16	**29**	9	20	**2**	13	23	4	16	27	8	18	30	12	22	**2**	13	26	**6**	17	29	**10**	**20**	1	**13**	**24**
9	5	16	26	7	17	30	10	21	3	14	24	5	17	28	9	19	1	13	23	3	14	27	7	18	30	11	21	2	14	25
10	**6**	17	27	8	**18**	1	11	22	4	15	25	**6**	18	29	**10**	**20**	2	**14**	**24**	4	15	**28**	8	19	**1**	12	22	3	15	26
11	7	18	28	9	19	2	12	23	5	16	26	7	19	30	11	21	3	15	25	5	16	29	9	20	2	13	23	4	16	27
12	8	19	29	**10**	20	3	13	**24**	6	17	27	8	20	1	12	22	4	16	26	6	**17**	30	10	**21**	3	14	24	**5**	17	28
13	9	20	30	11	21	4	**14**	25	7	**18**	**28**	9	**21**	**2**	13	23	**5**	17	27	7	18	1	11	22	4	15	25	6	18	29
14	10	21	1	12	22	5	15	26	8	19	29	10	22	3	14	24	6	18	28	8	19	2	12	23	5	16	26	7	19	30
15	11	**22**	**2**	13	23	**6**	16	27	**9**	20	30	11	23	4	15	25	7	19	29	**9**	20	3	**13**	24	6	**17**	**27**	8	**20**	**1**
16	12	23	3	14	24	7	17	28	10	21	1	12	24	5	16	26	8	20	30	10	21	4	14	25	7	18	28	9	21	2
17	**13**	24	4	15	**25**	8	18	29	11	22	2	**13**	25	6	**17**	**27**	9	**21**	**1**	11	22	**5**	15	26	**8**	19	29	10	22	3
18	**14**	**25**	**5**	**16**	**26**	**9**	**19**	**30**	**12**	**23**	**3**	**14**	**26**	**7**	**18**	**28**	**10**	**22**	**2**	**12**	**23**	**6**	**16**	**27**	**9**	**20**	**30**	**11**	**23**	**4**
19	15	26	6	**17**	27	10	20	**1**	13	24	4	15	27	8	19	29	11	23	3	13	**24**	7	17	**28**	10	21	1	**12**	24	5
20	16	27	7	18	28	11	**21**	2	14	**25**	**5**	16	**28**	**9**	20	30	**12**	24	4	14	25	8	18	29	11	22	2	13	25	6
21	17	28	8	19	29	12	22	3	15	26	6	17	29	10	21	1	13	25	5	15	26	9	19	30	12	23	3	14	26	7
22	18	**29**	**9**	20	30	**13**	23	4	**16**	27	7	18	30	11	22	2	14	26	6	**16**	27	10	**20**	31	13	**24**	**4**	15	**27**	**8**
23	19	30	10	21	31	14	24	5	17	28	8	19	31	12	23	3	15	27	7	17	28	11	21	1	14	25	5	16	28	9
24	**20**	31	11	22	**1**	15	25	6	18	29	9	**20**	1	13	**24**	**4**	16	**28**	**8**	18	29	**12**	22	2	**15**	26	6	17	29	10
25	21	1	12	23	2	16	26	7	19	30	10	21	2	14	25	5	17	29	9	19	30	13	23	3	16	27	7	18	30	11
26	22	2	13	**24**	3	17	27	**8**	20	31	11	22	3	15	26	6	18	30	10	20	**31**	14	24	**4**	17	28	8	**19**	31	12
27	23	3	14	25	4	18	**28**	9	21	**1**	**12**	23	**4**	**16**	27	7	**19**	31	11	21	1	15	25	5	18	29	9	20	1	13
28	24	4	15	26	5	19	29	10	22	2	13	24	5	17	28	8	20	1	12	22	2	16	26	6	19	30	10	21	2	14
29	25	**5**	**16**	27	6	**20**	30	11	**23**	3	14	25	6	18	29	9	21	2	13	**23**	3	17	**27**	7	20	**31**	**11**	22	**3**	**15**

Figures in **black type** denote Sabbaths.
18th, 33rd Day Omer, Scholars' Festival.

SIVAN (30 days)

Sivan	88	87	86	85	84	83	82	81	80	79	78	77	76	75	74	73	72	71	70	69	68	67	66	65	64	63	62	61	60	5759
	28	27	26	25	24	23	22	21	20	19	18	17	16	15	14	13	12	11	10	09	08	07	06	05	04	03	02	01	2000	1999
	May-Jn	Jn-July	May-Jn	May-Jn	Jn-July	May-Jn	May-Jn	May-Jn	May-Jn	Jn-July	May-Jn	May-Jn	Jn-July	May-Jn	May-Jn	May-Jn	May-Jn	Jn-July	May-Jn	May-Jn	Jn-July	May-Jn	May-Jn	Jn-July	May-Jn	June	May-Jn	May-Jn	Jn-July	May-Jn
1	26	6	17	28	7	21	31	12	24	4	15	26	7	19	30	10	22	3	14	24	4	18	28	8	21	1	12	23	4	16
2	27	7	18	29	8	22	1	13	25	5	16	27	8	20	31	11	23	4	15	25	5	19	29	9	22	2	13	24	5	17
3	28	8	19	30	9	23	2	14	26	6	17	28	9	21	1	12	24	5	16	26	6	20	30	10	23	3	14	25	6	18
4	29	9	20	31	10	24	3	15	27	7	18	29	10	22	2	13	25	6	17	27	7	21	31	11	24	4	15	26	7	19
5	30	10	21	1	11	25	4	16	28	8	19	30	11	23	3	14	26	7	18	28	8	22	1	12	25	5	16	27	8	20
6	31	11	22	2	12	26	5	17	29	9	20	31	12	24	4	15	27	8	19	29	9	23	2	13	26	6	17	28	9	21
7	1	12	23	3	13	27	6	18	30	10	21	1	13	25	5	16	28	9	20	30	10	24	3	14	27	7	18	29	10	22
8	2	13	24	4	14	28	7	19	31	11	22	2	14	26	6	17	29	10	21	31	11	25	4	15	28	8	19	30	11	23
9	3	14	25	5	15	29	8	20	1	12	23	3	15	27	7	18	30	11	22	1	12	26	5	16	29	9	20	31	12	24
10	4	15	26	6	16	30	9	21	2	13	24	4	16	28	8	19	31	12	23	2	13	27	6	17	30	10	21	1	13	25
11	5	16	27	7	17	31	10	22	3	14	25	5	17	29	9	20	1	13	24	3	14	28	7	18	31	11	22	2	14	26
12	6	17	28	8	18	1	11	23	4	15	26	6	18	30	10	21	2	14	25	4	15	29	8	19	1	12	23	3	15	27
13	7	18	29	9	19	2	12	24	5	16	27	7	19	31	11	22	3	15	26	5	16	30	9	20	2	13	24	4	16	28
14	8	19	30	10	20	3	13	25	6	17	28	8	20	1	12	23	4	16	27	6	17	31	10	21	3	14	25	5	17	29
15	9	20	31	11	21	4	14	26	7	18	29	9	21	2	13	24	5	17	28	7	18	1	11	22	4	15	26	6	18	30
16	10	21	1	12	22	5	15	27	8	19	30	10	22	3	14	25	6	18	29	8	19	2	12	23	5	16	27	7	19	31
17	11	22	2	13	23	6	16	28	9	20	31	11	23	4	15	26	7	19	30	9	20	3	13	24	6	17	28	8	20	1
18	12	23	3	14	24	7	17	29	10	21	1	12	24	5	16	27	8	20	31	10	21	4	14	25	7	18	29	9	21	2
19	13	24	4	15	25	8	18	30	11	22	2	13	25	6	17	28	9	21	1	11	22	5	15	26	8	19	30	10	22	3
20	14	25	5	16	26	9	19	31	12	23	3	14	26	7	18	29	10	22	2	12	23	6	16	27	9	20	31	11	23	4
21	15	26	6	17	27	10	20	1	13	24	4	15	27	8	19	30	11	23	3	13	24	7	17	28	10	21	1	12	24	5
22	16	27	7	18	28	11	21	2	14	25	5	16	28	9	20	31	12	24	4	14	25	8	18	29	11	22	2	13	25	6
23	17	28	8	19	29	12	22	3	15	26	6	17	29	10	21	1	13	25	5	15	26	9	19	30	12	23	3	14	26	7
24	18	29	9	20	30	13	23	4	16	27	7	18	30	11	22	2	14	26	6	16	27	10	20	1	13	24	4	15	27	8
25	19	30	10	21	1	14	24	5	17	28	8	19	1	12	23	3	15	27	7	17	28	11	21	2	14	25	5	16	28	9
26	20	1	11	22	2	15	25	6	18	29	9	20	2	13	24	4	16	28	8	18	29	12	22	3	15	26	6	17	29	10
27	21	2	12	23	3	16	26	7	19	30	10	21	3	14	25	5	17	29	9	19	30	13	23	4	16	27	7	18	30	11
28	22	3	13	24	4	17	27	8	20	1	11	22	4	15	26	6	18	30	10	20	1	14	24	5	17	28	8	19	1	12
29	23	4	14	25	5	18	28	9	21	2	12	23	5	16	27	7	19	1	11	21	2	15	25	6	18	29	9	20	2	13
30	24	5	15	26	6	19	29	10	22	3	13	24	6	17	28	8	20	2	12	22	3	16	26	7	19	30	10	21	3	14

In the left-hand margin figures in **black type** denote major Holy-days; elsewhere they denote Sabbaths. 6th and 7th, Pentecost; 30th, First day of New Moon of Tammuz.

TAMMUZ (29 days)

Tam	5759 / 1999 (Jn-July)	60 / 2000 (July-Au)	61 / 01 (Jn-July)	62 / 02 (Jn-July)	63 / 03 (July)	64 / 04 (Jn-July)	65 / 05 (July-Au)	66 / 06 (Jn-July)	67 / 07 (Jn-July)	68 / 08 (July-Au)	69 / 09 (Jn-July)	70 / 10 (Jn-July)	71 / 11 (July)	72 / 12 (Jn-July)	73 / 13 (Jn-July)	74 / 14 (Jn-July)	75 / 15 (Jn-July)	76 / 16 (July-Au)	77 / 17 (Jn-July)	78 / 18 (Jn-July)	79 / 19 (July-Au)	80 / 20 (Jn-July)	81 / 21 (Jn-July)	82 / 22 (Jn-July)	83 / 23 (Jn-July)	84 / 24 (July-Au)	85 / 25 (Jn-July)	86 / 26 (Jn-July)	87 / 27 (July-Au)	88 / 28 (Jn-July)
1	15	4	22	11	1	20	8	27	17	4	23	13	3	21	9	29	18	7	25	14	4	23	11	30	20	7	27	16	6	25
2	16	5	23	12	2	21	9	28	18	5	24	14	4	22	10	30	19	8	26	15	5	24	12	1	21	8	28	17	7	26
3	17	6	24	13	3	22	10	29	19	6	25	15	5	23	11	1	20	9	27	16	6	25	13	2	22	9	29	18	8	27
4	18	7	25	14	4	23	11	30	20	7	26	16	6	24	12	2	21	10	28	17	7	26	14	3	23	10	30	19	9	28
5	19	8	26	15	5	24	12	1	21	8	27	17	7	25	13	3	22	11	29	18	8	27	15	4	24	11	1	20	10	29
6	20	9	27	16	6	25	13	2	22	9	28	18	8	26	14	4	23	12	30	19	9	28	16	5	25	12	2	21	11	30
7	21	10	28	17	7	26	14	3	23	10	29	19	9	27	15	5	24	13	1	20	10	29	17	6	26	13	3	22	12	1
8	22	11	29	18	8	27	15	4	24	11	30	20	10	28	16	6	25	14	2	21	11	30	18	7	27	14	4	23	13	2
9	23	12	30	19	9	28	16	5	25	12	1	21	11	29	17	7	26	15	3	22	12	31	19	8	28	15	5	24	14	3
10	24	13	1	20	10	29	17	6	26	13	2	22	12	30	18	8	27	16	4	23	13	1	20	9	29	16	6	25	15	4
11	25	14	2	21	11	30	18	7	27	14	3	23	13	1	19	9	28	17	5	24	14	3	21	10	30	17	7	26	16	5
12	26	15	3	22	12	1	19	8	28	15	4	24	14	2	20	10	29	18	6	25	15	4	22	11	1	18	8	27	17	6
13	27	16	4	23	13	2	20	9	29	16	5	25	15	3	21	11	30	19	7	26	16	5	23	12	2	19	9	28	18	7
14	28	17	5	24	14	3	21	10	30	17	6	26	16	4	22	12	1	20	8	27	17	6	24	13	3	20	10	29	19	8
15	29	18	6	25	15	4	22	11	1	18	7	27	17	5	23	13	2	21	9	28	18	7	25	14	4	21	11	30	20	9
16	30	19	7	26	16	5	23	12	2	19	8	28	18	6	24	14	3	22	10	29	19	8	26	15	5	22	12	1	21	10
17	1	20	8	27	17	6	24	13	3	20	9	29	19	7	25	15	4	23	11	30	20	9	27	16	6	23	13	2	22	11
18	2	21	9	28	18	7	25	14	4	21	10	30	20	8	26	16	5	24	12	1	21	10	28	17	7	24	14	3	23	12
19	3	22	10	29	19	8	26	15	5	22	11	1	21	9	27	17	6	25	13	2	22	11	29	18	8	25	15	4	24	13
20	4	23	11	30	20	9	27	16	6	23	12	2	22	10	28	18	7	26	14	3	23	12	30	19	9	26	16	5	25	14
21	5	24	12	1	21	10	28	17	7	24	13	3	23	11	29	19	8	27	15	4	24	13	1	20	10	27	17	6	26	15
22	6	25	13	2	22	11	29	18	8	25	14	4	24	12	30	20	9	28	16	5	25	14	2	21	11	28	18	7	27	16
23	7	26	14	3	23	12	30	19	9	26	15	5	25	13	1	21	10	29	17	6	26	15	3	22	12	29	19	8	28	17
24	8	27	15	4	24	13	31	20	10	27	16	6	26	14	2	22	11	30	18	7	27	16	4	23	13	30	20	9	29	18
25	9	28	16	5	25	14	1	21	11	28	17	7	27	15	3	23	12	31	19	8	28	17	5	24	14	31	21	10	30	19
26	10	29	17	6	26	15	2	22	12	29	18	8	28	16	4	24	13	1	20	9	29	18	6	25	15	1	22	11	31	20
27	11	30	18	7	27	16	3	23	13	30	19	9	29	17	5	25	14	2	21	10	30	19	7	26	16	2	23	12	1	21
28	12	31	19	8	28	17	4	24	14	31	20	10	30	18	6	26	15	3	22	11	31	20	8	27	17	3	24	13	2	22
29	13	1	20	9	29	18	5	25	15	1	21	11	31	19	7	27	16	4	23	12	1	21	9	28	18	4	25	14	3	23

Figures in **black type** denote Sabbaths.

17th, Fast of Tammuz (if on Sabbath, postponed to Sunday).

AB (30 days)

88 / 28 July-Au	87 / 27 Au-Sep	86 / 26 July-Au	85 / 25 July-Au	84 / 24 Au-Sep	83 / 23 July-Au	82 / 22 July-Au	81 / 21 July-Au	80 / 20 July-Au	79 / 19 August	78 / 18 July-Au	77 / 17 July-Au	76 / 16 Au-Sep	75 / 15 July-Au	74 / 14 July-Au	73 / 13 July-Au	72 / 12 July-Au	71 / 11 August	70 / 10 July-Au	69 / 09 July-Au	68 / 08 August	67 / 07 July-Au	66 / 06 July-Au	65 / 05 Au-Sep	64 / 04 July-Au	63 / 03 July-Au	62 / 02 July-Au	61 / 01 July-Au	60 / 2000 August	5759 / 1999 July-Au	Ab
24	4	15	26	5	19	29	10	22	2	13	24	5	17	28	8	20	1	12	22	2	16	26	6	19	30	10	21	2	14	1
25	5	16	27	6	20	30	11	23	3	14	25	6	18	29	9	21	2	13	23	3	17	27	7	20	31	11	22	3	15	2
26	6	17	28	7	21	31	12	24	4	15	26	7	19	30	10	22	3	14	24	4	18	28	8	21	1	12	23	4	16	3
27	7	18	29	8	22	1	13	25	5	16	27	8	20	31	11	23	4	15	25	5	19	29	9	22	2	13	24	5	17	4
28	8	19	30	9	23	2	14	26	6	17	28	9	21	1	12	24	5	16	26	6	20	30	10	23	3	14	25	6	18	5
29	9	20	31	10	24	3	15	27	7	18	29	10	22	2	13	25	6	17	27	7	21	31	11	24	4	15	26	7	19	6
30	10	21	1	11	25	4	16	28	8	19	30	11	23	3	14	26	7	18	28	8	22	1	12	25	5	16	27	8	20	7
31	11	22	2	12	26	5	17	29	9	20	31	12	24	4	15	27	8	19	29	9	23	2	13	26	6	17	28	9	21	8
1	12	23	3	13	27	6	18	30	10	21	1	13	25	5	16	28	9	20	30	10	24	3	14	27	7	18	29	10	22	9
2	13	24	4	14	28	7	19	31	11	22	2	14	26	6	17	29	10	21	31	11	25	4	15	28	8	19	30	11	23	*10*
3	14	25	5	15	29	8	20	1	12	23	3	15	27	7	18	30	11	22	1	12	26	5	16	29	9	20	31	12	24	*11*
4	15	26	6	16	30	9	21	2	13	24	4	16	28	8	19	31	12	23	2	13	27	6	17	30	10	21	1	13	25	*12*
5	16	27	7	17	31	10	22	3	14	25	5	17	29	9	20	1	13	24	3	14	28	7	18	31	11	22	2	14	26	*13*
6	17	28	8	18	1	11	23	4	15	26	6	18	30	10	21	2	14	25	4	15	29	8	19	1	12	23	3	15	27	*14*
7	18	29	9	19	2	12	24	5	16	27	7	19	31	11	22	3	15	26	5	16	30	9	20	2	13	24	4	16	28	*15*
8	19	30	10	20	3	13	25	6	17	28	8	20	1	12	23	4	16	27	6	17	31	10	21	3	14	25	5	17	29	*16*
9	20	31	11	21	4	14	26	7	18	29	9	21	2	13	24	5	17	28	7	18	1	11	22	4	15	26	6	18	30	*17*
10	21	1	12	22	5	15	27	8	19	30	10	22	3	14	25	6	18	29	8	19	2	12	23	5	16	27	7	19	31	*18*
11	22	2	13	23	6	16	28	9	20	31	11	23	4	15	26	7	19	30	9	20	3	13	24	6	17	28	8	20	1	*19*
12	23	3	14	24	7	17	29	10	21	1	12	24	5	16	27	8	20	31	10	21	4	14	25	7	18	29	9	21	2	*20*
13	24	4	15	25	8	18	30	11	22	2	13	25	6	17	28	9	21	1	11	22	5	15	26	8	19	30	10	22	3	21
14	25	5	16	26	9	19	31	12	23	3	14	26	7	18	29	10	22	2	12	23	6	16	27	9	20	31	11	23	4	22
15	26	6	17	27	10	20	1	13	24	4	15	27	8	19	30	11	23	3	13	24	7	17	28	10	21	1	12	24	5	23
16	27	7	18	28	11	21	2	14	25	5	16	28	9	20	31	12	24	4	14	25	8	18	29	11	22	2	13	25	6	24
17	28	8	19	29	12	22	3	15	26	6	17	29	10	21	1	13	25	5	15	26	9	19	30	12	23	3	14	26	7	25
18	29	9	20	30	13	23	4	16	27	7	18	30	11	22	2	14	26	6	16	27	10	20	31	13	24	4	15	27	8	26
19	30	10	21	31	14	24	5	17	28	8	19	31	12	23	3	15	27	7	17	28	11	21	1	14	25	5	16	28	9	27
20	31	11	22	1	15	25	6	18	29	9	20	1	13	24	4	16	28	8	18	29	12	22	2	15	26	6	17	29	10	28
21	1	12	23	2	16	26	7	19	30	10	21	2	14	25	5	17	29	9	19	30	13	23	3	16	27	7	18	30	11	29
22	2	13	24	3	17	27	8	20	31	11	22	3	15	26	6	18	30	10	20	31	14	24	4	17	28	8	19	31	12	30

Figures in **black type** denote Sabbaths.

9th, Fast of Ab (if on Sabbath, postponed to Sunday); 30th, First Day of New Moon of Elul.

ELUL (29 days)

Elul	5759 1999 Au-Sep	60 2000 Sept	61 01 Au-Sep	62 02 Au-Sep	63 03 Au-Sep	64 04 Au-Sep	65 05 Sep-Oct	66 06 Au-Sep	67 07 Au-Sep	68 08 Sept	69 09 Au-Sep	70 10 Au-Sep	71 11 Au-Sep	72 12 Au-Sep	73 13 Au-Sep	74 14 Au-Sep	75 15 Au-Sep	76 16 Sep-Oct	77 17 Au-Sep	78 18 Au-Sep	79 19 Sept	80 20 Au-Sep	81 21 Au-Sep	82 22 Au-Sep	83 23 Au-Sep	84 24 Sep-Oct	85 25 Au-Sep	86 26 Au-Sep	87 27 Sep-Oct	88 28 Au-Sep
1	13	1	20	9	29	18	5	25	15	1	21	11	31	19	7	27	16	4	23	12	1	21	9	28	18	4	25	14	3	23
2	**14**	**2**	21	**10**	**30**	19	6	**26**	16	2	**22**	12	1	20	8	28	17	5	24	13	2	**22**	10	29	**19**	5	26	**15**	**4**	24
3	15	3	22	11	31	20	7	27	17	3	23	13	2	21	9	29	18	6	25	14	3	23	11	30	20	6	27	16	5	25
4	16	4	23	12	1	**21**	8	28	**18**	4	24	**14**	**3**	22	**10**	**30**	19	7	**26**	15	4	24	12	31	21	**7**	28	17	6	**26**
5	17	5	24	13	2	22	9	29	19	5	25	15	4	23	11	31	20	8	27	16	5	25	13	1	22	8	29	18	7	27
6	18	6	**25**	14	3	23	**10**	30	20	**6**	26	16	5	24	12	1	21	9	28	17	6	26	**14**	2	23	9	**30**	19	8	28
7	19	7	26	15	4	24	11	31	21	7	27	17	6	**25**	13	2	**22**	**10**	29	**18**	**7**	27	15	**3**	24	10	31	20	9	29
8	20	8	27	16	5	25	12	1	22	8	28	18	7	26	14	3	23	11	30	19	8	28	16	4	25	11	1	21	10	30
9	**21**	**9**	28	**17**	**6**	26	13	**2**	23	9	**29**	19	8	27	15	4	24	12	31	20	9	**29**	17	5	**26**	12	2	**22**	**11**	31
10	22	10	29	18	7	27	14	3	24	10	30	20	9	28	16	5	25	13	1	21	10	30	18	6	27	13	3	23	12	1
11	23	11	30	19	8	**28**	15	4	**25**	11	31	**21**	**10**	29	**17**	**6**	26	14	**2**	22	11	31	19	7	28	**14**	4	24	13	**2**
12	24	12	31	20	9	29	16	5	26	12	1	22	11	30	18	7	27	15	3	23	12	1	20	8	29	15	5	25	14	3
13	25	13	**1**	21	10	30	**17**	6	27	**13**	2	23	12	31	19	8	28	16	4	24	13	2	**21**	9	30	16	**6**	26	15	4
14	26	14	2	22	11	31	18	7	28	14	3	24	13	**1**	20	9	**29**	**17**	5	**25**	**14**	3	22	**10**	31	17	7	27	16	5
15	27	15	3	23	12	1	19	8	29	15	4	25	14	2	21	10	30	18	6	26	15	4	23	11	1	18	8	28	17	6
16	**28**	**16**	4	**24**	**13**	2	20	**9**	30	16	5	26	15	3	22	11	31	19	7	27	16	5	24	12	**2**	19	9	**29**	**18**	7
17	29	17	5	25	14	3	21	10	31	17	6	27	16	4	23	12	1	20	8	28	17	6	25	13	3	20	10	30	19	8
18	30	18	6	26	15	**4**	22	11	**1**	18	7	**28**	17	**5**	24	**13**	2	21	**9**	29	18	7	26	14	4	**21**	11	31	20	**9**
19	31	19	7	27	16	5	23	12	2	19	8	29	18	6	25	14	3	22	10	30	19	8	27	15	5	22	12	1	21	10
20	1	20	**8**	28	17	6	**24**	13	3	**20**	9	30	19	7	26	15	4	23	11	31	20	9	**28**	16	6	23	**13**	2	22	11
21	2	21	9	29	18	7	25	14	4	21	10	31	20	**8**	27	16	**5**	**24**	12	**1**	**21**	10	29	**17**	7	24	14	3	23	12
22	3	22	10	30	19	8	26	15	5	22	11	1	21	9	28	17	6	25	13	2	22	11	30	18	8	25	15	4	24	13
23	**4**	**23**	11	**31**	**20**	9	27	**16**	6	23	**12**	2	22	10	29	18	7	26	14	3	**23**	**12**	31	19	**9**	26	16	**5**	**25**	14
24	5	24	12	1	21	10	28	17	7	24	13	3	23	11	30	19	8	27	15	4	24	13	1	20	10	27	17	6	26	15
25	6	25	13	2	22	**11**	29	18	**8**	25	14	**4**	**24**	12	**31**	20	9	28	**16**	5	25	14	2	21	11	**28**	18	7	27	**16**
26	7	26	14	3	23	12	30	19	9	26	15	5	25	13	1	21	10	29	17	6	26	15	3	22	12	29	19	8	28	17
27	8	27	**15**	4	24	13	**1**	20	10	**27**	16	6	26	14	2	22	11	30	18	7	27	16	**4**	23	13	30	**20**	9	29	18
28	9	28	16	5	25	14	2	21	11	28	17	7	27	**15**	3	23	**12**	**1**	19	**8**	**28**	17	5	**24**	14	1	21	10	30	19
29	10	29	17	6	26	15	3	22	12	29	18	**8**	28	16	4	24	13	2	20	9	29	18	6	25	15	2	22	11	1	20

Figures in **black type** denote Sabbaths.

ARTICLES IN FORMER ISSUES OF THE YEAR BOOK

Below is a list of the essays that have appeared in the Jewish Year Book

GREEN, Geoffrey L. - *The Two-Hundredth Anniversary Of The Battle Of Trafalgar*
KLUG, Brian - *The Other Balfour: Recalling The 1905 Alien Act*

2006
JOLLES, Michael - *British Jews: Their Biographical Record*

2007
LANGHAM, Raphael - *Suez 1956*
SCHMOOL, Marlena - *Pointers To The Future Of The Community: Ethnicity, Mariage And Migration*
WITTENBERG, Jonathan - *Rabbi Dr Louis Jacobs*

2008
BECKMAN, Jonathan - *Sigmund Freud In London, 1938*
BLACK, Gerry - *Frank Cass Publisher, 1930-2007*
DAVIS, Bernard - *'Judaism Without Enforcement' - Reflections On The Clapton Jewish Youth Centre Sixty Years On*
DUNN, A. J. - *Wolf Mankowitz, 1924-1998 An Appreciation*
MOONMAN, Eric - *Reflections On Liverpool Jewry*

2009
APELOIG, Yitzchak - *Israel And Science*
CONWAY, David - *Short Dark And Jewish Looking': Felix Mendelssohn In Britain*
MASSIL, Stephen & Winston, Willow - *Ruth Winston Fox And The Jewish Way Of Life*
SHINDLER, Colin - *The Centenary Of Tel Aviv Founded In 1909*

2010
BUDD, Sidney – *Edgware & District Reform Synagogue*
GRUNWALD, Henry - *The Board Of Deputies at 250*
LEVY, Elkan D. - *The Communities That Nobody Knows About*
NEWMAN, Col. Martin & MORRIS, Henry - *The Jews In The British Armed Forces*
PINNICK, Jeffrey - *Yom Hashoah - The Annual Jewish Remembrance Day For Victims Of The Holocaust*
TAYLOR, Derek - *The Chareidim*
ZIMMELS, Erla – *The Jews' College Library: 1860-2010*

2011
CHINN, CVO, Sir Trevor – *Well done the British community*
GARDNER, Mark - *CST and the history of Jewish self-defence*
LEVY, Rabbi Abraham - *The way things are now*
SCHMOOL, Marlena - *Reflections on the 2011 Census of England and Wales*
WINEMAN, Vivian - *Getting on with the neighbours*

2012
SACKS, CHIEF RABBI LORD – *Community Transformation*
TAYLOR, Derek - *Shechita*
LAWTON, Clive - *Limmud*
BRAYBROOKE, Revd Dr Marcus - *CCJ: Seventy Years On*
LEVY, Elkan D. - *The Next Chief Rabbi*
LEE, PETER – *Plymouth: The Oldest Synagogue in the English-speaking World*
TAYLOR, Derek - *Cambridge Synagogue: 75th Anniversary*
BLOOM, Cecil - *The Jewish Libraries of Leeds*

Entries beginning 'Friends of' and 'British Friends of' will be filed under the first significant word.

Jerusalem Botanical Gardens,
Friends of 89
Jerusalem Foundation 90
Jewish Affiliates of the
UN Association 133
Jewish Aged Needy
Pension Society 169
Jewish Agency for
Israel 81, 270
Jewish Aid Committee
See One to One Project
Jewish Appreciation Group
Tours 174
Jewish Association for
Business Ethics 122
Jewish Association for the
Mental Illness 74
Jewish Association of
Cultural Societies 174
Jewish Association of Spiritual
Healers 122
Jewish Bereavement
Counselling Service 169
Jewish Blind and Disabled ..169
Projects 170
Jewish Blind in Israel
Association 90
Jewish Book Council 97
Jewish Calendar 447
Jewish Calendar for 30
years 469-82
Jewish Care 75, 170
Jewish Children's Holidays
Fund 170
Jewish Child's Day 75
Jewish Committee for H.M.
Forces 68
Jewish Community Centre
for London 162
Jewish Community Day
School Advisory Board ...97
Jewish Community Housing
Association 170
Jewish Community
Information, Board of
Deputies 57
Jewish Community Services,
Board of Deputies 57
Jewish Connection, Board of
Deputies 57
Jewish Council for Racial
Equality 122
Jewish Crisis Helpline
Miyad 171
Jewish Deaf Association ...171
Jewish Film Festival (UK) ..102
Jewish Friendly Societies ..123
Jewish Gay and Lesbian
Group 123
Jewish Genealogical Society

of Great Britain 97
Jewish Genetic Disorders
(JGD UK) 75
Jewish Guide Advisory
Council 108
Jewish Helpline 76
Jewish Heraldic Foundation ..98
Jewish Heritage UK
.............98, 315-17
Jewish Historical Society
of England 98
Jewish Information Services .66
Jewish Institute for the
Blind 90
Jewish Labour Movement ...81
Jewish Lads' and Girls'
Brigade 108
Jewish Leadership Council ..60
Jewish Learning
Exchange 162
Jewish Literary Trust 98
Jewish Marriage Council
Head Office 76
Jewish Medical Association 176
Jewish Memorial Council ..68
Jewish Military Museum ..116
Jewish Museum 116
Jewish Music Institute 98
Jewish Nurses & Midwives
Association 120
Jewish Organisations having
Consulative Status with
Economic and Social
Council of the United
Nations 127
Jewish Police Association ..176
Jewish Press (UK) 64-65
Jewish Radio Programmes ..66
Jewish Representative
Councils (UK) 58-59
Jewish Rescue and Relief
Committee 127
Jewish Resource Centre ...162
Jewish Scout Advisory
Council 108
Jewish Secondary Schools
Movement 164
Jewish Servicemen and
Women, Friends of 122
Jewish Socialists' Group ...123
Jewish Statistics 300-05
Jewish Students, Organisations
concerned with 122
Jewish Students, Union of ..112
Jewish Studies Courses ..436-37
Jewish Studies Library,
UCL 119
Jewish Teachers
Association 98

Jewish Visiting 176
Jewish Volunteering
Network 123
Jewish Women, International
Council of 132
Jewish Women, League of ..61
Jewish Women's Aid (JWA) ..76
Jewish Women's Organisations,
Association of 60
Jewish Year 449
Jewish Youth, Friends of ...107
Jewish Youth Fund 108
Jewish Youth, Organisations
concerned with 107-11
Jews & Christians, London
Society of 177
Jews' College Library 116
Jews for Justice for
Palestinians 123
Jews' Temporary Shelter ...171
JFS School 164
JHSE Essex Branch 174
JMC Pensions Fund 69
John Rylands Library 116
Joint Burial Committee 124
Joseph Interfaith
Foundation 63
JSENSE 76
JTA 98
Judith Lady Montefiore
College Trust...........151
JW3 ....124, 174

K

KabbalahUK.com 174
Kadima 264
Kathmandu (Nepal) 278
Kazakhstan 273
Kedassia *see* Joint
Kashrus Committee
Kashrus Committee -
Kedassia 71
Kashrut Division 67
Kehal Chareidim Beth
Hamedrash 147
Kehal Chasidim
D'Munkatch Synagogue ..147
Kehal Chassidim Beth
Hamedrash 147
Kehillah North London 155
Kehillas Ohel Moshe 147
Kent 192
Kenton Synagogue 138
Kenya 273
Keren Hatorah Book
and Tape Library 116
Kerem Schools 164
Keren Kayemeth Lelsrael ...270
Kesher - The Learning

Please complete and return the form to us by
28th August 2015

Please reserve the following advertising space in
The Jewish Year Book 2016:

FULL COLOUR AVAILABLE

☐ Full Page   £675   182 x 115 mm

☐ Half Page   £395   90 x 115 mm

☐ Quarter Page   £225   90 x 55 mm

(UK advertisers please note that the above rates are subject to VAT)
Special positions by arrangement

☐ Please insert the attached copy (If setting is required a 10% setting charge will be made.)

☐ Copy will be forwarded from our Advertising Agents (*see below*)

Contact Name: _____

Advertisers Name: _____

Address for invoicing: _____

_____

Tel: _____ Fax: _____

Signed: _____ Title: _____

VAT No: _____

Date: _____

Agency Name (if applicable): _____

Address: _____

_____

Tel: _____ Fax: _____

All advertisements set by the publisher will only be included if they
have been signed and approved by the advertiser.

To the Advertising Department
The Jewish Year Book
Vallentine Mitchell
Middlesex House, 29/45 High Street, Edgware, Middlesex HA8 7UU
Tel: +44 (0)20 8952 9526   Fax: + 44(0)20 8952 9242
www.vmbooks.com

Update for Jewish Year Book 2016

PUBLISHERS REQUEST

Readers are asked kindly to draw attention to any omissions or errors. If errors are discovered, it would be appreciated if you could give up-to-date information, referring to the appropriate page, and send this form to the Editor at the address given below. Alternatively, you can email us: info@vmbooks.com

With reference to the following entry:

Page:

Entry should read:

Kindly list on separate sheet if preferred.

Signed: _____ Date: _____ .

Name (BLOCK CAPITALS) _____

Address: _____

_____

Telephone: _____ .

The Editor

Jewish Year Book

Vallentine Mitchell & Co. Ltd.
Middlesex House, 29/45 High Street,
Edgware, Middlesex HA8 7UU
Tel: + 44(0)20 8952 9526   Fax: + 44(0)20 8952 9242
www.vmbooks.com